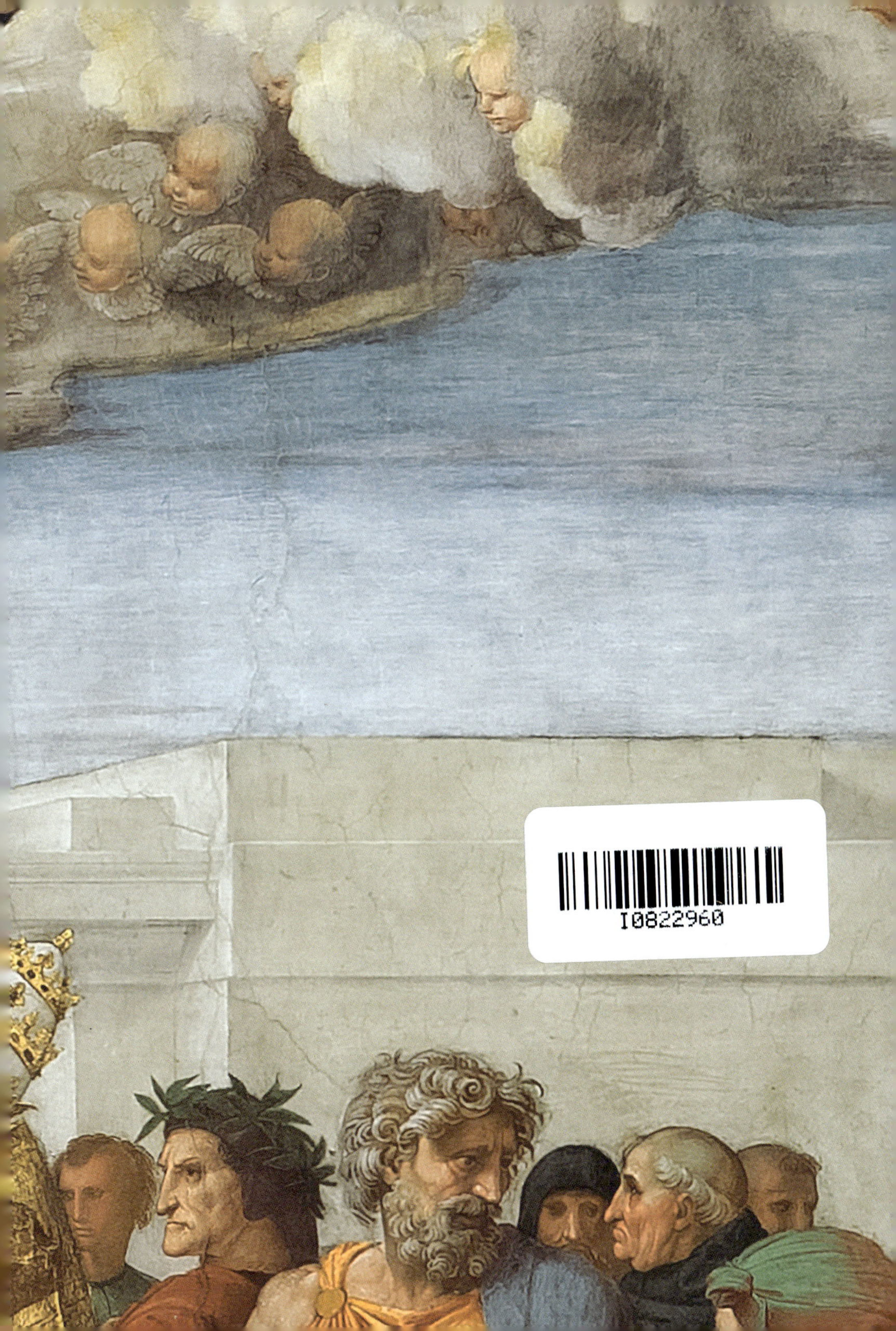
I0822960

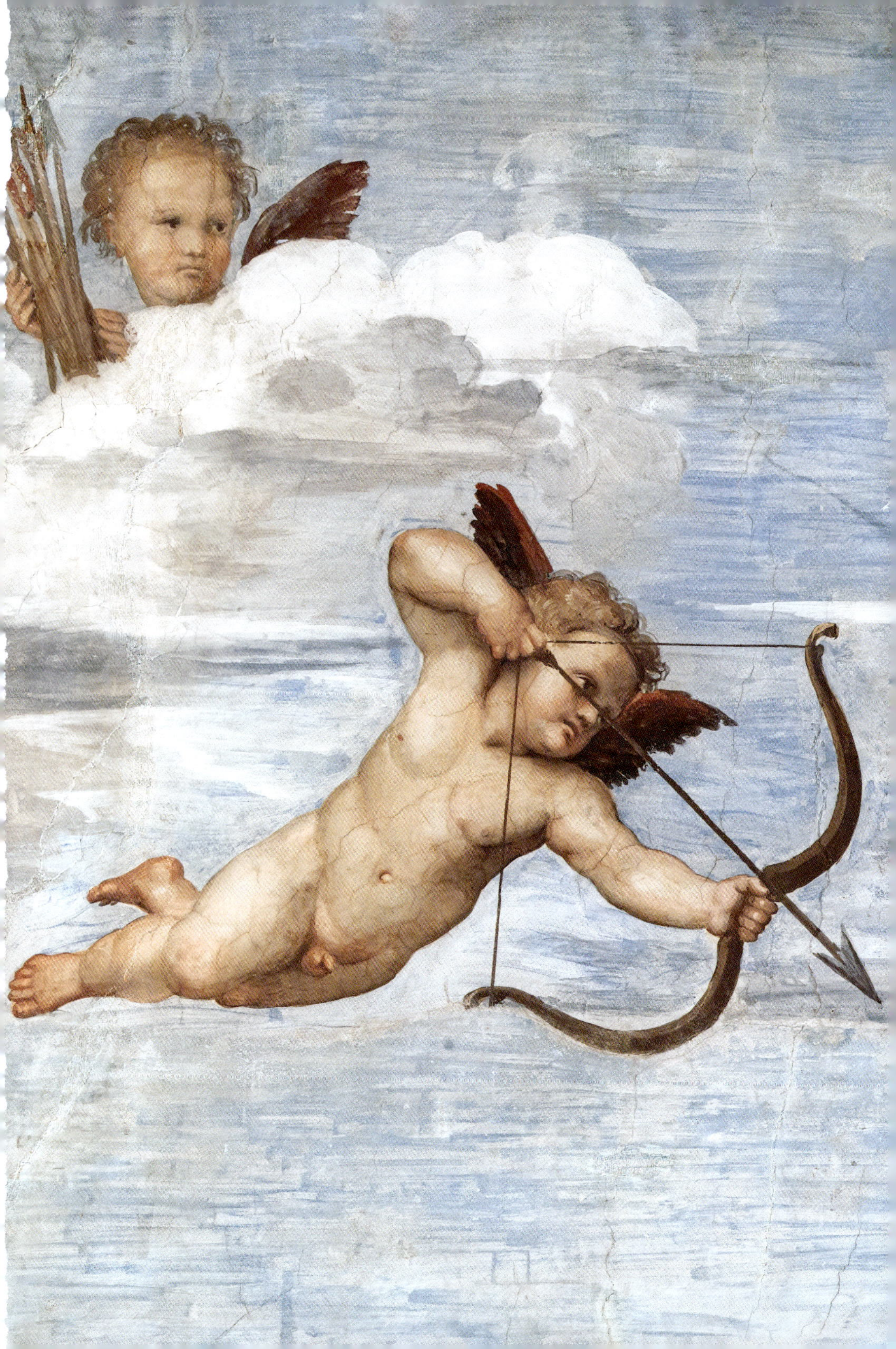

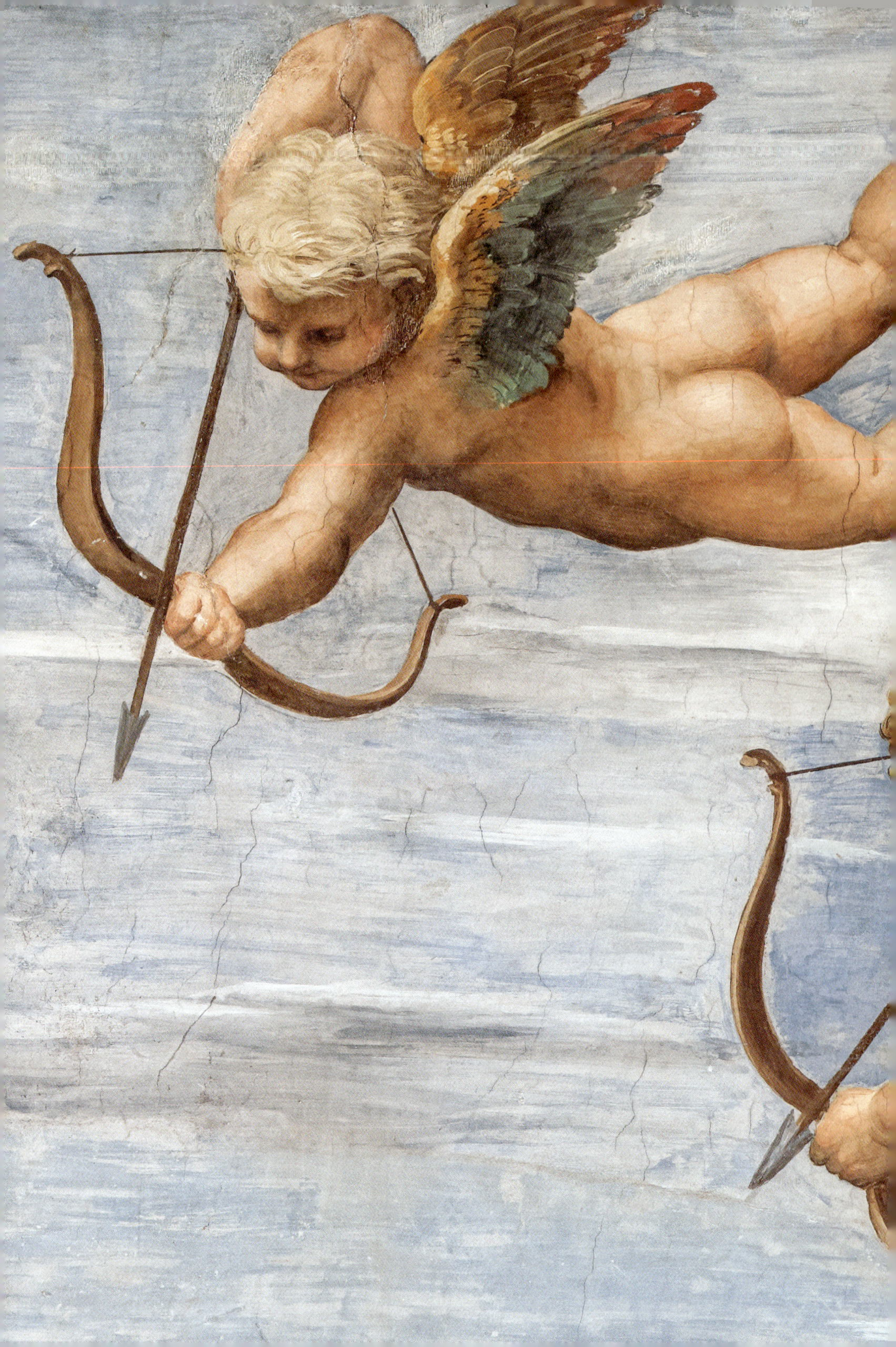

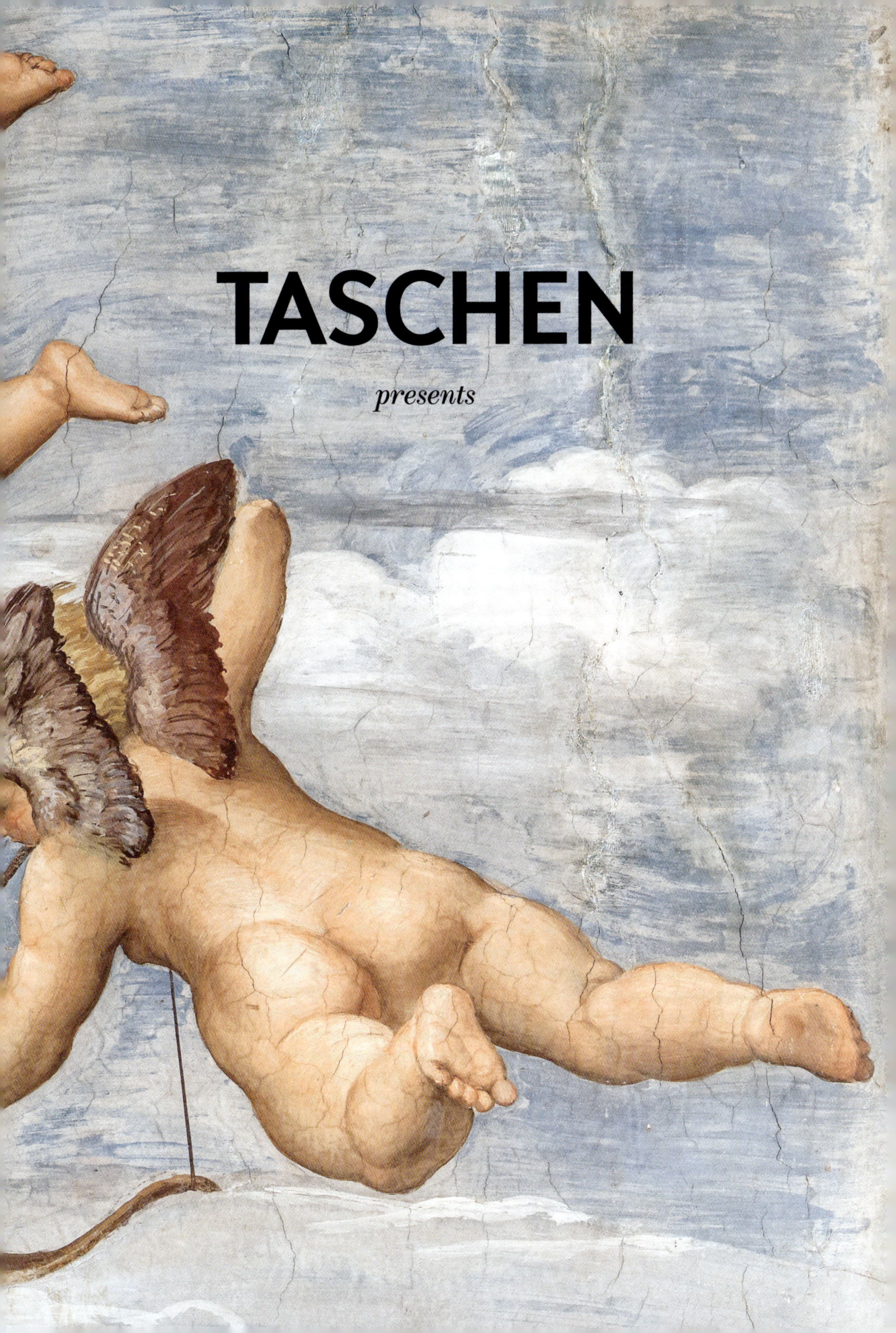
TASCHEN
presents

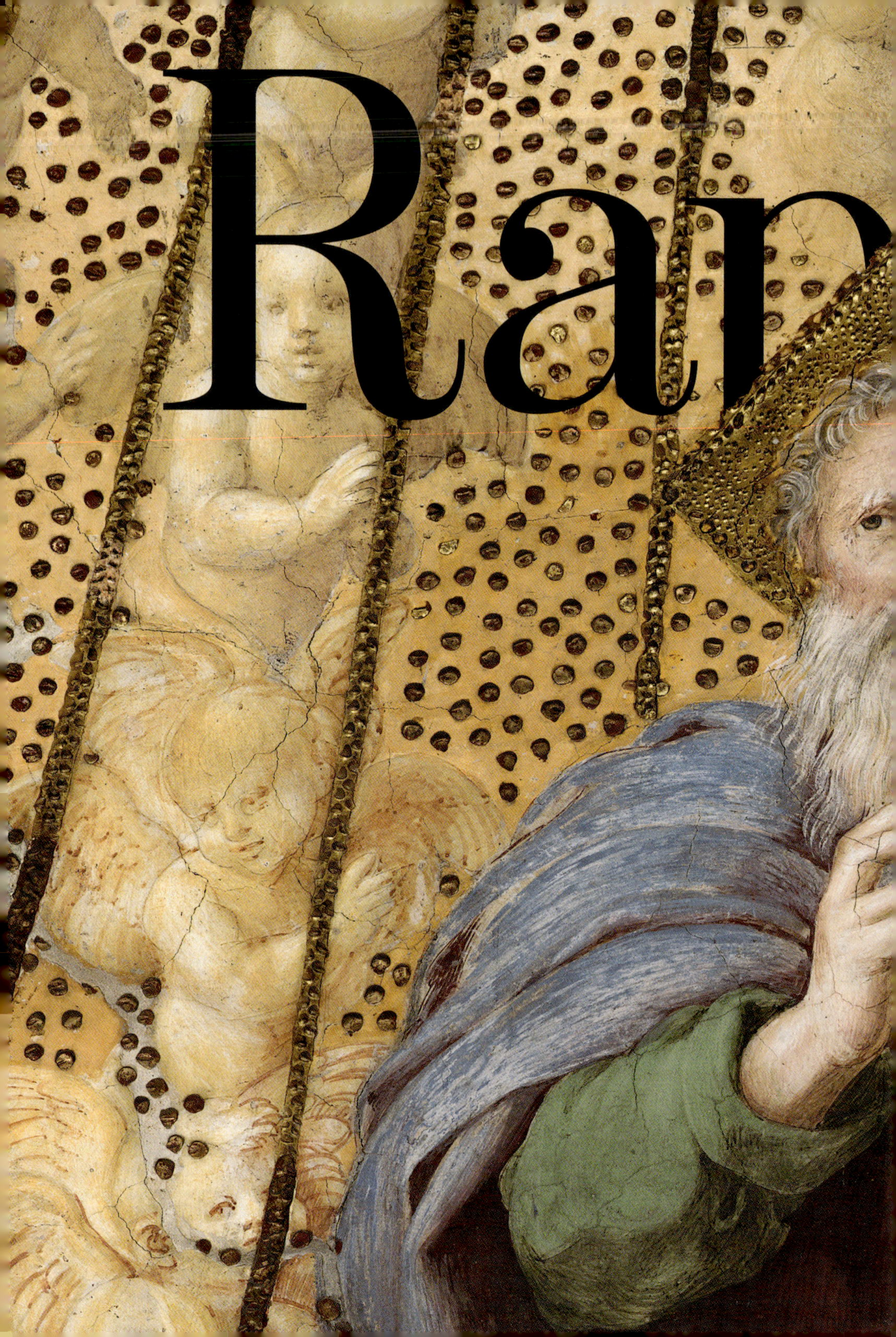
Ra

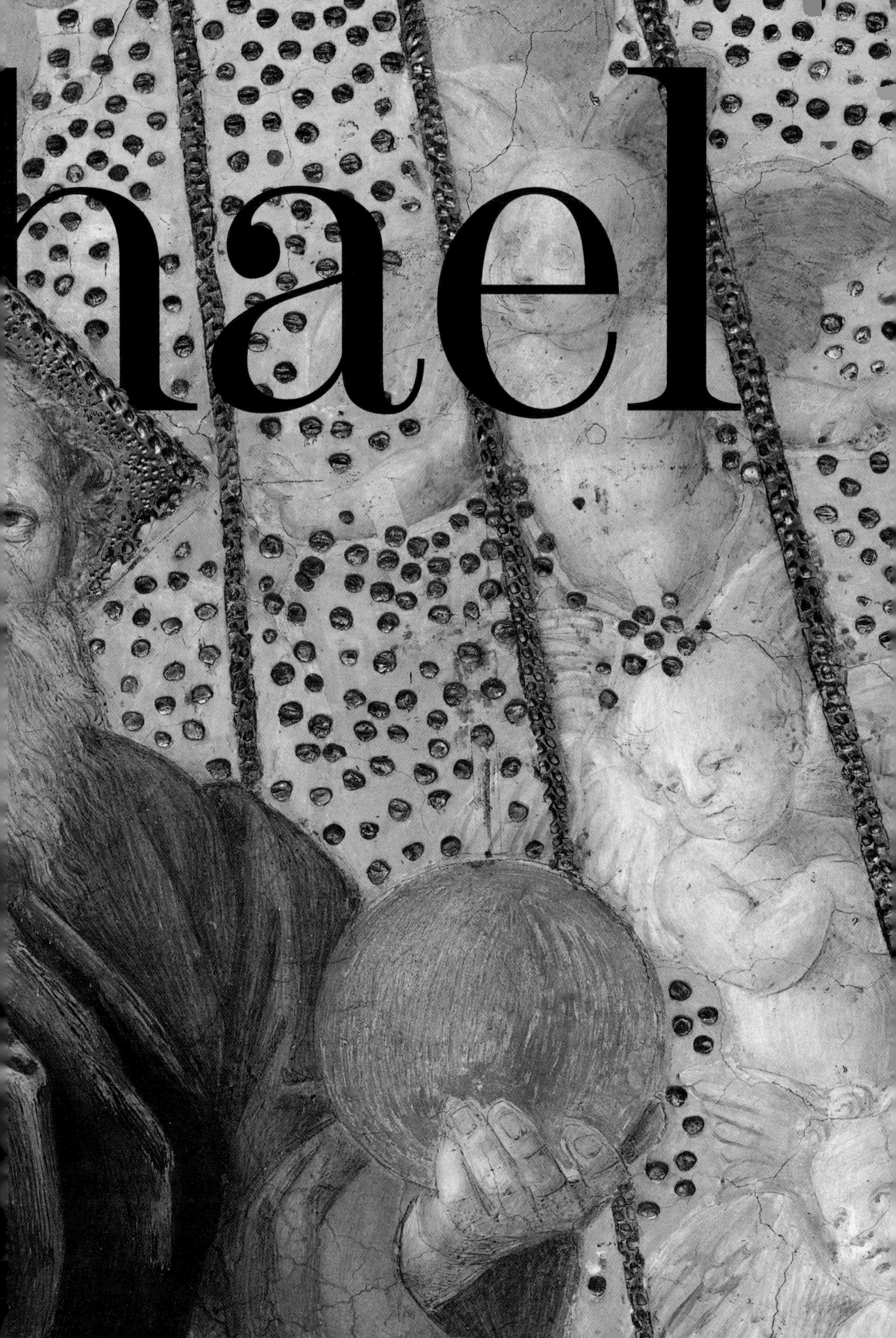

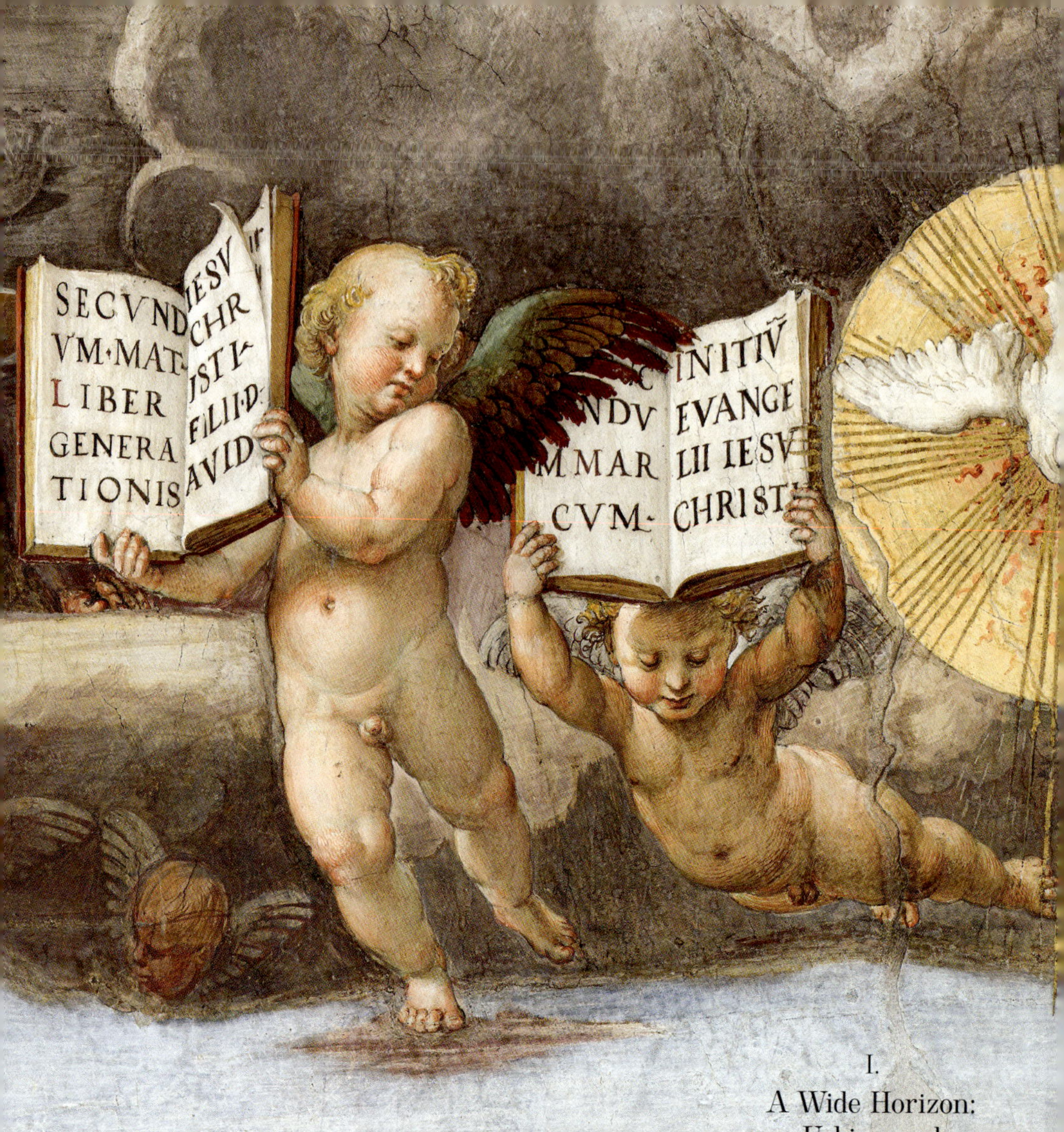

Paintings, Frescoes, Tapestries

Michael Rohlmann

Directed and produced by
Benedikt Taschen

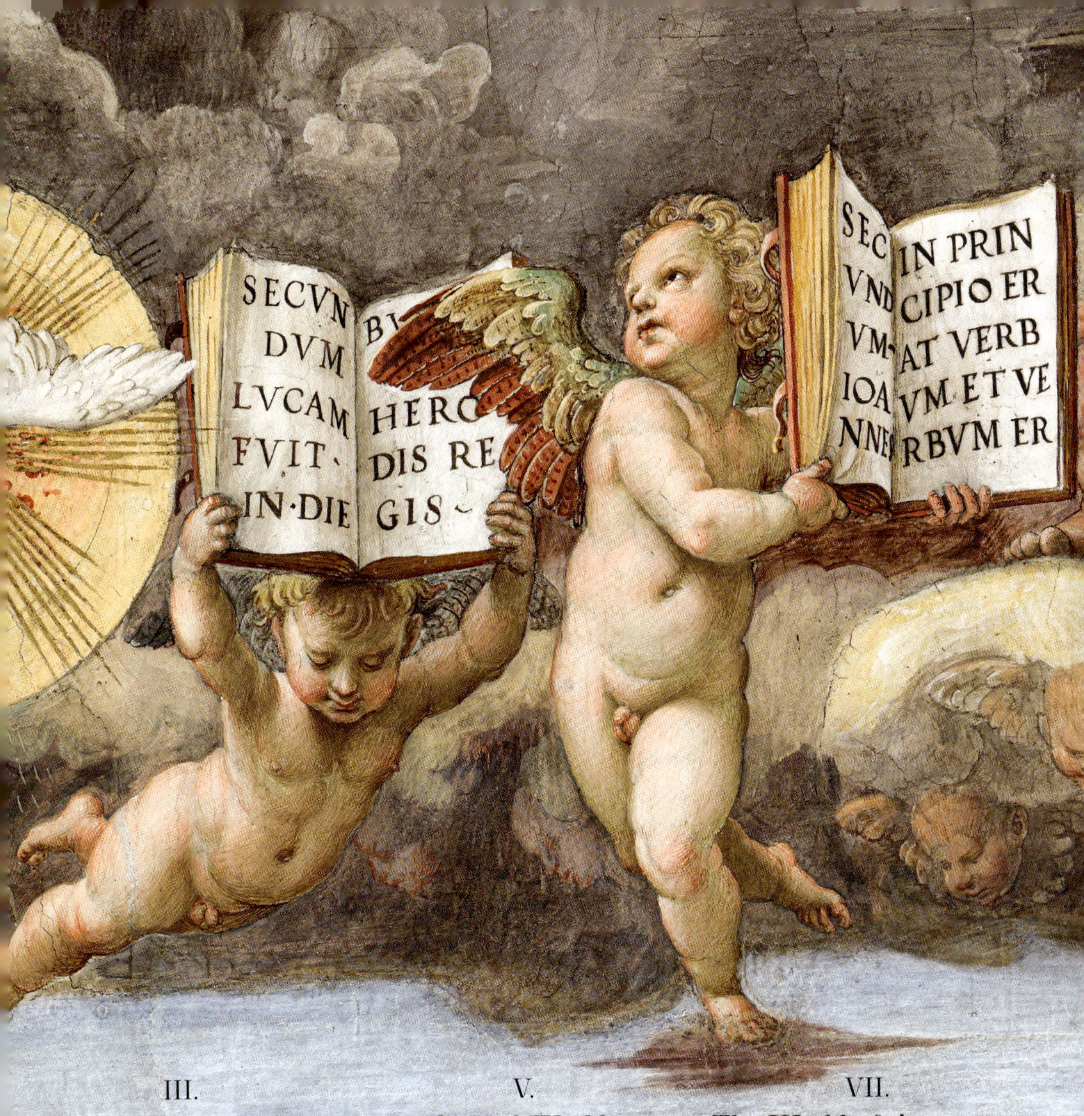
SECVN
DVM
LVCAM
FVIT·
IN·DIE
HERO
DIS RE
GIS
SEC
VND
VM-
IOA
NNE
IN PRIN
CIPIO ER
AT VERB
VM ET VE
RBVM ER

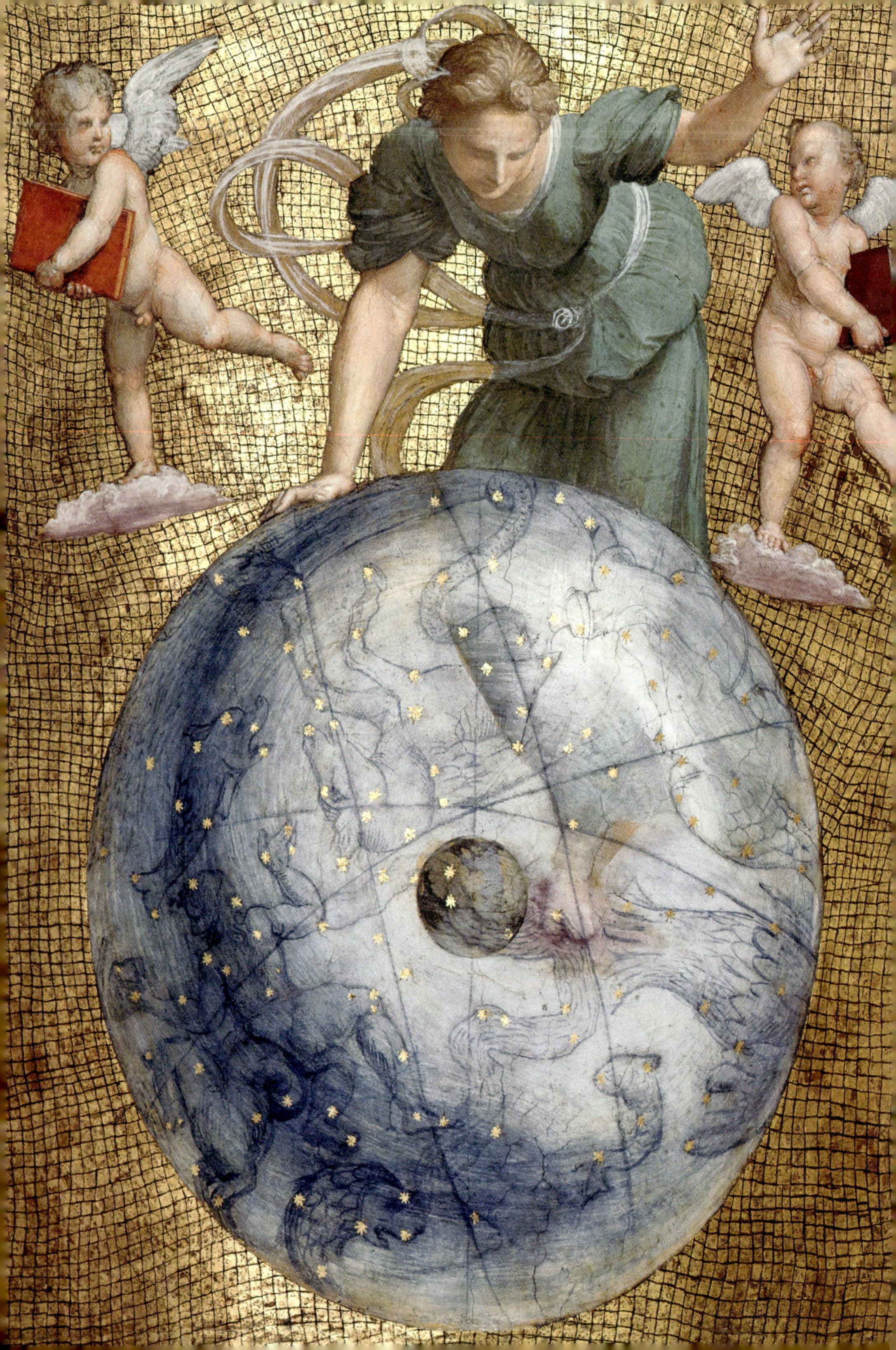

Foreword

Raphael's fame has glittered for five centuries. The beauty and uniqueness of his art appear astonishing, even inconceivable to this day: mysterious grace is combined with masterly lightness, elegance with naturalness, animate humanity with lofty ideal. The charm and melodiousness of the individual merges with the unmatched harmony of the whole. Raphael's *venustà*, his loveliness, warms our heart, his *poesia* makes us dream, his rhetoric moves us and his drama grips us. How versatile, how rich and varied is Raphael's oeuvre! From subdued, gentle and delicate beginnings, there proceed smiling grace and unfettered artistic freedom, then wealth of invention, grandeur, dignity and power. A dramatic world opens up; crowd scenes swell to the point of intense, theatrical clarity. Calm beauty gives way to sought-after artifice, balance becomes rhythm. The miraculous draughtsman and painter genius now also becomes the great decorator, the supplier of ideas and designer, the head, controller and teacher of a professional workshop. Raphael's life seems to be a never-ending course of study, an unceasing adaptation, improvement and enrichment. No one was as capable as he of transforming the most diverse external sources into something wholly his own. His much vaunted universality encompasses the fullness of human life, activity and feeling, the entire beauty, variety and spirit of art, nature and the world of things, and the fantasy and play of ornament. All of this is placed, in a deliberately selective fashion, in the service of the artistic task at hand and precisely tailored to the concrete functions and intentions of individual works and the content they aim to express.

Raphael's artistic variety and wealth of expression have inspired a vast body of art literature from the sixteenth century onwards. Early highlights are Vasari's *Life of Raphael* (1550/68) and Bellori's inspired interpretations of Raphael's oeuvre (1695), the first

Observation of the Cosmos, 1508/09
Representation in the Stanza della Segnatura ceiling fresco
(see ill. pp. 186/187)

complete critical survey by Passavant (1839/58), and, in the late nineteenth century, the great biographies by Grimm (1872-1896), Springer (1878-1883), Crowe/Cavalcaselle (1882/85) and Müntz (1881). These were followed by masterly formal and stylistic analyses by Wölfflin (1899), Hetzer (1932, 1947) and Freedberg (1961, 1971). The monographs by Fischel (1948) and Schöne (1958) still remain full of insights into Raphael's art. Numerous studies by Shearman (as from 1961) and Oberhubers (as from 1962) broke new ground. Large catalogues raisonnés appeared: of the drawings (Fischel as from 1913; Knab/Mitsch/Oberhuber/Ferino 1983; Joannides 1983), the paintings (Dussler 1966, 1971; Meyer zur Capellen 2001–2008) and the documents (Shearman 2003). Among the many treatments of Raphael's complete works in more recent times, the forthright Oberhuber (1982, 1999), the balanced Jones/Penny (1983) and the thoughtful Williams (2017) stand out. Countless individual studies, conference proceedings, exhibition and inventory catalogues, scientific investigations and restoration programmes have enriched and corrected our image of Raphael – and will undoubtedly continue to do so in the future.

This text originated in 2018/19 as an overview of Raphael's life and major works. It was originally supposed to be available in 2020 for the 500th anniversary of his death, but this was prevented by the consequences of the pandemic. Its first publication in 2022 was accompanied with studies of Raphael's architecture by Georg Satzinger and Nicole Riegel, but especially by a comprehensive annotated catalogue of works, mainly prepared by Frank Zöllner and Rudolf Hiller von Gaertringen (Rohlmann/Zöllner/Hiller von Gaertringen/Satzinger 2022). It includes additions and explanations, important evidence, and a summary of the current state of research. The dates and attributions of works in the present edition were taken from this publication. The extensive bibliography has been reduced to a few key titles, but supplemented for this purpose with current studies.

Many other publications and projects planned for the Raphael anniversary could be realised only after a delay due to the pandemic. Meanwhile, the literature survey by Ferino-Pagdens (2024) provides an overview of exhibitions and scientific results. I would like to emphasize the catalogues of the major Raphael exhibitions in Rome (2020, 2023) and London (2022), or the monographs by Farinella (2021), Turner (2022) and Joannides (2022). Some new collections on Raphael's activity in the Vatican offer important information (Cosgriff/Wingfield 2021, Jatta/Cimino 2023).

The world has changed since 2020, while Raphael's art seems more welcome than ever. It glorifies and transfigures a beautiful, thoughtful humanity that with calm equanimity and dignity still feels deeply and sympathises even more deeply. Love radiates from it with endless nuances, swirling around mother and child, man and wife, friends and companions. The pictures luxuriate in the allure of female and male bodies. The individual figures act with inner freedom, yet always in terms of their neighbours and the whole while intertwined in a web of social, reciprocal consideration and effect. The shapes and buildings also harmonise respectfully with the forms of the increasingly opulent landscape – man and nature attuned to each other.

Countless figures of children embody a compelling ideal of innocent happiness. The advancement of education leads the people in the Stanza della Segnatura to seek and contend for knowledge and truth. Thinking, teaching and learning appear as a never-ending task shared by all. Poetry and music imbue community with greater harmony. In the tapestries of the Apostles, individuals are raised from humiliation to become leaders – not of their own volition, but because they are called to the role. Property relieves the distress of the needy. Rulership aims for justice, strength, wisdom and moderation. The imperial lawmaker seeks wise counsel; the old, determined Pope considers the transience of all existence.

However, Raphael's art not only enriches its viewers with a profusion of models of desire, but demands and encourages empathy and emotional compassion because the pleasant order is often endangered. Age, illness and physical afflictions call for care. Painting lets the lame walk again, heals the sick, rescues the attacked. *Morbetto* even brings us to face a deadly plague. We see war and violence, banishment and flight, the city and countryside burning, the horrific details of combat, privation, suffering and death. We hear children's cries for help and their mothers' pleading. But a powerful individual forcefully resists during the *Bearing of the Cross*. In *Attila* a Pope fearlessly rides towards the conquest-seeking warmonger with the sign of peace. In *The Fire in the Borgo*, the catastrophic fire is fought as a collective effort. How rich and multifaceted are the laments and suffering as Christ is borne to the grave in *The Deposition*. Raphael's subjects often help and support one another. Their belief in a higher power gives them strength: may the bars not hold, and the prison burst open. In the *Transfiguration*, however, the painter's last great work before his death, even the heroes of the Church are powerless and helpless in facing their distress, while the transfigured Christ shines above as a sign of hope and consolation. It is like a vision of that higher beauty, of an idealised, desirable existence, of a nature and world with whose perspective Raphael's work for five hundred years has given its admirers moments of happiness and hope as if by a gentle urge.

Michael Rohlmann

I.

A Wide Horizon: Urbino and Umbria

1500/01–1504

Michael Rohlmann

"The heavens in their infinite generosity sometimes seem to bestow their endlessly abundant treasures, favours and rarest gifts on a single person rather than dividing them over time between many different individuals. This was clearly the case with Raphael Sanzio from Urbino."

GIORGIO VASARI, 1550

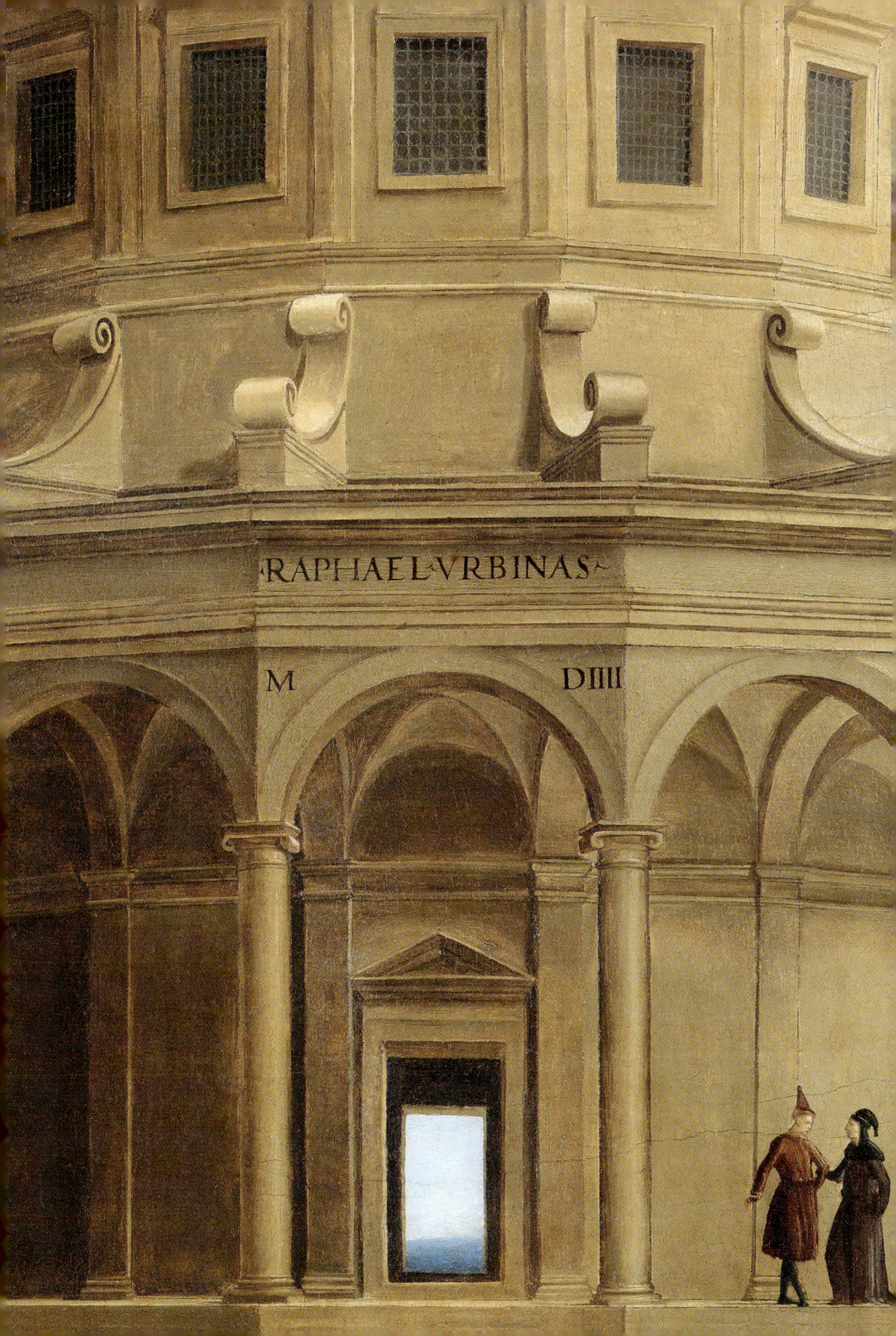
RAPHAEL VRBINAS
M
DIIII

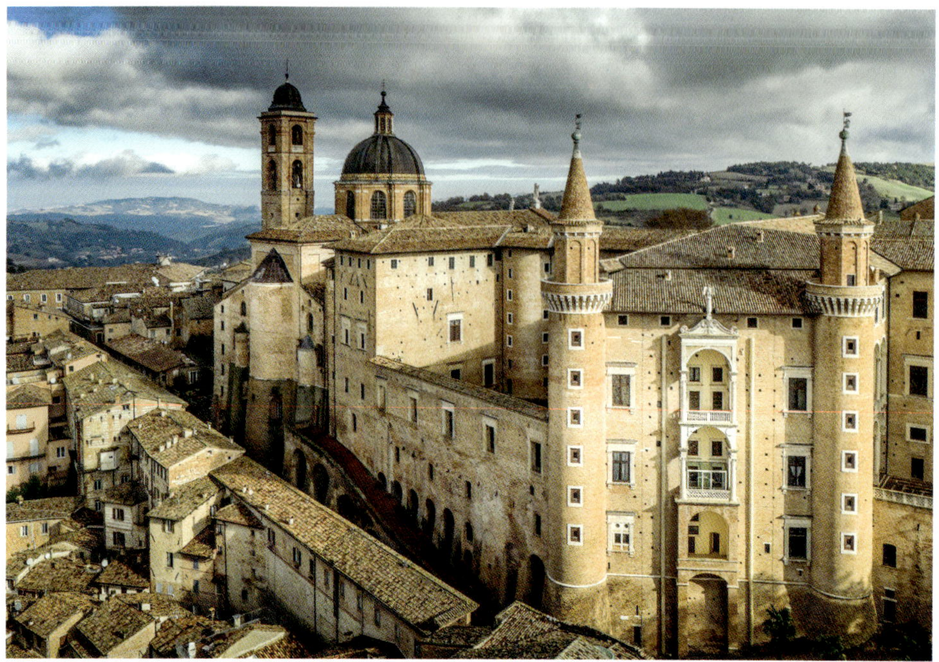

Raphael from Urbino – RAPHAEL VRBINAS: with this signature, which he used from his early days in Umbria, then in Florence and finally in Rome, the artist linked himself and his oeuvre with the hillside town in Italy's Marche region, where he was born in the spring of 1483 (on 28 March or 6 April). Then as now, the streets and narrow flights of steps between the old, dark brick houses lead, from Urbino's central square, south to the hilltop with the cathedral and ducal palace, and north to the rise with the old papal fortress. From the Palazzo Ducale, the sweeping view offers a panorama of the Apennines, whose distant peaks remain covered in snow late into spring. As if it had sprung from the dream of an ancient or medieval knight, the façade of the Palazzo, with its loggia balconies framed between two round towers, rises above the road to Umbria and on to Rome, once the centre of the Papal States to which the duchy of Urbino at that time belonged as a papal fief. From this northern elevation, narrow strips of blue sea can be seen on clear

Page 13
Detail from **The Marriage of the Virgin (Lo Sposalizio/Pala Albizzini)**, 1504
(see ill. p. 61)

View of Urbino and the façade of the Palazzo Ducale

Loggia of the Palazzo Ducale in Urbino

days: glittering in the east between the mountains and hills, they belong to the Adriatic, with its chain of wealthy coastal towns lying along the old Roman road.

The house in which Raphael was born still stands on the main road leading to the northern hill, diagonally opposite the monastery and church of the Franciscans, where his parents were buried after their early death. Raphael's great-grandfather, Peruzzolo di Piero, had brought the family to Urbino from the small town of Colbordolo before the middle of the fifteenth century. Raphael's grandfather Sante (died 1484), a merchant and gilder, after whom his descendants called themselves "Santi", had bought the house. Two daughters and two sons grew up. Raphael's father Giovanni (before 1439–1494) became painter and court artist to the ducal family, while Bartolomeo became parish priest of the *pieve* (parish) of San Donato just outside the city, next to which the ducal mausoleum church of San Bernardino, with its idealised design, was built.

The ruler of Urbino until his death in 1482 was Federico da Montefeltro (born 1422), the illegitimate offspring of a dynasty of counts that had ruled Urbino for two centuries. As a military entrepreneur and the most famous condottiere of his epoch, Federico – left one-eyed after a jousting accident – played a part in Italian politics and stood behind the wealth and heyday of the hillside town. Through him Urbino became a mythical site of Renaissance culture. In a new, vast Renaissance palace, Federico created a glittering court of the Muses, true to the humanist concept that military weapons and literary education, *arma et litterae*, belonged together. Federico's son Guidobaldo (1472–1508) was raised by his uncle Ottaviano della Carda after his father's death. In 1488 he married Elisabetta Gonzaga (1471–1526), daughter of the Marquis of Mantua. Since their union remained childless, in 1504 Guidobaldo adopted his nephew Francesco Maria della Rovere (1490–1538), the son of his sister Giovanna (1463–1513) from her marriage to a relative of Pope Sixtus IV (born Francesco della Rovere, 1414–1484; in office from 1471). Julius II (born Giuliano della Rovere, 1443–1513), elected pope in 1503, was Francesco Maria's uncle. Guidobaldo's

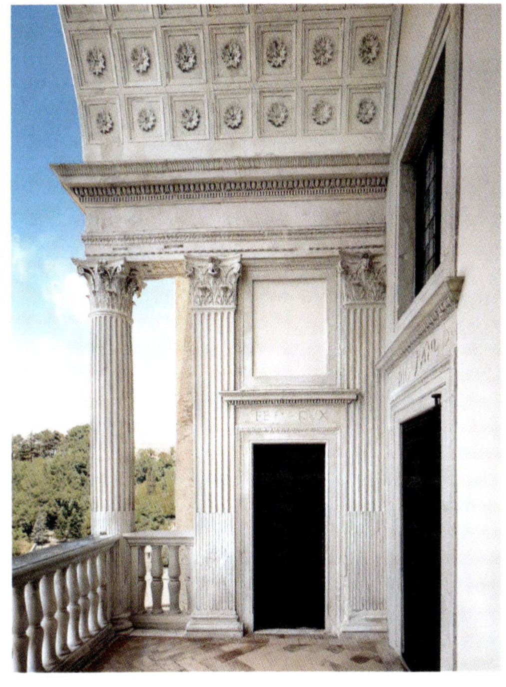

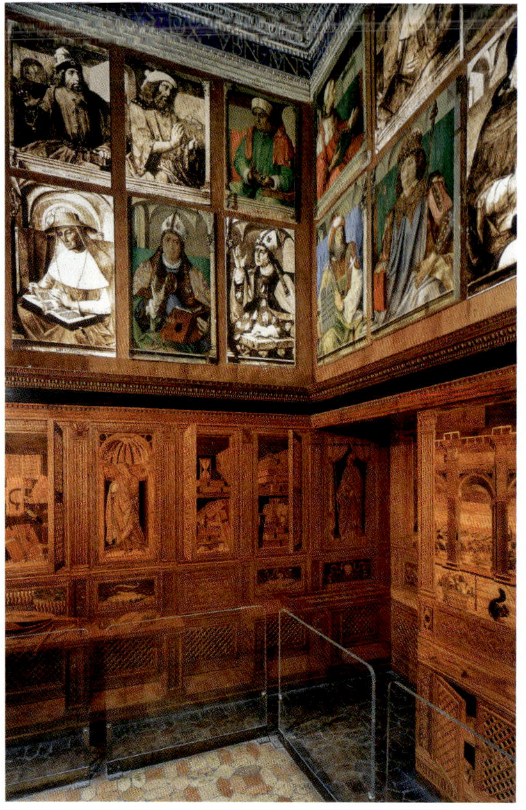

court also included Baldassare Castiglione (1478–1529), who later painted an ideal picture of intellectually learned and inspired evening conversations between the ducal family and their guests in his *Book of the Courtier*, and thereby outlined the qualities of the perfect courtier that would become a model for aristocratic elites throughout Europe.

In 1480 Giovanni Santi married Magia Ciarla, who came from a merchant family. Apart from Raphael, the couple had two other children, both of whom died young. On 7 October 1491, Raphael lost his mother; in May 1492 his father married Berardina (Bernardina), the daughter of a goldsmith. At the end of 1493 the Duchess of Urbino sent Giovanni Santi to Mantua, where he was to paint her sister-in-law, Isabella d'Este (1474–1539) – Elisabetta Gonzaga had not been satisfied with a portrait by Andrea Mantegna (1431–1506). Ill, Giovanni returned to Urbino at the end of July 1494 and died on 1 August. He had appointed his brother Don Bartolomeo as guardian ("tutor" and "curator") of his young son. Bartolomeo initiated legal proceedings against Giovanni's widow over her right to live in the Santi family home, which only ended with a settlement in 1500.

Giovanni Santi was not only a gifted painter of religious devotional panels and altarpieces, but also a man of letters with a humanist education. For special occasions at the ducal court, he wrote and staged plays and pageants in an antique style, in which the figures of gods and allegories appeared. After Federico da Montefeltro's death, he

Palazzo Ducale in Urbino: the Studiolo

Pedro Berruguete, **Federico da Montefeltro and His Son Guidobaldo**, *c.* 1476/77
Oil on panel, 138.5 × 82.5 cm (54 ½ × 32 ½ in)
Urbino, Palazzo Ducale, Galleria Nazionale delle Marche

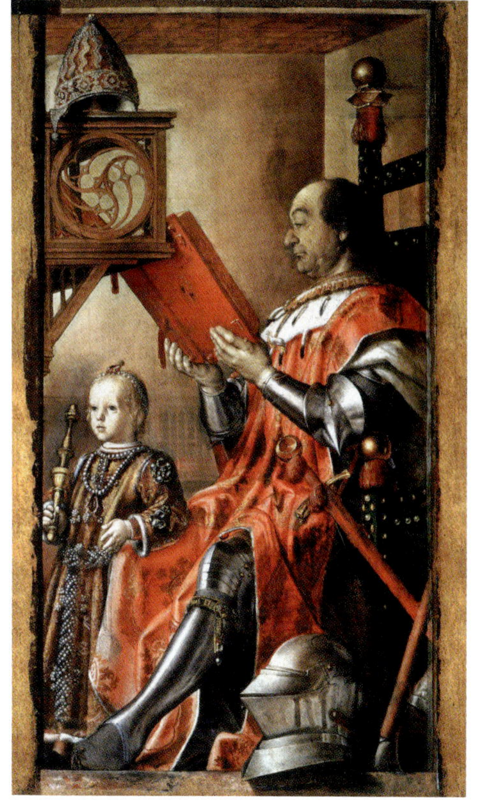

spent many years composing a rhymed *Chronicle* of the duke's life and achievements. It includes a section on painting, in which Santi offers an astonishing panorama that represents the most comprehensive and soundly judged list of artists to have come down us from the fifteenth century. It begins with Andrea Mantegna, the greatest master of all areas of painting in Italy and beyond. Next come the famous Early Netherlandish masters Jan van Eyck (*c.* 1390–1441) and Rogier van der Weyden (1399/1400–1464), who with their painting and colour technique – claims Santi – surpassed nature many times over ("che han superati molte volte il vero"). In Italy, Gentile da Fabriano (*c.* 1370–1427) and Fra Angelico (*c.* 1395–1455) stood out, along with Pisanello (1395–1455), Filippo Lippi (*c.* 1406–1469), Pesellino (1422–1457), Domenico Veneziano (*c.* 1410–1461), Masaccio (1401–1428), Castagno (*c.* 1419–1457), Uccello (1397–1475), Antonio (*c.* 1431–1498) and Piero Pollaiuolo (1443–1496) – the brothers described as outstanding draughtsmen ("si gran designatori") – and Piero della Francesca (*c.* 1416–1492) from Borgo San Sepolcro. Next come two illustrious young men of the same age, Leonardo da Vinci (1452–1519) and the divine painter Pietro Perugino (1445/48–1523), then Domenico Ghirlandaio (1448–1494), Filippino Lippi (1457–1504), Botticelli (1445–1510) and the talented, ingenious Luca Signorelli (1445–1523). Living outside Tuscany, meanwhile, were Antonello da Messina (*c.* 1430–1479), Giovanni (*c.* 1430–1516) and Gentile Bellini (*c.* 1429–1507), Cosme Tura (*c.* 1430–1495) and his rival Ercole de' Roberti (*c.* 1450–1496), along with many others ("e molti ch'hor trapasso"). The list ends with Melozzo da Forlì (1438–1494), who was so dear to Santi ("a me si caro") and so advanced in the art of perspective. Here, as in no other contemporary source, we gain a palpable sense of a breadth of horizon, a knowledge of the diversity of artistic personalities in different parts of Italy and even beyond. As a painter, Santi followed first and foremost Piero della Francesca, Perugino, Melozzo da Forlì and the Early Netherlandish masters. Raphael would later

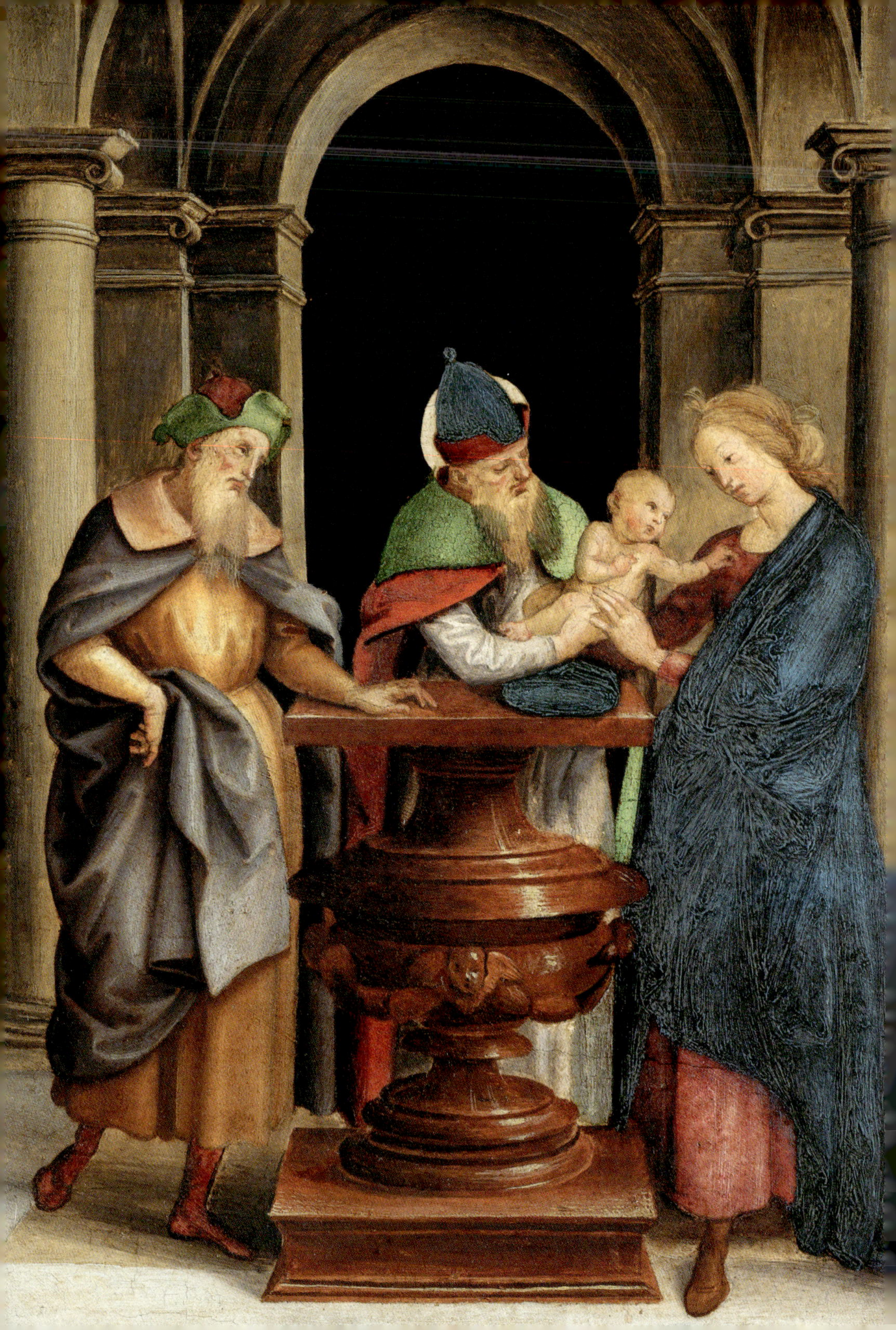

study, copy and imitate many of the artists named by Santi. The father's knowledge would only truly bear fruit in the work of the son.

Santi was aware that Urbino, its palace, churches and the surrounding area offered an unusually broad spectrum of outstanding art to study: not only paintings in local traditional styles, but also Umbrian, Florentine and Venetian art imports, and even works by the Early Netherlandish masters. In fifteenth-century Italy, these last were the most prized of all on account of their oil-painting technique, with its naturalistic details, gleaming depth of colour and breathtaking suggestion of materiality. Raphael must have studied all of these and would draw inspiration, even many years later, from the memories of his childhood and youth. Federico's brother, Ottaviano della Carda, owned the particularly admired painting of women bathing by the famous Jan van Eyck. The picture, which is today lost, showed naked female bodies seen from various sides (see Cat. F11; the catalogue references refer to the original edition's catalogue [TASCHEN, 2022]), as well as mirror effects and views into distant landscapes painted in minute detail. A Crucifixion triptych in the collection of Federico's father-in-law in Pesaro testified to Rogier van der Weyden's art of portraying emotions. In order to be able to commission works himself in the exquisite oil technique of the North, Federico engaged Justus van Gent (Joos van Wassenhove; *c.* 1410–*c.* 1480) to come to Urbino from Flanders. Joos did not stay long, and a Flemish-trained Spanish colleague, probably Pedro Berruguete (*c.* 1450–1504), appears to have completed many of the projects. The highlight of their work in Urbino, and at the same time of the palace decorations commissioned by Federico, was the Duke's small Studiolo. The lower part of the walls were lined with magnificent intarsia (inlaid wood) panels: Florentine marvels of linear perspective, they conveyed the illusion of latticework cabinets filled with books and objects. Above them ran two horizontal rows of paintings of learned men. The lower row, distinguished by its taller format, showed three-quarter-length portraits of religious scholars, the upper row half-length portraits of secular scholars. It was recognised early on that this room, with its intarsia and its evaluative juxtaposition of secular and spiritual knowledge, served as a decisive model for Raphael's Stanza della Segnatura in the Vatican Palace in Rome (Cat. F3.1). The Muses and Apollo likewise depicted in the Stanza della Segnatura could be found in Urbino one floor below the Studiolo as a series of paintings by Giovanni Santi and Timoteo Viti (1469–1523). The palace's large reception hall was adorned with a vast cycle of Flemish tapestries over 100 metres in length, which Federico had managed to acquire in 1476 for an enormous sum of money. The theme of the cycle was the Trojan War, and its tightly packed

Detail from **The Presentation at the Temple (Oddi Altarpiece, predella)**, 1503/04
(see ill. pp. 56/57)

representations showed cavalry battles as crowd scenes. Raphael later designed such battle scenes – in this case *all'antica* – as simulated tapestries for the large reception room at the Vatican Palace (Cat. F4). A landscape-format painting showing a view of an ideal city in the antique style probably served as a sopraporte; its attribution remains the subject of dispute even today (pp. 24/25). This miracle of perspective construction, with its illusion of space and light, must have made a deep impression on Raphael. Its influence can be traced from the early *Sposalizio* (Cat. P13) to the Acts of the Apostles tapestries in Rome (Cat. T8, T10) and late theatre designs. Under Guidobaldo, the mathematician Luca Pacioli (*c.* 1445–*c.* 1517) resided at the Urbino court, where Jacopo de' Barbari (c. 1460/70–*c.* 1516) painted him in a double portrait probably with the young duke (p. 23). The work became a model for Raphael's late group portraits (Cat. P79, P83). The combination of idealised architecture and groups of figures, and its effect, could be studied in the Santa Maria della Bella altarpiece by Fra Carnevale (*c.* 1420/25–1484) and – in a more solemn and sublime form – in Piero della Francesca's *Brera Madonna* (p. 21), which was installed in the Montefeltro burial church near the parish of Raphael's uncle (see Cat. F3.1j). Piero della Francesca even stayed with Giovanni Santi as a guest, when he came to Urbino to negotiate the production of an altarpiece for the confraternity of Corpus Christi. In the end, however, the *Communion of the Apostles* altarpiece was painted by Justus van Gent. Giovanni Santi, who – like Raphael later – was also a member of the confraternity, copied the figure of Christ in the painting, and Raphael himself quoted it in a *Procession to Calvary* predella panel (pp. 104/105; Cat. P22g) in Perugia. This list of Urbino's stylistically so wide-ranging holdings of paintings could easily be continued. Raphael would fall back on them all his life. And yet it is plain that his earliest identifiable works have their most important source not in Urbino.

The documents are silent about Raphael's path to painting, his training, and his first works. Reliable historical sources are found only as from 1500, when the young Raphael appears as a painter in Umbria. His father Giovanni, before his death in 1494, would undoubtedly have had time to teach the child the basic foundations and first steps in art. A Vatican document dated 1511 describes Raphael as a pupil of John (i. e. Giovanni) of Urbino ("Johannis de Urbino scolari"). Art historians have identified isolated examples, in Raphael's early oeuvre in Umbria, of motifs adopted from his father's representational formulae and workshop props. Raphael later received his first major commission in Città di Castello together with his father's former colleague, Evangelista da Pian di Meleto (*c.* 1458–1549). Some authors suspect that Evangelista took over the running of Santi's workshop, but there is no firm evidence for this. Timoteo Viti, who had trained in Bologna, returned to Urbino soon after Santi's death, and some art historians consider that he became Raphael's teacher as from this point. No clear idea can be gained of Viti's

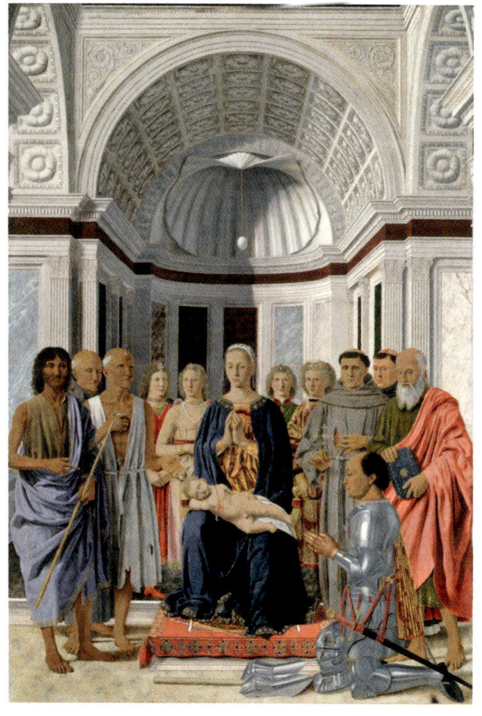

Piero della Francesca
Virgin and Child with Saints and Federico da Montefeltro (Brera Madonna), *c.* 1470/75
Oil and tempera on panel, 251 × 172 cm (98 ⅞ × 67 ¾ in)
Milan, Pinacoteca di Brera

early work in Urbino, it is true, but Raphael is said to have engaged him later on in Rome as an assistant for the frescoes in Santa Maria della Pace. There is a single mention, after 1592, of one Benedetto Coda in Rimini as the young Raphael's teacher.

Giorgio Vasari (1511–1574), on the other hand, in his *Life of Raphael* published in 1550 and in a second edition in 1568, names the Umbrian painter Pietro Perugino as Raphael's teacher. Perugino had trained in Florence and maintained a workshop there as well as in Perugia. He had painted important frescoes for Pope Sixtus IV in Rome. In 1488 he was described by a notary as the leading painter in all Italy ("pictor in Italia tota primus") and in 1500 by the merchant Agostino Chigi (1466–1520) as Italy's best master ("il miglior maestro d'Italia"). His painting style, with its gently moving, refined, slender figures inclining their heads in meditative fashion, was considered angelic ("aria angelica"), sweet and gentle ("molto dolce"). He had developed hallmark images of a celestially beautiful, pious world filled with soulfully graceful figures, which he successfully repeated as devotional paintings in a large workshop. The stylistic affinity between Raphael's first identified works and Perugino's forms and motifs is profound and unmistakable and has been regularly analysed in the literature. But for contemporary patrons of the arts, too, the young Raphael's proximity to Perugino was common fact. Thus Pope Leo X (born

Giovanni di Lorenzo de' Medici, 1475–1521; in office from 1513) observed in 1520 that, before he had seen works by Michelangelo (1475–1564), Raphael painted in the manner of Perugino. Ascanio Condivi (1525–1574) reported in 1553 that Raphael learned a different style from Michelangelo than from his father Giovanni Santi and from Perugino, his master ("suo maestro"). Vasari embellishes his account of this master-pupil relationship in literary fashion, recounting that Giovanni Santi himself asked Perugino to train his son and then – "not without many tears from his mother" – took the boy to Perugia in person. In Santi's will, however, there is no mention of his son being apprenticed to Perugino, and the mother had died when Raphael was still far too young for an apprenticeship outside Urbino. In his rhymed *Chronicle*, however, Giovanni Santi calls Perugino a divine painter ("divin pictore"), which implies that he held him in exceptional esteem.

Santi clearly borrowed from Perugino's inventions in his own works and would also have known him personally. Perugino had not only been commissioned, in 1488, to produce the high altarpiece for the newly built church of Santa Maria Nuova at Fano, a town not far from Urbino on the Adriatic, but was also asked – probably in 1489 – to paint an Annunciation for a side altar. Santi complemented the church's programme of Marian iconography, culminating in the birth of Christ, with a Visitation about this same time. Perugino completed the high altarpiece only in 1497, and some suspect Raphael's involvement in the preliminary drawings for its predella. If true, this would place Raphael's apprenticeship with Perugino in the late 1490s. Those art historians, on the other hand, who believe that Raphael received his training solely in Urbino, consider that Raphael made an intensive study of Perugino's work and style only after 1500, i. e. at the same time as his own first major documented commissions in Umbria.

In addition to training with Perugino, Raphael probably also received an education at the Urbino court. Sebastiano Serlio (1475–*c.* 1554) reports in 1544 that Elisabetta – as the wife of Guidobaldo da Montefeltro, the Duchess of Urbino – had educated and supported Raphael in his youth. His particular talent must thereby have struck those around him, for when he is recorded on 4 May 1500, at the court case against his stepmother, as being present in Urbino, the young man is described as famous ("illustris"). On 10 December he was in Città di Castello, where as a master ("magister"), together with Evangelista, he concluded the contract for an altarpiece commissioned by Andrea di Tommaso Baronci for the church of Sant'Agostino (pp. 40–42; Cat. P2). It is his first documented work and the prelude to a whole series of altarpieces, initially in Città di Castello and subsequently also in Perugia.

Città di Castello lies in a wide valley on the upper reaches of the Tiber, north of Perugia and closer to Urbino. At that time, it was still ruled by the Vitelli, who – like their Montefeltro friends and neighbours – were a condottiere family. Urbino and Città

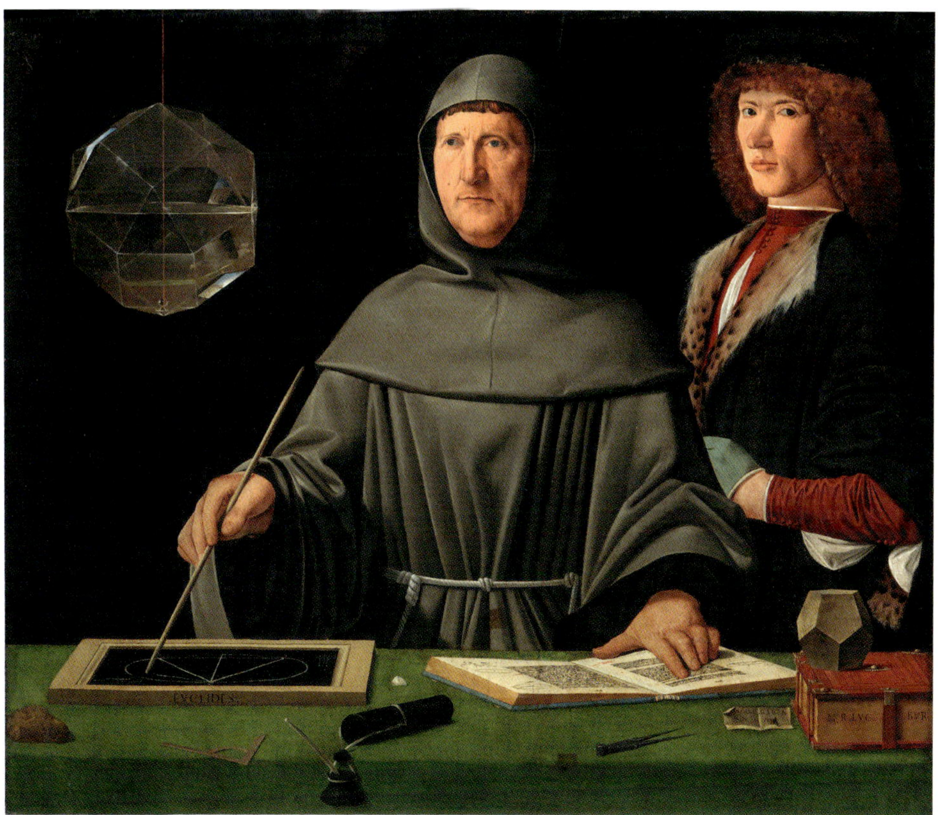

Jacopo de' Barbari, **Portrait of Luca Pacioli with a Companion (Guidobaldo da Montefeltro?)**, 1495
Oil on panel, 99 × 120 cm (38 ⅞ × 47 ¼ in). Naples, Museo e Gallerie Nazionali di Capodimonte

di Castello were linked by old and close ties. Indeed, the Umbrian town had even given Urbino its patron saint, when in the eleventh century it made a present of the relics of Saint Crescentianus (Crescentino) to the bishop of Urbino. That Raphael was first active in Città di Castello is undoubtedly also connected with the fact that Luca Signorelli, who for years had dominated the city's artistic production and supplied its altarpieces, in 1497/99 moved to Monteoliveto and then to Orvieto. In 1789 Sant'Agostino was destroyed by an earthquake and the Baronci altarpiece severely damaged, after which it was sold and the panel sawn into pieces. Fragments are today preserved in Naples, Brescia and Paris. Raphael's compositional study in Lille (p. 40 top left) and a partial copy made for the rebuilt church give us an idea of what was lost. Almost four metres in height, it was a monumental altarpiece even taller than Signorelli's high altarpiece in

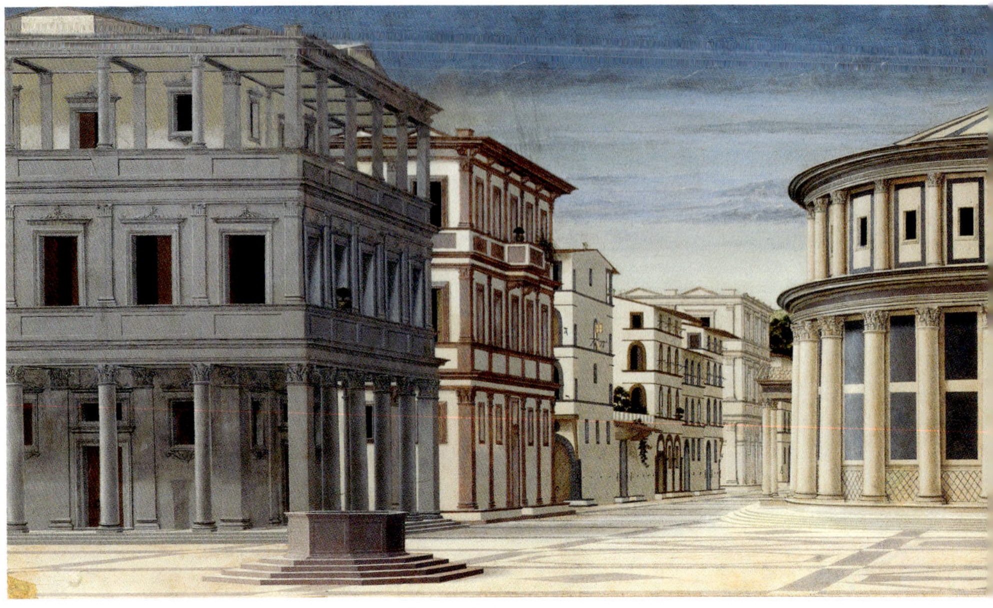

the same church. This latter showed the *Adoration of the Magi* and thus celebrated, in the worship of Christ by the Three Kings, the piety of the noble Vitelli elite. In competition with Signorelli's painting, Raphael's altarpiece was intended to represent the interests of the Augustinian Hermits at Sant'Agostino – propaganda for the Order in a prominent place opposite the side entrance of the church. The theme and iconography would have been decided by clerics, even if the commission was awarded by a member of the local upper class. Baronci had no children and was evidently dependent on the Order to ensure that his memory lived on – and so he placed his donation at the service of the Order and its interests. For the abbey, Nicholas of Tolentino (*c.* 1245–1305), who was only canonised in 1446, was to be celebrated in his virtues as the ideal of the Order. With his open book and crucifix, the saint stood elegantly and effortlessly triumphant on a devil stretched out on the ground. He was accompanied to the left and right by two angels, each with banderoles. Texts extolled the poverty, chastity and obedience of Nicholas, who brought honour to the Augustinian Order with miraculous signs and virtues; those who observed the Father's commandments remained in his favour. Floating overhead were the half-length figures of God the Father, the Virgin and Saint Augustine;

Anonymous, **Città ideale**
Oil on panel, 67.5 × 239.5 cm (26 5/8 × 94 1/4 in). Urbino, Palazzo Ducale, Galleria Nazionale delle Marche

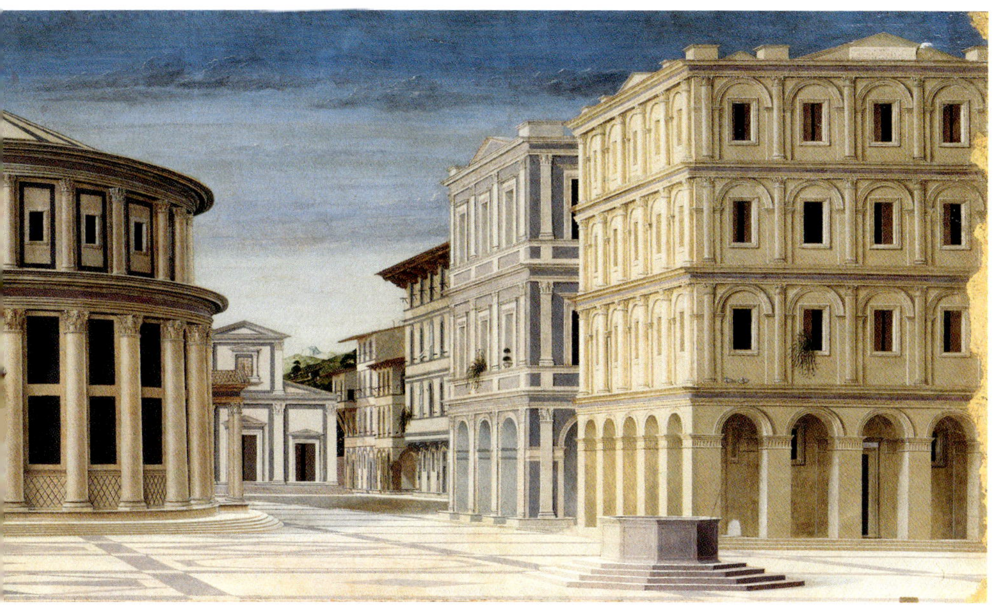

the latter is said to have appeared to Nicholas at his death. In the painting, they held three crowns over the saint as a reward for his various virtues and acts of service.

The composition was anchored by the pictorial architecture: the saint stood in the arch of a gatehouse with a view of the landscape and sky beyond. The two registers of angels and celestial figures were coordinated with the sides and vaulting of the architecture to form a framework around him. The painted building was probably taken up and extended by the architecture originally framing the altarpiece in real life, which thus lent the two-dimensional image a three-dimensional façade. Raphael seems to have adopted the painted architecture from Perugino, who had designed it previously for an altarpiece for Santa Maria degli Angeli in Perugia, not completed until 1502 and today in Marseille. Only in Raphael's hands, however, was it combined for the first time into a compelling functional whole with the figural composition and the pictorial frame. Raphael's figures likewise closely corresponded to Perugino's stylistic ideal in their dreamy soulfulness, graceful poses and the quiet rhythm of their subtle animation. How different Signorelli's high altarpiece must have appeared, with its earthly physicality and colourful throng. For the Augustinian Hermits, Raphael countered this with an image of a higher order: the gateway to a perfect world full of holiness beyond. Despite the kinship with Perugino in terms of motifs, there are striking differences in painting technique, something that may be due to the fact that large parts of Raphael's design were evidently executed by Evangelista.

Another commission unusually ambitious theologically was the processional banner that Raphael painted for the confraternity of the Trinity in Città di Castello. The front and back are today separated (Cat. P3a, b). The front shows the Crucifixion in a landscape. It is complemented with the Dove of the Holy Spirit and God the Father as symbols of the so-called Throne of Grace Trinity, and in this way illustrates the patronage of the confraternity. At the foot of the cross, kneeling in worship on either side, are the plague saints Sebastian and Roch – an epidemic of 1499 may have prompted the commission. When the banner was held up on its pole above the pious members of the confraternity, the Throne of Grace raised on the shaft of the cross above the kneeling figures in the picture was intended to mirror the appearance of the banner itself. The Trinity itself thus becomes a banner. In line with traditional biblical typology, the reverse shows an Old Testament antitype of the Crucifixion in a similar landscape. Once again God the Father appears, and once again a male nude is the focus of his concern. God has come down from heaven and bends over the sleeping Adam in order to take a rib from his side. From it, he will create Eve. Death and sleep are parallelised. Blood and water flowed from the wound in the side of Christ, the "new Adam". According to theological exegesis, this was to be understood as the birth of the redeeming institution of the Church, and was prefigured by the emergence of Eve from Adam's side. Such interpretative frameworks were spread from the thirteenth and fourteenth centuries onwards by the *Biblia pauperum* (Pauper's Bible) type of picture Bibles, including the *Bible moralisée* and *Armenbibel* (see Guldan 1966).

The stone frame of Raphael's second altarpiece commission in Città di Castello (Cat. P8) still stands in its original place, at the end of the right-hand side wall of the wide nave of the Dominican Church of San Domenico. An inscription on the frame names Domenico de' Gavari as the donor and the date as 1503. Gavari not only belonged to the same local ruling class as Baronci, but the two families must also have been close friends, since Baronci's widow appointed Gavari as her universal heir. The frame is inspired by that of Signorelli's *Martyrdom of Saint Sebastian*, which was located exactly opposite Raphael's retable on the left wall of the church. The main panel of Gavari's altarpiece shows the Christ's Crucifixion with the Virgin Mary, saints and angels (p. 45; Cat. P8a) and – as in the case of Raphael's Baronci altarpiece – was conceived as a deliberate pendant to Signorelli. The two works are directly connected in terms of theme: Signorelli's Sebastian, bound naked to the top of a wooden stake, is presented with Raphael's Christ on the Cross, the holy model whom the martyr, in his agony, is following. While Signorelli stages Sebastian's suffering as a savage thronging in a crowded composition with multiple

Detail from **The Annunciation (Oddi Altarpiece, predella)**, 1503/04
(see ill. pp. 54/55)

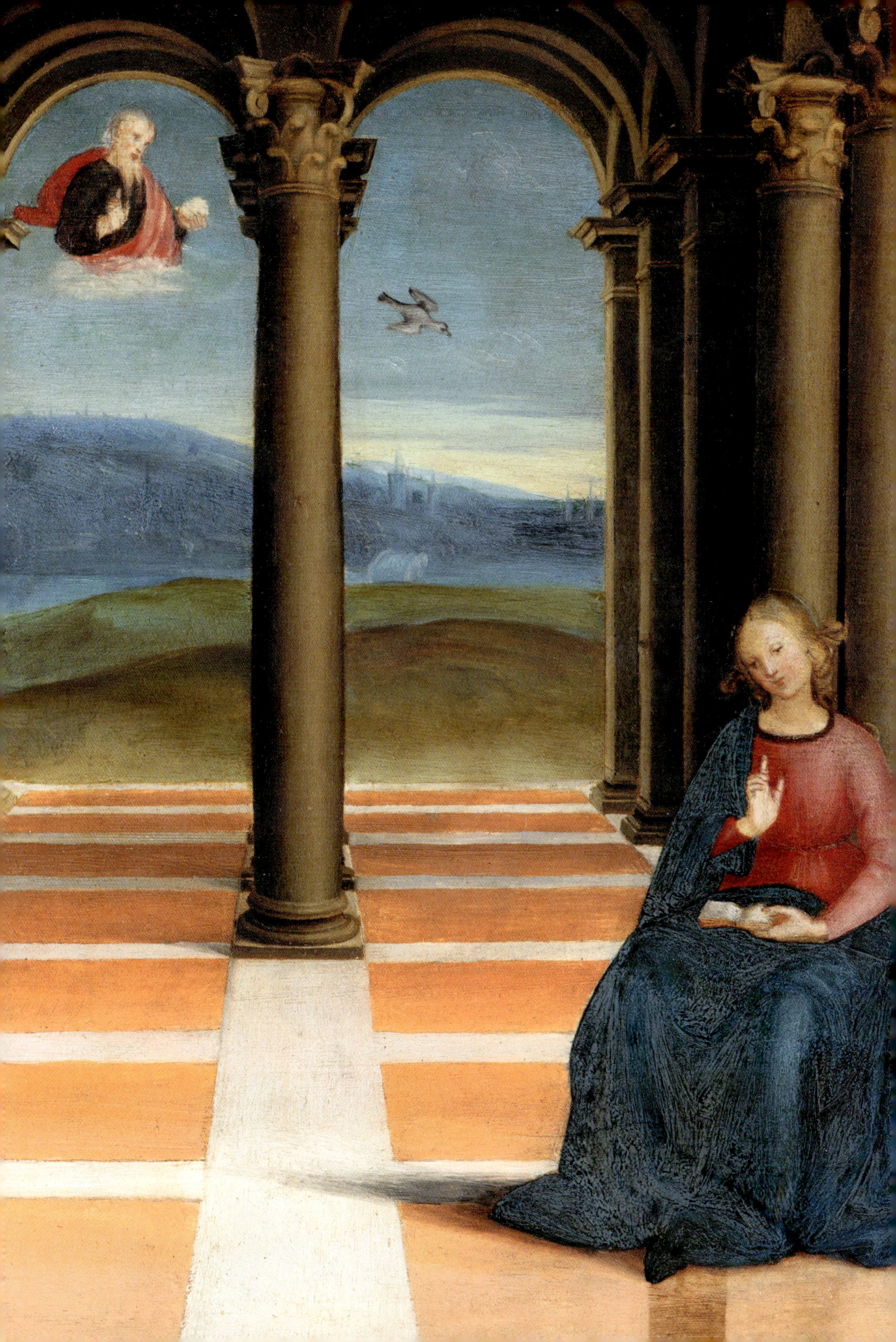

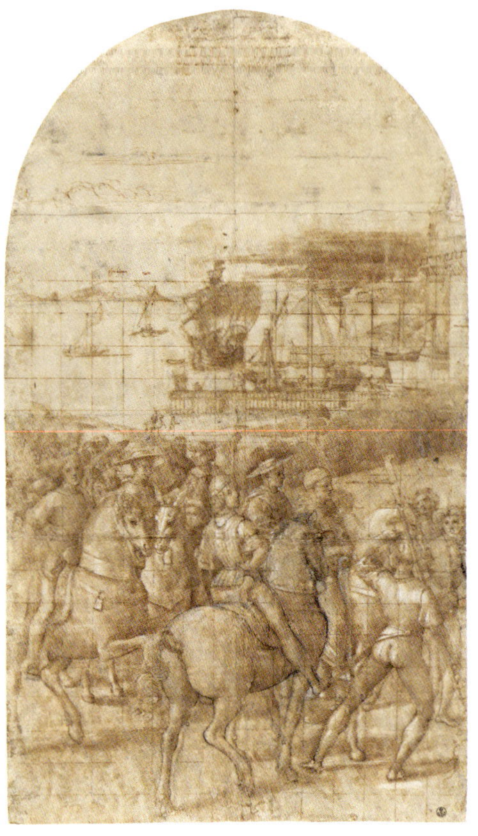

elements and deliberately difficult details, Raphael's Christ is already dead, the work of salvation has been accomplished and, as if in consequence, a magical stillness of supernatural transfiguration and harmony infuses the painting.

The quality of the picture has often been praised: the adaptation of the composition to the architectural surround, the delicate, free symmetry of forms and colours, and the integration of the semicircular top – dictated by the carved frame – into the circle of celestial motifs around Christ, the semicircle of the saints below and the gentle descent of the hills in the background towards the middle. The ornament of the angel's ribbon-like bands marks a celestial two-dimensionality of unreal, otherworldly beauty. By contrast, the pictorial space below gains earthly depth as a body of water leads calmly away into the far, infinite distance. The kinship with Perugino's style in terms of vibrancy of colour, elegance and delicacy of form has been analysed – as in the case of the motifs of the Trinity processional banner – many times. Indeed, Vasari himself had already been struck by the similarity.

Among Raphael's sources of inspiration for the *Crucified Christ* was another Perugino altarpiece that was still in the course of production in the latter's workshop (the Monteripido altarpiece). Unlike in Perugino's large-format Crucifixions, however, Raphael's Christ is shifted slightly to the left on the cross and, in the inclination of his head, is also directed towards Saint Jerome kneeling on the ground below and looking up.

Enea Silvio Piccolomini Leaves for the Council of Basel, 1503
Pen with wash, heightened with white, over traces of black metalpoint, squared in pen, 70.5 × 41.5 cm (27 ¾ × 16 ⅓ in). Florence, Gallerie degli Uffizi, Gabinetto dei Disegni e delle Stampe

Detail from **Resurrection of Christ**, *c.* 1499–1500
(see ill. p. 37)

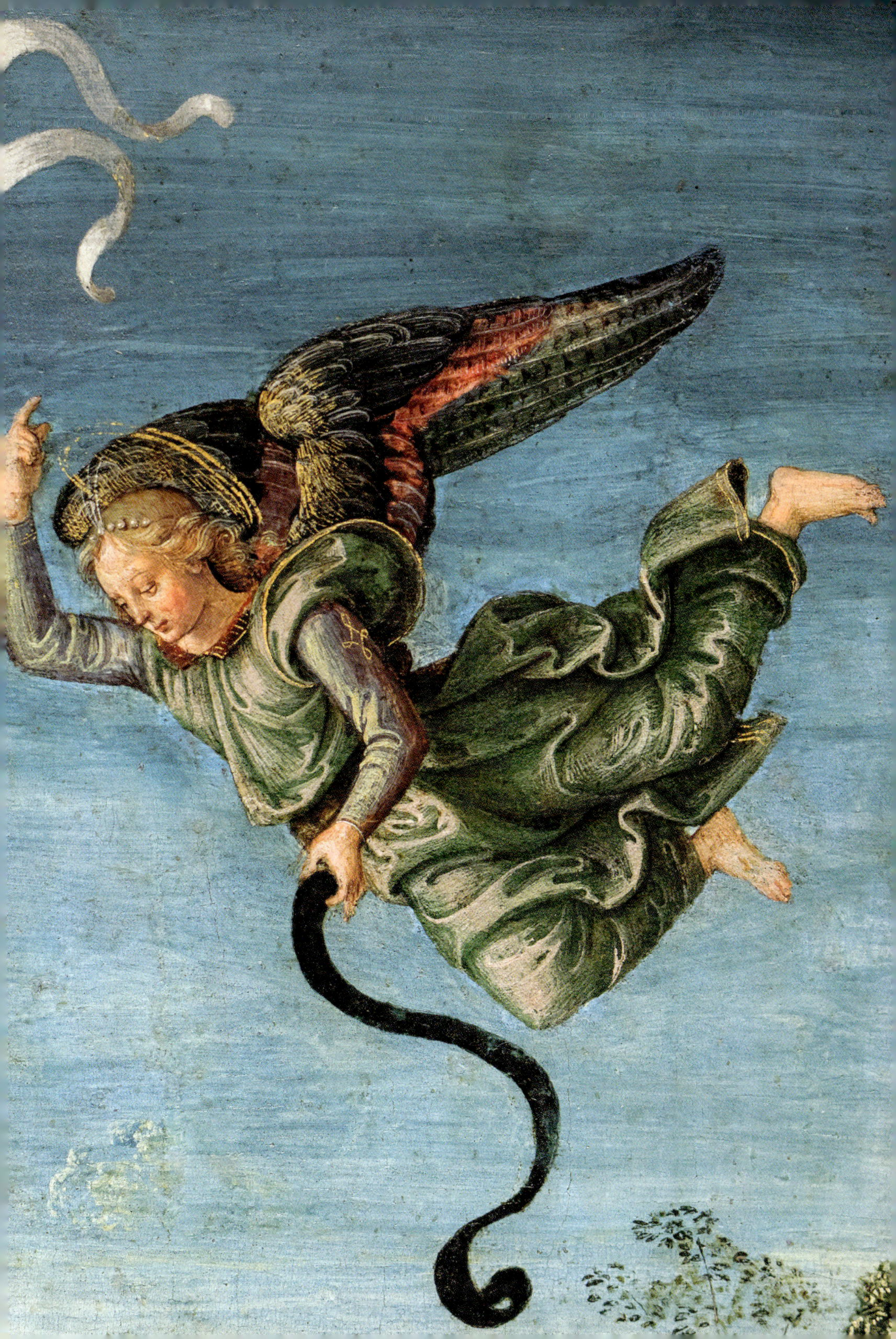

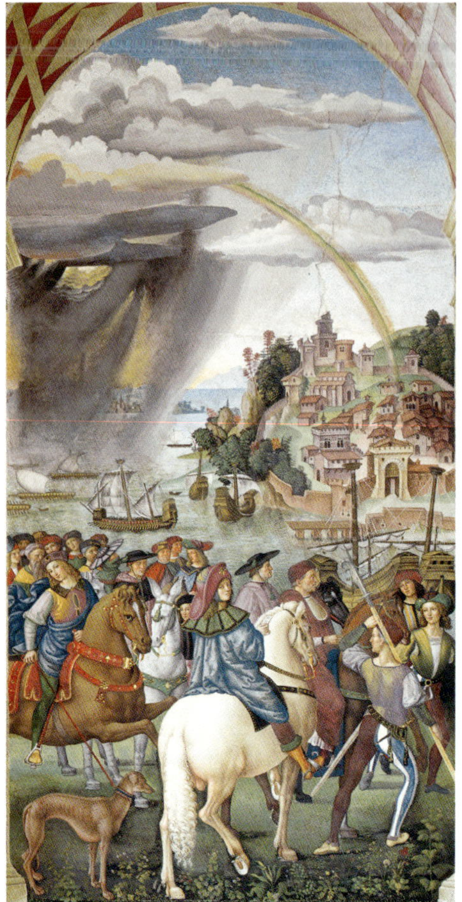

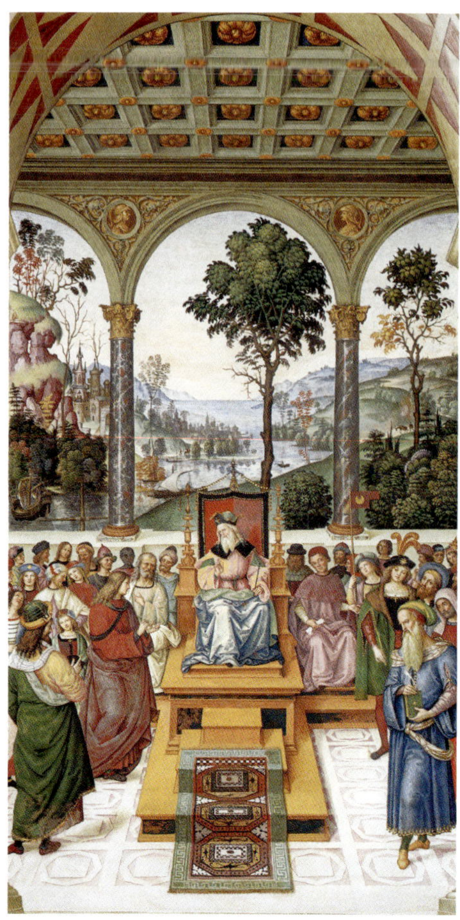

The altar was dedicated to Saint Jerome, whence his presence and prominence among the biblical figures on Calvary Hill. He appears as a penitent, ready to strike his bared breast with a stone in physical mortification and so follow the sufferings of Christ. In pictorial tradition he is often showing praying in this posture before a crucifix. Raphael heightens Jerome's devotion by transporting the saint to the foot of the cross, so that his meditation

Pinturicchio (after designs by Raphael)
Enea Silvio Piccolomini Leaves for the Council of Basel (1431), 1502–1508
Enea Silvio Piccolomini Delivers a Speech before King James I of Scotland (1435), 1502–1508
Enea Silvio Piccolomini is Crowned Poet Laureate by Emperor Frederick III (1442), 1502–1508
Enea Silvio Piccolomini Pays Homage to Pope Eugenius IV (1445), 1502–1508
Frescoes. Siena, Cathedral, Libreria Piccolomini

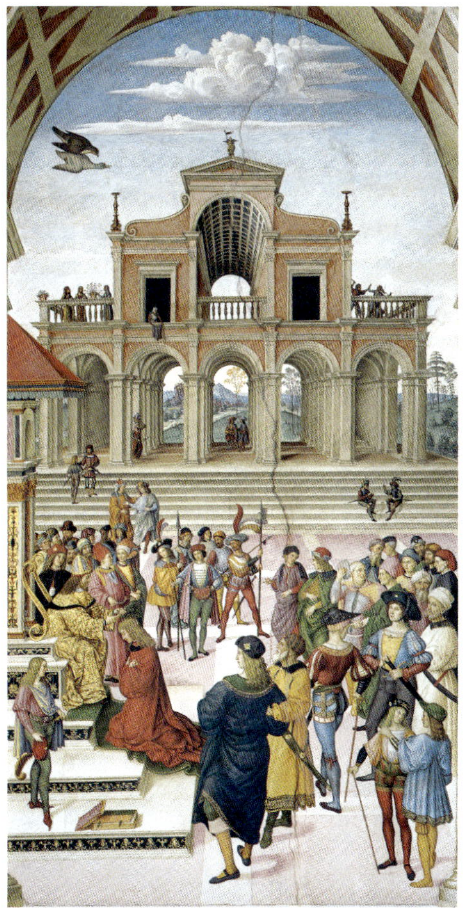

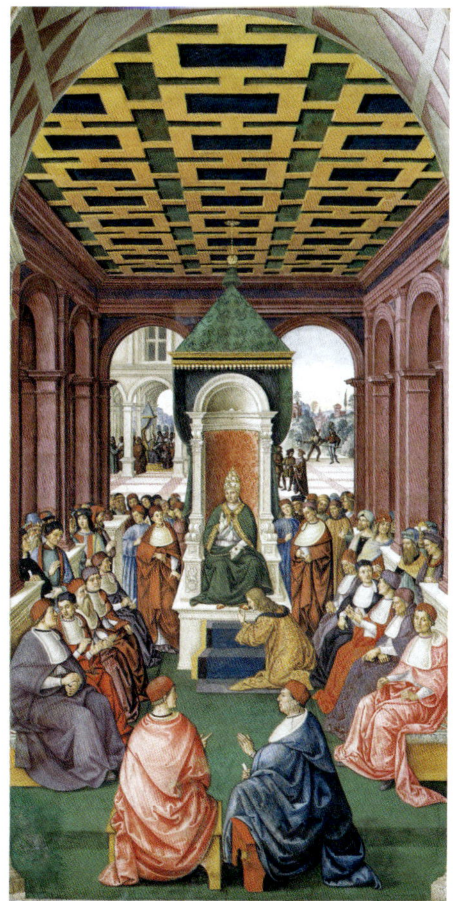

becomes a real witnessing of the Crucifixion, as it were. Gavari's coat of arms on the altarpiece frame shows a hand holding a crucifix. The symbol of the abstract heraldic device is transformed in the painting into a dramatic miraculous image: Jerome's emphatically spot-lit open hand is directed, as if gesturing, close to the base of the cross, as if a crucifix he had been holding before him had just turned into the real cross. Raphael modestly and proudly placed his signature at the foot of this cross.

Two predella panels of posthumous miracles by Saint Jerome have survived (pp. 46/47, 48/49; Cat. P8b, 8c). They show Raphael for the first time as a master of dramatic visual narration. Consecutive events are united simultaneously in one scene via a play with roles assigned to different figures (Wagner 1999). Raphael was concerned increasingly at this time with the representation of historical episodes, since he was concurrently involved on

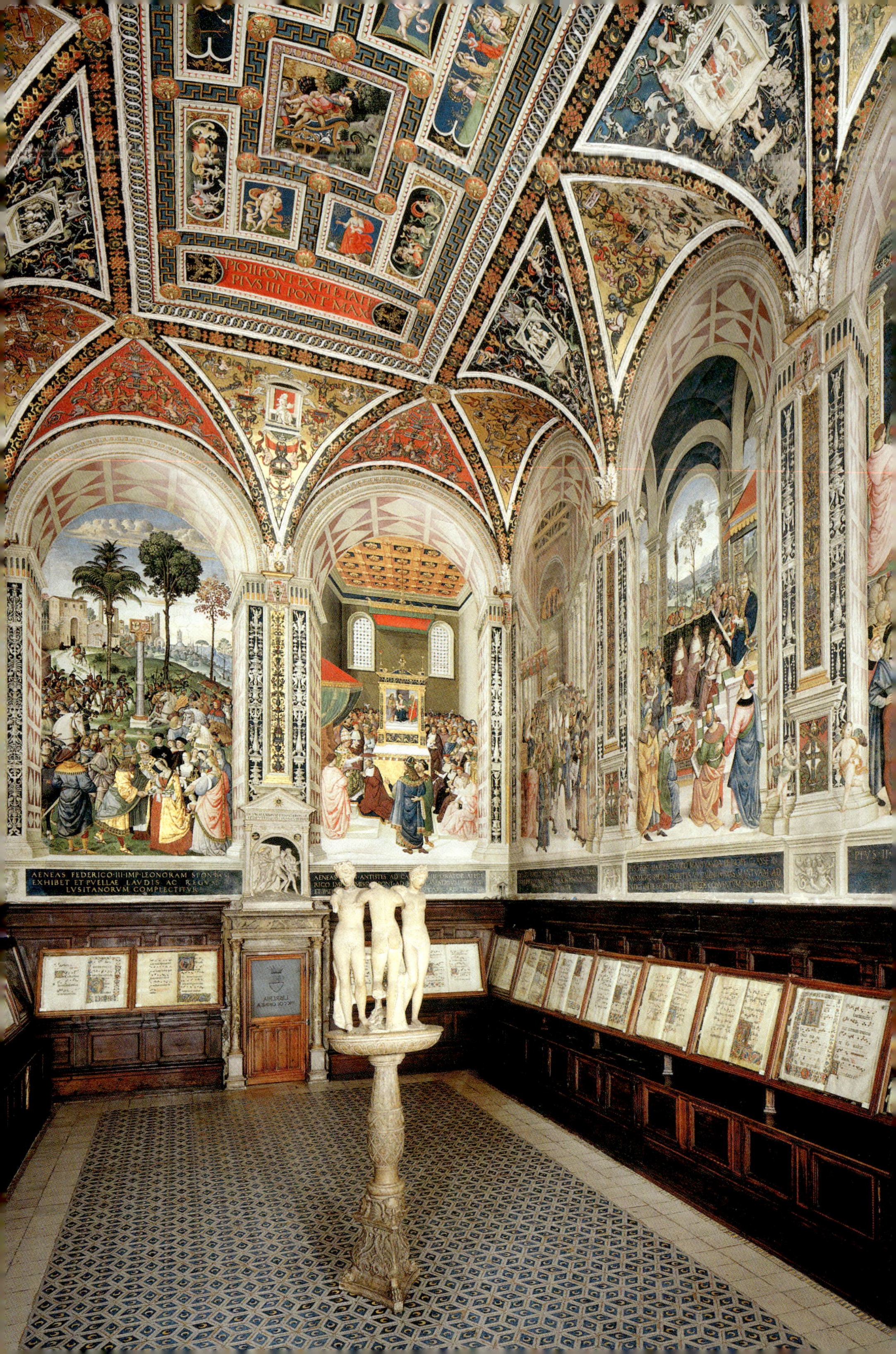
PIO II PONT EX PIETATE
PIVS III PONT MAX
AENEAS FEDERICO·III·IMP·LEONORAM
EXHIBET ET PVELLAE LAVDIS AC
LVSITANORVM COMPLECTITVR

one of the great narrative fresco cycles of the Early Renaissance, which was being designed in Perugia for execution in Siena. In January and March 1503, Raphael is documented at the court of law in Perugia, and in January 1504, he is described as a resident of the city. The Umbrian metropolis, enthroned on hilltop ridges above the wide valley floor, was officially part of the Papal States, but was at that time ruled by the Baglioni family. Alongside Perugino, who also maintained a workshop in Florence, the city's painters were dominated above all by Bernardo Pinturicchio (*c.* 1454–1513). Pinturicchio had returned to Perugia after a long and successful career working for the Borgia Pope Alexander VI (1431–1503; in office from 1492) in Rome. Raphael seems to have formed a friendship with him and later made regular references in his own art to Pinturicchio's great fresco cycles in the Vatican and in Spello. On 29 June 1502, Pinturicchio received a new large-scale fresco commission in Siena. He was to decorate the Library (p. 32) inside Siena Cathedral on behalf of its donor, Cardinal Francesco Todeschini Piccolomini (1439–1503). The Cardinal wished to see the life of his uncle, Pope Pius II (born Enea Silvio Piccolomini, 1408–1464; in office from 1458), glorified in large-scale history paintings. Vasari reports that Raphael designed some of the scenes for Pinturicchio. This information is confirmed by several Raphael drawings surviving in the original or as copies (KMOF 28–30, 62). Raphael appears to have designed at least the first five of the ten pictorial fields in the Library.

The starting point for the invention of the Library's visual programme was Pius II's dying words, which are inscribed in slightly modified form above the entrance as a fitting accompaniment to a relief of the Expulsion from Paradise: "I have offended against God and posterity. I owe a debt to both, neither to me" ("Deum Maximum et posteros offendi, utriusque debeo neuter mihi"). Pius thus humbly declared himself a poor, repentant sinner. The decorative scheme, however, was intended to rebut this self-accusation and turn it into even greater praise. For this purpose, a greatly admired ancient statuary group of the Three Graces was imported from Rome and erected in the centre of the room. In antique philosophy and ethics, the Latin word *gratia* means charity, alms, thanks and grace. The trinity of Graces was thereby seen as an illustration of the three steps that necessarily belong together in every act of charity: the giving of charity, the receiving of it, and lastly its repayment and reciprocation by the grateful recipient. The humanist Poliziano (Agnolo Ambrogini, 1454–1494) once alluded to this meaning of the statuary group in a letter to Todeschini Piccolomini. With his assertion that he had only received in life, but not given and re-given, Pius II seemed to have negated this meaning of the Graces, however. The Life of Pius II, alias Enea Silvio Piccolomini, which unfolds in frescoes on the walls

The Piccolomini Library in Siena Cathedral

around the marble group, was intended to show that his humble self-deprecation on his deathbed was untrue: on the contrary, the ideal of grace had stood – like the antique statuary group now – at the centre of Pius's life. Raphael made this clear in his four designs for the right-hand longitudinal wall of the Library (pp. 28, 30–31). In the first scene, Enea Silvio rides into the landscape of the narrative on his way to the Council of Basel (p. 28). In the second, he is standing up and delivering a speech in front of the Scottish king. The scene is now set in a loggia, through whose arches a landscape is visible. In the third scene, Enea is crowned poet laureate by Frederick III (1415–1493). He is kneeling in a square in front of a loggia, through which we see a distant landscape. In the fourth picture he kisses the foot of Pope Eugenius IV (1383–1447; in office from 1431). Enea has prostrated himself in an interior, through whose openings we look out onto a square where stands a loggia through which we in turn glimpse a landscape. In this way, the spatial situations cascade one behind the other in an increasingly elaborate manner from picture to picture. The protagonist Enea Silvio thereby constantly changes pose: first on horseback, then standing, then kneeling, finally kneeling and bowing. Step by step, Enea relinquishes his earthly pride, in order finally, through submission to the Pope, to humbly leave behind his secular life, enter the service of the Church and commence his rise as a cleric. Another aspect of his behaviour is even more important. In the first scene, as he rides into the picture Enea Silvio looks at the viewers and invites them to accompany him into the story. What then follows are the three steps of *gratia*: in his speech before the Scottish king, Enea is the giver, in his honouring by the emperor the receiver, and in kissing the Pope's foot once again the giver. The painted biography thus refutes the subject's dying words and proves that the antique group of the Three Graces is rightly in the centre of the room.

Gratia also possesses an aesthetic as well as a moral dimension of meaning. The Italian word *grazie* describes a style of casual, cheerful grace, sweetness, gentleness, lightness, endearing charm and elegance. Posterity has recognised a core stylistic feature of Raphael's art in this very quality. Perhaps it had already struck contemporaries in Raphael's very early work and was the reason why Pinturicchio engaged him to collaborate on the Library commission. The aesthetic *grazie* of the pictures was itself intended as an expression of the virtuousness of Enea Silvio's character. The frescoing of the Library took several years. In 1503 the patron himself became Pope (Pius III), but died just a few weeks later. Work on the project was subsequently broken off and the paintings completed only in 1508. Many authors have described how Pinturicchio and his workshop modified Raphael's designs in the final frescoes, for example reducing their spatial depth and increasing the ostentatious

Detail from **Resurrection of Christ**, *c.* 1499–1500
(see ill. p. 37)

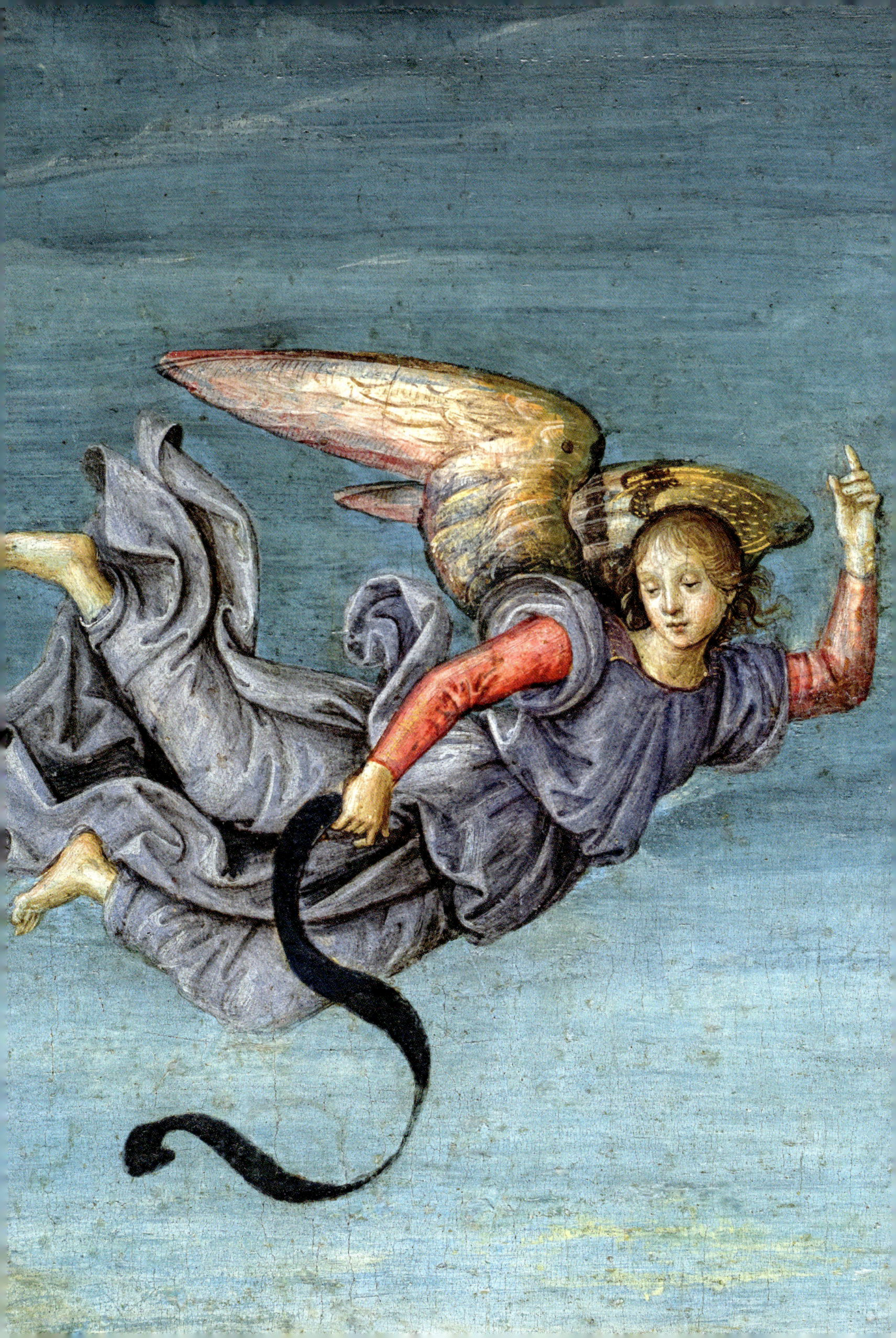

variety of their motifs. In the opening scene, *Enea Silvio Piccolomini Leaves for the Council of Basel* (p. 30), an elegant greyhound appears in the foreground, while the landscape assumes the recognisable form of the Sienese coastal town of Talamone, from where the party set sail. Pinturicchio shows, in impressive fashion, the storm gathering in the skies that will drive the ships to Libya. It is thus made clear that, here at the start of the cycle, Enea is following the fate of the ancient Aeneas, who was driven by a tempest to North Africa at the beginning of *The Aeneid* by Virgil (70–19 BC) (Esche 1992). Raphael will later make a similar reference to the story of Aeneas in his *Fire in the Borgo* fresco (Cat. F3.3l).

Raphael contributed preliminary drawings to another of Pinturicchio's projects, namely an altarpiece of the Assumption of the Virgin commissioned on 17 December 1502 by the Franciscans of Santa Maria dei Fossi, north of Perugia. The painting was completed in summer 1503 as the *Coronation of the Virgin* (p. 50), for which two silverpoint drawings of the saints kneeling in the foreground (KMOF 56, 57) have come down to us from Raphael's hand. The possibility that Raphael participated on other areas of the composition is supported by the series of five heads in the left-hand row of apostles, which is found in identical form in an altarpiece on the same theme that Raphael commenced probably around 1503. This altarpiece was produced on behalf of the Oddi family for a chapel in the Franciscan church of San Francesco al Prato in Perugia (p. 51; Cat. P11). The chapel lay along the left wall of the church, immediately before the transept. Raphael's painting was evidently commissioned by Alessandra Baglioni, the wife of Simone degli Oddi; her tomb is later documented in front of the altar. The men of the Oddi family had been expelled from the city in 1489 by their Baglioni rivals, but this exile was not imposed on the women. It is uncertain whether the altarpiece commission was related to a temporary return of the Oddi from exile in 1503. Payment for the carved wooden frame was made only in 1505. As drawings (KMOF 34, 35) show, this Coronation of the Virgin, too, was first begun as an Assunta, i. e. an Assumption of the Virgin – the Assumption and Coronation of the Virgin are celebrated on the same feast day. The composition is thematically concentrated and well thought-out in terms of narrative chronology. Thomas stands in the middle of the apostles gathered around the empty tomb and holds out the girdle that the Virgin has thrown down to him from above, as proof of her assumption into heaven. The Assumption has already taken place. Transfixed by the miracle, some disciples gaze in amazement heavenwards, where the Virgin is enthroned next to her son and is being crowned by him. The celestial zone is magnificently imbued with a solemn symmetry, culminating in the subtly varied ornament of a formation of seraphim heads. Beneath them, elegant youthful angel musicians flank the seated pair, who seem to float between them, almost as if an apse, beneath the semi-circular upper edge of the picture (cf. Cat. F3.1r). A divine breath causes the angel's robes to billow outwards – melodious figures of artistic grace.

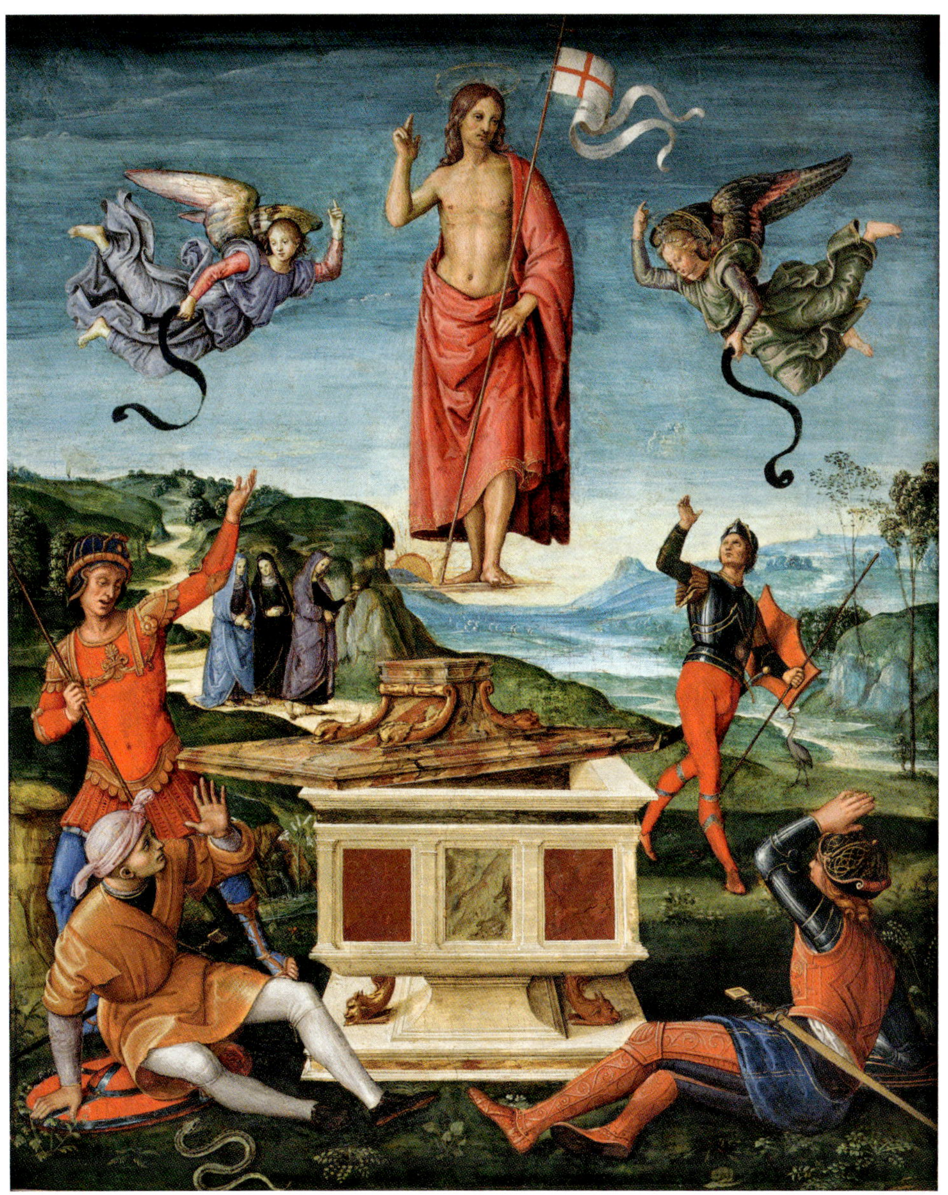

Resurrection of Christ, *c.* 1499–1500
Oil on panel, 56.5 × 47 cm (22 ¼ × 18 ½ in)
São Paulo, Museu de Arte de São Paulo Assis Chateaubriand
(Details pages 29, 35)

Below, the string of animated character heads follows the horizon of the landscape. Like the angels around the heavenly pair above, the apostles cluster around the empty tomb, from which lilies and roses have sprung up. The representation of the tomb is not only a reference to the miracle of the Assumption of the Virgin, but also an aesthetic showpiece of difficult perspective. For it is seen at an unprecedented diagonal, foreshortened on two sides. Only following a cleaning of the painting in 2020 did it become clear that the diagonals of the sarcophagus are taken up by the luminous blue and red lower bodies, angled towards each other, of the Virgin and Christ, in order to bring the upper and lower halves of the composition into greater harmony. The front of the sarcophagus is turned towards the right, from where the visitors inside the church formerly approached the altarpiece at an angle. At the same time, the altar block that originally stood in front of the painting seems to have shifted into the picture in the chest-like shape of the tomb. The semicircle formed by the apostles behind the tomb reflected the semicircle of the congregation gathered in front of the altar during Mass. Realities were thus interwoven.

Between the altar block and the main altarpiece were three predella panels (pp. 54–59; Cat. P11b–d). Raphael clearly took his inspiration for these from the predella of Perugino's high altarpiece in Fano. This is evident above all in the *Annunciation* and *The Presentation at the Temple*. These two scenes, set in *all'antica* halls, framed the central landscape of the *Adoration of the Magi*. Contrasting with the splendour of the immaculate halls is the humble, dilapidated stable with its masonry and timberwork, borrowed from an engraving by Albrecht Dürer (1471–1528). The royal procession with its trappings of pomp sinks down before it. The Magi kneel and worship Christ in the ruined stable, like the simple shepherds opposite them. The Franciscan Order's ideal of poverty has here found visual expression. The Assumption of the Virgin, too, was held in particular reverence by the Franciscans. For the women of the Oddi family, on the other hand, the theme of the Coronation of the Virgin may have reflected their female identity as heads of families while their menfolk were in exile. Even more importantly, the Assumption of the Virgin illustrated the women's hope of their own resurrection in their burial chapel.

The last altarpiece that Raphael produced for Città di Castello is dated 1504. *Lo Sposalizio* (also known as *The Marriage of the Virgin*, p. 61; Cat. P13) was destined for Filippo Albizzini's altar, which was located in San Francesco on the left-hand side of the nave. Albizzini had acquired the patronage rights to the chapel in 1501. At his request, it was dedicated to Saint Joseph and the Most Holy Name of Jesus. Perhaps Filippo identified himself with Joseph: just as this latter espoused Mary from the temple under the eyes of the high priest, Filippo had assumed care of the chapel from the Church and clergy in a formal contract. He had, as it were, betrothed himself to his religious endowment in a legal act. This would make Raphael's painting the visual documentation of an act of endowment and the obligations arising out of it. As Traeger has shown, Saint Joseph was also venerated for his significance in a wide range of other contexts.

Raphael oriented himself in his altarpiece towards a painting of the same subject by Perugino (p. 60) at that time still under production in the latter's workshop, to which Raphael evidently had constant access for many years. Commenced in 1499 and completed in 1504, Perugino's *Marriage of the Virgin* was to adorn the chapel in Perugino Cathedral housing the city's most important holy relic, the Virgin's engagement ring, which had been acquired in 1474. As appropriate to the relic, Perugino portrays the scene in which Joseph is betrothed to the Virgin Mary before the high priest and the temple. The temple brackets the betrothal and rises upwards out of the picture. Here, on the altarpiece frame, stood the tabernacle containing the ring. Perugino seems to point towards it with his temple and to mirror its form in the picture. In his own painting, Raphael portrays the relic, which was especially venerated by the Franciscans, in recognisable form in Joseph's hand.

The ways in which Raphael competes artistically with Perugino in his *Marriage of the Virgin* are famous and have often been described. The suggestion of homogeneous three-dimensionality in place of layered, shallow planes, the suction of the viewer's gaze into the depths of the picture, the infusion of figural groups with lively and graceful rhythm, and the greater harmony of the palette are just some of Raphael's new qualities. For his own, more elegant and more graceful figures, Raphael thereby also oriented himself towards other works by Perugino, such as the latter's Fano predella (mirrored: Mary and the High Priest from the *Presentation*, as well as two suitors on the left from the *Marriage*). Perhaps he felt challenged to such a competition, a *paragone*, because rivalry is a key element of the story portrayed. According to legend, Joseph prevailed over his fellow suitors for the hand of Mary because his was the only staff to burst into flower. Raphael stresses this rivalry, insofar as the losing suitors hold up their staffs and two of them even set about breaking them in half. Delicate blossoms sprout on all sides from the tip of Joseph's staff. Perhaps Raphael makes an illusion to this in the artistic showpiece of his composition: a flawless work of architecture, shimmering in the subtlest nuances of light and shadow, burgeons like a bud on the far side of the temple square and blossoms into an airy ambulatory. Raphael here proves himself an architect of supreme harmony and beauty, and at the same time displays his virtuoso handling of perspective of a heightened degree of difficulty. He has signed the building and the picture in a simulated frieze inscription in the central axis of the ambulatory. It is the coronation of his early work in Umbria.

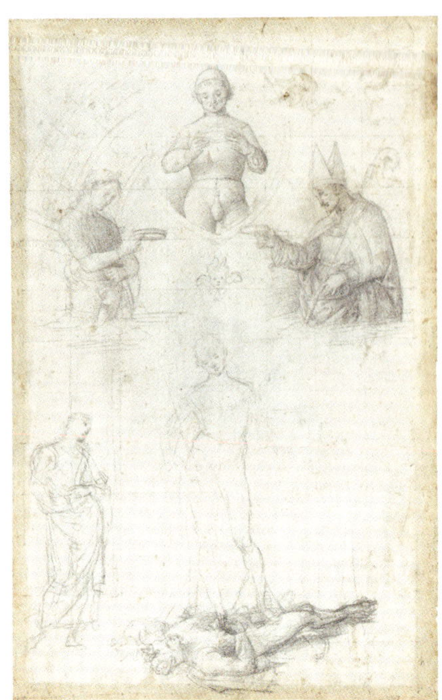

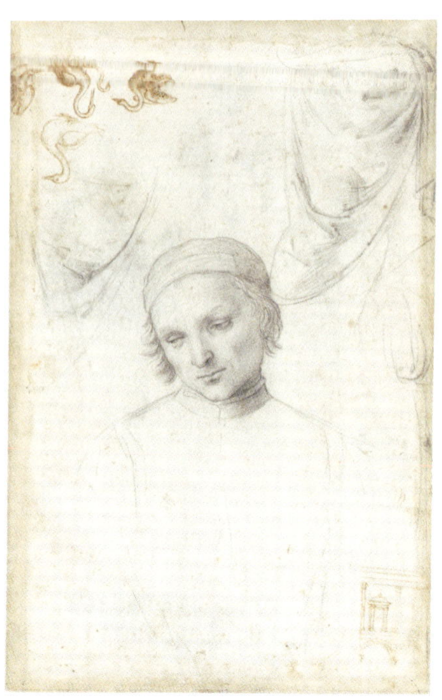

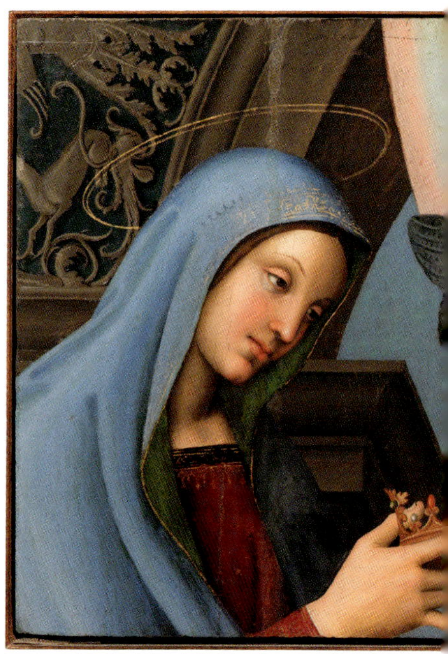

Compositional study for the *Coronation of Saint Nicholas of Tolentino*, 1500/01
Metalpoint heightened with white, squared,
39.4 × 26.3 cm (15 ½ × 10 ⅜ in)
Lille, Palais des Beaux-Arts

Head of Saint Nicholas, drapery studies, aquatic birds, two bays of a two-storey palace building with portico, 1500/01
Black chalk and pen, 39.4 × 26.3 cm (15 ½ × 10 ⅜ in)
Lille, Palais des Beaux-Arts

God the Father with Crown and **Madonna (Altarpiece of San Nicola da Tolentino/Pala Baronci)**, 1500/01
Oil on poplar panel, 112 × 116 cm
(44 ⅛ × 45 ⅔ in) /51 × 41 cm (20 ⅛ × 16 ⅛ in)
Naples, Museo e Gallerie Nazionali
di Capodimonte

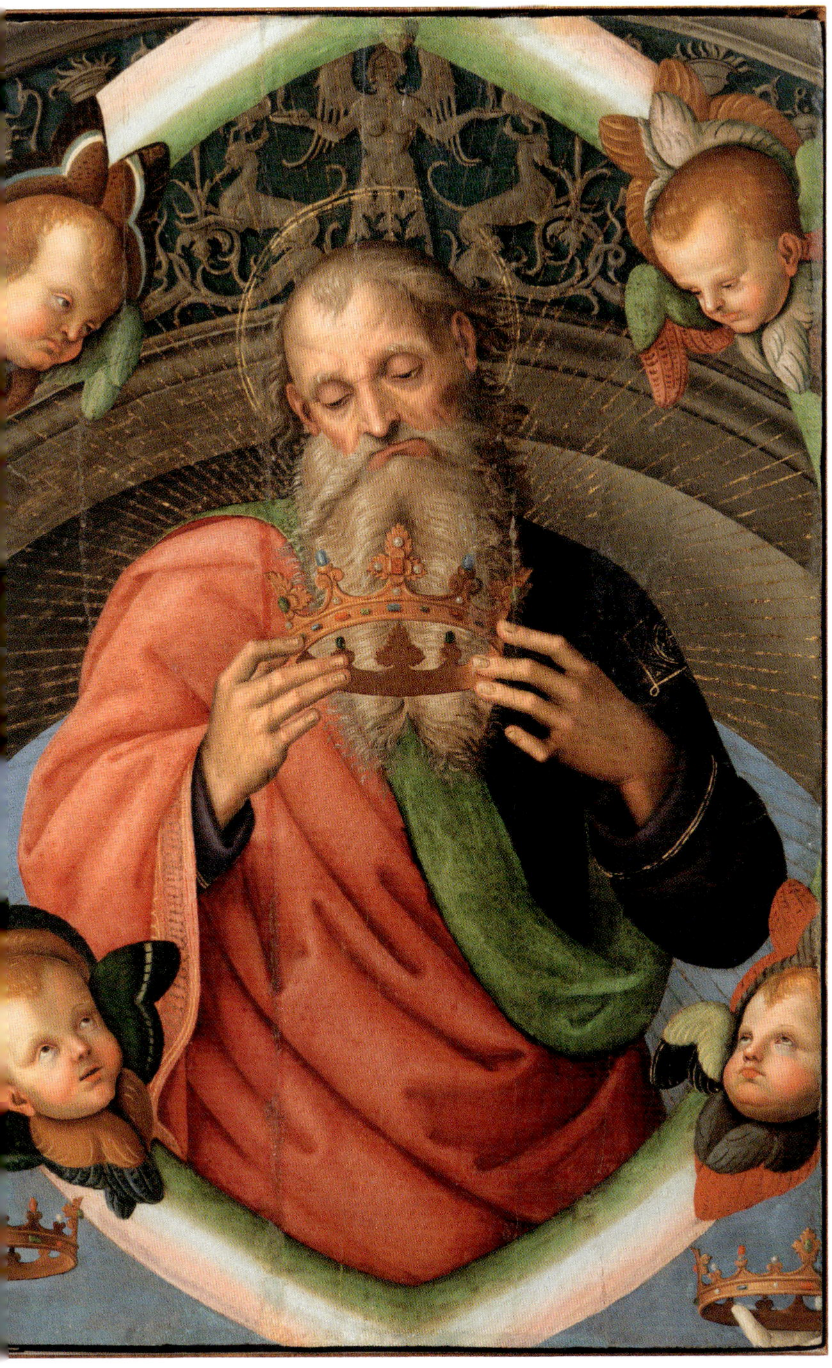

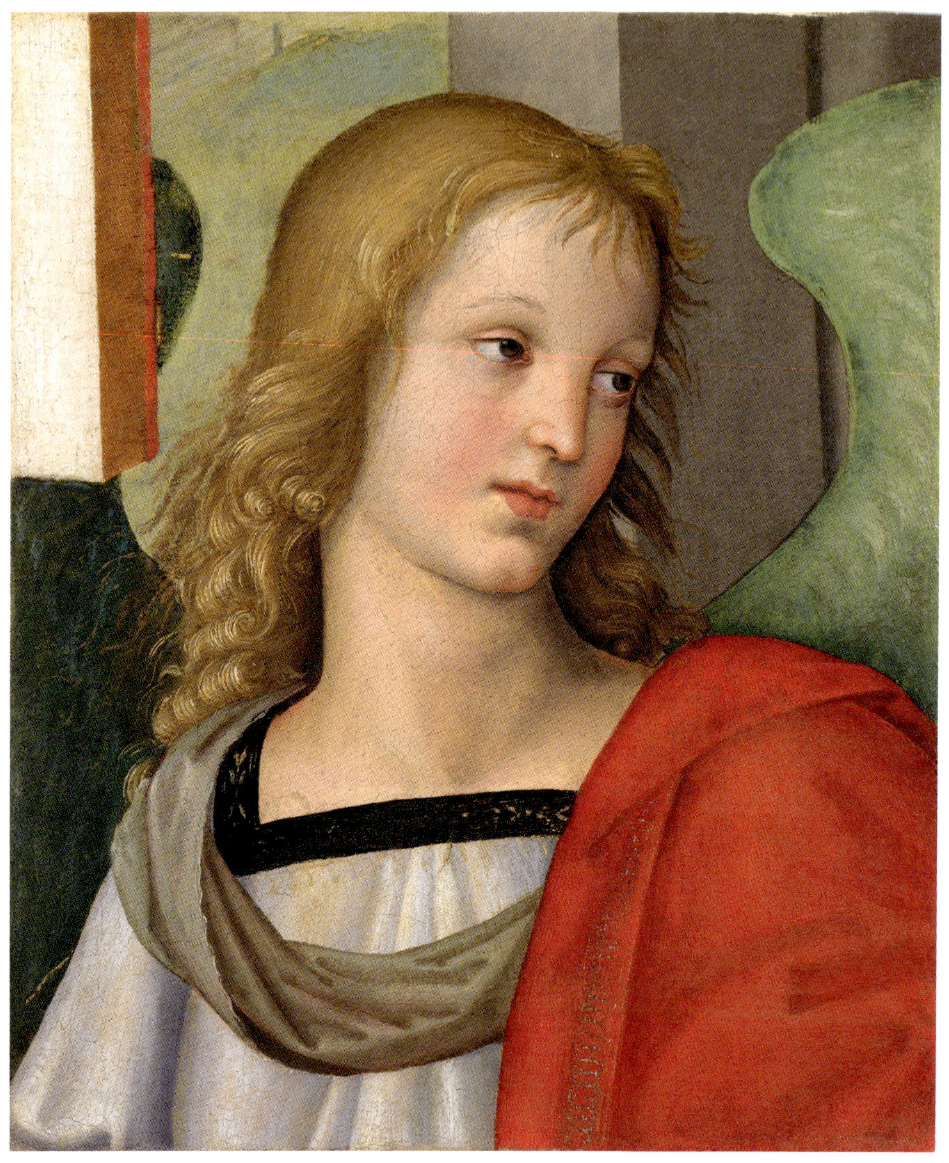

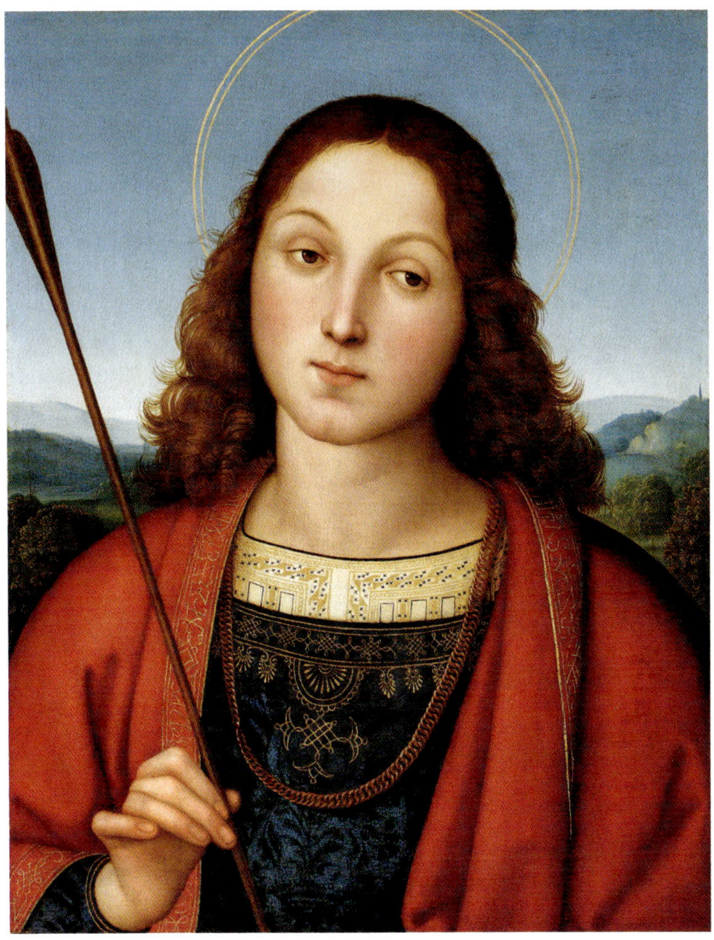

Head of an Angel (Altarpiece of San Nicola da Tolentino/Pala Baronci), 1500/01
Oil on poplar panel, transferred to canvas, 31 × 27 cm (12 ¼ × 10 ⅝ in)
Brescia, Pinacoteca Tosio Martinengo

Saint Sebastian, *c.* 1502
Oil on panel, 45.1 × 36.5 cm (17 ¾ × 14 ⅜ in)
Bergamo, Accademia Carrara

Reconstruction of the Gavari Altarpiece
(Mond Crucifixion) in its original frame of 1503
Città di Castello, San Domenico

Christ's Crucifixion with the Virgin Mary and Saints John the Evangelist,
Jerome and Mary Magdalene (Gavari Altarpiece), 1502/03
Oil on poplar panel, 280.7 × 165 cm (110 ½ × 64 ⅞ in)
Inscription on the cross: *RAPHAEL / VRBINAS P[inxit]*
London, The National Gallery

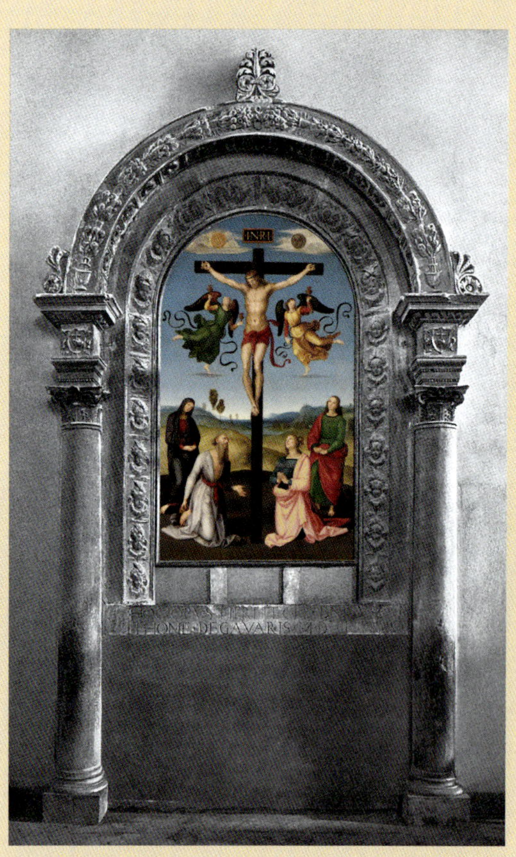

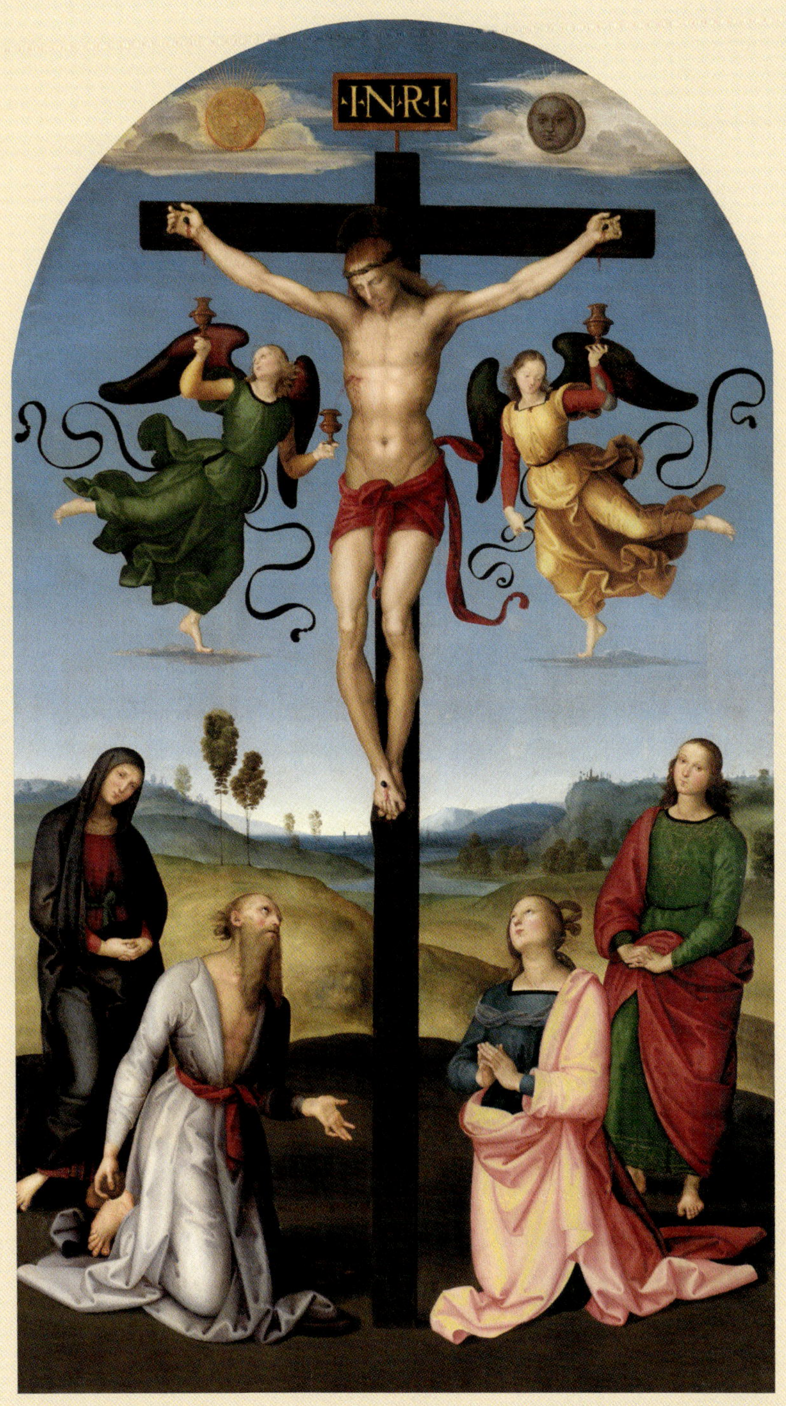
·I·N·R·I·

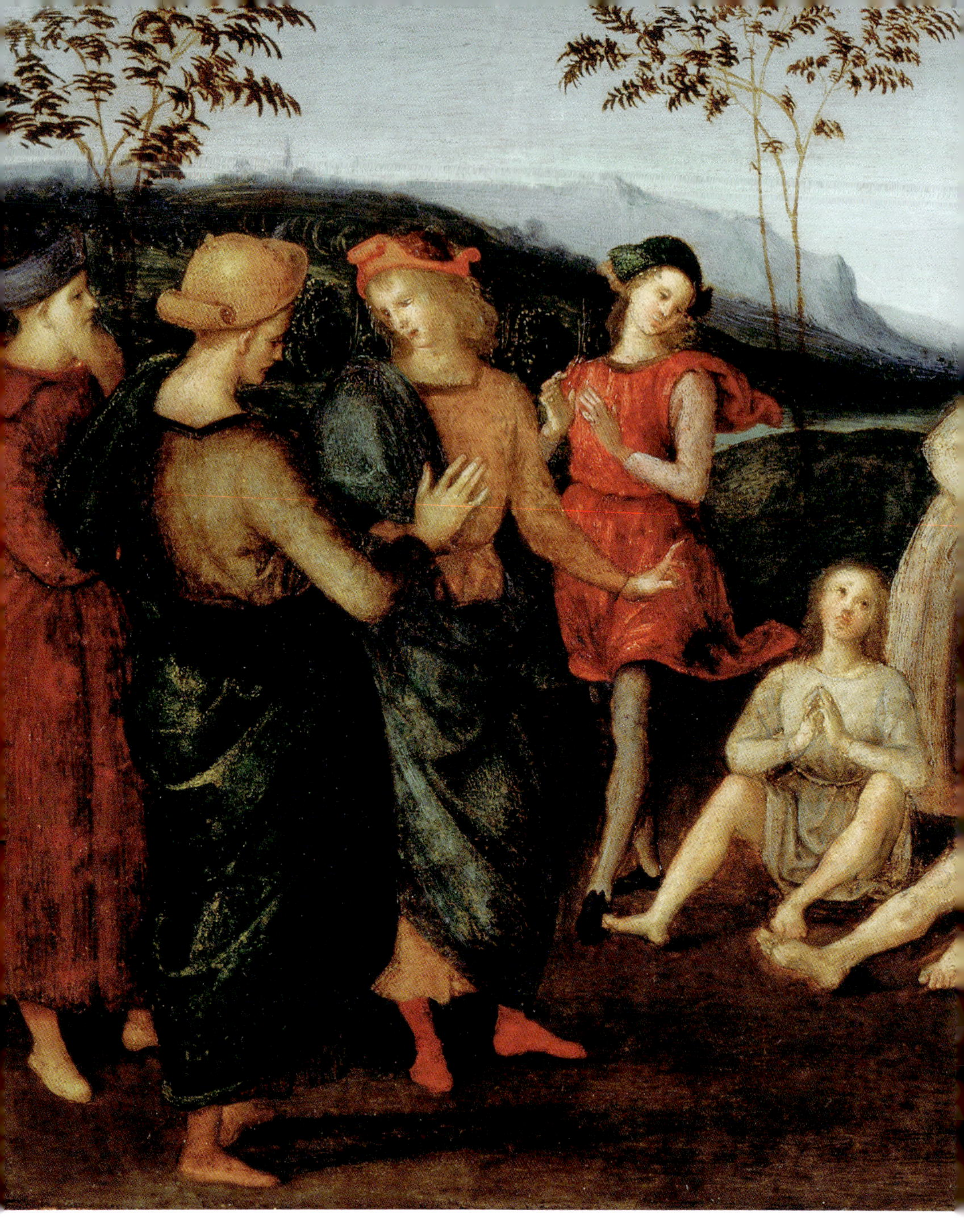

Eusebius of Cremona Raises Three Men from the Dead with the Cloak of Saint Jerome (Gavari Altarpiece, predella), 1502/03
Oil on poplar panel, 26 × 44 cm (10 ¼ × 17 ⅓ in). Lisbon, Museu Nacional de Arte Antiga

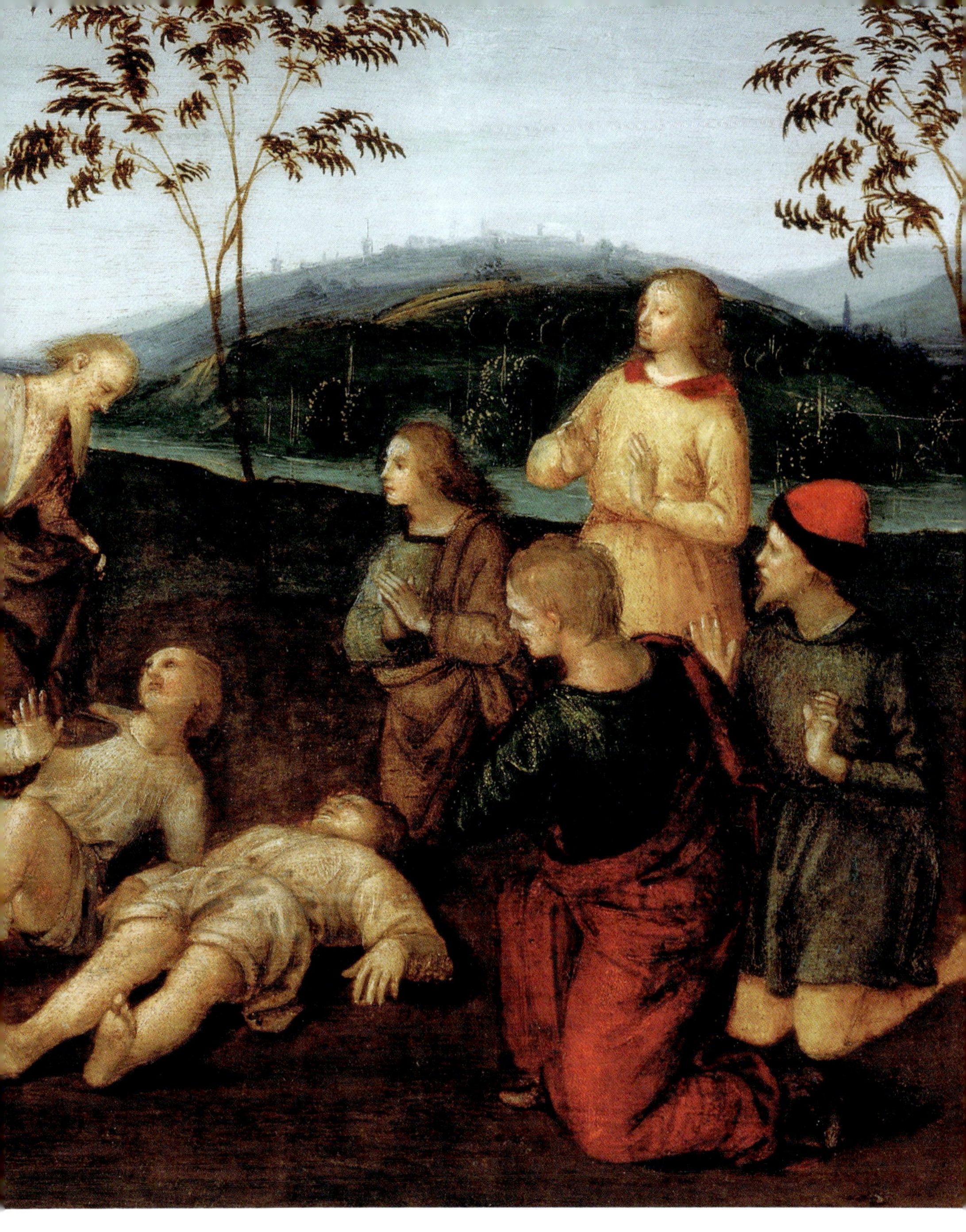

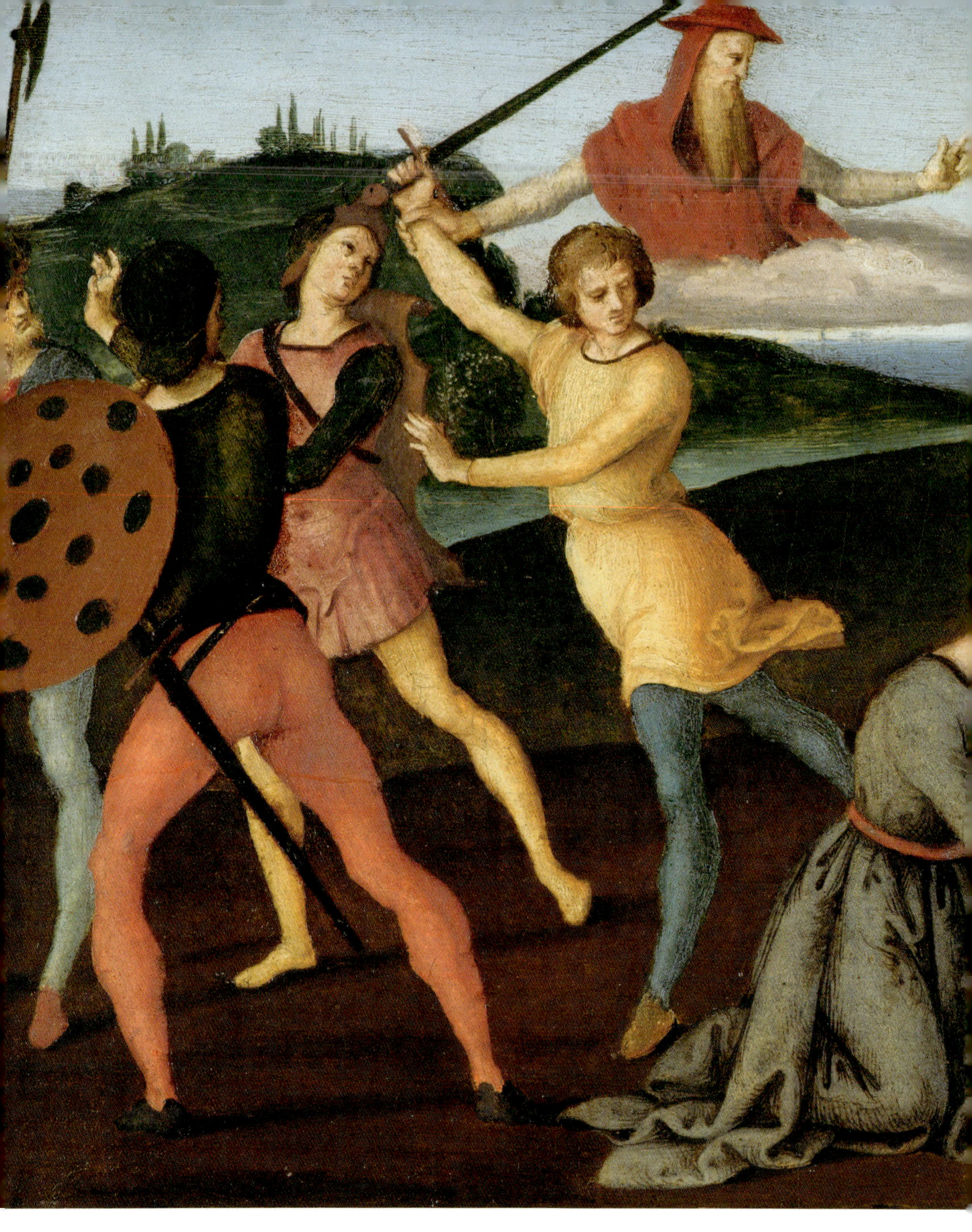

Saint Jerome Rescues Silvanus and Punishes the Heretic Sabinianus
(Gavari Altarpiece, predella), 1502/03
Oil on poplar panel, 23 × 41 cm (9 ⅛ × 16 ⅛ in). Raleigh, North Carolina Museum of Art

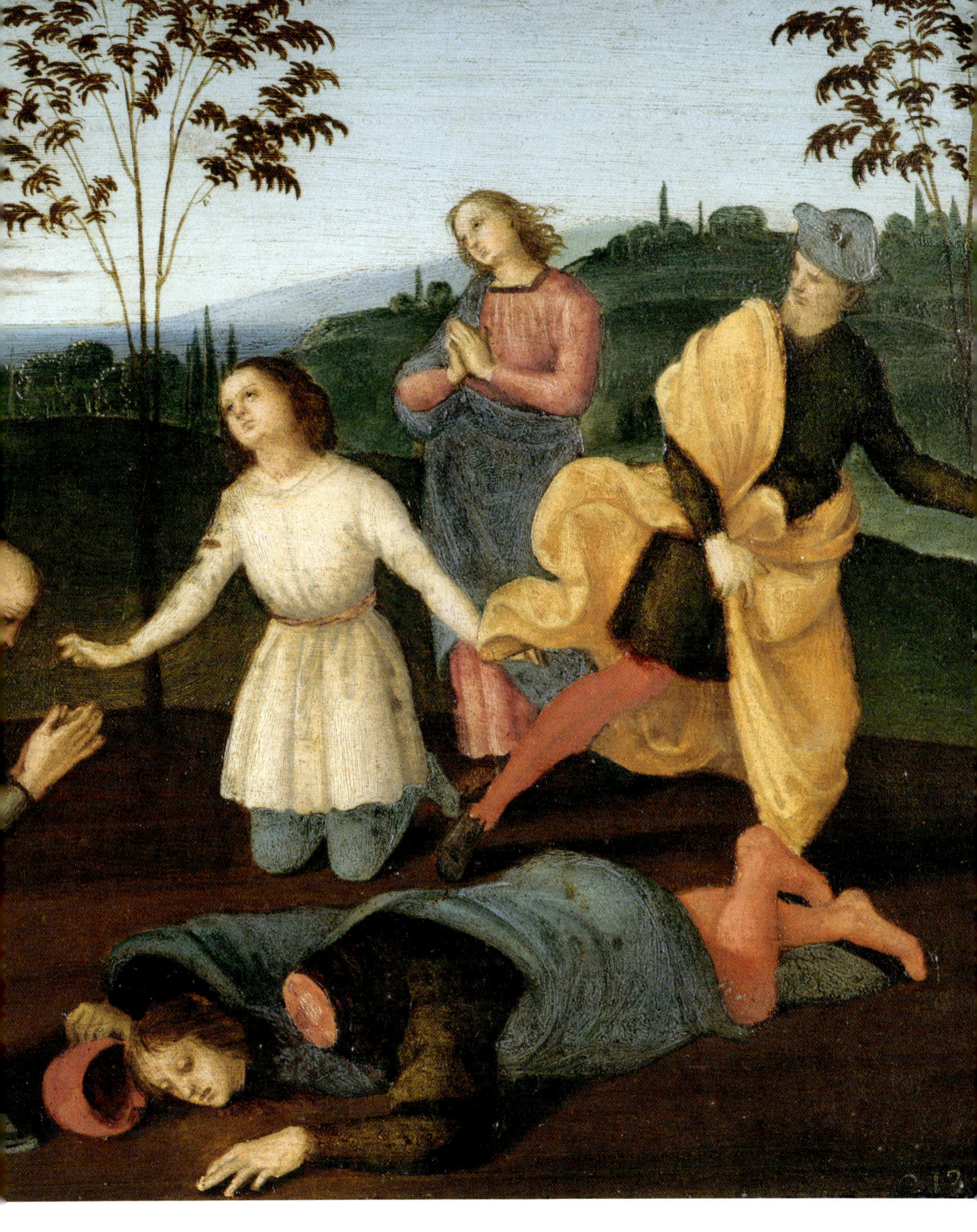

Pinturicchio
Coronation of the Virgin (Pala della Fratta), 1502/03
Tempera on panel, 330 × 200 cm (129 ⅞ × 78 ¾ in)
Vatican City, Musei Vaticani, Pinacoteca

The Coronation of the Virgin (Oddi Altarpiece), 1503/04
Oil on panel, transferred on canvas, 267 × 163 cm (105 ⅛ × 64 ⅛ in)
Vatican City, Musei Vaticani, Pinacoteca
(Detail pages 52/53)

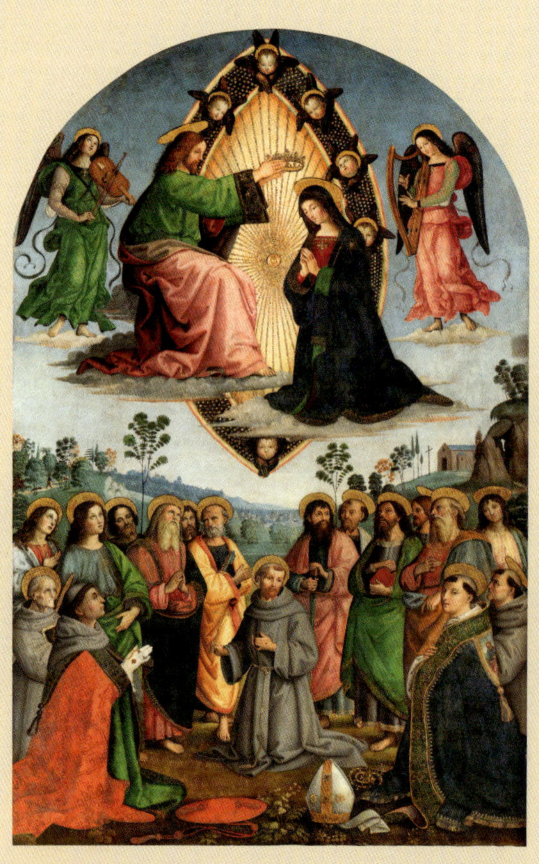

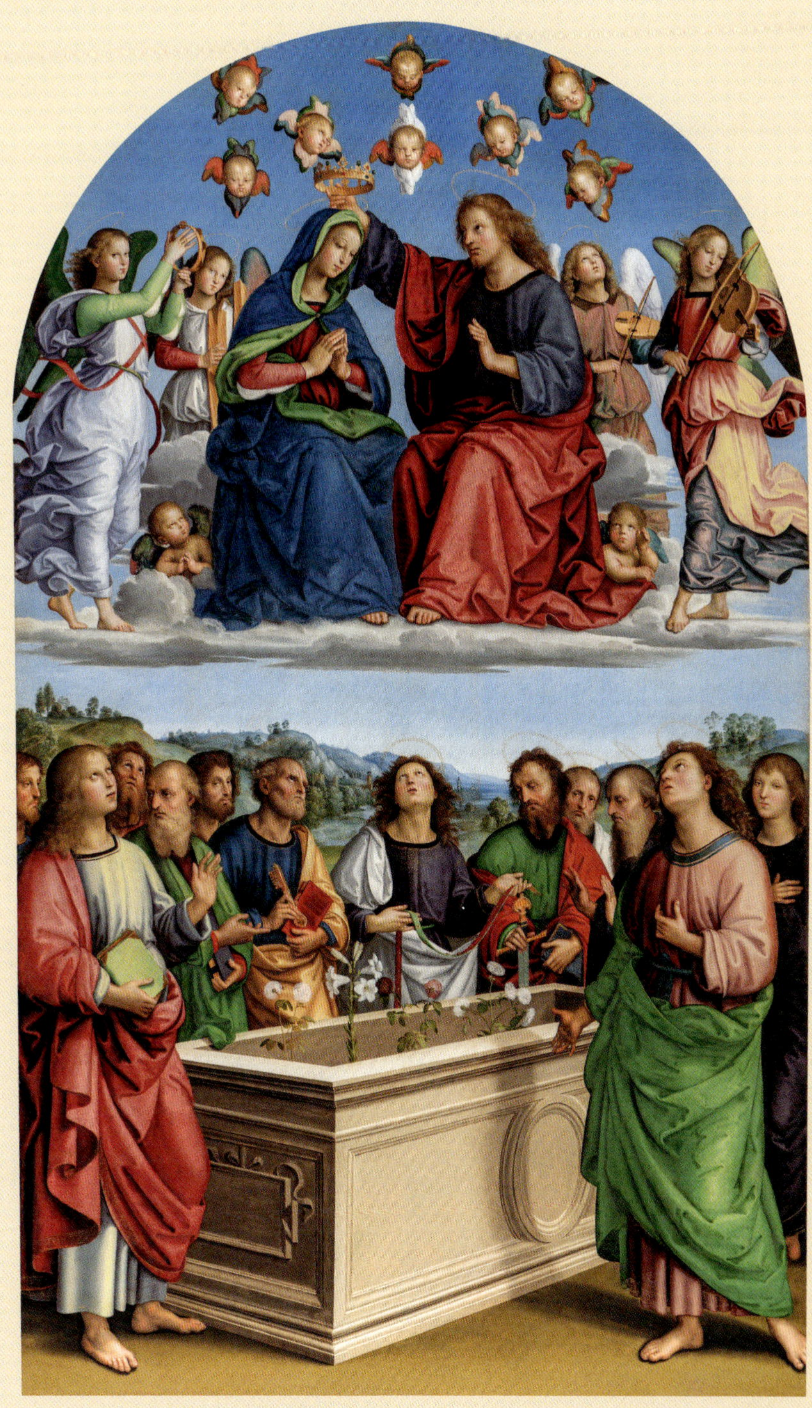

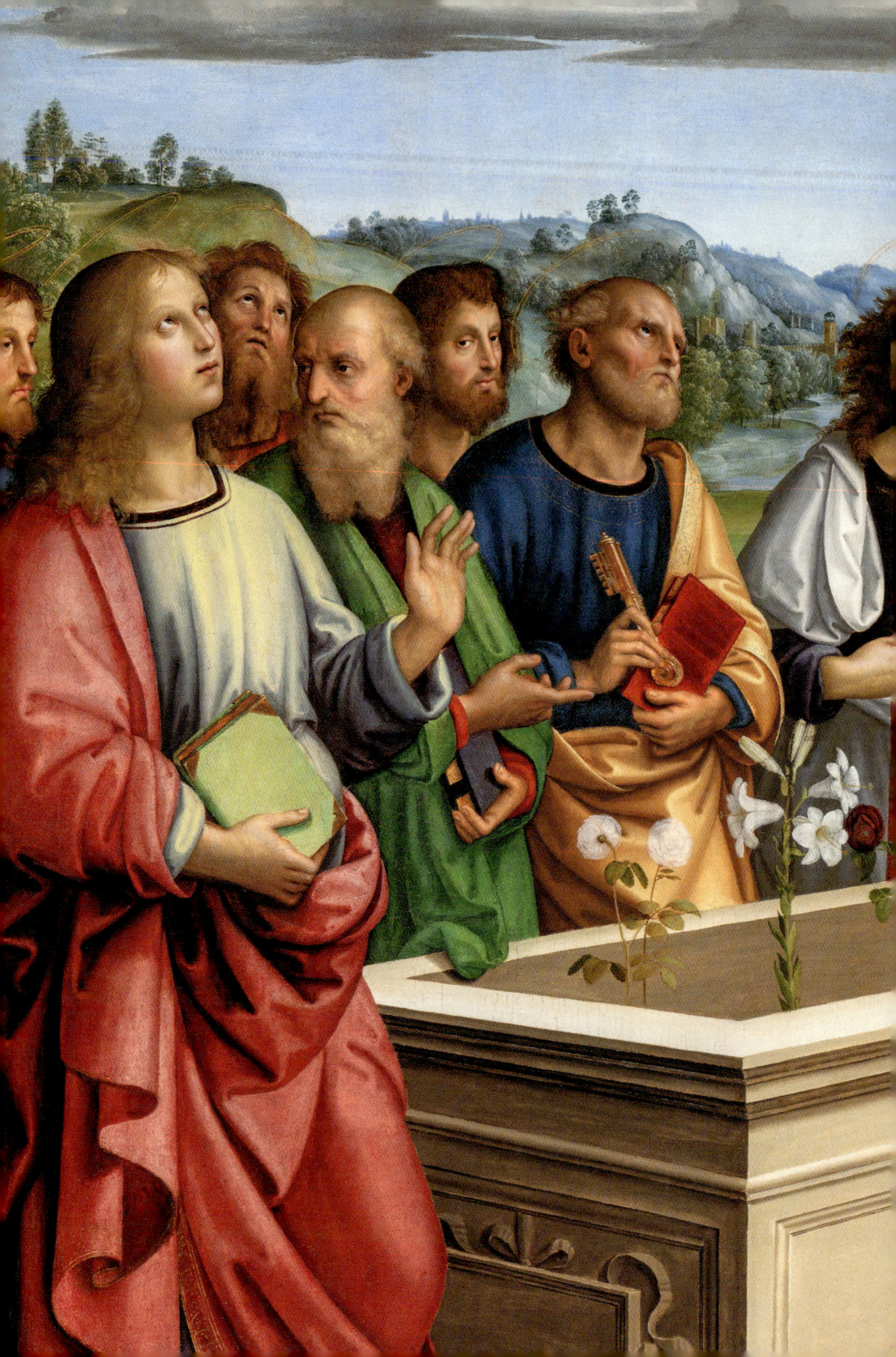

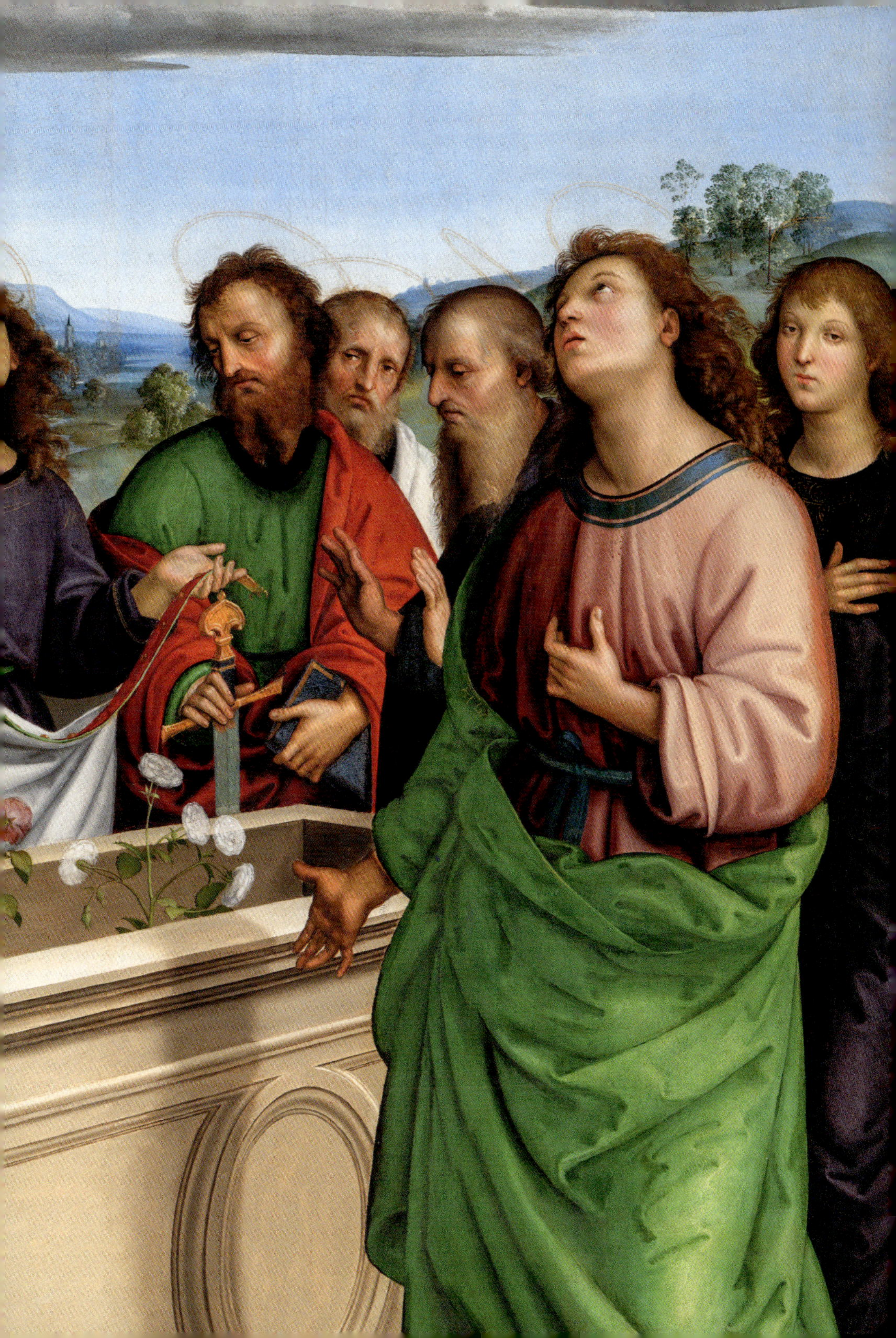

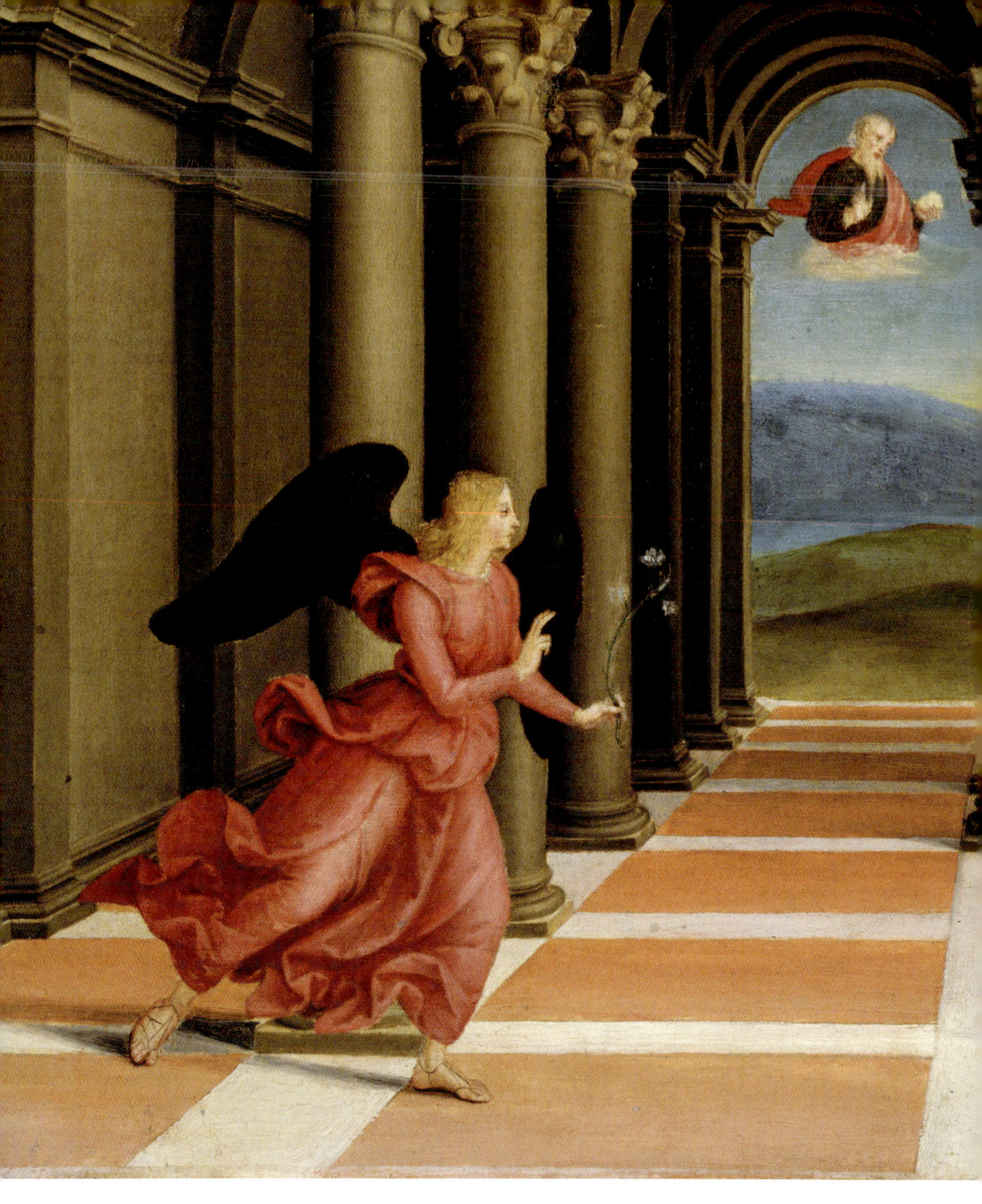

The Annunciation (Oddi Altarpiece, predella), 1503/04
Oil on panel, 39 × 190 cm (15 ⅜ × 74 ¾ in)
Vatican City, Musei Vaticani, Pinacoteca
(Detail page 27)

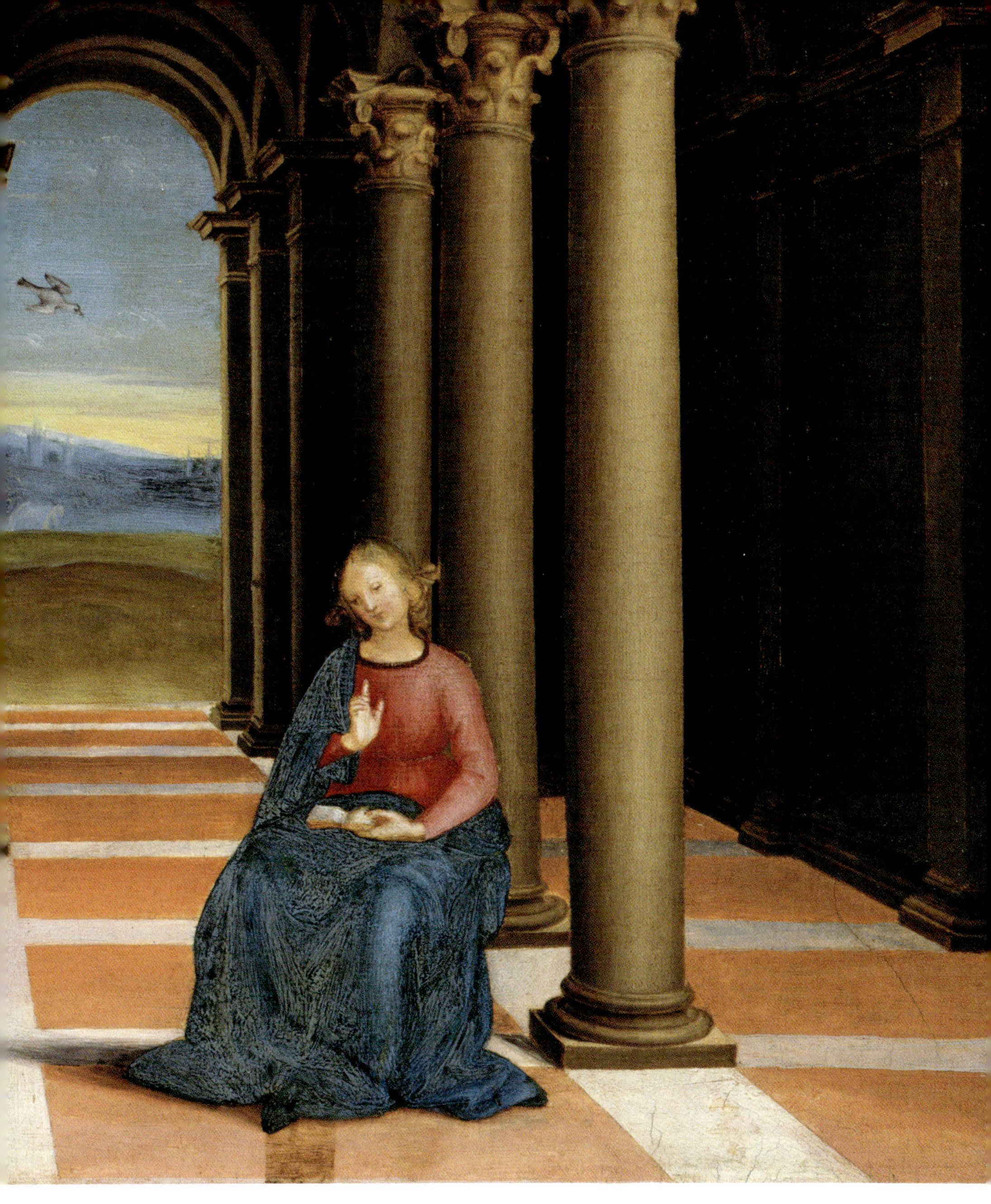

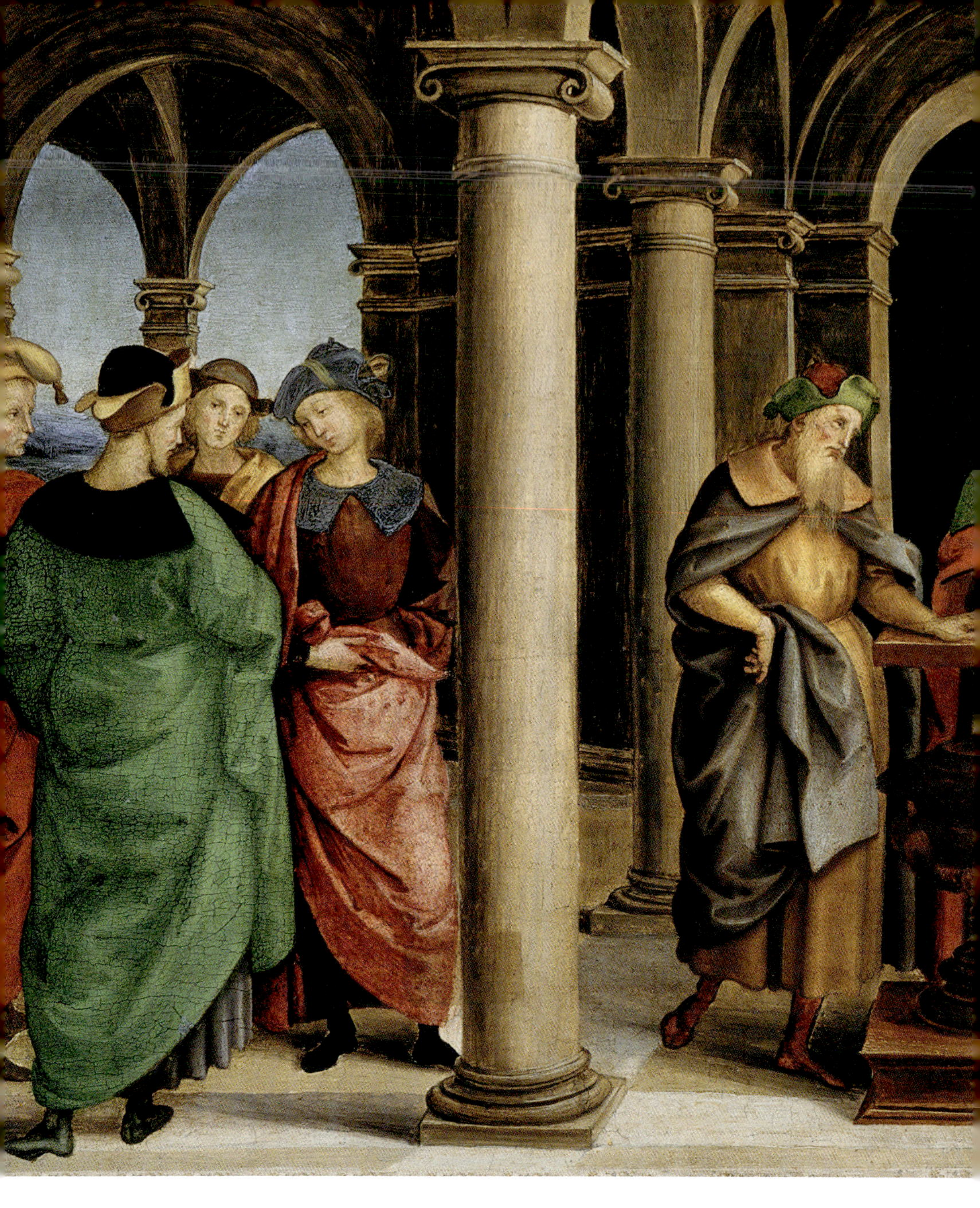

The Presentation at the Temple (Oddi Altarpiece, predella), 1503/04
Oil on panel, 39 × 190 cm (15 3/8 × 74 3/4 in)
Vatican City, Musei Vaticani, Pinacoteca
(Detail page 18)

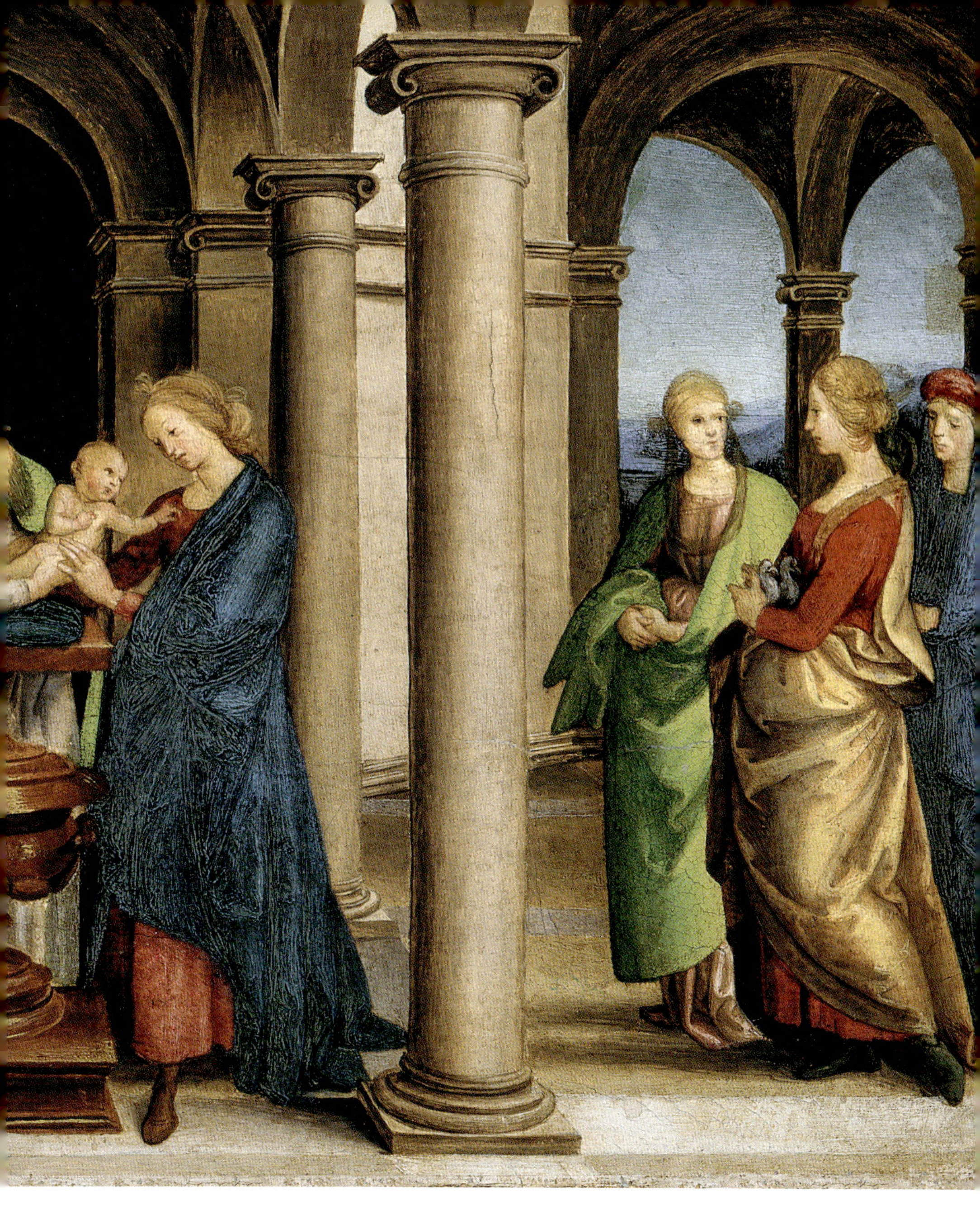

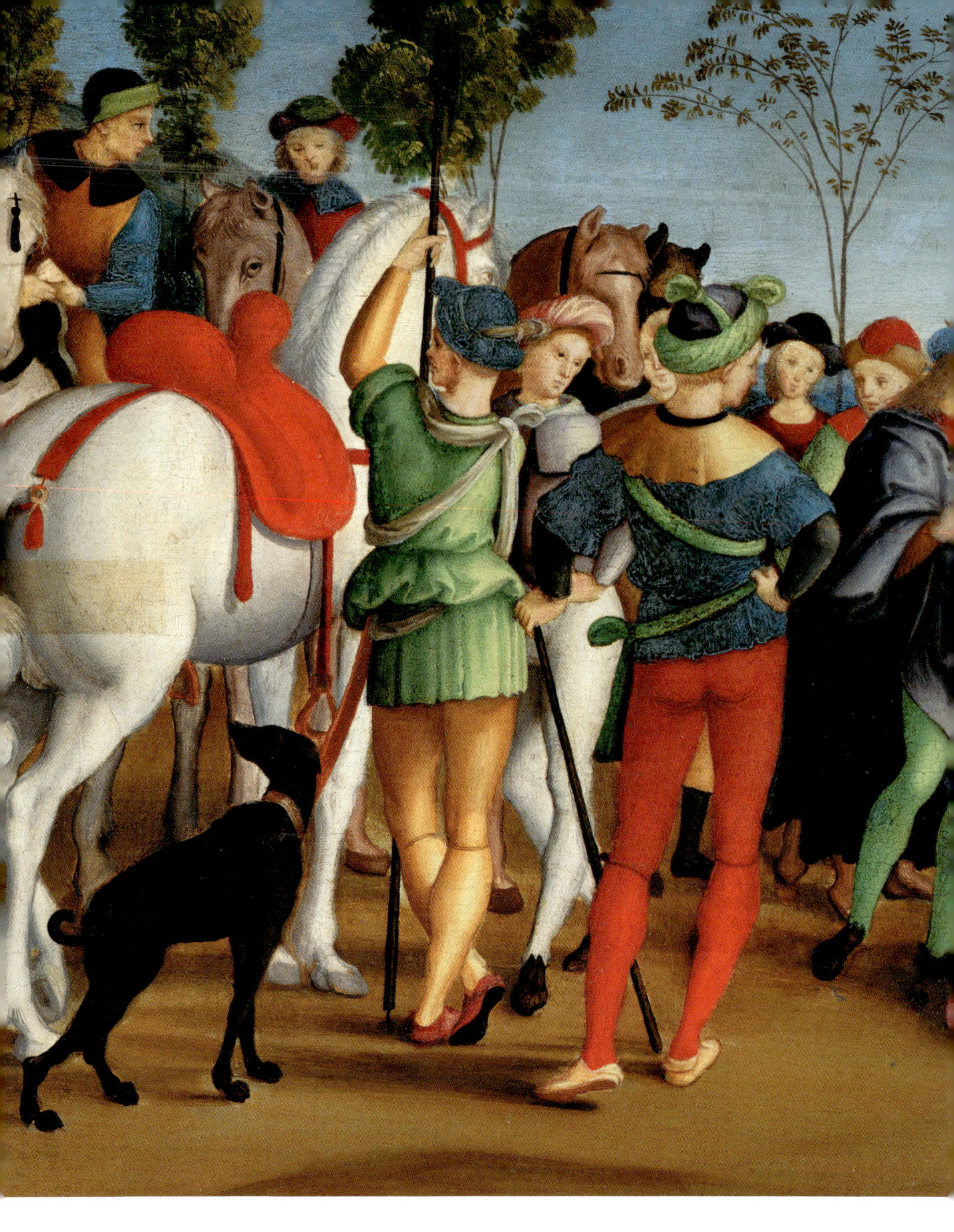

Adoration of the Magi (Oddi Altarpiece, Predella), 1503/04
Oil on panel, 39 × 190 cm (15 3/8 × 74 3/4 in). Vatican City, Musei Vaticani, Pinacoteca

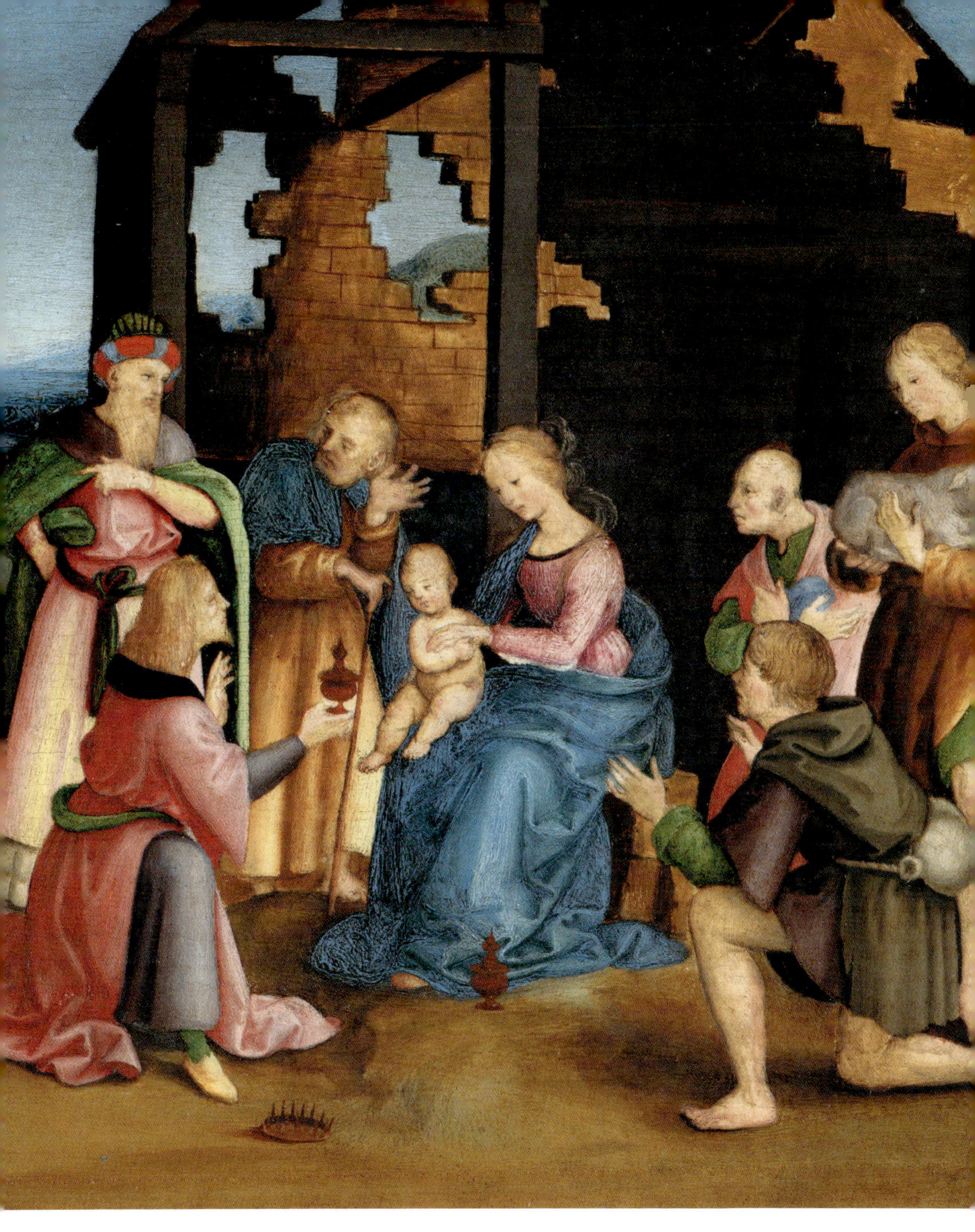

Pietro Perugino
Marriage of the Virgin, 1499/1501–1504
Oil on panel, 236 × 186 cm (92 7/8 × 73 1/4 in)
Caen, Musée des Beaux-Arts

The Marriage of the Virgin (Lo Sposalizio/Pala Albizzini), 1504
Oil on panel, 170 × 118 cm (66 7/8 × 46 1/2 in)
Inscription: *.RAPHAEL. VRBINAS. MDIIII*
Milan, Pinacoteca di Brera
(Detail page 13)

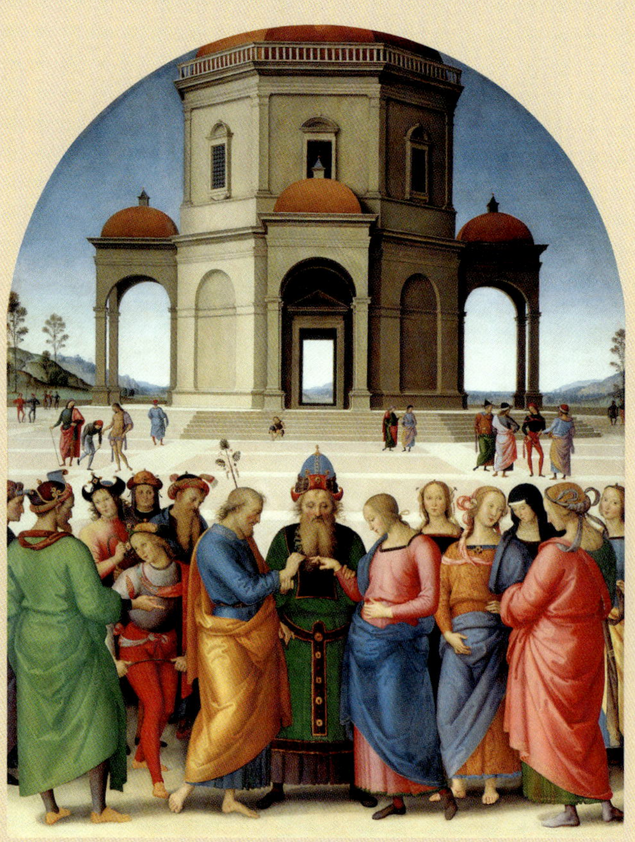

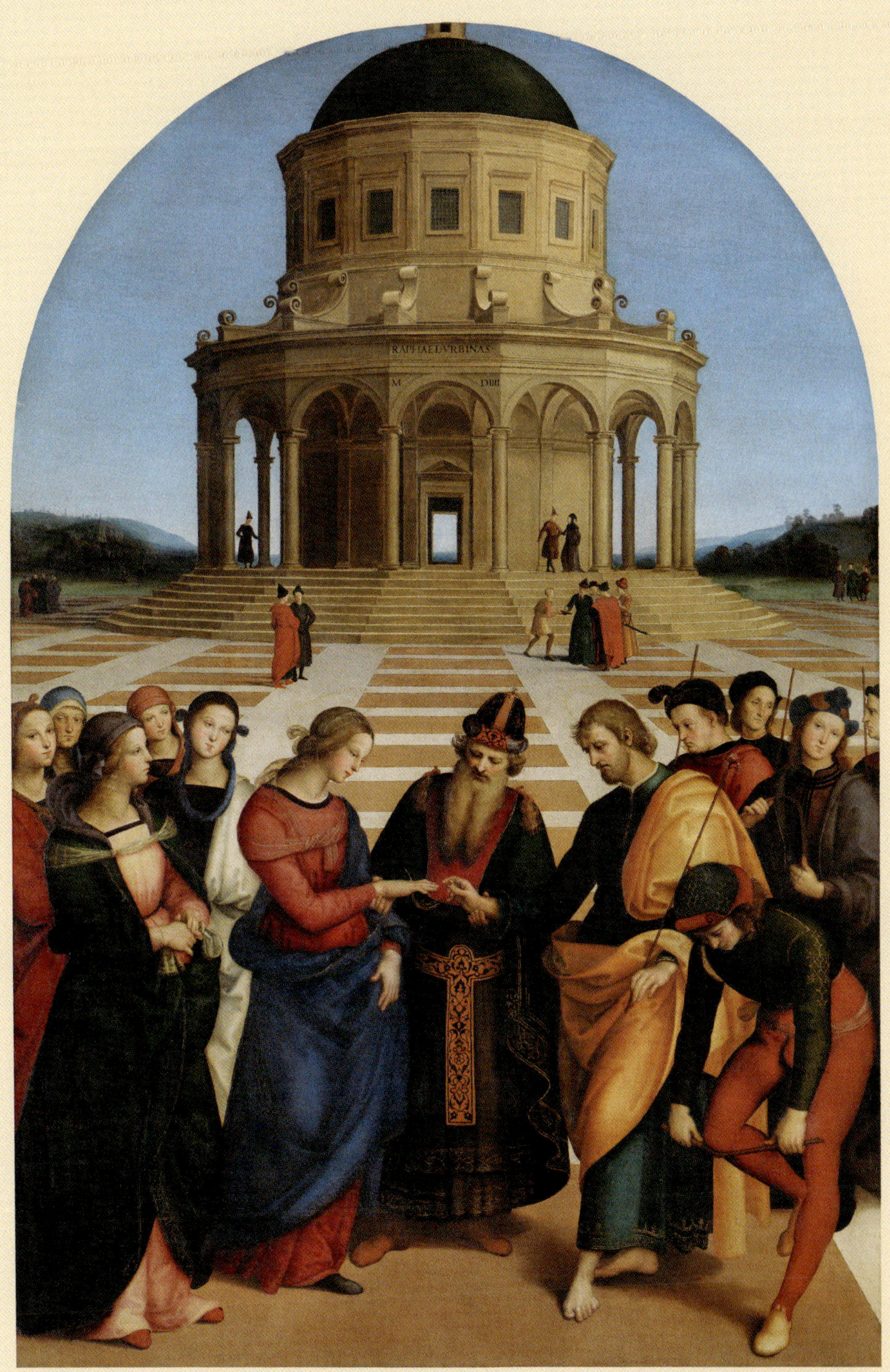
RAPHAEL VRBINAS
M
DIIII

II.

The New Art: From Florence to Urbino and Umbria

1504–1508

Michael Rohlmann

"From his first beginnings, however shy, he paints people of a divine race, over whom a sweetness is poured like a glimmer of light from the lost Paradise. His figures fill those who pursue them with a profound yearning for a higher nature."

JACOB BURCKHARDT, 1844/45

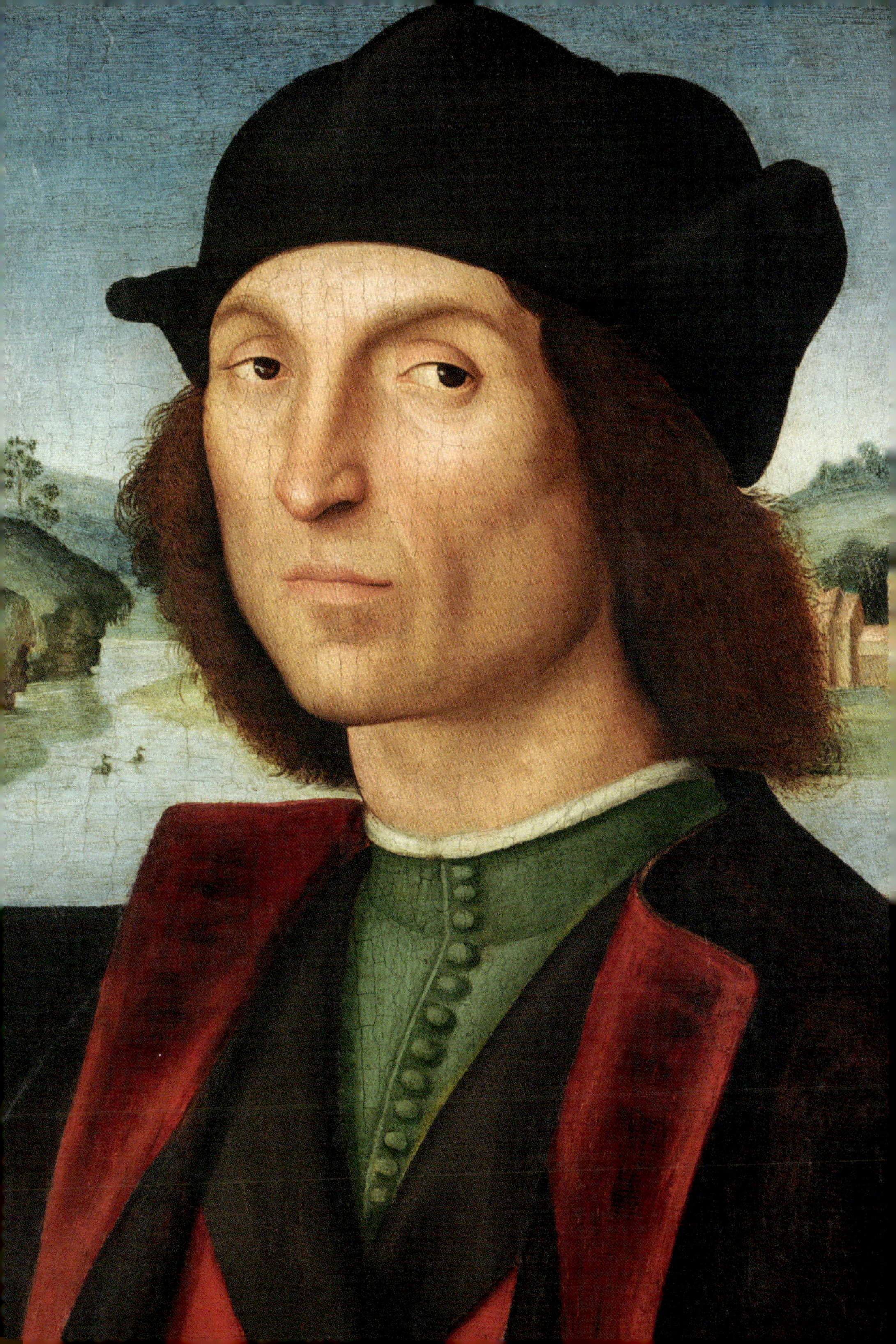

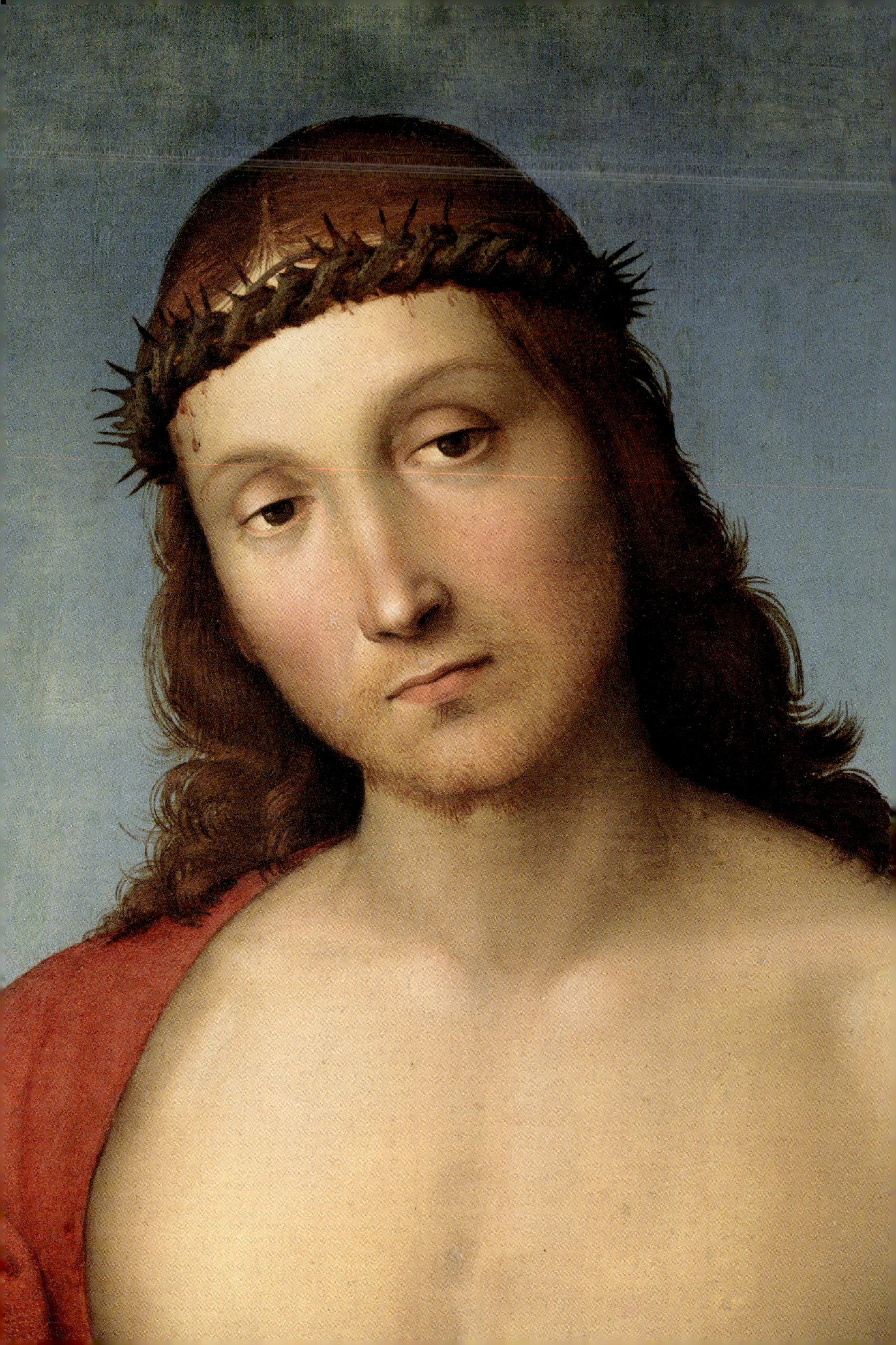

A letter of recommendation from Giovanna Feltria della Rovere, the sister of Duke Guidobaldo da Montefeltro, is dated 1 October 1504. From Urbino, she addressed a special request to the Florentine head of state Piero Soderini (1452–1522): Raphael wished to spend some time in Florence in order to study there. The authenticity of this letter, first documented in 1754, is disputed. According to Vasari, following the *Sposalizio* (Cat. P13), dated 1504, Raphael went to Siena, where he executed the drawings for the Piccolomini Library. From here, the fame of the battle cartoons created by Leonardo and Michelangelo for the Florentine council chamber led him to the city on the Arno. A letter of recommendation to Soderini, who had commissioned the council chamber frescoes, would thereby surely have seemed desirable to Raphael. This is also supported by a document written a few years later: in a letter to his uncle dated 21 April 1508, Raphael mentioned that he was hoping for a recommendation addressed to Soderini from Giovanna's son, Francesco Maria della Rovere. At that time, he signed himself "Your Raphael, painter in Florence" ("El vostro Raphaello dipintore in Fiore[n]za").

It is certain that, after 1504, Raphael was increasingly based in Florence, before in 1508 moving to the papal court in Rome. The economic and artistic metropolis of Florence was at that time a republic under Soderini's leadership; the Medici family, who had long dominated politics, had been overthrown and expelled in 1494. Vasari speaks of close friendships formed by Raphael during this Florentine period with Fra Bartolomeo (1472–1517), as well as with the young Aristotele da Sangallo (1481–1551) and Ridolfo Ghirlandaio (1482–1561). In winter, artists met in the workshop of Baccio d'Agnolo (1462–1543) and talked: Raphael, the sculptor Andrea Sansovino (*c.* 1460–1529), the architect Cronaca (1457–1508), Antonio (1455–1534) and Giuliano da Sangallo (*c.* 1445–1516), Granacci (*c.* 1469–1543), occasionally Michelangelo, many young Florentines and others from farther afield. A number of merchants also became good friends, such as Lorenzo Nasi and Taddeo Taddei (1470–1529). The latter, a cultivated merchant with contacts in Urbino, was constantly inviting Raphael to his house. Raphael himself wrote in 1508 that there was no other living person to whom he was more attached.

To observe Raphael over these four years of Florentine inspiration is to witness one of the most astonishing phenomena in art history. An established painter with a successful, recognisable style sets off to learn more, and avidly processes and absorbs qualities,

Page 63
Detail from **Portrait of a Man**, *c.* 1503/04
(see ill. p. 115)

Detail from **Christ Blessing (Pax Vobiscum)**, *c.* 1505/06
(see ill. p. 109)

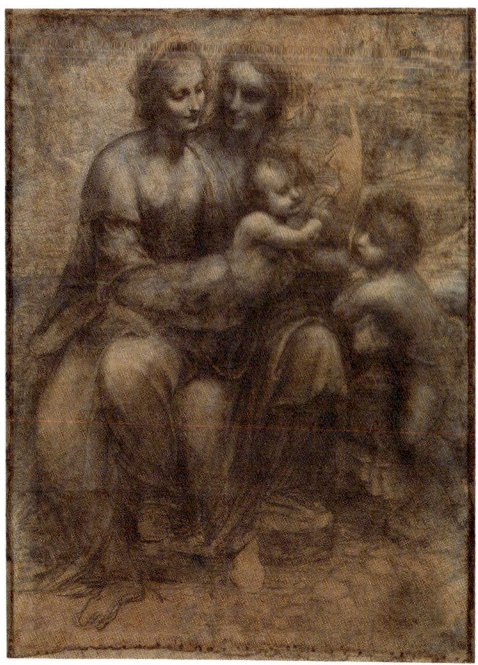

Leonardo da Vinci
Virgin and Child with Saint Anne and the Infant Saint John the Baptist ("The Burlington House Cartoon"), 1499/1500 or *c.* 1508 (?)
Charcoal heightened with white on brownish paper, mounted on canvas, 141.5 × 106.5 cm (55 ¾ × 41 ⅞ in) (max. dimensions)
London, The National Gallery

inventions and motifs from a unique variety of sources. He copies, varies, combines and experiments and thereby arrives at ever new solutions. Here we meet a fundamental trait that will characterise Raphael's art all his life: the ability to keep on developing and evolving and, with insatiable curiosity, to absorb everything unfamiliar and make it his own. No standing still, no repeating of formulae that were successful in the past, but the constant forging ahead of a boundless imagination. No other artist of the Renaissance travelled a similar path or underwent a similar development. After four years, Raphael had completely transformed his style. The early Peruginesque painter of a pious, delicate gracefulness has become the master of the new style of heroic gravitas, the companion of Leonardo and competitor of Michelangelo in a "classical art" (Wölfflin 1899).

The scale on which Raphael assimilated the great Florentine artistic tradition of the fifteenth century can only be briefly indicated here. A small number of surviving drawings show Raphael making copies of works by other artists, but what he studied in Florence is primarily witnessed by reflections in his own art. These reflections extend even into his late Roman period. Raphael's study of Masaccio's frescoes in the Brancacci chapel is specifically mentioned by Vasari; he would later compete with their powerful, dignified figures and groups in his own designs for the Acts of the Apostles (Cat. T) and in the Stanze (Cat. F3.1j, F3.1s). Raphael took up the statue and relief of Saint George by Donatello

(1386–1466) in drawing (KMOF 165) and painting (p. 99; Cat. P27). Copy drawings of playing putti from the bronze pulpits in San Lorenzo also survive (Bambach 2007). Raphael must also have been familiar with Donatello's *Life of Saint Anthony* reliefs in Padua (cf. Cat. F3.1j, F3.2a, T6, P46). The reliefs on the Florence Baptistery doors by Ghiberti (1378–1455) also served as a model (e. g. for *Solomon and the Queen of Sheba*: Cat. F6.12d). Raphael was fascinated by Pollaiuolo's manner of portraying naked male figures in violent movement, above all in his *Battle of the Naked Men* engraving (cf. KMOF 30, 61, 134, 135, 516). Domenico Ghirlandaio's monumental fresco cycles for the Sassetti and Tornabuoni chapels became major sources of inspiration, both in their overall composition and in their details (cf. Sassetti: Cat. F3.3; Tornabuoni: KMOF 207, Cat. P35a, F3.1j, F3.1r). In his 1505 contract for the Monteluce altarpiece in Perugia, Raphael was asked to imitate Ghirlandaio's *Coronation of the Virgin* in Narni. Of Filippino Lippi's frescoes in the Strozzi Chapel, copy drawings survive of two scenes on the vault (KMOF 276, 277). Fra Bartolomeo's *Last Judgement* offered examples of celestial groups (cf. Cat. F2, F3.1r).

The artists most important of all for Raphael, however, were Leonardo and Michelangelo, who at that time in Florence were revolutionising the art of composition, anatomy and expression. Leonardo lived in Florence from 1500 to 1502 and again in 1503. Still here, too, was his early, unfinished *Adoration of the Magi* (p. 271), whose world of figures Raphael would imitate from the *Disputa* (Cat. F3.1r) and the *School of Athens* (Cat. F3.1j) to the *Transfiguration* (Cat. P85) – in part combined with motifs from the *Last Supper* in Milan. Raphael transformed Leonardo's early *Benois Madonna* into the *Madonna of the Pinks* (Cat. P38). Raphael also processed Leonardo's *Madonna of the Yarnwinder* (see Cat. P19), and subsequently various designs for the *Virgin and Child with Saint Anne* (p. 134; cf. Cat. P30, P34a, P39). The *Mona Lisa* became the basis of his Florentine portraiture (KMOF 125, Cat. P25, P29b, P36, P45). Raphael made a drawing of Leonardo's *Leda* (p. 69), whose sinuous *figura serpentinata* established a new ideal of beauty in terms of graceful posture (cf. Cat. P33, P37, P43, F3.1a, F3.1g, F3.1k, F10, KMOF 346).

In 1503 Leonardo started work on his most important Florentine commission: the extremely large-format representation of a cavalry battle for the grand council chamber. Leonardo prepared the *Battle of Anghiari* (p. 98), with its furious mêlée of horses and soldiers and its portrayal of extreme emotions, in drawings, but its execution on the wall barely got beyond the first stages. Raphael made a sketch of the composition (KMOF 112) and used it again and again in dramatic equestrian scenes (Cat. F3.2a, F3.2g, F4.5, T6). Raphael here had access – as in the case of other works by Leonardo, too – to the latter's preliminary drawings, which points to a close relationship between the two. This is supported by Raphael's adoption of Leonardo's agile, sketch-like drawing technique, which circumscribes a motif with numerous rapid lines in an open and searching manner, and only arrives at the final form as it corrects and varies itself in the course of drawing. Raphael was likewise influenced by Leonardo's handling of colour and light, his distinctive chiaroscuro, which also lent new weight to the dark zones in Raphael's work and new corporeality to his human figures.

Raphael's personal contact with Michelangelo, who in 1501 returned to Florence from Rome, seems to have been less close. The inspiration he took from Michelangelo seems to have come chiefly from the latter's works (on the following, see Forlani Tempesti in: Florence 1984c). Following the installation of the *David* in 1504 (p. 76), Raphael drew and thereby modified the marble colossus (p. 77; KMOF 226, cf. KMOF 166, 167, 169, 174). He likewise copied Michelangelo's unfinished *Saint Matthew* from the planned series of marble Apostles for Florence Cathedral (KMOF 206), and subsequently took inspiration from its powerful figure and head on several occasions (see Cat. P35a, F3.2q, KMOF 215, 223, 369, 390). From the marble *Bruges Madonna*, Raphael adopted and varied the Christ Child standing and moving between his mother's legs (cf. KMOF 158, 184, Cat. P31, P39). He also studied the pose of the Christ Child in the *Taddei Tondo* (Chatsworth House, Collection of the Duke of Devonshire, inv. 723b, see KMOF 133, 161, 162, Cat. P41; cf. also the Infant John in Cat. P31). The *Pitti Tondo* (p. 154) served as a model for Raphael's *Charity* (Cat. P35c; see KMOF 218). In the case of Michelangelo's painted *Doni Tondo* (p. 269), Raphael was interested in the Virgin's complicated twisting turn (see Cat. P35a, F3.1h, F3.3l) as well as in the climbing pose of the Infant Christ (cf. Cat. P37, P58, F3.1b, F9b). Raphael adopted the Infant John peering out from the background in the *Pitti Tondo* and *Doni Tondo* on multiple occasions (see Cat. P61, P62).

Undoubtedly Raphael's most important source, however, was Michelangelo's cartoon of the *Battle of Cascina* (p. 74) for the Florentine council chamber. Awarded in 1504, the commission was conceived as a pendant to Leonardo's *Battle of Anghiari*. Michelangelo was to depict troops getting ready for battle, responding to a sham warning alarm as they bathed without a care. Just as the *David* sculpture gazing intently outwards, ready for action beside the entrance to the town hall, publicly proclaimed vigilance as a given virtue of the Florentine Republic, so the fresco inside was to challenge and rouse the city council to the same vigilance and readiness for war. A correlation was thus established between the art decorating the palace inside and outside. In both works, sculpture and painting, Michelangelo created a new, heroic image of man. The gallery of interwoven athletic male nudes, elaborated for the fresco in a huge cartoon, illustrated the ideals of a superior, more muscular physical beauty, represented by figures seen from all angles and in a host of different and deliberately hard-to-render movements. For artists, the cartoon represented "a school for all the world" (Cellini). Raphael copied this new, artificial art of the human body and returned to it again and again (p. 75; cf. KMOF 136, 180, 234–236, 340, 345, 471, 476–479, 586; Cat. F3.1j, T1).

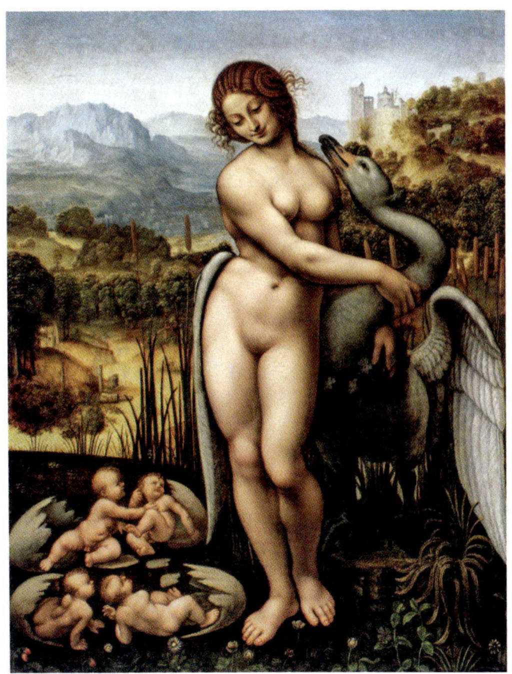

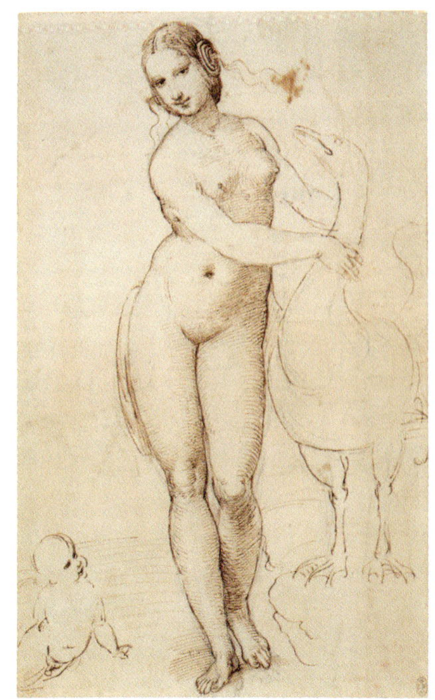

Major commissions were not immediately forthcoming for Raphael in Florence. Orders from Urbino and Umbria, on the other hand, were plentiful. Raphael interrupted his stay in Florence several times, on occasions for extended periods, in order to return to his hometown or to travel to Perugia. He had maintained his close contacts with the Urbino court and supplied it with numerous works. In 1507 his personal presence in Urbino is documented by two sources. According to Vasari, Raphael painted two small Madonnas for Duke Guidobaldo. For the Duke's wife, Elisabetta, Raphael executed a devotional painting of the Agony in the Garden, which was intended as a gift for a monk in Camaldoli. Guidobaldo's sister Giovanna possessed a Madonna picture, whose lid Raphael mentions in a letter of 1508. He probably also painted a portrait of Pietro Bembo (1470–1547) in Urbino in 1507. It has not been possible to identify any of these works with certainty. Early portraits survive of various members of the ducal family.

Cesare da Sesto (?) after Leonardo, **Leda and the Swan**, 1515–1520
Oil on panel, 96.5 × 73.7 cm (37 ⅞ × 29 ⅛ in)
Salisbury, Wilton House, Collection of the Earl of Pembroke and Montgomery

Leda and the Swan (after Leonardo), 1505/06
Pen over stylus underdrawing, 30.8 × 19.2 cm (12 ⅛ × 7 ½ in). Windsor Castle, Royal Library

In the seventeenth century, some of them were taken from Urbino to Florence. In some cases, their attribution or identification is disputed (pp. 93–95; Cat. P12, P20, P21).

Among the works for Urbino, five small, exquisite panels stand out. They probably served as a folding diptych, a picture with an accompanying painted lid, and a diplomatic gift. The works are cabinet pieces designed to be held in the hand and admired close up. The diptych shows two sword-wielding saints doing battle with monstrous dragons (Cat. P16). The saints in question are patrons of knights and chivalric orders. Federico da Montefeltro was a member of a Neapolitan Order of Saint Michael and a Knight of the English Order of the Garter, whose patron was Saint George (Marcelli 2020). In 1504 Federico's son, Duke Guidobaldo, was also admitted to the Order of the Garter, and in 1503 the young Francesco Maria della Rovere was made a Knight of Saint Michael by the King of France. Raphael perhaps also links the two saints with the Montefeltro and Rovere families via the colours of their dress: Saint Michael wears a blue skirt over his golden armour and thus displays the two heraldic colours of the Della Rovere coat of arms. Saint George wears a suit of black and gold armour and hence presents the Montefeltro colours. These latter are also found in the sitter's dress in Raphael's portrait of Guidobaldo's wife, the Duchess Elisabetta (p. 95; Cat. P20).

The *Saint Michael* (p. 97; Cat. P16a) is a quite astonishing reformulation of old biblical theme. The young Raphael here demonstrates the richness of his imagination when it comes to inventing wondrous and terrible monsters never seen before. Only in the case of a few details has he borrowed from Dürer's *Apocalypse* woodcut. The colourfully shimmering angel displays grace in an elegant twisting pose. And in the background, the painter becomes a poet, designing a Hell pervaded by motifs from Dante Alighieri (1265–1321). The infernal city burns, fire strikes out of tombs, and the punished hypocrites struggle past in their heavy leaden coats, only gilded on the outside (*Divine Comedy*, Hell, XXIII). To the right, in the next chasm of Hell, are the naked thieves, who are constantly tormented by snakes (XXIV). Through their gilded coats and serpent adversaries, the two groups of sinners establish a deliberately chosen foil to the celestial knight in his gleaming golden armour, effortlessly trampling on the serpent-dragon. Saint Michael is thus portrayed as a virtuous hero who triumphs over the vices.

Saint George (p. 96; Cat. P16b) is defending the king's daughter, in what appears to relate to the safeguarding of power – the Borgia occupation of Urbino had only recently ended. The dragon is a serious opponent. A first strike with a lance (its splintered pieces are red and white, like Saint Michael's shield opposite) has provoked the beast to attack

Detail from **Portrait of Elisabetta Gonzaga**, *c.* 1504–1506
(see ill. p. 95)

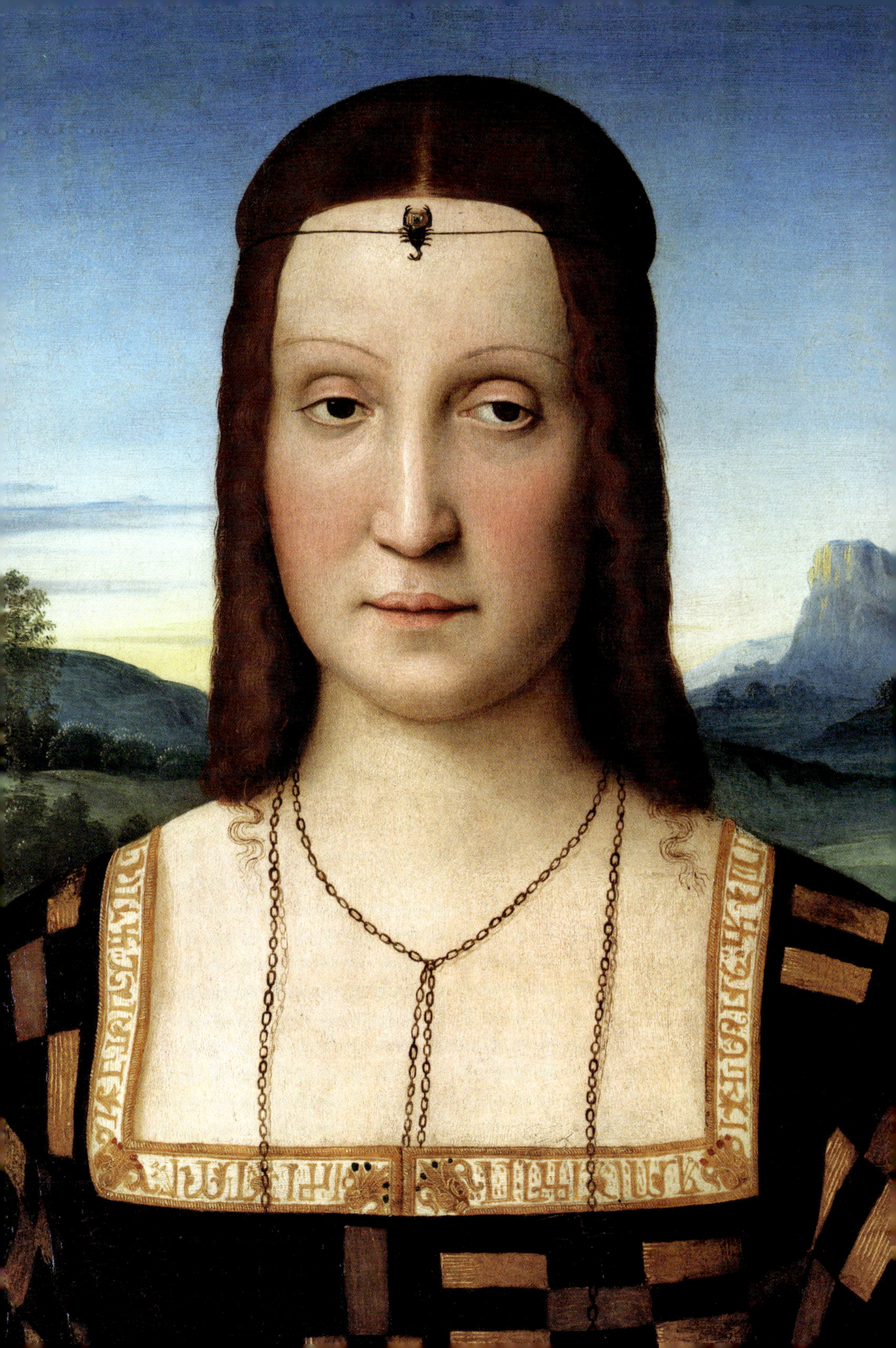

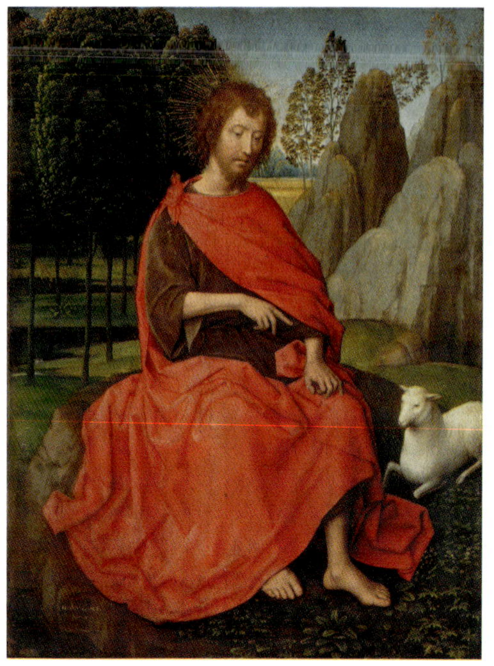

with increased ferocity. On the right, the terrified horse rears while the princess desperately attempts to escape. The calmness with which the holy knight raises his sword to deliver the decisive stroke appears all the more composed and sublime. What Raphael learned in Florence from Leonardo in terms of movement and emotion is clearly visible here.

Raphael also represented Saint George and the Dragon with reference to the English Order of the Garter in a second, even smaller painting (p. 99; Cat. P27). The landscape assumes greater significance: it shows plants in detail, the dragon's dark lair in the rocks, and in the distance the Roman Torre delle Milizie. Handsome groups of trees gleam in the sunlight – Raphael has here studied the detailed manner of the Early Netherlandish painter Hans Memling (1433/40–1494; p. 72). In comparison with the *Saint George* of the diptych, Raphael here shows an earlier moment in the battle and lends the duel a different character: the lance pierces the already fleeing dragon, the horse looks joyfully out at us, and the princess has transformed into a praying saint. Saint George here has to ride towards the left so that we can see the blue Garter of the Order worn below his left knee. Raphael was thereby able to orient himself towards the composition of Donatello's Saint George relief in Florence. If Clough's (1984/85) assumption is correct, Castiglione, as Guidobaldo's envoy, presented the painting to Gilbert Talbot (*c.* 1452/55–1517/18; a member of the Order since 1495) during his visit to England in 1506. Talbot had previously invested the Duke into the Order in Italy on behalf of the English king.

Even smaller is the jewel-bright gem of painting depicting the *Vision of a Knight* (p. 101; Cat. P17a). Raphael here once again proves himself a poet. He modifies the antique thematic

Hans Memling, **Saint John the Baptist**, 1470s/1480s
Oil on panel, 31.8 × 24.4 cm (12 ½ × 9 ⅝ in). Munich, Bayerische Staatsgemäldesammlungen, Alte Pinakothek

Circle of Raphael (?), **Portrait of a Young Man**, *c.* 1505 (?)
Oil on panel, 53.5 × 41.2 cm (21 ⅛ × 16 ¼ in). Munich, Bayerische Staatsgemäldesammlungen, Alte Pinakothek

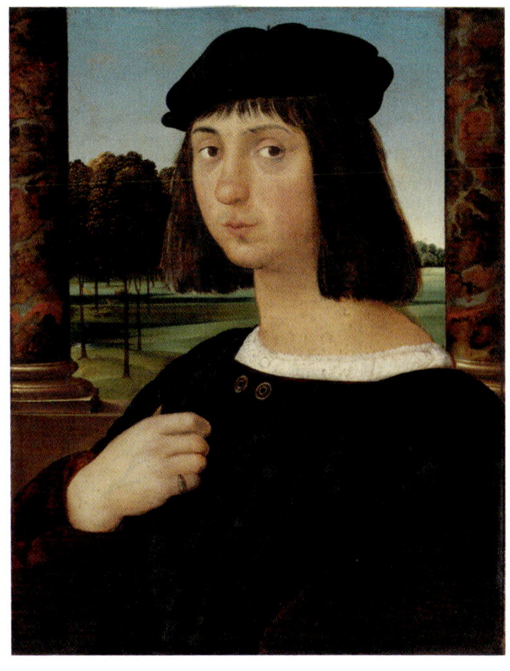

tradition of Hercules at the Crossroads between Virtue and Vice and does not have his hero decide between two life paths. Rather, the sleeper is shown what he needs to do in order for the laurel tree of glory to grow out of him and up towards heaven. On the left, a plainly and soberly dressed personification of Virtue holds out a sword and a book. *Arma et litterae* was an ideal already propagated earlier by Federico da Montefeltro. On the right, a sprightly beauty dressed in luminous colours and bathed in sunlight offers a sprig of myrtle. The flower, which is traditionally found in wedding bouquets, tells us that she is a bride. Wagner (1999) suspects that the panel celebrates the engagement of Francesco Maria della Rovere, the heir to the throne of Urbino, to Eleonora Gonzaga (1493–1550) of Mantua, which took place in 1504/05. This is confirmed by the landscape: the long, covered bridge in the right-hand background, bounded by a church and towers, is of the type only found in Mantua, where it connected the city surrounded by lakes with the outside world. It was a well-known and highly admired marvel of engineering. Mantegna had depicted the Ponte di San Giorgio as a vedutà in his *Death of the Virgin*, where it serves as a metaphor for the Mother of God's passage from this life into the world beyond, into the heavenly arms of Christ. Rubens (1577–1640) later incorporated a view of the bridge into his *Self-Portrait in a Circle of Friends from Mantua* as a connecting "friendship bridge" between the sitters. Raphael creates a parallel to the bridge with the outstretched arm of the beautiful young woman, who presents the bridal bouquet as if from Mantua across to the mainland. The city perched on the rock on the left could then be understood as representing Urbino or *mons Feretri*, the ancestral seat of the Montefeltro family. Raphael shows no vedute here, and his landscape is perhaps inspired compositionally, too, by Botticelli's Florentine *Cestello Annunciation* (Gould 1978). Nevertheless, the meaning of the symbolic landscape would have been obvious at the court of Urbino: via the bridge, Mantua offers a link to a mountainous landscape. Duke Guidobaldo had already led a Gonzaga daughter from Mantua into the mountains of the Marches when he married Elisabetta, Raphael's patroness.

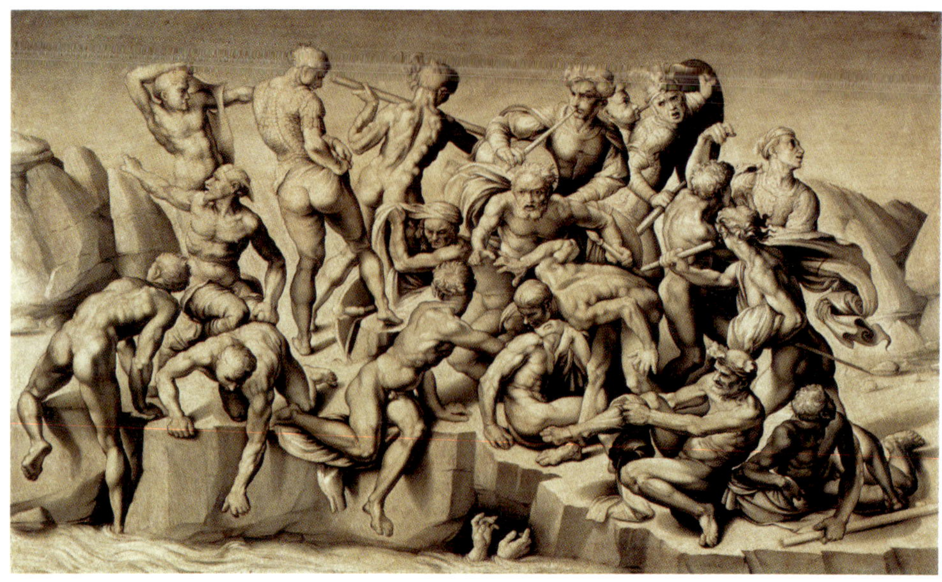

Executed in a simpler mode of painting, *The Three Graces* (p. 100; Cat. P17b) probably served as the lid to the *Vision of the Knight*. Raphael was here competing with Sienese antiquity. The three beauties all look alike and rest one hand on another's shoulder while holding a golden apple like a gift in the other hand. They thus suggest the unity and parity of a trinity, which the viewer is evidently meant to transfer to the three attributes belonging to the sleeping knight in the pendant panel: sword, book and love are not opposites, but unite in the young hero into graceful harmony. Above and beyond the emphasis on a courtly philosophy of life, however, the painting with its suggestive, soft carnality, and its display of female buttocks at the very centre of the picture, promised the young Francesco Maria first and foremost sensual erotic pleasure. This was indeed a necessity, because in the case of Guidobaldo and Elisabetta, the Montefeltro dynasty had produced no heirs owing to the husband being unable to father a child: "Nulla cum foemina coire umquam in tota vita potuisse" ("Never in his whole life was he able to mate with a woman"), as Pietro Bembo put it. On the occasion of Guidobaldo and Elisabetta's

Aristotile da Sangallo (?), ***Battle of Cascina* after Michelangelo's cartoon (1505/06)**, before 1519
Grisaille on panel, 76.4 × 130.2 cm (30 ⅛ × 51 ¼ in). Norfolk, Holkham Hall, Collection of the Earl of Leicester

Studies of figures in motion, 1506/07
Pen, 20.2 × 14.8 cm (7 ⅞ × 5 ⅞ in). Vatican City, Biblioteca Apostolica Vaticana

wedding, Raphael's father had written and performed a mythological play, in which Juno, the goddess of marriage, and Diana, the goddess of chastity, argued which way of life was better. Jupiter finally decided in favour of marriage. Raphael succeeded his father not as a poet with words, but with his painting and the ambition to craft his own poetry in pictures. In *Vision of the Knight*, he thereby took up and continued one of his own works: the knight lies asleep in the landscape like Adam, from whom God takes a rib in order to create Eve, so that he can subsequently present Adam with a welcome companion (Cat. P3b). The beautiful young woman has already approached the knight, and the laurel springs, as if from his side, as the family tree of a new, glorious dynasty.

In 1505 Raphael spent an extended period in Perugia. There he probably completed two altarpieces, frescoed an altar wall and at the end of the year accepted a commission for another large altarpiece. The first fruits of Raphael's experiences in Florence are plainly visible in these works. The *Colonna Altarpiece* (pp. 102–105; Cat. P22) presents the old, standard type of altarpiece known as a *sacra conversazione*: the assembly of the saints particularly venerated at the altar in question around the enthroned Virgin and Child. It was intended for Sant'Antonio, a small convent of nuns following the rule of the Franciscan Third Order. Perhaps Raphael owed the commission to the convent's most prominent resident: Ilaria Baglioni, the elder sister of Alessandra Baglioni Oddi, for whom Raphael had painted the *Oddi Altarpiece* (Cat. P11). Raphael seems to have embarked on the retable a few years before 1505. The throne with steps is borrowed from Perugino's *Decemviri Altarpiece* (1483–1495) in the chapel in Perugia's town hall. The group of the Virgin and Child with the Infant Baptist drawing near one side follows Pinturicchio's model. Although Raphael's palette is still dominated by the strong colours of his early works (Wagner 1999), the multiple references in the predella panels to Florentine works by Perugino, as well as the new monumentality of the powerful drapery figures of Saint Peter and Saint Paul in the main picture, support the completion date of 1505 given in a nineteenth-century source. The two apostles flank the group of holy women like guards, as

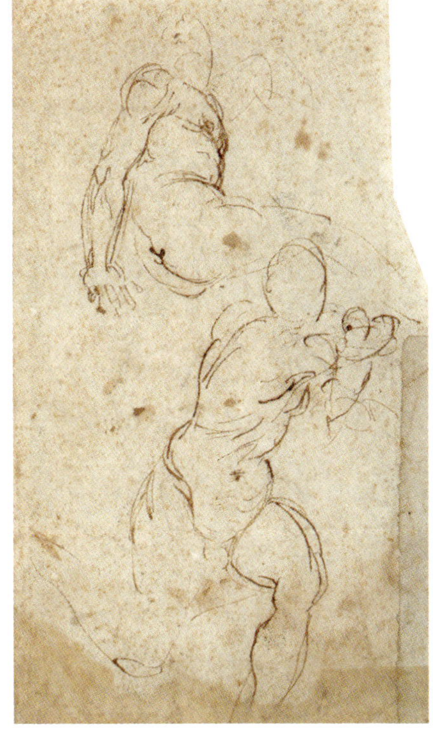

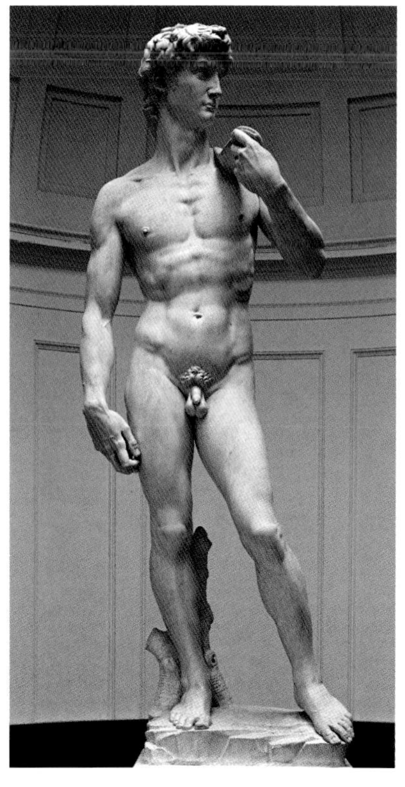

if to reinforce the support of the papacy for the community of nuns, whose autonomy was under threat. Rising above the two apostles are Saint Catherine, who betrothed herself to Christ, and Saint Cecilia, who chose a life of chastity. Shifted closer to the Virgin and Child, the female saints, like Mary herself, served to a certain extent as figures of identification for the convent's nuns.

With its saints, Raphael's retable complemented the polyptych by Piero della Francesca in the public church of Sant'Antonio. The public church and the separate, inner church used by the nuns met at their altar ends, so that Piero and Raphael's paintings effectively stood back to back. In Piero's altarpiece, Saint Anthony of Padua – as the saint to whom the church was dedicated – appeared in a suitably prominent position within an entirely Franciscan programme of saints. Raphael's only allusion to this are two small Franciscan saints on the sides of his predella (pp. 104, 105; Cat. P22c, 22f). His focus lay not on the patron saints of the church and the Order, but on the interests of the community of women. Vasari tells us that the simple, pious nuns had wished the Infant Jesus to be fully clothed. Perhaps this was not an expression of conservative, prudish taste (after all, Piero's Christ child is naked!), but a deliberate part of the forms of meditation practised in convents, concentrating on maternal care for the Child. Well protected by clothing, the Infant Christ blesses the praying young Baptist approaching within the picture – just as God the Father, from the lunette above the main panel, blesses the nuns originally gathered in front of it (Cat. P22b).

The date on Raphael's *Ansidei Altarpiece* (pp. 106, 107; Cat. P23) can probably be read as 1505. In 1483 the wool merchant Filippo Ansidei, who died in 1490, had erected an

Michelangelo Buonarroti, **David**, 1501–1504
Marble, height 5.16 m (203 1/8 in). Florence, Galleria dell'Accademia

Male nude seen from behind, after Michelangelo's *David*, 1507/08
Pen over traces of a black chalk underdrawing, 39.6 × 21.9 cm (15 5/8 × 8 5/8 in)
London, British Museum, Department of Prints and Drawings

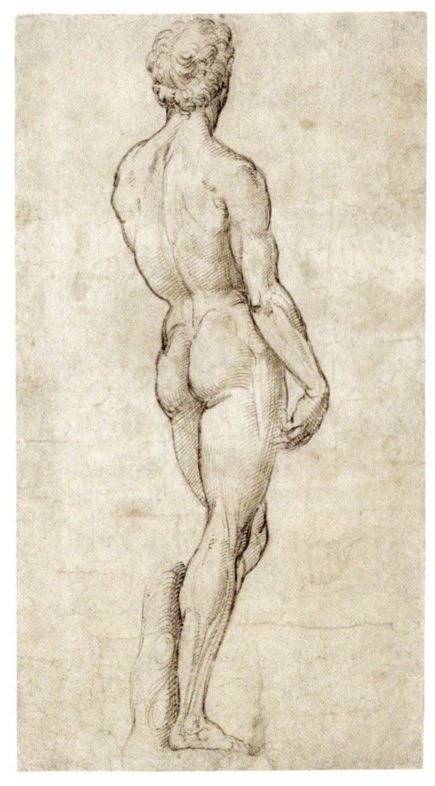

altar dedicated to Saint Nicholas in the Servite church of San Fiorenzo in Perugia. Filippo's son Niccolò commissioned Raphael to paint a *sacra conversazione* as its altarpiece. Here, too, borrowings from earlier local painting have been identified in its composition, in particular from works by Perugino and Signorelli. As in Perugino or in Raphael's *Colonna Altarpiece* (Cat. P22), steps invite the viewer to ascend in their imagination to the throne of the Virgin and Child. Their rhythm carries that of the real altar steps, the altar block and the predella rectangle into the picture, leading from our world into the heavenly throne room. The Mother of God, enthroned like a sovereign, and her child are flanked on either side by a saint: on the right, wholly lost in his reading, stands Saint Nicholas of Bari, patron saint of the altar and name saint of Niccolò Ansidei. Since a lost predella panel from the altarpiece showed Saint Nicholas' miraculous rescue of a merchant ship in a storm at sea, his veneration by the donor family is probably related to their business. On the left, John the Baptist poses with his right foot stepping elegantly forward. As an aesthetic pendant and *contrapposto* to Nicholas, he opens himself fully outwards. He is the name saint of Niccolò's son Giovanni Battista and probably also of his mother Giovanna, wife of the chapel's donor Filippo.

An inner spiritual connection between the figures, whose respective individuality is made emphatically clear on the outside, reveals itself in the consonance of their four inclined heads. All wear an expression of concentration and thus invite us to likewise look more deeply. Transported in ecstasy, the Baptist has combined his pointing gesture, traditionally associated with the message "Behold the Lamb of God", with the contemplation of his exquisite crystal cross, the symbol of the Sacrificial Lamb, as if he were seeing a vision of Christ's Passion. At the same time, he directs our attention towards the salutation to Mary that can be read across the top of the throne: SALVE MATER CHRISTI. Reading is a theme in the case of the other figures, too: in the book open on her lap, Mary is showing her child a special passage whose text is marked in red. Is the red also a reference to the Passion, which is already leaning towards the Child in the crystal cross? Nicholas reads, completely absorbed in his book. Its content is concealed from us and so remains open for our meditation. Raphael differentiates between various modes of perception and showing. The silent image encourages us to "read" the painting itself.

In the surviving predella panel, *Saint John the Baptist Preaching* (Cat. P23b), the public to which the holy message is addressed itself appears in the picture. John points upwards towards heaven and the main picture. It is marvellous how the different reactions of those assembled are imbued with a psychological dimension, and how the groups are infused with rhythm and fall more and more under the Baptist's spell to the right! As a concluding ornament, his fluttering red draperies convey his spiritual state of excitement.

In the *Ansidei Madonna*, Raphael's figures acquire an enhanced bodily structure and spatial presence, balanced weight, dignified solemnity and inner greatness. A new, majestic aura envelops them. The cohesion of the whole is much greater than in the *Colonna Altarpiece*. The widening throne steps find their visual response in the baldachin narrowing towards the top. The two columns supporting the arch seem to rest, symmetrically left and right, on the shoulders and necks of the saints: architecture and figures correspond. In the clear, crisp light, the palette is more muted. Colours are repeated, vary in nuance and together sound a melodious chord. The goal is harmony.

In 1505, in his first surviving fresco, Raphael decorated the wall zone above a side altar in the Camaldolese church of San Severo (p. 108; Cat. F2) in Perugia. Viewers are given the impression that the heavens have opened up above them and that the blessed are seated there quite naturally on banks of cloud. Their bright, voluminous draperies, modelled in light and shade, are the main constituent of their bodies and are intended to exude powerful dignity – Fra Bartolomeo has been rightly named as a source. Lofty symmetry structures the sky: the vertical tripartite group of the Trinity is flanked to the left and right respectively by a horizontal group of three beatified monks in a foreground spatial plane. The genealogy, holiness and unity of the Camaldolese are propagated. The group on the right, consisting of Romuald and two followers, takes up the model of the first Benedictines on the left. Both groups of monks feature one long-bearded father figure, in line with the Trinity. Three groups of three thus combine into a theologically carefully devised formation in which the San Severo monks' image of themselves is lent expression.

In addition to all these commissions executed in Florence for Urbino and Perugia, Raphael also produced paintings for the Florentine market itself – initially almost exclusively on the standard religious theme of the Madonna and Child. These paintings, which

Detail from **Lady with a Unicorn**, *c.* 1505
(see ill. p. 143)

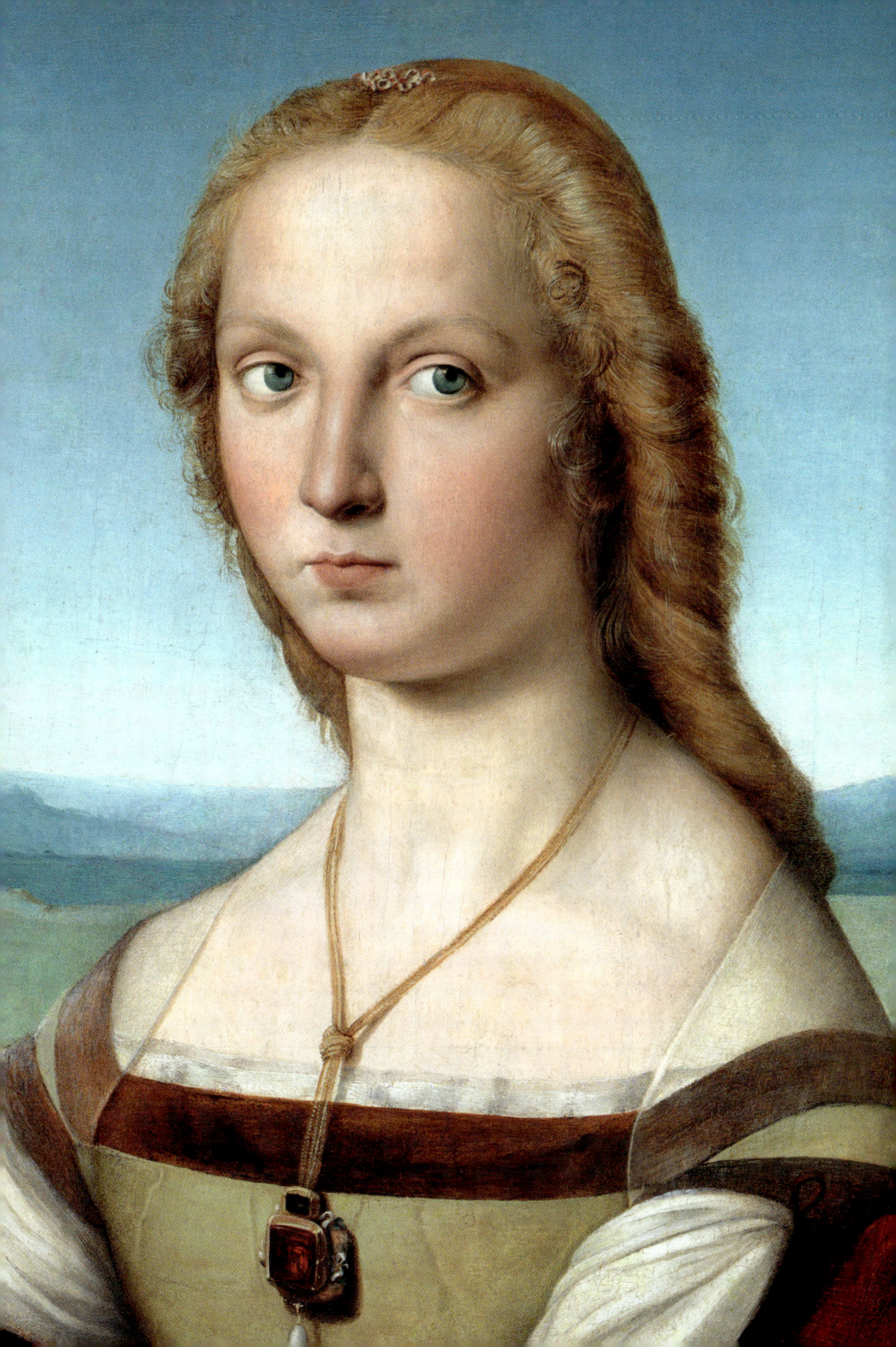

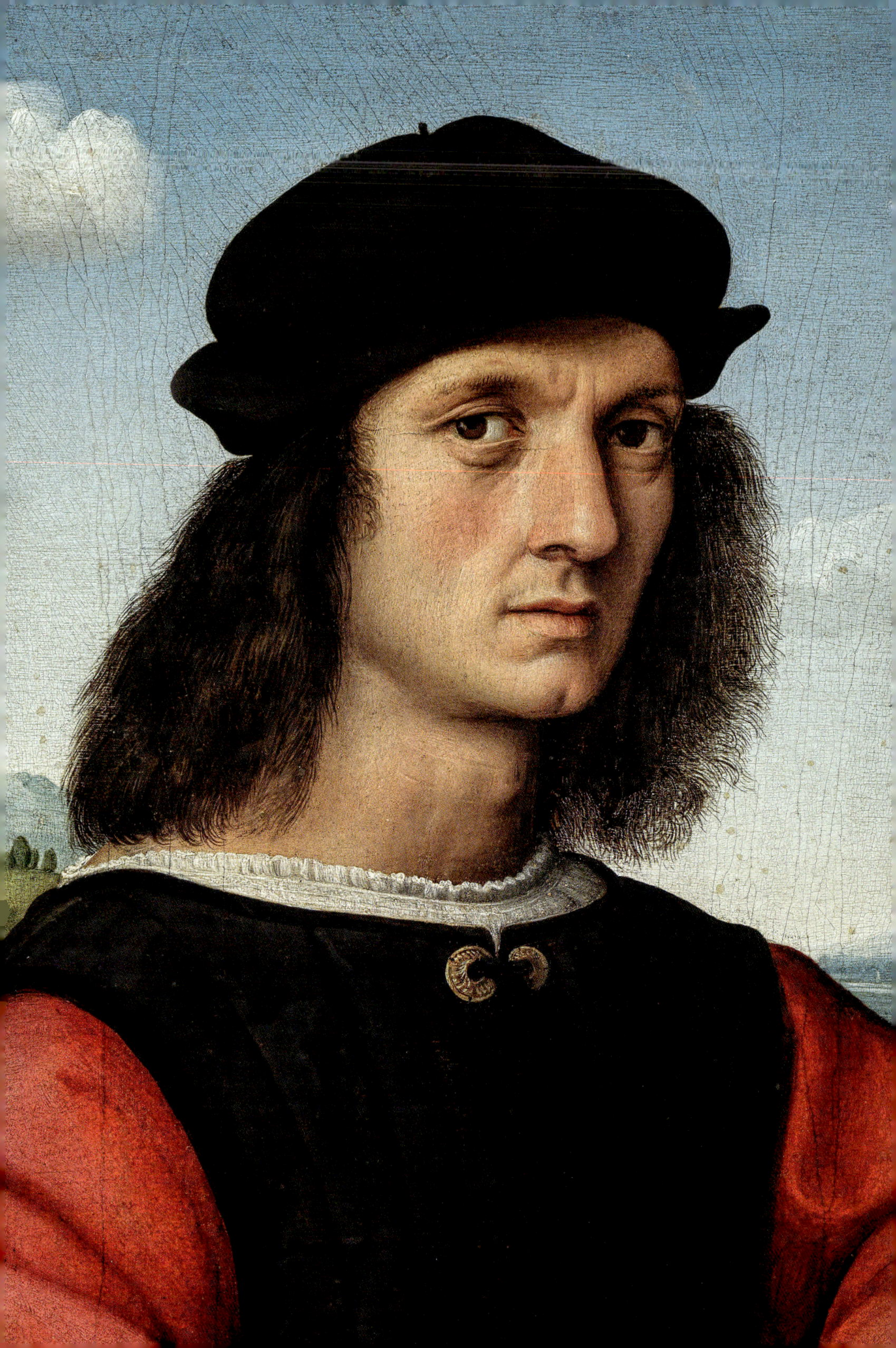

served as domestic devotional images, could evidently also be sold on the open market without an advance client commission. They provided the real-life families residing in Florence's *palazzi* with paradigms in the form of the Holy Family. They presented role models for mothers and children and celebrated beauty, intimacy and piety. Often purchased on the occasion of a marriage or childbirth, they held the promise of hoped-for offspring or were a permanent reminder of the service rendered by the wife through motherhood. Raphael had already painted a number of Madonnas at an early date in Umbria (pp. 111–114; Cat. P4–P6, P10). They are exclusively half-length figures that follow traditional formulas: the Madonna is in every case presented frontally with her head humbly inclined, while at the same time rising majestically into the sky against a landscape backdrop. Her mantle is draped over her head and usually fastened over her chest as in Pinturicchio and Santi, lending the representation a nun-like severity. The Christ Child is always naked, wherein God incarnate reveals himself – human right down to his uncovered sex. Initially the Christ Child sits stiffly at a right angle with his legs first parallel, then more animated, and in the *Solly Madonna* (Cat. P5) even with a slight overlap of one foot. He makes the sign of blessing or looks up, seized with emotion. In one instance the Madonna and Child are accompanied by saints (Cat. P6), in another by the Infant John (Cat. P4). Attributes such as a book, a bird or a cross-staff provide symbolic accents that introduce further layers of meaning. They refer to prophetic knowledge and point to Christ's future role and Passion. A tiny, wonderful tondo (p. 116; Cat. P14), painted with exquisite delicacy, shows mother and child immersed in an equally small book – mirroring the viewer's contemplation of the picture (Wagner 1999). A winter landscape leads away to snow-covered mountains in the background, while the meadows in the foreground are already turning green with the Saviour's incarnation. Christ's pose has become more complex: he leans back, semi-reclining, and the sole of one foot is seen foreshortened from below. This jewel-like tondo was probably intended for the Alfani family in Perugia and evidently deliberately demanded a close-up, in-depth look at its quality – one member of the family was a painter friend of Raphael's.

In Florence, the Umbrian formula relaxes. The Virgin's clothing becomes freer; her body is never again enclosed by a cloak fastened over her chest. Only where the Madonna is standing does her mantle still cover her head (pp. 119, 126; Cat. P26, P46). Where she is seated, she is allowed to take it off, so that her beautiful hair is revealed. A delicate veil always plays around it, as befits a married woman. Her head remains inclined, her eyes lowered in a contemplative fashion. As if liberated, however, her body

Detail from **Portrait of Agnolo Doni**, *c.* 1505/06
(see ill. p. 146)

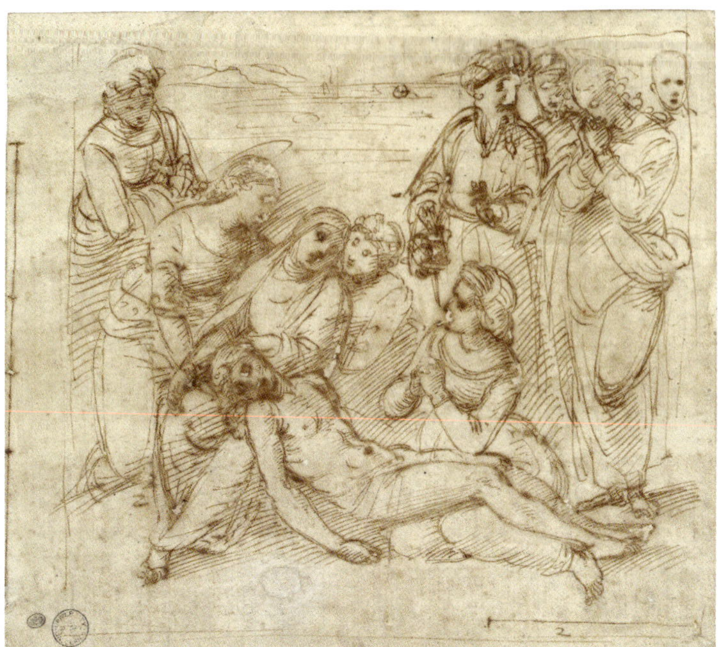

Compositional study for the *Lamentation of Christ*, 1506/07
Pen over stylus underdrawing, 17.9 × 20.6 cm (7 ⅛ × 8 ⅛ in)
Oxford, Ashmolean Museum

Compositional study for the *Entombment*, 1507
Pen, 21.5 × 32 cm (8 ½ × 12 ⅝ in)
London, British Museum, Department of Prints and Drawings

is permitted to turn, and soon her upper body and legs are angled in different directions. Her corporeality becomes palpable within the pictorial space. The Virgin thereby takes a passive, reactive role, sheltering and tenderly caring for the Child. He is suddenly given unrestricted mobility: he turns, stretches, clambers up, lies down, crosses his legs, spreads them apart or stands with one behind the other. He seems to turn actively towards the world and only rarely looks back at his mother. A premonition of separation becomes visible. Raphael aims to convey the appearance of naturalness and increases the sense of vivacity. The bounds of a certain restraint are nevertheless preserved – only once is the Child violently agitated in a Michelangelesque manner (p. 124; Cat. P41). The feeling of emotions is not to be drowned out by action; gracefulness is associated with greater dignity and sacred, more profound knowledge. Raphael studied the motif of the mother and child group in countless sketches, constantly varying their poses. We sense the pleasure he took in seeking after ever new and endless possibilities, his savouring of beauty in the life of the animated body and in the capturing of psychological nuances between child and mother. Attributes now become less important, with the book and flowers appearing just once. The women of the Florentine upper class did not nurse their children themselves, and in Raphael's body of paintings, too, there is no *Maria lactans*. On three occasions, nevertheless, the child reaches for his mother's bodice. In two cases

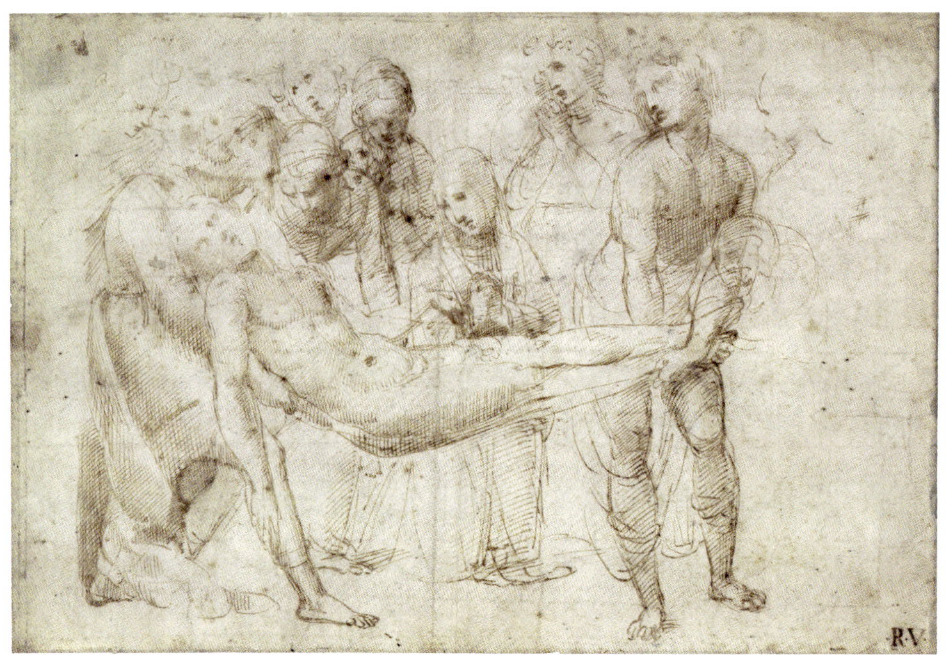

her dress can evidently be unfastened in this spot (pp. 122, 125; Cat. P32, P42), while in the third the mother raises her hand in an impeding manner to her breast (p. 127; Cat. P47). The security of a domestic interior occasionally appears in place of a background landscape. In clear emulation of the Early Netherlandish pictures imported with such success into Florence, Raphael in places embellishes his natural settings with fine details. San Bernardino, the burial church of the ruling dynasty recently constructed on a hill opposite Urbino, is prominently recognisable in one painting (p. 118, 120/121; Cat. P24). The mausoleum appears next to the Child like a *memento mori*. The burial church is at the same time commended to the Infant Christ as a plea for salvation. The picture was undoubtedly destined for the Montefeltros.

Only in Florence does Raphael for the first time also portray the Madonna as a full-length figure. She sits humbly on a bare rock in a peaceful idyllic landscape. These compositions almost always include Saint John, the patron saint of Florence, who as a child hermit once met the Holy Family on their flight to Egypt. Narrative and a dialogue with gestures immediately take shape. The cross-staff is angled towards Christ, a bird is held and stroked, a book is held, and arms reach out towards the prophetic text. The composition becomes more architectural: in three famous pyramidal groups, Mary rotates a little further round each time (pp. 129, 132, 133; Cat. P30, P31, P39). The constellation of the children reinforces the directional axes. The Virgin's head is no longer inclined to one side, but raised upright to form the tip of the pyramid and lent additional significance by a blue, celestial nimbus framed on either side by clouds. The addition of Joseph gives rise to multi-figural groups. The narrative is amplified into a Rest on the Flight to Egypt (p. 135; Cat. P34a): the Infant Jesus – tenderly held by his mother – seated astride a lamb, and exchanging deep, knowing glances with his parents, is an allusion to Christ's later decision to accept the role of sacrificial lamb. The family's flight to Egypt can be seen directly above the Christ Child, in the landscape on the left. Mary and her child are here riding on a donkey to escape – for now, at least – suffering and the threat of death. The viewer is invited to meditate on the parallels between these riding motifs: Christ had to be saved at an infant so that he would be able accomplish his work of salvation later on through his Passion. Where the group is joined by Elizabeth as John's mother (p. 137; Cat. P33), the scene assumes a "convivial, if not social" dimension (Schöne 1958). Even groups of cherubs converse in the clouds. Christ has unknotted John's twisted banderole and in so doing revealed the mystery of the prophecy and read the inscription – already prepared by what he has been reading with his mother. Mary still has one finger in the page they have just been studying. The message shocks and stuns the Infant Baptist. Like an ancient sibyl, the elderly Elisabeth explains its contents to the contemplative Joseph: the child is AGNUS DEI, the Lamb of God. Here a devotional painting has virtually transformed into a history painting.

How strongly Raphael, in his late Florentine period, imbues even a single-figure devotional painting with a narrative charge is demonstrated by *Saint Catherine of Alexandria* (p. 141; Cat. P43). The martyr leans against her wooden instrument of torture but looks in the opposite direction up towards the sky. There, as if a consolation and reward, sunlight breaks through the clouds in a natural atmospheric phenomenon. But as fine golden rays reveal, it is a divine apparition. In the light, Catherine is permeated by heavenly grace, *gratia*. She has already transformed her stance into a graceful *figura serpentinata*. The fulfilment of divine *gratia* is thus visible in an aesthetic image of grace (Kleinbub 2011; Cosgriff 2019b). According to the *Golden Legend*, at her place of execution, the saint raised her eyes to heaven and prayed to God to grant divine mercy to all who invoked her at their hour of death or in any need. A voice answered and promised this divine aid. Through golden rays and celestial light, Raphael's painting renders the hearing of this voice visible. It presents the saint to us for devotion and at the same time certifies, by means of these divine signs, the effectiveness of this devotion.

Only in the case of the costly full-length figural paintings do we know some of the patrons who commissioned them. They were all closely connected and part of a young generation. Raphael's friend Taddeo Taddei (cf. Cat. P30) also owned a marble tondo by

Michelangelo. Taddeo's brother had married a Nasi. In 1506 Lorenzo Nasi (cf. Cat. P31) married a Canigiani. Domenico Canigiani (1486–1548; cf. Cat. P33) lived not far from Nasi in the same street.

Raphael's Florentine commissions also included a small number of portraits. The composition of *Lady with a Unicorn* (p. 143; Cat. P25) is clearly inspired by Leonardo's *Mona Lisa* (p. 142). The balustrade with flanking columns had also been laid down by Leonardo in his painting. Raphael, however, ties the young woman more closely into the architectural setting. Thus the neckline of her dress is matched to the height of the parapet. The same is true of the preparatory drawing (p. 142), whereby the sitter's bodice here ends closer to her throat and the balustrade is correspondingly higher. Her flawless bare skin was intended to establish an association with the sphere of nature. The blue of her eyes is also echoed in the landscape and sky. The bright bust-length figure is framed by the architectural elements like a picture within a picture. The beautiful young woman with blonde locks is oriented towards the ideals of love poetry, and Raphael initially portrayed her with a little dog of Fidelity (perhaps an allusion to the name of the Canigiani family, who used such a dog as a heraldic device; Cat. P31 and P33 were produced in the context of Canigiani weddings). Only later, by means of overpainting, did Raphael let a unicorn take refuge in the arms of the mythically pure virgin. It lends her the magic of the imaginary and the fairy-tale.

The identity of the sitters is known only in the case of the portraits of Agnolo and Maddalena Doni (pp. 146/147; Cat. P29). The married couple who commissioned the painted *Doni Tondo* from Michelangelo also ordered a portrait diptych from Raphael. In his initial concept for the project, Raphael evidently wanted to differentiate the pictorial settings occupied by husband and wife – a scheme for which models existed in Florence. Only Agnolo, as a professionally active merchant, was to be assigned to the open world via a landscape background, whereas Maddalena was to be shown in an interior and thus associated with the domestic sphere. In the final version, however, the two appear in front of a continuous backdrop of landscape and sky. United in the same place and with their bodies angled towards each other, husband and wife form – in aesthetic terms, too – an ideal, inseparable pair of equal partners (see Witte 2012). It is true that Agnolo, on the left, pushes more forcefully against the edges of the picture with his arm and has his hands in a more open position, ready to act. But his head is shifted too far to the left for his picture to exist without a balancing counterweight on the right. Maddalena's head rises slightly above that of her husband and – for the right-hand side of a diptych – her portrait is more self-contained. Raphael has somewhat corrected this by introducing a tall tree silhouetted against the sky on the left, and thus makes the picture thrust almost imperceptibly towards the left.

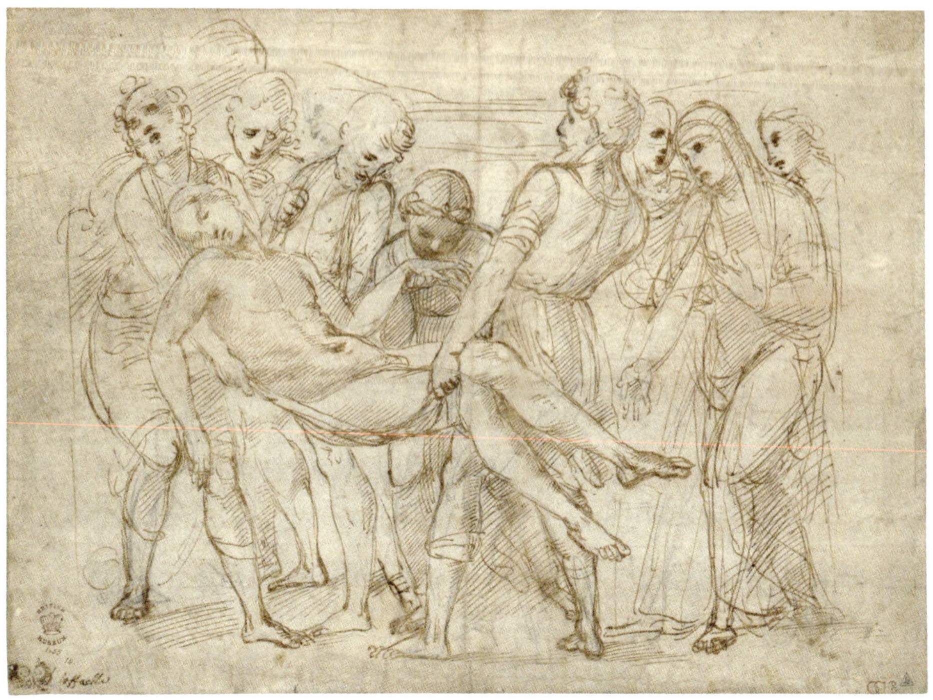

Following the Flemish example, the backs of the panels are decorated with grisaille paintings by another hand (Cat. P29c, 29d). Two scenes illustrate the Greek myth of Deucalion and Pyrrha: the gods destroy sinful humankind in a flood. Only the pious ancients Deucalion and his wife Pyrrha survive. They found a new race by throwing rocks over their shoulder, which transform into new people. These grisailles not only lend expression to the Doni couple's wish for children, but also pay compliment to the quality of Raphael's portraiture: just as life springs from inanimate stones behind the backs of Deucalion and Pyrrha, so the grisaille painting on the back of the diptych turns, when it is opened, into the colourfully dazzling illusion of two living people (see Wood 2005, Bolzoni 2010). Agnolo and Maddalena seem to be brought to life before us in a painting of breathtaking materiality, right down to the finest tips of their hair.

Only one Florentine family ordered an altarpiece from Raphael. It remained incomplete, however, when the artist left for Rome in 1508. Bernardo Dei had endowed one of the left-hand side chapels in the Augustinian church of Santo Spirito and dedicated it to his name saint, Bernard. His son Rinieri Dei, who died in 1506, stipulated in his will that the chapel should be furnished with an altarpiece. Rinieri's wish was respected by his son and heir, who gave the commission to Raphael (p. 151; Cat. P44). The side

Compositional study for the *Entombment*, 1507
Pen over black chalk underdrawing, 23 × 31.9 cm (9 ⅛ × 12 ½ in)
London, British Museum, Department of Prints and Drawings

Raphael (?)
Study for the group of the swooning Virgin, 1507
Pen, 28.9 × 20.1 cm (11 ⅜ × 7 ⅞ in)
Inscription below left in pen: *R. V.*
London, British Museum, Department of Prints and Drawings

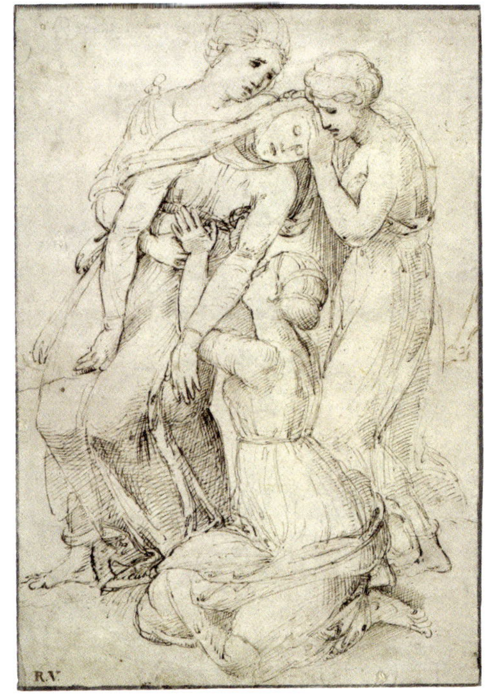

chapel in the Renaissance basilica by Brunelleschi (1377–1446) is laid out as a semi-circular niche. Raphael takes up this motif and locates the Virgin's throne in an apse, albeit one inspired – with its flat pilasters subdividing the rear wall – by the niches in the ancient Roman Pantheon. The throne is flanked by columns in the same Corinthian order as Brunelleschi's columns in front of the altar. Raphael thus seeks a harmonisation between the painting and its architectural surroundings, so that the scene it shows appears as real as possible to the chapel's visitors. Just as the architecture in Raphael's painting takes precise account of the actual interior of Santo Spirito, so the four saints surrounding the Virgin closely reflect the interests of the donors and the circumstances of the altarpiece's creation. Bernard, in his pale Cistercian habit, stands in place of honour on the Virgin's right as the patron saint of the chapel and the name saint of Bernardo Dei, the original donor. Bernard directs our attention to his neighbour, Peter, the name saint of Raphael's patron, Pietro. Peter looks across at the Virgin, where the Christ Child's attention is directed toward him. Peter is thus particularly distinguished among all the saints. On the other side of the throne, the hermit saint Ranieri of Pisa gazes up at the Madonna. He is the name saint of Rinieri Dei, Bernardo's son and Pietro's father, who had made financial provision for the painting in his will. Beside him, Saint Augustine looks directly out at us and gestures us towards the Virgin and Child. Here he represents the Augustinians of Santo Spirito, who celebrated Mass at the altar, and thus becomes a conduit, like them, of salvation for the faithful gathered in front of the picture. The grand, majestic pictorial architecture and the powerful drapery figures of the saints lend the composition a grave dignity. By way of contrast, the Infant Jesus in the centre plays almost shyly with his toe – a genre motif that gives the child a particularly natural air.

The second altarpiece (Cat. P35) that Raphael designed in his late Florentine period was destined one last time for Umbria. Raphael once again returned to Perugia to paint it. Dated to 1507, the retable shows the *Entombment of Christ* (p. 152) in its main panel and was produced – like almost all of Raphael's altarpieces for Perugia – for a woman. Had Atalanta Baglioni already commissioned the work during Raphael's stay in Perugia in 1505? The widow of Grifone Baglioni was the sister-in-law of Alessandra Baglioni Oddi and Ilaria Baglioni, both of whom had ordered altarpieces from Raphael, probably before Atalanta. The terrible events of the "bloody night" of 1500 are invariably cited, probably correctly, as the reason behind the new altarpiece, even though they lay some years in the past. On that occasion, members of the Baglioni family who controlled the city had murdered each other. Atalanta's only son, Grifonetto (1477–1500), died in his mother's arms. Her husband Grifone had already been murdered in 1477. In the anguish of the Virgin over her son being carried to the tomb, Atalanta's grief seems to be preserved forever as a visual motif. Atalanta had purchased the chapel in 1499, when Grifonetto was still alive. It was officially dedicated to Saint Matthew, but Atalanta's endowment inscription names Christ the Redeemer as the patron of the altarpiece.

As a work of art, Raphael's *Entombment* exhibits a distinctly programmatic character. Raphael wants to show that he has attained Michelangelo's new style with its pantheon of heroic figures, its dignity, pathos and ethos, and its new image of humankind and athletic physical ideal, and that he has mastered the large-format art of history painting (Locher 1994). The picture's artistic sources have often been analysed and range from antique sculpture, via Mantegna, Ghirlandaio, Signorelli and Perugino, to Michelangelo. Indeed, Raphael may even have intended connoisseurs to recognise some of his sources (such as an antique relief of the transport of the dead Meleager, or the figure of Christ from Michelangelo's *Pietà* in Rome). He thereby interwove these motifs into his evolving design in a step-by-step process that is quite astonishing in other respects, too, and which we can follow via a number of surviving compositional studies (KMOF 187, 193, 195, 196, 199, 203). Raphael started out with a design for a Lamentation based on Perugino's multi-figural *Lamentation over the Dead Christ* for Santa Chiara in Florence. In Raphael's initial studies, the dead Christ is lying in the lap of his swooning mother in a circle of loyal followers. Over subsequent drawings, an action sequence unfolds as if in a film (pp. 82, 83, 86): Christ's body is lifted up from the ground by devout bearers and then held before the Virgin, who has regained consciousness and now kneels in worship before her son. Standing up, she then gazes in farewell at Christ as he is carried away. Overwhelmed by grief, she once again faints away into the arms of figures standing around her, who catch and support her. The Virgin's swoon links the first draft with the final execution, like the beginning and end of a narrative. Mary Magdalene is initially seated on the ground holding Christ's legs, then bends in adoration over his hand as he is lifted up, and finally hurries after Christ as he is carried away. The history painting that Raphael finally produced was thus only the final stage of a narrative journey taken in the mind of the artist and in his drawings. Raphael's imagination thereby follows the religious meditational practice of visualising a biblical event in vivid detail and reliving it: a compositional process as a meditation on the Passion!

A sequence of events is also suggested by the final painting. Christ's body is being transported from right to left: in the right-hand background, the three crucifixion crosses, including the ladder required for the Deposition, rise upwards against a dark cloud. Below them, further forward, the Virgin Mary sinks downwards, tended by others just as the body of Christ was supported as it was taken down from the cross. At the very front of the picture, Christ is being carried towards the left, where – once again a little further back – the dark opening of the tomb awaits. The narrative goes hand in hand with an invitation to devotion: the company of mourners has gathered exclusively *behind* the body of Christ, as if to present it for worship in an uninterrupted view. The beautiful divine body lies relaxed as if in sleep; only the ashen skin characterises it as a corpse. Its weight is heavy in the arms of its athletically braced bearers. Full of reverence, they do not touch Christ's holy body directly. Even where Christ's hand rests on that of Mary Magdalene, a fine veil lies between them. The expressions of grief in the various faces rise to an emotional climax towards the central figure of Mary Magdalene, whose loud cry of despair is accompanied by painted tears. Just as she draws near Christ on the far side of his body, we can do so from the front and, in our imagination, clasp his other hand, still hanging down loosely. The representation makes clear Eucharistic reference to the Mass and the Elevation *(elevatio)* of the Host, the culminating moment at which the holding up of the Body of Christ before the congregation was associated with an almost magical power of salvation.

On the right, the Virgin sinks in a pose which is a mirror image of that of Christ. In her compassion *(compassio)*, she is correlated with Christ and, according to theological exegesis, plays a part in the work of salvation as co-redemptrix. The compassionate Mary is herself treated with compassion by the women around her. On the left, the bearer dressed in blue leans his head backwards and thereby repeats, like an echo, the position of Christ's head. His eyes are directed upwards in a lamenting and beseeching manner. From another reality, beyond the top of the frame with its frieze, there formerly came a consoling reply: in the lunette originally crowning the altarpiece, God the Father appears between cherubim, raising one hand in blessing as he directs a gaze full of compassion towards his dead son on the left, and extending his other hand as if protectively in the direction of the swooning Virgin (p. 153; Cat P35e). This expression of divine solicitousness could also be read in conjunction with the representations on the frieze (Cat P35f) between the lunette and the main painting, where small gryphons *(grifoni, grifonetti)* are receiving crowns and food from putti – an allusion to rewards and joys in Heaven (for the deceased Grifonetto). On the predella at the bottom, the three Theological Virtues of Faith, Hope and Charity (p. 155; Cat P35b–d) appeared in the form of painted reliefs, i. e. as fictive works of sculpture, to represent, as it were, the stone foundation upon which to have a share in Christ's work of salvation and the step leading up to the pictorial stage on which the holy scene is taking place. Within the picture, the simulated stone is continued in the rock steps up which Christ's body is carried to the tomb. Raphael has placed his signature on the bottom step.

The viewer in front of the retable in its original location would have been able to extend the conceptual links between its individual components to other elements of the church's decoration. Atalanta's altar was located in San Francesco al Prato in the chapel to the right of the transept. The *Entombment of Christ* thus stood as a pendant to the *Coronation of the Virgin* displayed on the left, painted by Raphael a few years earlier as part of the *Oddi Altarpiece* (Cat. P11). There the tomb motif was already formulated and the Assumption had already taken place. While in the Baglioni altarpiece the Virgin is correlated with the dead Christ in the pallor of her unconscious face, in the Oddi altarpiece she floats, resurrected, above her tomb. As if in reward for the excess of suffering she endures in one retable, she receives her crown in the other. Just as the figures of the Virgin and Christ mirror each other in the Baglioni altarpiece in their suffering, so they do the same in the Oddi altarpiece, now resurrected and enthroned in heavenly joy: their falling away from each other in separation is followed by their reunion facing towards each other. In this programmatic fusion of the Oddi and Baglioni altarpieces, Raphael re-enacted in art what Pope Julius II had sought to achieve in 1506, when he officiated at a celebration of Mass at the main altar located exactly halfway between the two family chapels: the reconciliation of the two families competing for power in Perugia (see Luchs 1983). At the same time, Raphael showcased his own artistic progress in an unparalleled manner. The arranger of graceful, elegant and joyful spiritual harmony had become a director of heroic human drama.

Detail from **Portrait of Maddalena Doni**, *c.* 1505/06
(see ill. p. 147)

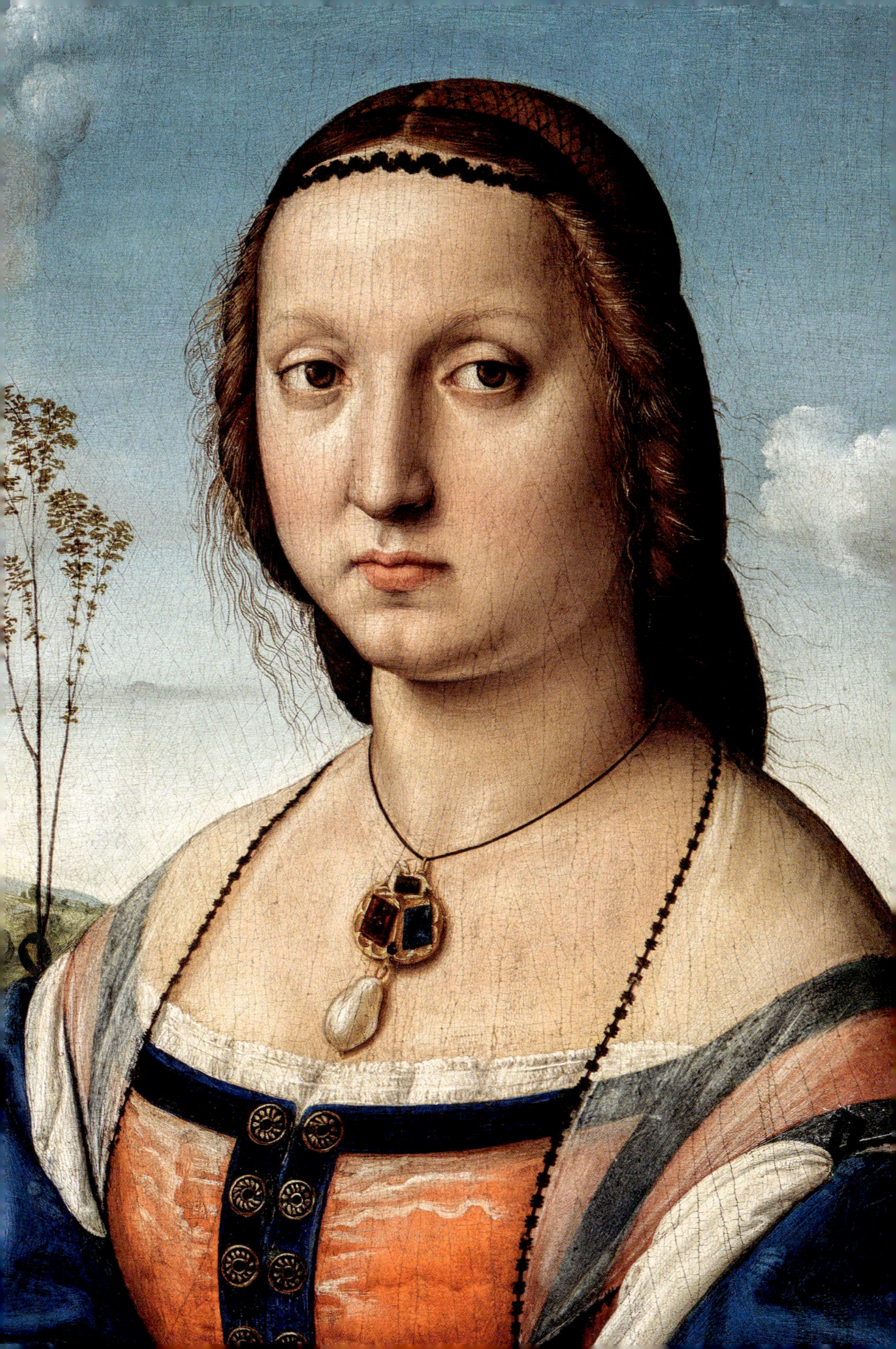

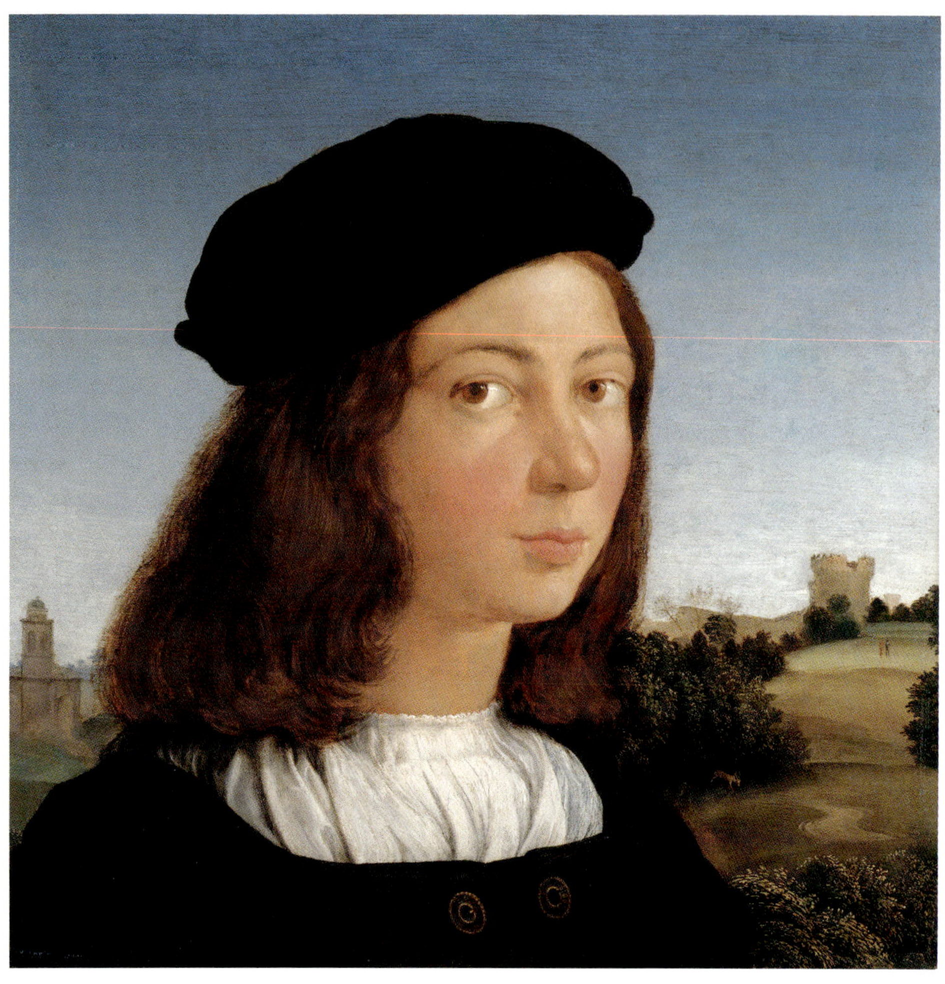

Portrait of a Young Man, *c.* 1504/05
Oil on panel, 37 × 40 cm (14 5/8 × 15 3/4 in). Inscription: *RAFFAELLO VRBINAS*
Windsor Castle, Collection of Her Majesty Queen Elizabeth II

Portrait of a Young Man (Francesco Maria della Rovere), *c.* 1504
Oil on poplar panel, 47.4 × 35.3 cm (18 2/3 × 13 7/8 in)
Florence, Gallerie degli Uffizi

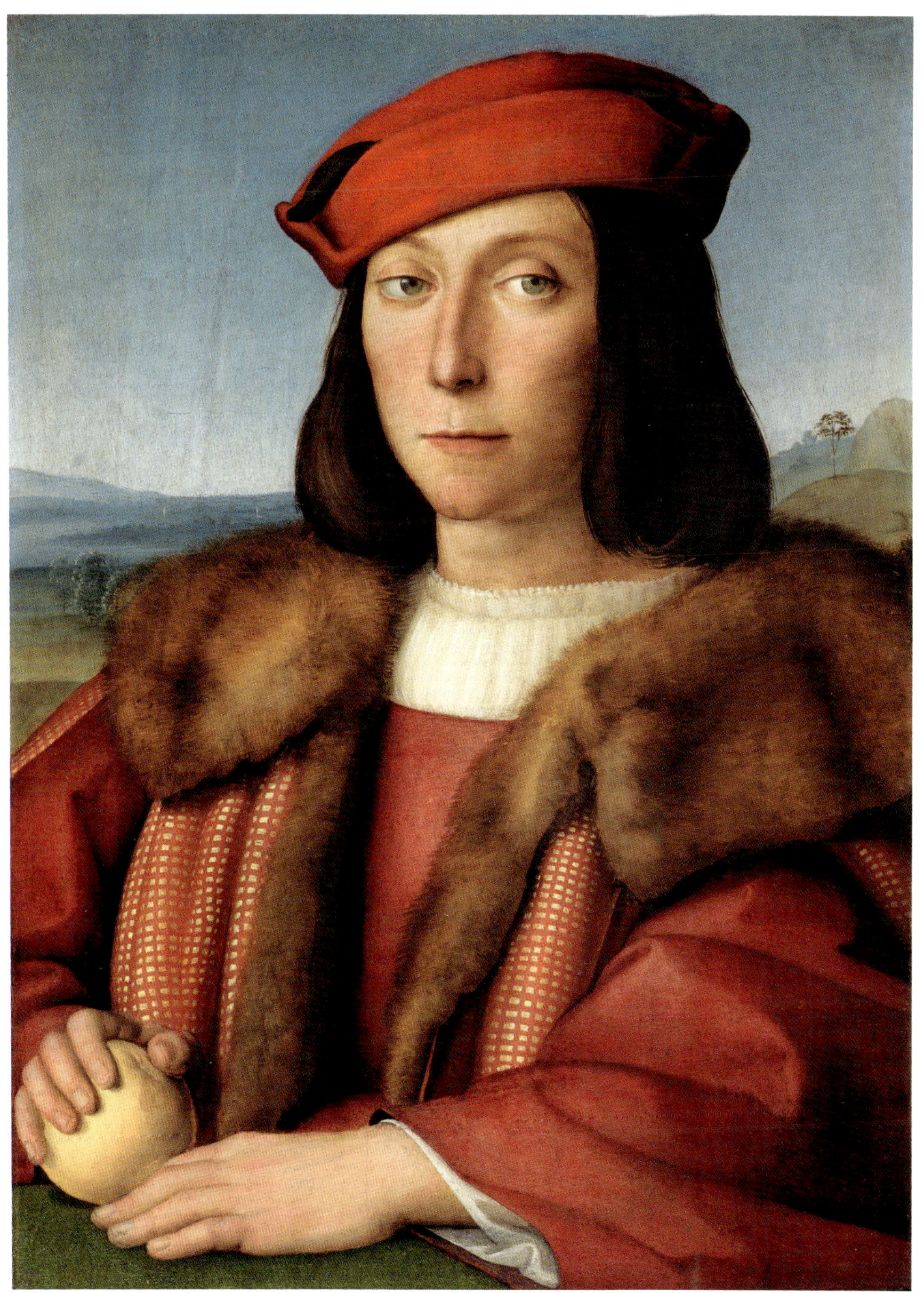

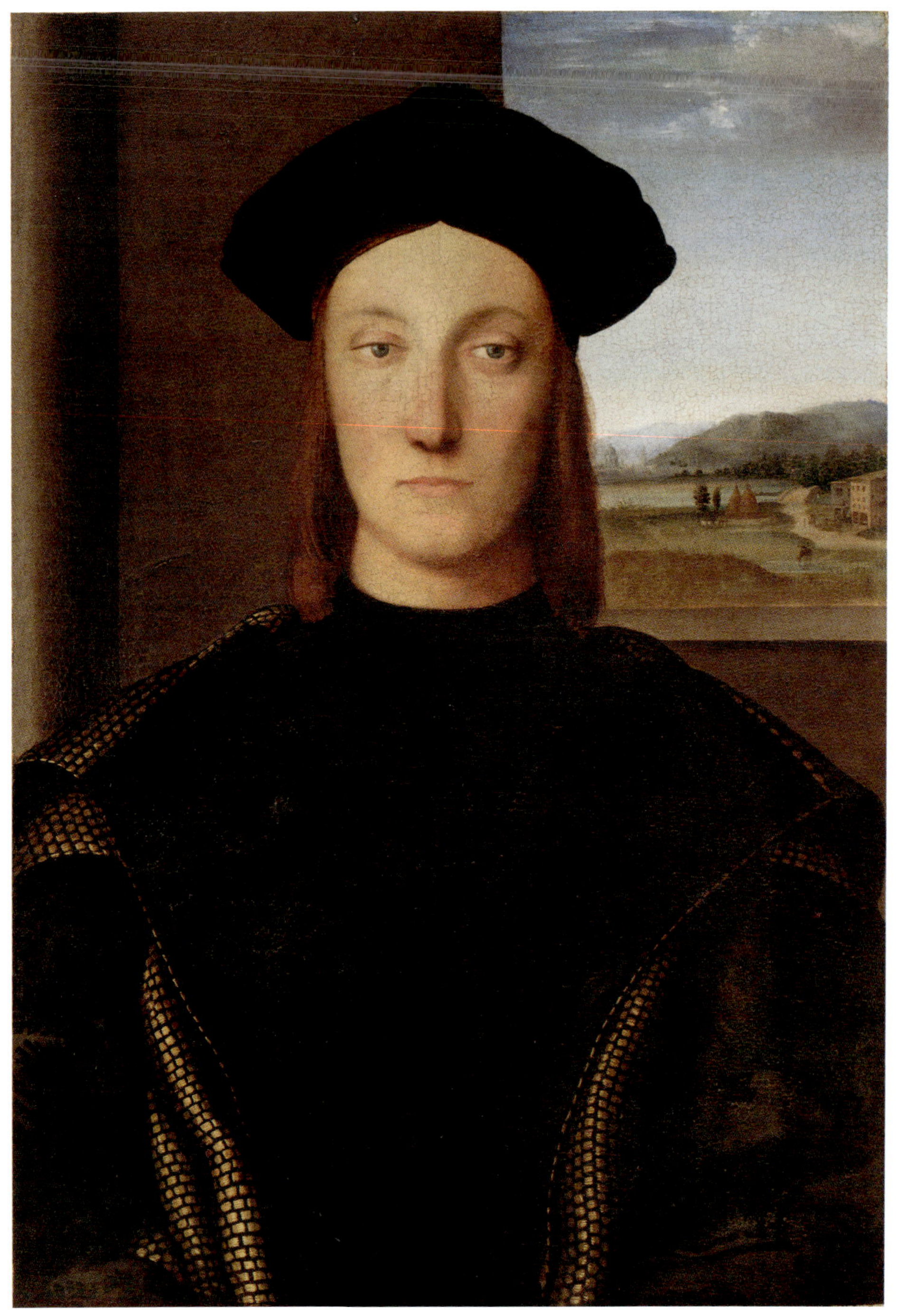

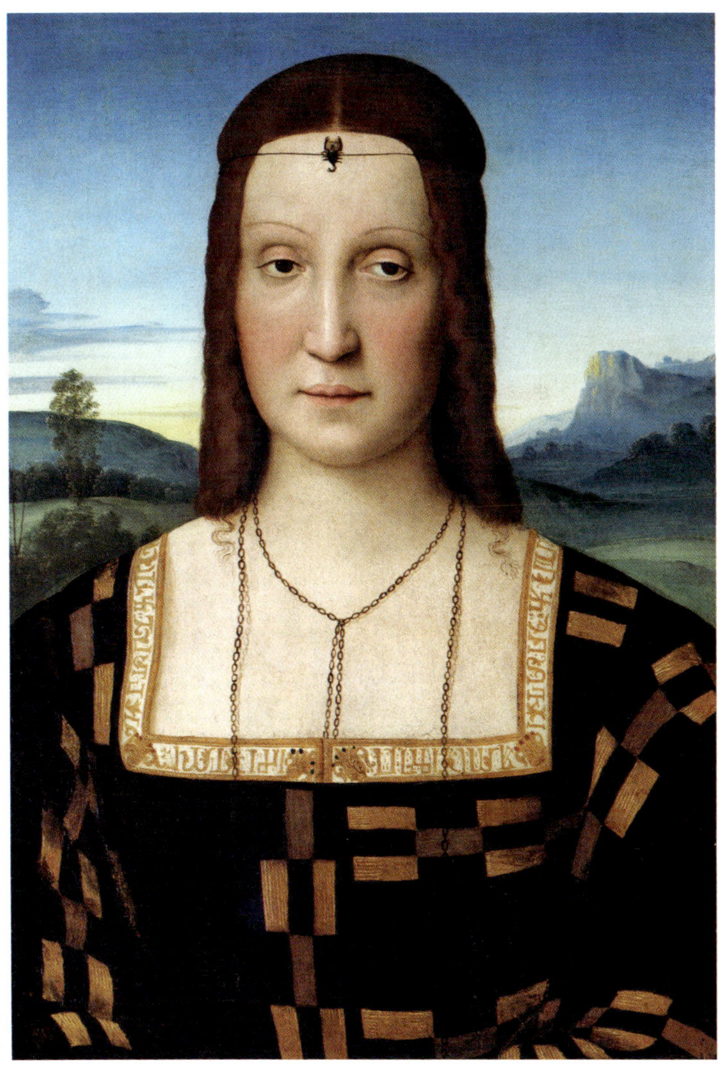

Portrait of Guidobaldo da Montefeltro, *c.* 1504–1506
Oil on panel, 70 × 51.6 cm (27 ½ × 20 ⅓ in). Florence, Gallerie degli Uffizi

Portrait of Elisabetta Gonzaga, *c.* 1504–1506
Oil on panel, 52.9 × 37.4 cm (20 ⅞ × 14 ¾ in). Florence, Gallerie degli Uffizi
(Detail page 71)

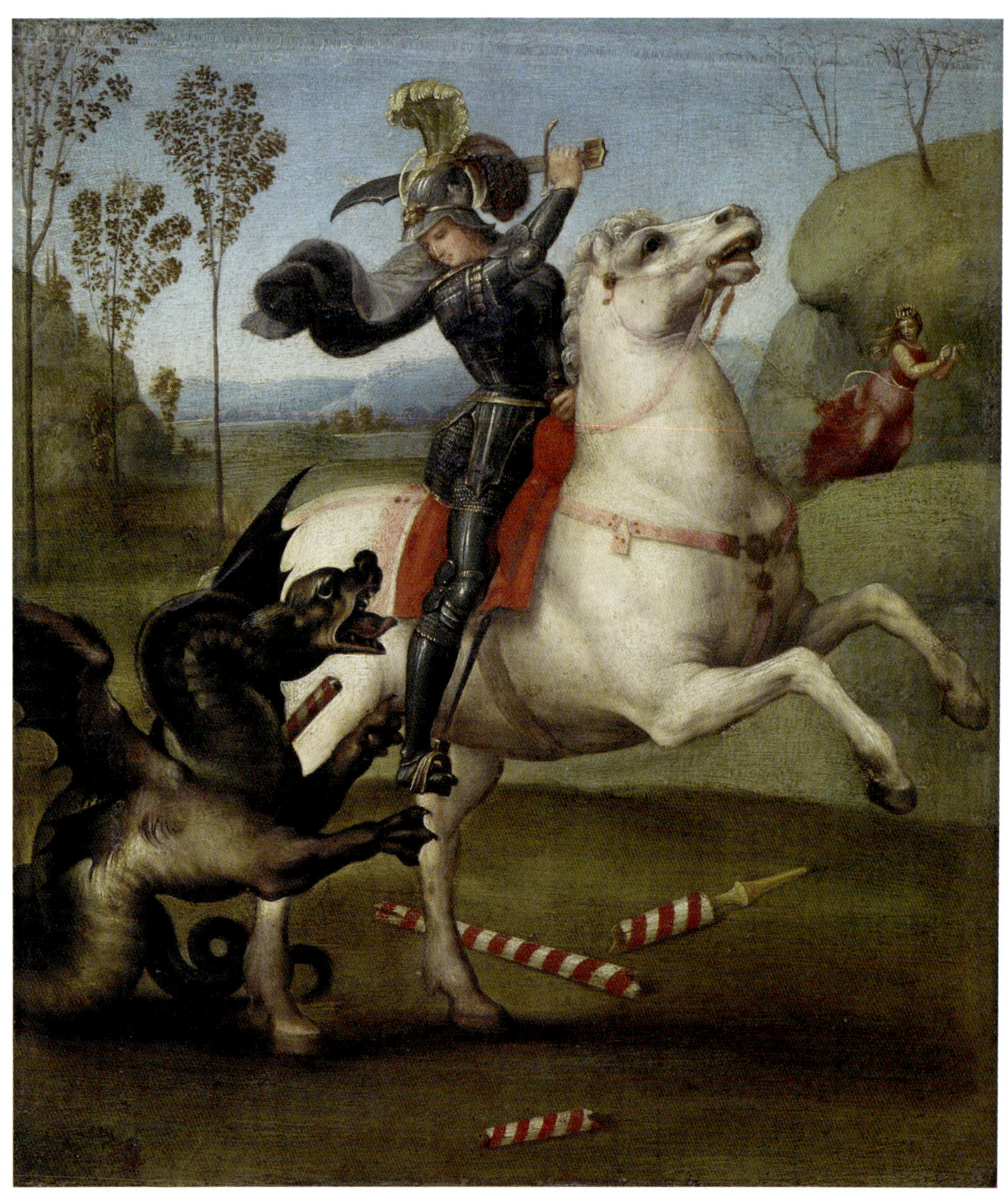

Saint George, *c.* 1504/05
Oil on poplar panel, 30.7 × 26.8 cm (12 ⅛ × 10 ½ in)
Paris, Musée du Louvre

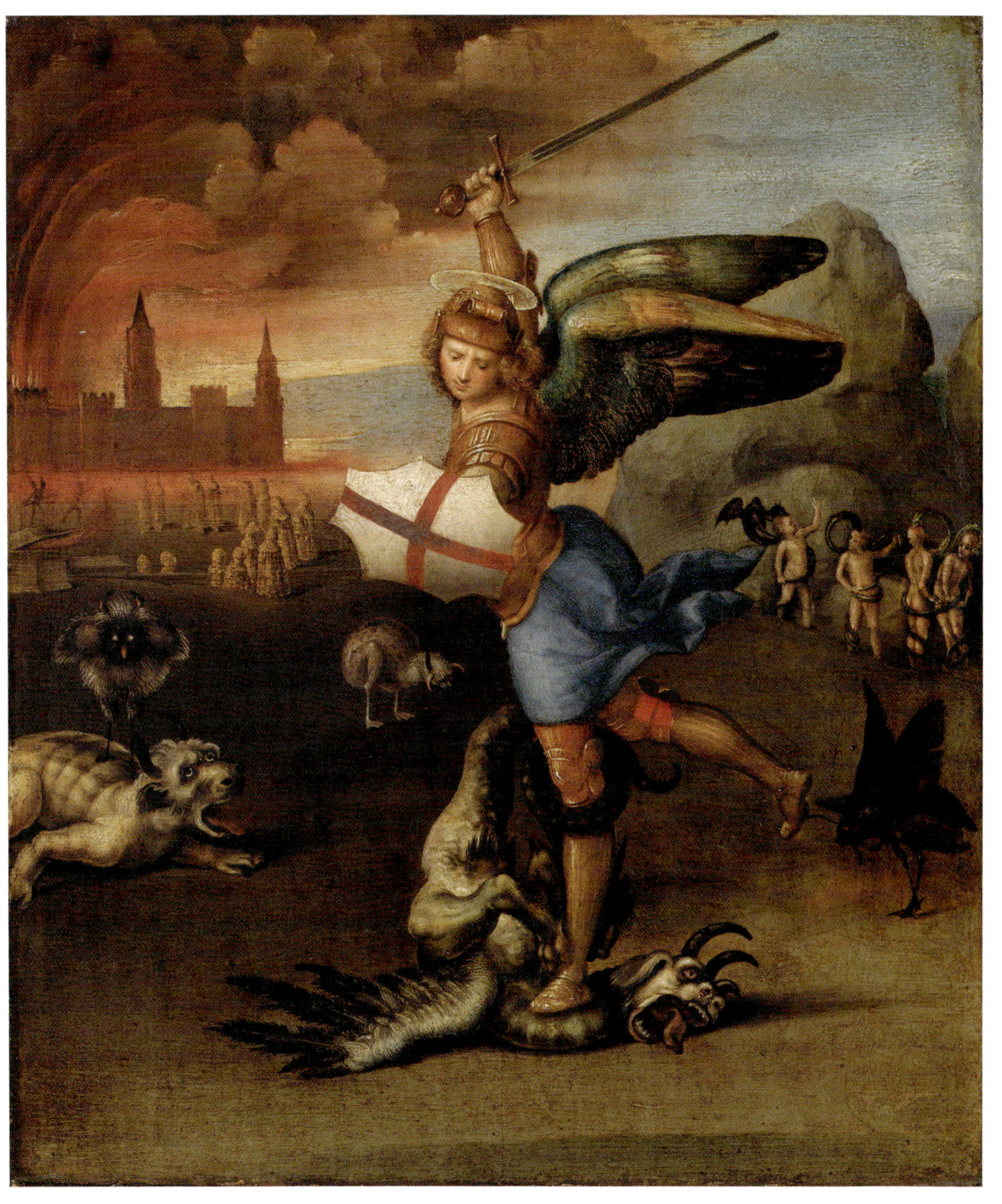

Saint Michael, *c.* 1503/04
Oil on poplar panel, 30.9 × 26.5 cm (12 ⅛ × 10 ⅜ in)
Paris, Musée du Louvre

Unknown artist/Peter Paul Rubens
Copy after Leonardo's *Battle of Anghiari*, before 1550 and around 1603
Black chalk, pen and ink, heightened with lead white,
reworked with watercolour, 45.2 × 63.7 cm (17 ¾ × 25 ⅛ in)
Paris, Musée du Louvre

Saint George and the Dragon, *c.* 1505/06
Oil on panel, 29 × 21 cm (11 ⅜ × 8 ¼ in). Inscription on the horse's breast strap:
RAPHELLO, and on a girth under Saint George's knee: *HONI*
Washington, D.C., National Gallery of Art

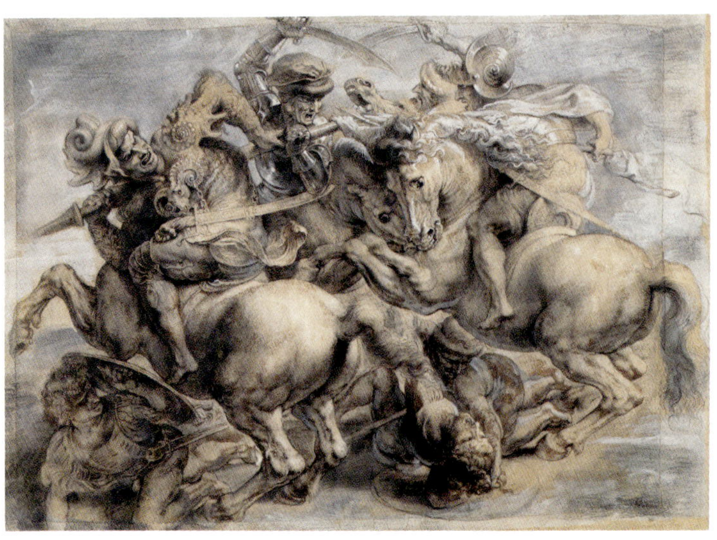

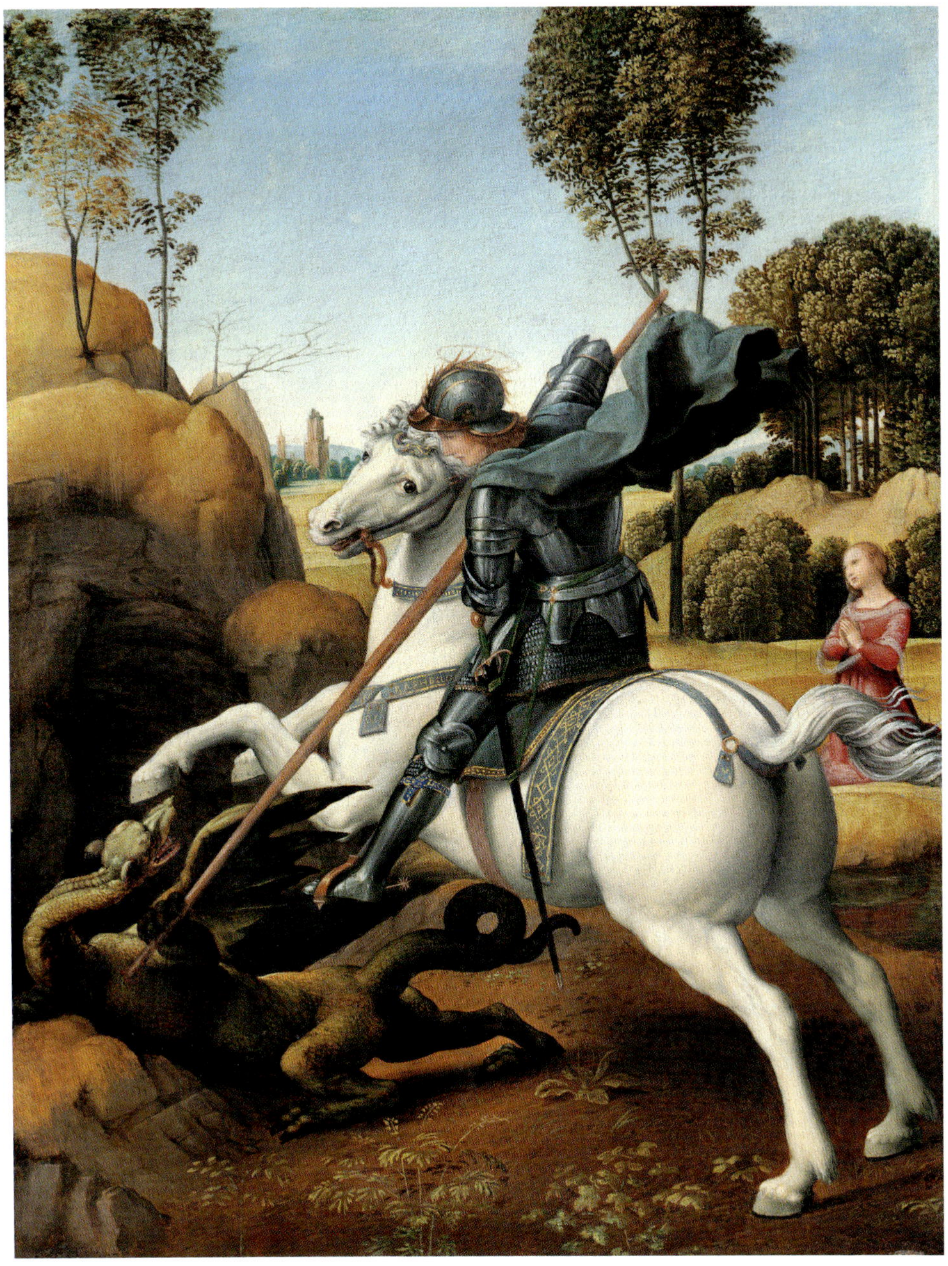

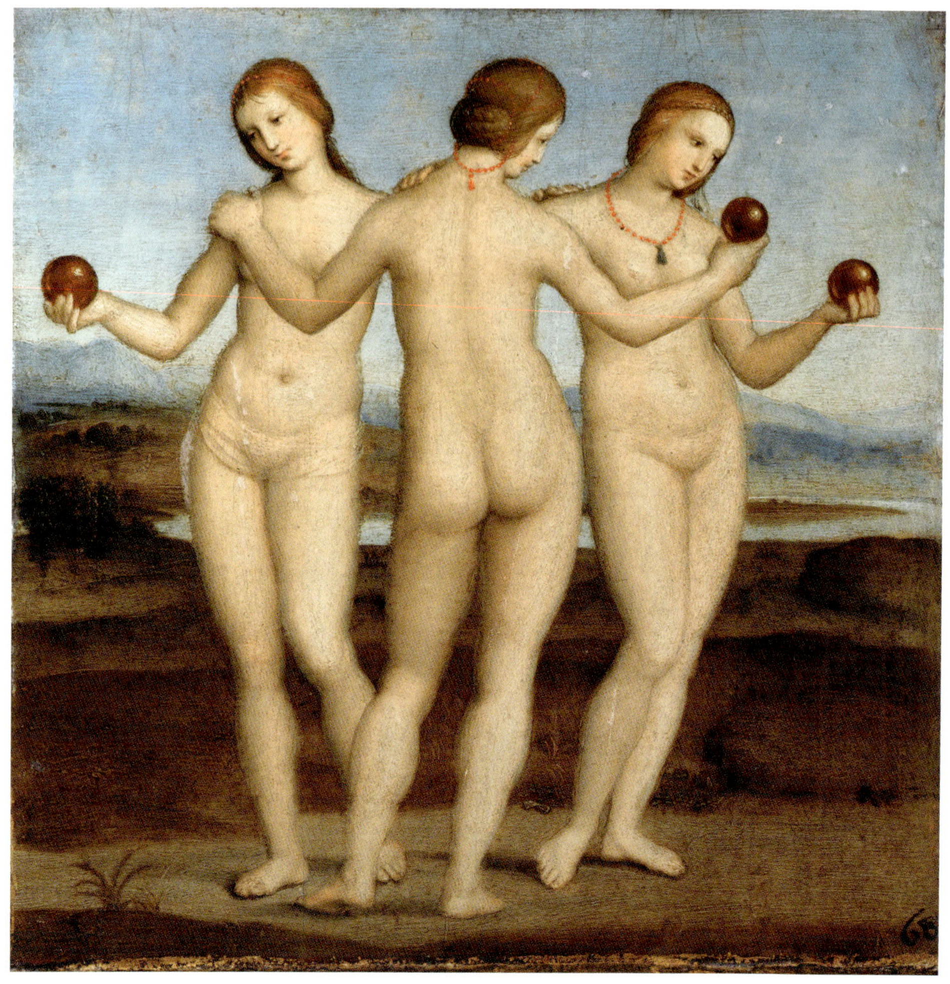

The Three Graces, *c.* 1504
Oil on poplar panel, 17.5 × 17.4 cm (6 7/8 × 6 7/8 in)
Chantilly, Musée Condé

Vision of a Knight
Oil on poplar panel, 17.5 × 17.5 cm (6 7/8 × 6 7/8 in)
London, The National Gallery

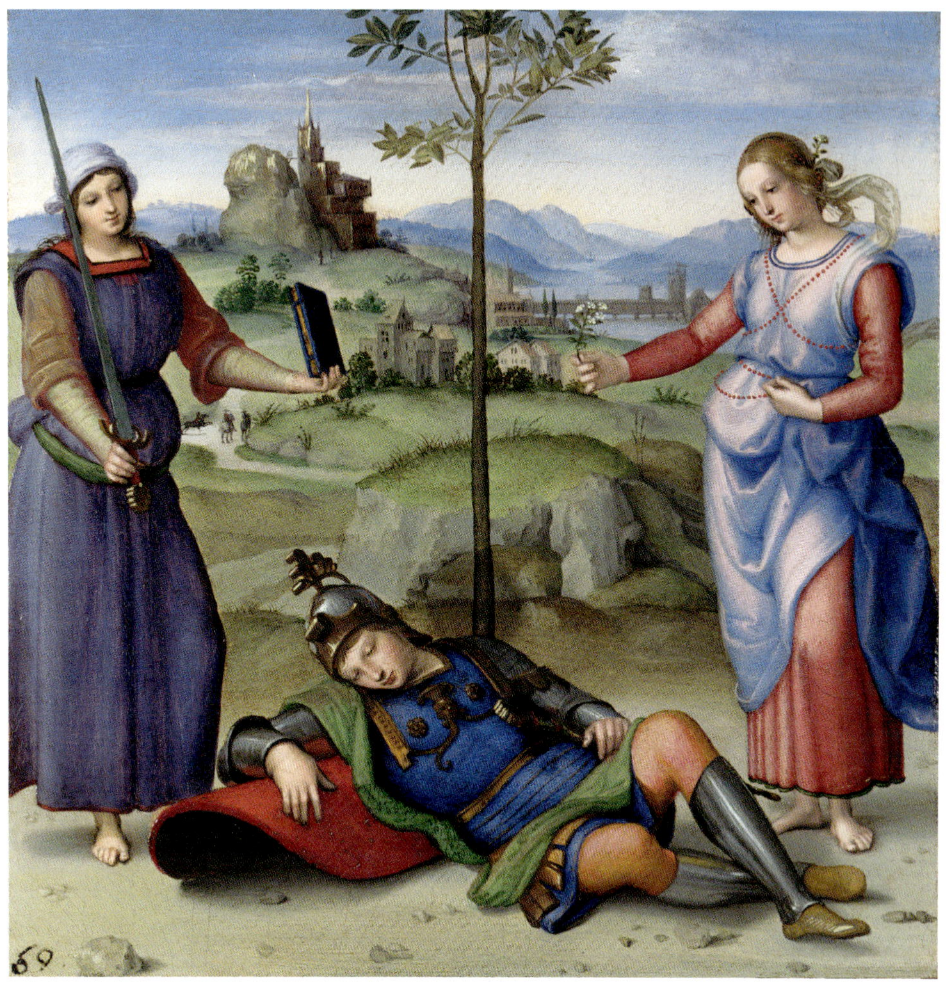

Reconstruction of the Colonna Altarpiece

Enthroned Madonna and Child with the Infant Saint John the Baptist and Saints Peter, Paul, Catherine and Cecilia and **God the Father Blessing between Two Angels (Colonna Altarpiece)**, *c.* 1504/05
Oil and gold on panel, main panel: 172.4 × 172.4 cm (67 ⅞ × 67 ⅞ in),
lunette: 74.9 × 180 cm (29 ½ × 70 ⅞ in)
New York, The Metropolitan Museum of Art

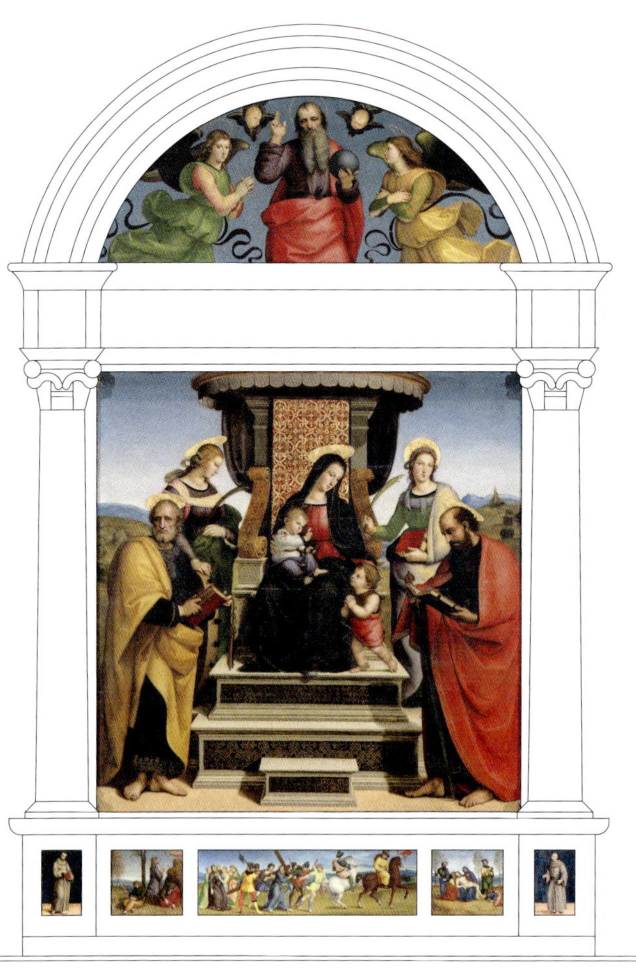

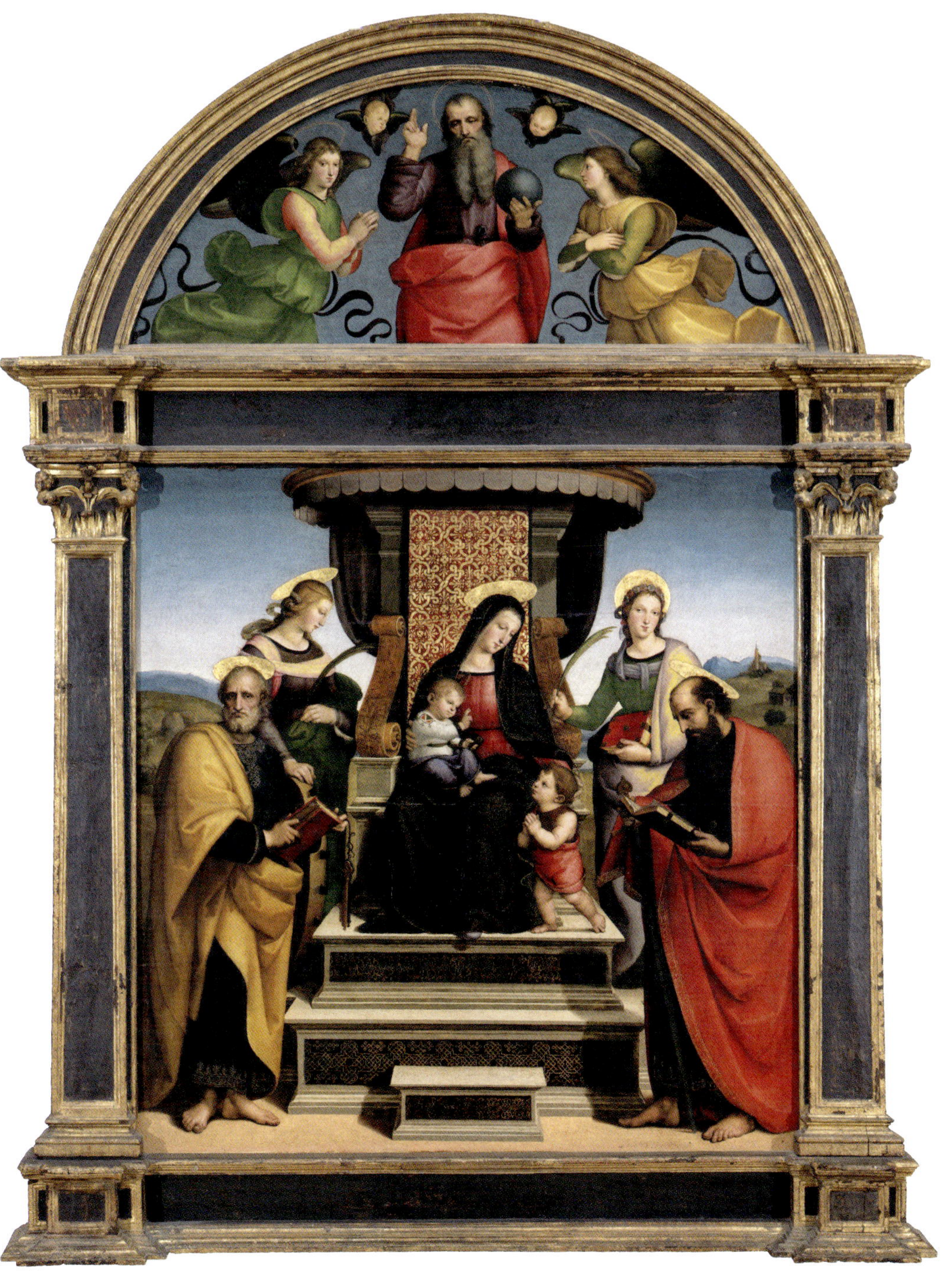

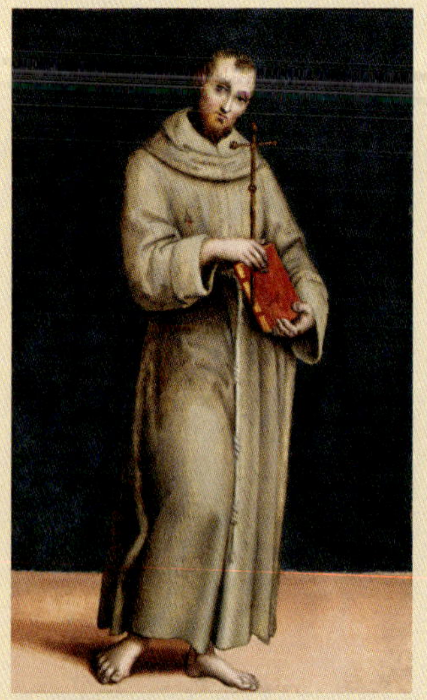

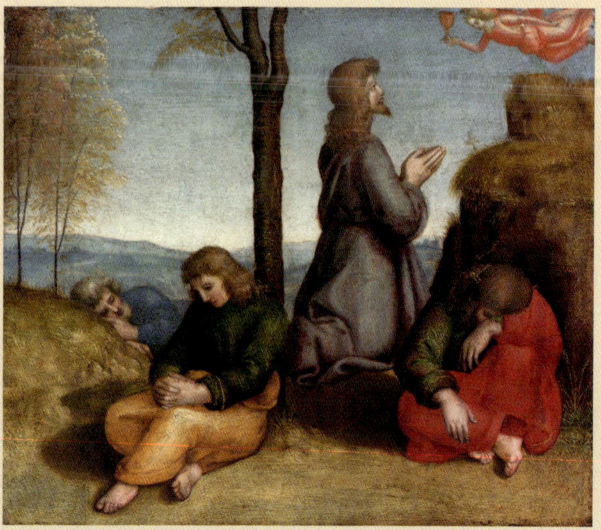

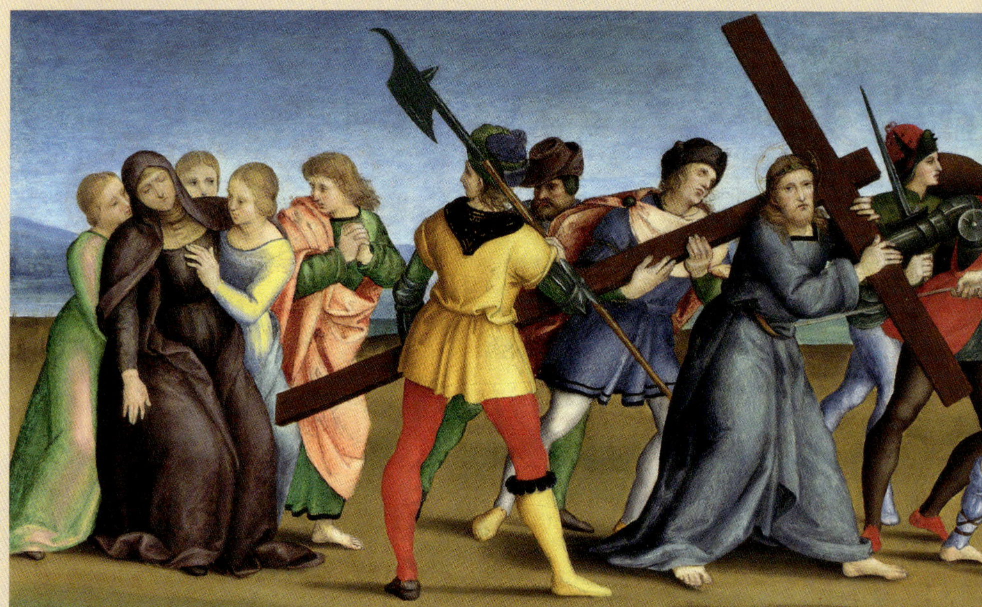

Saint Francis (Colonna Altarpiece, predella), *c.* 1505
Oil on panel, 25.8 × 16.8 cm (10 ⅛ × 6 ⅝ in)
London, Dulwich Picture Gallery

Christ on the Mount of Olives (Colonna Altarpiece, predella), *c.* 1505
Oil on panel, 24 × 29 cm (9 ½ × 11 ⅜ in)
New York, The Metropolitan Museum of Art

Procession to Calvary (Colonna Altarpiece, predella), *c.* 1505
Oil on panel, 24.1 × 85.1 cm (9 ½ × 33 ½ in). London, The National Gallery

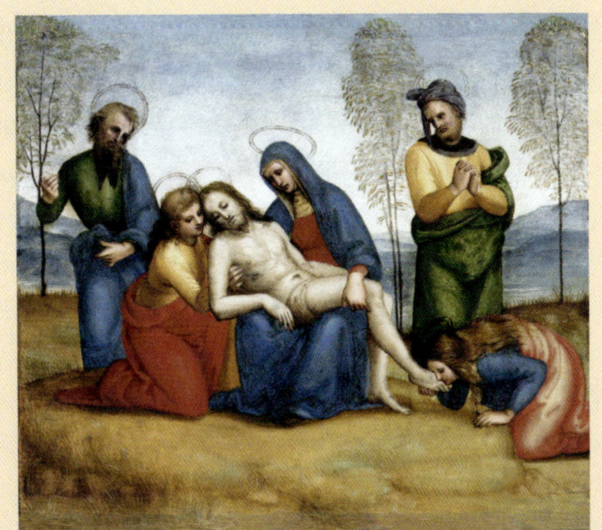

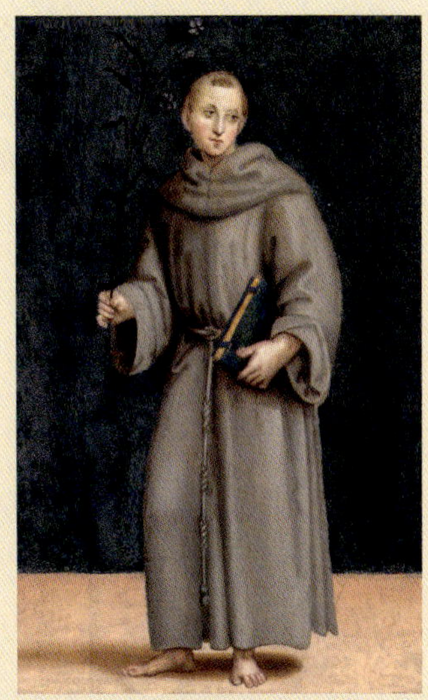

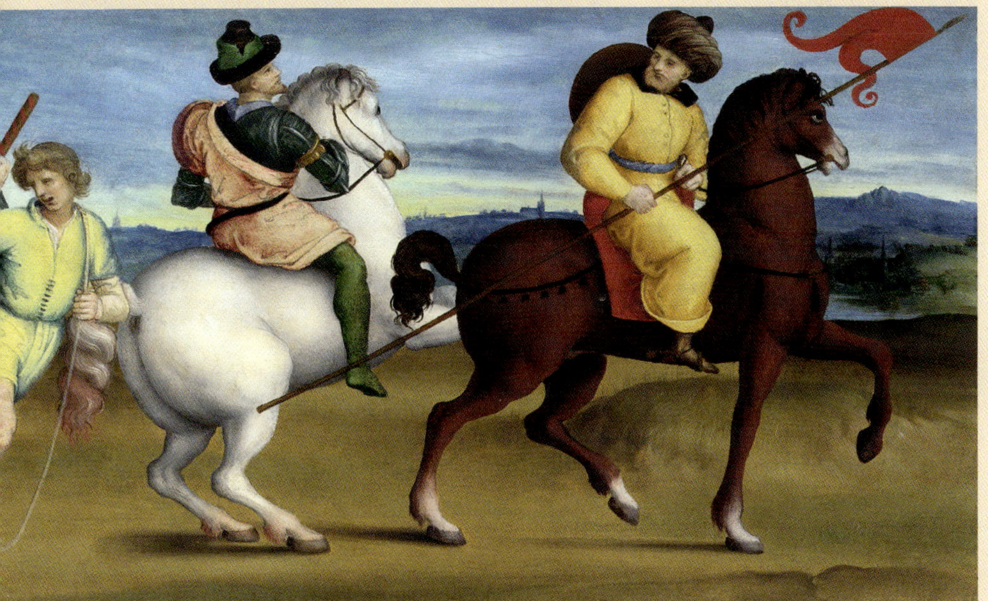

Pietà (Colonna Altarpiece, predella), *c.* 1505
Oil on poplar panel, 23 × 28 cm (9 ⅛ × 11 ⅛ in)
Boston, Isabella Stewart Gardner Museum

Saint Anthony of Padua (Colonna Altarpiece, predella), *c.* 1505
Oil on panel, 25.6 × 16.4 cm (10 ⅛ × 6 ½ in)
London, Dulwich Picture Gallery

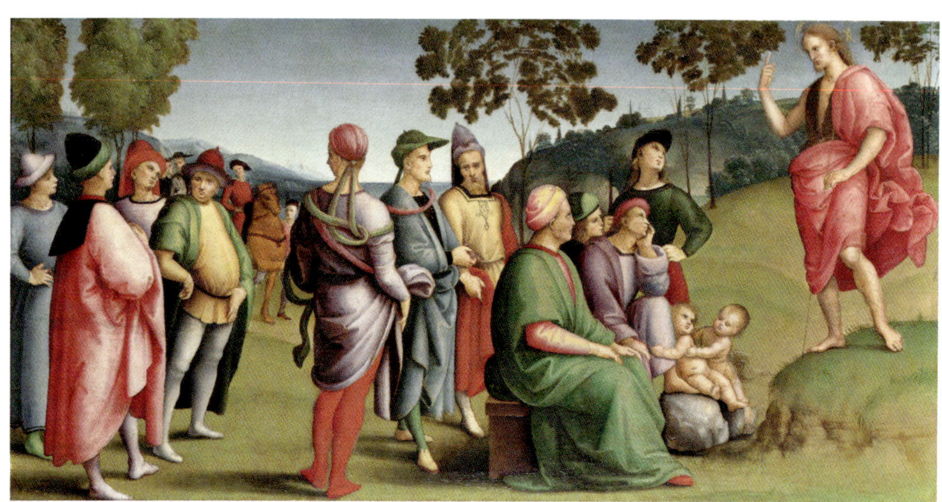

Saint John the Baptist Preaching (Ansidei Altarpiece, predella), *c.* 1504–1506
Oil on poplar panel, 26 × 53 cm (10 ¼ × 20 ⅞ in)
London, The National Gallery

Madonna and Child with Saint John the Baptist and Saint Nicholas of Bari (Ansidei Altarpiece), *c.* 1504–1506
Oil on poplar panel, 209 × 148 cm (82 ¼ × 58 ¼ in)
London, The National Gallery

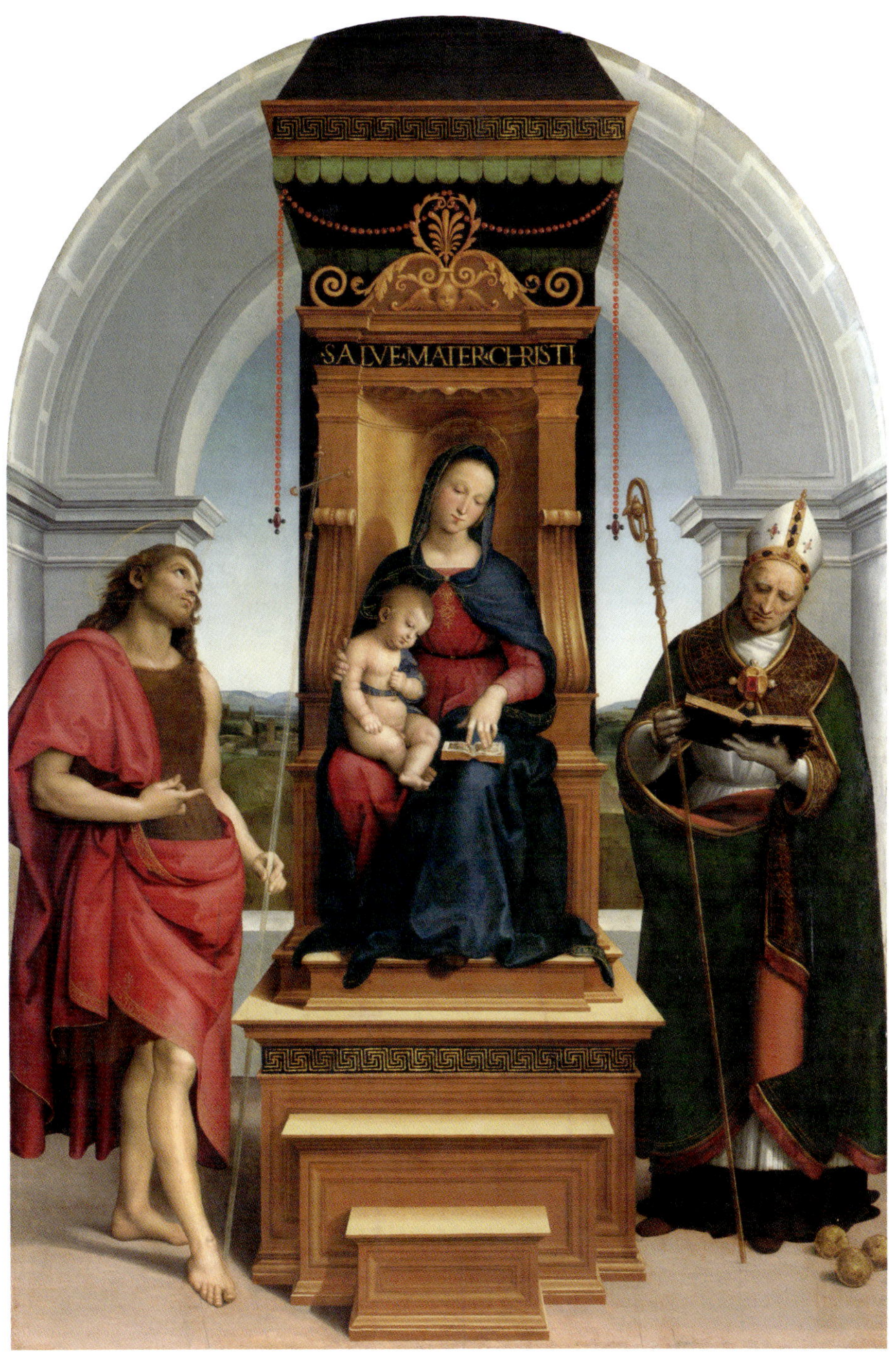
SALVE MATER CHRISTI

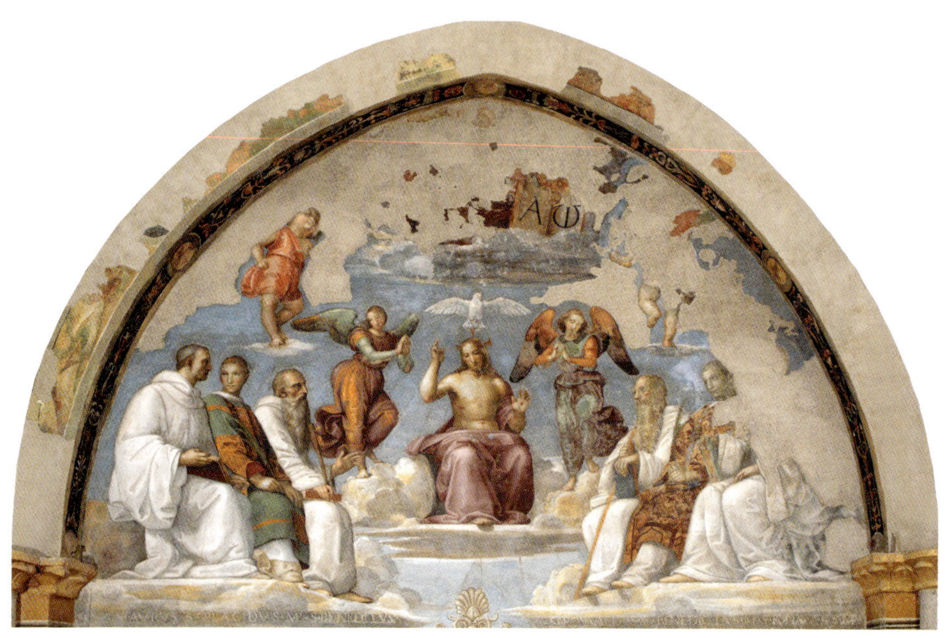

Trinity with Saints, 1505
Fresco, 275 × 390 cm (108 ¼ × 153 ½ in)
Perugia, San Severo

Christ Blessing (Pax Vobiscum), *c.* 1505/06
Oil on panel, 31.7 × 25.3 cm (12 ½ × 9 ⅞ in)
Brescia, Pinacoteca Tosio Martinengo
(Detail page 64)

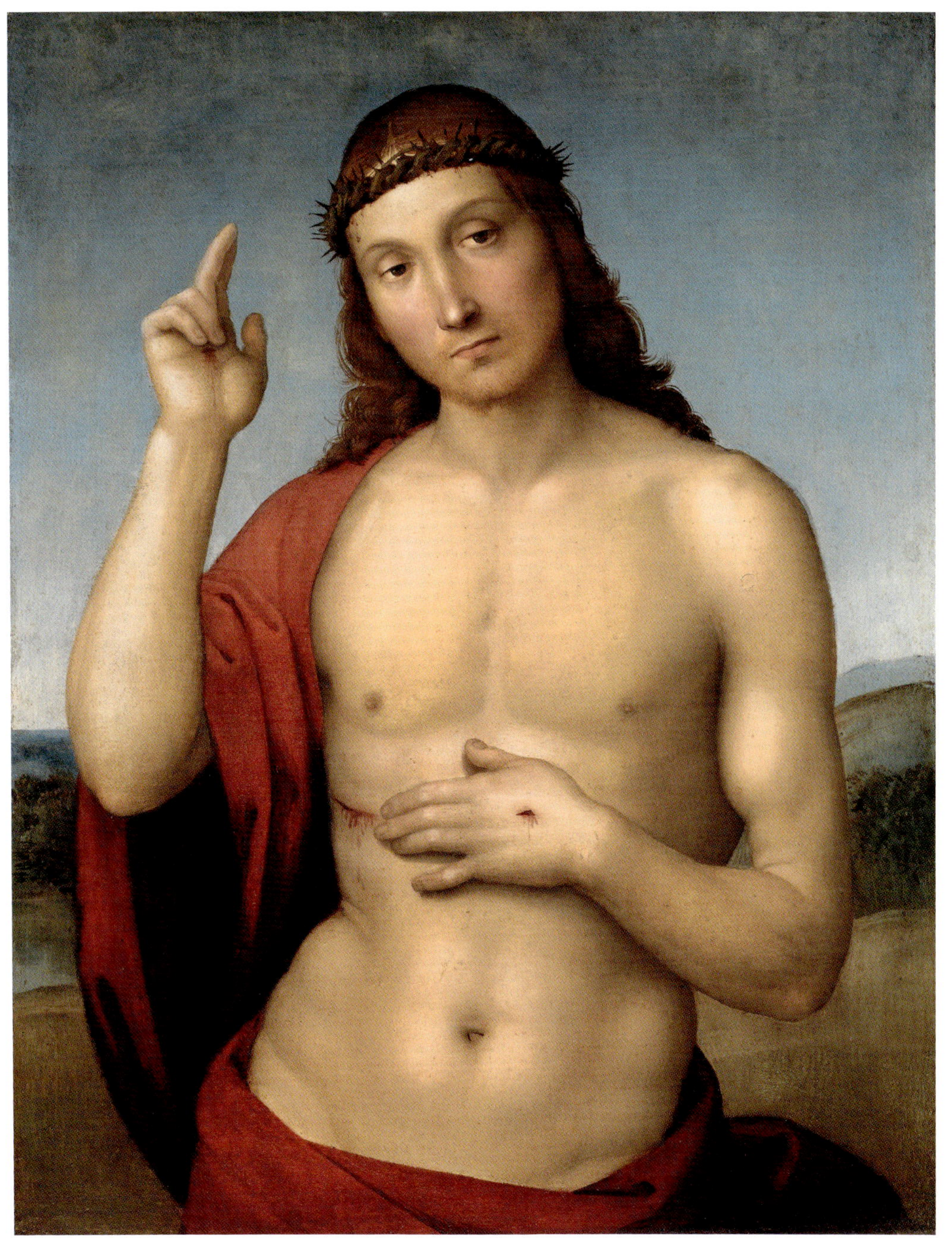

Pinturicchio
Virgin and Child with Saint John the Baptist, 1490–1495
Oil on panel, 56.7 × 40.7 cm (22 ⅓ × 16 ⅛ in)
Cambridge, Fitzwilliam Museum

Diotalevi Madonna (Madonna and Child with the Infant Saint John), *c.* 1500–1502
Oil on poplar panel, 69 × 50 cm (27 ⅛ × 19 ⅔ in)
Staatliche Museen zu Berlin, Gemäldegalerie

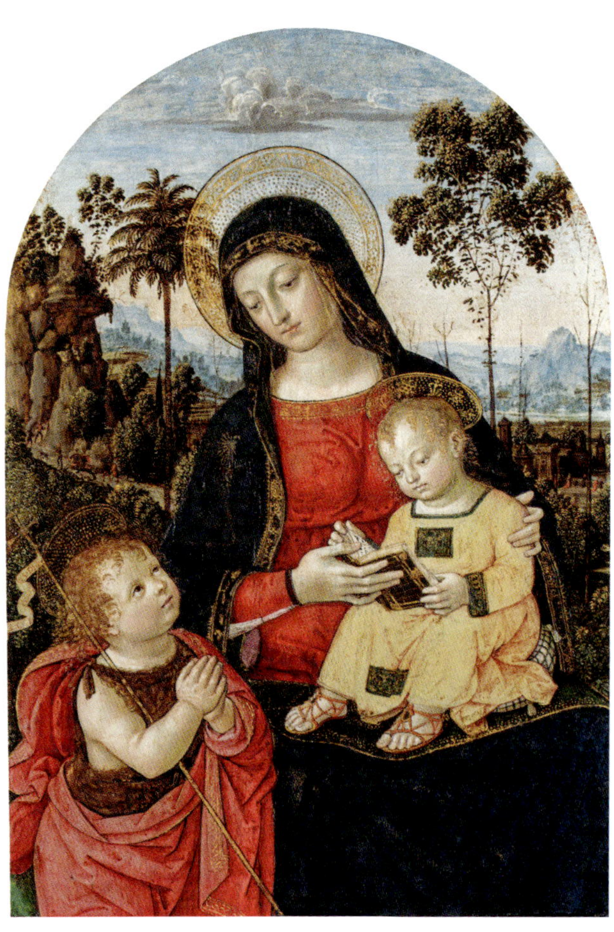

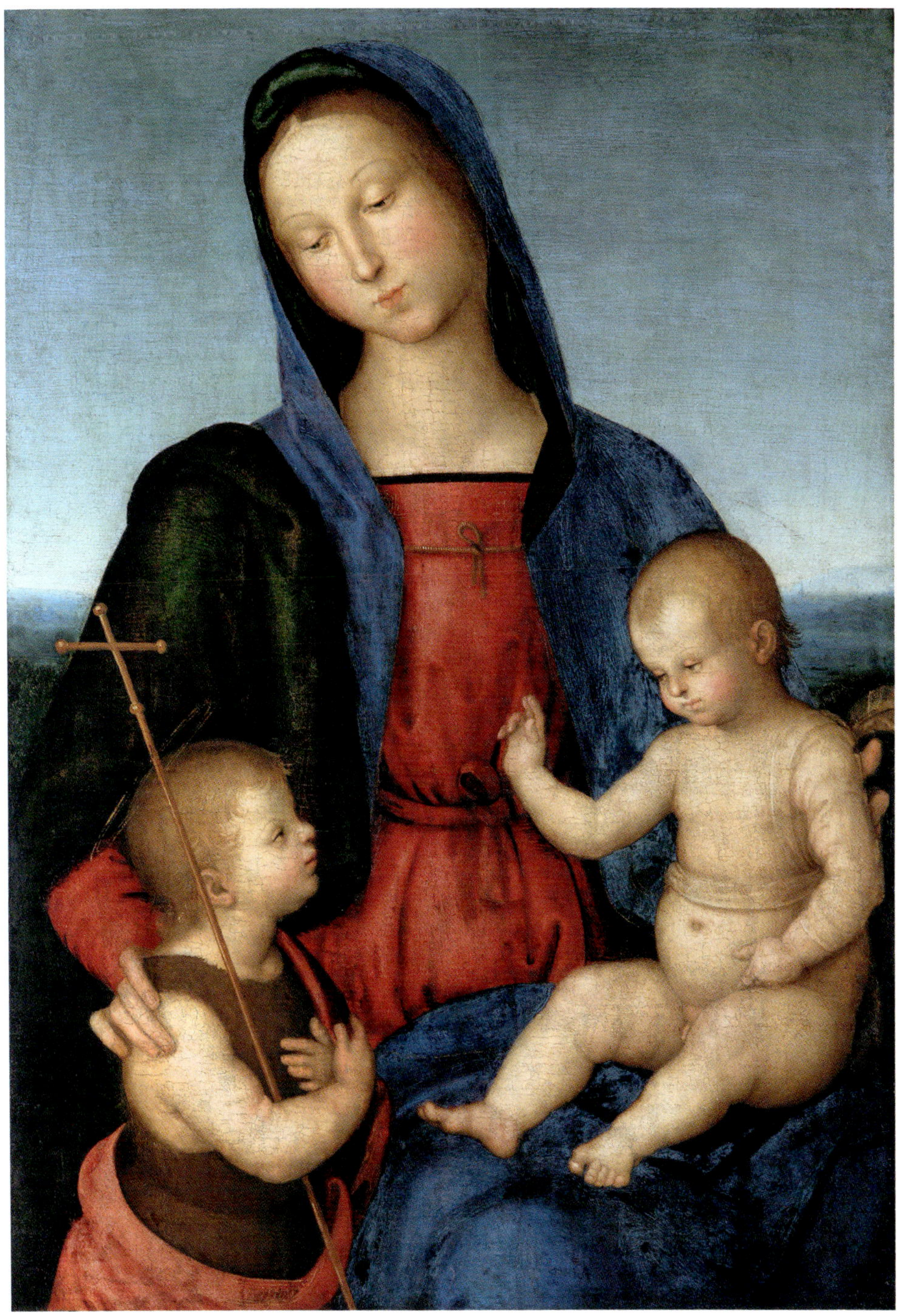

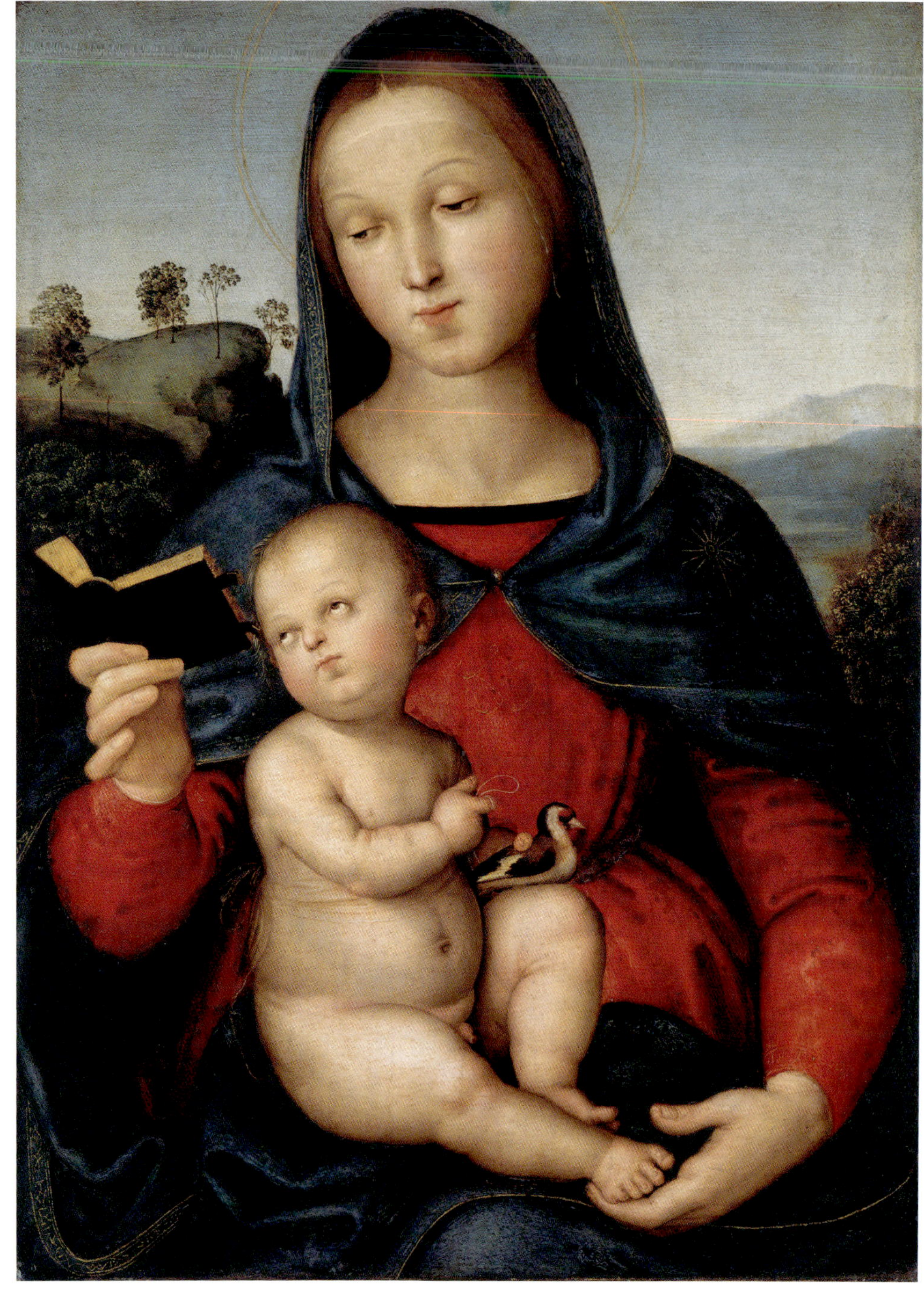

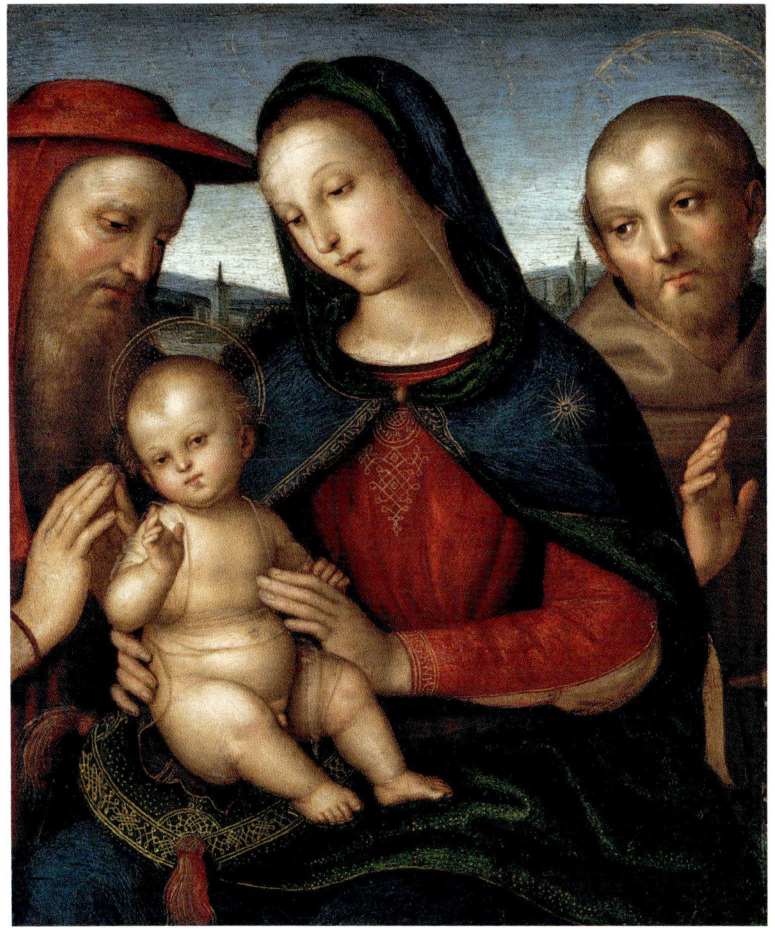

Solly Madonna (Madonna and Child Holding a Goldfinch), *c.* 1501/02
Oil on poplar panel, 52 × 38 cm (20 ½ × 14 ⅞ in)
Staatliche Museen zu Berlin, Gemäldegalerie

Madonna with Child and Saints (Saints Jerome and Francis), *c.* 1502
Oil on poplar panel, 34 × 29 cm (13 ⅜ × 11 ⅜ in)
Staatliche Museen zu Berlin, Gemäldegalerie

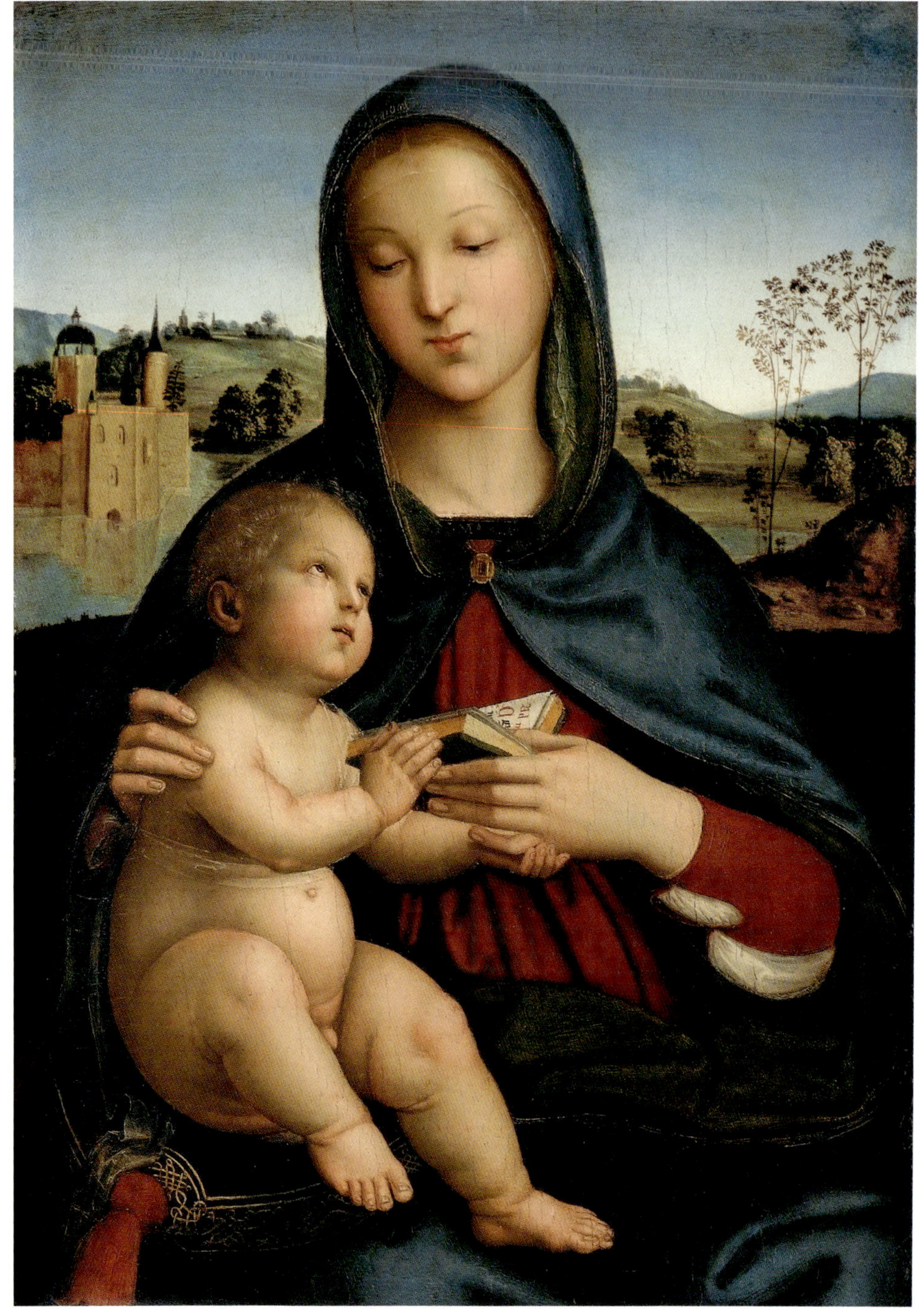

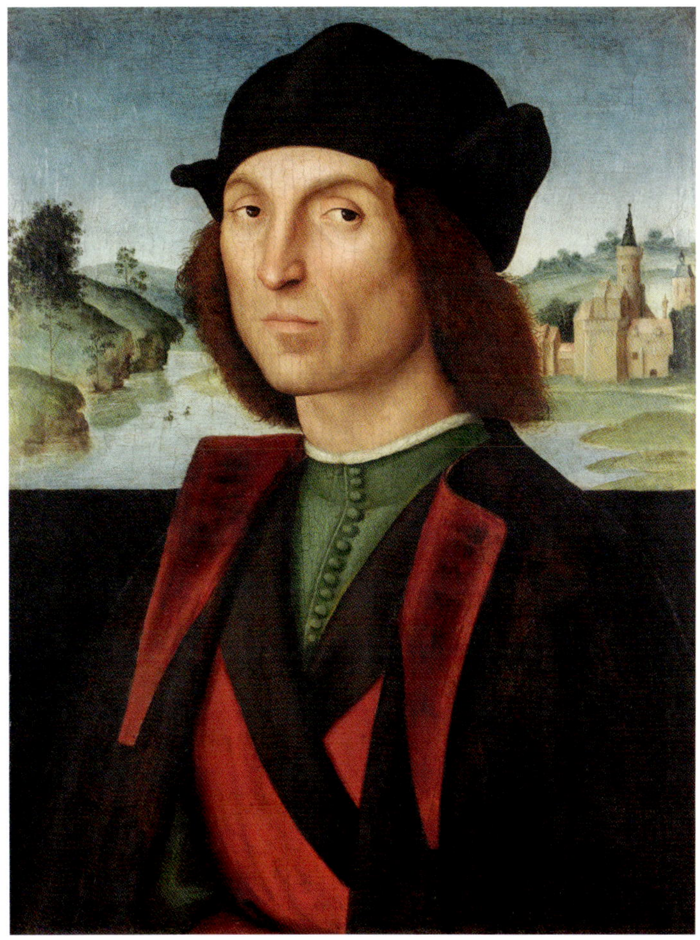

Madonna and Child with Book (Norton Simon Madonna), *c.* 1503/04
Oil on poplar panel, 52.7 × 40 cm (20 ¾ × 15 ¾ in)
Pasadena, California, Norton Simon Museum of Art

Portrait of a Man, *c.* 1503/04
Oil on panel, 47.5 × 37.2 cm (18 ¾ × 14 ⅝ in)
Vaduz–Vienna, Liechtenstein. The Princely Collections
(Detail page 63)

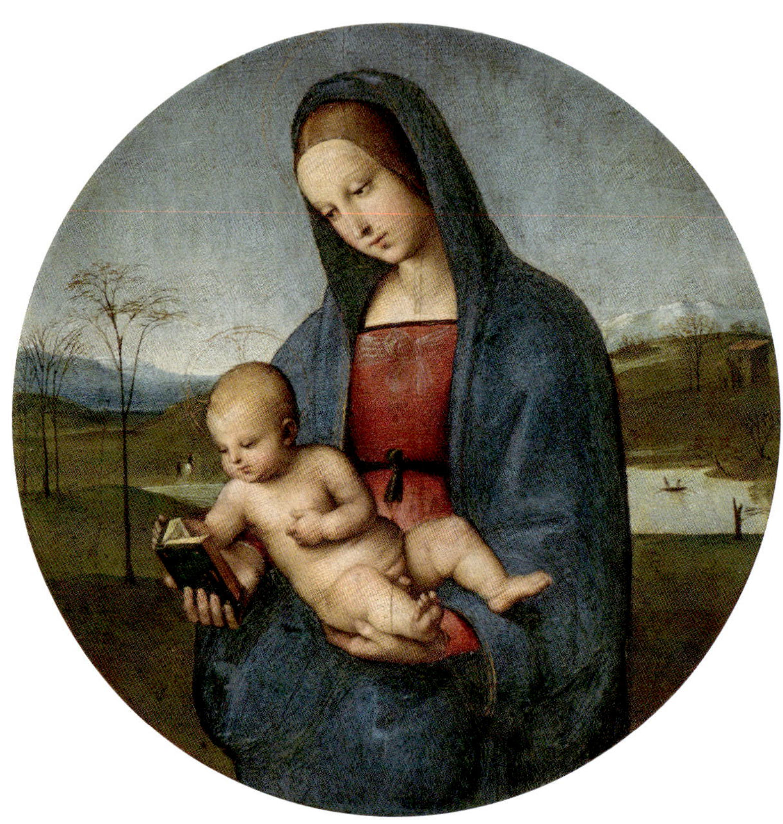

The Madonna Conestabile, *c.* 1504
Tempera on panel, transferred to canvas, tondo, dia. 17.5 × 18 cm (6 ⅞ × 7 ⅛ in)
St Petersburg, Hermitage

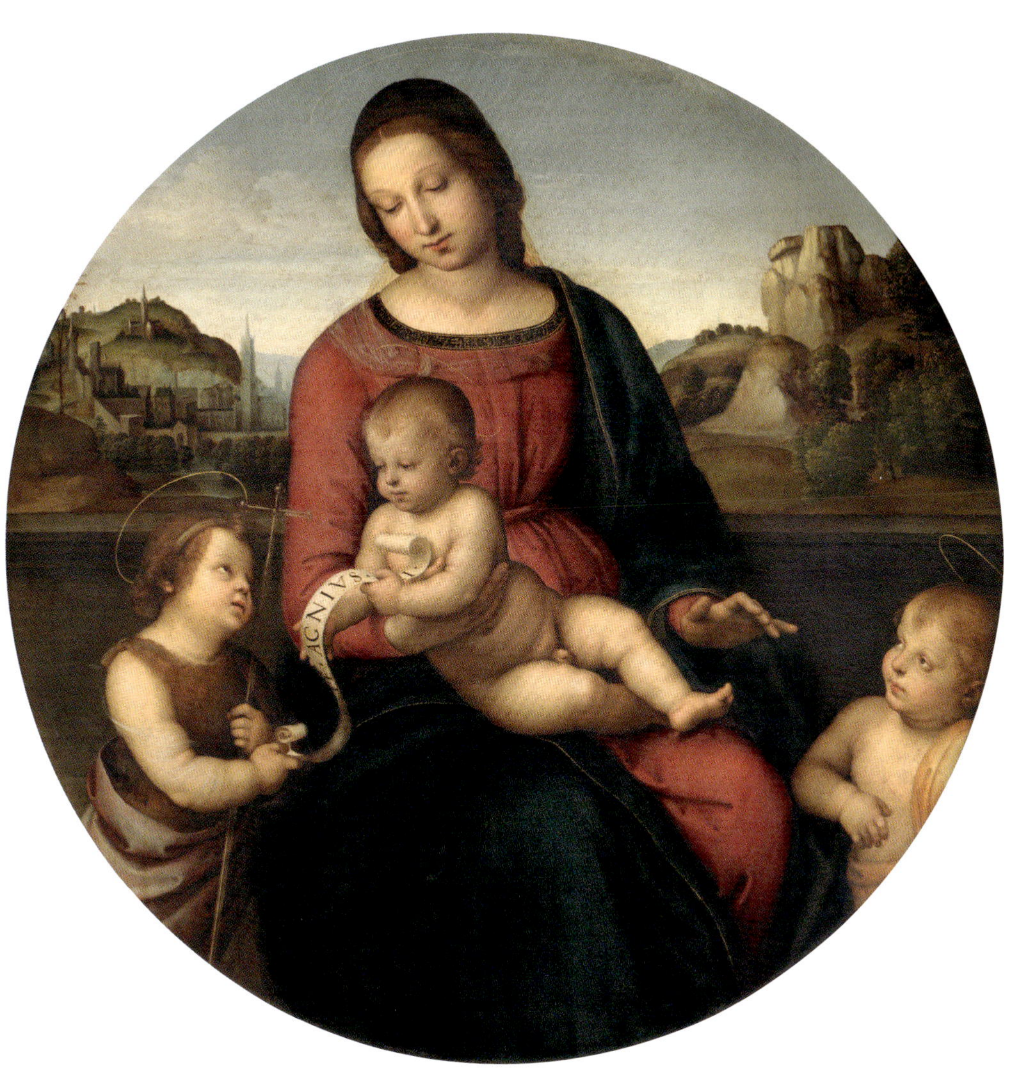

Terranuova Madonna, *c.* 1504/05
Oil on poplar panel, tondo, dia. 88.4 × 88.9 cm (34 ¾ × 35 in)
Staatliche Museen zu Berlin, Gemäldegalerie

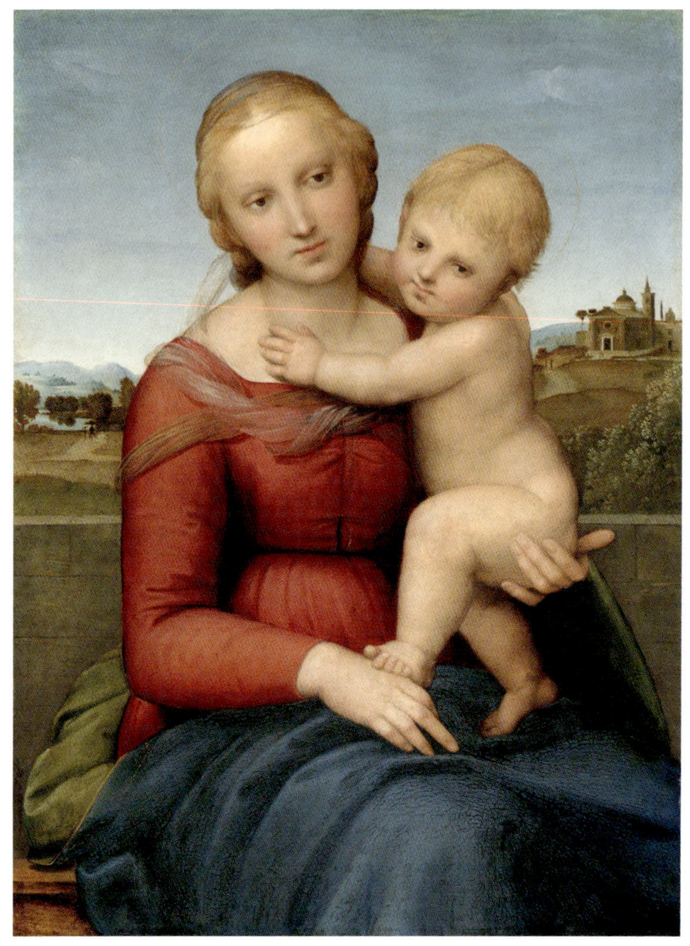

Small Cowper Madonna, *c.* 1505
Oil on poplar panel, 60 × 44 cm (23 5⁄8 × 17 1⁄3 in)
Washington, D. C., National Gallery of Art
(Detail pages 120/121)

Madonna del Granduca, *c.* 1505/06
Oil on panel, 84.4 × 55.9 cm (33 1⁄4 × 22 1⁄8 in)
Florence, Palazzo Pitti

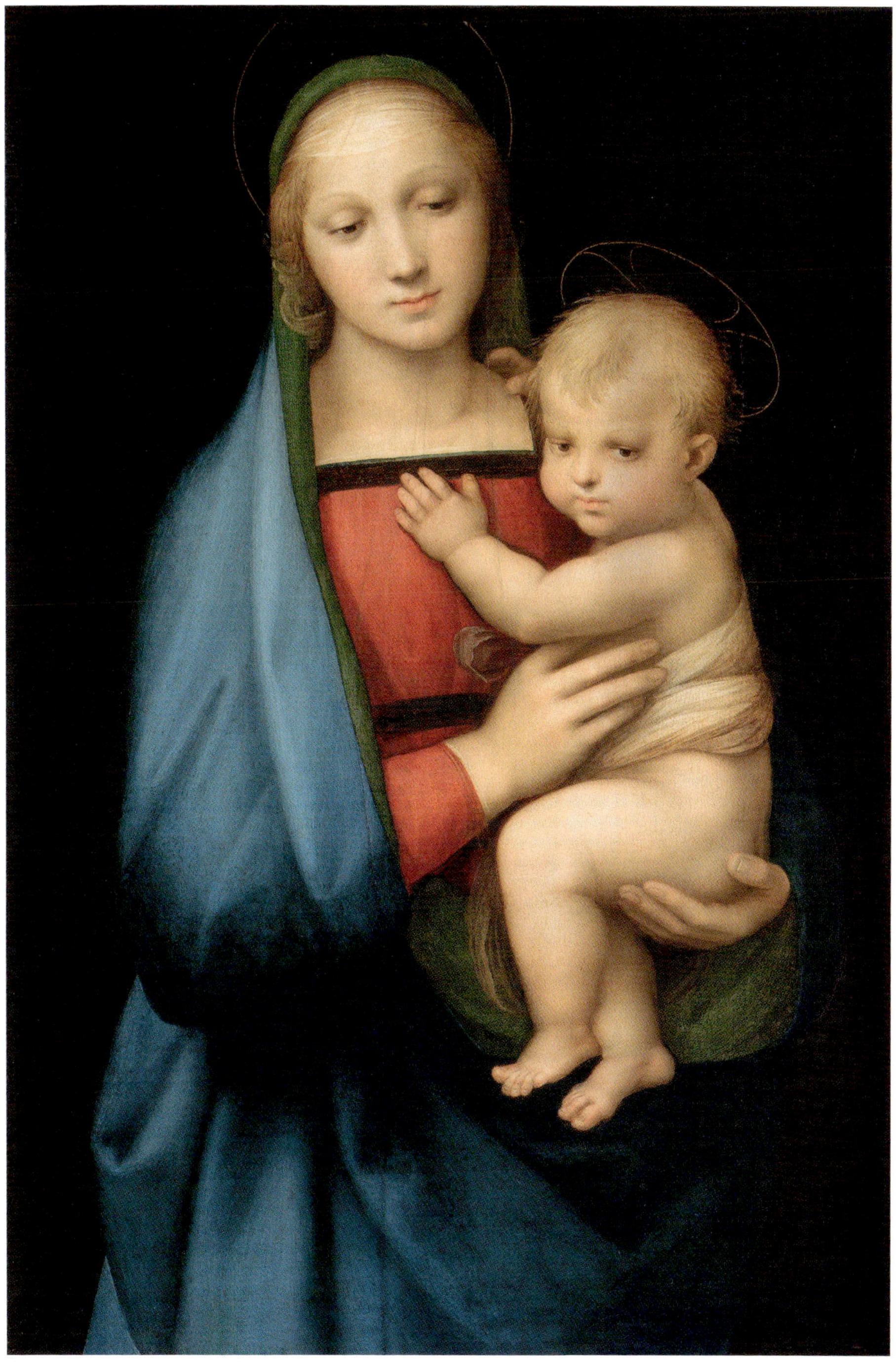

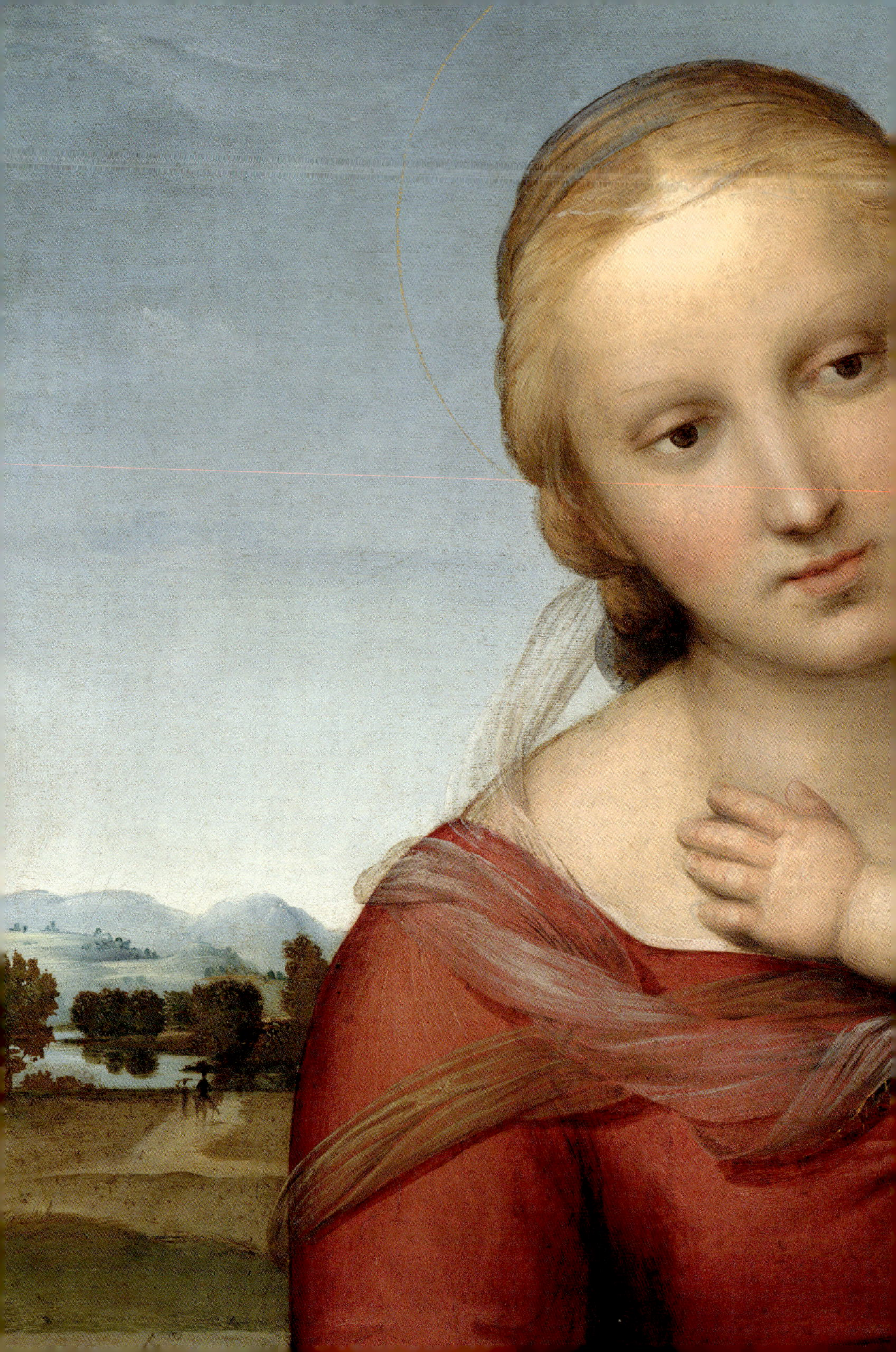

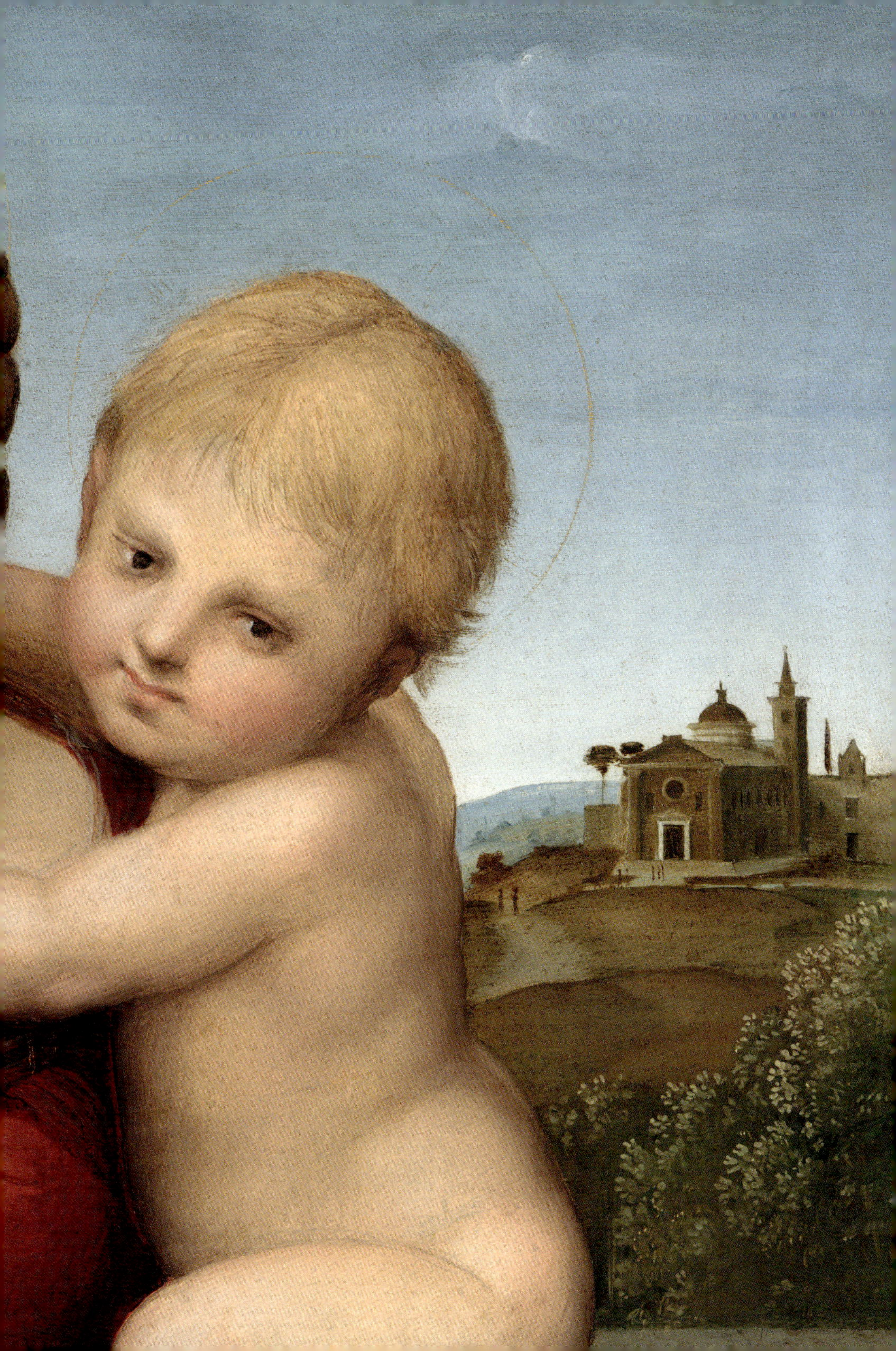

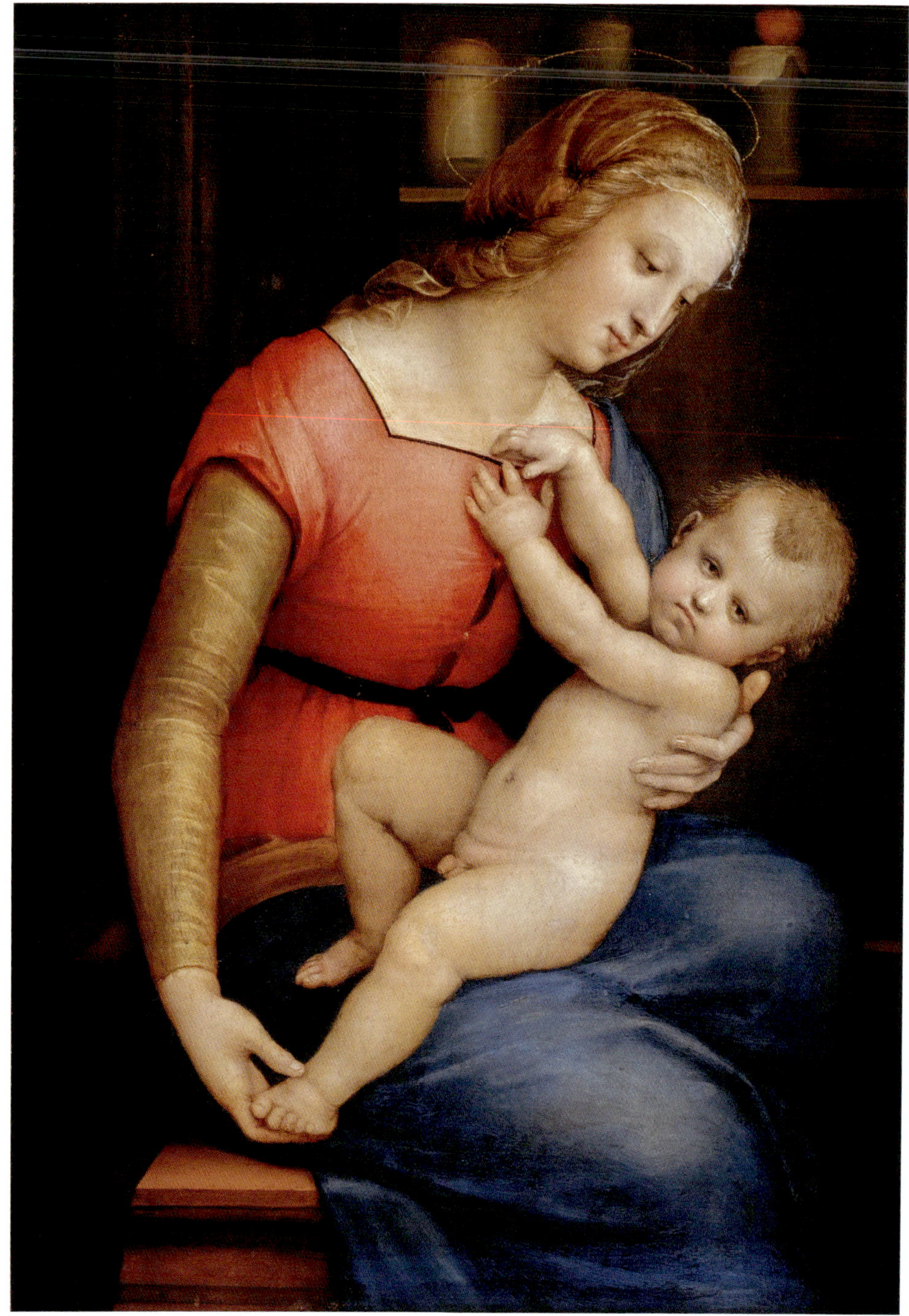

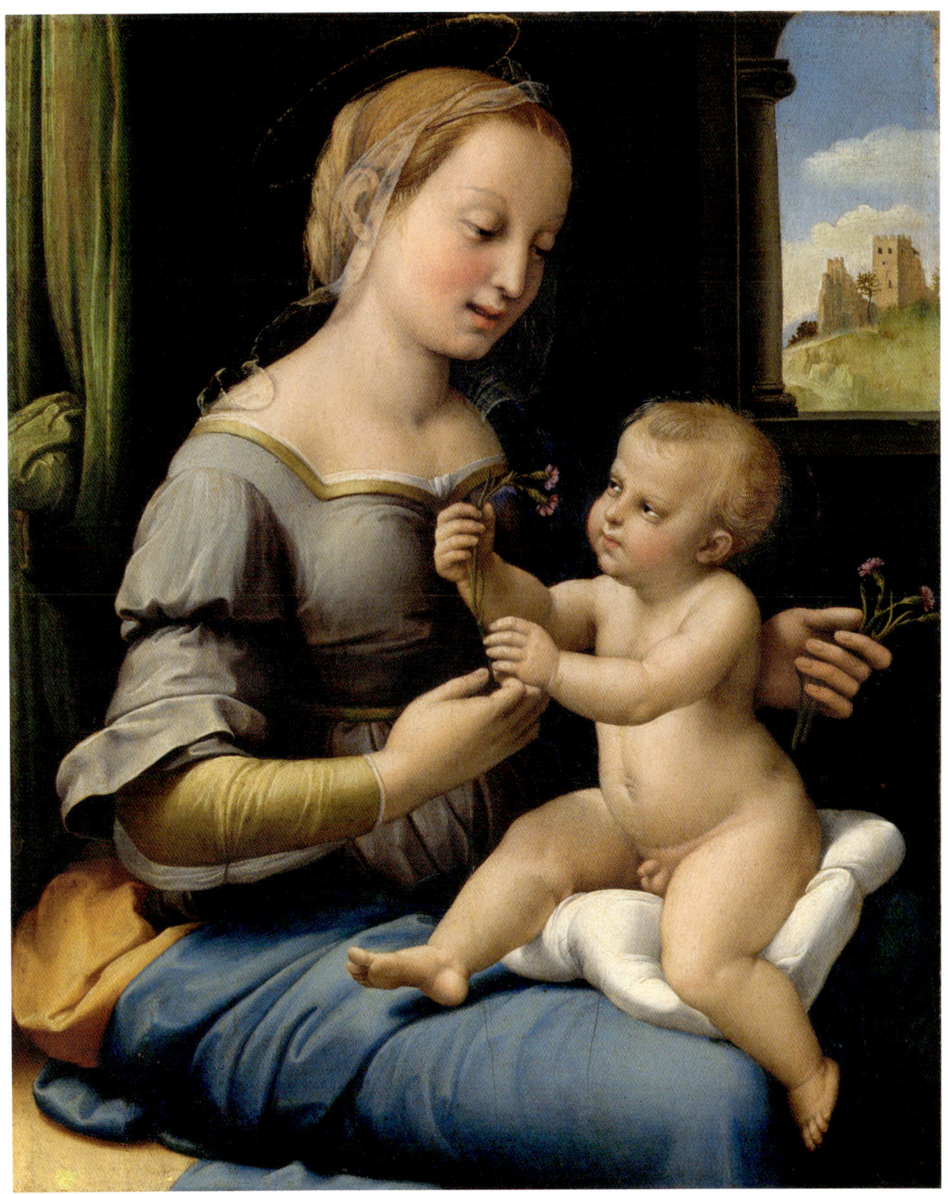

Orléans Madonna, *c.* 1506/07
Oil on panel, 31.7 × 23.3 cm (12 ½ × 9 ⅛ in). Chantilly, Musée Condé

Madonna of the Pinks
(Madonna dei Garofani/Northumberland Madonna), *c.* 1507/08
Oil on yew, 28.8 × 22.9 cm (11 ⅓ × 9 ⅛ in). London, The National Gallery

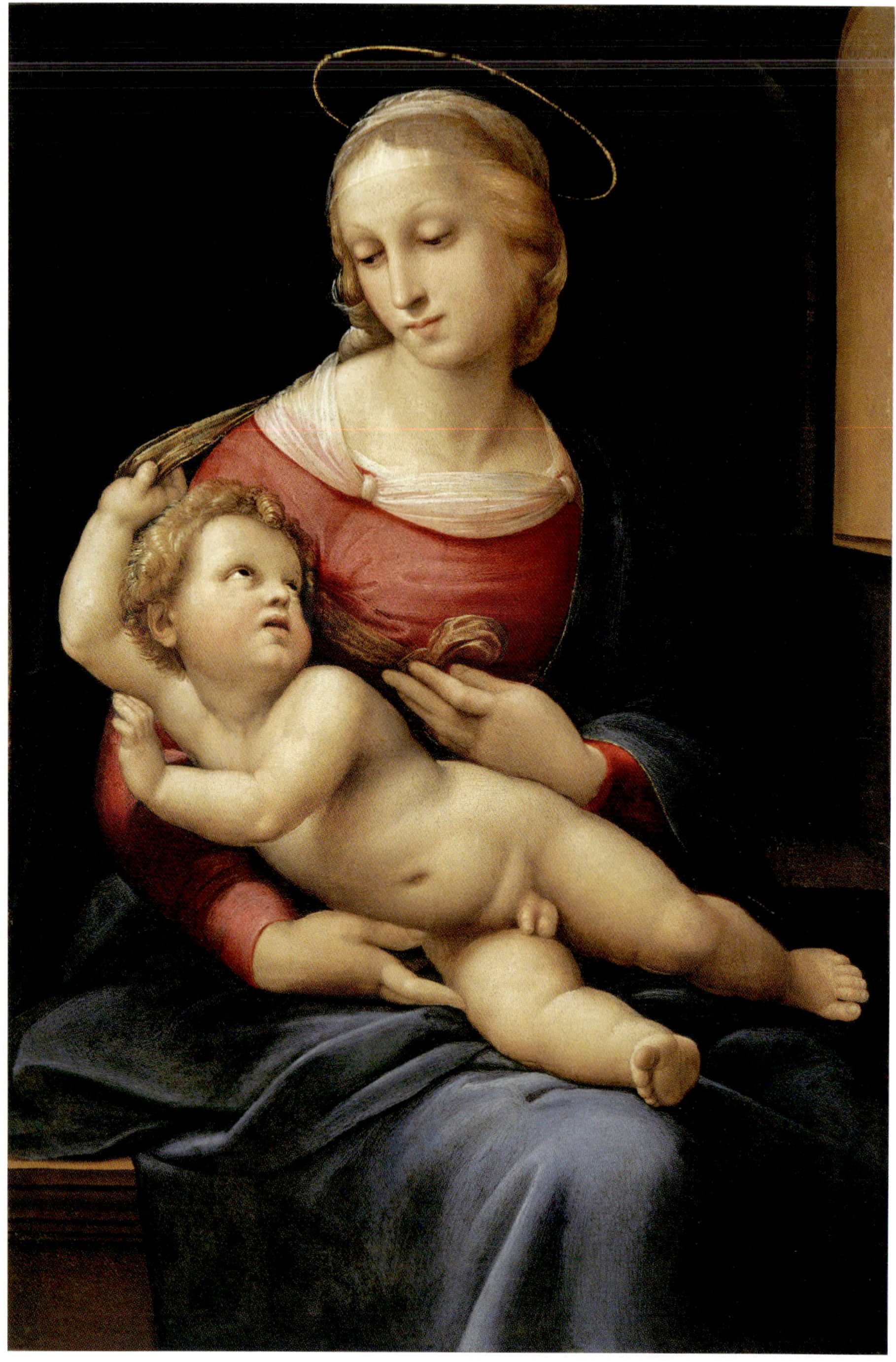

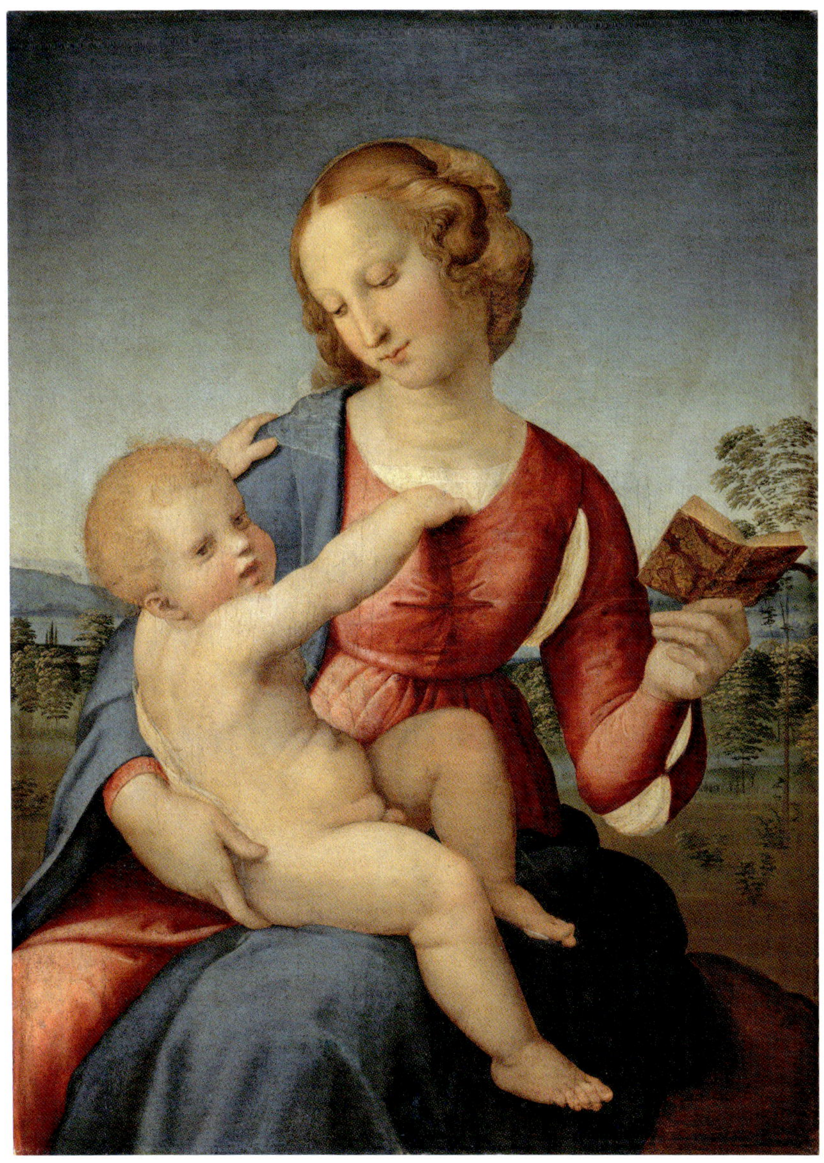

Madonna and Child (Bridgewater Madonna), *c.* 1507/08
Oil on panel, transferred to canvas, 82 × 57 cm (32 ¼ × 22 ½ in)
Edinburgh, Scottish National Gallery, Bridgewater Collection Loan

Madonna Colonna (The Virgin Mary Reading with the Child), *c.* 1507/08
Oil on poplar panel, 77 × 56 cm (30 ⅓ × 22 ⅛ in). Staatliche Museen zu Berlin, Gemäldegalerie

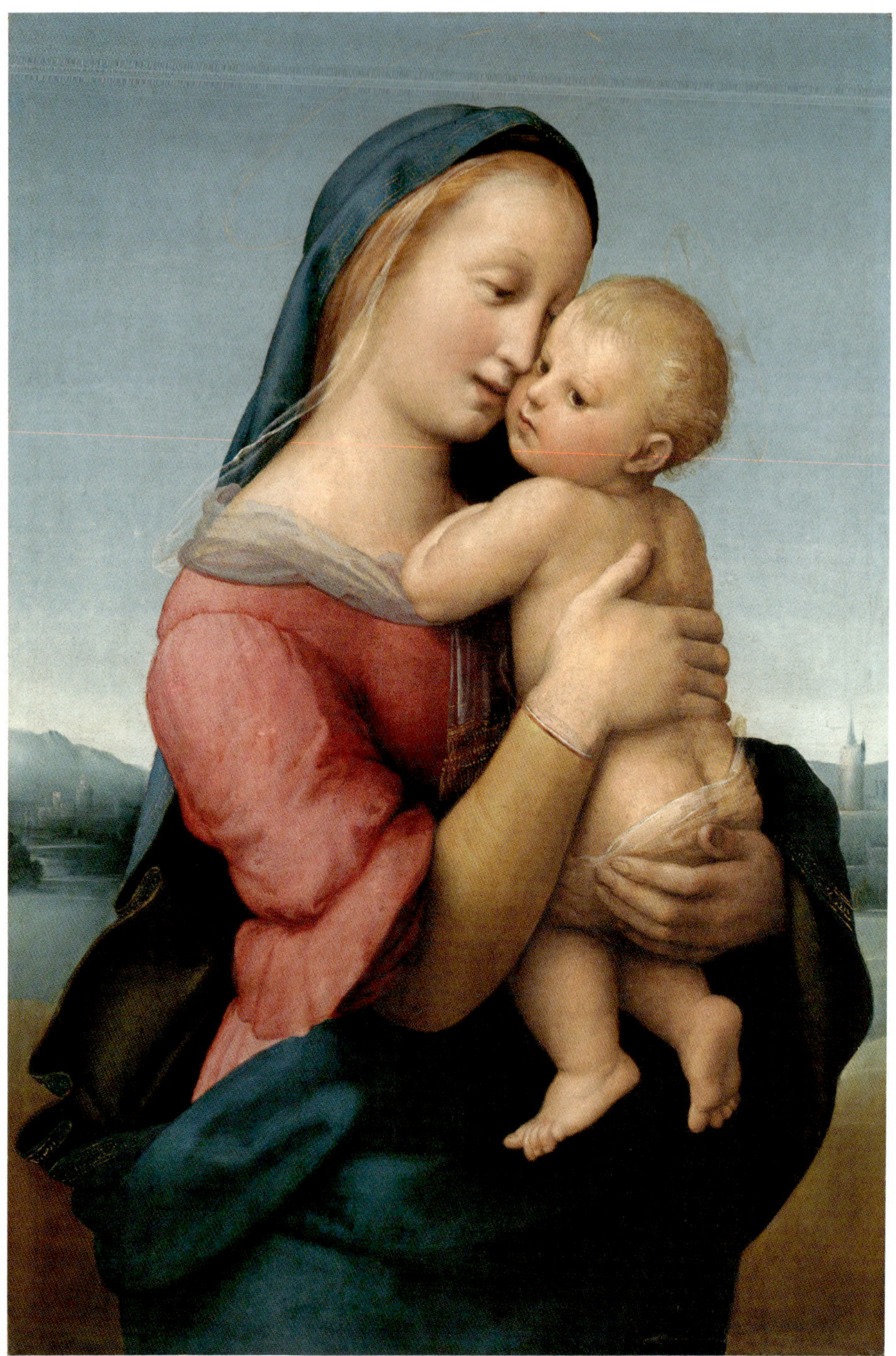

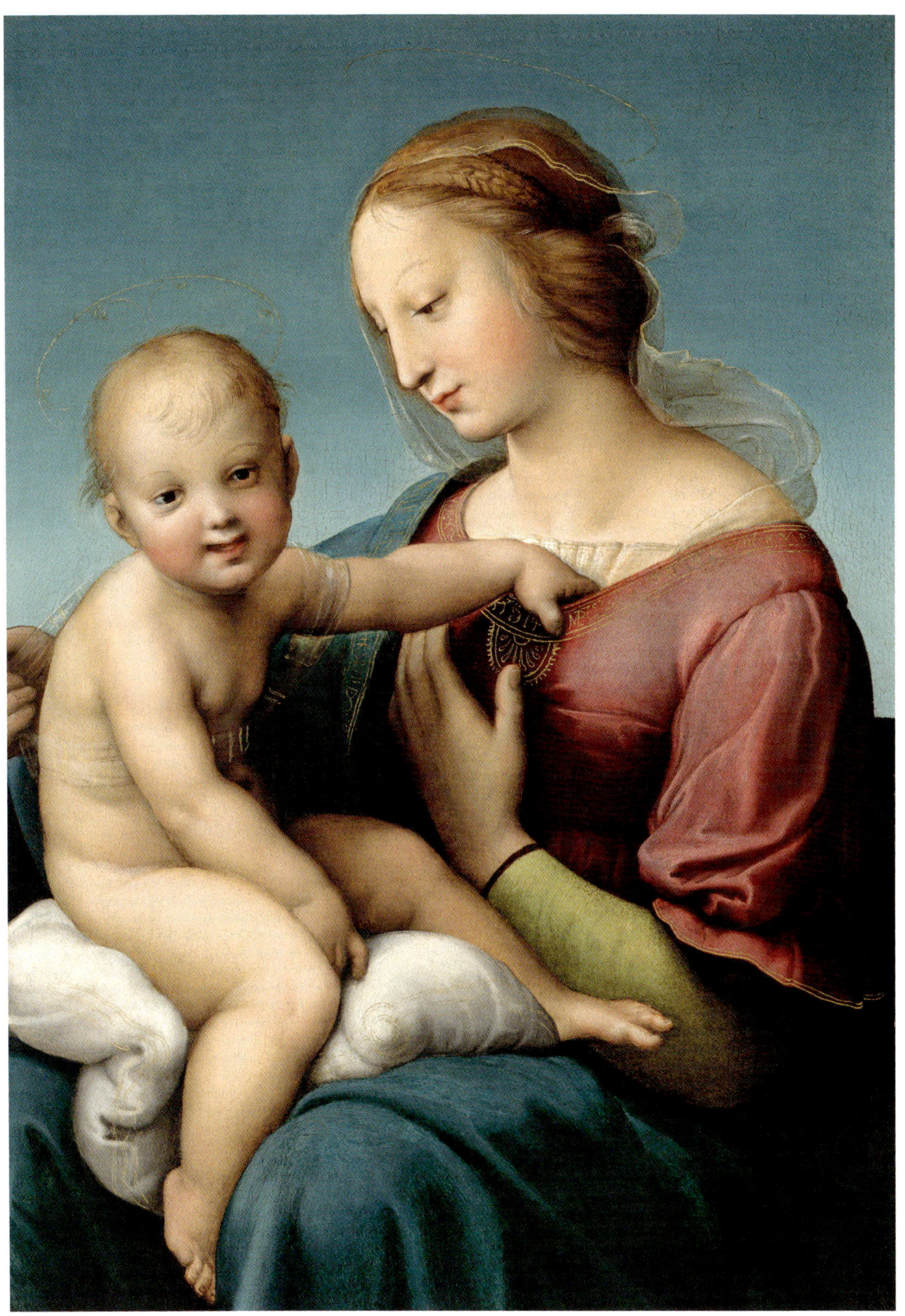

Page 126
Tempi Madonna (The Madonna and Child), *c.* 1508
Oil on poplar panel, 75 × 51 cm (29 ½ × 20 ⅛ in)
Munich, Bayerische Staatsgemäldesammlungen, Alte Pinakothek

Page 127
Large Cowper Madonna (Niccolini-Cowper Madonna), *c.* 1508
Oil on (poplar?) panel, 81 × 57 cm (31 ⅞ × 22 ½ in)
Inscription on the hem of the robe: *MD.VIII. R[APHAEL]. V[RBINAS]. PIN[XIT]*
Washington, D. C., National Gallery of Art

Studies for the *Madonna of the Meadow*, 1505/06
Pen, 24.6 × 36.4 cm (9 ⅔ × 14 ⅓ in)
Vienna, Albertina

Madonna del Prato/Madonna Belvedere (Madonna of the Meadow), *c.* 1505/06
Oil on poplar panel, 113 × 88 cm (44 ½ × 34 ⅝ in)
Vienna, Kunsthistorisches Museum
(Detail pages 130/131)

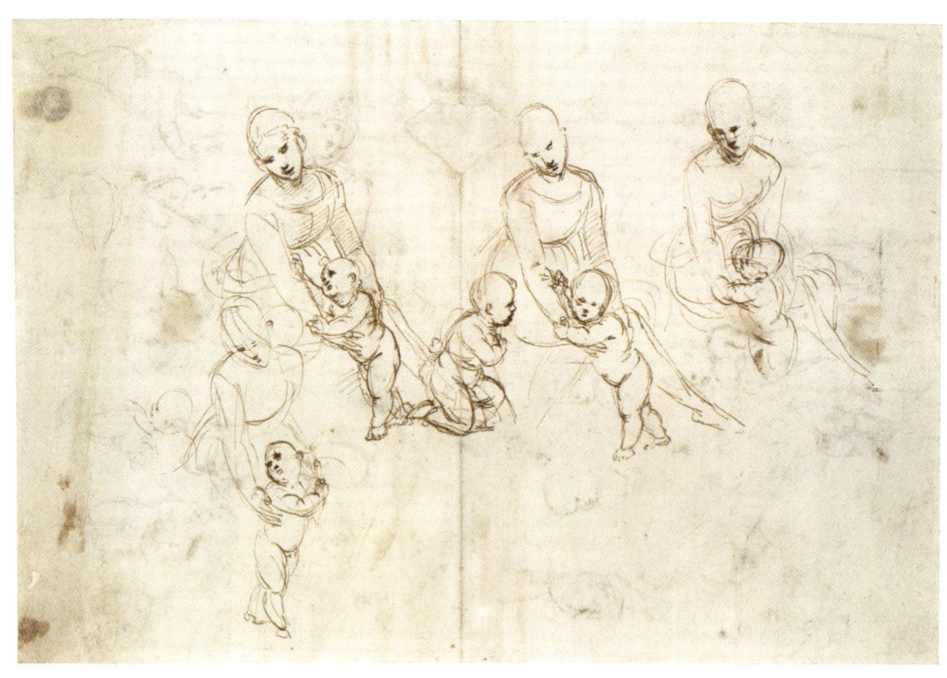

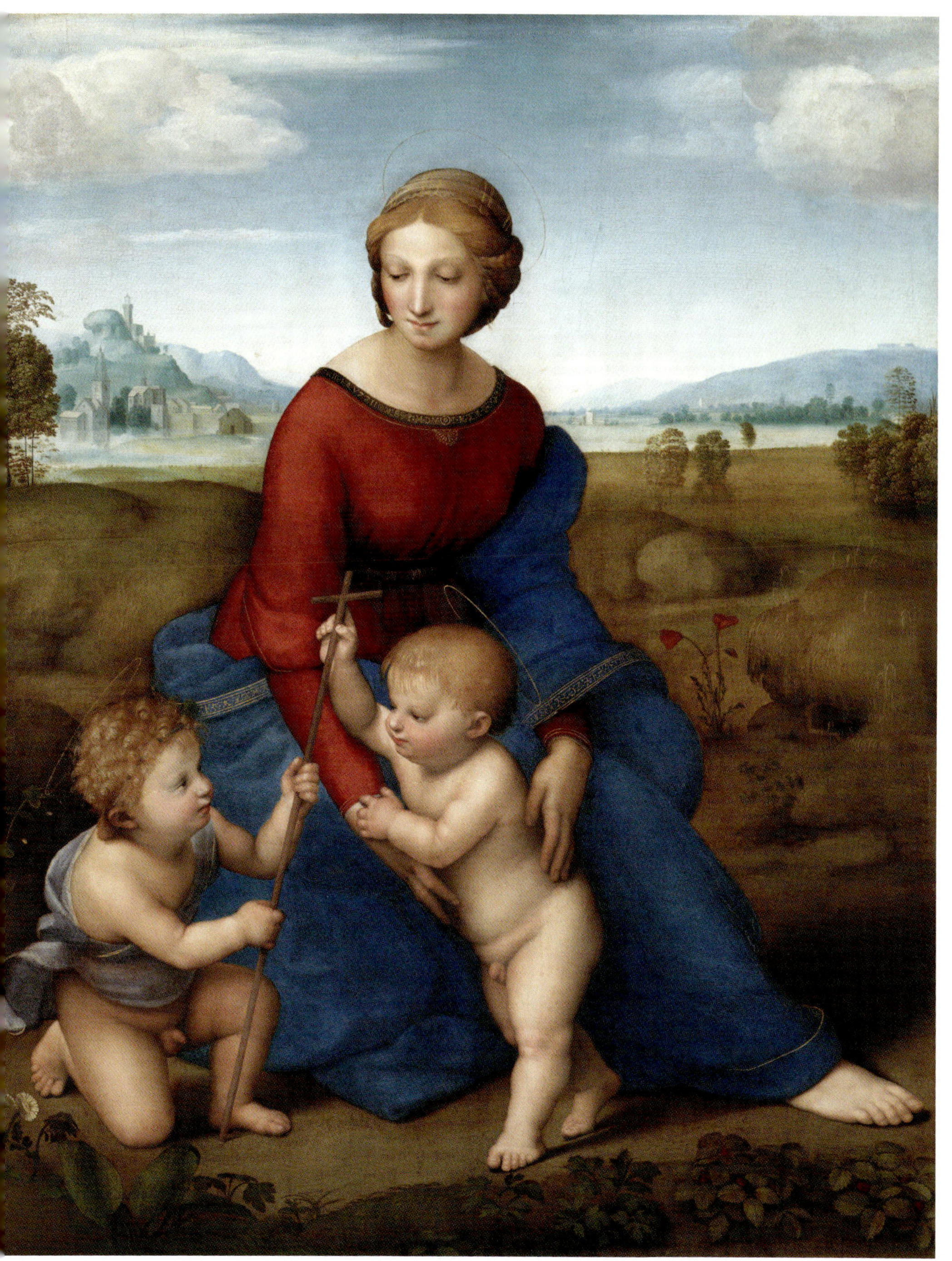

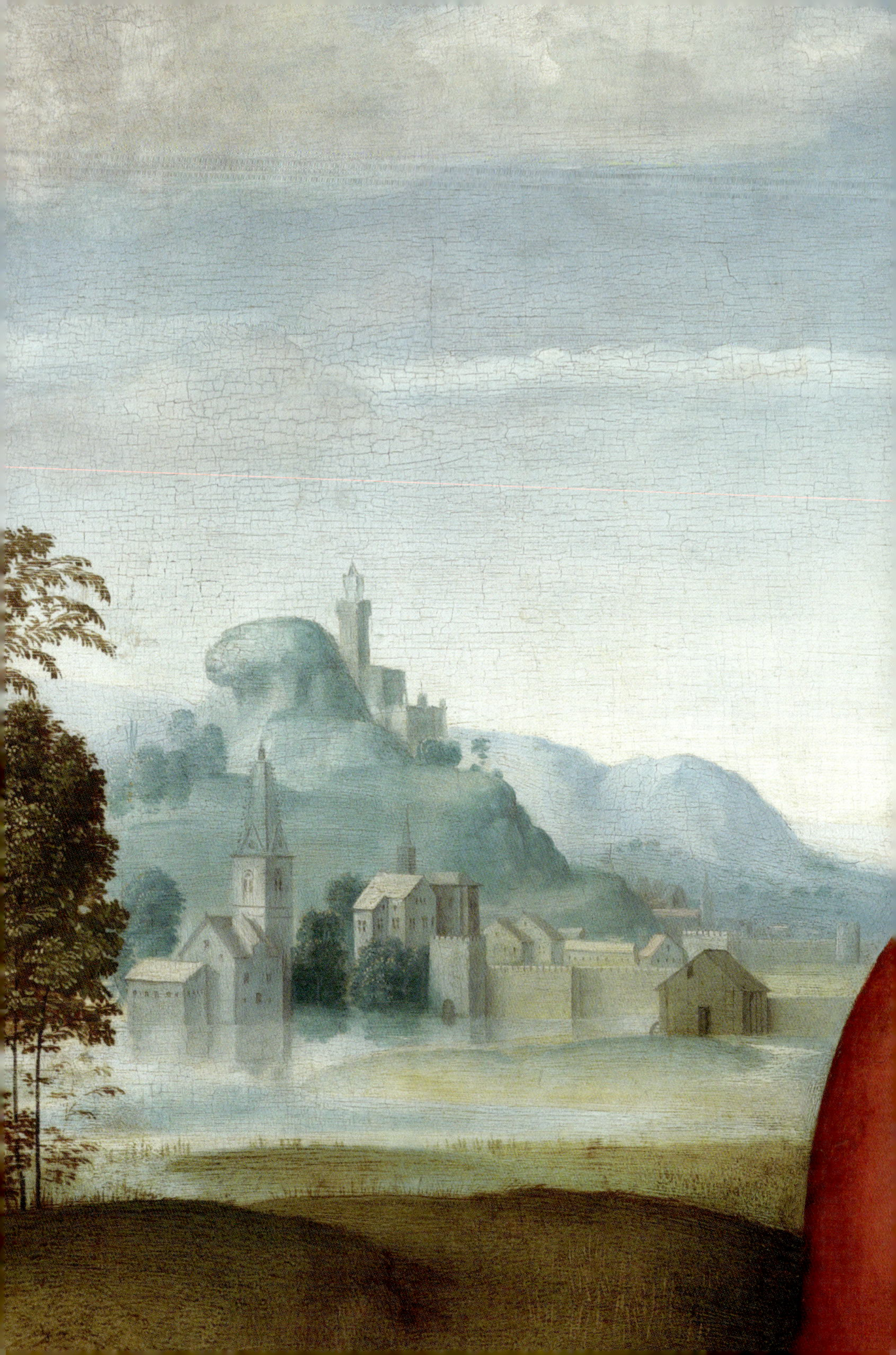

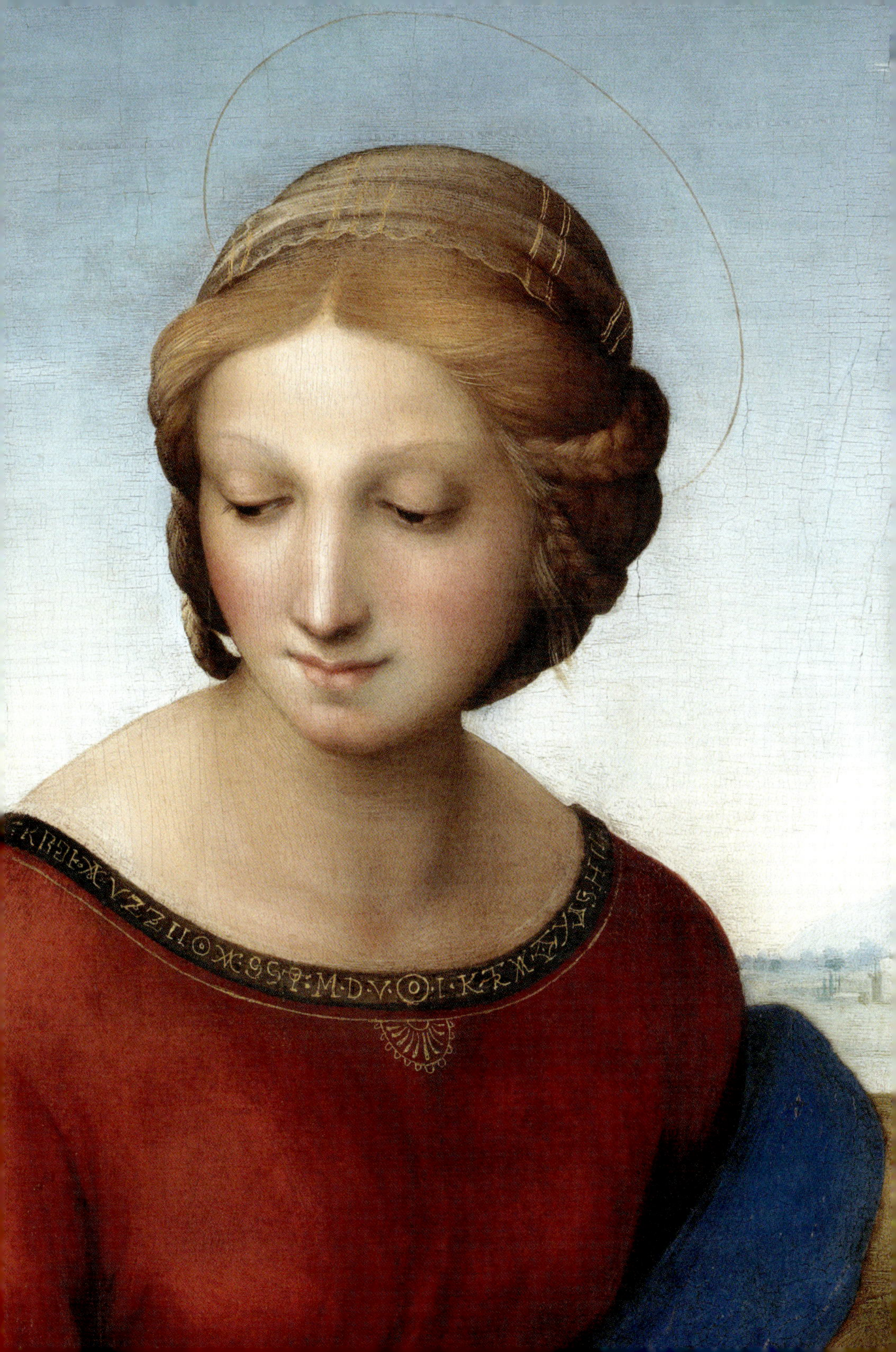

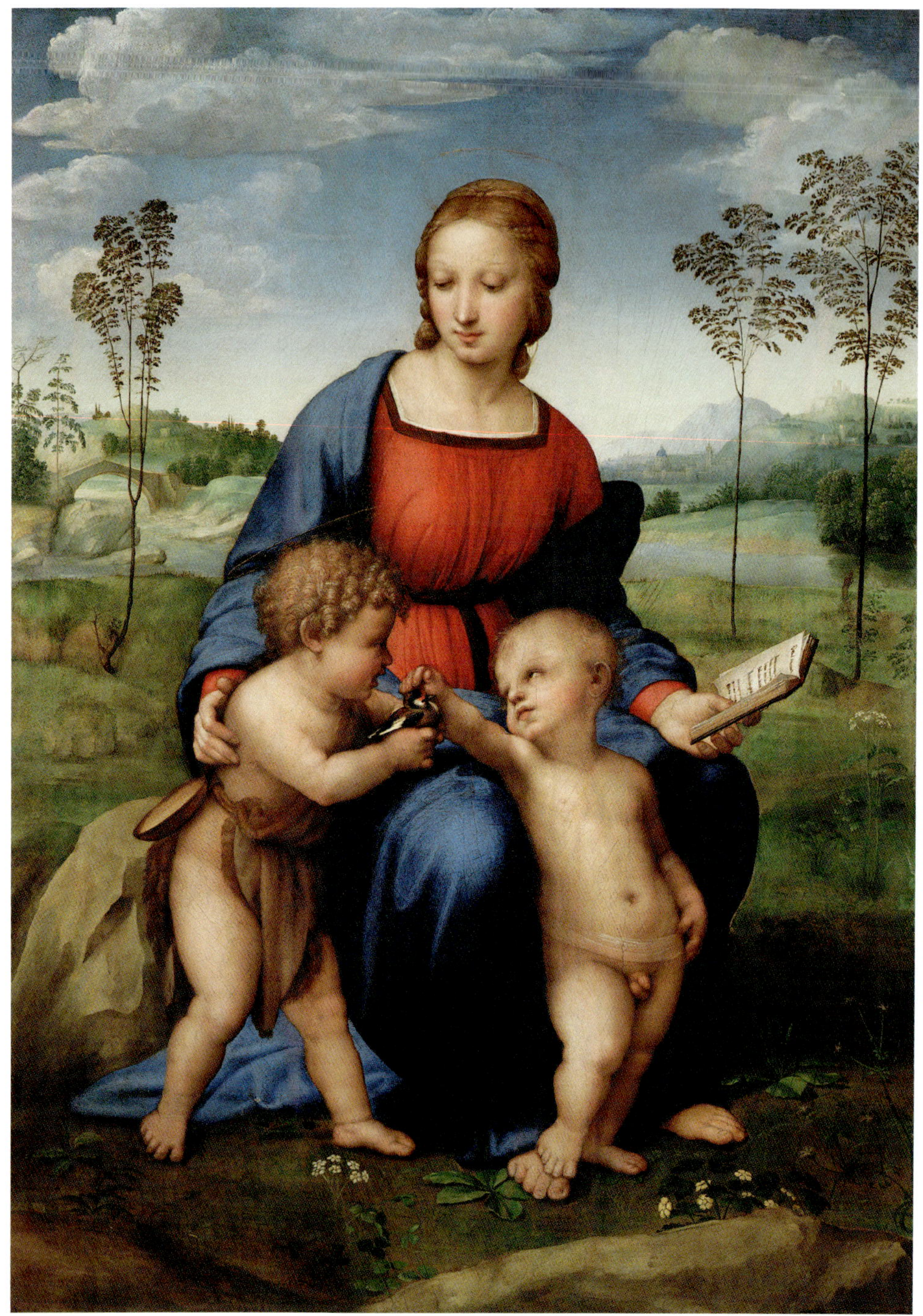

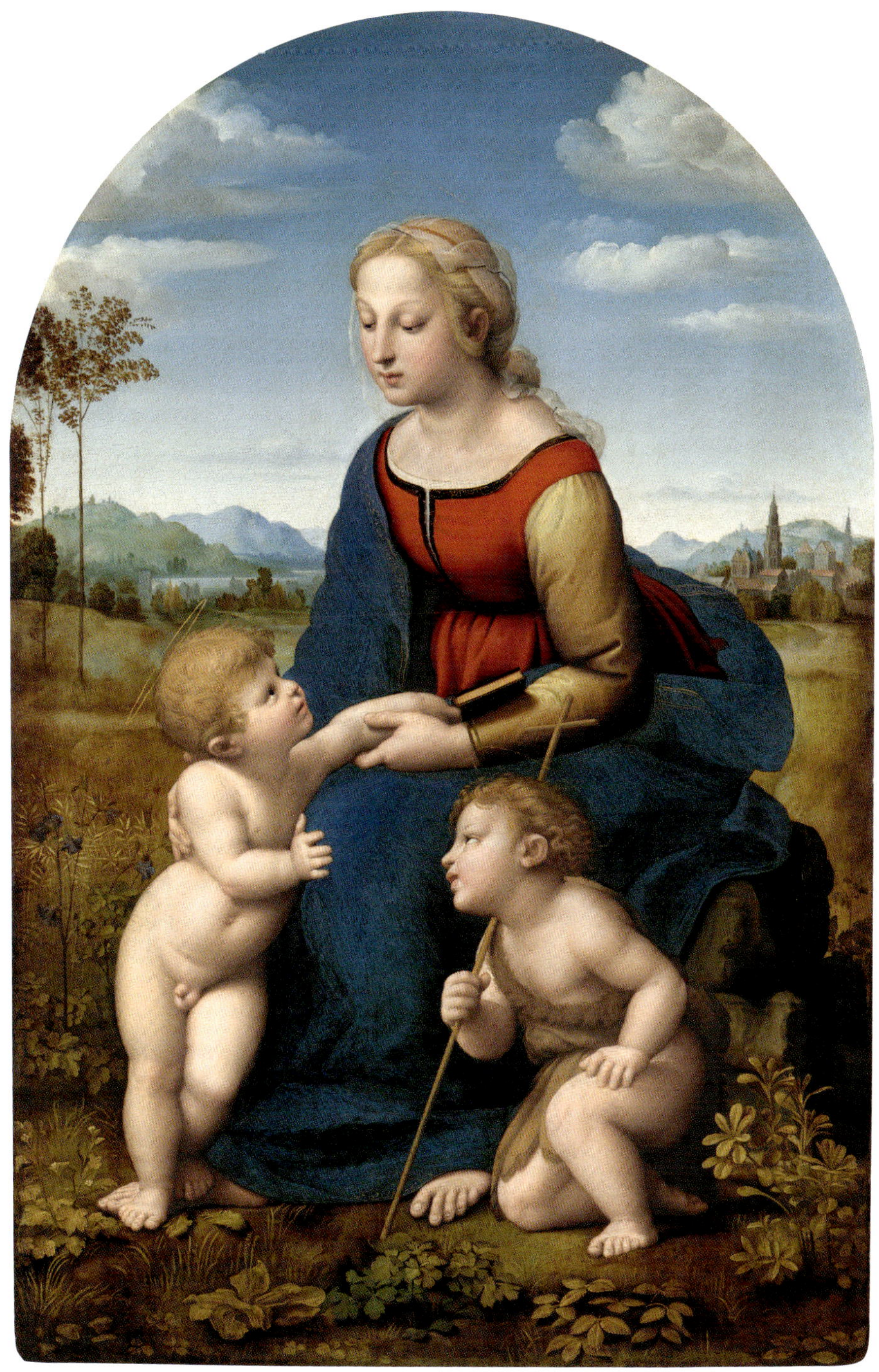

Page 132
Madonna of the Goldfinch (Madonna del Cardellino), *c.* 1506
Oil on panel, 107 × 77.2 cm (42 ⅛ × 30 ⅜ in). Florence, Gallerie degli Uffizi

Page 133
Madonna and Child with the Infant Saint John (La Belle Jardinière), *c.* 1507/08
Oil on poplar panel, 122 × 80 cm (48 ⅛ × 31 ½ in)
Inscription on the hem of the cloak: *RAPHAELLO VRB.[INAS] .M.DVII* or *.M.DVIII*
Paris, Musée du Louvre

Leonardo da Vinci
Virgin and Child with Saint Anne, *c.* 1503–1519
Oil on poplar panel, 168.4 × 113 cm (66 ¼ × 44 ½ in). Paris, Musée du Louvre

Holy Family with Lamb, 1507
Oil on panel, 29 × 21 cm (11 ⅜ × 8 ¼ in)
Inscription on the hem of the gown: *RAPHA[E]L.VRBINAS. MDVII*
Madrid, Museo Nacional del Prado

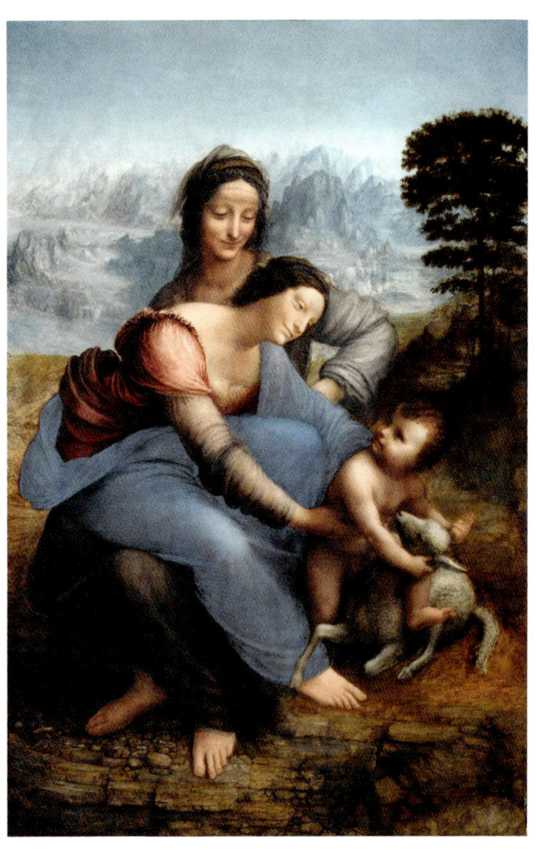

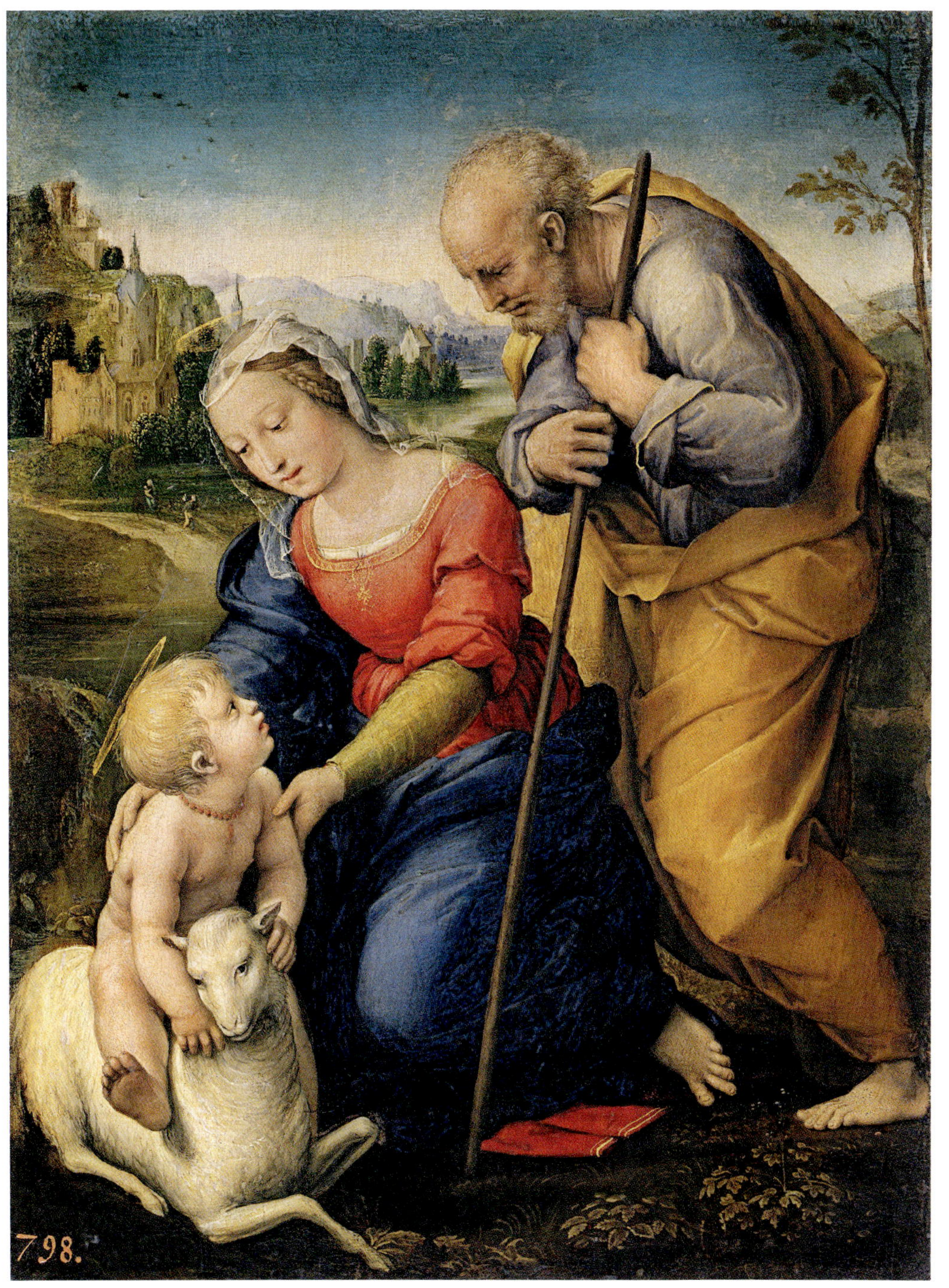
798.

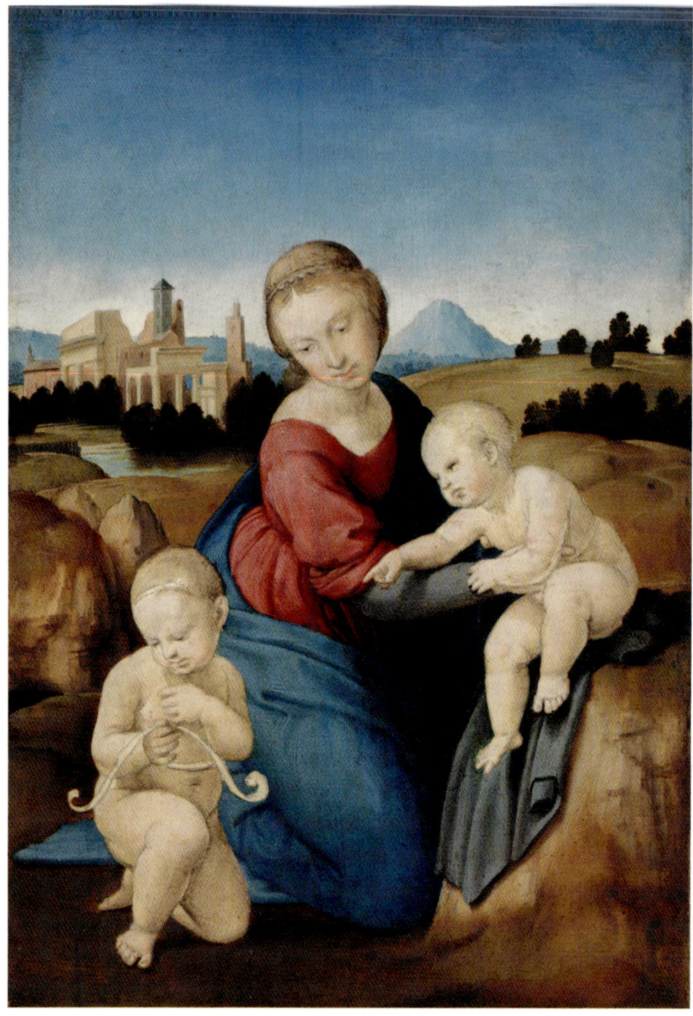

The Virgin and Child with the Infant Saint John (Esterházy Madonna), *c.* 1508
Oil on poplar panel, 28.5 × 21.5 cm (11 ¼ × 8 ½ in)
Inscription on the banderole: *ECCE AGNUS DEI*
Budapest, Szépművészeti Múzeum

Madonna and Child with Saint Joseph, Saint Elizabeth and the Infant Saint John (Canigiani Holy Family), 1507
Oil on poplar panel, 131 × 107 cm (51 ⅝ × 42 ⅛ in)
Munich, Bayerische Staatsgemäldesammlungen, Alte Pinakothek

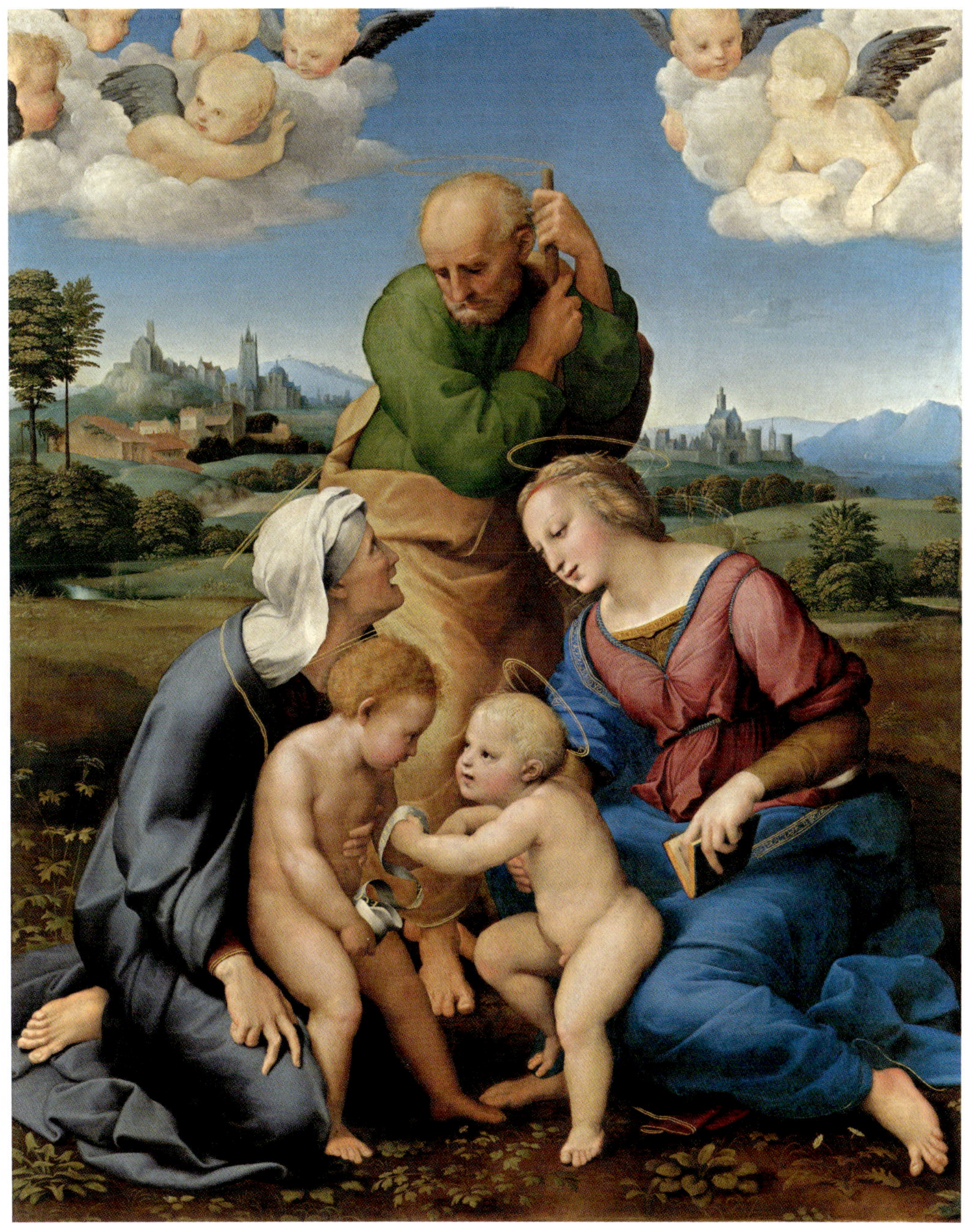

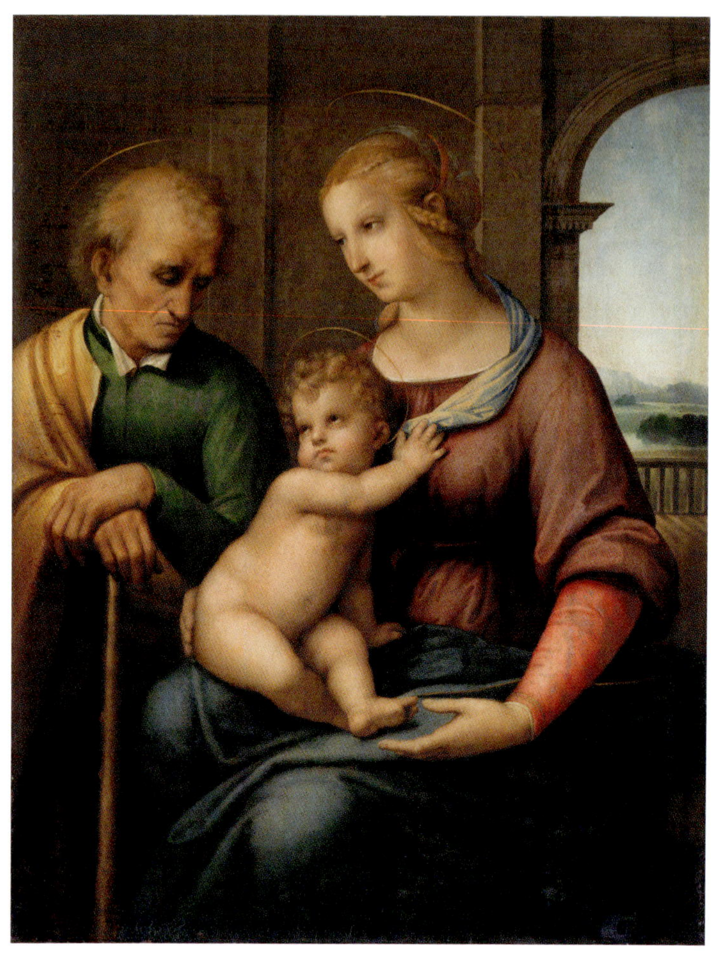

The Holy Family, *c.* 1507/08 (?)
Oil on panel, transferred to canvas, 72.5 × 56.5 cm (28 ½ × 22 ¼ in)
St Petersburg, Hermitage

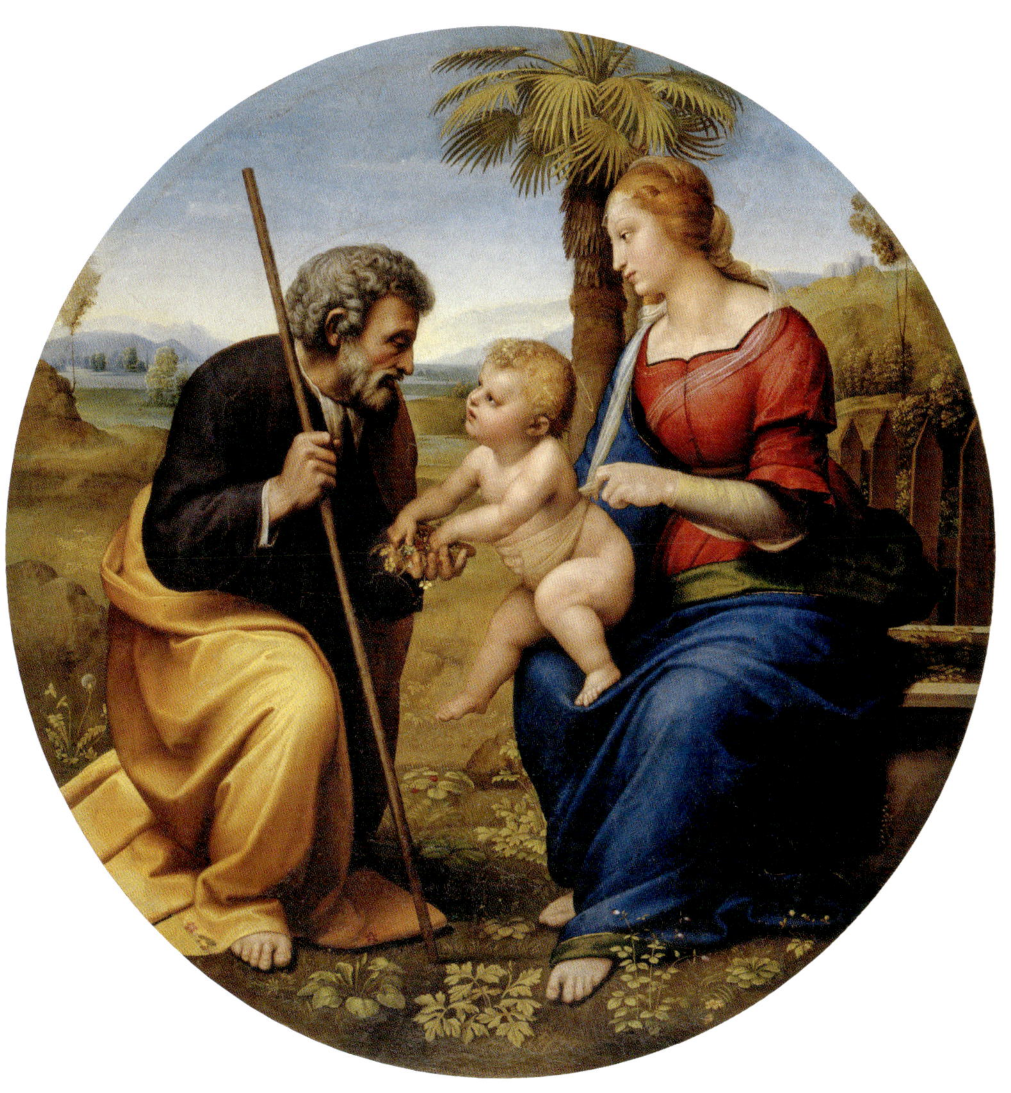

The Holy Family with a Palm Tree, *c.* 1507/08
Oil on panel, transferred to canvas, tondo, dia. 101.5 cm (39 ⅞ in)
Edinburgh, Scottish National Gallery, Bridgewater Collection Loan

Saint Catherine, 1507/08
Cartoon, black and white chalk, pricked outlines, 58.5 × 43.6 cm (23 ⅛ × 17 ⅛ in)
Paris, Musée du Louvre, Département des Arts graphiques

Saint Catherine of Alexandria, *c.* 1507/08
Oil on poplar panel, 71.5 × 55.7 cm (28 ⅛ × 21 ⅞ in)
London, The National Gallery

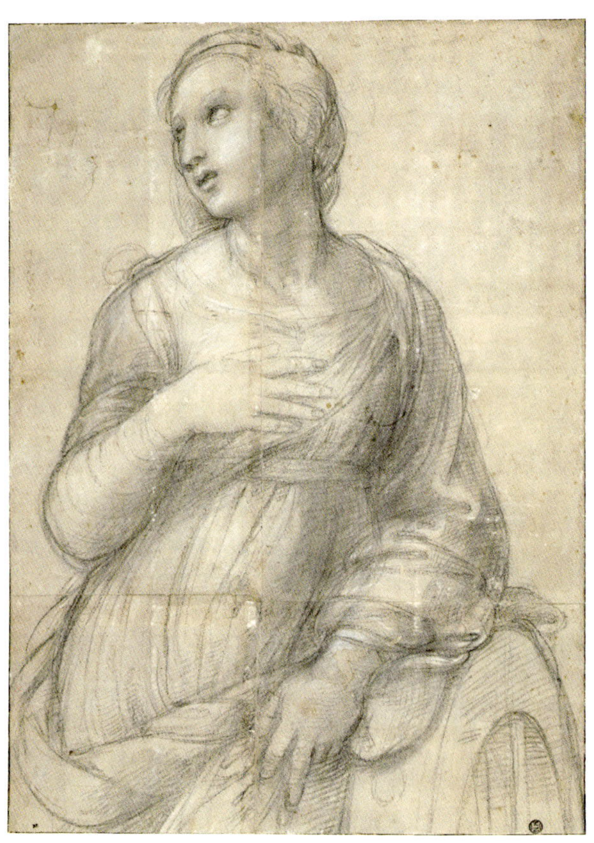

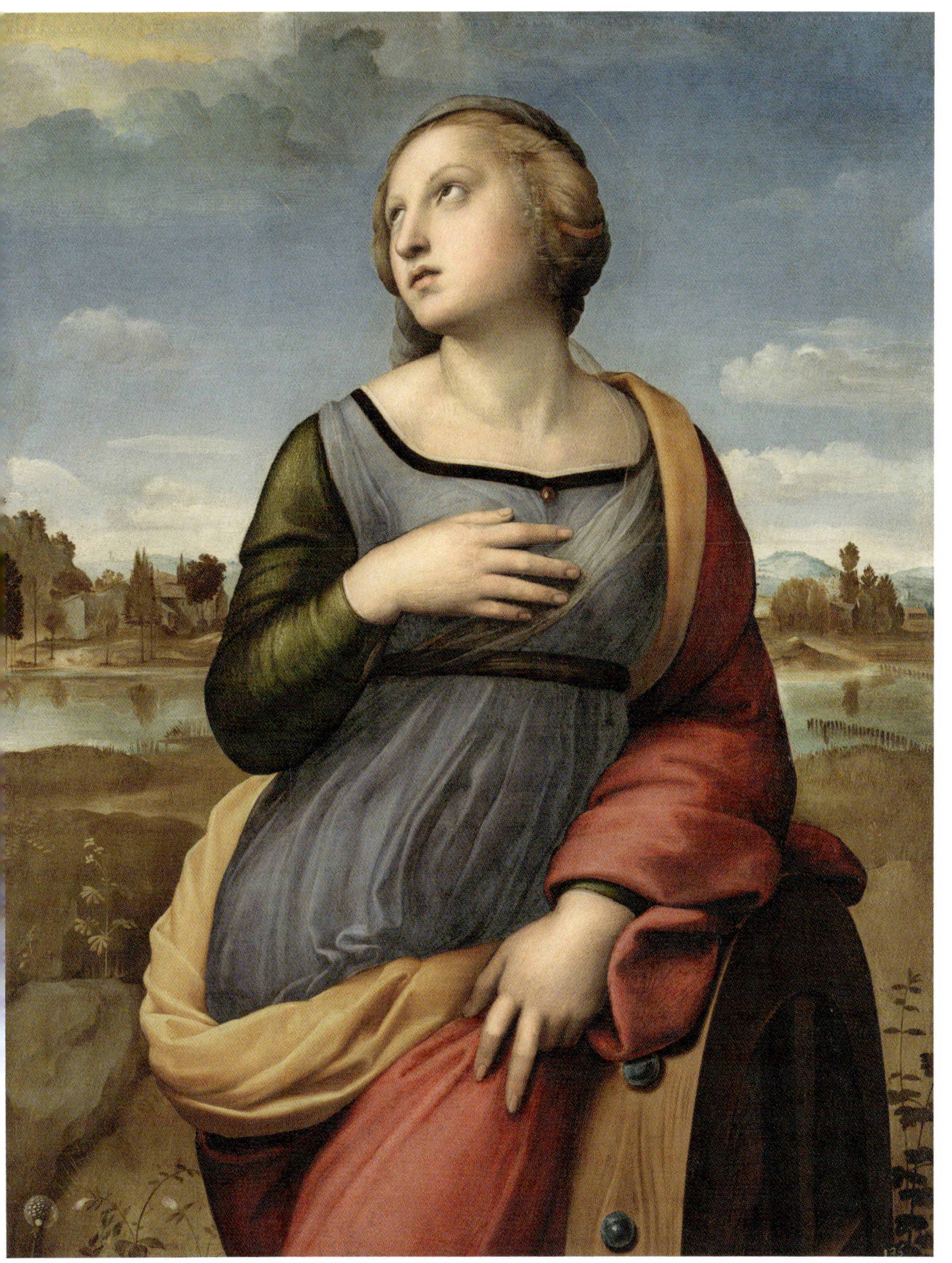

Leonardo da Vinci
Portrait of Lisa del Giocondo (Mona Lisa), 1503–1506 and later (1510?)
Oil on poplar, 77 × 53 cm (30 ⅓ × 20 ⅞ in)
Paris, Musée du Louvre

Portrait of a Lady (after Leonardo's *Mona Lisa*), *c.* 1505
Pen over traces of stylus and chalk, 22.2 × 15.8 cm (8 ¾ × 6 ¼ in)
Paris, Musée du Louvre, Département des Arts graphiques

Lady with a Unicorn, *c.* 1505
Oil on panel, transferred to canvas, 65 × 51 cm (25 ⅝ × 20 ⅛ in)
Rome, Galleria Borghese
(Detail page 79)

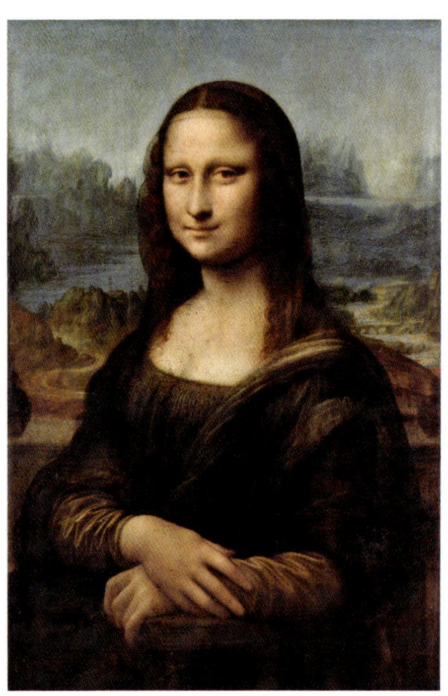

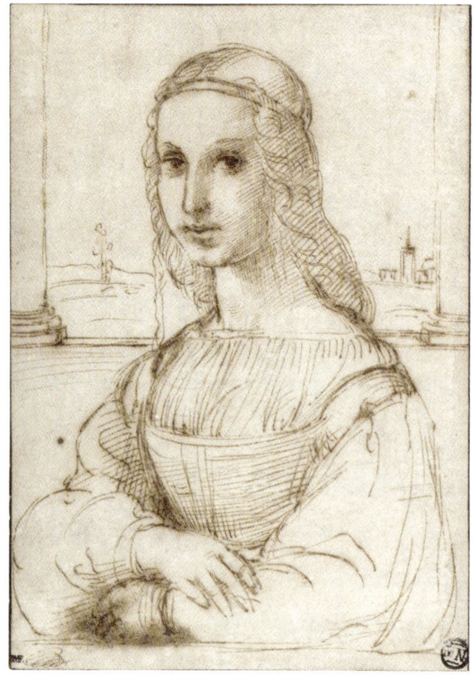

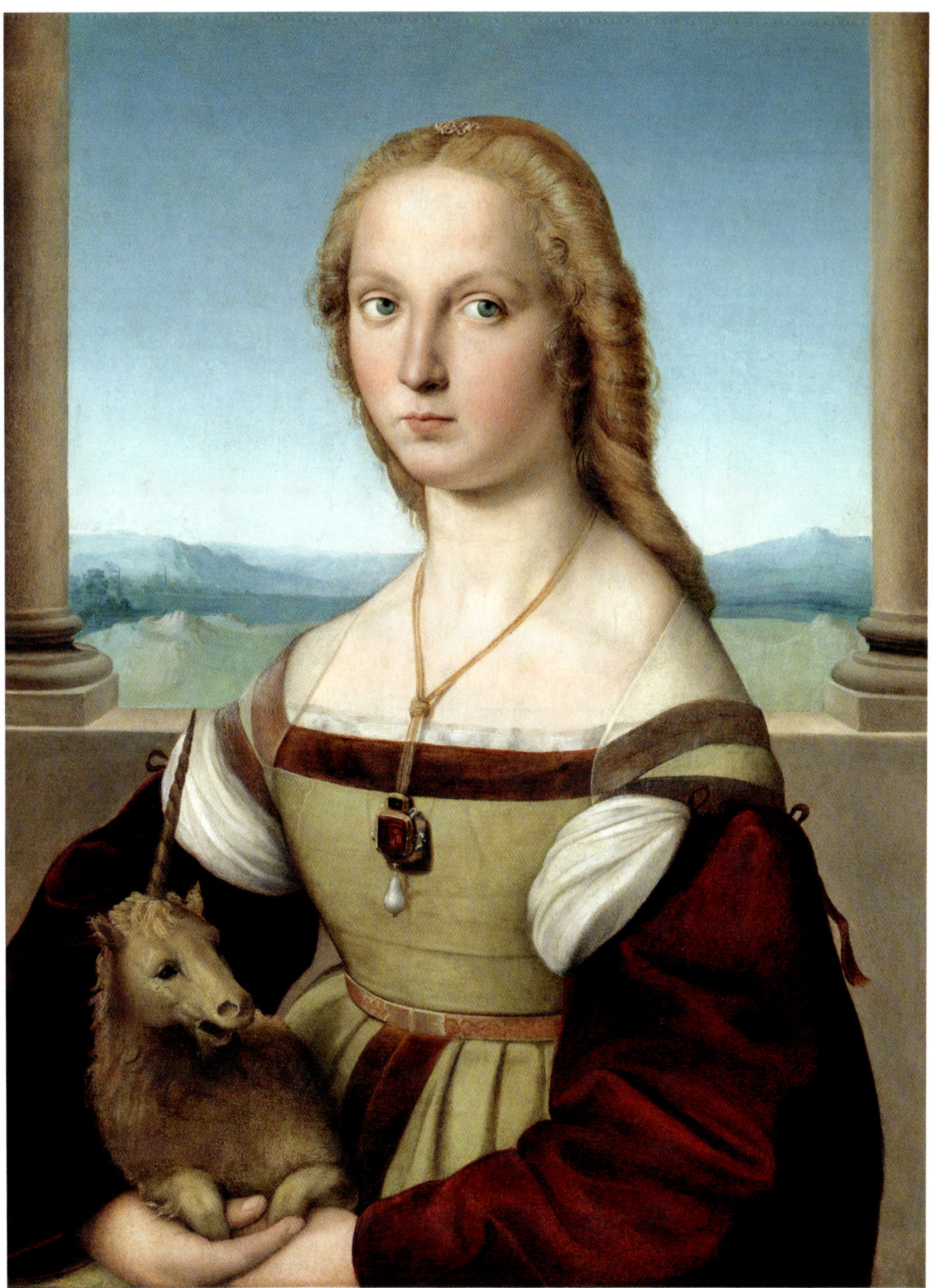

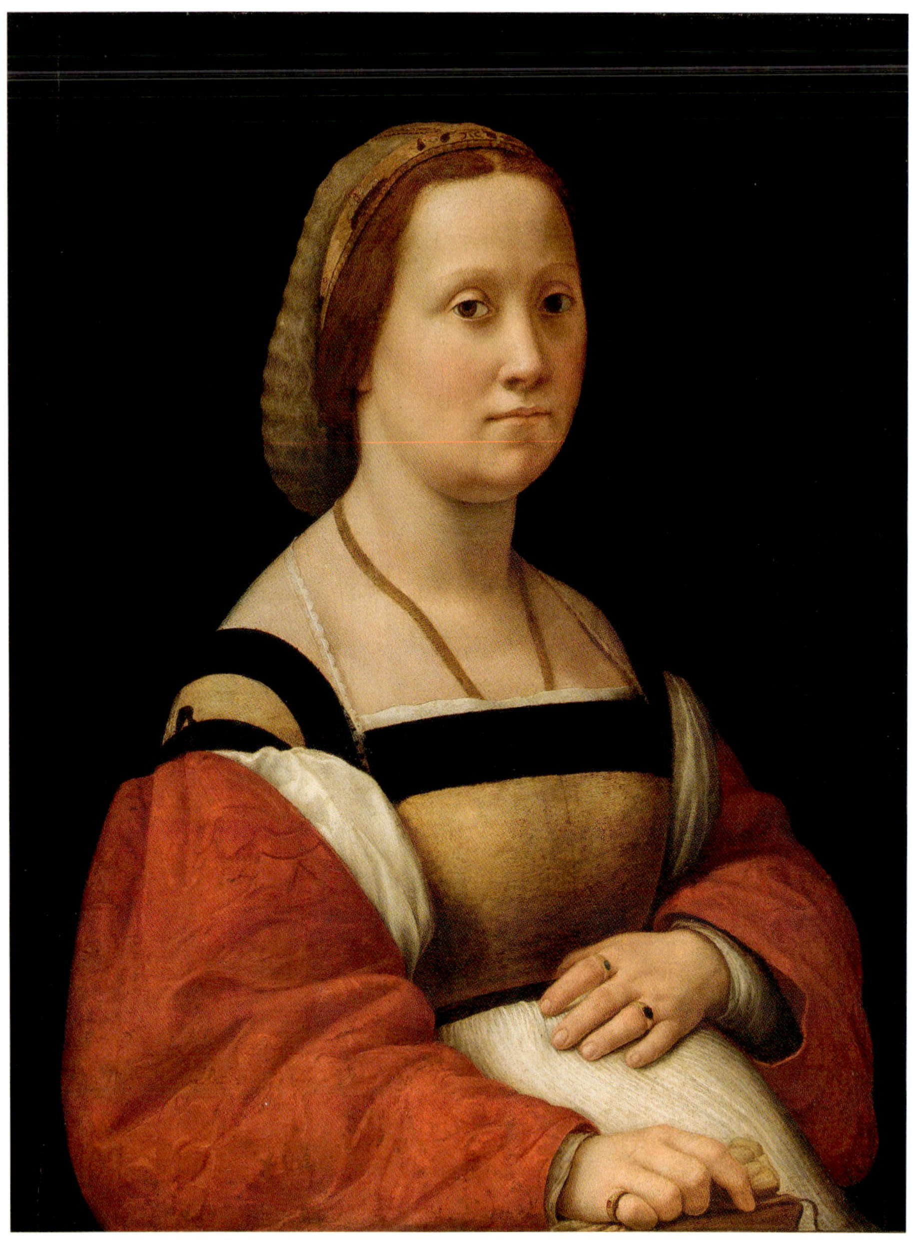

La Donna Gravida (The Pregnant Woman), *c.* 1507/08
Oil on panel, 66.8 × 52.7 cm (26 ¼ × 20 ¾ in)
Florence, Palazzo Pitti

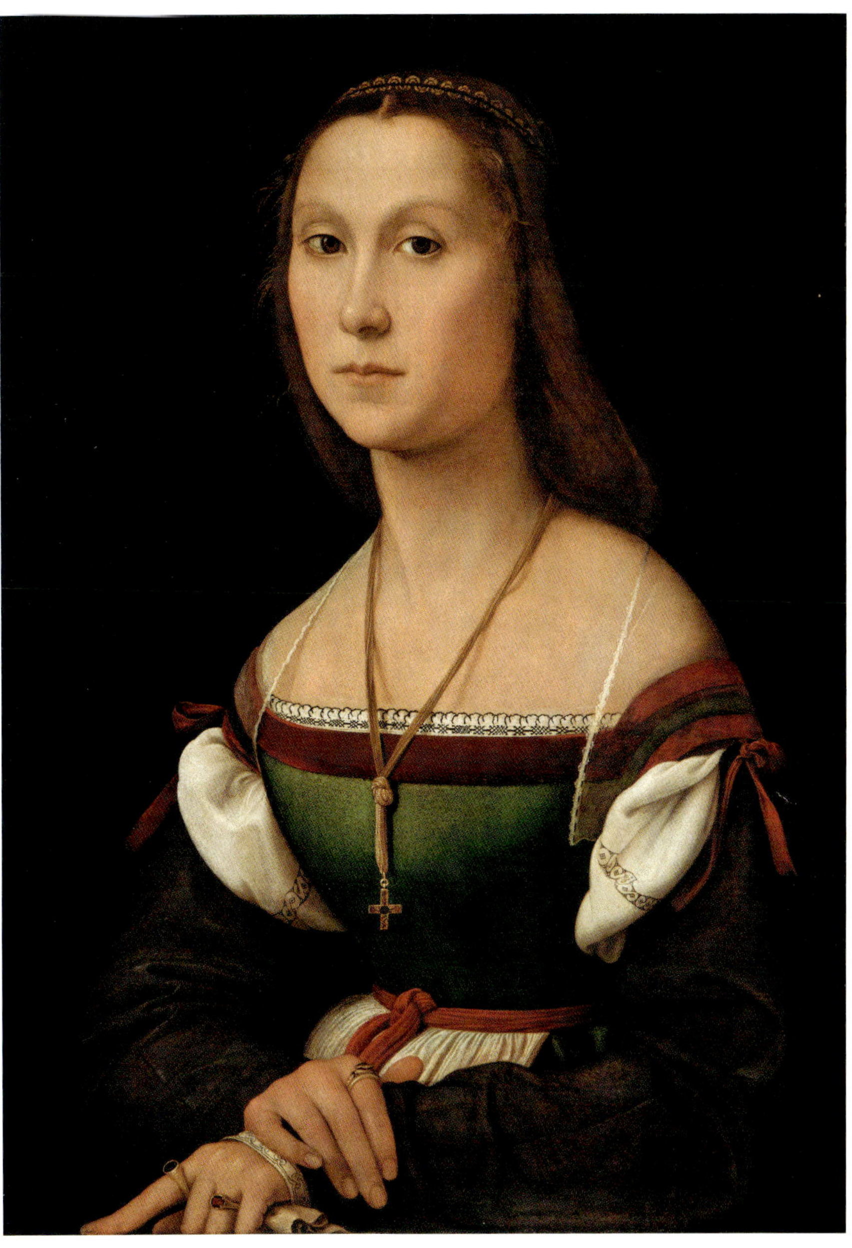

Portrait of a Woman (La Muta), *c.* 1506/07
Oil on panel, 64 × 48 cm (25 ¼ × 18 ⅞ in)
Urbino, Palazzo Ducale

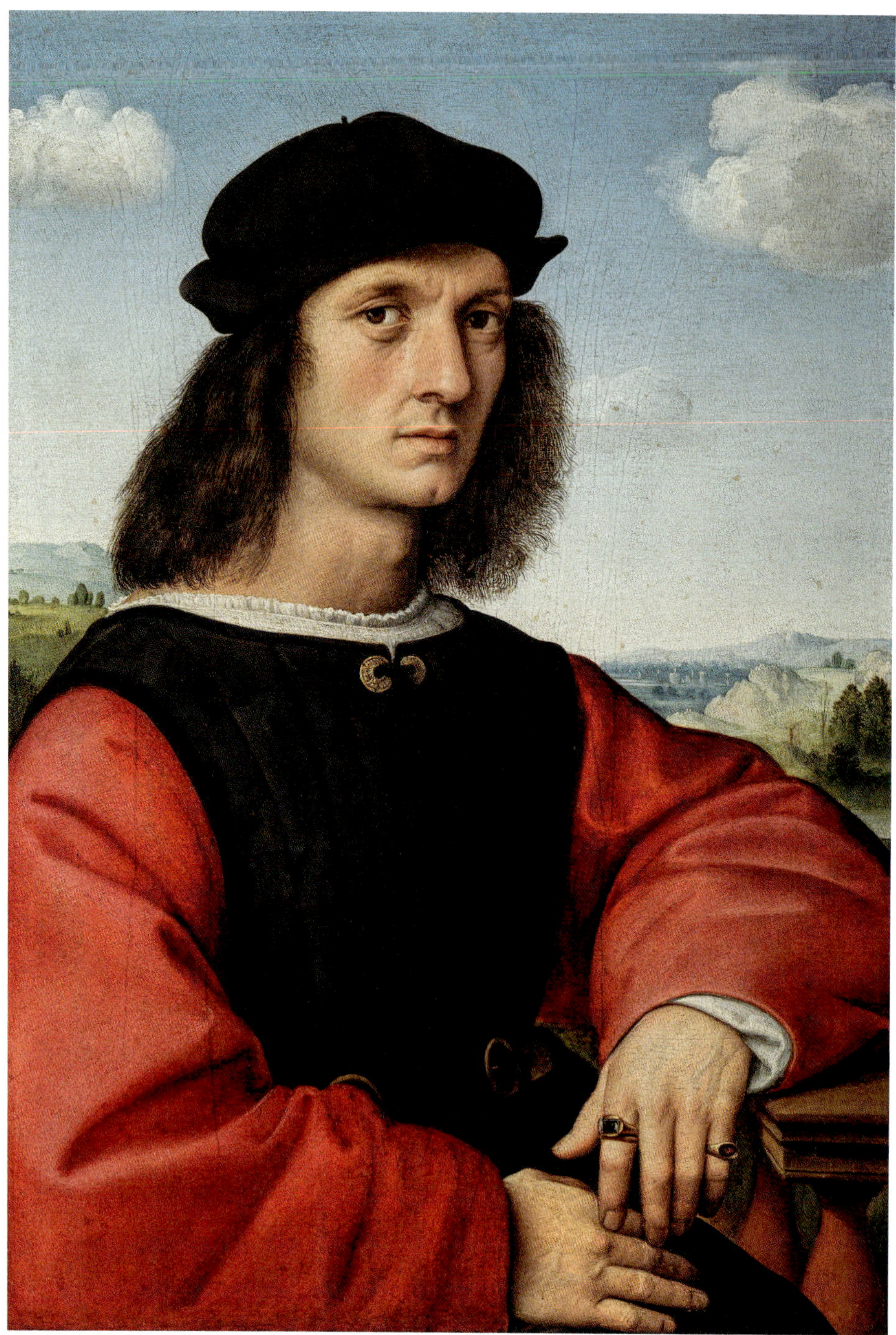

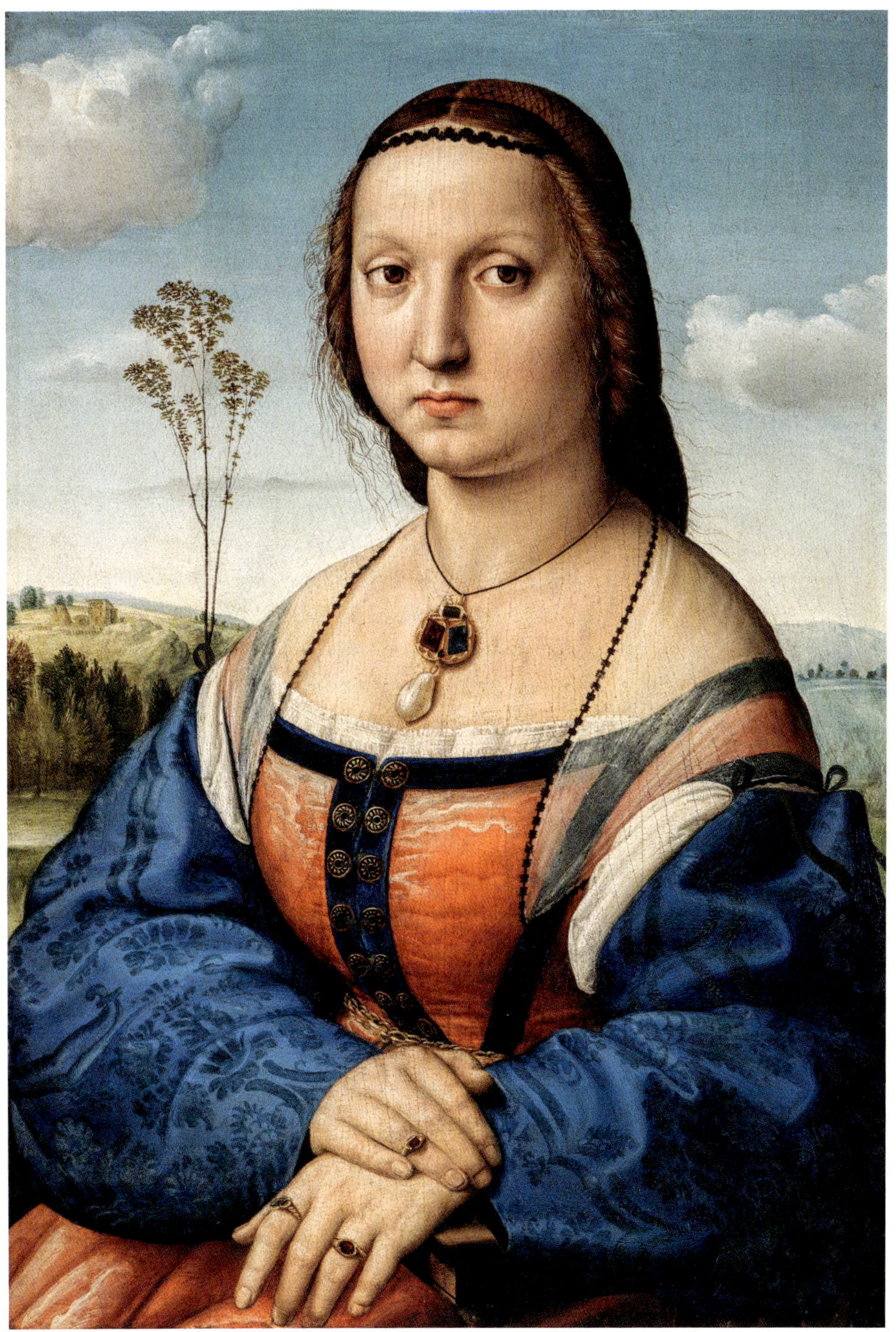

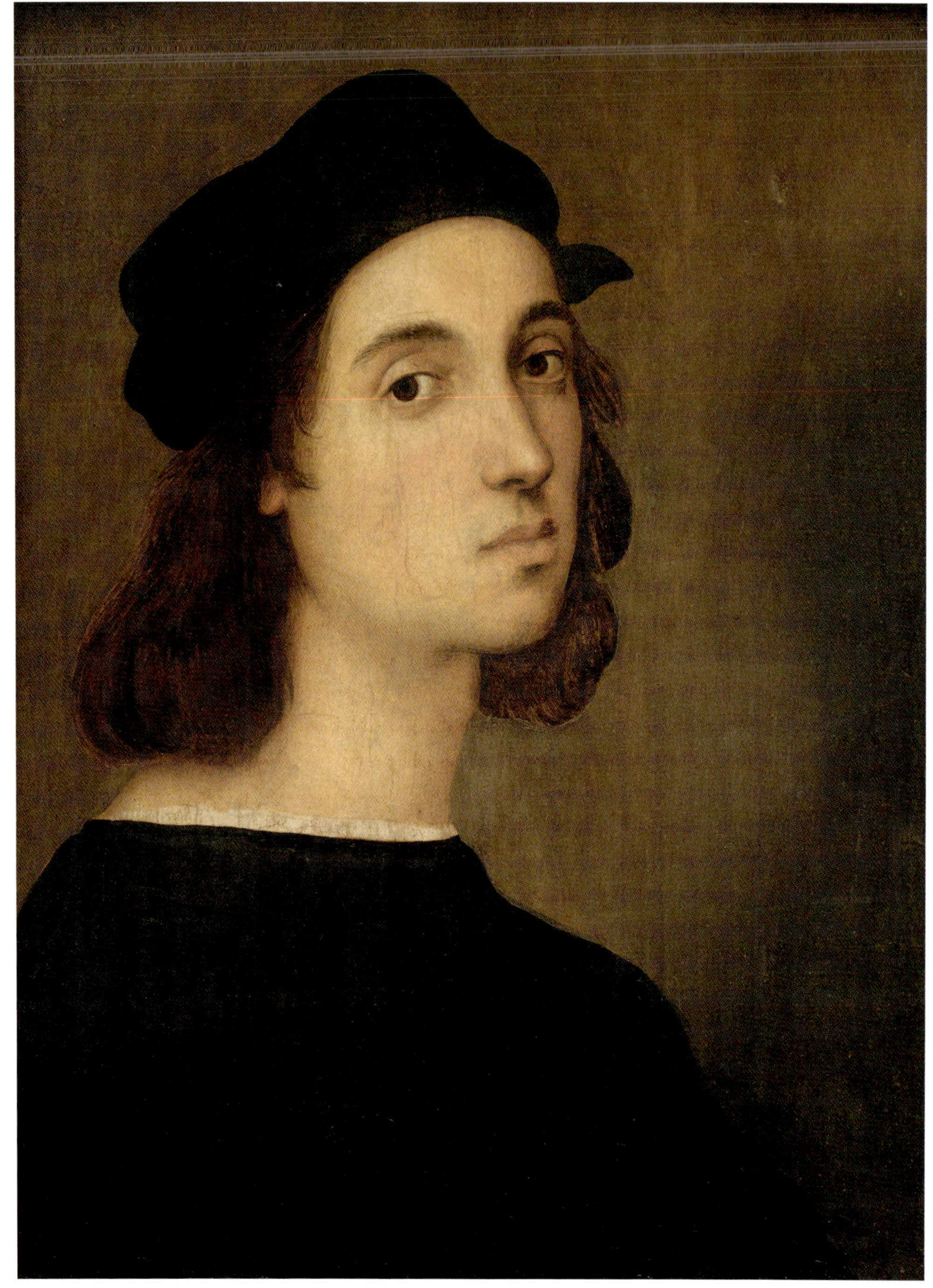

Pages 146/147

Portraits of Agnolo Doni and Maddalena Doni, *c.* 1505/06
Oil on panel, 65 × 45.7 cm (25 ⅝ × 17 ⅞ in) / 65 × 45.8 cm (25 ⅝ × 18 ⅛ in)
Florence, Palazzo Pitti
(Details pages 80, 91)

Portrait of a Young Man (Self-Portrait of Raphael), *c.* 1508 (?)
Oil on poplar panel, 47.3 × 34.8 cm (18 ⅝ × 13 ¾ in)
Florence, Gallerie degli Uffizi

Self-Portrait of Raphael in the *School of Athens*, *c.* 1509
(see ill. p. 184)

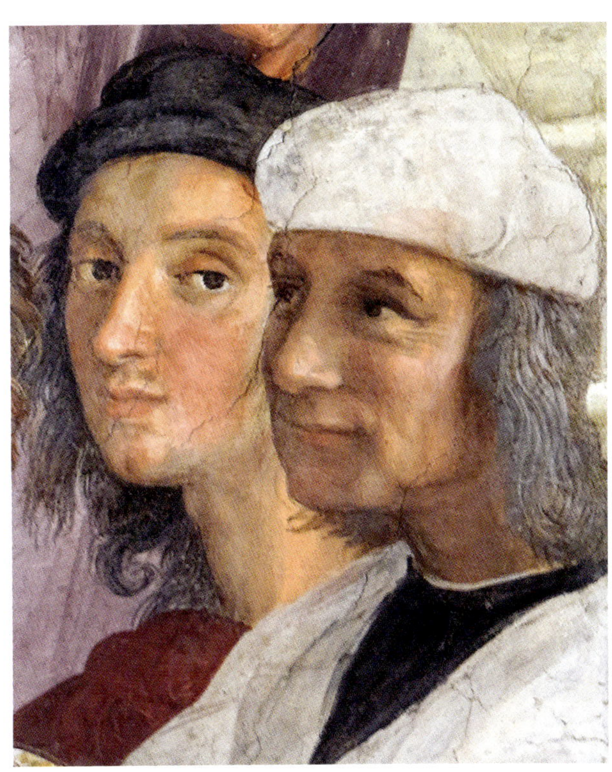

Madonna del Baldacchino (The Virgin Mary and Child with Saints Peter, Bernard, Rainerius and Augustine/Pala Dei), *c.* 1507/08
Oil on poplar panel, 280 × 217 cm (110 ¼ × 85 ⅜ in). Florence, Palazzo Pitti

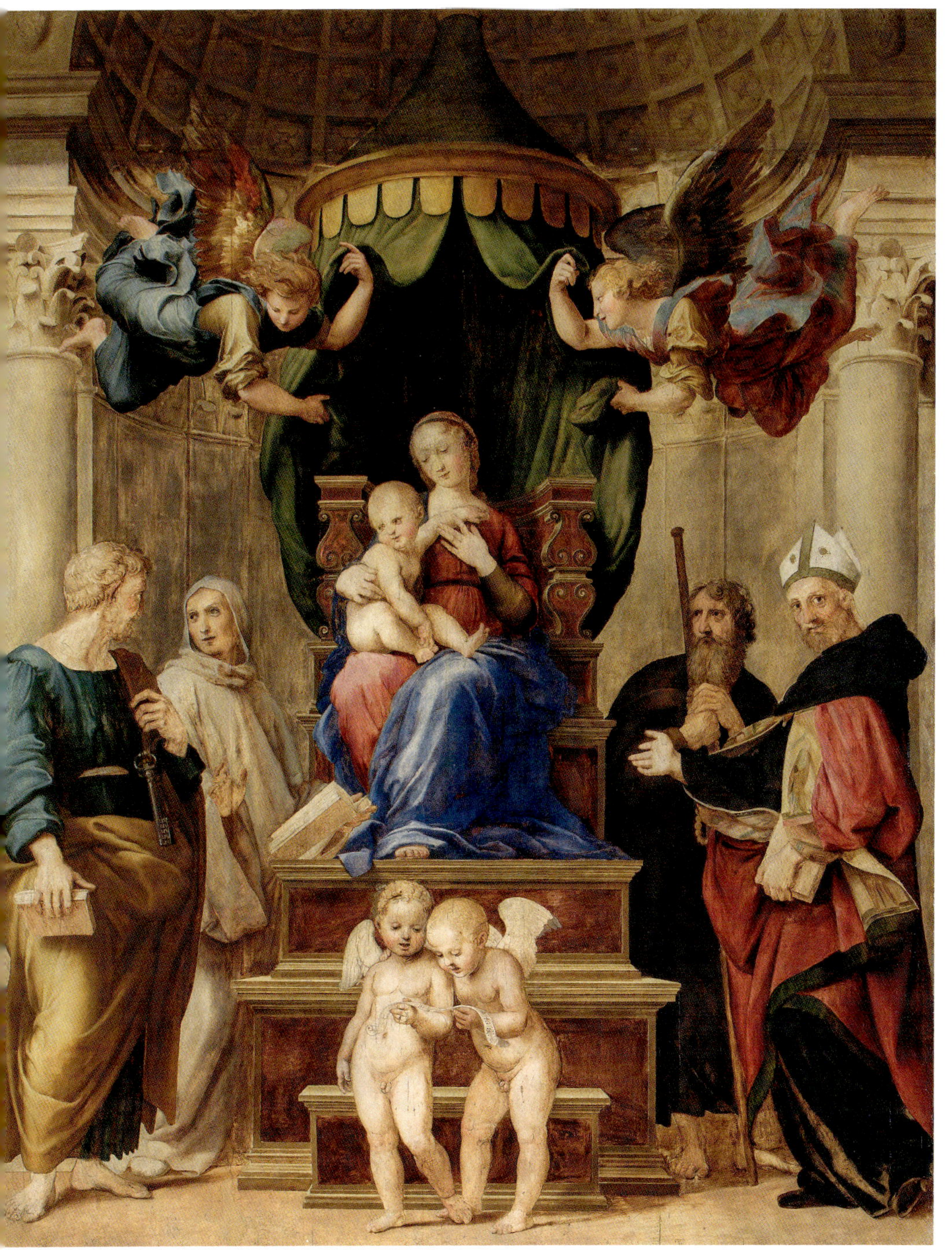

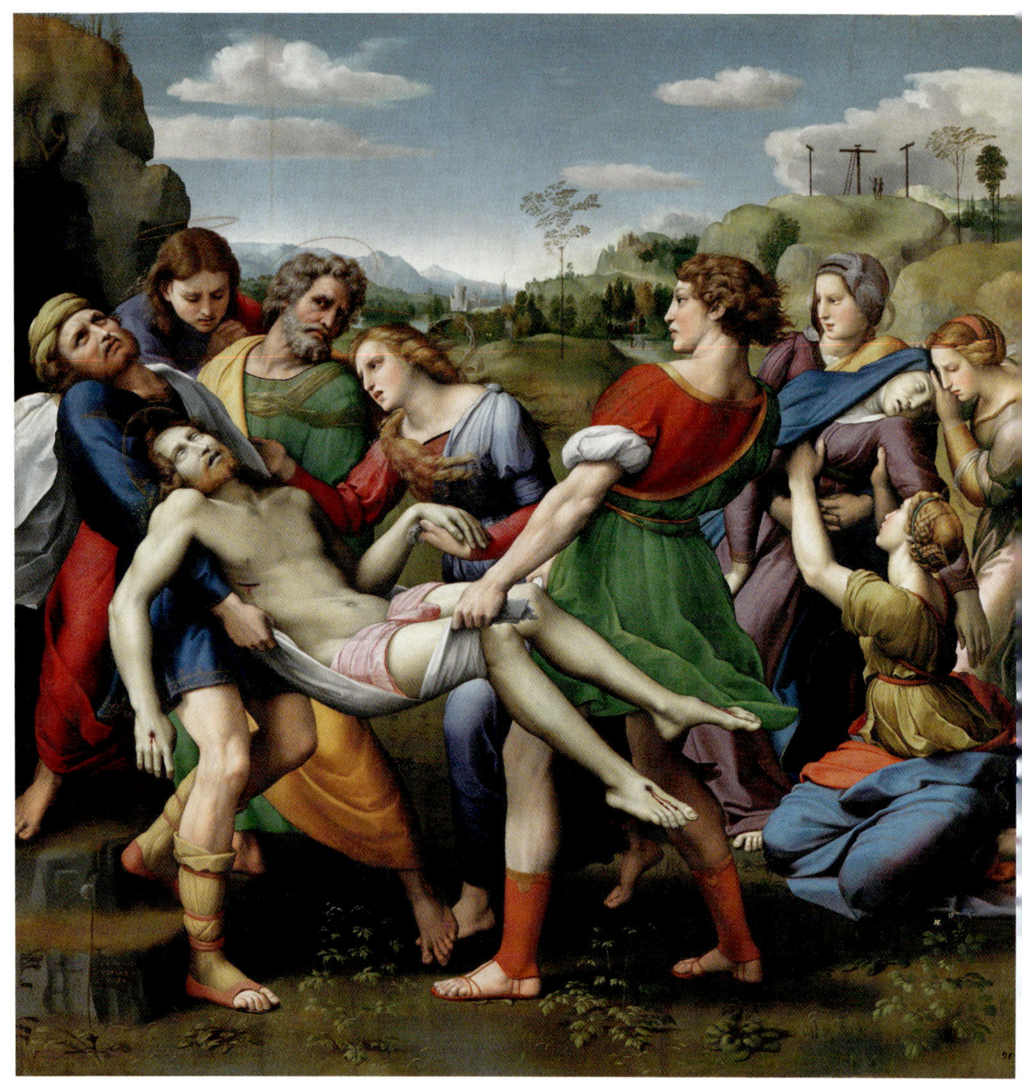

Entombment of Christ (Baglioni Altarpiece), 1506/07
Oil on panel, 184 × 176 cm (72 ½ × 69 ¼ in)
Inscription on the stone: *.RAPHAEL. / VRBINAS. /.M.D.VII.*
Rome, Galleria Borghese

Reconstruction of the Baglioni Altarpiece

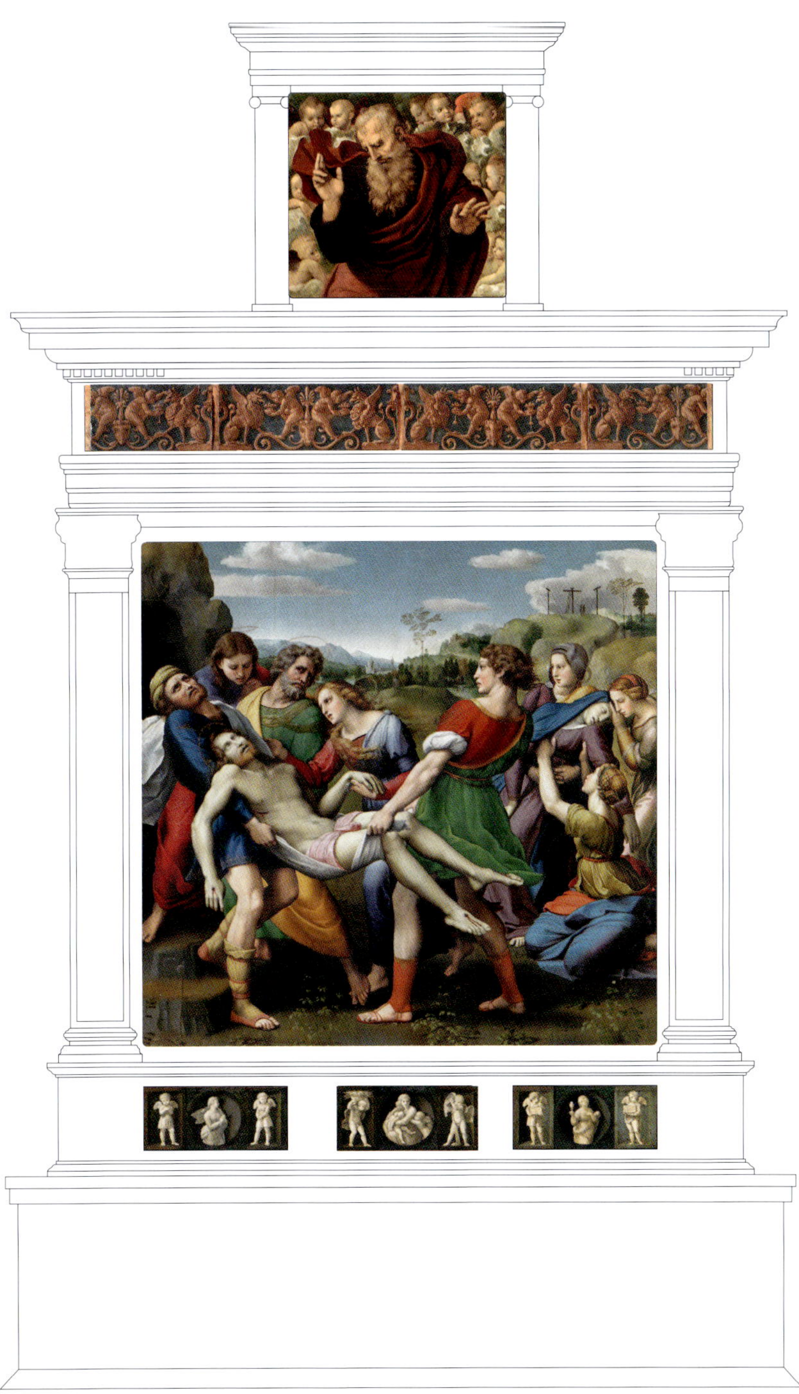

Charity, 1507
Pen over silverpoint underdrawing, 33.9 × 24.1 cm (13 ⅓ × 9 ½ in)
Vienna, Albertina

Michelangelo Buonarroti
Virgin and Child with the Infant St John (Pitti Tondo), *c.* 1504–1506
Marble, height 85.5 cm (33 ⅔ in), width 82 cm (32 ¼ in)
Florence, Museo Nazionale del Bargello

Predellas of the Baglioni Altarpiece: Hope – Charity – Faith, 1506/07
Oil on panel, each 16 × 44 cm (6 ¼ × 17 ⅓ in)
Vatican City, Musei Vaticani, Pinacoteca

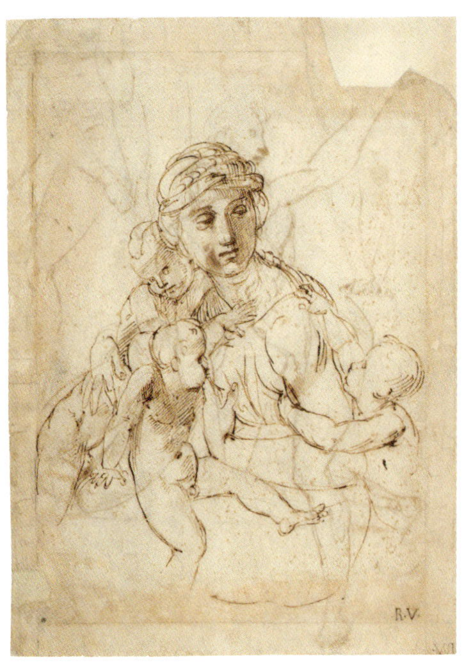

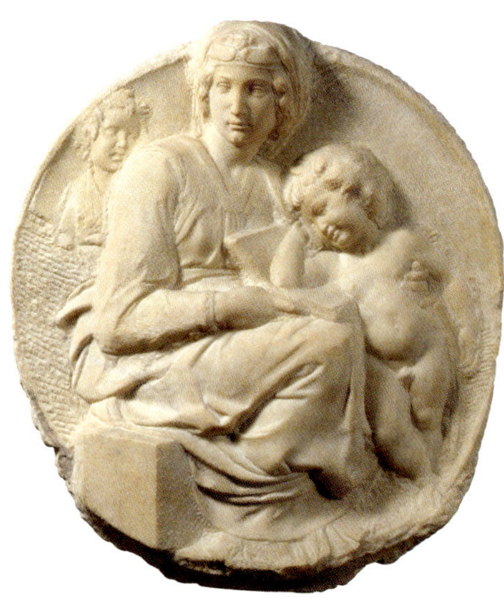

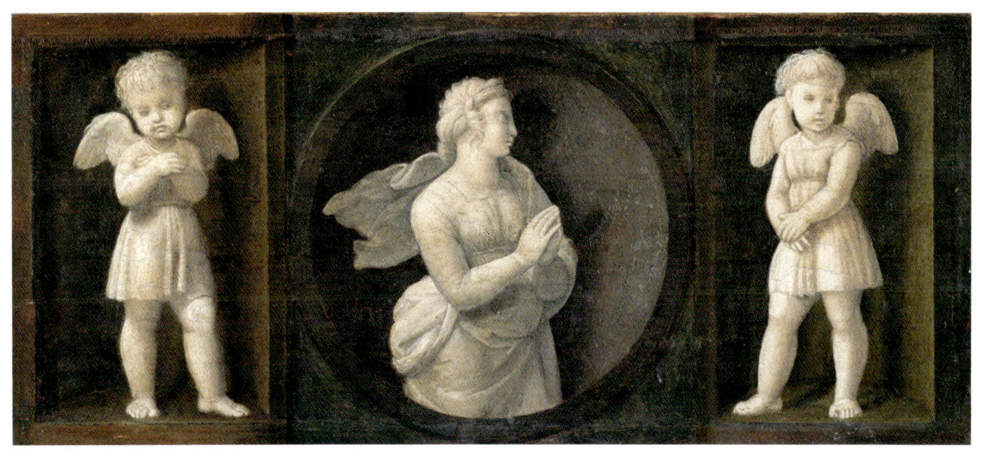

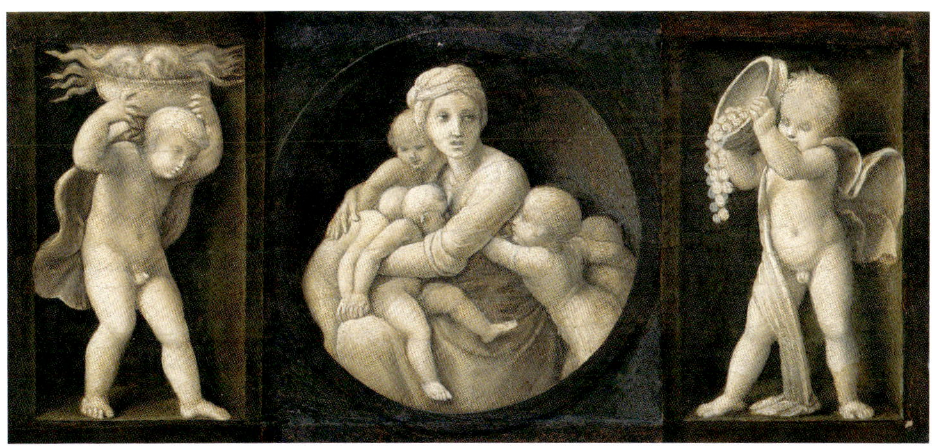

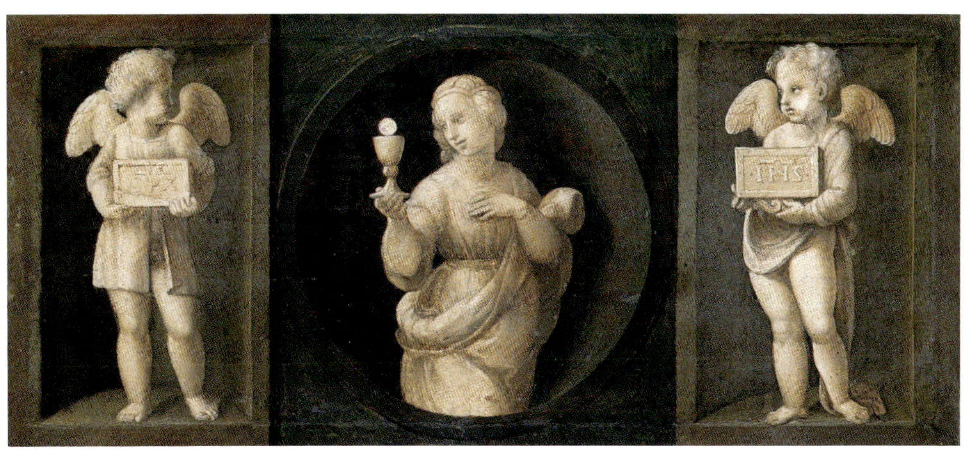
·IHS·

III.

The Great Tradition: Rome and the Stanze for Pope Julius II

1508/09–1513/14

Michael Rohlmann

"By him large theoretic conceptions are addressed, so to speak, to the intelligence of the eye."

WALTER PATER, 1892

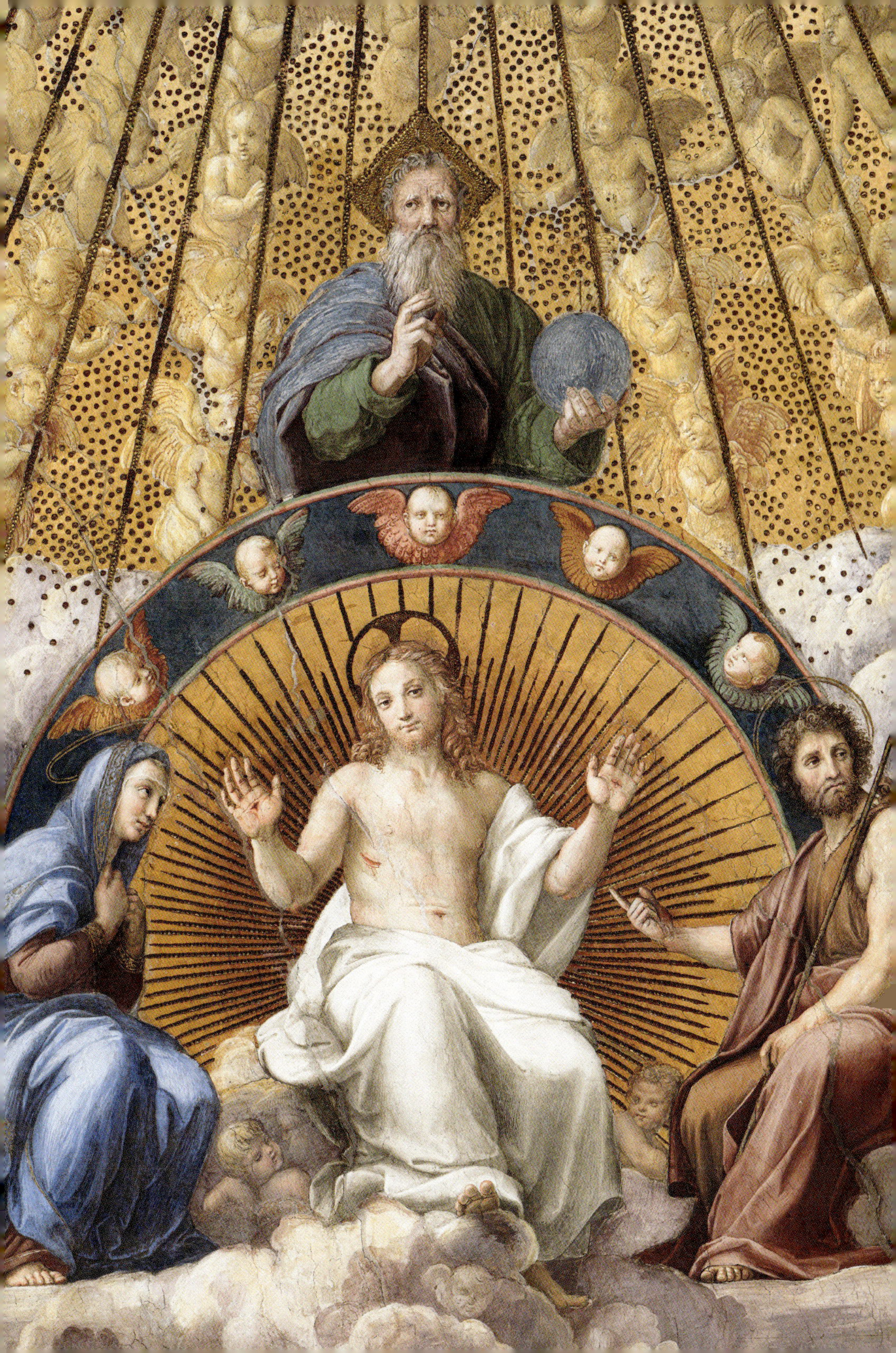

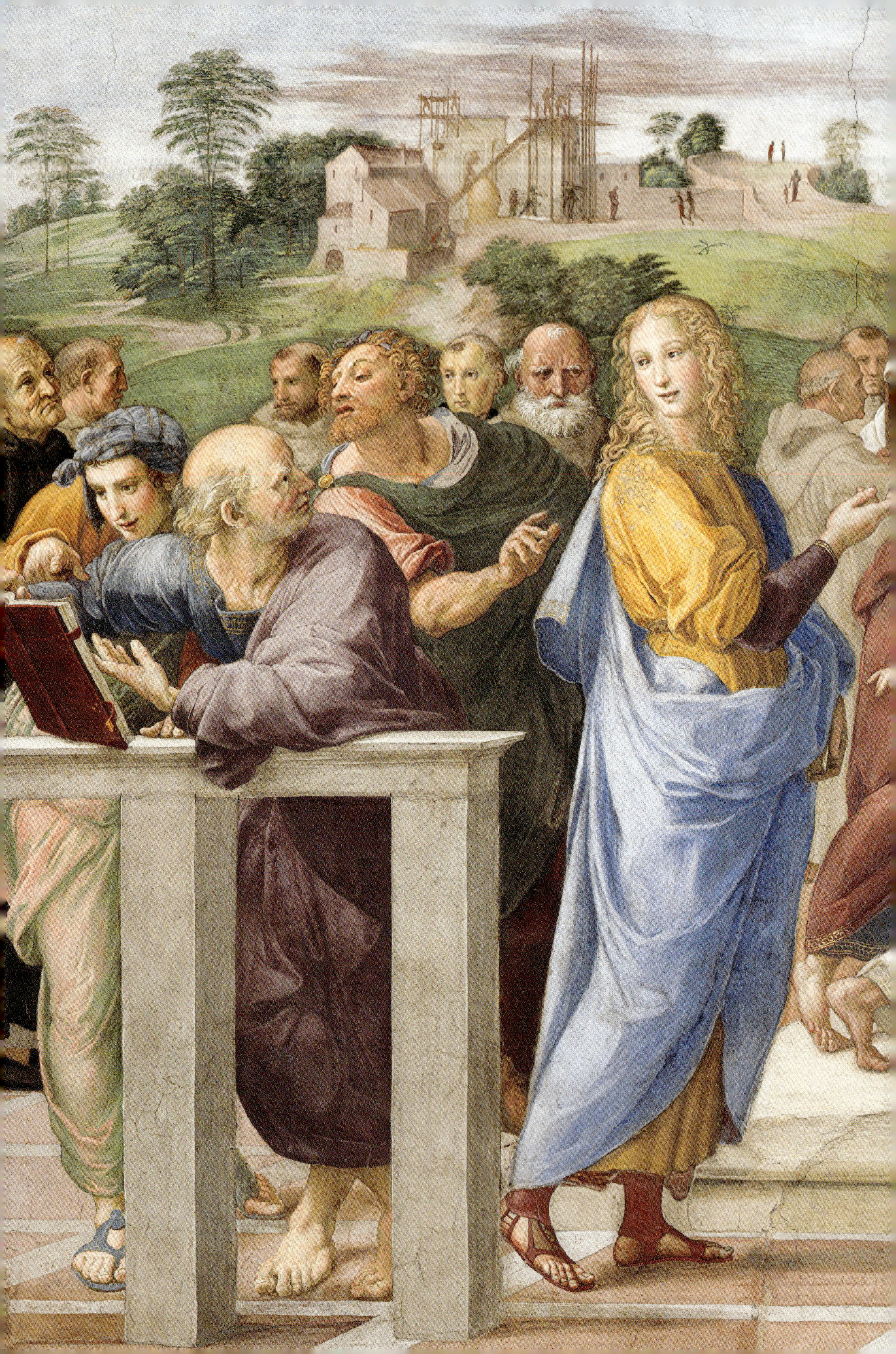

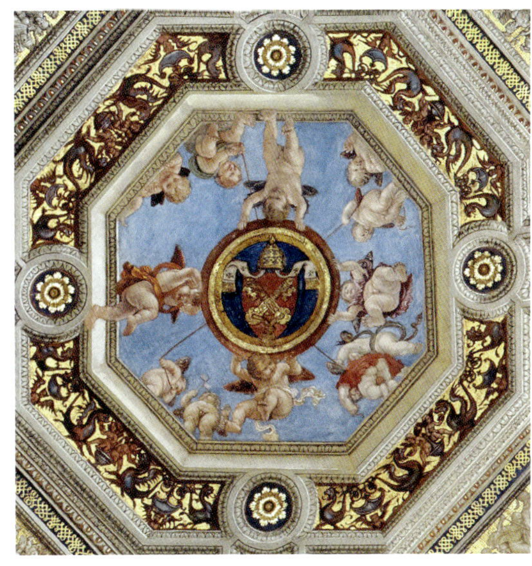

With the start of the pontificate of the elderly Della Rovere pope Julius II in 1503, it seemed as though a new epoch had dawned in Rome. Restless, irascible, ruthless, assertive and prepared to use force, the old man was considered *terribile* – terrifying. His very name evoked memories of imperial ambitions: as Julius II, he laid claim to the succession not only of the beatified Pope Julius I (died 352; in office from 337), but above all of the Roman emperor Julius Caesar (100–44 BC). The Pope wished to assert his secular power in Rome over the long-established, powerful noble houses. In the Papal States, he ended the rule of individual powers such as the Baglioni in Perugia and the Bentivoglio in Bologna. The intensification of his state power at home went hand in hand with its consolidation abroad. In the power play between the Italian and European states, the Pope did not hesitate to assume personal command of his troops. He waged war against Venice as well as against the French king, who had invaded Italy. In response to a council of renegade cardinals, who threatened to depose him, he convened his own council in the Lateran in Rome. In 1506, on the site of the venerable Basilica of St Peter dating back more than a thousand years, he laid the foundation stone for a vast new cathedral surmounted by a dome, as a visible sign of the primacy of the Roman Church headed by Peter's successor. The Vatican Palace was enlarged and a vast courtyard laid out, connecting the papal palace with the Villa Belvedere. Here, in a garden of antiquities, Julius displayed magnificent statues including the *Apollo Belvedere* and the *Laocoön* group (p. 358), the latter having been discovered in 1506. A new road axis, on which a huge palace of justice was to be built, was laid out through Rome's historical centre. In staged festivities, inscriptions,

Pages 157, 158
Details from **Disputa**, *c.* 1509/10
(see ill. p. 185)

Sodoma, **Putti Surrounding the Papal Coat of Arms**, 1508
Fresco (sculptural heraldic shield with crossed keys from the pontificate of Nicholas V, *c.* 1447–1455)
Vatican City, Musei Vaticani, Stanza della Segnatura

medallions and poems, panegyric art sought to glorify the Della Rovere reign as the return of a Golden Age.

As part of the Pope's new claim to power, it was necessary to redesign, artistically and programmatically, the political stage: the rooms that were the setting for day-to-day diplomacy, meetings with ambassadors and envoys, discussions and counsels. To this end, in 1508 work began on the redecoration of three adjacent, vaulted rooms in the Vatican's papal apartments, which adjoined the large state room behind the ceremonial and private rooms. In these Stanze, as they are known, a whole group of painters of various degrees of celebrity set to work, among them Signorelli, Perugino and Sodoma (1477–1549). Raphael is first mentioned in the documents on 13 January 1509, in conjunction with a payment for paintings in the middle room.

How had Raphael become involved in the Vatican commission? The previous year he had sought a letter of recommendation from the new Duke of Urbino, Francesco Maria della Rovere, who was the Pope's nephew. From the Florentine head of state, *gonfaloniere* Piero Soderini, Raphael wished to obtain the commission that was due to be awarded for the decoration of a room ("una certa stanza da lavorare, la quale t[oc]ha a sua S. de alocare"). It is unclear whether the commission was for a project for Florentine government (sua S[ignoria]) or for the Pope (sua S[antità]) in Rome, for which Soderini possibly supplied artists from Florence (Shearman 2003). Vasari tells a different story: in his version, it was Bramante (1444–1514), the architect working on the papal apartments, who summoned his Urbino compatriot Raphael to Rome. Or did Raphael's old teacher Perugino and his friend Signorelli perhaps play a role? Was Julius already acquainted with Raphael's art from his visits to Perugia and Urbino in 1506? Or did Pinturicchio, who had long been the Pope's favourite painter, open up Raphael's path to Rome? Pinturicchio had decorated the Vatican apartments of the Borgia pope Alexander VI, who died in 1503, and for Julius II had frescoed the vault of the choir in the Roman church of Santa Maria del Popolo, a project completed only in 1510. For Julius's immediate predecessor, Pius III, Pinturicchio had already engaged Raphael to design parts of the large-scale decorative scheme devoted to the Piccolomini pope Pius II in Siena (pp. 24–25, 28, 30–32). It seems almost inevitable that Raphael, who thus already had first-hand experience of producing a papal cycle, should also be involved in the frescoing of Julius II's papal apartments – all the more so given that Raphael was the outstanding painter of the ruling house of Urbino, of which Julius's nephew Francesco Maria became head, as the new Duke, following Guidobaldo's death in 1508.

After only a short time, Julius II transferred responsibility for the Stanze fresco project entirely to Raphael. Vasari attributed this decision to the overwhelming impression made upon Julius by the first fresco Raphael painted for the Stanze. Decorations executed by other artists were preserved only on the vaulted ceilings and in some of the painted elements framing the large wall frescoes. Raphael concentrated first of all on the middle Stanza, which he was essentially able to complete in 1511 (Cat. F3.1). Today called the Stanza della Segnatura (pp. 184–195), this was already the main room when the palace wing was built under Pope Nicholas V (1397–1455; in office from 1447), since it is the only one to have a floor of magnificent stone intarsia. A geometric pattern surrounds the large central motif of the crossed keys. Nicholas used this official insignia of the papacy as his personal device as well. It is also found overhead in the coat of arms in relief on the keystone of the vault (pp. 186/187). Julius not only retained both but even made the pontifical emblem the symbolic centre of the entire new decoration scheme and the starting point from which the main intellectual themes of the room's programme were developed. Just as the pictorial cycle in the Piccolomini Library in Siena revolves around the theme of *gratia* established by the sculptural group the *Three Graces* installed in the centre of the room, so it revolves here around the axis of the crossed keys in the centre of the floor and the ceiling. The power of the keys is the foundation of the papal claim to authority: with the keys, Christ gave Peter and his successors the power of binding and loosening and of passing judgements that would be ratified in Heaven. The two keys awarded to the pope were the key of discerning truth from falsehood in matters of faith *(clavis discernendi scientia)* and the key of power of judgement *(clavis potentia judicandi)*. The divine mandate of the power of the keys was to be legitimised and fulfilled by a power of judgment based on education and comprehensive knowledge. Justice, who judges expertly and fairly on the basis of knowledge, is the foundation of every good government. The frescoes in the Stanza della Segnatura illustrate the areas of knowledge upon which Julius II, in exercising his power of the keys, wanted to draw for support in order to achieve the goal of just governance. On the ceiling and walls of the room, Raphael therefore portrayed Justice in company with three different types and areas of knowledge acquisition.

Emphasis is placed on the window wall facing the enfilade entrance, which is dedicated to Justice (Cat. F3.1s). Unlike the other wall frescoes, the pictorial surface above and on either side of the window opening is transformed into fictive architecture, which divides three main scenes and at the same time lends them a particular, illusionistic presence. Depicted on either side of the window are the two legislative acts laying the basis of secular and ecclesiastical law: the Roman Emperor Justinian (*c.* 482–565, reigned from 527) approves the body of civil law, the *Corpus Iuris Civilis*, and Pope Gregory IX (*c.* 1167–1241; in office from 1227) the canon law of the Decretals. Enthroned above them, in the pictorial field over the window, are the personifications of three of the four cardinal virtues required by every judge: Fortitude, Prudence and Temperance. Justice, as the fourth of the virtues, completes the series in the ceiling field overhead (Cat. F3.1d). There

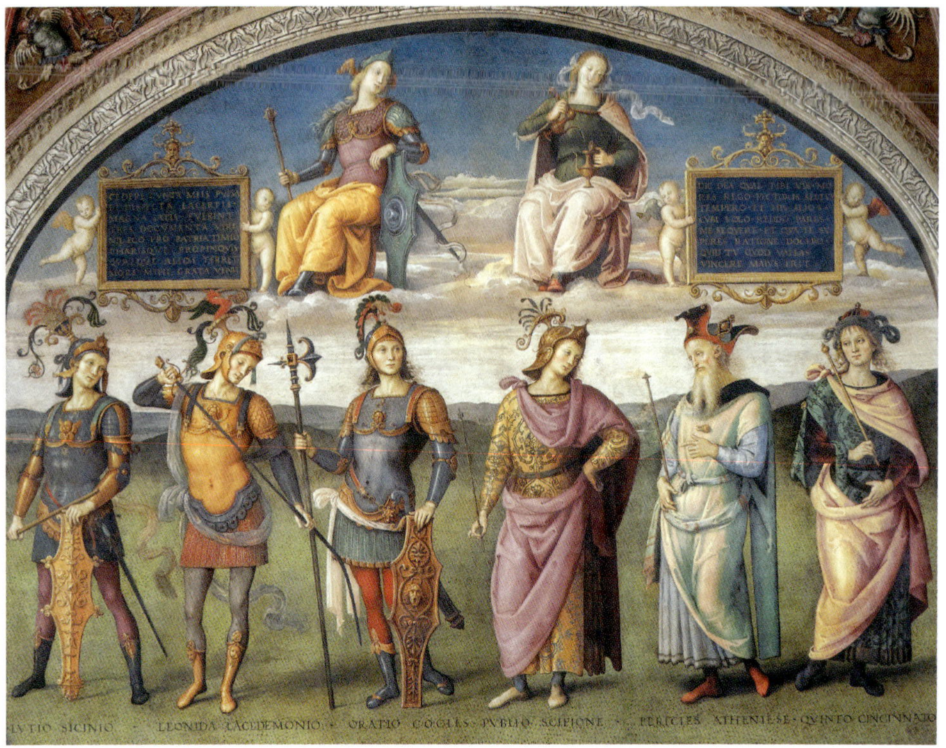

she is raised above her three sisters on the wall below and at the same time establishes the Justice theme of this entire side of the room. The inscription accompanying her personification proclaims that the law renders to everyone their due. In the two lower frescoes, Justinian is assigned the narrower space and the lower seat, Gregory IX the wider space and the higher throne – as if this hierarchy between Emperor and Pope had been justly assigned by Justice, true to her motto.

The role of Gregory IX is played by Julius II. Only here in the Stanza is the Della Rovere pope prominently present life size. The Pope undoubtedly had his real seat near this portrait and against this same wall, where he would thus have appeared as a ruler under the protection of the secular virtues painted above him. For his representation of Pope Gregory approving the decretals, Raphael drew not only on Vatican and Florentine

Pietro Perugino, **The Virtues Fortitude and Temperance with Six Famous Men**, 1496–1500
Fresco, 293 × 418 cm (115 3/8 × 164 5/8 in). Perugia, Collegio del Cambio, Sala di Udienza

Pinturicchio and Workshop, **Geometry**, 1492–1494
Fresco. Vatican City, Musei Vaticani, Appartamento Borgia, Sala delle Arti Liberali

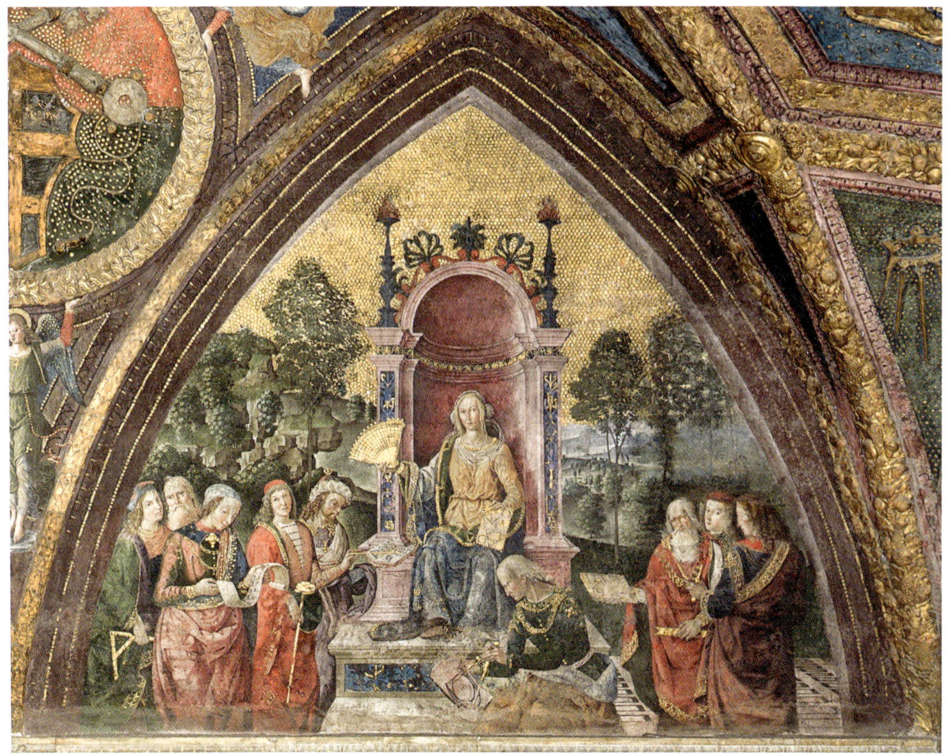

models, but also on a memory from his youth. The handing over of a book against an architectural backdrop clearly follows an Early Netherlandish painting from the study in the Montefeltro palace in Gubbio, which showed the personification of Grammar presenting a codex to Duke Federico.

The ceiling paintings (pp. 186/187) above the room's three other walls complement Justice with female personifications of Philosophy, Poetry and Theology. The primacy of Justice among the four fields is made clear by the fact that she has four *genii* to hold her inscription tablets, whereas the other women are assigned just two small companions, one per tablet. Philosophy's *genii* have no wings – the "knowledge of causes" evidently counts as secular thought (Cat. F3.1a). Poetry is "breathed upon by the spirit" and her *genii* correspondingly feature the wings of divine inspiration (Cat. F3.1b). The same is true in the case of Theology, who receives "knowledge of divine things" (Cat. F3.1c). Justice, with her secular and ecclesiastical legal sides, suitably combines two wingless and two winged *genii* (Cat. F3.1d). It is striking that the wingless *genii* each support the tablets on their shoulder, from underneath, in a subservient manner. The winged genii, on the other hand, in both cases hold the inscriptions in front of their torso, with their head appearing over the top. In this way, too, the secular is subordinated to the spiritual.

In the Stanza della Segnatura ceiling paintings, Philosophy, Poetry and Theology appear as the assistants of Justice. To render to everyone their due *(ius suum unicuique tribuit)*, the judge must recognise the causes of an incident *(causarum cognitio)*, possess knowledge of the divine, right order of things *(divinarum rerum notitia)* or reach his verdict through divine inspiration *(numine afflatur)*. Three of the four Latin inscriptions are taken verbatim or in slightly modified form from the beginning of the *Corpus Iuris Civilis*. Three of the episodes portrayed in the rectangular fields assigned to the personifications also clearly introduce the field of law: *The Fall (Theology)* is the first crime (Cat. F3.1g), *The Judgement of Solomon (Justice)* shows the process of establishing the truth (Cat. F3.1h), and *The Punishment of Marsyas (Poetry)* depicts, in the coronation of one and the punishment of the other, the carrying out of a verdict (Cat. F3.1f). The fourth personification *(Philosophy)* is illustrated by an angel-like figure who is contemplating the cosmos (Cat. F3.1e). Raphael here achieves a particular painterly *tour de force*: the outermost moving sphere *(primum mobile)* appears as a transparent, shimmering crystal universe with the globe of the earth at its centre. We see an angel of the prime movement, who is setting the cosmos into first motion with his hand. In the world view of that time, this is the first cause, the *primum movens* or *prima causa*, as it is called in the popular Mantegna Tarocchi tarot cards (p. 314). Raphael shows, as a visualization of Philosophy and its activity of "recognizing the causes" *(causarum cognitio)*, the outermost identifiable cause *(prima causa)*. The moment of insight into the causes fits, like the other three scenes, into the thematic context of a court of law. Read clockwise, the four examples could be understood as consecutive aspects of a single legal process, leading from the deed, via the establishing of the truth and knowledge of the causes, to the enforcement of the judgement.

The three walls below the personifications of Philosophy, Poetry and Theology all show grand-scale, multi-figural assemblies of scholars and outstanding representatives of the individual faculties on which Pope Julius II purported to base his judgements. Below Philosophy, the philosophers of antiquity seek the "knowledge of the causes" in the interior of a spacious and clear imaginary edifice (*School of Athens*, Cat. F3.1j). Beneath Poetry, Apollo makes music on Mount Parnassus, the home of the Muses, and inspires the Greek, Latin and Italian poets "moved by the divine spirit" (*Parnassus*, Cat. F3.1k). Below Theology, theologians have gathered around an altar on a spacious square (*Disputa*,

Detail from **Disputa**, *c.* 1509/10
(see ill. p. 185)

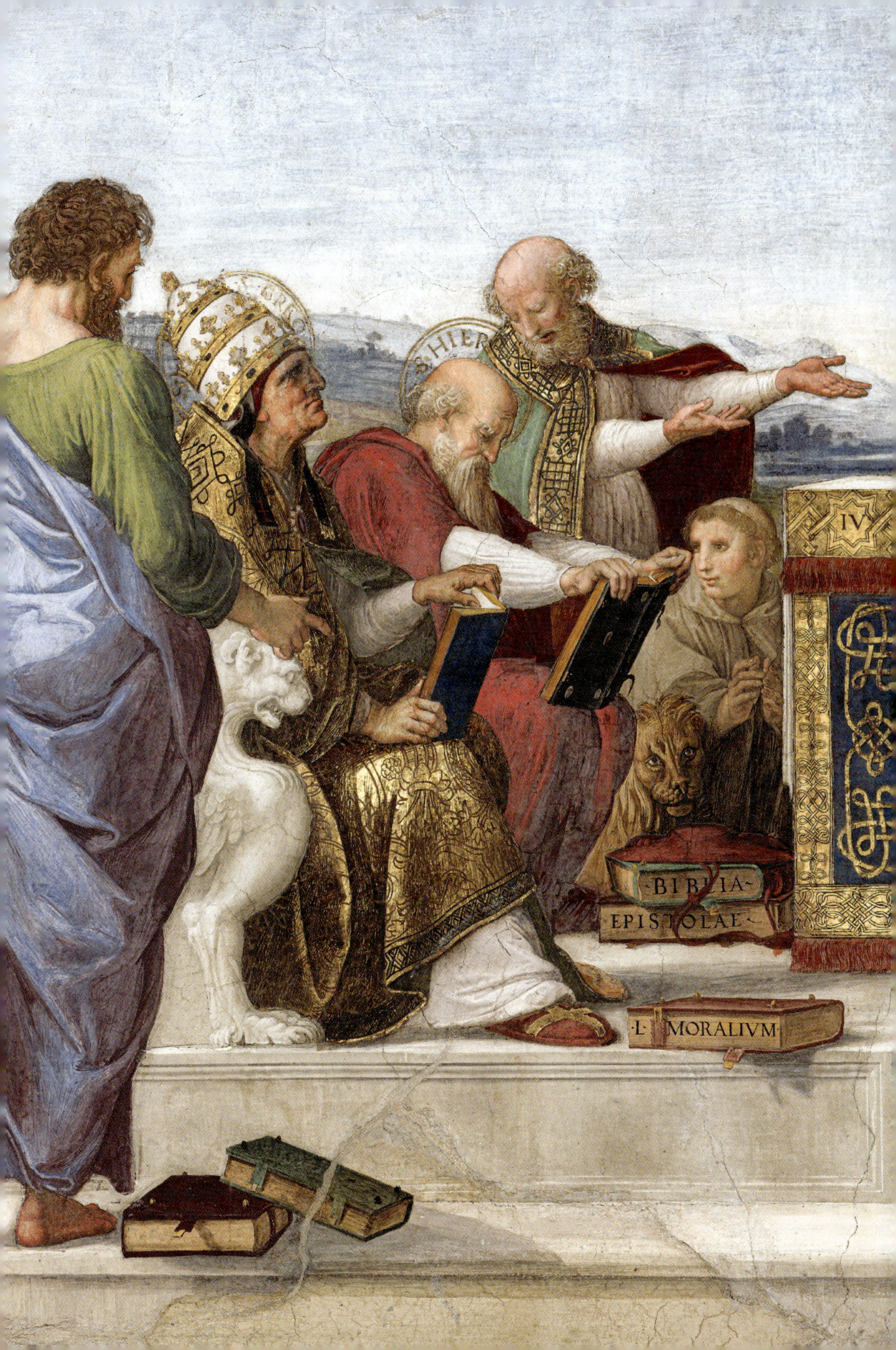
IV
BIBLIA
EPISTOLAE
L· MORALIVM

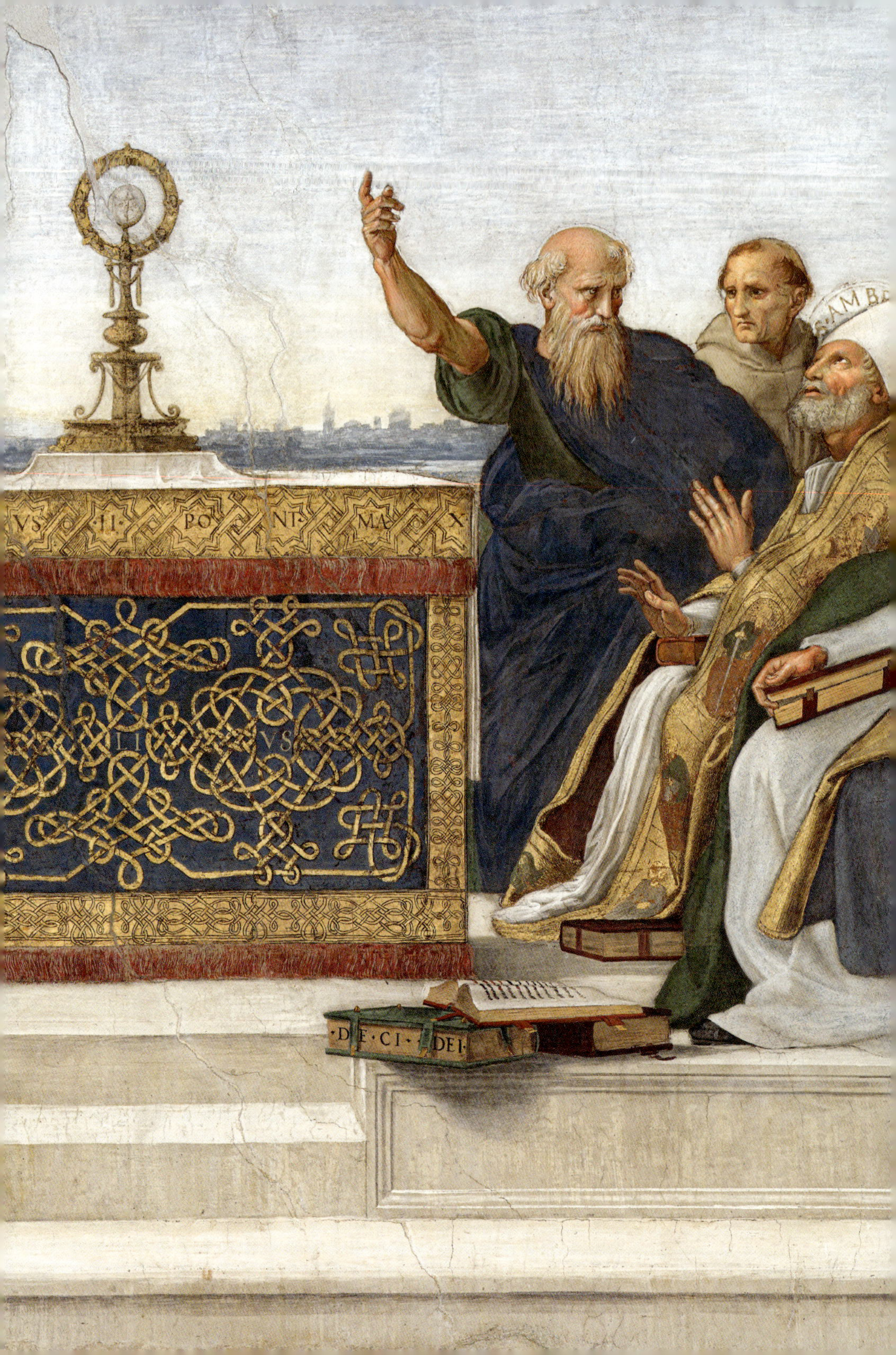
VS ·II· PO NT· MA X
LI VS
·DE CI· DEI·
AMB

Cat. F3.1r). Here they receive the "knowledge of the doctrine of God" as a higher grace by means of a celestial apparition and the reception of the Gospel texts.

Cycles portraying series of famous models of virtue *(uomini famosi)*, scholars and intellectual giants, were part of artistic tradition in Italy, and were found in particular in studies and courtrooms. Neither in the Studiolo in Urbino, however, nor in Perugino's Collegio del Cambio (1496–1500, p. 162), do they unite in social interaction as in these frescoes by Raphael. It is true that in Pinturicchio's Sala delle Arti Liberali in the Vatican Borgia apartments (1493–1495; p. 163) representatives of the liberal arts are already combined into groups. Nowhere before, however, do we find dramatic scenes unfolding at specific imaginary places as here with Raphael; nowhere do the gatherings of intellectuals represented in large, uniform pictorial fields acquire such vivid presence. Nowhere are the single figures or groups brought so close to us, the viewer, as fictive extensions of our real-life surroundings. We are, as it were, surrounded by intellectuals in action. In the Stanza della Segnatura Raphael evidently draws upon another existing model: the tradition of narrative cycles in chapels. Pinturicchio's fresco decoration of the architecturally related Baglioni Chapel in Spello (1500/01) provided a concrete source for Raphael's differentiation of the settings of his individual scenes. On three walls of the Baglioni Chapel, the large-scale frescoes – bounded by painted pilasters and arches as in the Segnatura – likewise extend far down to a plinth zone (p. 170/171). As in Raphael, a spacious view of a natural landscape *(The Nativity)* is flanked on one side by an interior in which a series of arches leads away into the background *(The Annunciation)* and on the other by an open-air, square-like area with ecclesiastical connotations *(Christ Among the Doctors)*. A comparison of *Christ Among the Doctors* and the *Disputation of the Holy Sacrament*, in particular, reveals further clear parallels in terms of theme, figural composition and the motif of the books scattered on the floor.

Raphael thus enlivens the imaginary staff of advisors whom he has assembled around the Pope with elements developed in narrative painting. He expands the papal chamber into lofty halls and a sacred square, a rocky mountain and a celestial vision. He opens up visual access for the viewer to the great tradition of antique philosophy, poetry and Christian faith. All search for knowledge, all inspiration and all knowledge of God seem to be united before our eyes at the court of Julius II. Around the identifiable philosophers, more are clustered in front of every wall, their interpretation open to the viewer. There is thus no limit to the abundance of exemplary thinkers from whom the viewer can hope for imaginary inspiration. In the centre of the ceiling and thus at the apex of this realm

Detail from **Disputa**, *c.* 1509/10
(see ill. p. 185)

of thought and experience, a view of the heavens – painted earlier by Sodoma – opens up around the pre-existing heraldic shield. Cherubs look down from it. They are holding the old papal coat of arms with the crossed keys and seem to want to lower it into the room itself (p. 159). The coat of arms thus becomes the object of an action scene, in which – here in the Segnatura – the power of the keys is being bestowed upon the Pope anew by God from on high. This is happening, so the fresco decoration suggests, precisely because education, expertise and knowledge are here united in unique fashion. The wise, well-advised ruler is given the legitimating keys of office so that he may exercise his ideal governance, justly bind and loosen, and render to everyone their due.

Among the wall frescoes, the artistic quality of the *School of Athens* (p. 184 t.; Cat. F3.1j) has always been particularly admired. It has been the focus of many analyses (Springer 1883; Wölfflin 1899; Hetzer 1932 and 1947; Schöne 1958; Freedberg 1961; Kuhn 1980; Oberhuber 1983; Rosand 2000; Keazor 2012), whose findings may be summarised thus: Raphael shows an ideal assembly and figures full of inner greatness, ethos, dignity and *gravitas*. He achieves beauty as a central position between the individual and the general. The natural appears without the banal and the everyday; details play a subordinate role. Poses and movements unfold calmly and in great diversity. Figures interact with each other, react to their neighbours and fuse into narrative groups, which in turn form coordinated constellations. The individual lives in social community; everything is orchestrated into a lively balance between freedom and law and so brought into harmony.

The figural composition is thereby divided into two zones. The figures above the steps form a more serried row, while those at the bottom separate into two groups to the left and right. One man reclining on the steps, one ascending the stairs and another descending connect the two zones. The lower groups of seated, kneeling and bending figures are richer and more animated and flexed in form and in each case more firmly interwoven. Above, horizontal alignment predominates and everything is straightened upright to stand vertically. This figural composition grows calmer and more condensed from above to below and from outside to inside, and loosens towards the edges. Axial connections are generated in the lower groups and in the upper row. What is happening below finds a muted echo above. Directly above the philosopher standing in magnificent contrapposto at the bottom of the steps on the left, for example, gesturing to his open book and inviting the seated figure further left to read it, Socrates appears on the steps above, likewise turned towards the left as he presents his argument in speech and gestures to his audience. On the right, above the students bending forwards around the geometrician in the foreground, a young scribe, also bent forward, is seated in the upper row with an older man leaning over him in turn. In the centre, Plato (428/27–348/47 BC) and Aristotle (384–322 BC) rise above the seated thinker and the reclining Diogenes (*c.* 405–*c.* 320 BC) as a contrasting pair of figures.

In both rows, left and right are brought into a symmetrical equilibrium. Below, the group of older men gathered close around Pythagoras (*c.* 570–after 510 BC) on the left corresponds to that of younger figures gathered more loosely around the geometrician on the right. In the upper row, Plato and Aristotle dominate the centre as a pair, stepping between the left and right cordon of their listeners. One figure hurries into the picture on the far left, and on the far right, one hurries out. The symmetry here is quietly accompanied by a diagonal movement leading towards the right. This movement is taken up by two sequences of motifs. Firstly, three blocks of stone on the floor in the foreground successively increase in size from the left to the middle. Secondly, three figures looking out at us in the left-hand foreground grow successively older, bigger and more important: a carried child, a boy and a young man. The adult Raphael himself looks out of the picture on the far right, by way of conclusion – as if a process of education were completed in him.

Rising above the figures is a vast hall-like building, whose succession of arches repeatedly echoes the curved upper edge of the fresco. Lower down, the organisation of the architecture determines the arrangement of the figural groups. Thus erect figures stand in front of the pilasters, and two rows of listeners accompany the recession of the central arch towards the background. Between them Plato and Aristotle are presented in an open space, against the backdrop of a view of the sky and with multiple arches rising above. Beneath the soaring hall, the horizontals of the steps transfer themselves to the sitting and bending forwards of the foreground figures.

Between Plato and Aristotle lies the vanishing point of the architecture. From this point of convergence, the horizontals of the perspective construction radiate forwards and outwards parallel to the two philosophers striding forward out of the background. The movement of the figures thus corresponds to that infusing the surrounding space. Indeed, the physical gestures made by the two philosophers almost seem to determine the extension of the architecture upwards and outwards. Plato rises like a flame and the innermost arch seems to rise exactly behind his upward pointing arm. His book, too, is held vertically. Aristotle, by contrast, holds his book horizontally. He looks sideways, expands laterally, gestures forwards into the room. The majestic statues of Apollo and Minerva vary the poses of the two philosophers: Apollo that of Aristotle, Minerva that of Plato. Echoing the two philosophers in the vertical axis are a pair of columns visible in the cropped window high up in the rear domed interior. The whole architecture, symmetrically duplicated on the left and right, repeats the duality of the philosophers in the centre. The pair of philosophers and their books are taken up yet again, lastly, in two writing tablets in the foreground: like Plato's volume, the tablet of Pythagoras is held upright, while the geometrician's slate lies flat on the floor in keeping with Aristotle's tome.

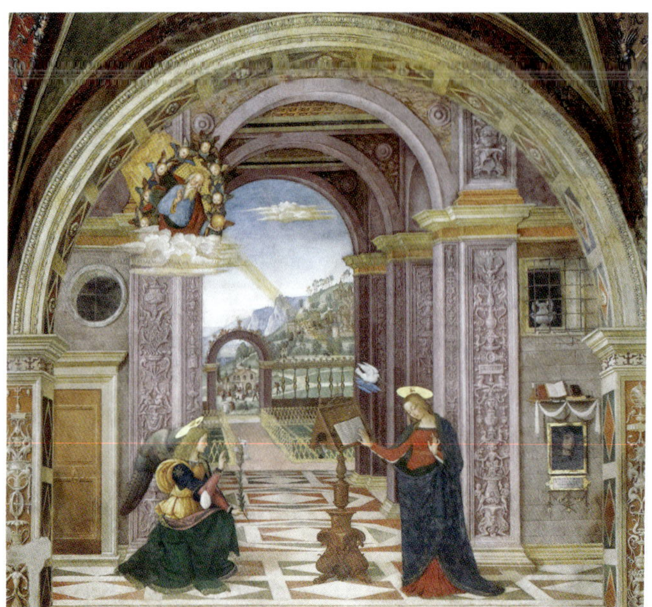

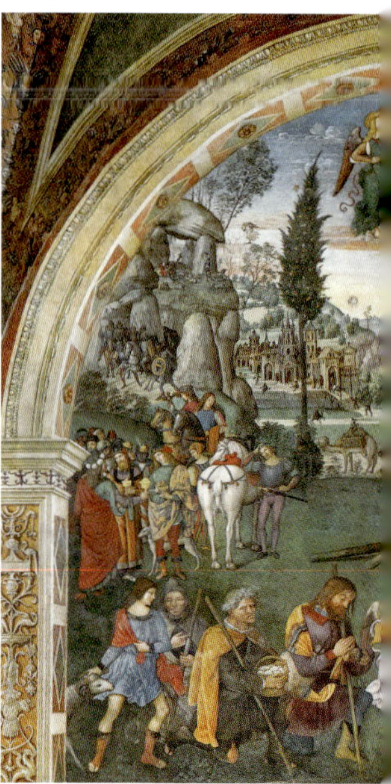

All these visual structures, correspondences and parallels are not purely aesthetic ends in themselves. In most cases they also carry an intellectual content, for example illustrating the development and structure of philosophical teachings, affinities between themes and ideas, and stages of learning and teaching. These meanings have been mapped out many times in the literature. Yet Raphael has at the same time succeeded in creating, in the *School of Athens*, the programmatic example of a rich, clear, logically transparent composition whose individual motifs are tightly interwoven at multiple levels, and which is characterised by a perfect balance between diversity and unity, and by the harmony of free and at the same time hierarchically ordered beings who fit together as a whole. Everything seems to blend with everything else.

In his fresco *Parnassus* (p. 184 b.; Cat. F3.1k), Raphael heightened the presence of contemporary elements. Portraits of the poets Bernardo Accolti (1458–1535) and Jacopo Sannazaro (1458–1530), for example, have been identified on the right-hand side. Just as Raphael had included his own portrait in the *School of Athens* and in so doing asserted the

Pinturicchio
Annunciation, Nativity and Adoration of the Shepherds, The Twelve-year-old Christ among the Doctors, 1500/01
Frescoes. Spello, Santa Maria Maggiore, Cappella Baglioni

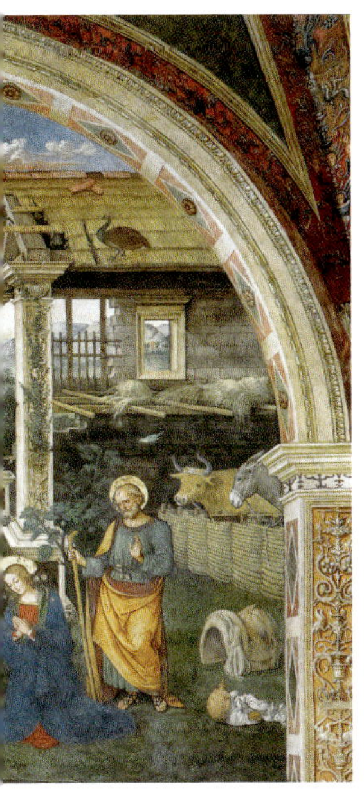

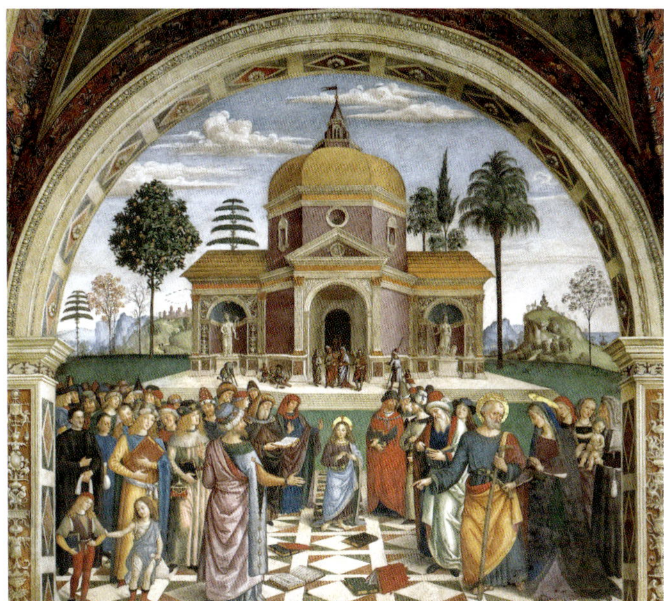

painter's place in the spheres of philosophy, the natural sciences, mathematics and geometry, so he declares himself a divinely inspired poet by also incorporating his portrait into *Parnassus*. To the left of the group of Muses, Homer (*c.* 8th century BC) is composing poetry, flanked by Virgil and Dante. Virgil, who in Dante's *Divine Comedy* had guided the poet through Hell and to the Mount of Purgatory, here directs him towards Apollo and the Muses as a source of artistic inspiration. Raphael looks out from the background behind Virgil's pointing hand, as if the gesture was also meant for him. Indeed, the motto assigned to *Poetry* is taken from Virgil's *Aeneid* – *numine afflatur*: solely in the case of the Muse standing on the left are her abundant draperies already billowing inspiringly in the direction of the group of poets.

Dante is also portrayed in the fresco of the *Disputation of the Holy Sacrament*, commonly known under its Italian title of *Disputa* (p. 185 t.; Cat. F3.1r). Just as the poet in the *Divine Comedy* must first climb the Mount of Purgatory before he can share in the vision of God in Paradise, so in the Stanza della Segnatura he takes the path, as it were, from the mountain sacred to the Muses in *Parnassus* to the vision of the divine in the *Disputa*. In this latter, too, Raphael seeks a comparison with Dante, albeit in a different way: above the *Disputa*, Theology (Cat. F3.1c) is the only one of the personifications on the ceiling to point downwards towards her mural field. Raphael models his personification of the knowledge of God on Dante's description of Beatrice in the *Divine Comedy*: a

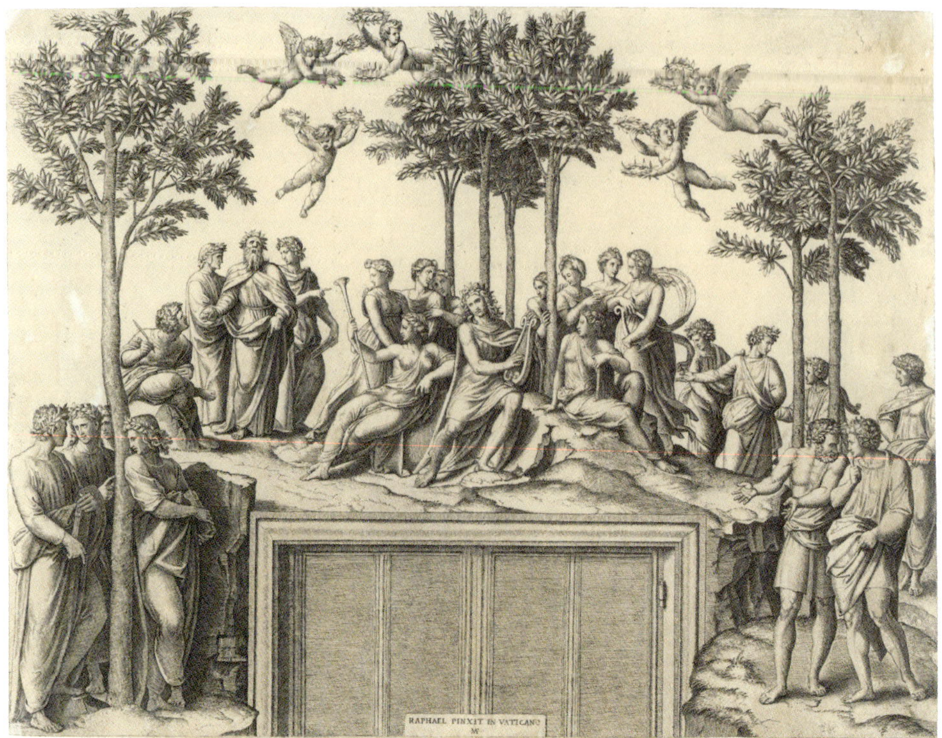

white scarf plays around her head, which is crowned with olive branches, and she wears a red gown beneath a green cloak. The colours of her dress refer to the three Theological Virtues: white symbolises the purity of Faith, red the flame of Charity, and green, Hope (Bellori 1695). In the case of Dante, Beatrice led the poet into the heavenly world of Paradise to the vision of God, which Dante then attempted to describe in his poetry. Insofar as Raphael's fresco has Beatrice-Theology point to the *Disputa*, her allegorical figure directs the viewer – like a guide, as it were – towards the contemplation of the divine vision which Raphael has portrayed there. Raphael thus creates a parallel with his own pictorial invention with Dante's verse portrait of the divine and reinforces his claim to be a poet of painting. As if he wished to show on this wall the vision previously inspired in him on Mount Parnassus.

Marcantonio Raimondi after Raphael, **Parnassus**, *c.* 1517–1520
Copperplate engraving, 35.6 × 47 cm (14 ⅛ × 18 ½ in). New York, The Metropolitan Museum of Art

Detail from **Disputa**, *c.* 1509/10
(see ill. p. 185)

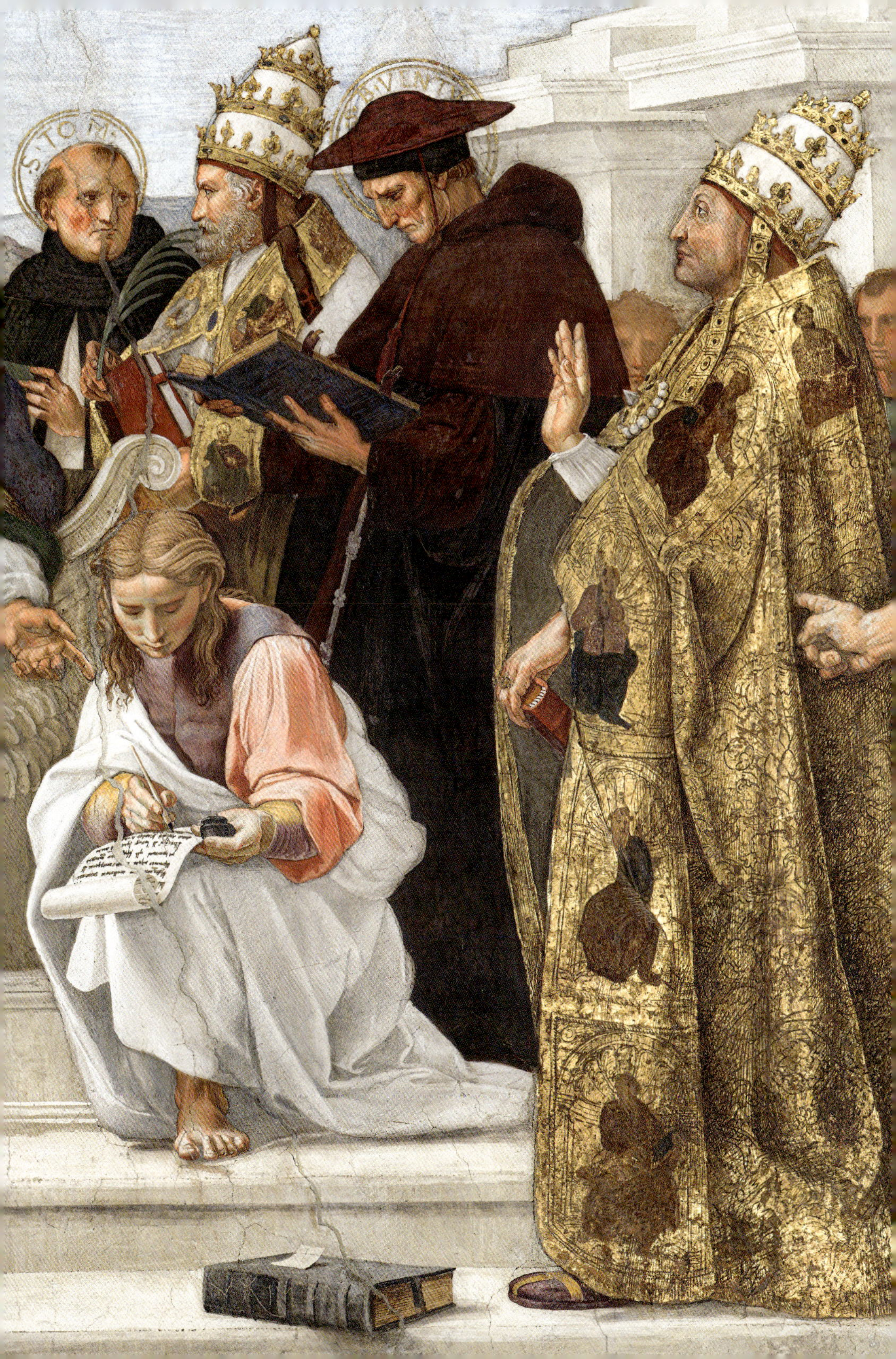
S·TOM·
S·B·VENT

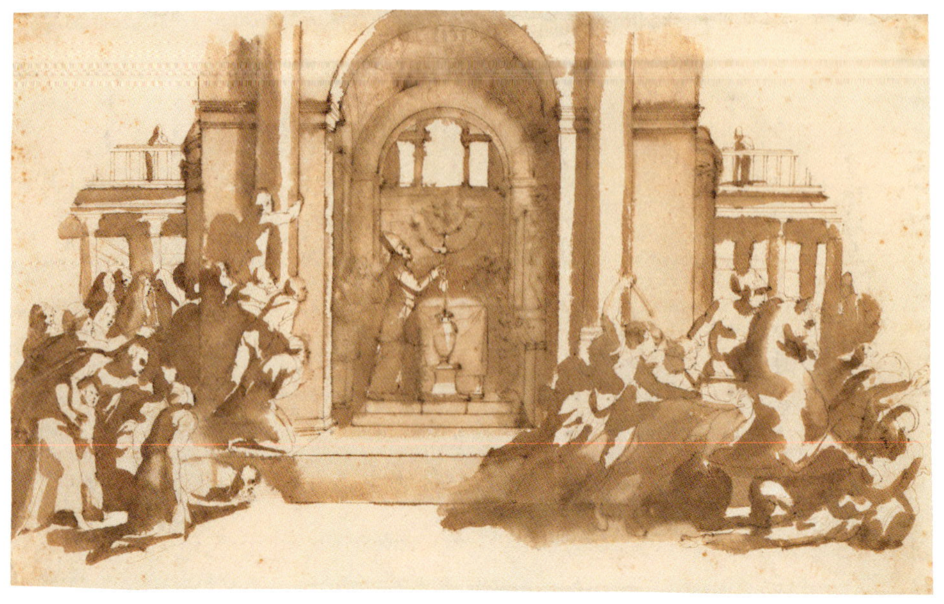

Raphael (copy)
The Expulsion of Heliodorus, first compositional draft, 16th/17th cent. (?)
Pen, wash, 25.2 × 41.5 cm (9 7/8 × 16 1/3 in). Vienna, Albertina

In the pictorial field of the cardinal virtues on the *Justice* wall (p. 185 b.; Cat. F3.1s), Raphael once again takes up the distinction – developed in the ceiling paintings of the personifications – between winged and wingless putti. The three cardinal virtues are accompanied by five *genii*, of which only three have wings. The distribution and staging of the various putti again follow the motto of "To everyone their due": clad in armour, Fortitude, a figure of courage and strength, drives away a wingless child with her lion, while bending her oak tree with its fruits towards a winged putto for harvesting. The wise Prudence, with her youthful countenance, looks into the mirror held up by a winged genius. A wingless putto with a torch attempts to illuminate the aged face in shadow on the back of her head. Here Raphael distinguishes the wisdom of the Christian present, which reflects and hence understands, from that of pagan antiquity in the past, which has yet to be brought to the light. Temperance, who represents moderation and restraint, holds her attribute of the bridle directly in front of the gleaming, wingless putto carrying the torch, while on her other side a winged child points heavenwards. The work of illuminating antiquity is evidently supposed to keep itself in check in accordance with the Christian faith. This represents a quite astonishing position statement on a fundamental problem of the Renaissance, namely the conflicting relationship between the desire for a rebirth of pagan antiquity and the demands of the Christian faith.

Consequences of this problem can be seen on the *Parnassus* wall opposite (Cat. F3.1k). Two fictive reliefs beneath the main fresco depict, as forerunners of the pope, two rulers from antiquity who prized ancient literature: Alexander the Great (356–323 BC), who honours the works of Homer with a place in a magnificent chest (Cat. F3.1l), and Augustus (63 BC–AD 14), who prevents the burning of Virgil's *Aeneid* (Cat. F3.1m), extend the sovereign's power of jurisdiction to the realm of literature. Antiquity here appears without qualification as a positive model. But in the final fresco of Mount Parnassus overhead (p. 172), Raphael implemented a number of noteworthy changes vis-à-vis his early design for the scene, which survives in an engraving. Originally, Dante was the only non-antique poet. In the fresco, however, at least five more were introduced. In the first design, moreover, Apollo played on an ancient lyre, not on a contemporary viola da braccio as in the fresco. Most significantly, however, the Olympian deity was initially portrayed as the sole source of inspiration, true to antique tradition. In the fresco, however, Apollo wears a "heavenwards gaze"; in other words he casts his eyes upwards, from where he is now inspired by an even higher power. The pagan god is subordinated to the Christian one. Upon the wishes of his papal patron, in the course of the design process Raphael evidently had to adjust the relationship between pagan antiquity and the Christian present, giving greater weight to this latter and placing a Christian curb on the revival of the antique doctrine of divine inspiration.

The two large frescoes on the long walls, the *School of Athens* (Cat. F3.1j) and the *Disputa* (Cat. F3.1r), are likewise by no means to be regarded as equal in value in terms of their content. On the contrary, Raphael scholarship has analysed the subtle hierarchy established between the two images. Similarities can be seen, for example, in the patterned flooring receding in perspective, the ascending flight of steps and the rows of scholarly figures. There are correspondences even between individual motifs, such as the pointing gestures – upwards and sideways – at the centre of the composition. But there are also deliberate differences. Where the philosophers stand beneath a spacious hall architecture with merely stone figures and partially obscured glimpses of the skies beyond, the heavenly realm of apparently living saints floats freely above the theologians against a backdrop of divine light. The philosophers' building is the work of human hands, unlike the celestial apse occupied by the hovering hosts of saints. The completed hall occupied by the ancient thinkers refers to the past, while the church whose building has only just commenced with the stone foundations in the *Disputa* belongs to the future. The dominant shape in the *Disputa* is the complete circle, which appears several times in a vertical alignment, as opposed to the semicircular form of the three vaulted arches in the *School of Athens*.

While the theologians congregate as a body towards the single centre of the altar, among the philosophers, individual groups remain separate; even the centre is characterised by Plato and Aristotle side by side. The philosophers' hall resembles the receding nave of a church, which is set against a heavenly apse formed by the altar and the curving ranks of the *Disputa*. Plato and Aristotle seem to be making their way out of their philosophers' interior towards the Christian altar of the theologians on the opposite wall. All this awards Theology primacy over Philosophy and subordinates the philosophers in the *School of Athens* to the theologians of the *Disputa*: knowledge arrived at via philosophy and based on scholarship is inferior – thus the message – to the revealed wisdom of Heaven.

Raphael's Stanza della Segnatura thus not only legitimises Pope Julius II's claim to possess, through a superior accumulation of education and culture, the decision-making ability of a just ruler necessary for the Office of the Keys, but at the same time combines the great educational tradition of past and present into a comprehensive system. The artist himself also finds his place within it, among the intellectual thinkers and inspired poets. Raphael must indeed have maintained an intensive dialogue with the intellectuals and literary figures assembled at Julius II's court at that time. Advisors inculcated him with the great educational traditions of the Renaissance Curia, knowledge which he then organised, as an artist arranging the motifs, into a rich visual system. Not only the Pope but also Raphael, too, acquired the power of judgement to "render to everyone their due".

In the fresco *Parnassus* (Cat. F3.1k), the blind Homer is composing verse on the left, his tall figure followed by Virgil behind him to the right. The writings of both authors are honoured by rulers in the grisaille paintings below the main picture: the work of Homer on the left, that of Virgil on the right. On Mount Parnassus, Raphael himself appears as another poet behind Virgil on the right. A sequence is thus established that begins with Homer and leads via Virgil to the artist. It is thus suggested to the viewer that the honour paid below by Alexander the Great to Homer, and by Emperor Augustus to Virgil, should also be extended further: Raphael is asking that he, too, should be honoured by the regent. On 4 October 1511, Julius II appointed Raphael *scriptor brevium* (papal "writer of letters", an honorary title), evidently as a reward for completing the Stanze. This honorary post carried a guaranteed permanent income. The office at the same time symbolically made Raphael a paid "scribe" who wrote down, in painting, the wishes of the Pope – a court painter to the Curia.

The two rooms on either side of the central Stanza della Segnatura are today called the Stanza d'Eliodoro and the Stanza dell'Incendio after themes treated in their frescoes. Work on their decoration began under Julius II but was only completed by his successor, Leo X, in some places with modifications. In 1511, under Julius, Raphael began in the Stanza d'Eliodoro (pp. 196–205; Cat. F3.2) with the large wall frescoes, finishing the

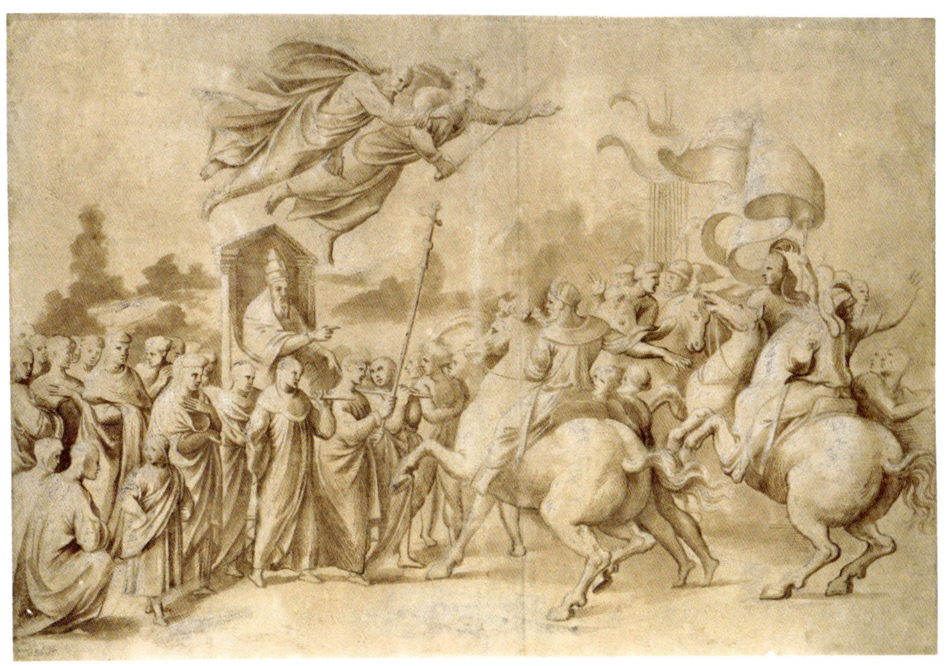

Workshop of Raphael, **Meeting of Leo I and Attila**, 1511/12
Brush in brown ink, with white heightening (oxidised), 38.8 × 58 cm (15 ¼ × 22 ⅞ in)
Oxford, Ashmolean Museum

cycle in 1514 after the pope's death. In addition, Leo X also had the decoration carried out for the Della Rovere pope on the ceiling largely replaced. The ceiling frescoes in the Stanza dell'Incendio (pp. 230–241; Cat. F3.3) had already been completed a few years earlier, around 1508, when they were executed for Julius II by Perugino (p. 210), whereas Raphael and his workshop carried out the wall paintings under Leo X. In terms of their themes, the frescoes created successively inside the three Stanze form a closely interrelated unity. The frescoes in the two lateral rooms complement the theme of the acquisition of knowledge in the Stanza della Segnatura with dramatic action scenes. Via a chronological series of examples from history, they show how the pontifical power of the keys founded on knowledge in the middle room is applied by the Pope in practical governance, how it takes effect and what divine protection it enjoys. The coat of arms bearing the crossed keys is again mounted at the apex of the ceiling in both rooms and thereby particularly embellished with wreaths and the heraldic device of the Della Rovere pope (pp. 198/199, 210). It is thus made clear that the power of the keys has here already been conferred and that the Della Rovere pope possesses it and uses it.

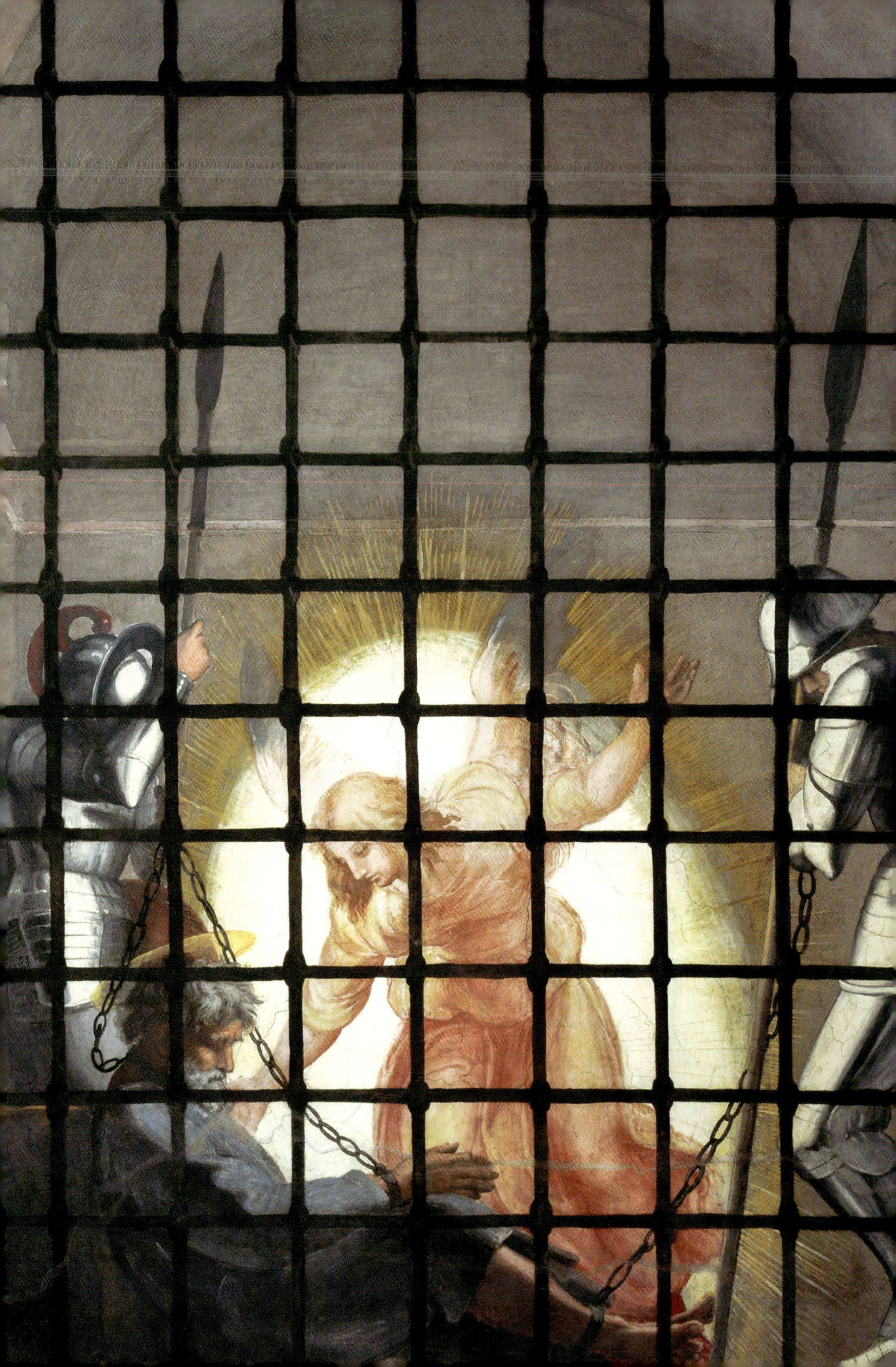

In the middle room, Raphael had assigned ceiling paintings of corresponding content to the wall paintings directly below. The same system is found in the two adjacent rooms, even if the ceiling programme of one and the mural programme of the other were altered under Leo X. There are many visual cross-references, moreover, between the frescoes of the two outer Stanze. From a comparison of the wall paintings in the Stanza d'Eliodoro and the ceiling scenes in the Stanza dell'Incendio, in other words the elements of the decoration in these two rooms that date from the reign of Julius II, it has been possible to reconstruct the systematic visual programme intended by Julius for the group of rooms as a whole (Rohlmann 2002 and 2013). The Stanza d'Eliodoro shows how the head of the Church has been repeatedly attacked by enemies in different epochs and in different territories, and how God thereby always comes to his aid and helps him to win victory and deliverance. The east wall presents an episode from the Old Testament (*Expulsion of Heliodorus*, Cat. F3.2a), the north wall one from the New Testament (*Liberation of Saint Peter*, Cat. F3.2b) and the west wall one from the history of the Church (*Leo I and Attila*, Cat. F3.2g). On the south wall, the initial plan was for a vision of the future Apocalypse (p. 181). This was subsequently replaced by the *Mass at Bolsena* (Cat. F3.2h). Above the corresponding walls in the Stanza dell'Incendio, the same epochs are invoked by different representations of God on the ceiling: in the east, an Old Testament God the Father, in the north Christ, in the west Christ together with God the Father, Dove and Apostles, and in the south Christ as Judge between Justice and Mercy.

These representations were conceived as celestial complements to planned wall paintings. Under Julius, these were probably intended to show occasions on which, thanks to the blessing and mercy of the corresponding figure of God on the ceiling, the Pope on earth below was not attacked, but aided. Leo X subsequently chose a different set of historical episodes, but his "Leo popes" are also able to act freely in different areas and so bestow their grace upon the people providing assistance, addressing their pleas or submitting themselves to papal authority. On either side of the middle room, the Stanze's political audience was thus confronted with examples of the negative consequences of any anti-papal behaviour in one Stanza, and with examples of the positive results of pro-papal policies in the other. What has been designed here, perhaps for the first time, is a multi-room programmatic statement of ruling power that does not simply present a series of arguments, but structurally combines them into a tightknit, overarching unity.

The wall frescoes of the Stanza d'Eliodoro presented Raphael with a new and challenging task. In place of beautiful poses, harmonious composition and a structure rich

Detail from **The Liberation of Saint Peter**, *c.* 1512/13
(see ill. p. 196)

in allusions and connections, their vast pictorial fields now demanded dramatic narration, immediacy and a storyline, accompanied by movement and affects. The aim was to stir the emotions of the viewer and secure the latter's inner participation in events. How Raphael achieved this in the four pictures has often been described. The *Expulsion of Heliodorus* (p. 196 t.; Cat. F3.2a) leads into the interior of the plundered temple in Jerusalem. Beneath gleaming golden cupolas, lights and candlesticks flicker. The terrified women and children huddle together into a crowd. The agitated commotion surges upwards, as it were, around the column. In the background, the high priest seems to be praying for God's assistance not only to the Ark of the Covenant, but to heaven itself, seen through the arch. With gale force, however, flying angels and a celestial horseman have already swept in towards the right from a centre from which everything seems to have been blasted away. As a falling cascade, they strike down the robber Heliodorus and his accomplices laden with the temple's treasures.

On the left-hand side, Julius II edges into the biblical scene: as if he were meant to be a spectator of and witness to divine aid, the Pope is carried onto the stage. He thus claims the assistance granted in the Old Testament as valid for his own policies, too. His calmness and steadfast strength are contrasted with the terror of the agitated populace, including in his darker colours and solid mode of execution. Julius wanted to see his papal motto, chosen at the start of his pontificate, represented in visual terms: *Dominus mihi adiutor, non timebo quid faciat mihi homo* ("With the Lord on my side I do not fear. What can man do to me?"; Psalm 118: 6). In the litter bearer on Julius's far side, Raphael has portrayed himself: his gaze becomes our direct access into the narrative that he has fashioned. At the same time, the artist carrying his patron also metaphorically declares himself a "pillar" of the pontifical throne. Raphael the papal employee thus makes one purpose of his art openly visible to us. The office held by the litter bearer closest to us may be politically more charged. If his recently proposed identification with Alberto Pio da Carpi (1475–1531) is correct (Minarelli 2015), the ambassador to the Holy Roman Emperor and hence imperial policy is here visually fixed on supporting Julius II.

Just as the contemporary figure of Julius II leads into the scene on the left, the biblical events on the right lead back out into the reality of the Stanza: the window in the wall to the right of the fresco is reflected on the armour of prone Heliodorus. The overturned pot of money also emerges out of the fiction of the picture and gains haptic presence through the addition of real gilding. Its seductive allure radiates outwards to us, too, in warning fashion. Heliodorus had succumbed to its temptation, and the reflection of the gold on his breastplate lies right over his heart.

The Liberation of Saint Peter (p. 196 b.; Cat. F3.2b) introduces the New Testament. The first pope is being held in prison in Jerusalem and is freed by an angel during the

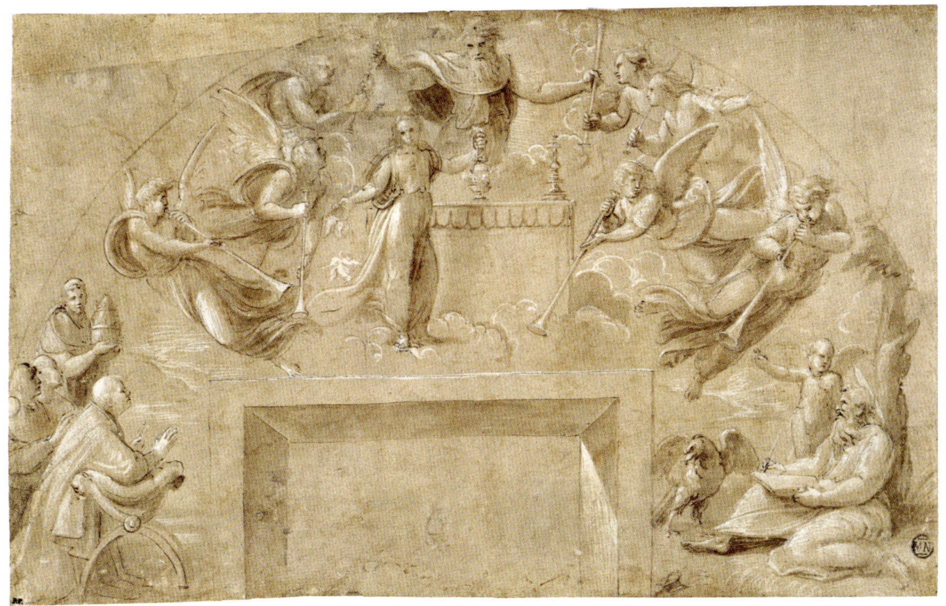

Apocalyptic vision, first sketch for the *Mass at Bolsena* wall, 1511/12
Pen, with wash and heightened with white, over underdrawing in black chalk and metalpoint, on beige prepared paper, 24.7 × 39.8 cm (9 ¾ × 15 ⅔ in)
Paris, Musée du Louvre, Département des Arts graphiques

night. Raphael follows the biblical text very closely: he shows two of the four squads of four soldiers. Peter, in chains, is asleep between two guards, while a further two are supposed to be standing watch at the entrance. The angel appears and, with him, a bright light shines into the cell. He commands Peter to rise (middle). He leads him past the two outer guards (right). At daybreak the miracle is noticed and there is uproar among the soldiers (left). Raphael uses the window opening to construct his painted stage architecture. He responds to the backlighting effect of the window with a differentiated array of natural, artificial and supernatural light sources, particularly admired ever since Vasari. The grating of the cell opening, through which light arrives from behind, replies to the small leaded lights of the original window. It is possible that these even incorporated a stained-glass painting of angels bearing the papal coat of arms; one such is documented for the Stanza dell'Incendio. If so, the divine assistance lent to Peter would have been heraldically repeated in the holding up of the reigning pontiff's shield by angels.

Raphael faithfully reproduces the chains of Saint Peter which are venerated as relics even today in the Roman church of San Pietro in Vincoli – Julius II's titular church when he was still a cardinal. When the liberated Peter makes his appearance a second time on the right-hand side of the fresco, outside the prison cell, the chains on the Apostle's hands have turned into the papal key. An allusion is perhaps made here to Giuliano della Rovere's ascent to the papacy: from his titular church of San Pietro in Vincoli (Saint Peter in Chains), he was led with heavenly assistance to the office of the keys first held by Peter. If we look further right, past the painted framework to the adjacent wall, we see Julius II in painted person being carried into the *Heliodorus* fresco as Pope. This "entrance" motif fittingly appears directly above the real door into the Stanza. Raphael thus invites us to follow a line of argumentation interlinking reality and art. The successor of Christ transforms from the man lying down to the man walking forward and finally to the man enthroned on high: a step-by-step ascent to the present.

The encounter between *Leo I and Attila* (p. 197 t.; Cat. F3.2g) was frescoed under Leo X. The subject had been planned by Julius II, however, as evidenced by a preliminary drawing (p. 177). The sheet shows Julius in the role of Saint Leo being carried in his *sedia gestatoria* towards the Huns. Protected by the sword-wielding Saint Peter and Saint Paul, who appear in the sky overhead, the pontiff convinces the invaders laying waste to Italy to withdraw. The development of the composition shows the great degree to which Raphael had to take political developments into account in his artistic design. The repulse of Attila with divine assistance was intended to serve as an example of God's help against any attack on the territories under papal rule. But on 11 April 1512, on the very feast day of Saint Leo I and with the fresco not yet painted, the French invading army inflicted a crushing defeat on Julius II at the Battle of Ravenna. The papal cardinal legate Giovanni de' Medici was even taken prisoner. This is perhaps why the fresco was not executed under Julius. A second surviving compositional study (KMOF 449) draws attention away from Leo I by relegating the papal group to the background, where it is so small as to be barely noticeable. Now the attackers are driven back by the celestial apparition alone. It is unclear whether Raphael has here produced a corrected design for the fresco or whether he wanted to use the reworked theme independently for a print. But the death of Julius II and the election of the new pontiff changed the plan again. Giovanni de' Medici had succeeded in escaping from French captivity and was elected Leo X. The Medici pope held his *possesso* – the traditional ceremonial procession by the new pope through Rome to the Lateran – on the exact anniversary of the Battle of Ravenna and, on this Feast of Saint Leo, even rode the same horse on which he had been captured. It was only by a miracle that, through divine providence, he had risen from the lowest circumstances to the highest honour. The fresco in the Stanza d'Eliodoro was executed, and in the composition the papal group was restored to the foreground. Leo the Great, with the features of Leo X, now appears on horseback. The Medici *possesso* inserts itself into a political episode from the era of the Huns.

The visual concept for the fourth wall of the Stanza d'Eliodoro underwent an even more substantial change. Raphael painted the *Mass at Bolsena* (p. 197 b.; Cat. F3.2h) while Julius was still pope. It shows an episode that reportedly took place in 1263 and which pertains to the assurance of faith: during a Mass conducted by a visiting priest from the North, who doubted the doctrine of transubstantiation, the Host – transformed into the Body of Christ – began to bleed. In the fresco, Julius II and his retinue, firm in their faith, venerate the presence of God demonstrated in this Eucharistic miracle. Originally, however, a completely different event had been planned for this wall: a visionary scene showing the moment in the Book of Revelation in which God gives seven angels the seven trumpets of judgement, with which the enemies of the Church and persecutors of the faithful would be destroyed. The *modello* of this apocalyptic vision is preserved in the Louvre (p. 181). But when a number of cardinals with French support convened a council with the aim of deposing him, Julius evidently demanded that this subject be changed. Raphael was now to illustrate God's protection of the Christian faith and Church, in an example in which an attack against the doctrine of faith, led from within the institution of the Church itself, is repulsed. Doubts within the Church had to be fought, even if this meant weakening the stringency of Raphael's original programme for the room. Having started in the epoch of the Old Testament high priest, and having continued with Peter as the first pope and then with one of his early successors, the cycle of divine aid no longer extends to the end of days. Instead, the age of the popes is represented a second time with a later event. The continuous evolution of the settings of each scene, as planned by Raphael, also lost its culminating point. From an interior *(Expulsion of Heliodorus)*, the narrative was intended to emerge out of built architecture *(Liberation of Saint Peter)* into the open landscape *(Leo I and Attila)* and finally to lead to the scene of God in heaven *(Apocalyptic vision)*. In the *Mass at Bolsena*, Raphael instead had to show the altar area of a house of God as in the *Expulsion of Heliodorus* – albeit now that of a Christian church.

In February 1513 Julius II died. The new Pope, Leo X, propagated politically new priorities. He stood for compromise, reconciliation and clemency, a benevolent reign of peace, magnificence and abundance. This new image of the Pope needed to be made visible within the same two settings in which Julius II had sited his large, programmatic fresco cycles: in Raphael's Stanze and in Michelangelo's Sistine Chapel. Raphael now began working in both. In the Stanze as in the chapel, the new histories of the Medici pope were to be told.

Stanza della Segnatura

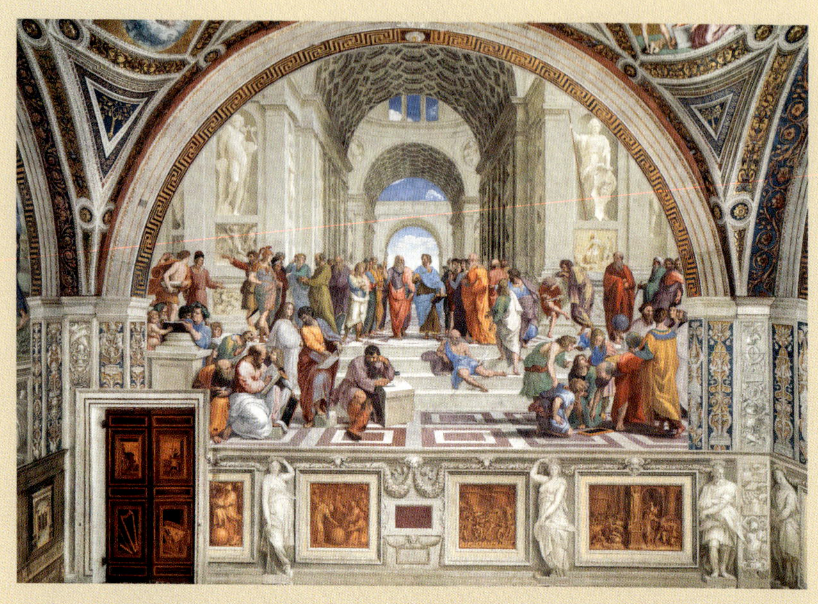

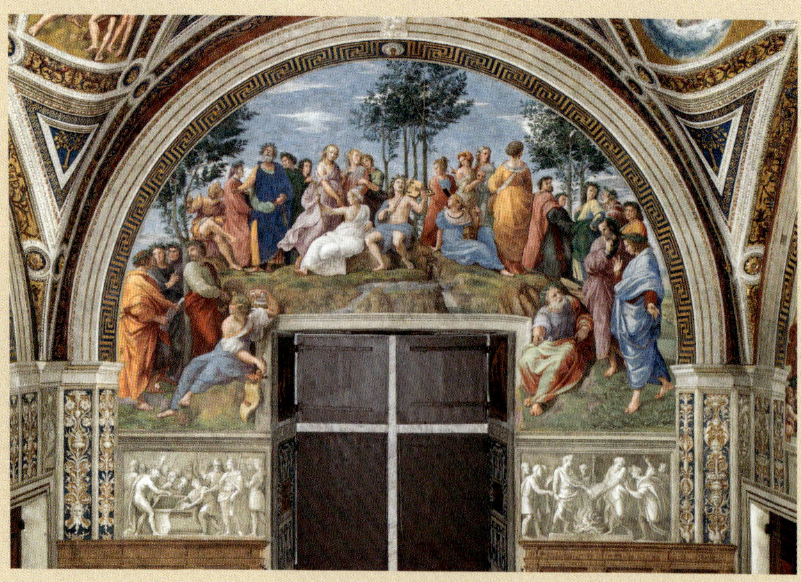

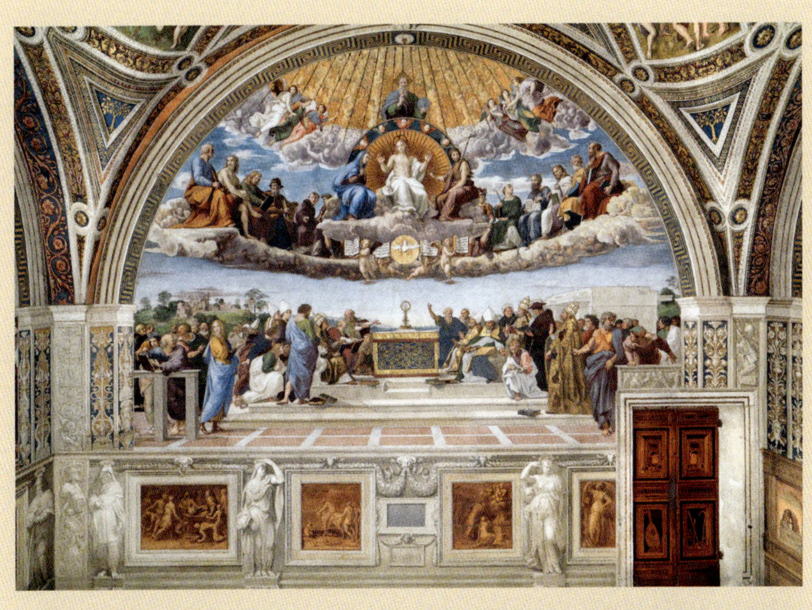

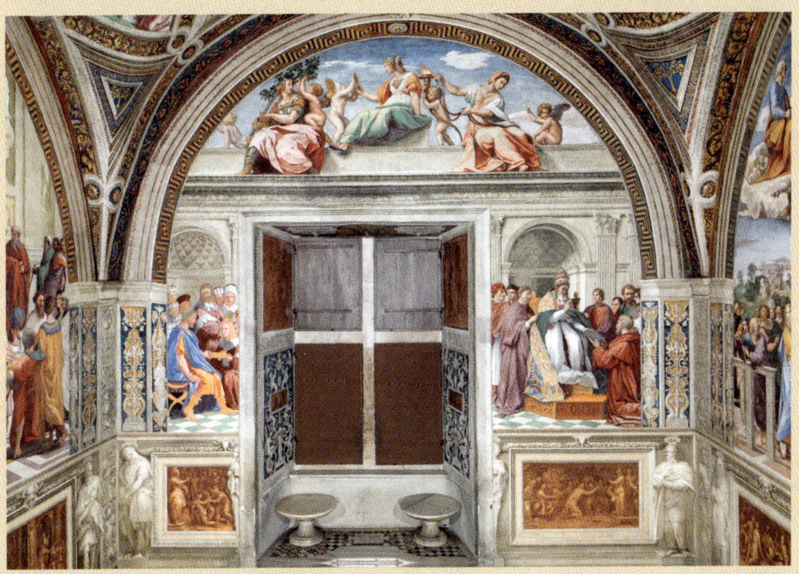

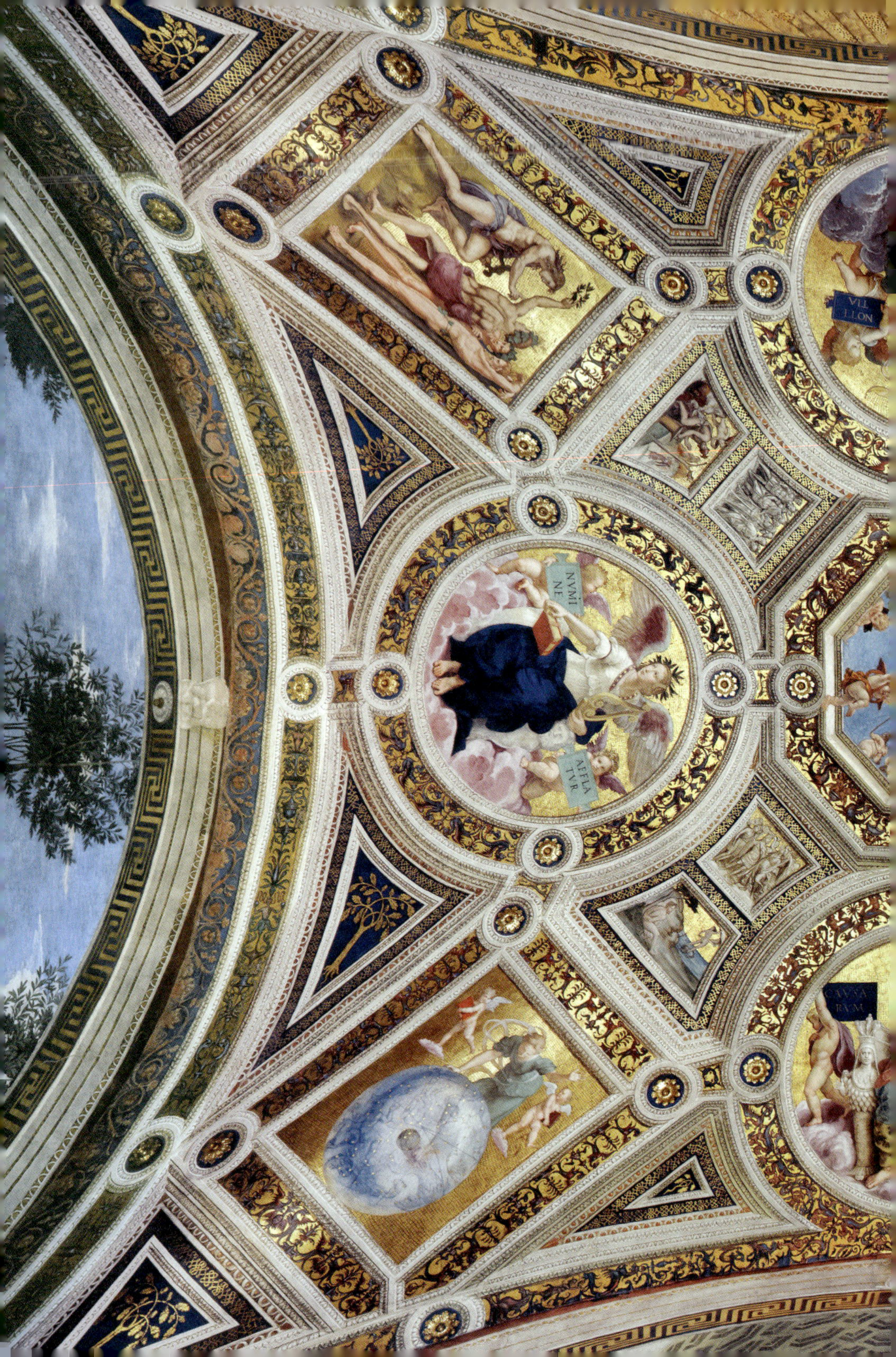

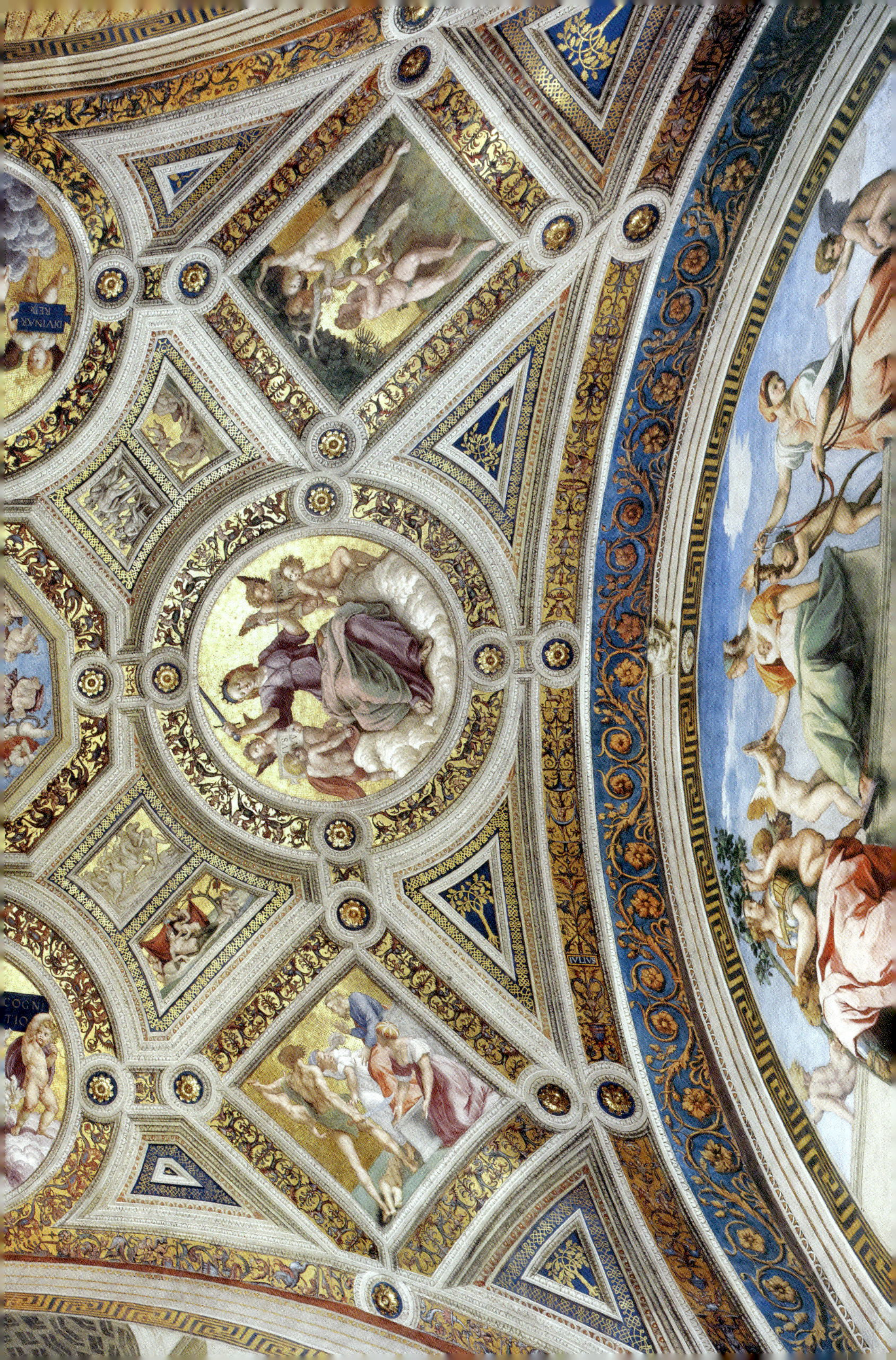

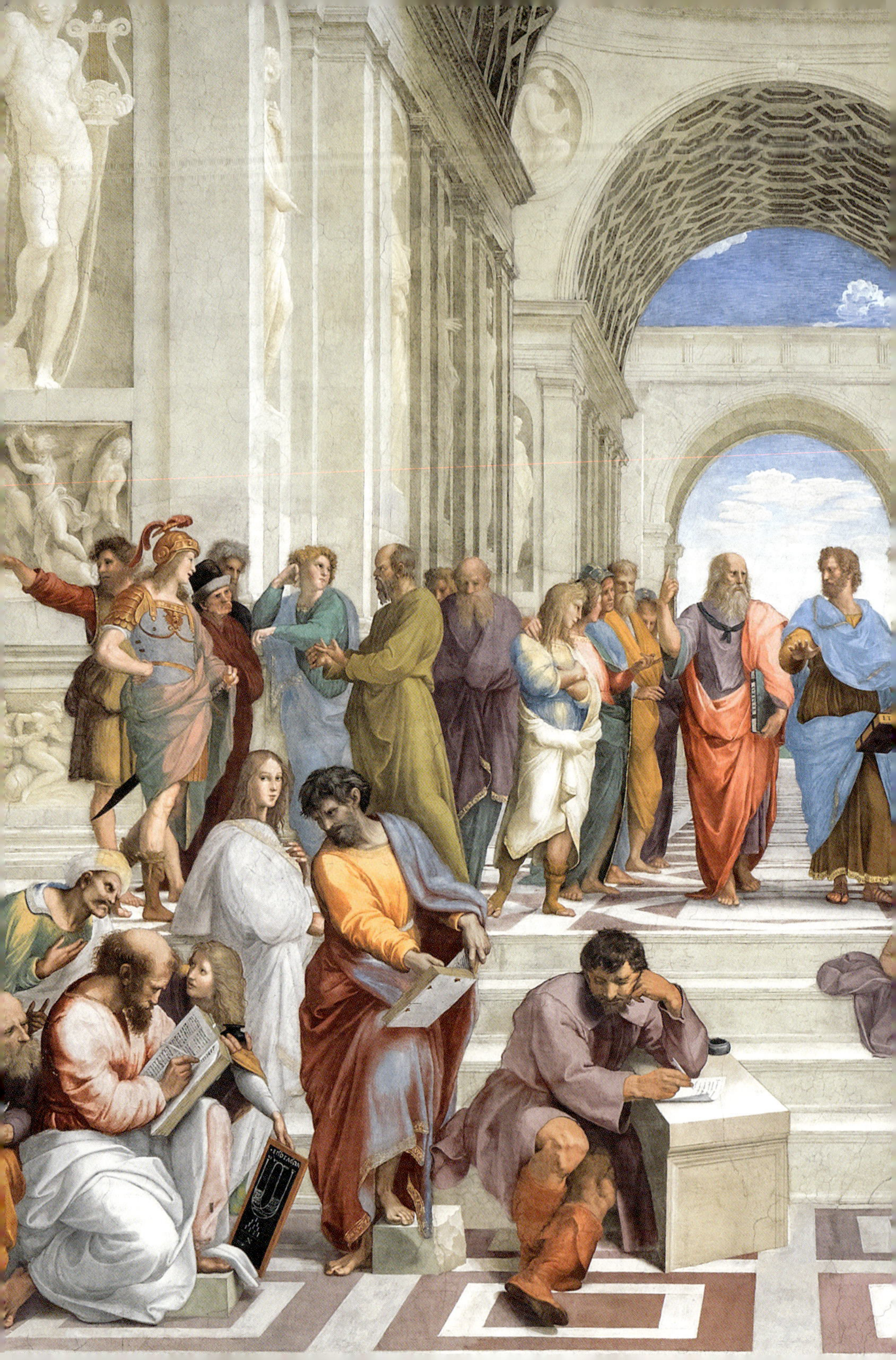

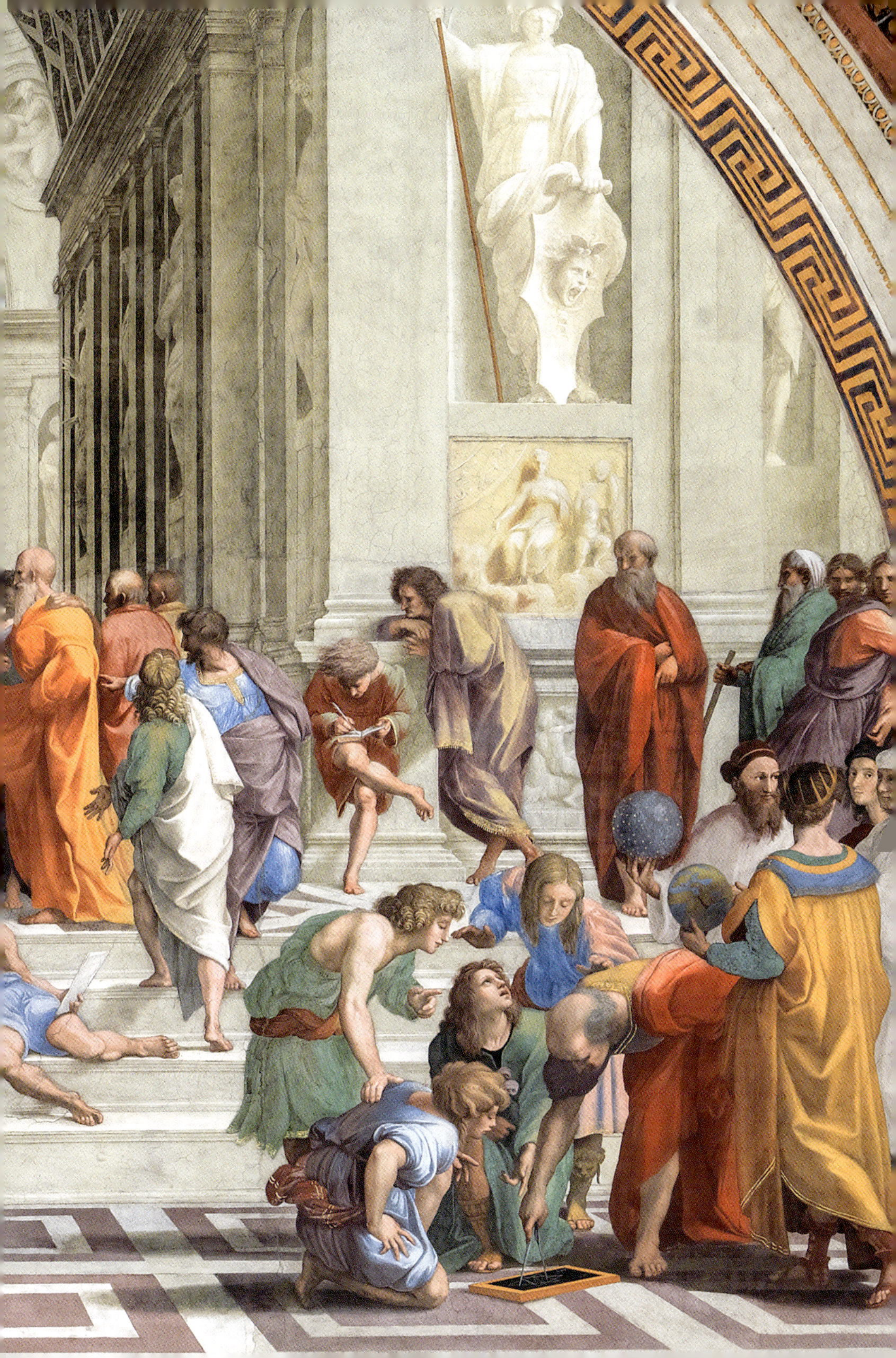

Page 184

School of Athens, *c.* 1509
Fresco, height 5.77 m, (227 ⅛ in), width of base: 8.14 m (320 ½ in)
Vatican City, Musei Vaticani, Stanza della Segnatura
(Detail pages 188/189)

Parnassus, 1508–1510/11
Fresco, width of base: 7.00 m (275 ⅝ in)
Vatican City, Musei Vaticani, Stanza della Segnatura
(Detail pages 194/195)

Page 185

Disputa, *c.* 1509/10
Fresco, height 5.88 m (231 ½ in), width at base 8.18 m (322 ⅛ in)
(Details pages 4–7, 157, 165, 166, 173, 192/193)

Inscriptions in the angels' books:
SECVNDVM MAT[thaeum] LIBER GENERATIONIS IESV CHRISTI FILII DAVID (Matthew 1:1):
According to Matthew, the book of the genealogy of Jesus Christ, the son of David
SECVNDVM MARCVM INITIVM EVANGELII IESV CHRISTI (Mark 1:1):
According to Mark, the beginning of the Gospel of Jesus Christ
SECVUNDVM LVCAM FVIT IN DIEBVS HERODIS REGIS (Luke 1:5):
According to Luke, there was in the days of Herod, the king
SECVNDVM IOANNEM IN PRINCIPIO ERAT VERBVM ET VER [bum erat apud Deum] (John 1:1):
According to John, in the beginning was the Word, and the Word [was with God]
Vatican City, Musei Vaticani, Stanza della Segnatura

Justice wall: the Cardinal virtues Fortitude, Prudence and Temperance;
Emperor Justinian Affirms the *Corpus Iuris Civilis*; Gregory IX Affirms the Decretals, 1508–1511
Fresco, width at base 7.00 m (275 ⅝ in)
Vatican City, Musei Vaticani, Stanza della Segnatura

Pages 186/187

Ceiling fresco with representations of *Philosophy*, *Poetry*, *Theology* and *Justice*, the *Observation of the Cosmos*, *The Punishment of Marsyas*, *The Fall* and *The Judgement of Solomon*, 1508/09
Frescoes. Vatican City, Musei Vaticani, Stanza della Segnatura
(Detail page 8)

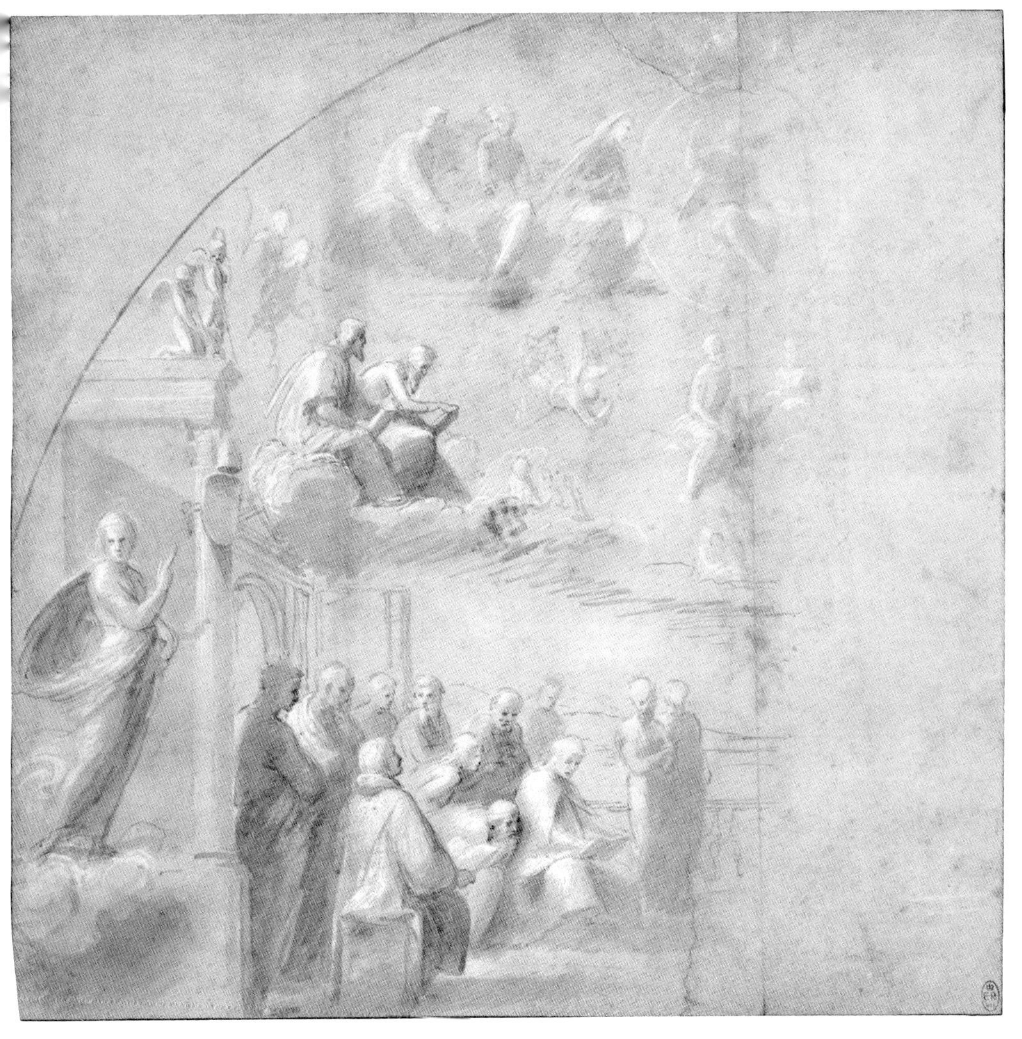

Design for the *Disputa*, 1509
Pen and brush with white heightening over stylus, 27.6 × 28.3 cm (10 ⅞ × 11 ⅛ in)
Windsor Castle, Royal Library

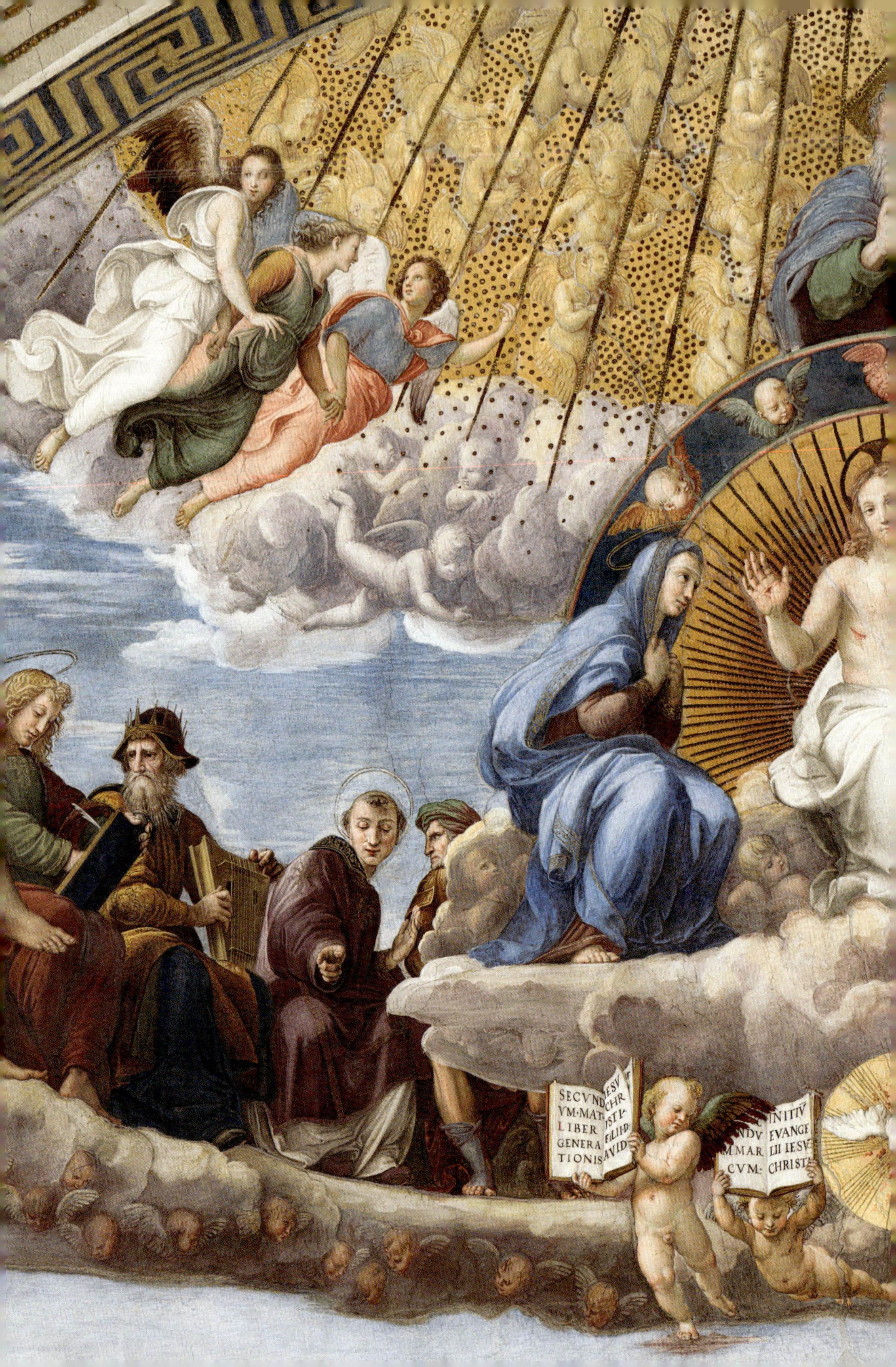
SECVND
VM·MAT
LIBER
GENERA
TIONIS
IESV
CHR
ISTI
FILII·D
AVID
NDV
MMAR
CVM·
INITIV
EVANGE
LII IESV
CHRISTI

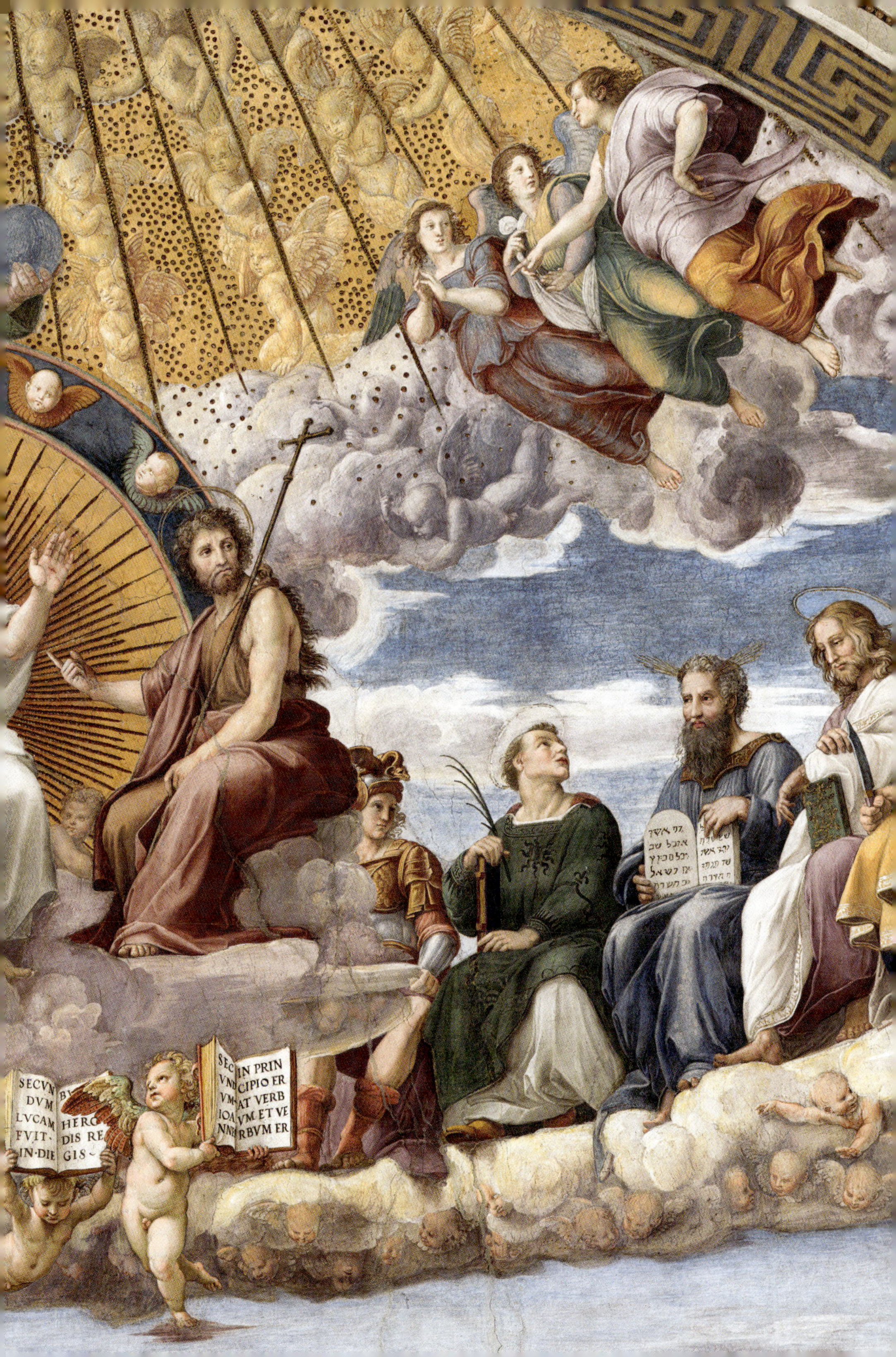
SECVN
DVM
LVCAM
FVIT·
IN·DIE
B
HER
DIS RE
GIS
SEC
VND
VM
IOA
NNE
IN PRIN
CIPIO ER
AT VERB
VM ET VE
RBVM ER

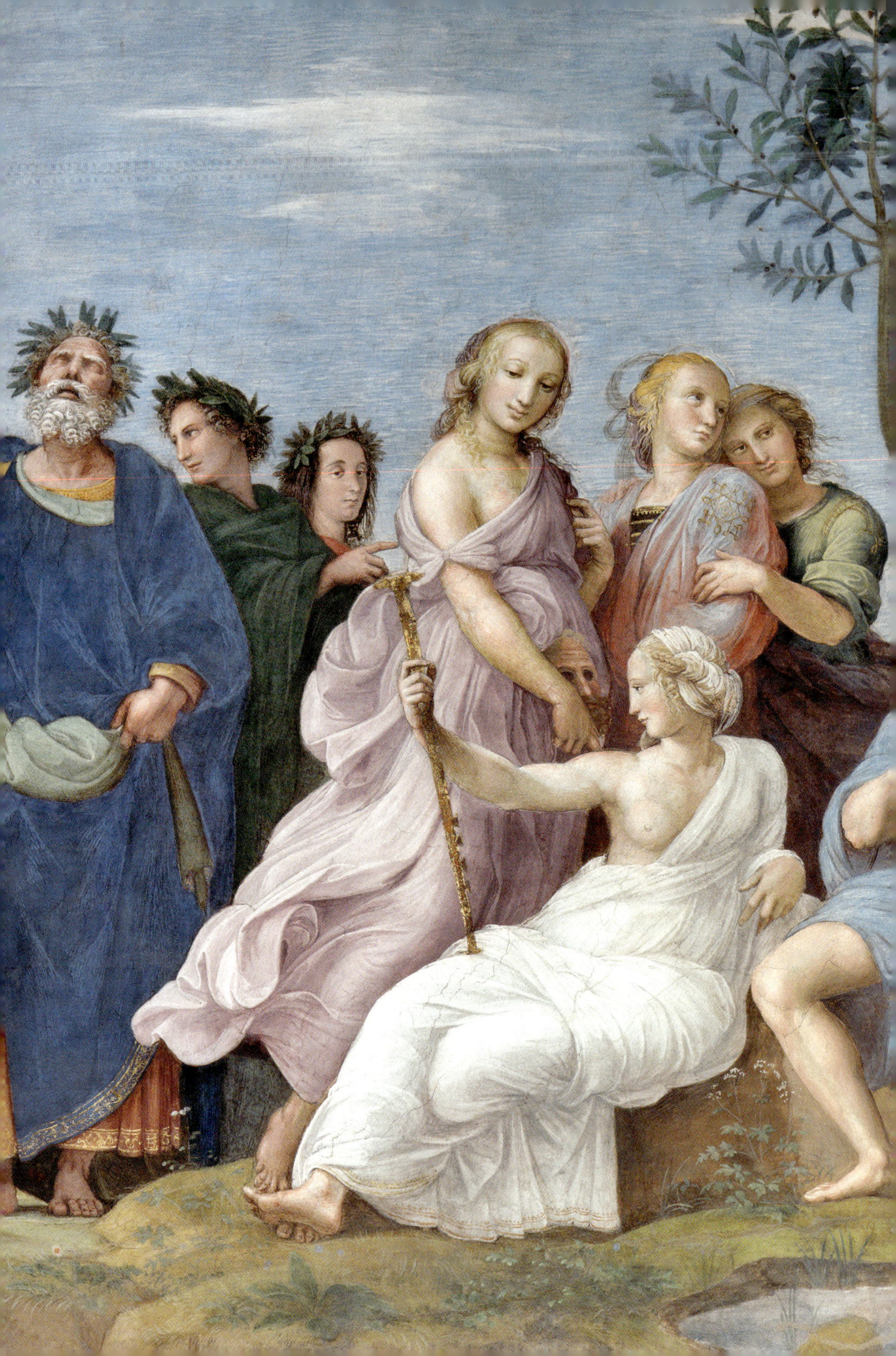

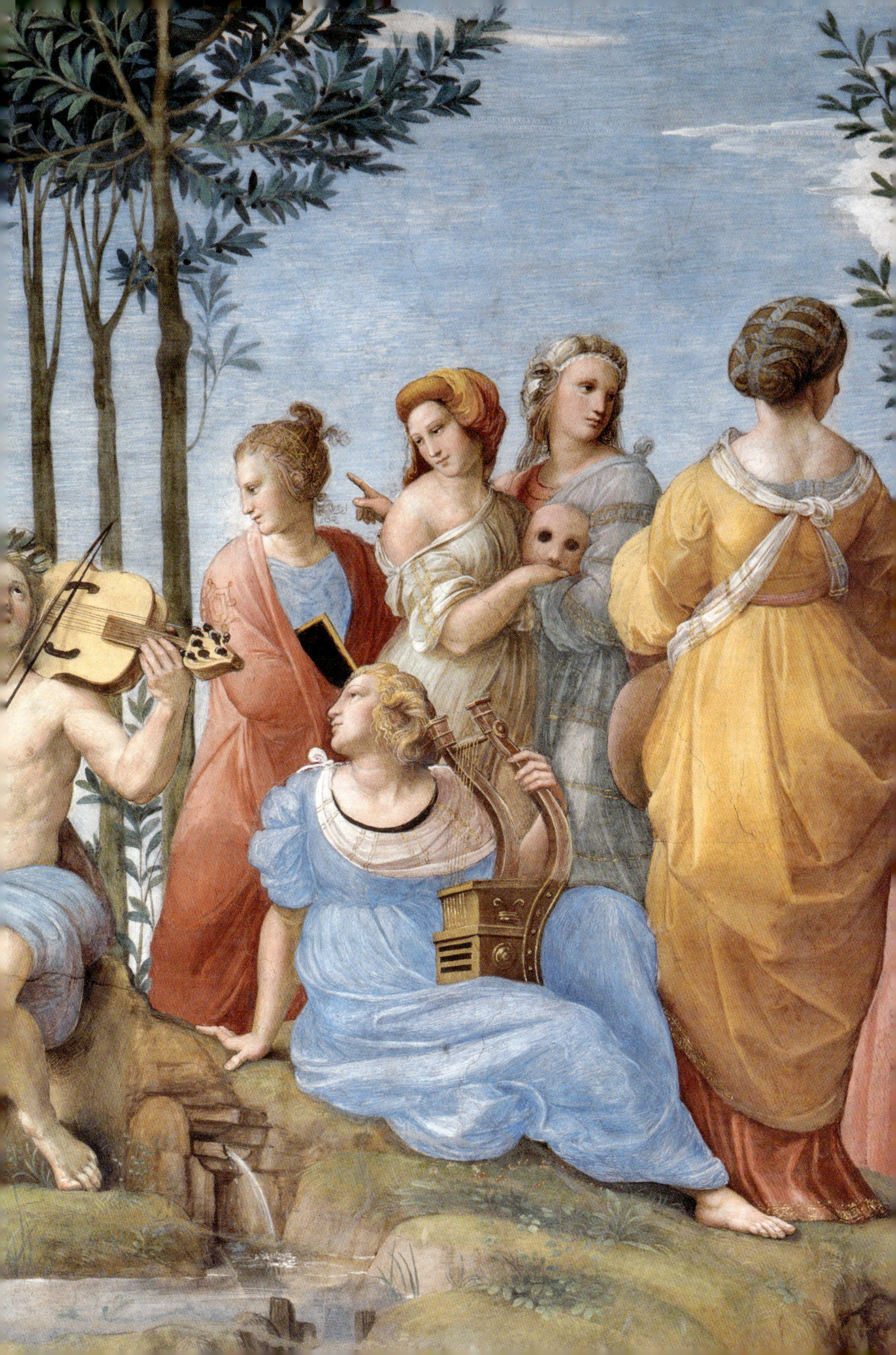

Stanza d'Eliodoro

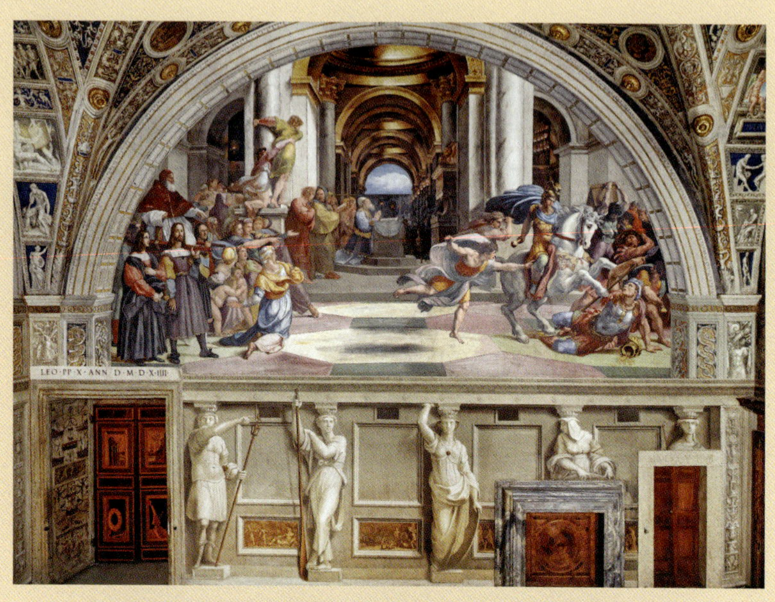

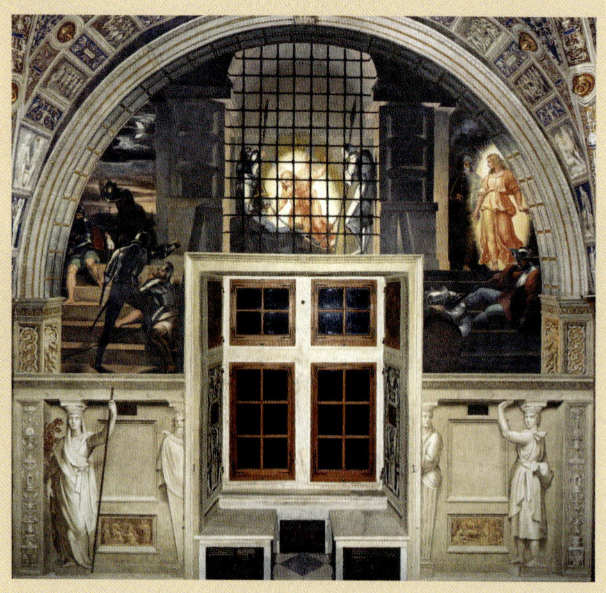

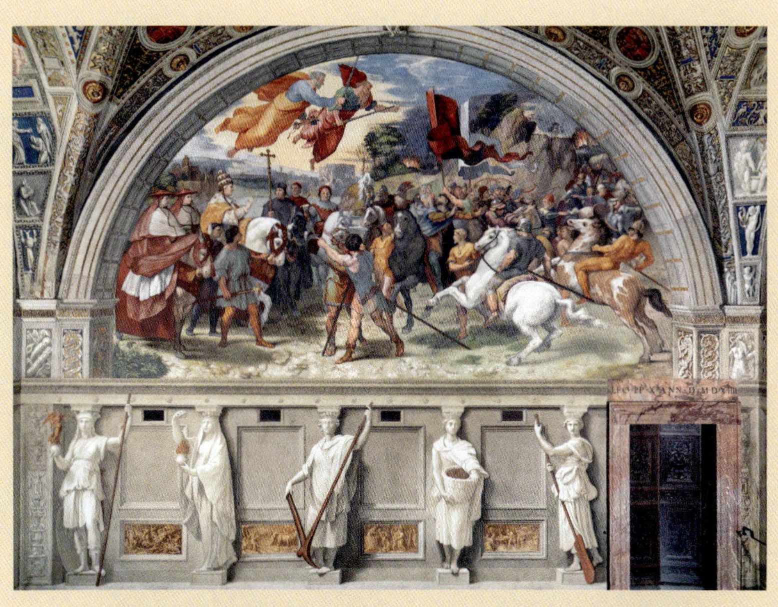

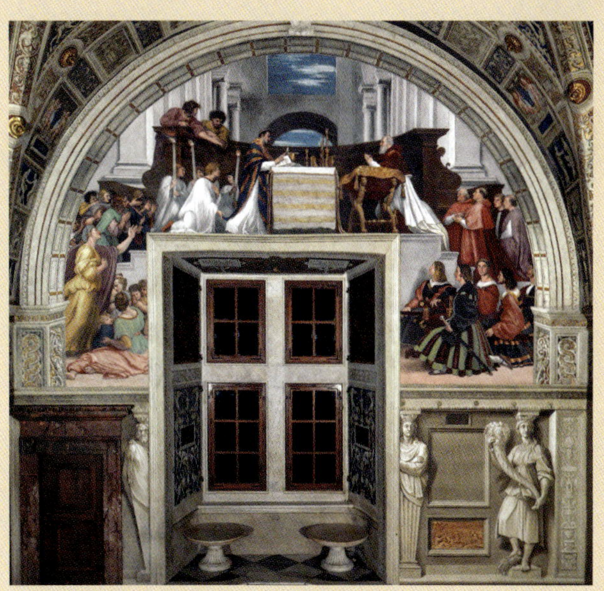

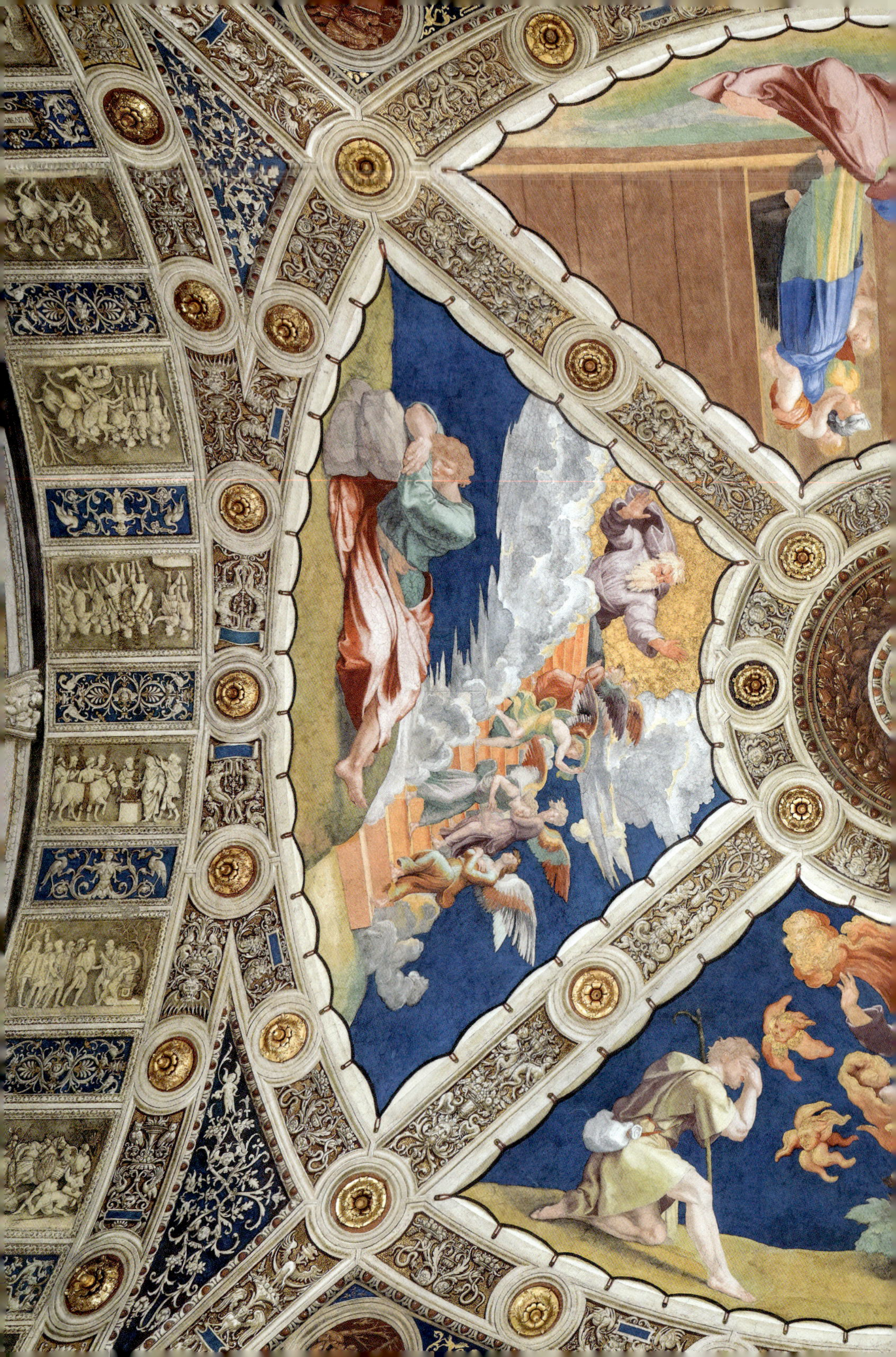

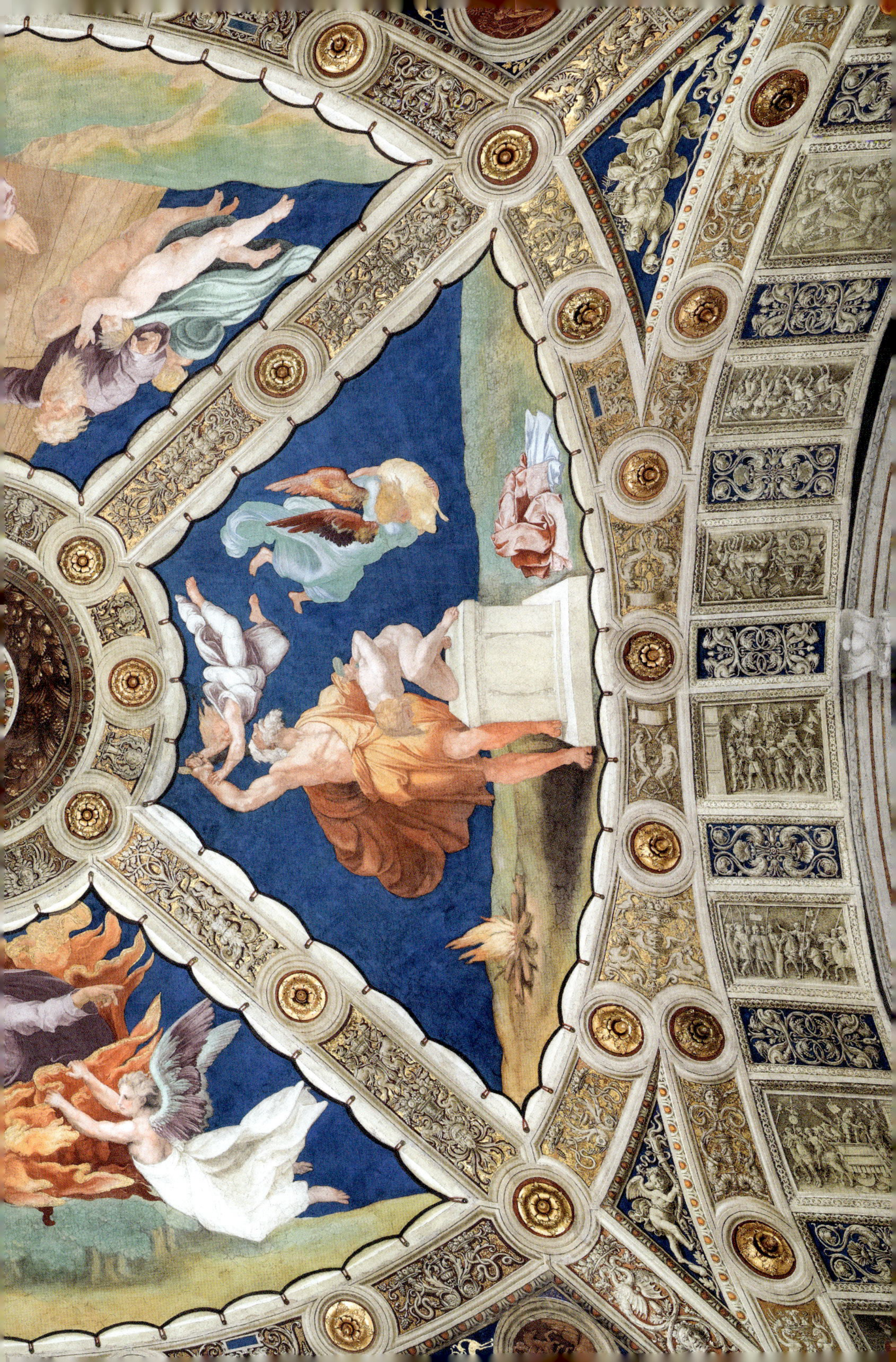

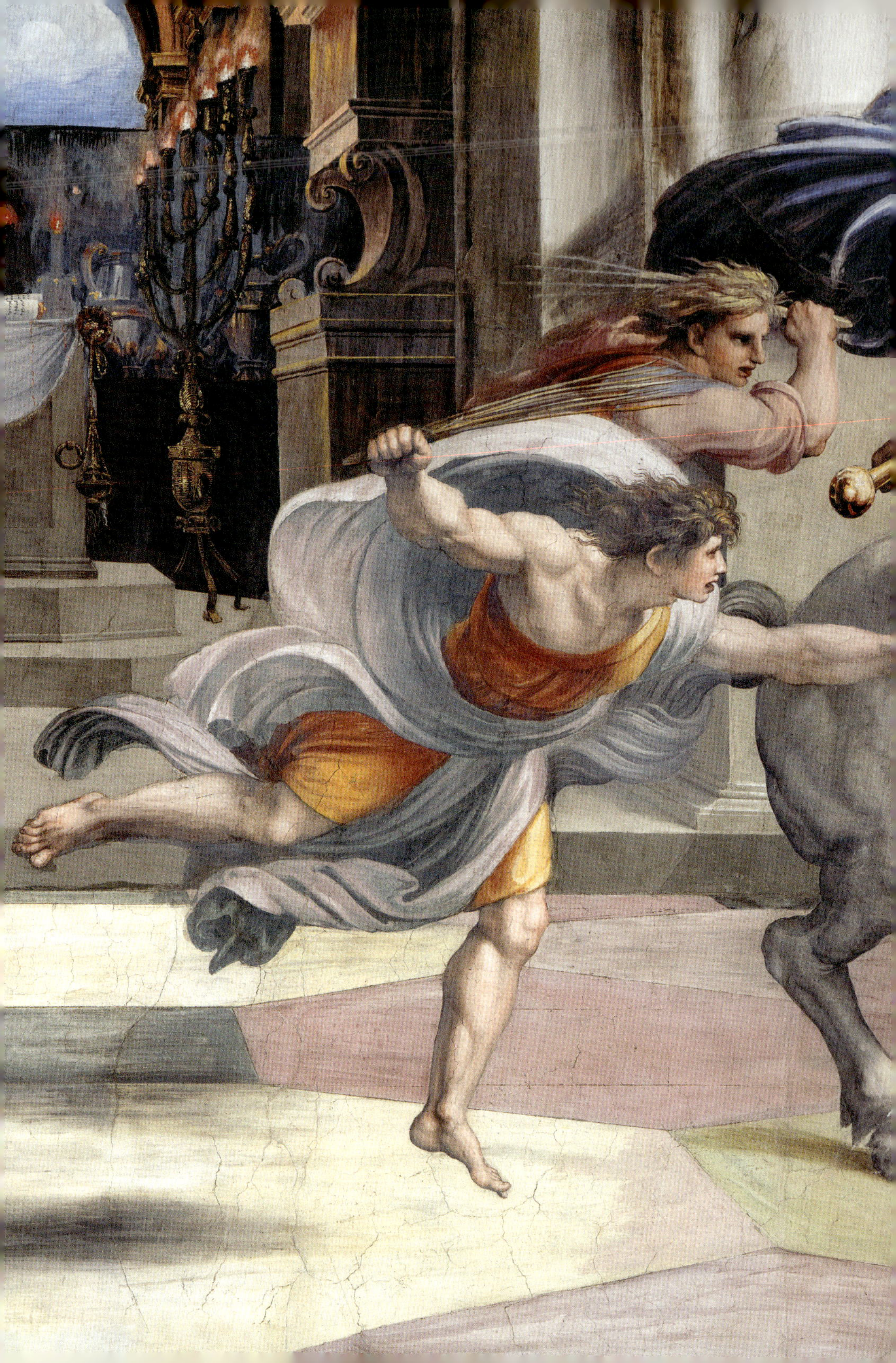

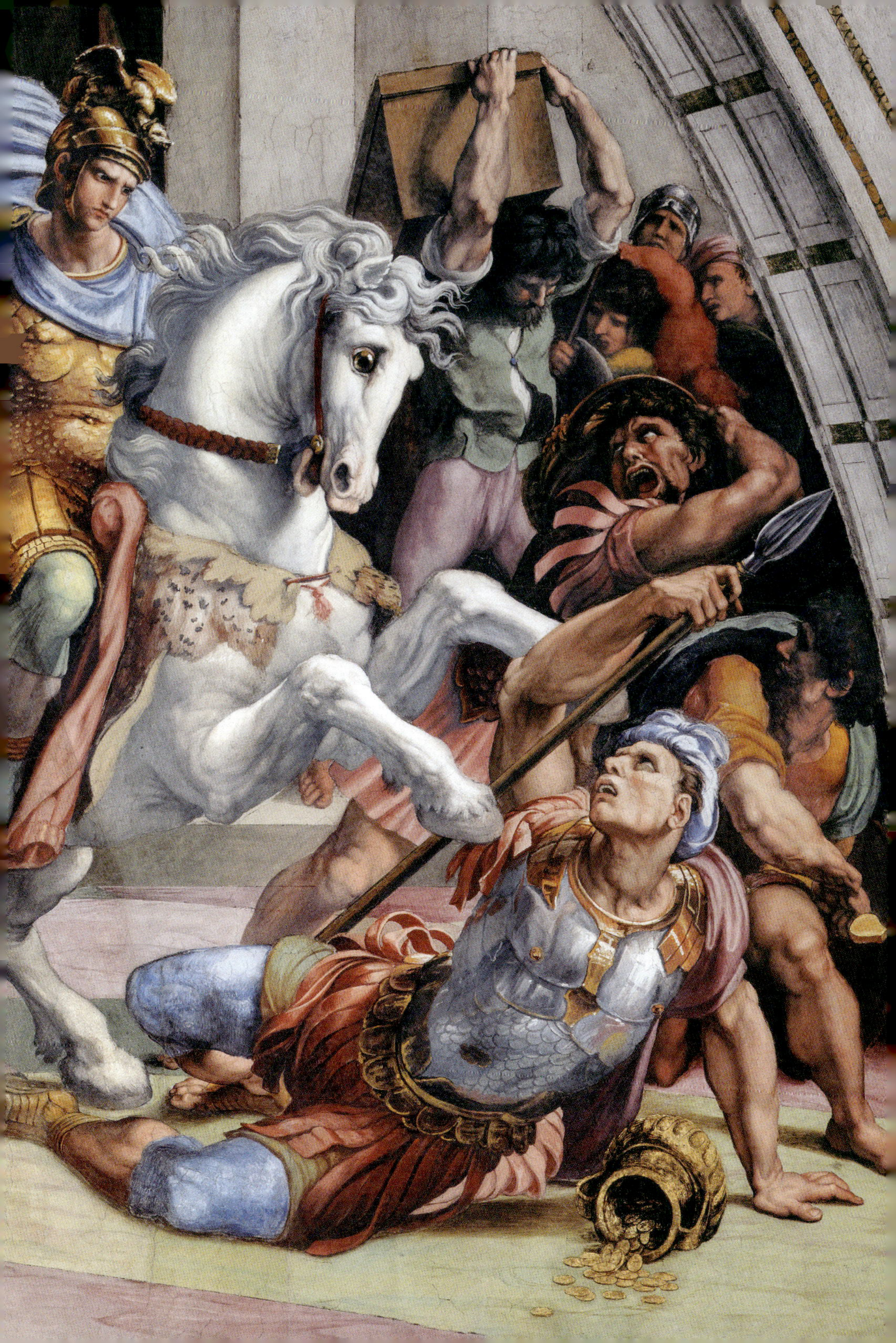

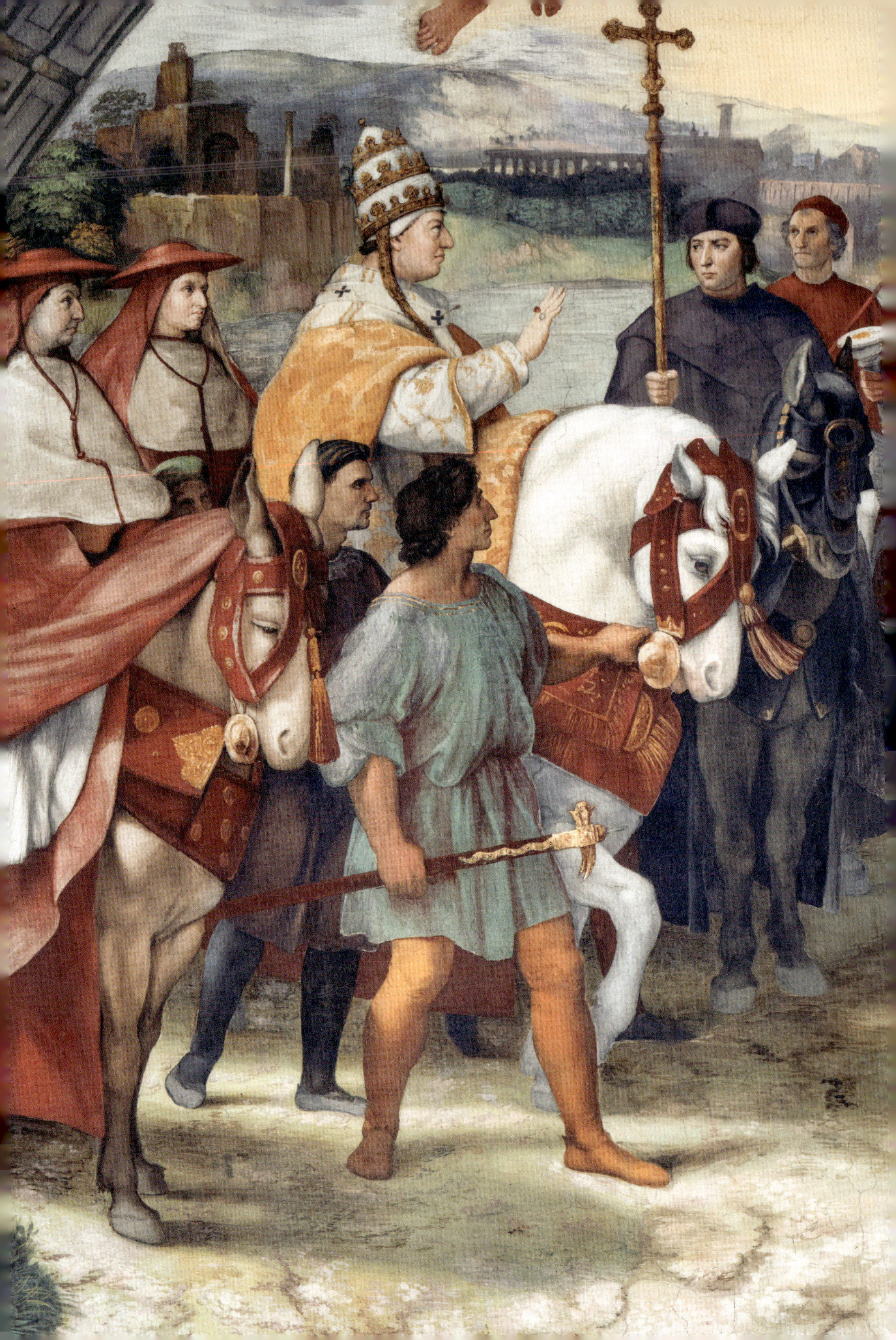

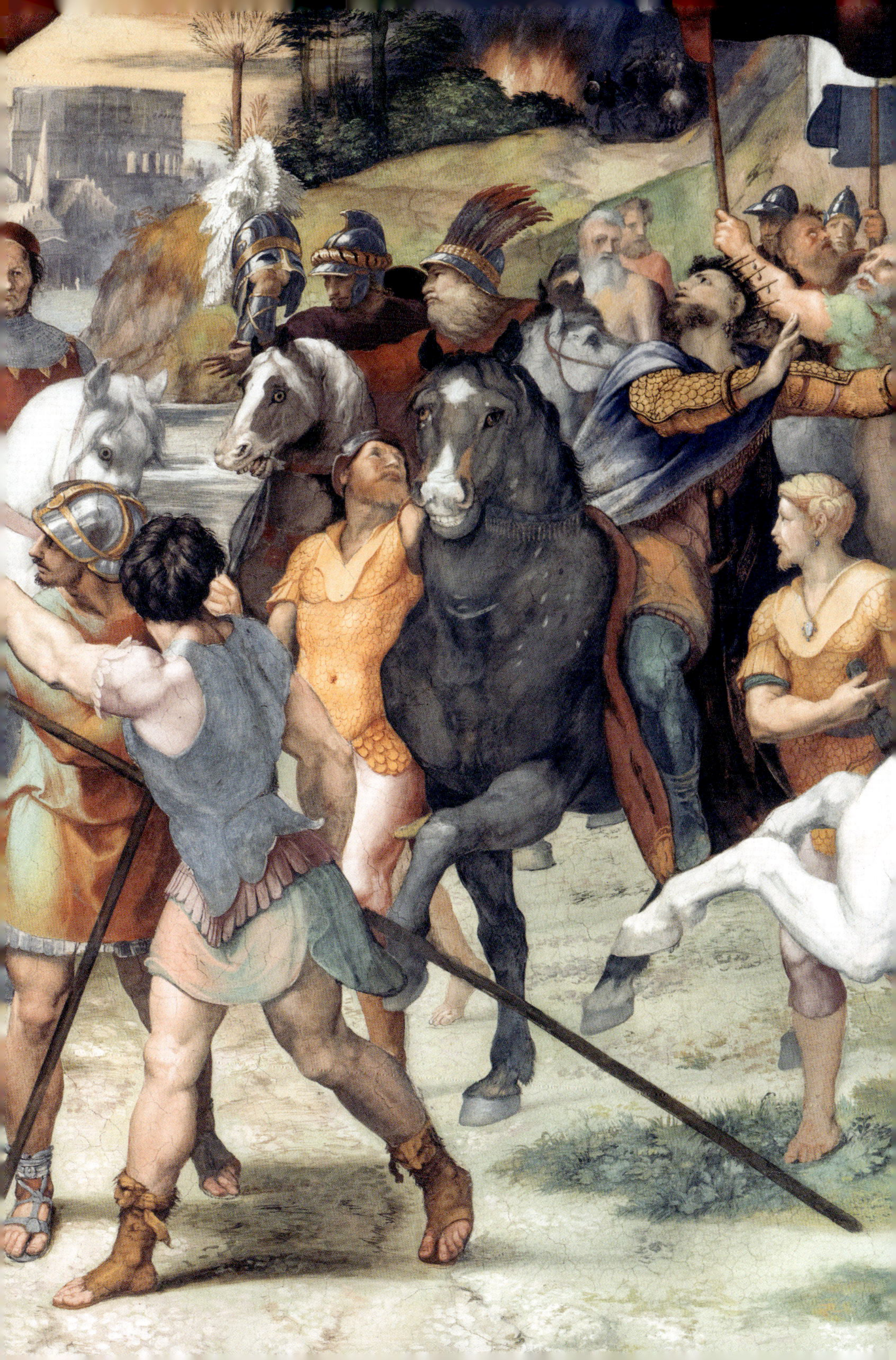

Page 196

The Expulsion of Heliodorus, 1511/12
Fresco, height 4.53 m (178 ⅓ in), width of base: 8.08 m (318 ⅛ in)
Vatican City, Musei Vaticani, Stanza d'Eliodoro
(Detail pages 200/201)

The Liberation of Saint Peter, *c.* 1512/13
Fresco, width of base 7.15 m (281 ½ in)
Vatican City, Musei Vaticani, Stanza d'Eliodoro
(Detail page 178)

Page 197

Leo I and Attila, *c.* 1513/14
Fresco, height 4.65 m (183 ⅛ in), width of base: 8.10 m (318 ⅞ in)
Vatican City, Musei Vaticani, Stanza d'Eliodoro
(Detail pages 202/203)

The Mass at Bolsena, 1511/12
Fresco, width of base 7.12 m (280 ⅓ in)
Vatican City, Musei Vaticani, Stanza d'Eliodoro
(Detail page 205)

Pages 198/199

Ceiling frescoes with the representations
Moses before the Burning Bush,
Jacob's Ladder, God Appears to Noah,
The Sacrifice of Abraham, 1513/14
Frescoes
Vatican City, Musei Vaticani, Stanza d'Eliodoro

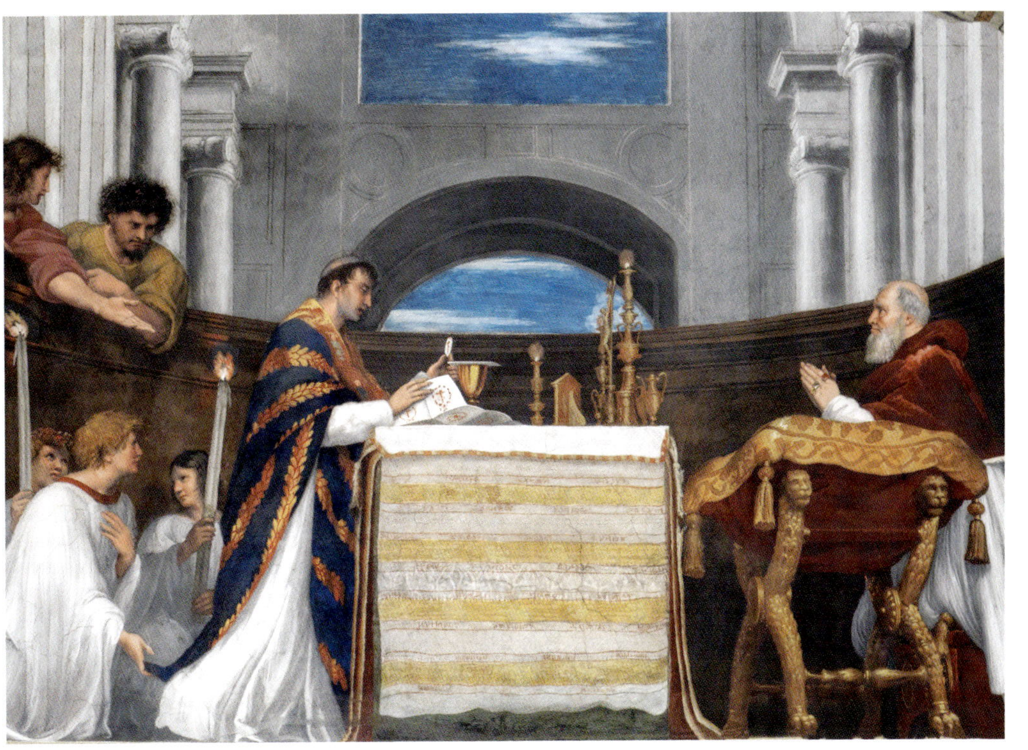

Detail from **The Mass at Bolsena**, 1511/12
(see ill. p. 197)

IV.

The Grand Style: Historical and biblical cycles in the Stanze and Sistine Chapel under Leo X

1514–1515/17

Michael Rohlmann

"He has invariably accomplished that which others wished in vain to accomplish..."

JOHANN WOLFGANG VON GOETHE, 1816

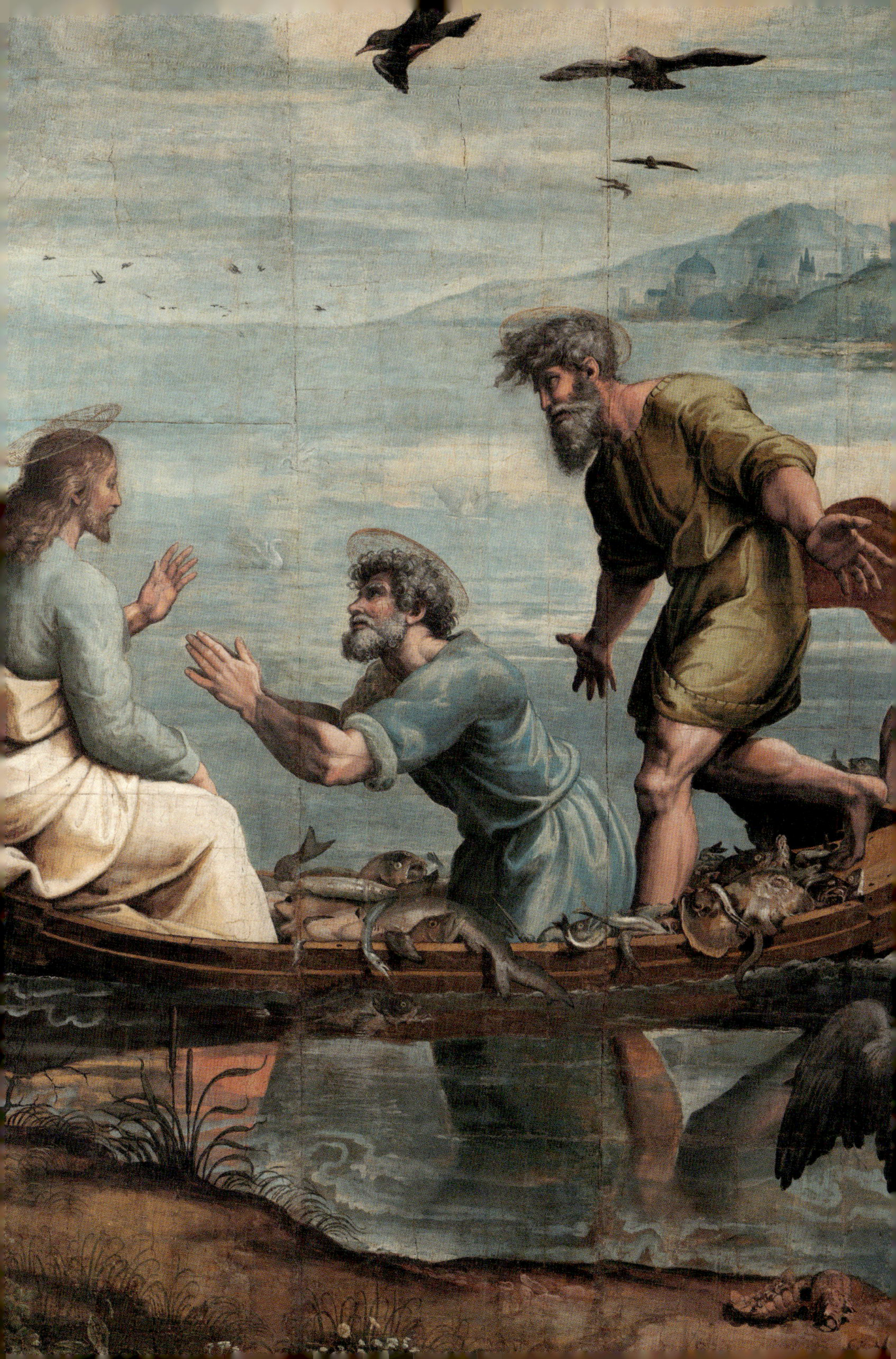

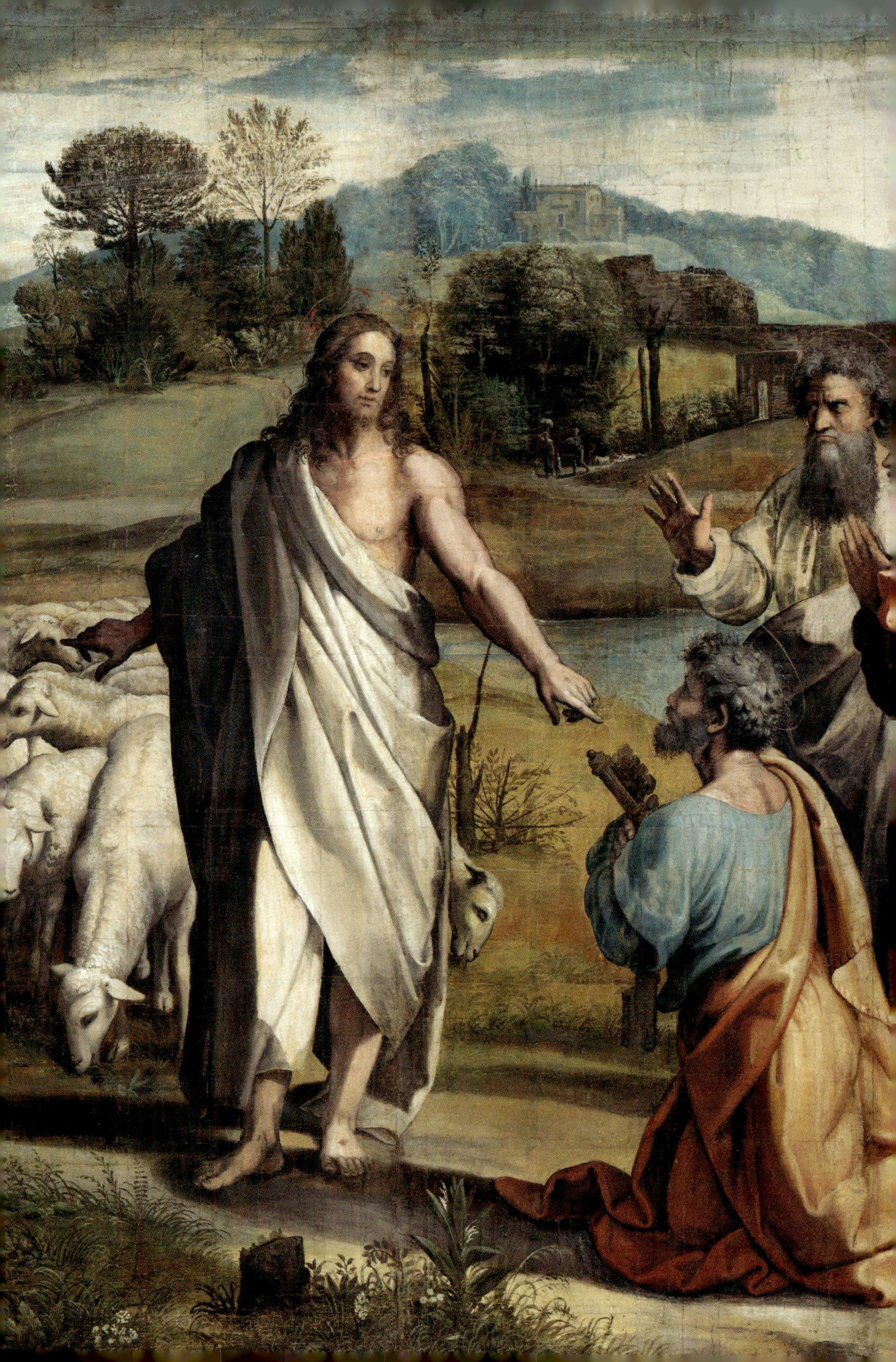

While Raphael was painting in the Stanza della Segnatura, Michelangelo was frescoing the ceiling of the Sistine Chapel (1508–1512). The force and inner greatness of the monumental prophets and sibyls, the differentiation and heightened characteristics of these spiritual heroes and heroines, the beauty of the *ignudi* posing above them, and the power of the Creation story told in the space between them, must have fascinated the Urbino artist. He had access to the work in progress even before it was officially unveiled. Vasari reports that Bramante, who had the keys to the chapel, gave him a secret viewing. With work still ongoing in the Stanza della Segnatura, Raphael reacted to what he saw in individual figures such as the two poets seated in expansive poses beside the *Parnassus* window (p. 184 b.; Cat. F3.1k), the three monumental Virtues on the *Justice* wall (185 b.; Cat. F3.1s), and the overtly muscular figure of the thinker belatedly inserted into the *School of Athens* (p. 184 t.; Cat. F3.1j). This competition continues in the frescoes of the Stanza d'Eliodoro, where Raphael seeks to rival Michelangelo's Genesis scenes. In the pair of flying angels and the prone Heliodorus in the *Expulsion of Heliodorus* (p. 196 t.; Cat. F3.2a) he tried to surpass Michelangelo's *Creation of Adam* in terms of movement and drama. In the painting that Raphael then carried out on the ceiling of the same Stanza, these references to the Sistine ceiling became programmatic. Soon after the start of his pontificate, Leo X had four scenes inserted into Julius II's existing decorative scheme (pp. 198/199). Painted to look as if a textile canopy was suspended across the ceiling, each scene shows an episode from the Old Testament in which a patriarch is promised divine assistance and protection by a celestial apparition. The themes refer in each case to the wall paintings commissioned by Julius II below: where these offer four examples of miraculous divine aid being provided to the heads of the Church, the scenes overhead show God's intervention and support for four worthy leaders from much earlier epochs. In the style of Michelangelo's ceiling frescoes, powerful figures dominate austere settings. Raphael goes even further, however: picture by picture, he varies the great aerial figures of God in the opening four scenes from Genesis in Michelangelo's Sistine Chapel. Thus the athlete reaching upwards in the *Creation of the Sun, Moon and Plants* is found in the *Sacrifice of Abraham* (Cat. F3.2q); the bearded figure (p. 289) positioning the sun and moon appears before Moses in the flames of the Burning Bush (Cat. F3.2n); the Creator advancing in foreshortened view over the sea raises his arms above the dreaming Jacob (Cat. F3.2o); and lastly the Father (pp. 264/265) creating Adam

Page 207
Detail from **The Miraculous Draught of Fishes and Christ's Charge to Peter**, 1515/16
(see ill. pp. 244/245)

Detail from **"Feed My Sheep"**, 1515/16
(see ill. pp. 246/247)

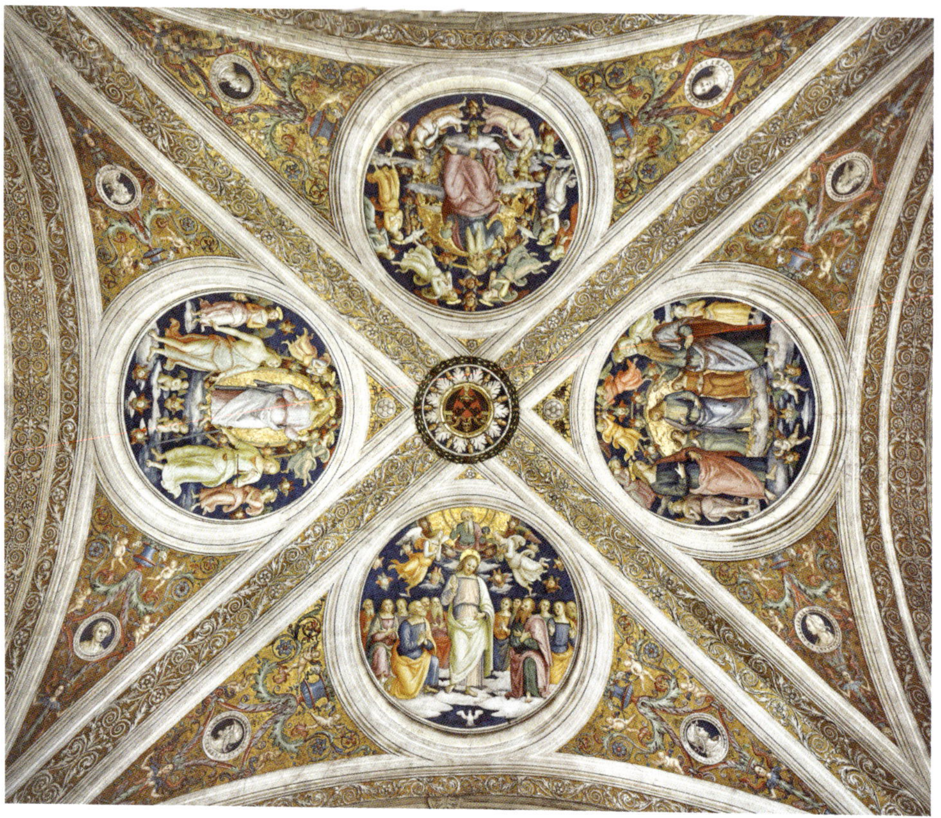

with outstretched arm flies in Raphael's fresco towards Noah (Cat. F3.2p). It seems as if the painted God the Creator, who in the Sistine Chapel acts solely over the ceremonial area reserved for the Pope, cardinals and Curia, was also intended to watch over the same public as it pursued papal politics in the Stanze.

In Raphael's large wall frescoes for the Stanza dell'Incendio (pp. 230–241; Cat. F3.3), created for Leo X between 1514 and 1517 below the ceiling paintings by Perugino, the political statements are couched in markedly more personalised terms of the Medici pope and

Pietro Perugino, **Ceiling fresco in the Stanza dell'Incendio**, 1508
Vatican City, Musei Vaticani, Stanza dell'Incendio

Ambrogio Brambilla after Lorenzo Vaccari, **Maiestas Pontificiae. View of a Capella Papalis Mass in the Sistine Chapel**, 1582 (1st state by Vaccari, 1578)
Copperplate engraving, 54.4 × 39.6 cm (21 3/8 × 15 5/8 in)
London, British Museum, Department of Prints and Drawings

his family. Raphael had already included a portrait of Giovanni de' Medici in the Segnatura fresco *Gregory IX Affirms the Decretals* (Cat. F3.1s): as throne assistant, the Cardinal stands in the worthiest position to the right of Pope Gregory, alias Julius II, as if already prepared to succeed him. In *Leo I and Attila* (p. 197 t.; Cat. F3.2g) in the Stanza d'Eliodoro, Leo X then replaces the originally planned Julius II in the role of Leo I and thus also becomes the Della Rovere's successor in the genesis of the picture. This role play as Pope Leo became a core strand running through the Stanza dell'Incendio, where the portrait of Leo X can be found in all four wall fields as his historical namesake: twice as Leo III (*c.* 750–816; in office 795–816) and twice as Leo IV (*c.* 790–855; in office 847–855). In Rome Pope Leo III was accused of having committed crimes. In the year 800, under the protection of Charlemagne (747/48–814; emperor from 800), he exonerated himself of these charges by taking an oath of purgation in St Peter's Basilica and thus affirmed his innocence. No one might judge the Pope (*Leo III's Oath of Purgation*, Cat. F3.3a). On Christmas Day Leo III proceeded to crown Charlemagne emperor. Secular power was subordinate to the Pope and obliged to pay tribute and provide help and protection (*Leo III Crowns Charlemagne*, Cat. F3.3f). In 847 a devastating fire broke out in the Borgo district near St Peter's in Rome. Pope Leo IV was able, through his act of blessing, to end the fire and with it the desperate plight of the populace (*Fire in the Borgo*, Cat. F3.3l). In 849 the threat loomed of an attack by marauding Saracens. In a naval battle off the port of Ostia, at the mouth of the Tiber, the papal troops defeated the invaders and Pope Leo IV thus overthrew the infidel (*Naval Victory of Leo IV at Ostia*, Cat. F3.3m). The frescoes thus contain a clear political content: they lend visual expression to ambitions and claims to power which – as Raphael scholarship has regularly shown – have a direct relevance for the pontificate of the Medici pope.

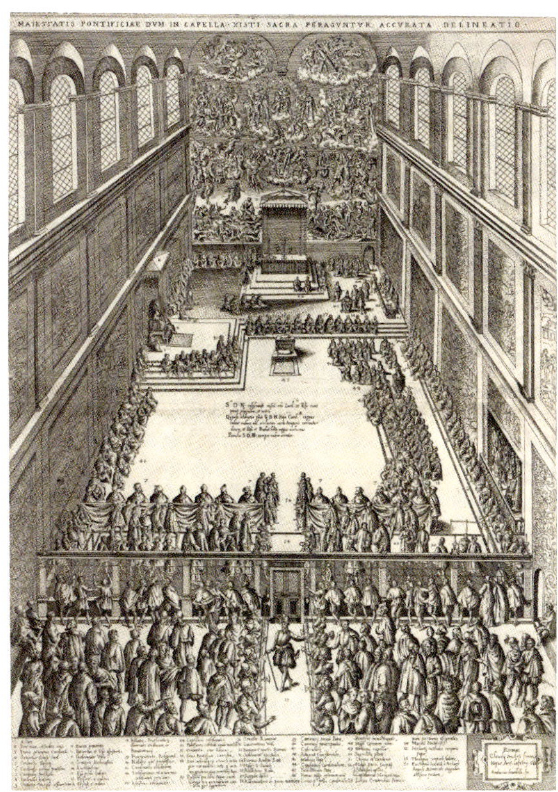

The themes of the four wall frescoes not only had to possess an updatable political significance for Leo X, however. They also had to fit into an intellectually complex, multi-layered network of existing frescoes. As in all the rooms, the wall and ceiling pictures were intended to complement or annotate each other in terms of content. It was furthermore necessary to take into account the symmetries planned between the two outer rooms, according to which the exercise of papal authority was to be illustrated via contrasting examples. In other words, Raphael's new frescoes in the Stanza dell'Incendio had to be thematically related to their respective ceiling paintings by Perugino, and at the same time correspond with their mural counterparts in the Stanza d'Eliodoro. Whereas Perugino had frescoed four celestial apparitions of God on the ceiling of the Stanza dell'Incendio (p. 210), in the case of Raphael on the walls of the Stanza d'Eliodoro it was four examples of divine assistance coming to the miraculous aid of Church leaders throughout history. Raphael combined both in new wall frescoes into a unique systematic programme.

Let us look more closely at the astonishingly tight relationships woven between the pictures in the example of *Leo III's Oath of Purgation* (p. 230 t.; Cat. F3.3a) in terms of the historical date of the earliest of the episodes represented on the walls of the Stanza dell'Incendio. In the fresco on the north side of the room, Leo III frees himself from calumnies and threats by taking the oath, while his soldiers stand guard on either side of the window opening. Here the Pope is no longer dependent on a divine miracle of the kind that is happening to Peter on the corresponding north wall of the Stanza d'Eliodoro. There an angel frees the Pope and leads him out of prison past enemy soldiers (p. 178; Cat. F3.2b). The two scenes are connected by the theme of the Pope's personal freedom and security, and the protection of the head of the Church against accusations and persecution. Above the *Oath of Purgation*, Perugino shows how Christ withstands the temptations of the devil and is then served by angels. If resistance to evil and freedom from sin make reference to the *Oath of Purgation*, the ministering of angels to Christ evidently takes up the *Liberation of Saint Peter* in the other Stanza. There, similar links exist between the *Liberation of Saint Peter* and the ceiling picture of *Jacob's Dream* overhead, in which God appears in a burst of dazzling light, from where angels ascend and descend a ladder to the sleeping Jacob (Cat. F3.20). Jacob has propped his head on a rock. He subsequently consecrates this stone as an altar and declares the place a house of God. This pictorial element of altar and house of God, however, finds its point of reference not in the *Liberation of Saint Peter* but only in the altar in the *Oath of Purgation* in the Stanza dell'Incendio.

Detail from **The Healing of the Lame Man**, 1515/16

(see ill. pp. 248/249)

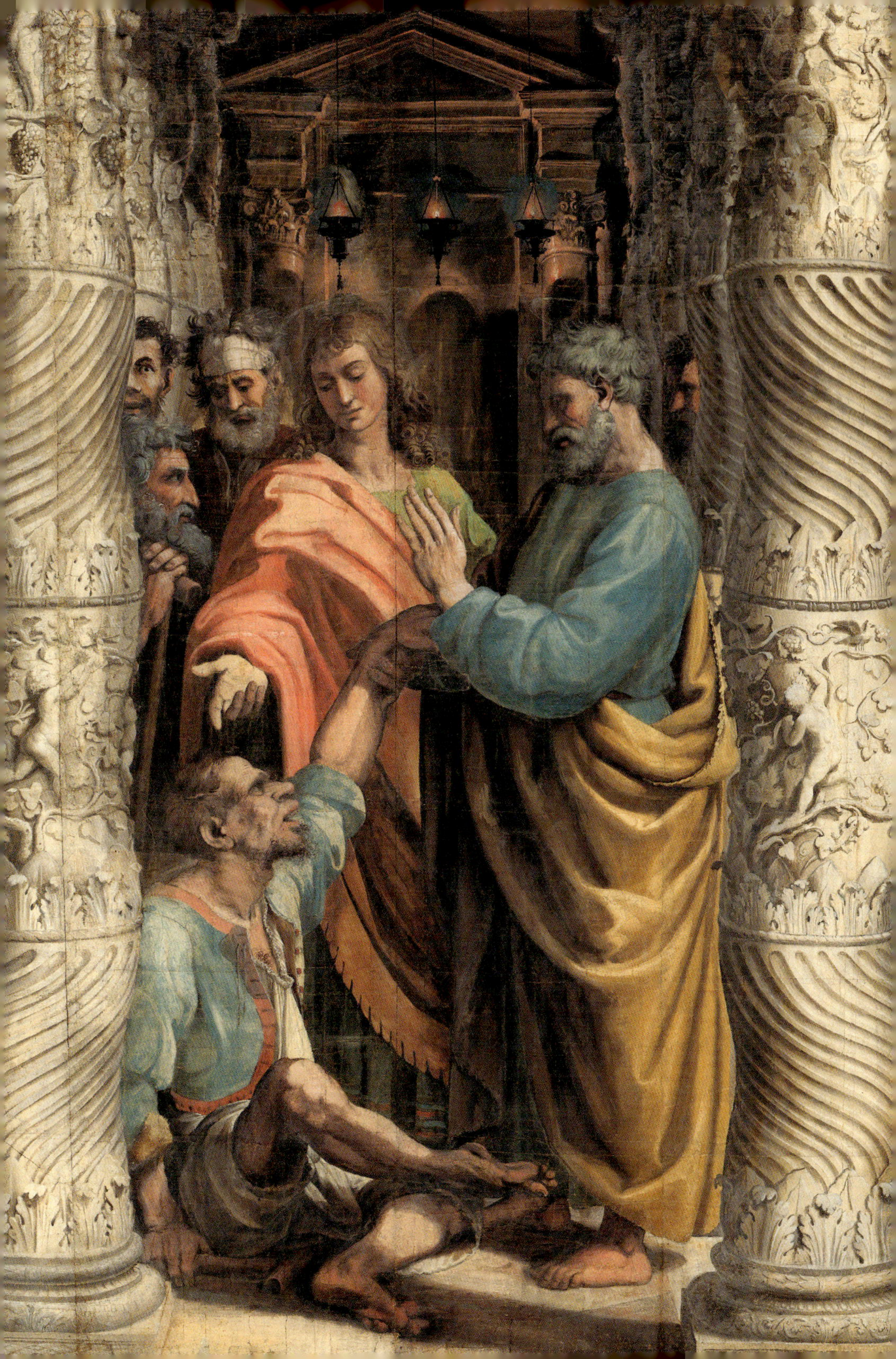

The other ceiling paintings in the Stanza d'Eliodoro (pp. 198/199) also possess a double reference system of this kind and establish links for the viewer between the new Stanza dell'Incendio frescoes and the existing decoration of the Stanza d'Eliodoro. In *Moses before the Burning Bush*, Moses – who has removed his shoes because he is standing on holy ground – is dazzled by the fiery vision of God's majesty (Cat. F3.2n). In the fresco on the wall below, Heliodorus, as a thief, has violated the sanctity of the Jewish Temple and been punished for it (Cat. F3.2a). On the symmetrically corresponding wall in the Stanza dell'Incendio, no such attempt at robbery is being made during the Papal Mass being conducted on the consecrated ground of the Christian house of God. On the contrary, treasures are being carried in as gifts. Charlemagne humbly approaches Leo III, who rewards him with the imperial crown (p. 230 b.; Cat. F3.3f). The solemnity of the Temple of Jerusalem is surpassed by the magnificence of the scene in St Peter's Basilica: in Rome, the seven candles on the altar burn in golden candlesticks. The church ceremony provides the setting for a sumptuous display of the majesty of the Pope, the so-called *maiestas papalis*, whose spectacular visibility is reminiscent of the dazzling appearance of God before Moses. In the *Sacrifice of Abraham* (Cat. F3.2q) on the Stanza d'Eliodoro ceiling, the young Isaac escapes death and the sacrificial fire. Abraham thereby proves himself at the altar to be obedient to God's will. The priest in the *Mass at Bolsena* (Cat. F3.2h) on the wall below had doubted what took place at the altar. The supplications addressed towards the priest by the people, including mothers with their children, is repeated in the corresponding Stanze dell'Incendio fresco of the *Fire in the Borgo* (p. 231 t.; Cat. F3.3l). Here a number of naked children are saved from the oncoming flames – just as Isaac was saved from death and sacrificial fire. Finally, in the fourth field on the Stanza d'Eliodoro ceiling, Noah gives thanks to God for having spared him from the devastating Flood (Cat. F3.2p). This alludes at the same time to the final halting of the "deluge of Huns" in *Leo I and Attila* (Cat. F3.2g), as well as to Leo IV's naval victory over the Saracens at Ostia (p. 231 b.; Cat. F3.3m). Just as Noah appears in front of the doorway to the safe ark, lifting his gaze to God in prayer, so Leo IV is to be seen in the same pose in front of the gates of Ostia's mighty papal fortress.

Of course, this pictorial network with its many cross-references is not visible to the same extent in all parts of the Stanze. Again and again, however, correspondences between motifs clearly refer us to the connections between their content. The aim was not just to present a series of examples from history, but to reveal a structure underlying them: God had planned this history in a meaningful and rigorous manner. Every current event in papal politics, every action by the power of the keys was to be integrated into a pattern pre-determined by law – an enforced higher order that remained constant even as the popes changed.

Simply by studying the series of Raphael's four large Leo frescoes on the walls of the Stanza dell'Incendio alone, the viewer can recognise in these, too, a cycle linking together the different historical episodes they show. Raphael here demonstrates the breadth of his stylistic ability and deploys widely differing means of narration – unlike Michelangelo in the heroic style of his Sistine ceiling, always animated and inspiring awe; Raphael consistently adapts his style to suit the pictorial theme in question. A continuous story unfolds. It starts with a seemingly frozen, solemnly subdued ceremony in the area immediately around the altar of an ideal St Peter's church. In a symmetrical, statically calm composition, the Pope avows his innocence (p. 230 t.; *Leo III's Oath of Purgation*, Cat. F3.3a). He is thereby able to ward off a threat coming from within the clergy and safeguard his position as Pope. In the next narrative step, the pictorial space inside St Peter's gains width and depth. Clerics and princes, clad in a variety of sumptuous fabrics and gleaming armour, are gathered in rows at different heights and angles in the choir area. The abundance, concentration and colourfulness of the church assembly increase. The solemn ceremony of the *Coronation of Charlemagne* (p. 230 b.; Cat. F3.3f) unfolds with much animation. The concord of the princes and the sovereignty of the Pope are here invoked as the Christian world order. Energetic muscled figures bearing gifts are already advancing into the ceremonial scene from the left-hand foreground.

In the *Fire in the Borgo* (p. 231 t.; Cat. F3.3l), the scene takes place in the square in front of St Peter's. The outdoor setting is furnished in the foreground with antique ruins and in the background with the medieval St Peter's Basilica and an idealised Renaissance papal palace. The architecture resembles a stage set and assigns different groups to their places within the picture. The only papal ceremonial still visible is distant and small. The foreground, by contrast, is dominated by anatomical art and dramatic storytelling – the art of the *historia*. While the fire continues to rage on the left, on the right it is already being extinguished. The harried populace turns imploringly to the Pope, who appears on the benediction loggia in the distant background and pronounces his saving blessing in front of the processional cross. After the cleansing of the institution of the Church and the establishment of a Christian system of government, the Pope can now bestow deliverance and salvation upon the people by means of the power of the keys. In the foreground, the people shown fleeing, beseeching, and putting out the fire are individually characterised and at the same time join together to form groups, each creating one small strand of the narrative. The figures do not merge into a single mass, but retain their individuality, with each one playing a meaningful and necessary role in the action as a whole. Raphael has here staged a dramatic piece of theatre that has rightly been admired and analysed many times.

Mantegna's engraving *The Entombment of Christ*, which Raphael had already consulted for the design of his *Baglioni Altarpiece* (Cat. P35), once again provides a source of

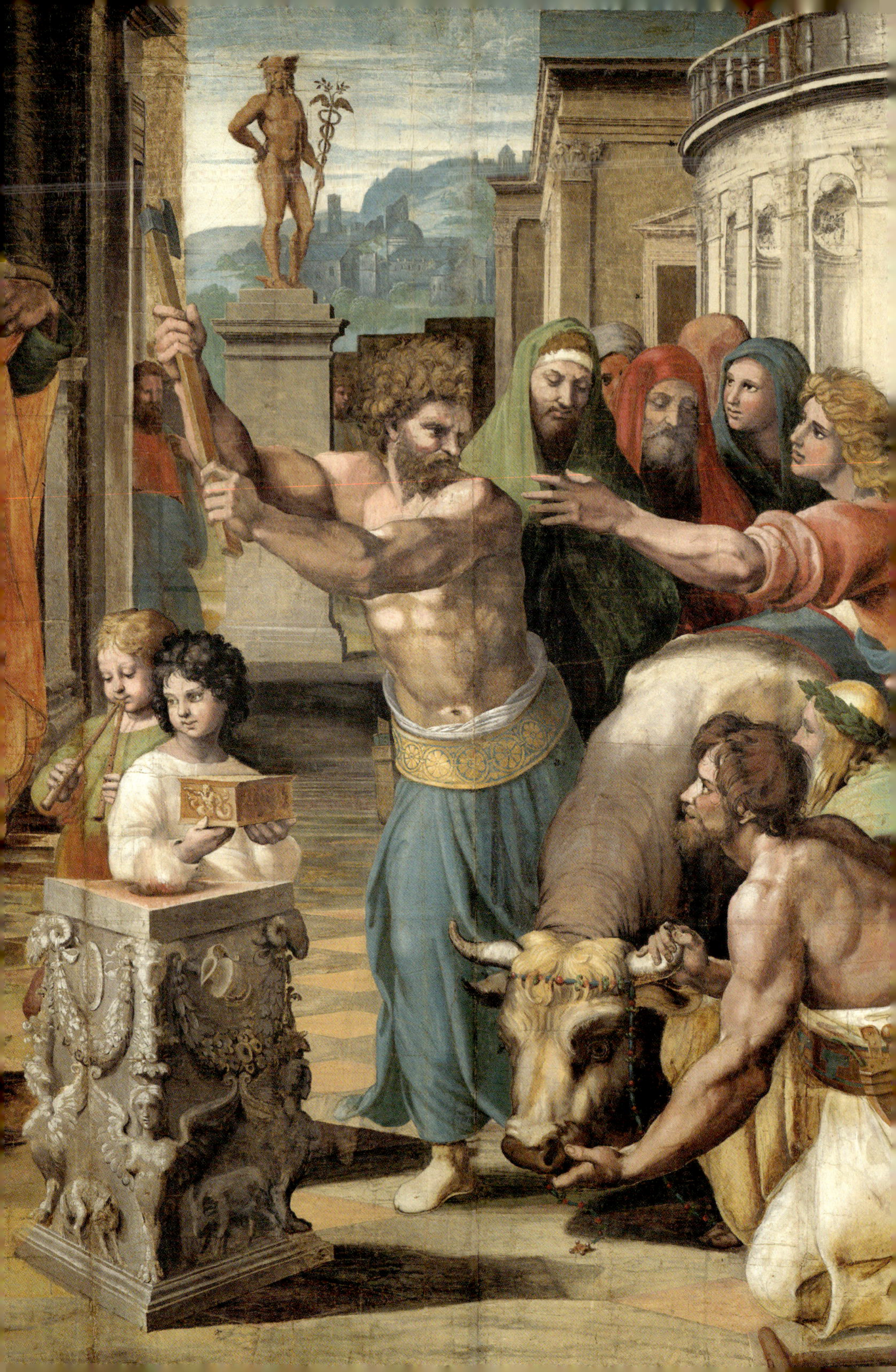

inspiration, this time for the sequence of the four foreground motifs: on the left, against a background seen at an angle, the carrying of the body, then the man looking over his shoulder to the right – in mid-stride in Mantegna, dangling in Raphael. Next the women crouching down with the body lying across their lap, and above them the recession into the depths of the picture towards the distant symbol of salvation in the shape of the cross. The sequence concludes on the right with the standing figure angled towards the centre and crying out. It is true that no figure is cited exactly; Raphael's figures in their dramatic poses are borrowed more closely from Michelangelo's Sistine ceiling and compete above all with *The Flood* and *The Sacrifice of Noah*.

Raphael thereby draws inspiration not only from a painter but also from a poet: the fleeing family on the left, in which an old man is carried by his son, invites comparison with Virgil's word painting of the flight of Aeneas from burning Troy. Raphael gives the wife the profile head of Michelangelo's Cumaean Sibyl (Forlani Tempesti, in: Florence 1984c), the seer who, in Virgil, later guides Aeneas through the underworld. In Raphael's fresco, the prophetic gaze that she directs upon the scene seems to refer us to a deeper dimension of meaning lying beneath the events depicted. In the final fresco in the Stanza, depicting Leo IV's naval victory, *The Battle of Ostia* (p. 231 b.; Cat. F3.3m), the Michelangelesque treatment of the human anatomy is heightened to a wild melee of muscular figures in violent movement (cf. Michelangelo's *The Fall* and *The Brazen Serpent*), and then finds a calming end in the densely clustered papal group on the left. In the *Battle of Ostia*, the action has moved away from Rome and takes place at the mouth of the Tiber. It was here, long ago, that Aeneas had landed in Italy and where the flight begun in the burning Troy had found its goal and happy ending. But the fate of the papacy elevates itself above the lot of the Trojans: just as Rome, unlike Troy, was not destroyed in the Borgo fire, so the land at the mouth of the Tiber no longer falls victim to the invaders from across the sea. After his achievements within Christianity, shown in the *Fire in the Borgo*, the Pope can protect its beneficial order from outside threats. Where secular powers fight under the banner of the Pope, the unbelievers can be defeated and forced to submit to the followers of Christ.

In four pictures, the viewer undertakes an imaginary journey that leads them from the high altar and the choir of St Peter's into the streets of Rome in front of its façade, and out into the countryside to the endless expanse of the sea. Raphael's style thereby metamorphoses from two-dimensional rigidity, via palpable and sumptuous materiality, to the most dramatic rendering of the human body and the greatest relief effect.

Detail from **The Sacrifice at Lystra**, 1515/16
(see ill. pp. 254/255)

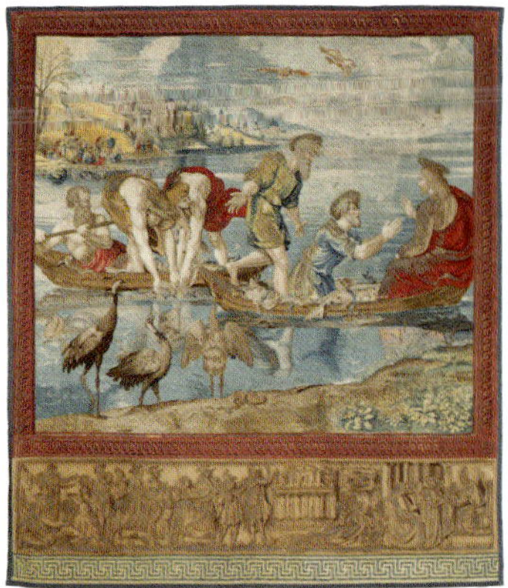

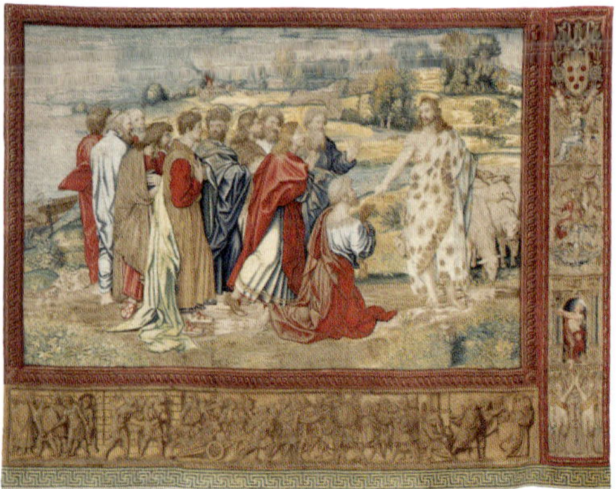

Step by step, the painter-dramatist supplants the master of ceremonies as arranger of the action. In his move from one setting, style of representation and type of theme to the next, Raphael demonstratively emphasises his artistry. With the breadth and wealth of his skill, he seeks to assert himself as a painter in the face of the dominance of Michelangelo's *terribilità*.

The plinth zone in the Stanza della Segnatura was formerly clad in exquisite intarsia. These marvels of wood inlay were commenced under Julius II by Fra Giovanni da Verona (*c.* 1457–1525), the greatest intarsia artist of the day. In the Stanza dell'Incendio, as in the Stanza d'Eliodoro, however, Raphael introduced a fictive stone plinth with *trompe l'œil* sculptural decoration below the large history paintings. The caryatid figures in the base zone in the Stanza d'Eliodoro personify aspects of an ideal papal rule (Cat. F3.2r). In the Stanza dell'Incendio, a series of a commemorative seated statues of exemplary rulers (Cat. F3.3n–s) leads from Emperor Constantine (270/88–337) to the Spanish sovereign Ferdinand the Catholic (1452–1516). Inscriptions allude to the services each rendered to the Pope. This triple layering of a painted plinth with fictive stone figures, followed by main paintings of colourful historical scenes and, at the very top, celestial apparitions in part connected to the scene below, was one that Raphael had already prepared in the predella, main panel and lunette of his *Baglioni Altarpiece* (Cat. P35).

On the ceiling of the Stanza d'Eliodoro, and in part on the walls of the Stanza dell'Incendio, Raphael left the execution of his designs to a workshop built up by himself, in which he gathered talented young painters around him. This enabled Raphael to handle a constantly growing number of commissions. Concurrently with the frescoes in the Stanza dell'Incendio, Leo X commissioned him to design an even larger historical cycle. The Medici pope had decided to adorn the lower walls of the Sistine Chapel, in the area occupied by the Pope and Curia, with a lavish series of narrative tapestries

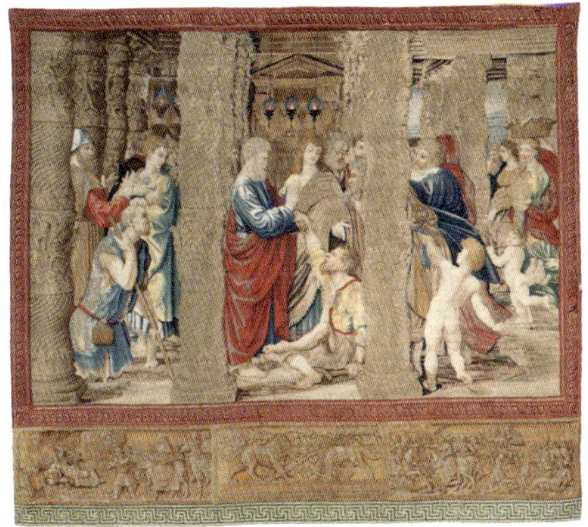

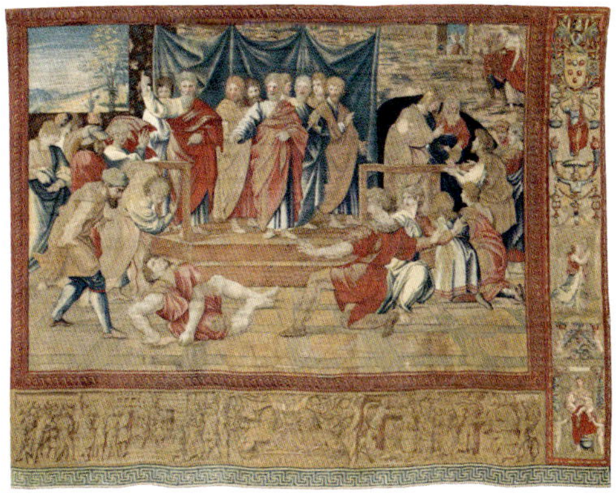

(pp. 242–259; Cat. T). The walls in this plinth zone had formerly been decorated with painted ornamental tapestries. The new textile representations were intended to introduce new Medici accents into the already fully frescoed space, enhance the splendour of papal ceremonies, and improve the acoustics for the choir. Raphael's painted cartoons of the individual scenes were translated into costly tapestries woven in gold, silver and silk thread by a specialist workshop in Brussels. They thereby had to take account of the fact that the design would be reversed in the process of weaving on the loom and hence that the final tapestries would appear as mirror images of the cartoon. For Raphael, the commission meant competing directly with Michelangelo's ceiling frescoes and with the wall cycles executed in 1481/82 by Perugino, Botticelli and others. Unlike in the Stanza dell'Incendio, Raphael opted for a consistently grand style with monumental figures, clear gestures and eloquent facial expressions on stages filled with large numbers of actors. The stately events are enlivened with countless details, to which the weavers added more of their own. The colourfulness of the older, fifteenth-century narrative fresco cycles running along the chapel's walls seems to coalesce, in Raphael's tapestries, with the dramatically heightened style of Michelangelo's ceiling scenes. For chapel visitors, the magnificence of its décor thereby continuously increased as their gaze descended from Michelangelo's ceiling frescoes far overhead to the quattrocento wall frescoes, with their more luminous colours and occasional areas of gilding, and finally to Raphael's tapestries shot with gold, hanging in close proximity. Appropriately, their respective visual content told the history of salvation in chronological order: from Michelangelo's world of the Creation, via episodes from the lives of Moses and Christ depicted in the wall frescoes, to Raphael's representations of the early apostles Peter and Paul – from above to below, from the distant, celestial realms of prehistory down, so it seemed, to the Roman Church's own present day.

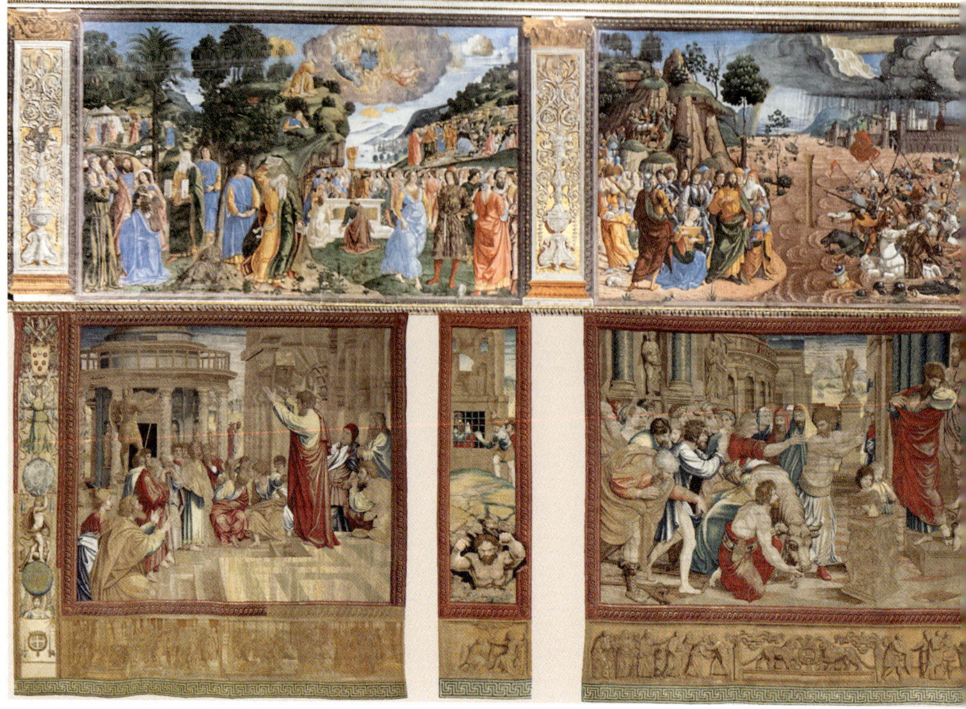

Raphael presents the lives of Saint Peter and Saint Paul in two series of cycles. Each began with a tapestry on the altar wall and from there continued along the longitudinal walls. The story of Peter unfolded on the right, that of Paul on the left. The central theme of each series is presented right at the start. The Peter cycle begins with *The Miraculous Draught of Fishes* (p. 218 l.; Cat. T1). The calling of the disciple is visualised via a series of figures as Peter stepping out of the secular boat of his earthly father into the boat of Christ. A continuous sequence of movement leads from left to right: next to the older helmsman, the first fisherman is bent low over the edge of the boat and is still focused entirely on drawing in the net. The fisherman bending down beside him has turned his head towards the right and appears more aware of the wider scene. The third figure has already stepped into the boat in front. His outspread arms and marvelling gaze show the moment of understanding. As if in consequence, Peter sinks to his knees and, with his hands clasped in prayer, leans towards Christ, who receives him. Raphael at the same time here tells the art history of his admired rival Michelangelo: the stooped fishermen in the

Reconstructed original sequence of the Pauline tapestries on the left-hand chapel wall (after White/Shearman 1958)

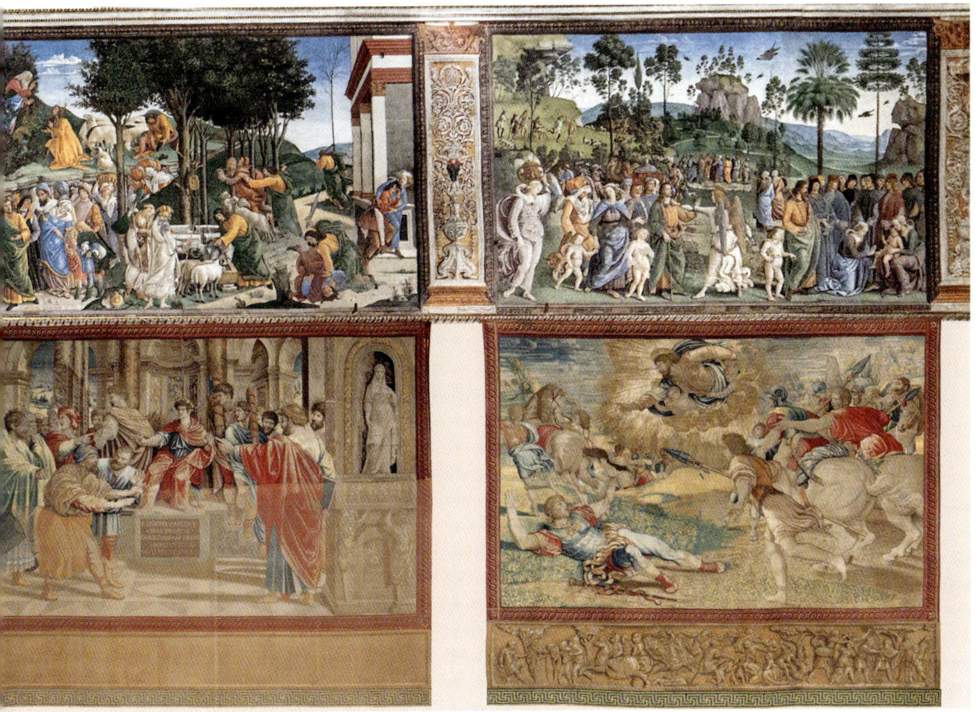

secular boat take up figures from Michelangelo's greatest secular commission, the *Battle of Cascina* in Florence (p. 74). Michelangelo had abandoned the latter project in order to enter the service of Pope Julius II, for whom he then frescoed the Sistine Ceiling as a new religious masterpiece. Raphael has consequently borrowed the way in which Peter leans towards Christ in the boat of the Church, and the way in which gestures and gazes meet against a backdrop of water and sky, from the fresco in the centre of Michelangelo's ceiling, the *Creation of Eve* (p. 228). There Eve symbolises Ecclesia, the institution of the Church, which was to orient itself entirely towards its head. It is wonderful to see how, in Raphael's composition, the colourful hilly real-world landscape on the left seems to weigh like a heavy earthly load on the stooping figures, how the land then transitions into water above Peter's upright figure, and finally how Peter is silhouetted freely against the foil of lake and sky, one flowing into the other, as he comes face to face with God.

Raphael alludes in a particular way to Christ's invitation to Peter to change from a fisherman to a fisher of men: the stooped fishermen seem to want to pull up with their hands not only the net, but also – in the illusion of the visual image – the reflection of their arms into the boat. The artist arrived at this idea, too, via Michelangelo's *Cascina* cartoon, in which the figures bending down want to help their colleagues still swimming back onto the bank; a pair of hands can be seen reaching out of the water in search of assistance.

The next tapestry, *"Feed My Sheep"* (p. 218 r.; Cat. T2), which follows on the longitudinal wall, expands upon Peter's task. The lake landscape continues, the boat appears to have landed, and the fishermen have got out and are gathered on the shore. It is true that this episode takes place much later in the biblical narrative, following another miraculous draught of fishes: the risen Christ stands before the apostles and charges Peter to "Feed my sheep" (John 21: 17). Raphael's art suggests a continuity of action, however, in order to reveal a structural connection between the two episodes. Christ's second charge to Peter necessarily builds on the first: fish must first of all be drawn up into the boat of the Church and thus a community established, and only then can the flock be guarded. Peter, as the first, the foremost, the humbly kneeling apostle, is given the task of leading the Church with his two keys. Both charges are successively fulfilled in the two following tapestries. Peter will thereby use his power of the keys first to bind and then to loosen. In front of the Jerusalem temple doors, he helps the lame man to stand up, healed, within the church nave formed by rows of columns (*The Healing of the Lame Man*; p. 219 l.; Cat. T3) – just as the fishermen had energetically heaved their catch on board. In the last tapestry of the series, the Church – as a congregation of the faithful, in the basic meaning of the Greek word *ecclesia* – is fittingly assembled in an ancient forum, where Peter is directing the work of the apostles: goods are received and distributed to the needy. The sinner Ananias, who defrauds this system, falls dead to the ground, punished by God and expelled from the Church (*The Death of Ananias*; p. 219 l.; Cat. T4). The faithful flock is protected and the Church is led.

Peter appears in all four scenes in visual dialogue with a pendant figure. Both change their pose continuously from tapestry to tapestry: first Peter bends forward as he kneels before the enthroned Christ (Cat. T1). Then he kneels upright before the standing Christ (Cat. T2). In the temple scene, Peter stands while the lame man sits before him (Cat. T3). Finally, the apostle is raised up on a podium, while Ananias is cast to the ground (Cat. T4). The viewer thus sees Peter undergo a step-by-step process of elevation, which continues with the orientation of his figure towards the right and thus in the direction in which the cycle is read. Insofar as he is turned to the right in all his actions, the hero drives the narrative onward. In the fourth and final tapestry, however,

The Stoning of Saint Stephen, 1515/19
Socle border: **Entry of Giovanni de' Medici into Florence after His Investiture in the Badia of Fiesole (10/3/1492)**. Tapestry, 450 × 370 cm (177 ⅛ × 145 ⅔ in)
Vatican City, Musei Vaticani, Pinacoteca

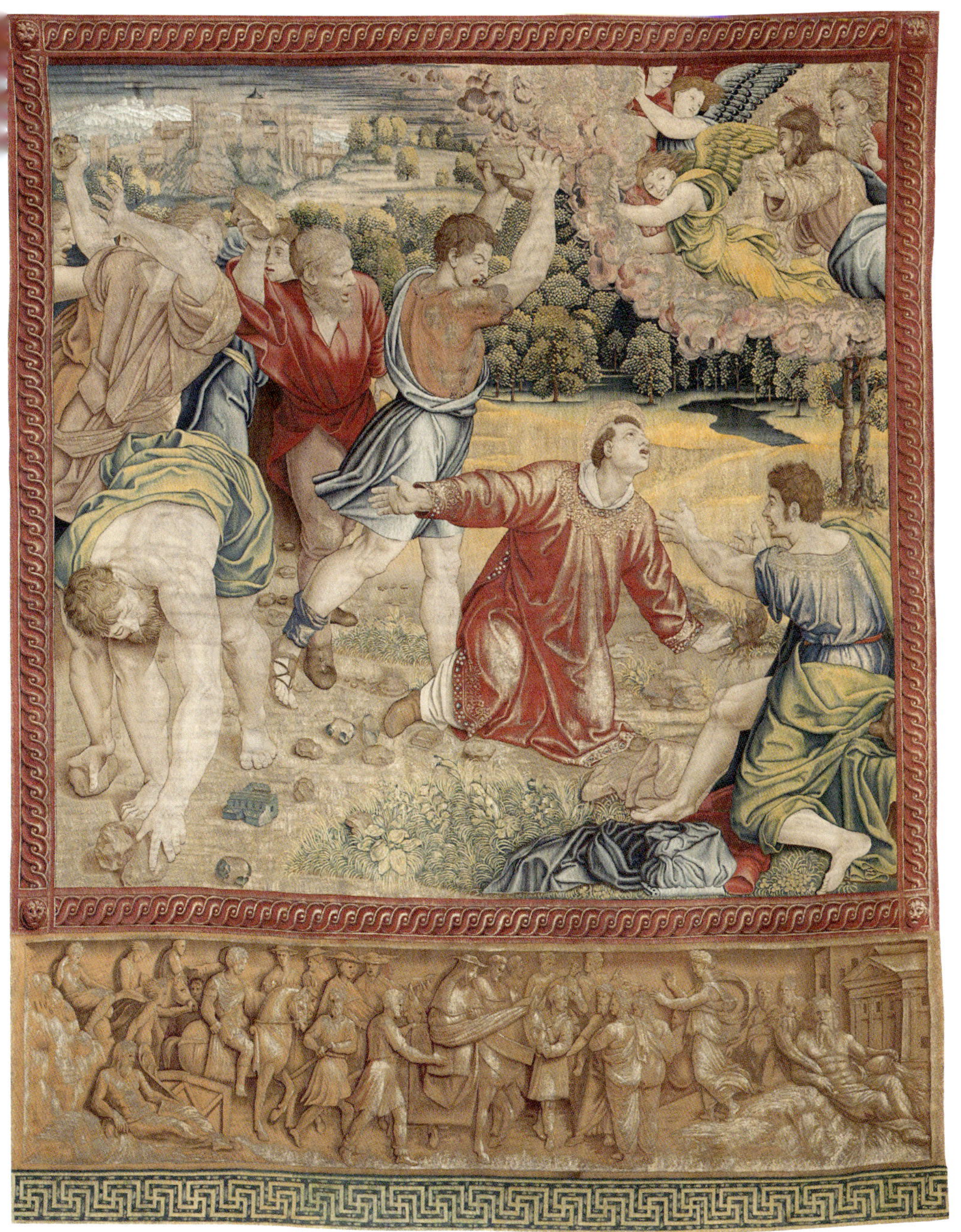

this movement towards the right ends and the narrative axis turns forward, towards our world. Peter faces us frontally, as if his administrative government of the gathering of the faithful extended into the viewer's present day. The course of the history of Peter's "rise" that has been unfolding towards the right thus comes to an end. Raphael clearly marks the conclusion of the series.

The continuous change in Peter's pose and angle recalls Raphael's staging of an incremental lowering of the protagonist in the frescoes of the Piccolomini Library (p. 30–32). A precedent lying even closer at hand, however, are the scenes from the life of Christ in the Sistine Chapel, beneath which the Peter tapestries were to hang. Let us examine the two protagonists in the centre of each fresco. In Perugino's *Baptism of Christ*, Jesus stands beside the Baptist and bends his head before him. In Botticelli's *Temptations of Christ*, the High Priest towers over the approaching servant. In Ghirlandaio's *Calling of the Apostles*, Christ stands before the now kneeling disciples. The ascent finally reaches its end and high point above the chancel screen and choir loft, where in the *Sermon on the Mount* by Cosimo Rosselli (1439–1507) Christ appears on a hill above his seated audience and thereby turns towards the space occupied by the viewer. Peter's development thus follows the example of Christ, who had appointed him as his successor on earth.

The *Peter* series is thus structured in a formally meaningful way and constitutes a self-contained whole. It portrays Peter in a single, continuous ascent. He is given a dual task by Christ and fulfils it in two steps: Peter must first build up the Church (catch fish) and then lead it as a shepherd (tend sheep). The miracle shown in *The Healing of the Lame Man* (Cat. T3) first of all brings the believers flocking together, while in *The Death of Ananias* (Cat. T4) the congregation of the Church is already fully established and the ecclesiastical distribution of alms – and by extension, salvation – can now be organised, and defended against disruption, within the institution of the Church.

A comparable rigour in terms of content and form characterises the Pauline tapestry cycle, too. It unfolds from right to left on the left-hand side of the chapel. The sequence starts beside the altar with *The Stoning of Saint Stephen* (p. 223; Cat. T5). Saul is seated in front of the first martyr as one of his persecutors, near garments discarded by some of the others. Raphael visualises the martyrdom of Stephen as a succession to the Passion of Christ, insofar as he borrows the pose of the kneeling Stephen from that of the fallen Christ in Dürer's *Christ Carrying the Cross* woodcut (p. 298). Both support themselves with one hand on the ground, and in both cases they are harried by a mob above left. It is true that Stephen looks up to the right, where the heavens have opened and Christ is visible at God's right hand. At the same time, the saint gestures with an outstretched arm towards his attackers. At the moment of death, Stephen asks the Son of God to forgive his tormentors and to show mercy. This representation of a plea during persecution is evidently intended to illustrate the papal motto of Leo X: *Ad Dominum cum tribularer clamavi, et exaudivit me* ("In my distress I cried unto the Lord, and he heard me"; Psalm 120: 1). How God hears Stephen's request, and how persecutors are gradually converted into believers, is the main theme of the Pauline series.

As if in response to the saint's intercession, Christ appears once again in the heavens in the very next tapestry, in order to overthrow and cast down one of the persecutors of the early Christians. The layout of *The Conversion of Saul* (p. 221 b. r.; Cat. T6) is a symmetrical mirror-image of *The Stoning of Saint Stephen*. The landscape and the massed group of muscular figures seem to continue from one tapestry leftwards into the next. In a visual contrapposto, the act of violence rebounds, as it were, onto the perpetrator. The persecution of Christians is stopped and Saul submits with open arms to God's command. In the adjacent tapestry on the left, *The Blinding of Elymas* (p. 221 b. l.; Cat. T7), a role reversal has taken place: Paul now does himself what Christ had done to him. In the throne room of the proconsul, Paul blinds the sorcerer Elymas, who had tried to discourage the Roman governor from converting to the Christian faith. The true preacher of God triumphs over the false one. In the next tapestry, *The Sacrifice at Lystra*, we see reactions to a miracle performed by Paul (p. 220 b. r.; Cat. T8). The apostle has healed a lame man, but the people – recognising his superior power – take him to be a god and want to make a sacrifice to him. Those present have not yet been converted. Raphael shows in this tapestry scene that, before understanding, there is misunderstanding. After the martyrdom *(Stoning of Stephen)*, the ending of persecution *(Conversion of Saul)*, the replacement of the false religious leader by the true messenger of God *(Blinding of Elymas)*, the seekers are now enlightened about what they must not do or believe: Paul is not a heathen god and hence they should not sacrifice to him. Before being taught the message of Christian salvation, the heathens must first learn that they must abandon their former religious practices of animal sacrifice and idolatry.

In *The Sacrifice at Lystra*, the goal of conversion has not yet been achieved and hence the narrative has to be continued on another section of wall. This was divided by the chancel screen (It. *cancellata*) into one narrow and one wider section, however. The narrow tapestry of *The Liberation of Paul from Prison in Philippi through an Earthquake* shows Paul imprisoned in Philippi for spreading unacceptable religious teachings (pp. 220 c., 243; Cat. T9). The depiction establishes an astonishing parallel with the adjacent chancel screen, or *cancellata*. The bars of Paul's dungeon cell are identical to the grating of the real *cancellata* that formerly stood next to it on the left. Anyone who looked at the tapestry from the chancel during a liturgical celebration saw not only Paul behind bars, but also the members of the public behind the dividing screen, which excluded them from this privileged area of the chapel, reserved for the Pope and clergy.

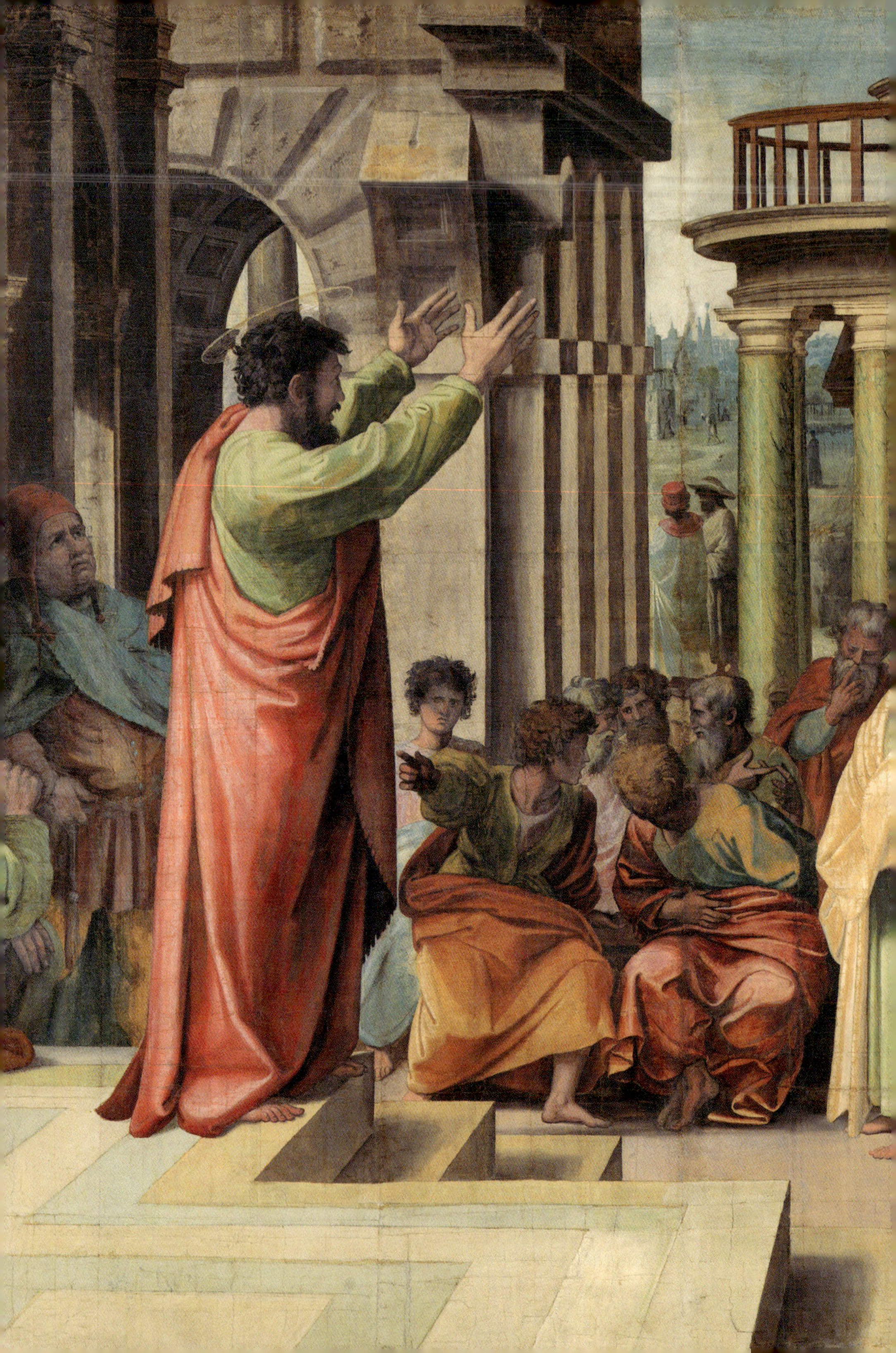

But salvation is at hand. A mighty earthquake brings liberation. Not only does the dungeon falls into ruins, but the personification of the earthquake punches with one fist through the fictive picture frame. The tapestry thereby alludes to the breaking through of real boundaries in the world of the viewer: together with the apostle, the tapestry series, too, can overcome the barrier of the chancel screen, as it were. It continues with one final tapestry beyond the screen, *Paul Preaching at Athens* (p. 220 b. l.; Cat. T10). In the wider half of the wall section divided by the *cancellata*, Paul can at last proclaim the Gospel freely. He gives the appearance of having stepped out of the chancel. With this tapestry, the stage on which Paul's story is set expands downwards: it drops down via steps to a lower level which formerly appeared to be an extension of the real floor on which the viewer was standing. The story of Paul – like that of Peter opposite – leads into the chapel space. Thus Paul's sermon is also directed, as it were, at the chapel's visitors. In the tapestry, the apostle's message is received, pondered, reviewed and digested by the audience gathered below. On the left, this leads finally to conversion: Dionysius and Damaris are seized with enthusiasm for the new doctrine and mount the steps to Paul's podium as if from the viewer's space. Paul's preaching seems to be able to exert its effect right up to the present.

With the conversion of the heathens, Stephen's request is fulfilled. Stage and tapestry cycle end. Like Peter, Paul undergoes a continuous development from scene to scene. In his case, however, the persecutor of Christians (Cat. T5) must first be cast down before his ascent begins. At his conversion, he is flung backwards to the ground before Christ floating overhead (Cat. T6). He then stands before the slightly stooped sorcerer on the same level (Cat. T7). At Lystra he ascends one step above the man bending over the sacrificial ram (Cat. T8). In Athens, lastly, he appears alone at the top of a flight of steps, elevated above everyone remaining below (Cat. T10). With the increasing success of his missionary work, in other words, Paul's position rises. Here, too, the direction in which the protagonist's body is facing drives the visual narrative onwards to the next tapestry. The viewer accompanies him leftwards on a journey from Jerusalem, via Damascus, Cyprus, Lystra in Asia Minor and Philippi in Macedonia, to Athens. At the individual stations along this biographical journey, Raphael portrays a differentiated variety of groups of converts, missionary activities, and means of power or social spheres of dominion of the Christian faith. Step by step, Christianity asserts itself against Roman military power and brute force, fights against wicked sorcery in front of the court of the Roman proconsul,

Detail from **Paul Preaching on the Areopagus in Athens and the Conversion of Dionysius Areopagita and Damaris**, 1515/16
(see ill. pp. 256/257)

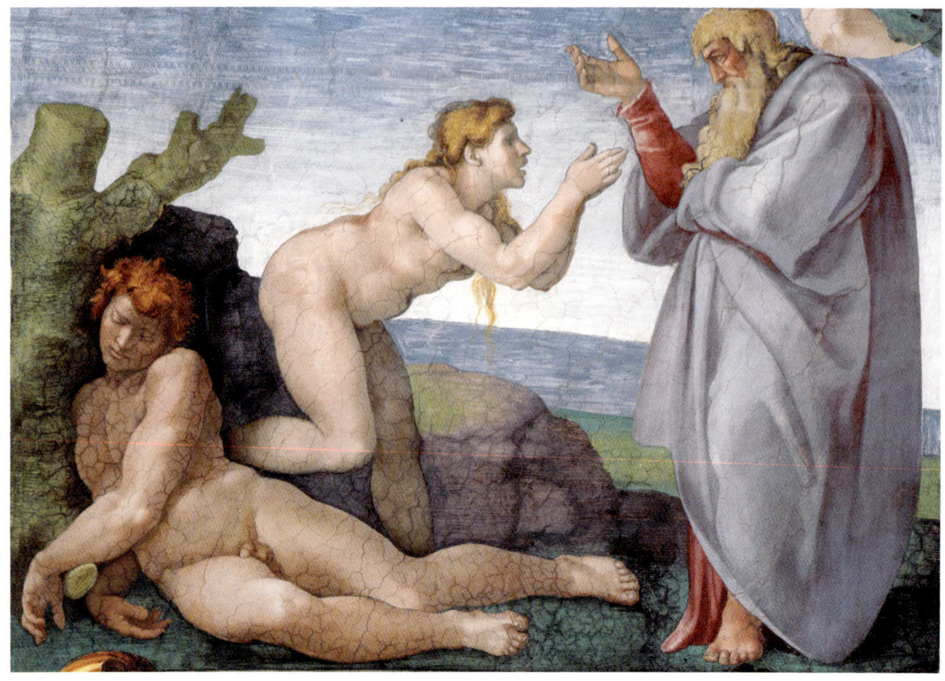

Michelangelo Buonarroti, **Sistine Ceiling: Creation of Eve**, 1509/10
Fresco, 170 × 260 cm (66 7/8 × 102 3/8 in). Vatican City, Musei Vaticani, Cappella Sistina

then against pagan idols, their priests and their animal sacrifices, and finally also against the highest powers of reasoning of the greatest ancient philosophers. Brute force, secular government, religion and wisdom – all submit to Christianity: the physically strongest, the politically most powerful, the educated as well as the common people. All these different scenes combine to form a single great narrative, which begins with the request of the persecuted and ends with the conversion of the persecutor. Just as the cycle of Peter thematises the leadership of the Church as the task of the Pope, so the cycle of Paul deals with the spread of faith and the conversion of non-believers through preaching.

Raphael's tapestries pay close attention to the liturgical organisation of the space, its areas of use and their décor. Only in the raised altar area, reached up a flight of steps, do the first two tapestry scenes on either side take place in a natural outdoor setting, whose landscape continues, moreover, from the first to the second tapestry respectively. Only in these four scenes does Christ himself appear. The *Peter* series runs as far as the choir loft set into the wall. In its concluding tapestry, *The Death of Ananias*, the fictive podium and balustrade lead formally to the choir loft's elevated position and balustrade. The *Pauline* series extends beyond the chancel area. It thereby thematises the breaking through of the latticework *cancellata* and ends opposite the choir loft, which likewise continues beyond the screen. This crossing of the barrier excluding unprivileged visitors is to be understood as a gesture of great significance, by means of which Leo X wished to distinguish himself from Michelangelo's ceiling frescoes for his predecessor Julius II. Michelangelo had also taken into account the position of the screen: the figure of God appeared only in the papal area inside the chancel. *The Fall* and the *Expulsion from Paradise* immediately beyond the *cancellata* made the exclusion of the non-clerical congregation look like the just expulsion of sinners from the paradise of the Pope's Church. By having his tapestry cycle extend into this public zone, and by letting Paul preach salvation beyond the dividing screen, Leo X declared that he set no limits to his benevolence and accessibility, that he cared for the excluded and the outcast and wished to carry redeeming salvation out into the sinful world. It is the same gesture which, in the Stanza dell'Incendio, leads the Leo popes out of the sphere reserved for liturgical ceremony and into the arena of the beseeching people in their distress, and from here to the conquest and conversion of the unbelievers. In both spaces, Raphael shows himself a magnificent designer of pictorial cycles. Their messages are not confined to the individual picture but unfold in the harmony of the whole. This harmony, so carefully orchestrated by Raphael, is a fundamental part of his artistic achievement.

Pages 218/219
The Miraculous Draught of Fishes and Christ's Charge to Peter, 1515/19
Socle border: **Entrance of Giovanni de' Medici into Rome (22/3/1492)** and **Enrolment in the College of Cardinals by Pope Innocent VIII (23/3/1492)**
Tapestry, 493 × 440 cm (194 ⅛ × 173 ¼ in). Vatican City, Musei Vaticani, Pinacoteca

"Feed My Sheep", 1515/17
Socle border: **Sack of the Medici Palace, Giovanni de' Medici Flees from Florence Disguised as a Franciscan Friar (9/11/1494)**. Vertical border: **Parcae (Fates)**
Tapestry, 466 × 634 cm (183 ½ × 249 ⅝ in). Vatican City, Musei Vaticani, Pinacoteca

The Healing of the Lame Man, 1515/19
Socle border: **Arrival of Giovanni de' Medici in Mantua (13/6/1512), Giovanni de' Medici Escapes French Captivity at Pieve del Cairo on the Po (4/6/1512)**
Tapestry, 501 × 575 cm (197 ¼ × 226 ⅜ in). Vatican City, Musei Vaticani, Pinacoteca

The Death of Ananias, 1515/21
Socle border: **Address of the *Gonfaloniere* Ridolfi to the Florentine *Parlamento* in front of the Palazzo della Signoria (16/9/1512), Entry of Giovanni de' Medici in Florence (14/9/1512)**
Vertical border: **Theological Virtues**. Tapestry, 488 × 631 cm (192 ⅛ × 248 ⅜ in)
Vatican City, Musei Vaticani, Pinacoteca

Stanza dell'Incendio

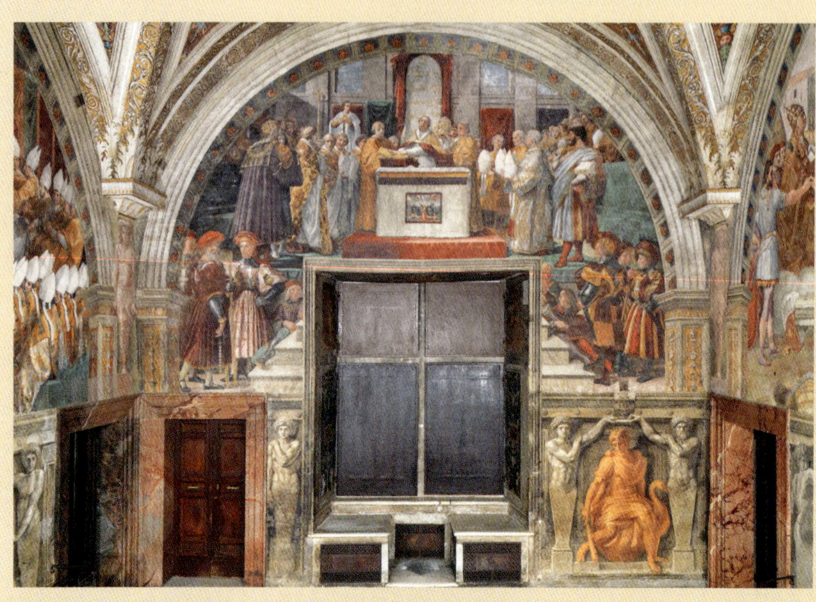

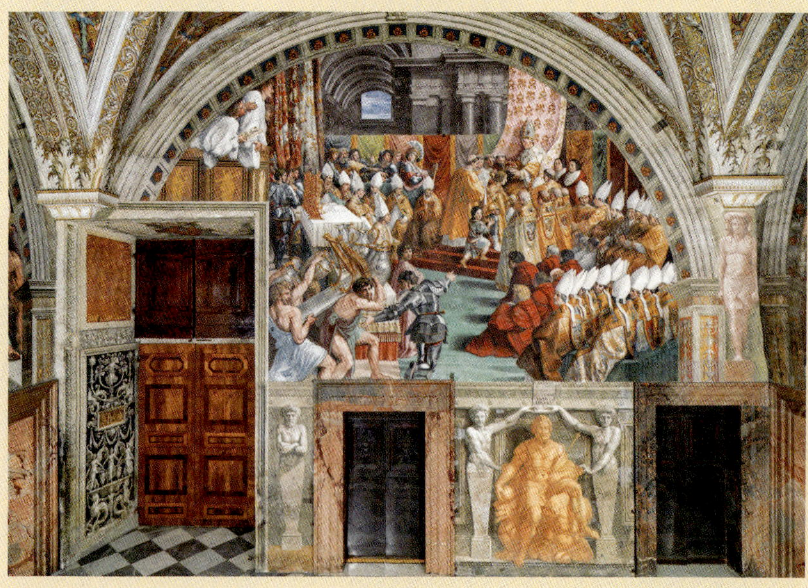

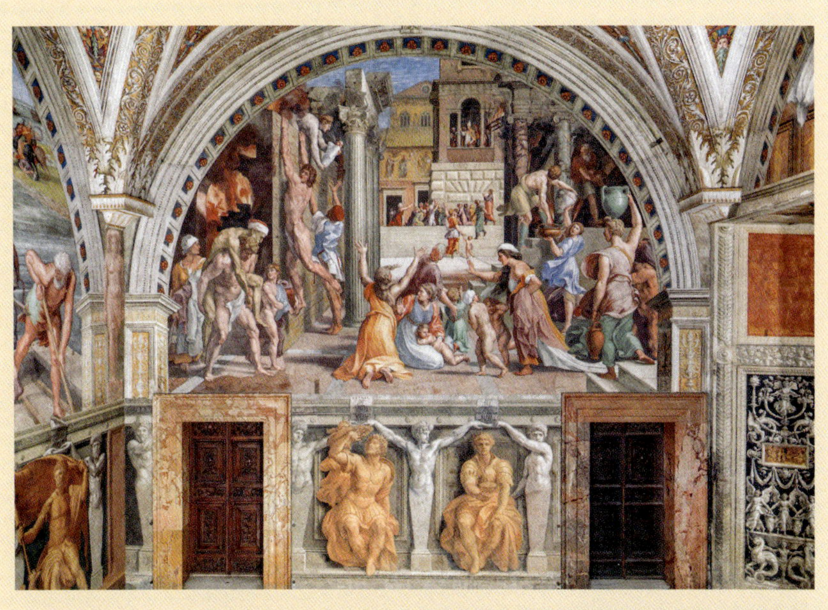

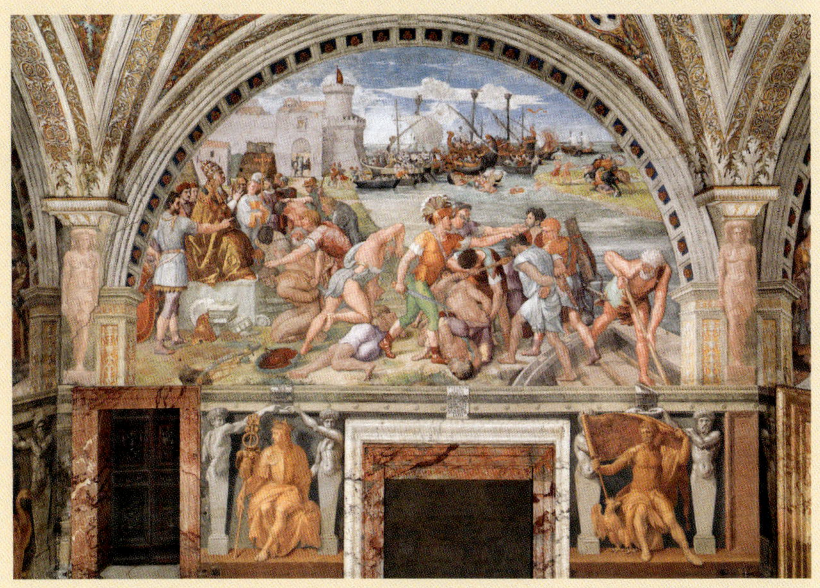

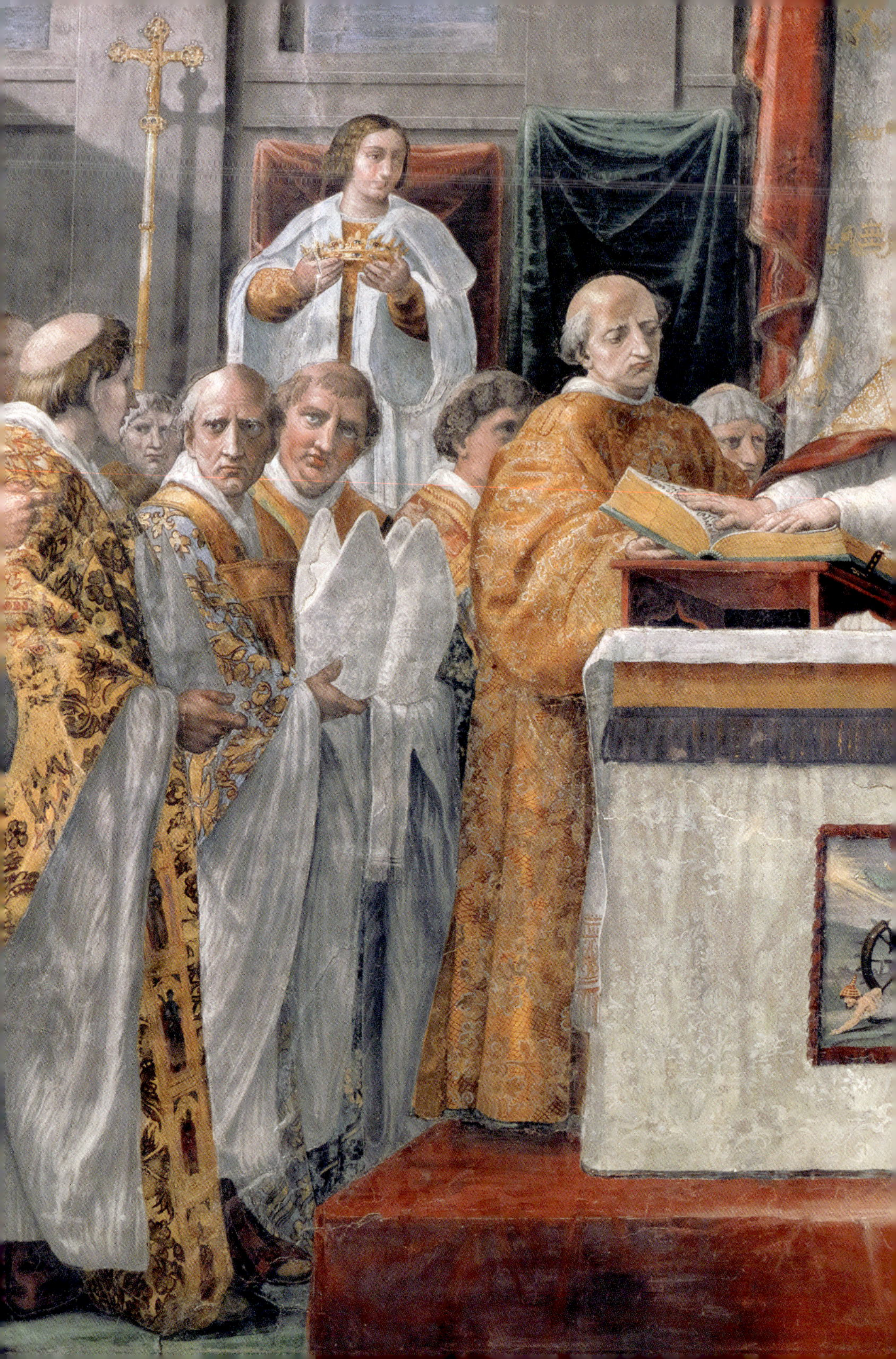

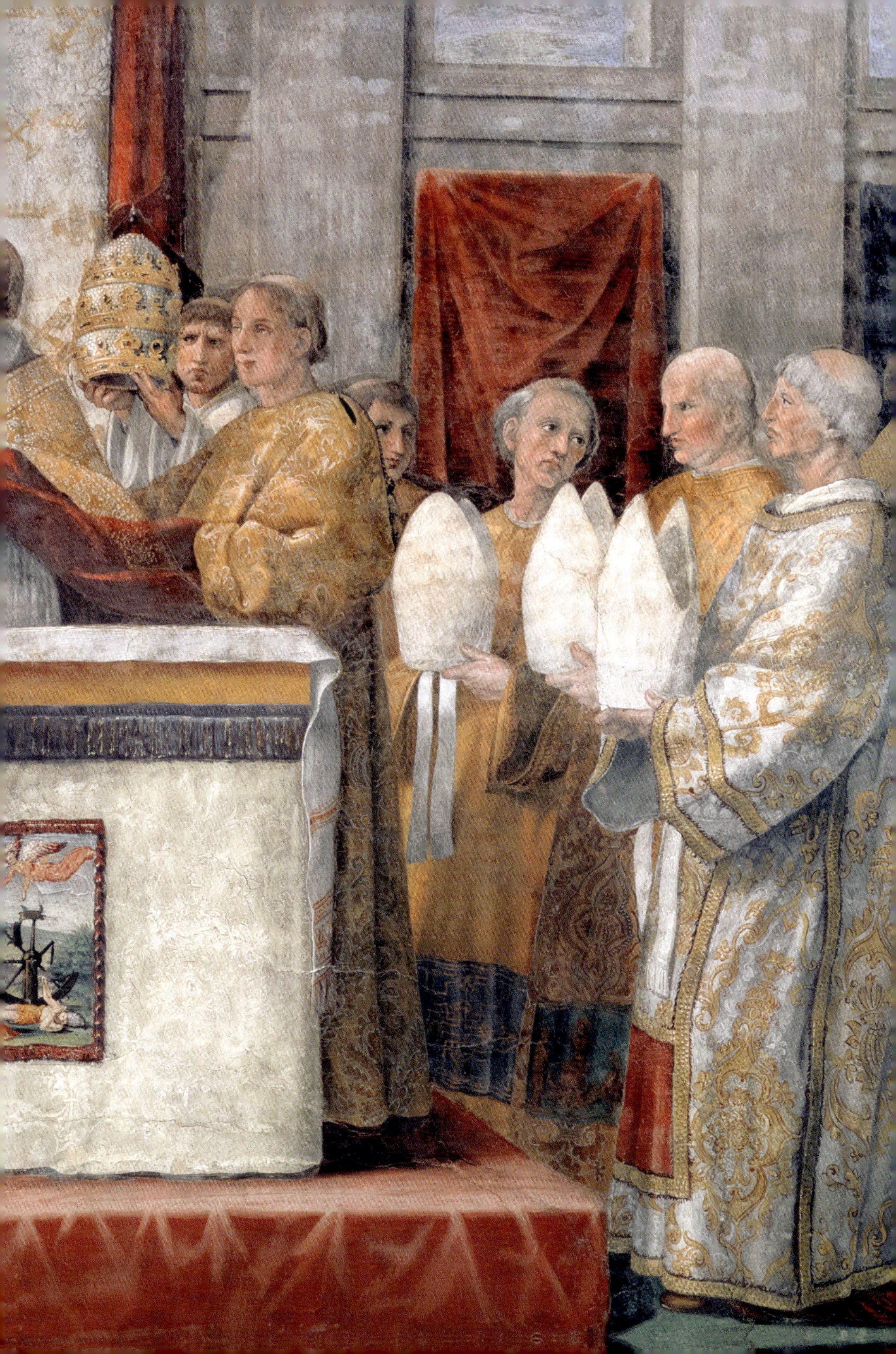

Page 230
Leo III's Oath of Purgation, 1514–1516/17
Fresco, width of base 7.15 m (281 ½ in)
Vatican City, Musei Vaticani, Stanza dell'Incendio
(Detail pages 232/233)

Leo III Crowns Charlemagne, 1514–1516
Fresco, height 5.08 m (200 in)
Vatican City, Musei Vaticani, Stanza dell'Incendio
(Details pages 235–237)

Page 231
Leo IV Extinguishes the Fire in the Borgo, 1514
Fresco, height 4.95 m (194 ⅞ in),
width of base 7.28 m (286 ⅝ in)
Vatican City, Musei Vaticani, Stanza dell'Incendio
(Detail pages 238/239)

Naval Victory of Leo IV at Ostia, 1514–1516/17
Fresco, width of base 7.28 m (286 ⅝ in)
Vatican City, Musei Vaticani, Stanza dell'Incendio
(Detail pages 240/241)

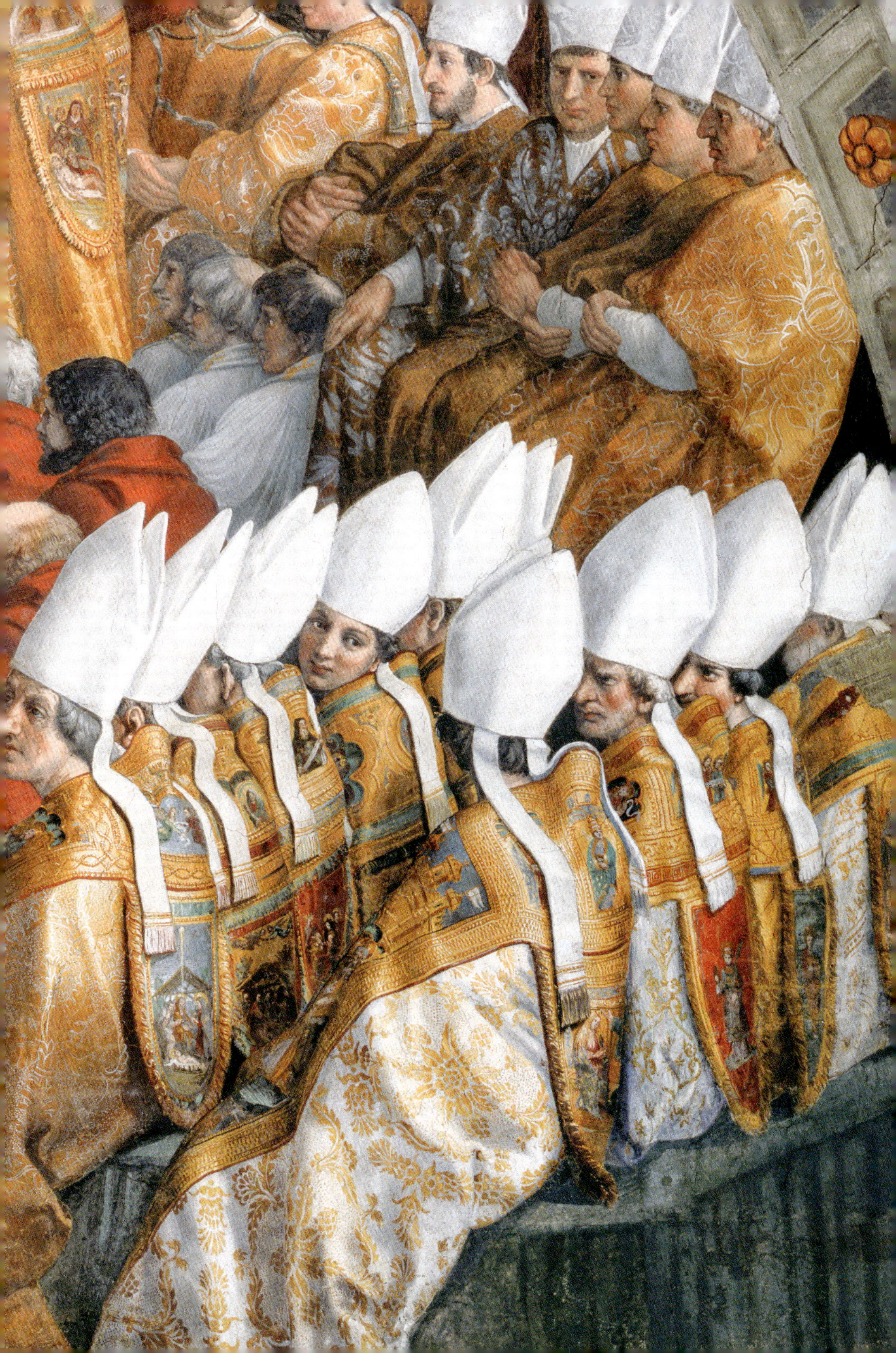

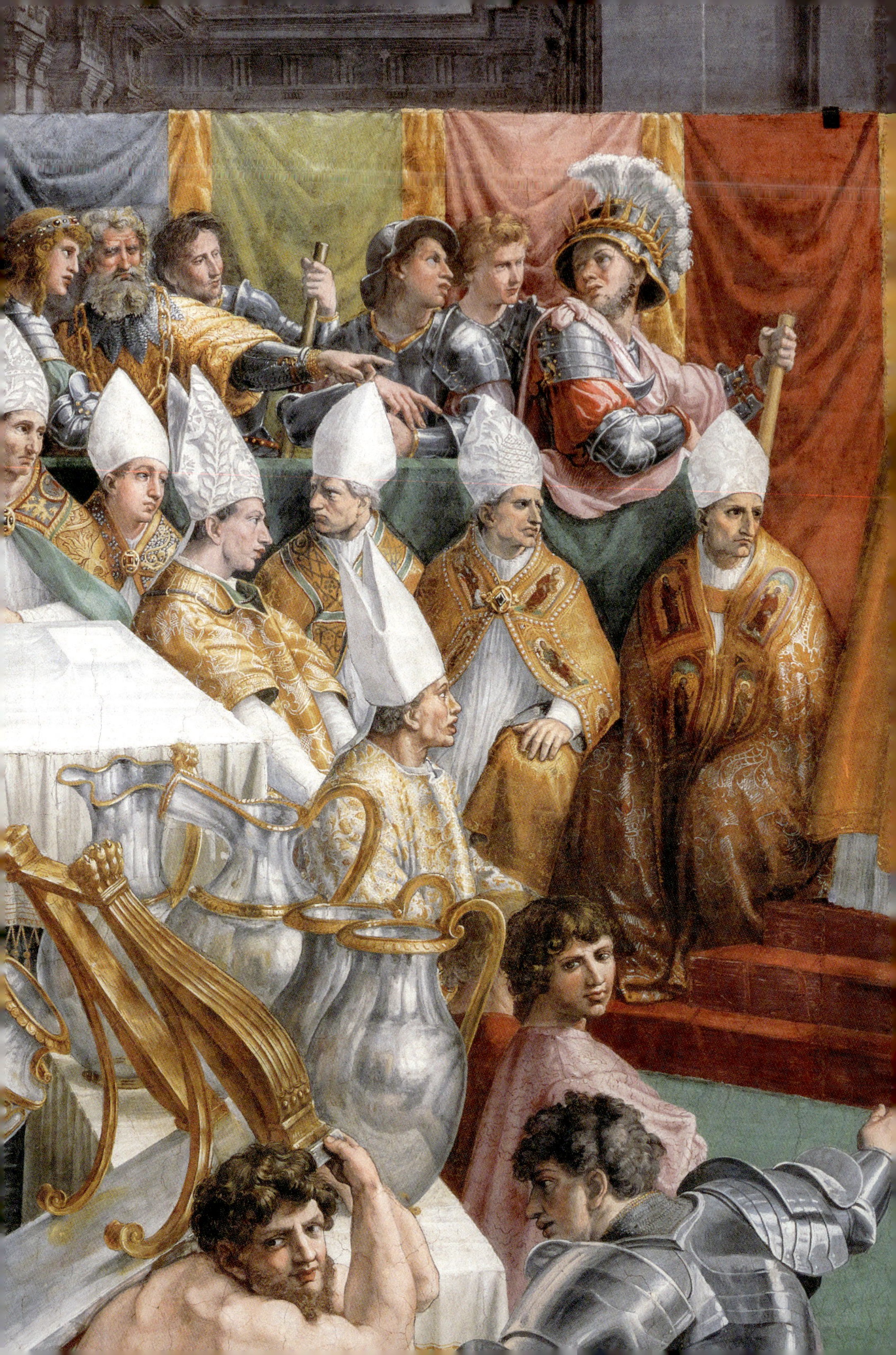

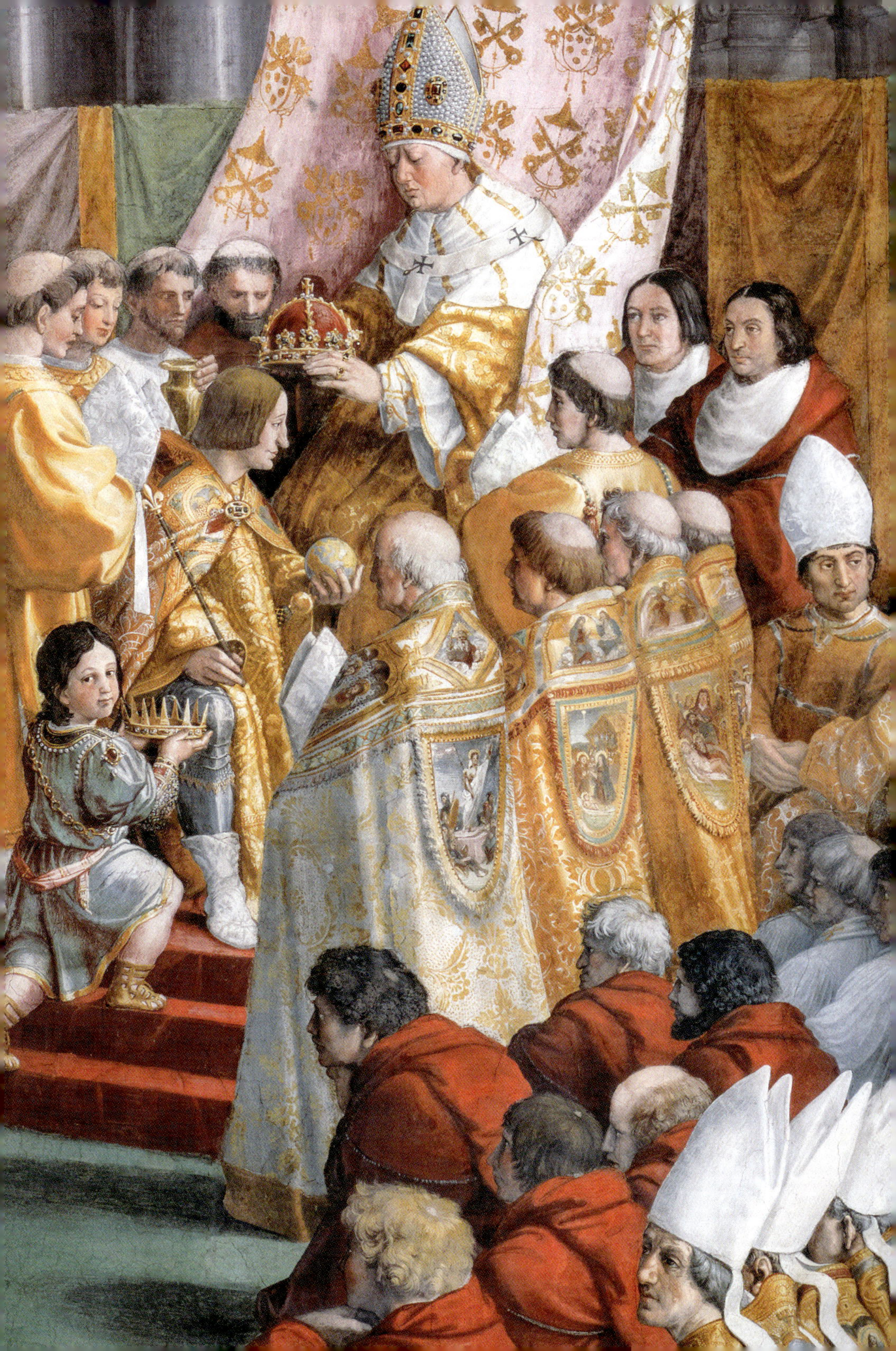

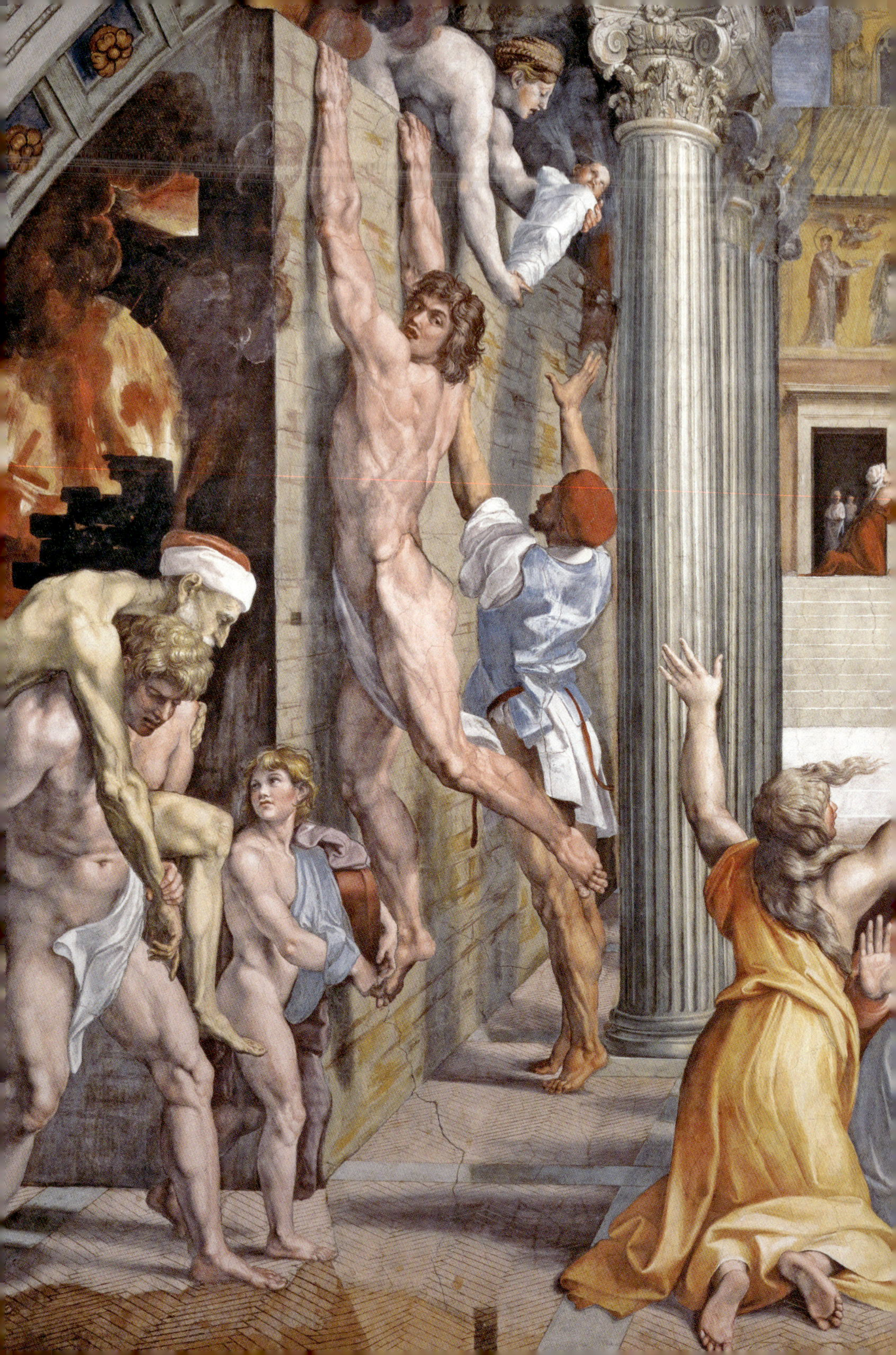

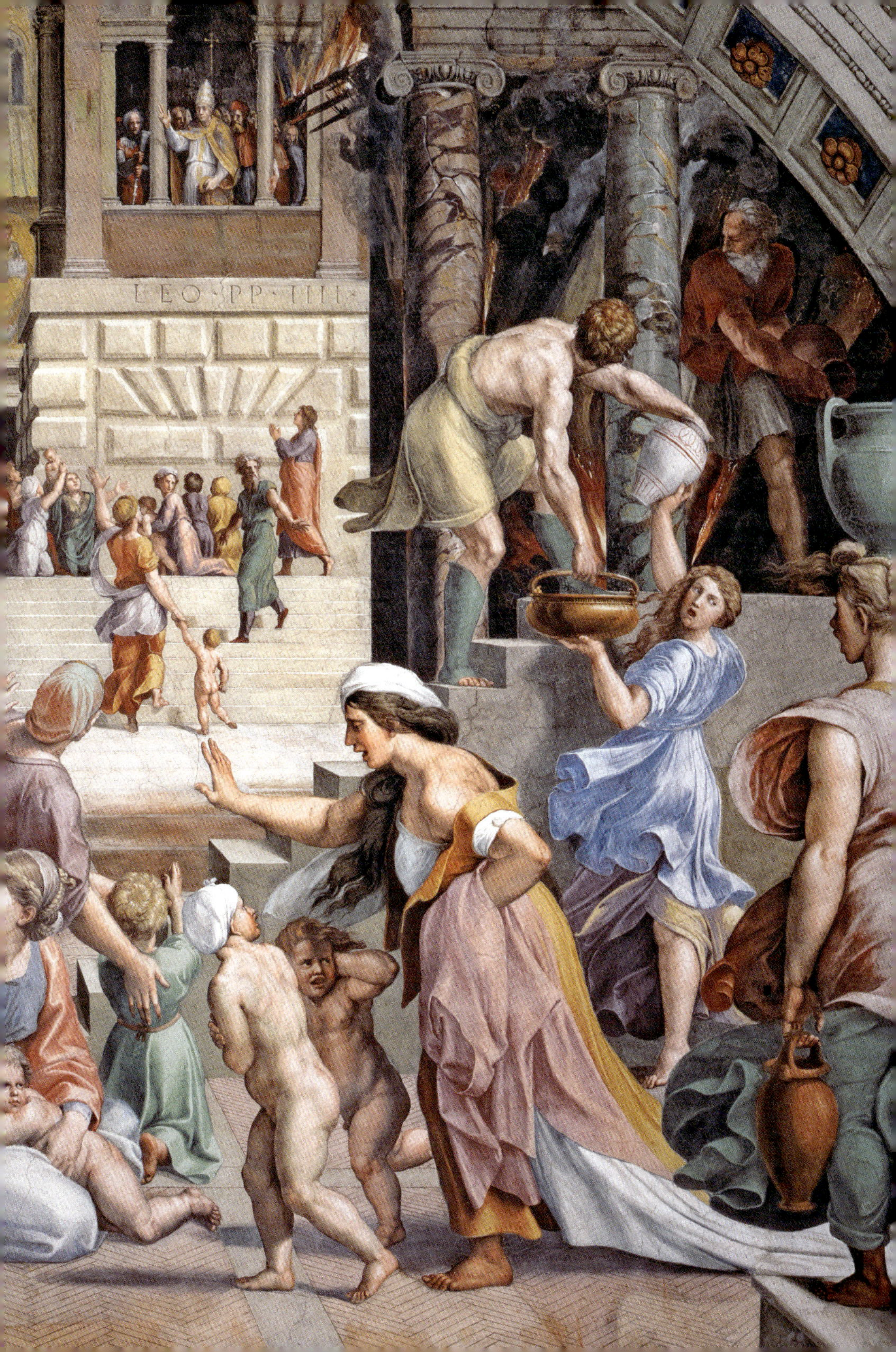
LEO·PP·IIII

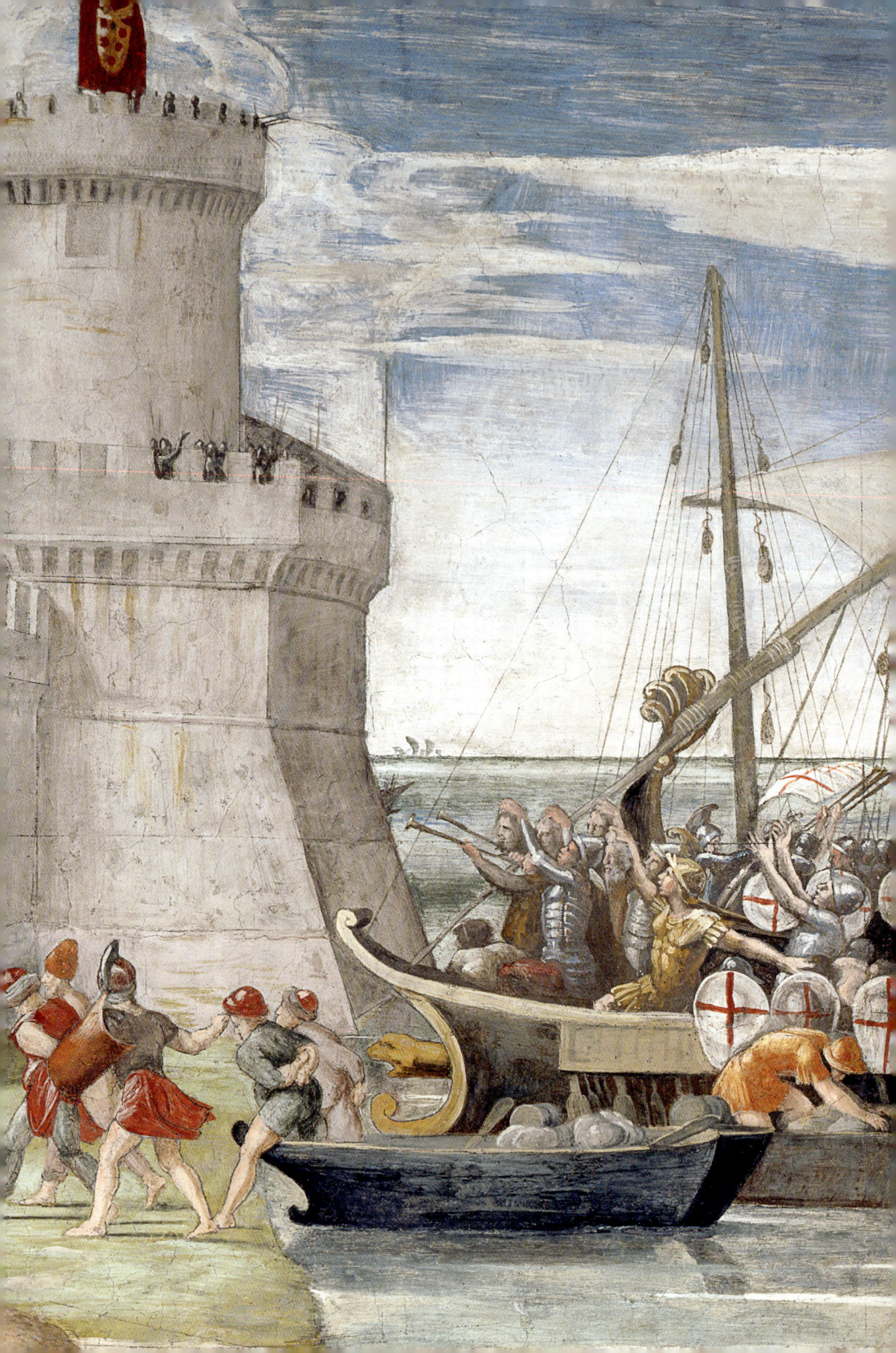

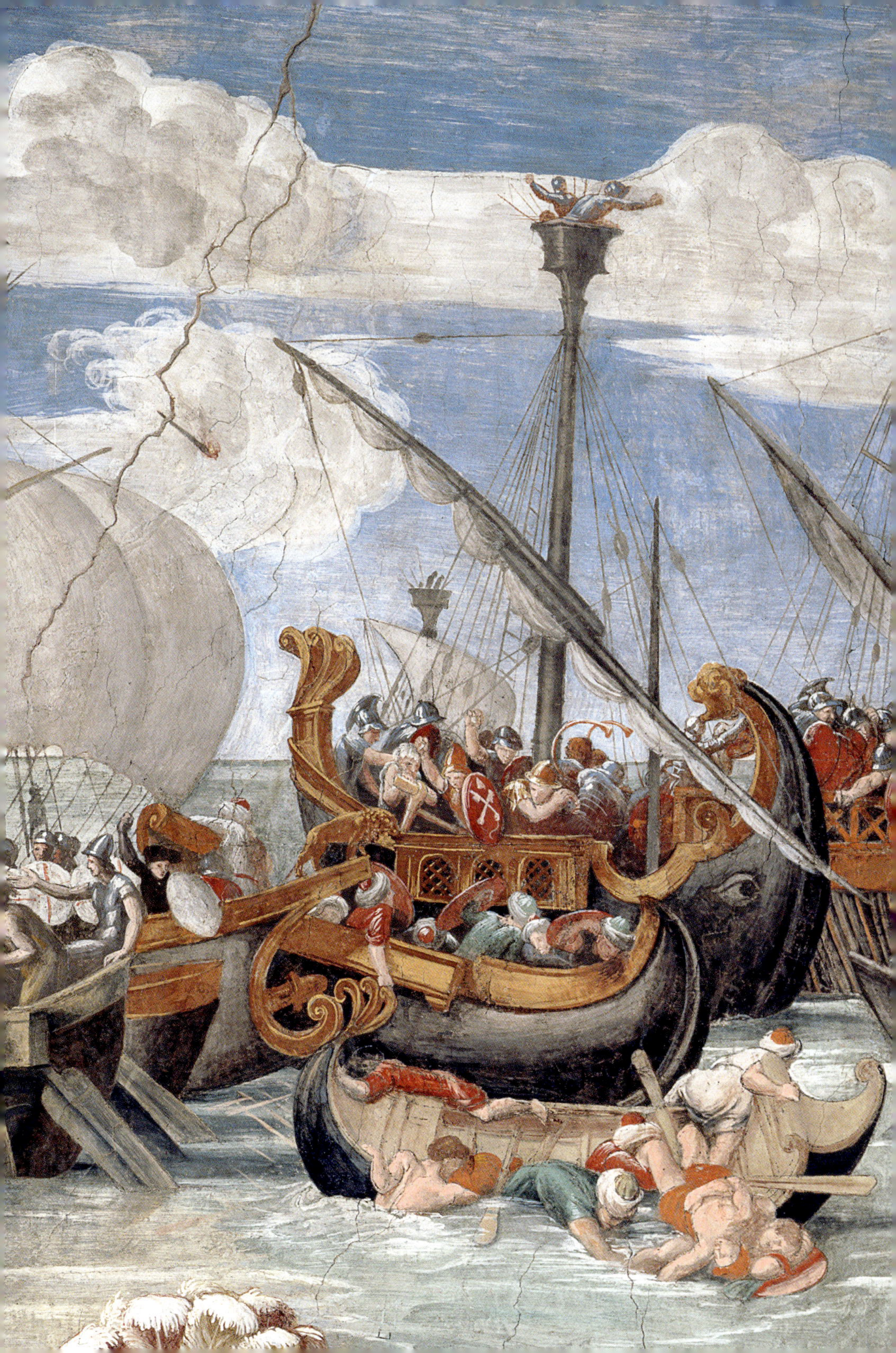

Raphael's Tapestries for the Sistine Chapel

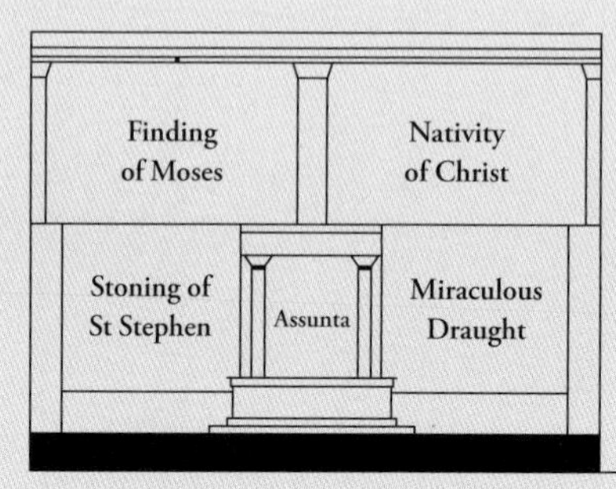

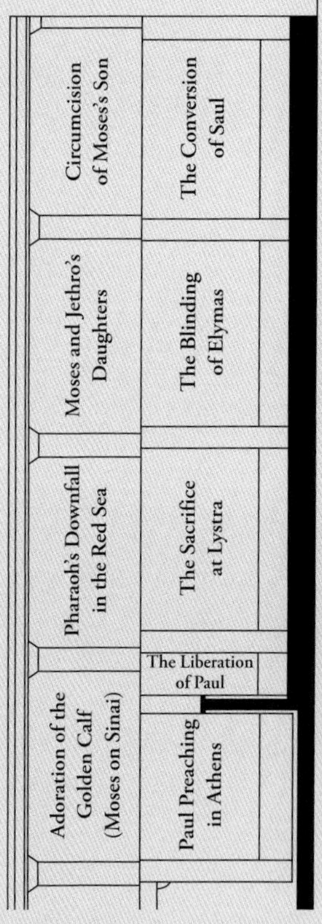

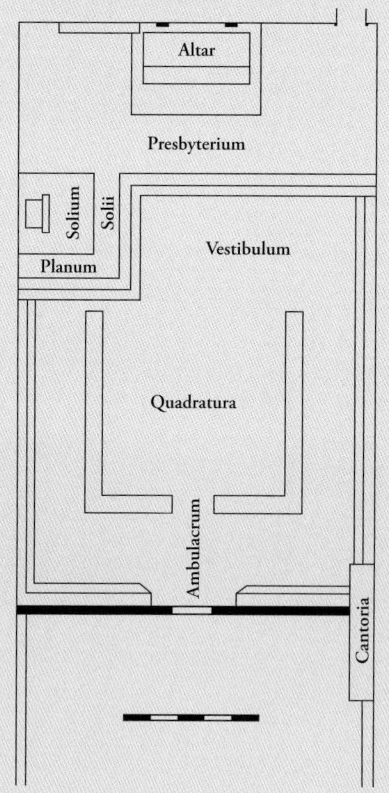

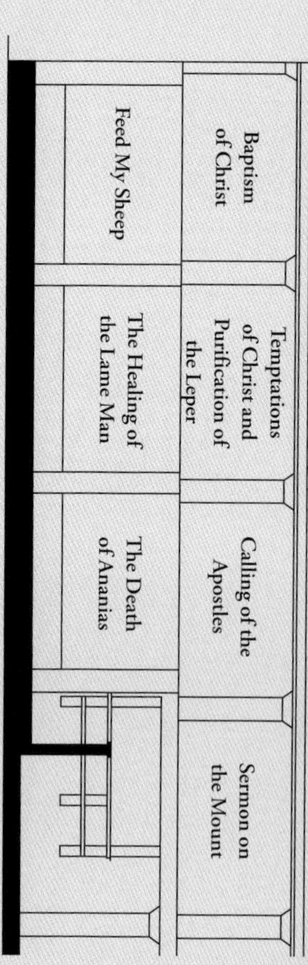

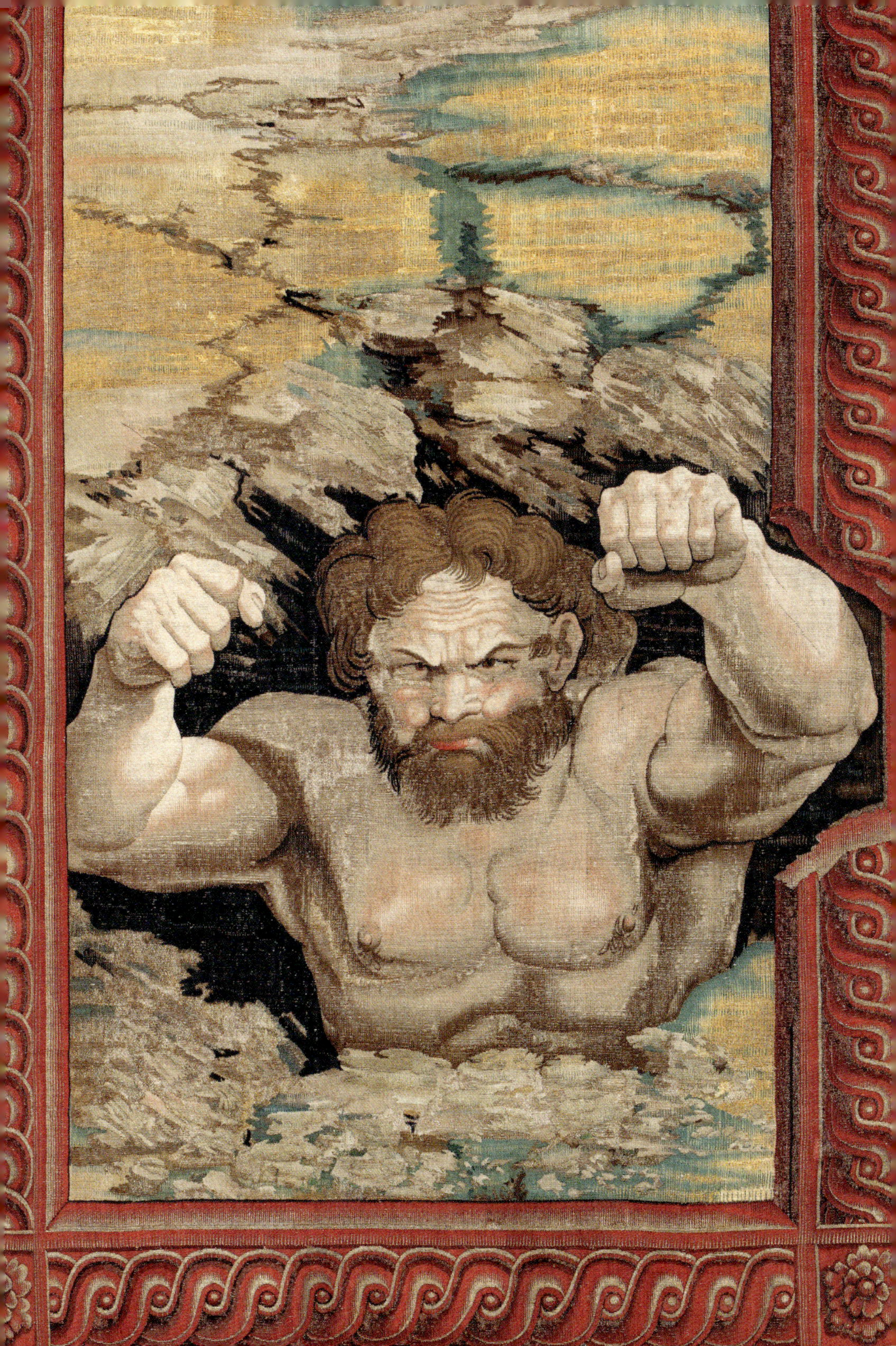

Page 242
Reconstruction of the original hanging of Raphael's tapestries in the Sistine Chapel (after Shearman 1972)

Page 243
Detail from **The Liberation of Paul from the Prison in Philippi through an Earthquake**, *c.* 1515/21
Tapestry
(see ill. p. 220 c.)

The Miraculous Draught of Fishes and Christ's Charge to Peter, 1515/16
Tapestry cartoon, gouache on paper, 319 × 399 cm (125 ⅝ × 157 ⅛ in)
London, Victoria and Albert Museum (on loan from the Royal Collection)
(Detail page 207)

Pages 246/247
"Feed My Sheep", 1515/16
Tapestry cartoon, gouache on paper, 343 × 532 cm (135 ⅛ × 209 ½ in)
London, Victoria and Albert Museum (on loan from the Royal Collection)
(Detail page 208)

Pages 248/249
The Healing of the Lame Man, 1515/16
Tapestry cartoon, gouache on paper, 342 × 536 cm (134 ⅝ × 211 ⅛ in)
London, Victoria and Albert Museum (on loan from the Royal Collection)
(Detail page 213)

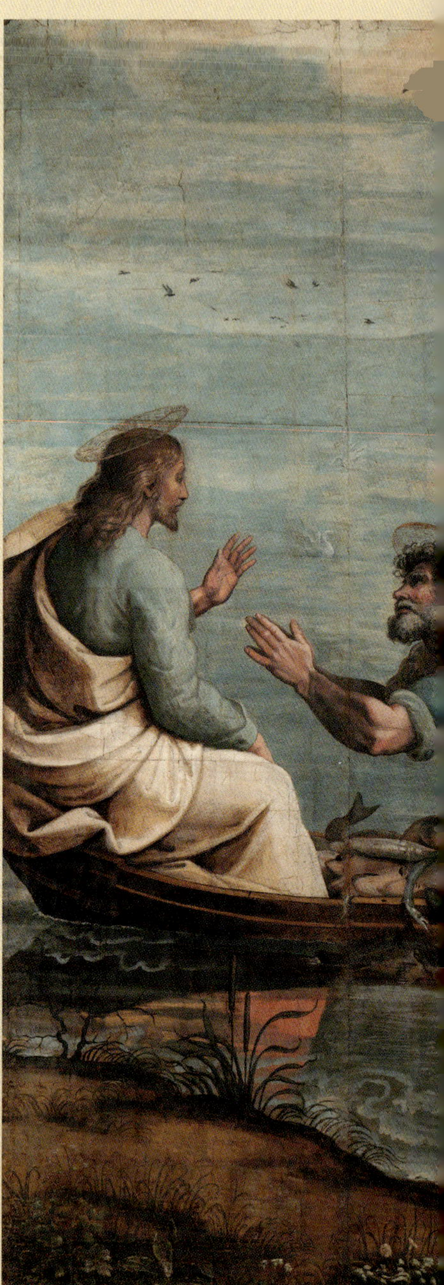

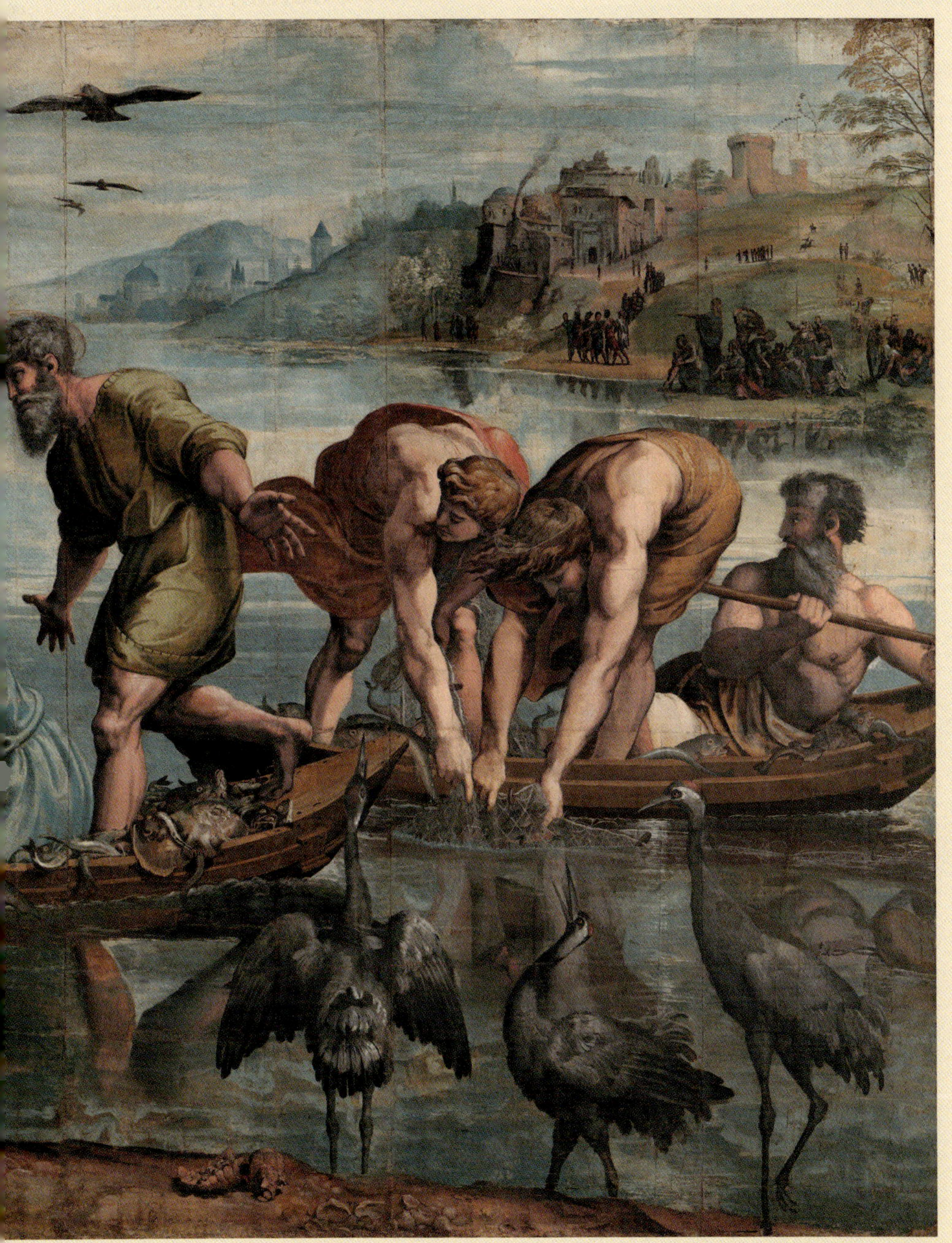

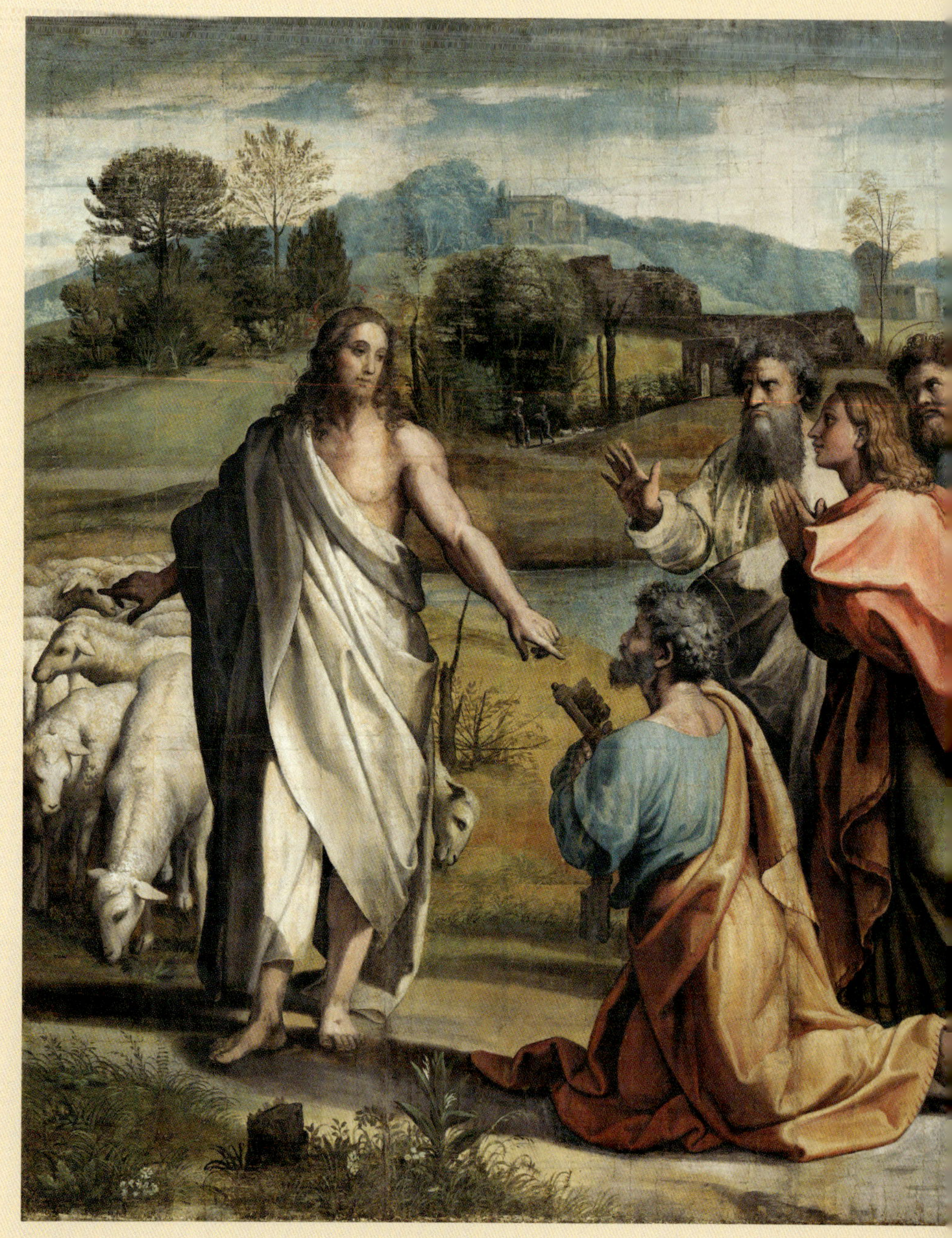

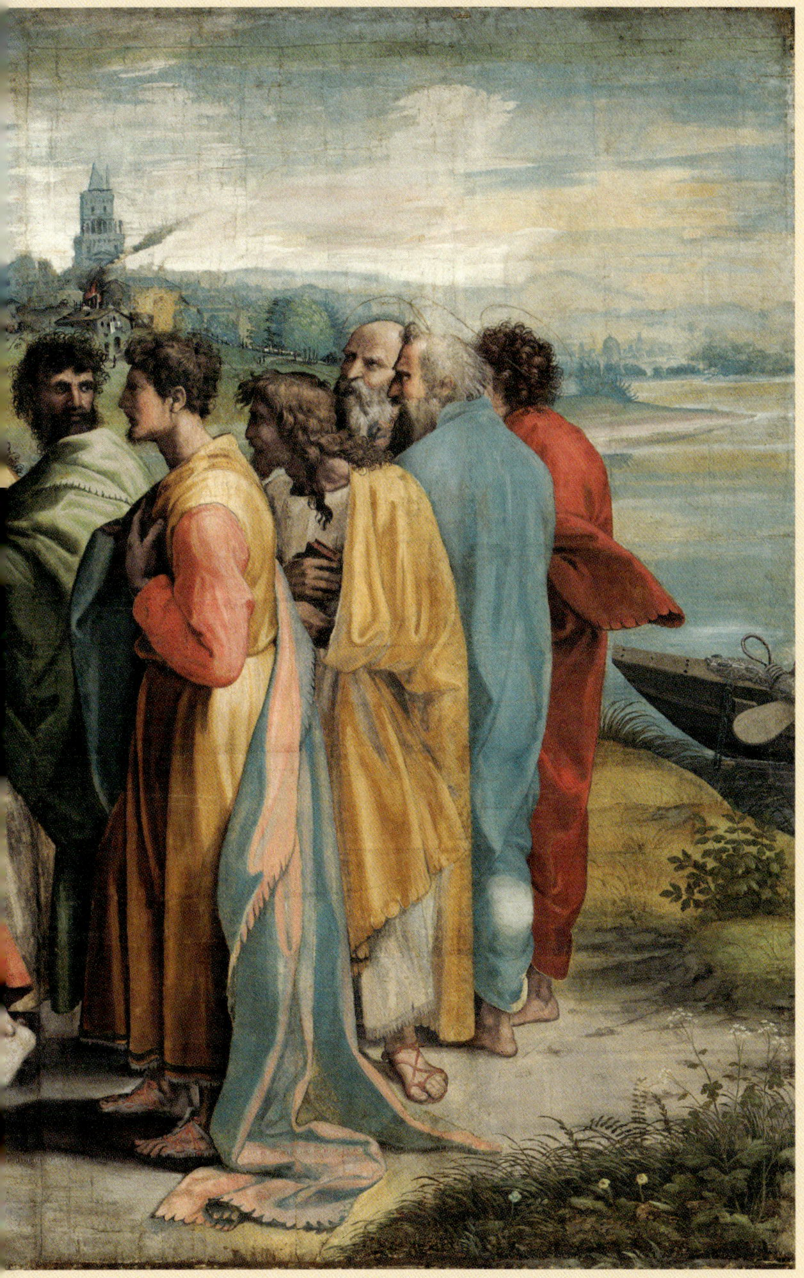

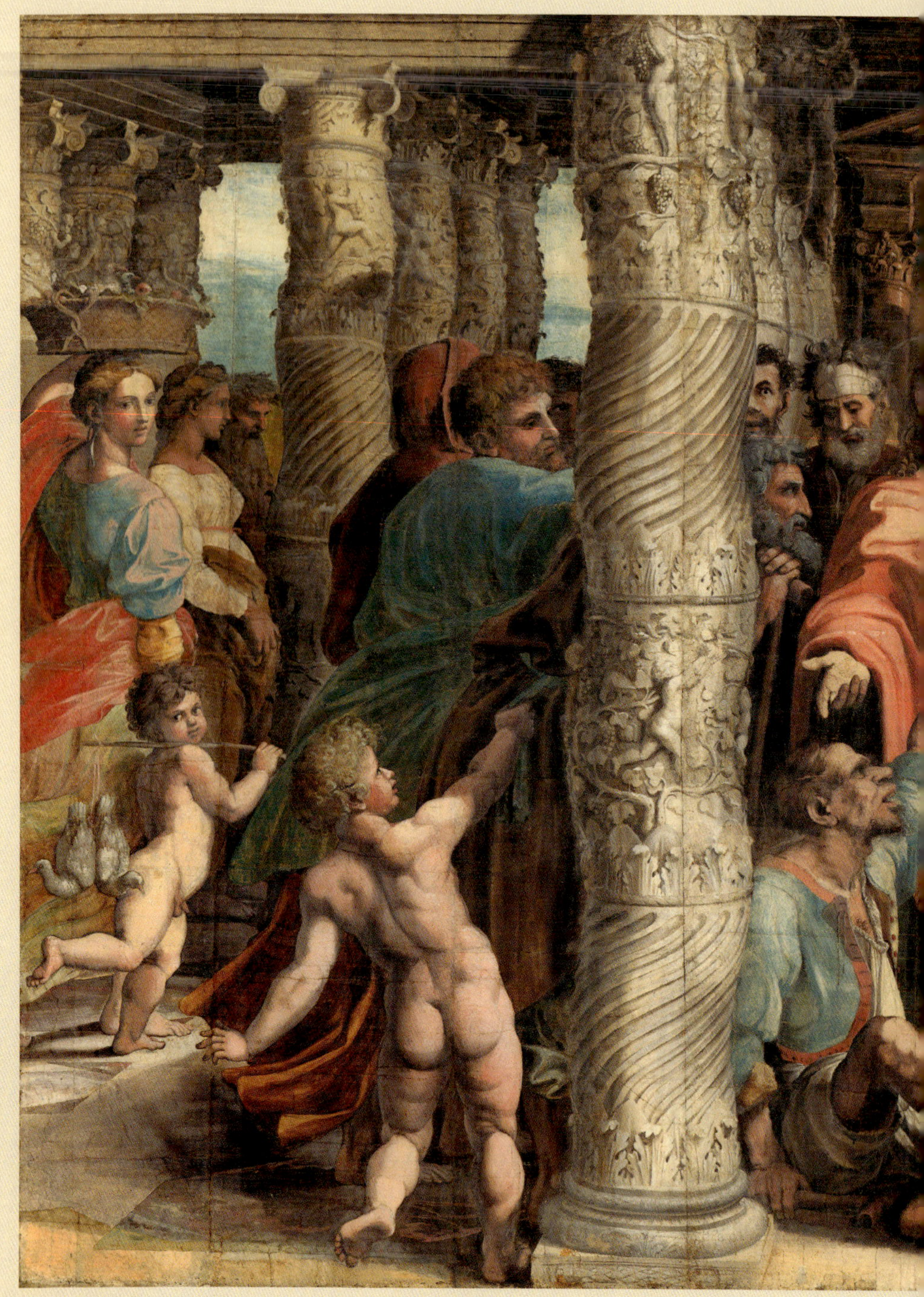

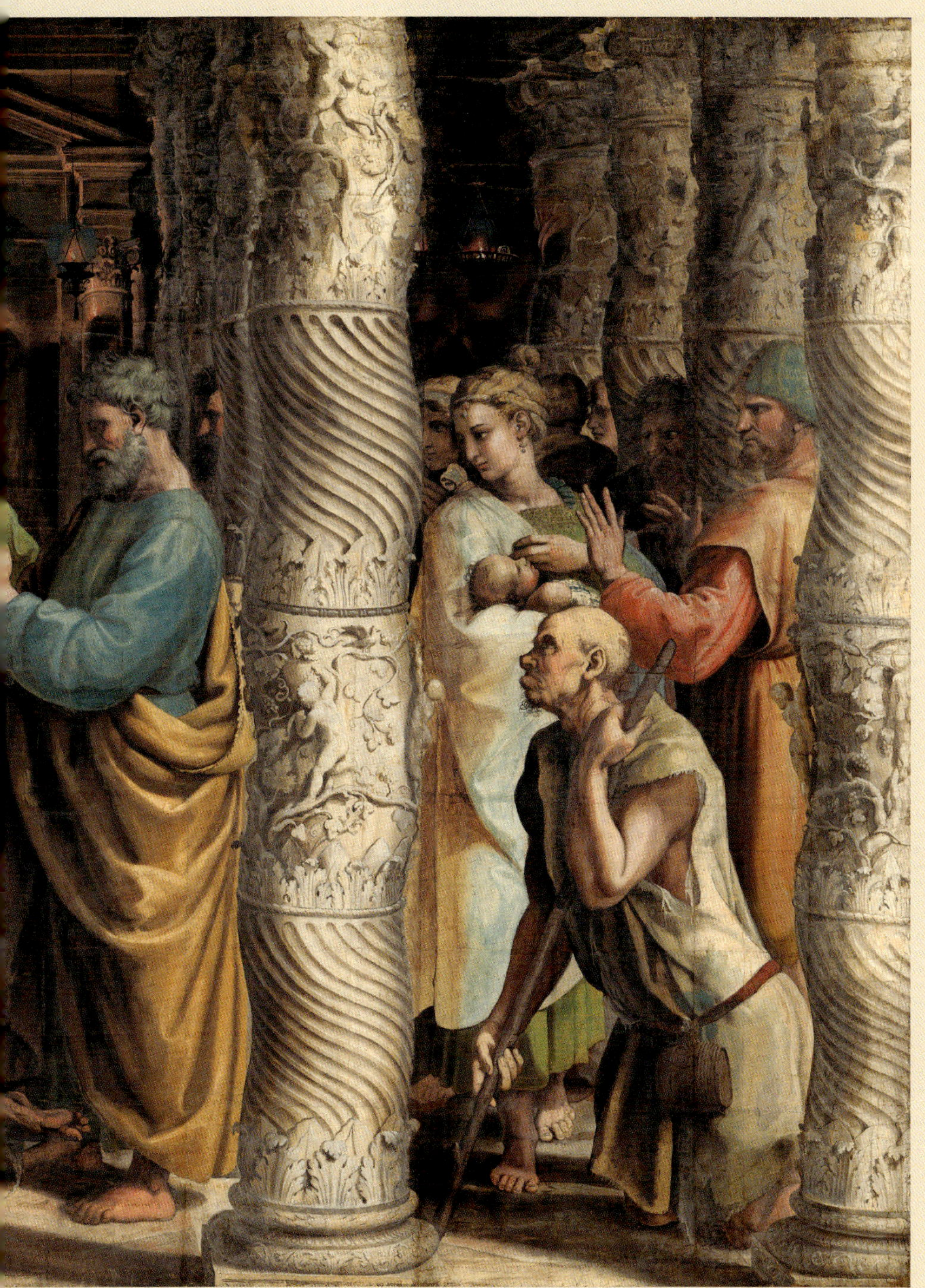

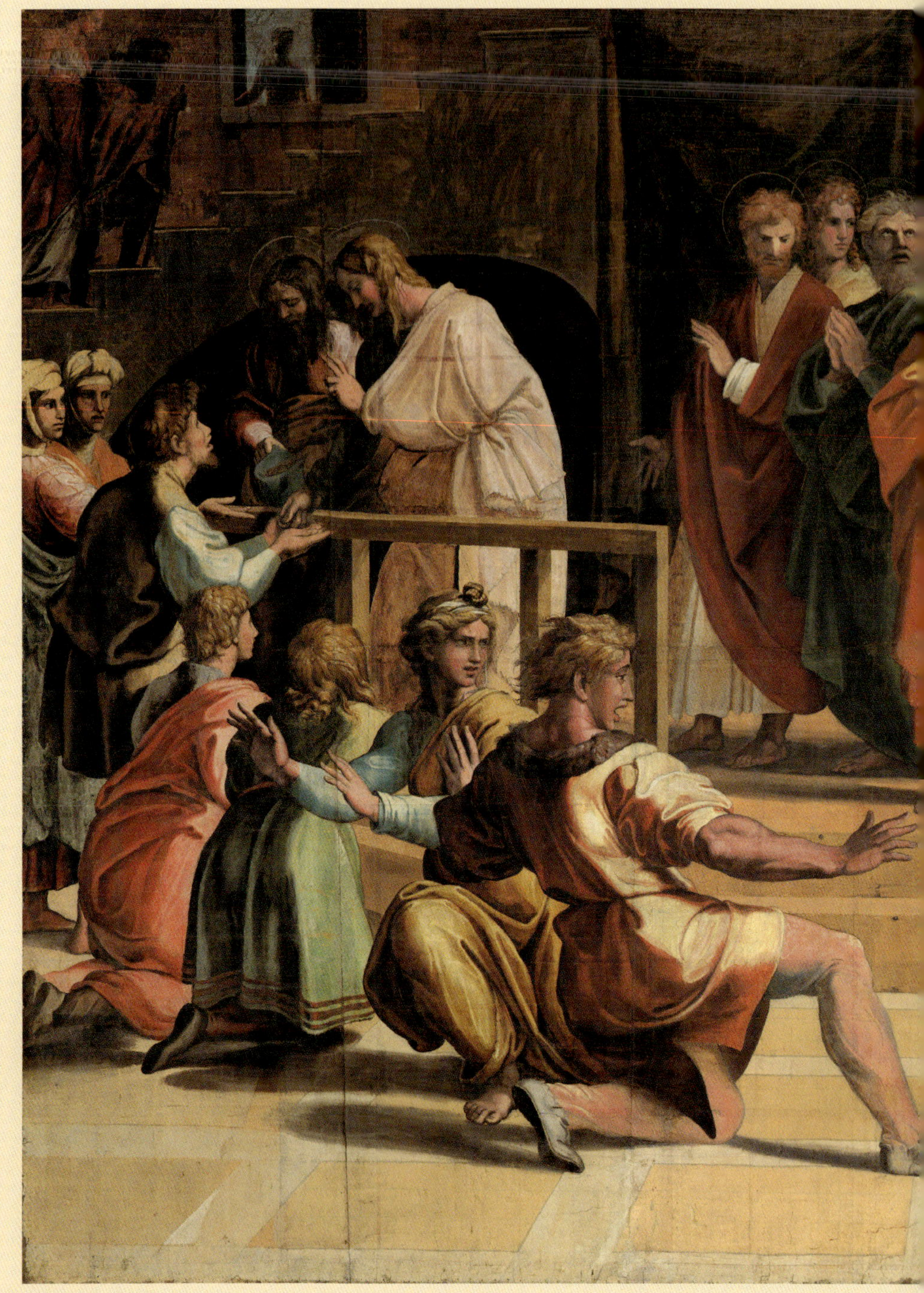

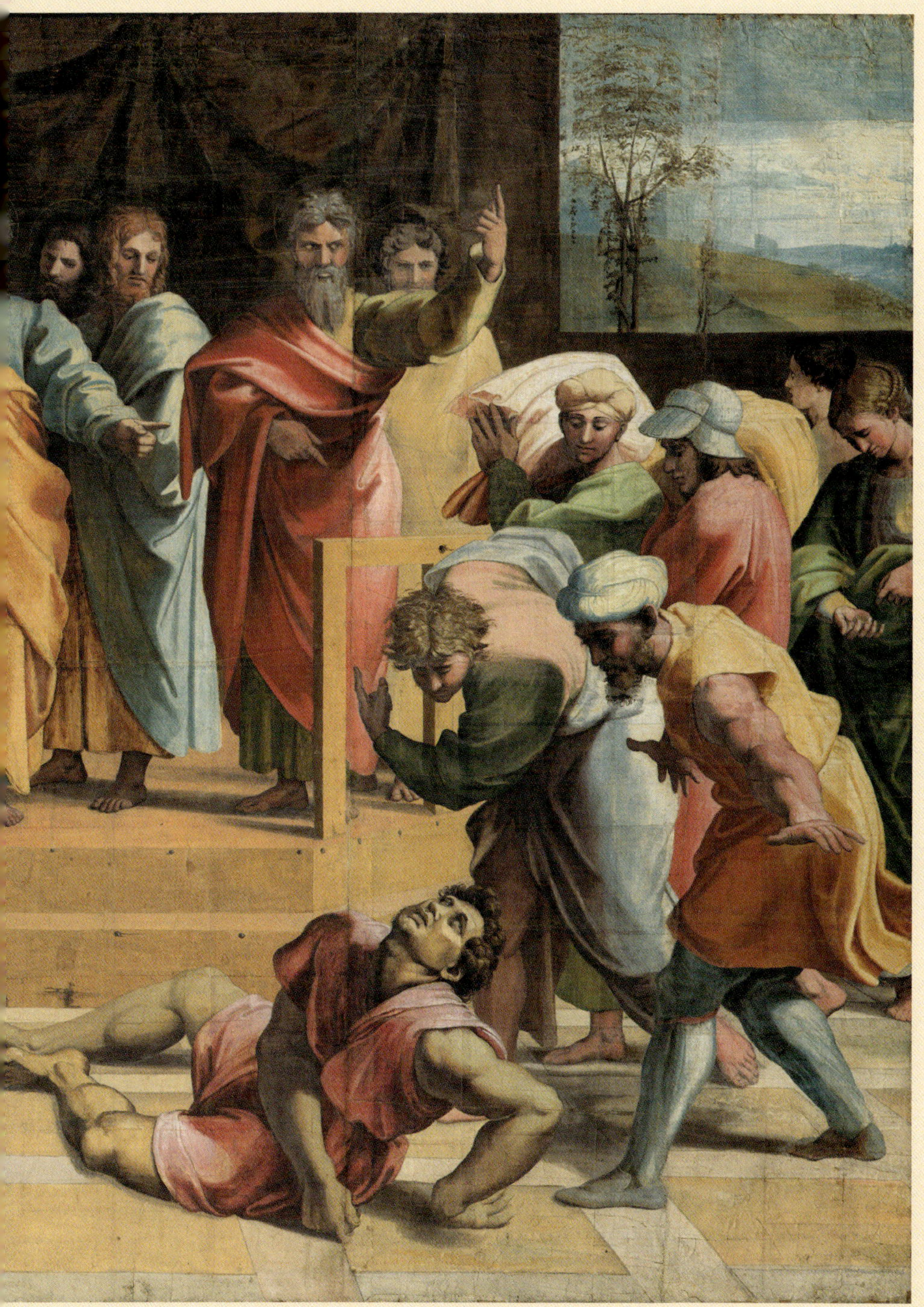

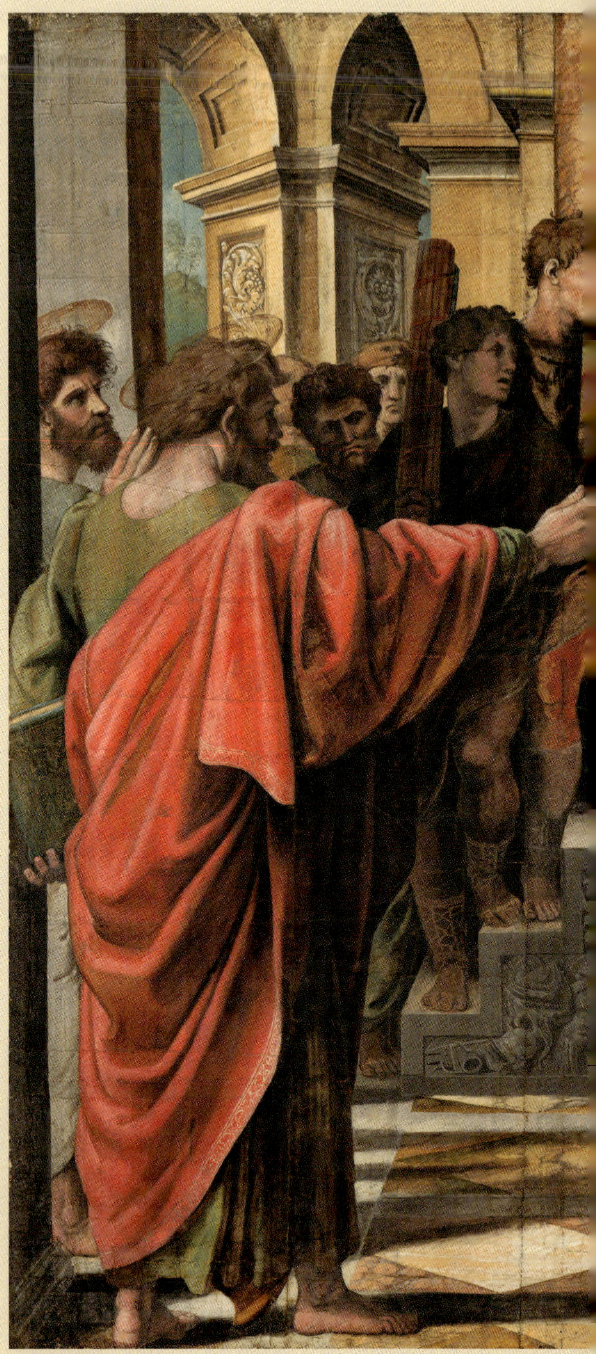

Pages 250/251
The Death of Ananias, *c.* 1515/16
Tapestry cartoon, gouache on paper,
342 × 532 cm (134 5/8 × 209 1/2 in)
London, Victoria and Albert Museum
(on loan from the Royal Collection)

The Blinding of Elymas and Conversion of the Roman Proconsul Sergius Paulus on Cyprus, *c.* 1515/16
Tapestry cartoon, gouache on paper,
342 × 446 cm (134 5/8 × 175 5/8 in)
London, Victoria and Albert Museum
(on loan from the Royal Collection)

Page 254/255
The Sacrifice at Lystra, *c.* 1515/16
Tapestry cartoon, gouache on paper,
347 × 532 cm (136 5/8 × 209 1/2 in)
London, Victoria and Albert Museum
(on loan from the Royal Collection)
(Detail page 216)

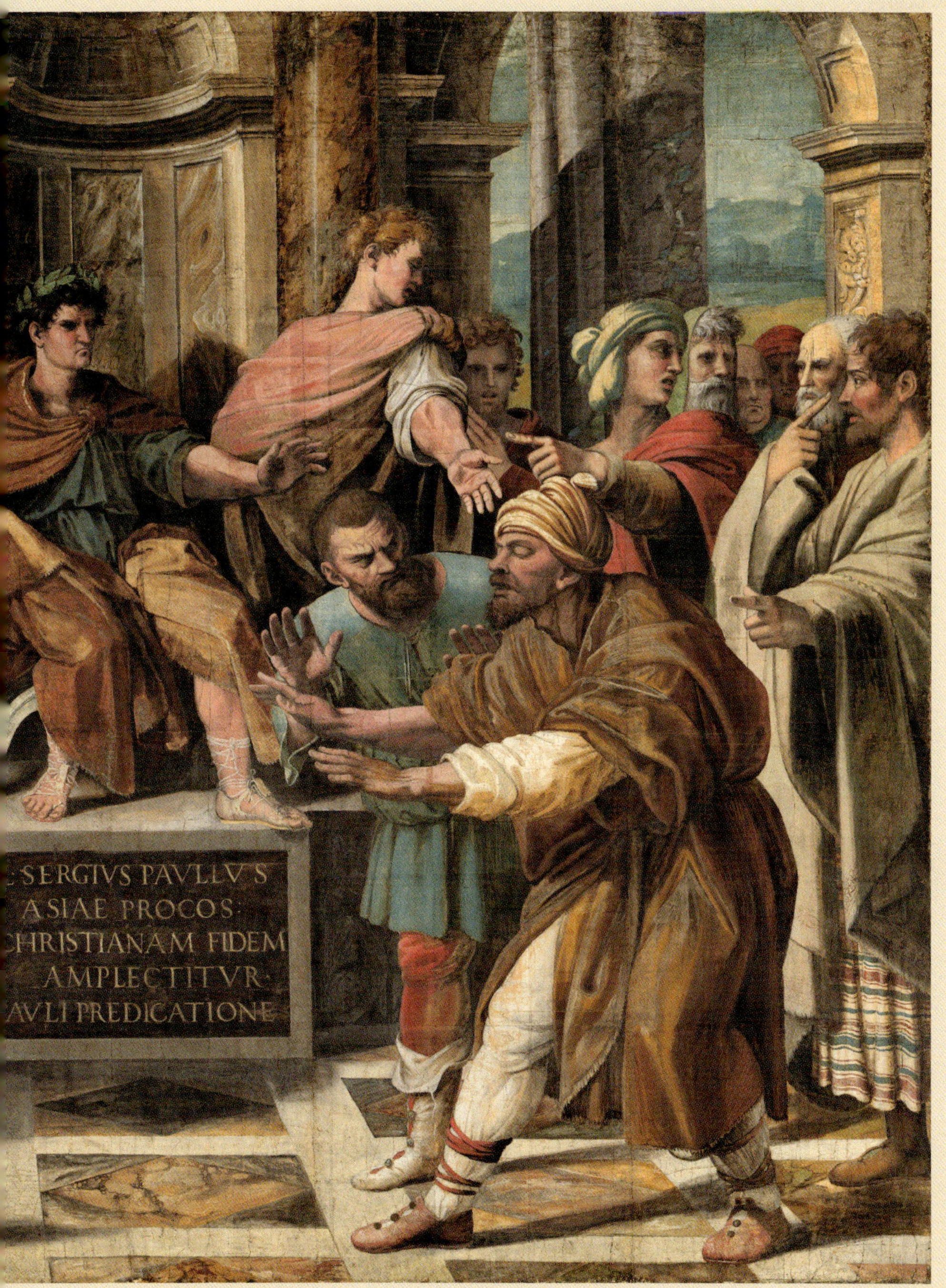
SERGIVS PAVLLVS
ASIAE PROCOS
HRISTIANAM FIDEM
AMPLECTITVR
AVLI PREDICATIONE

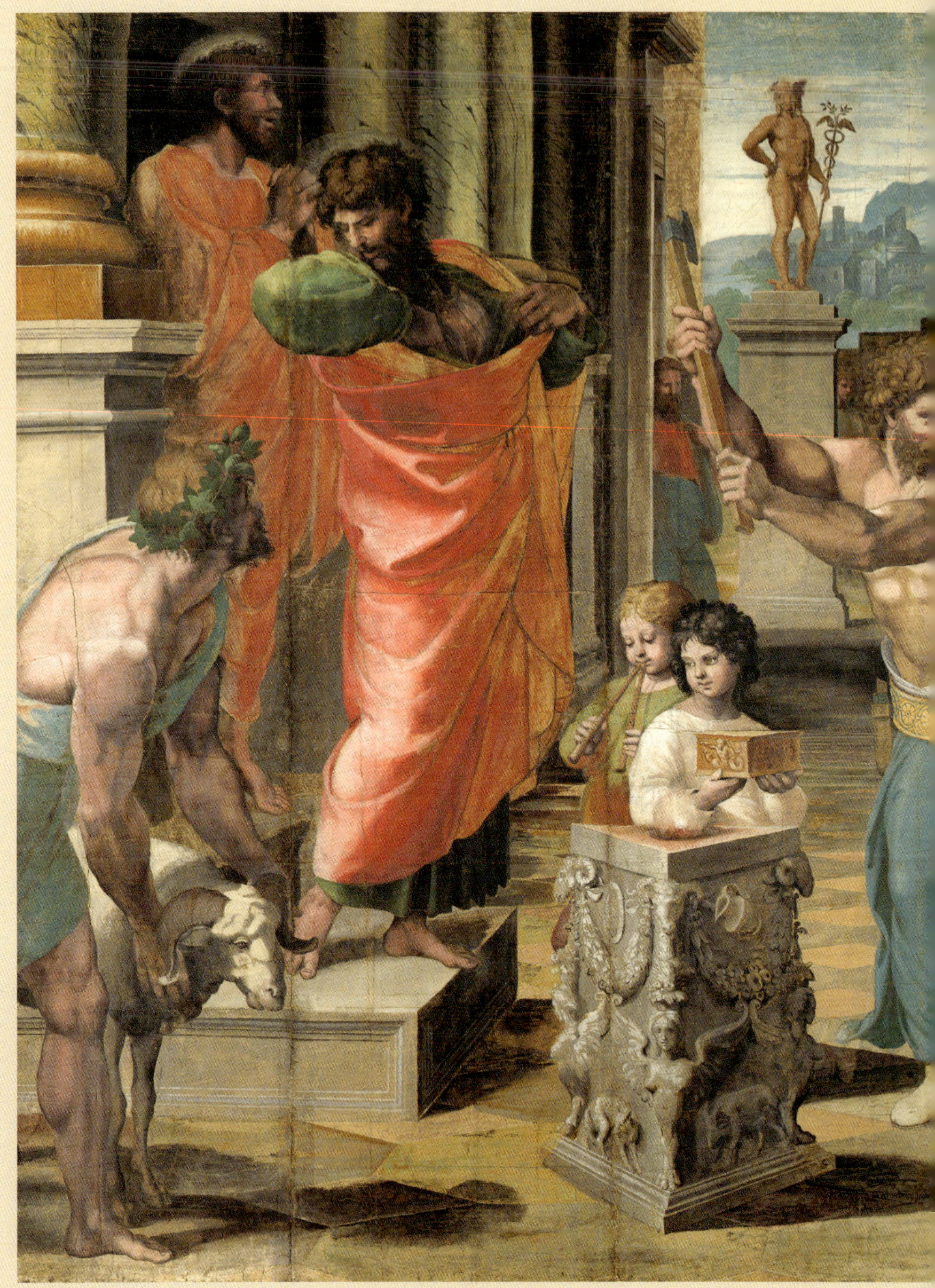

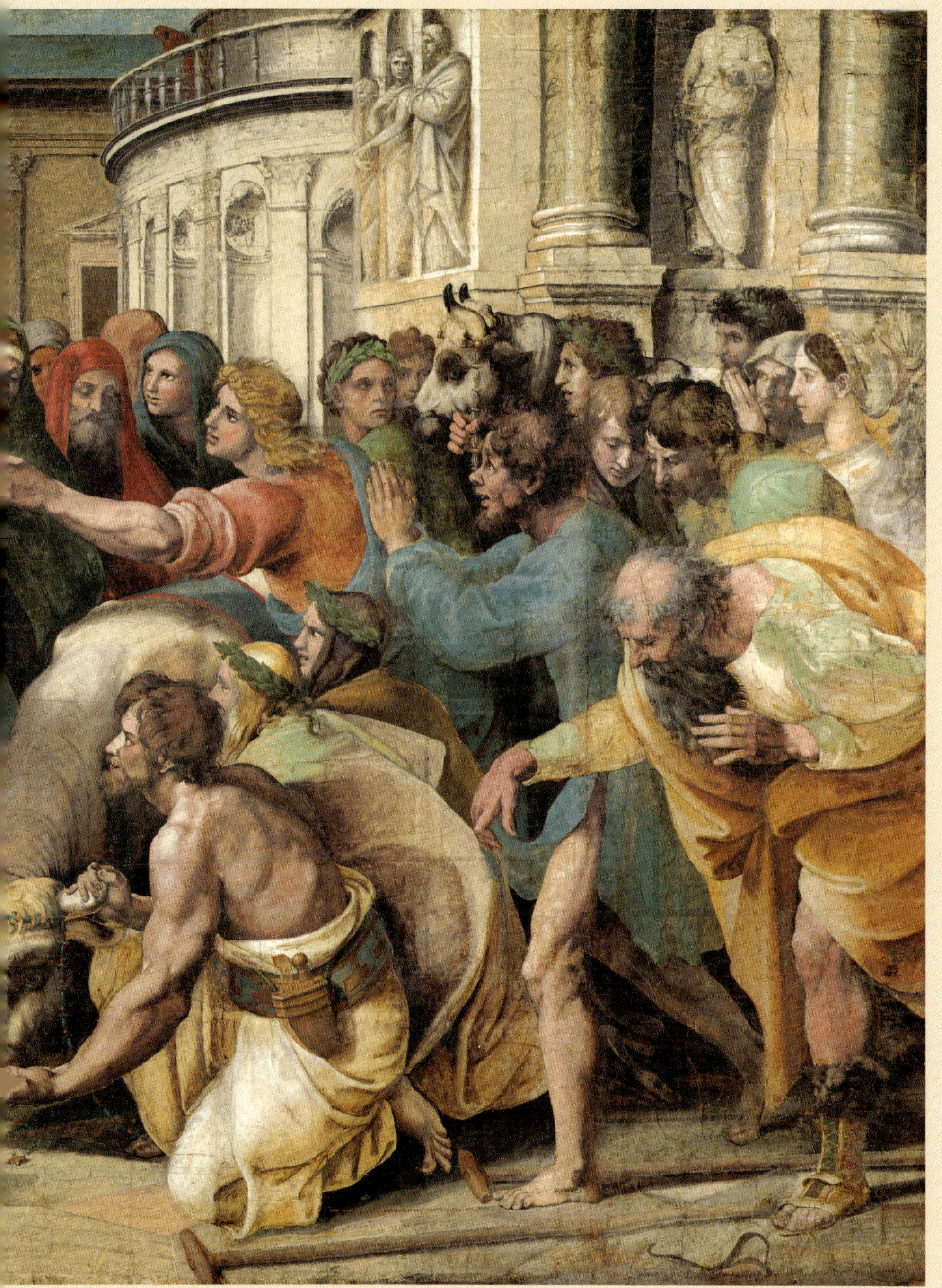

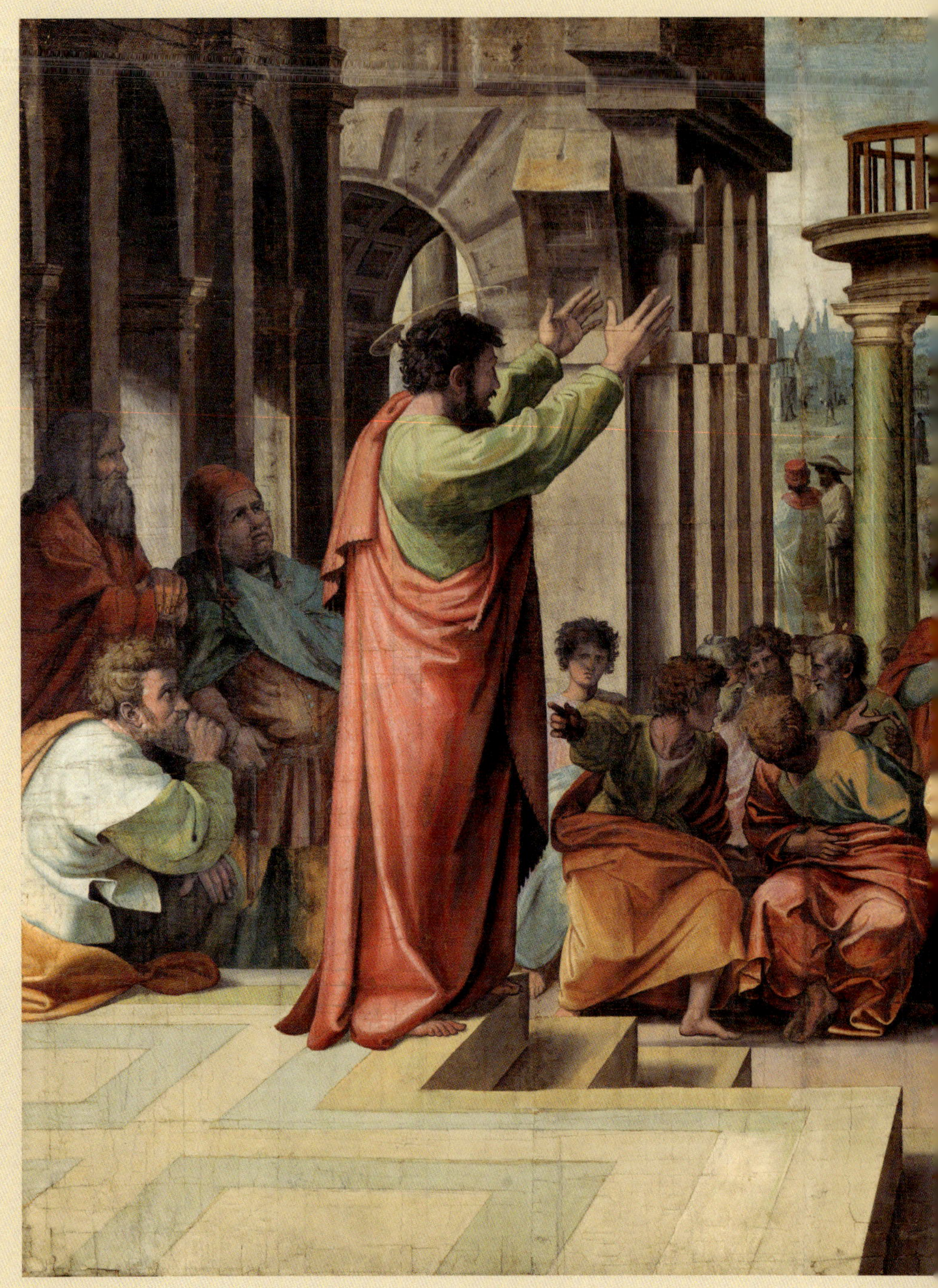

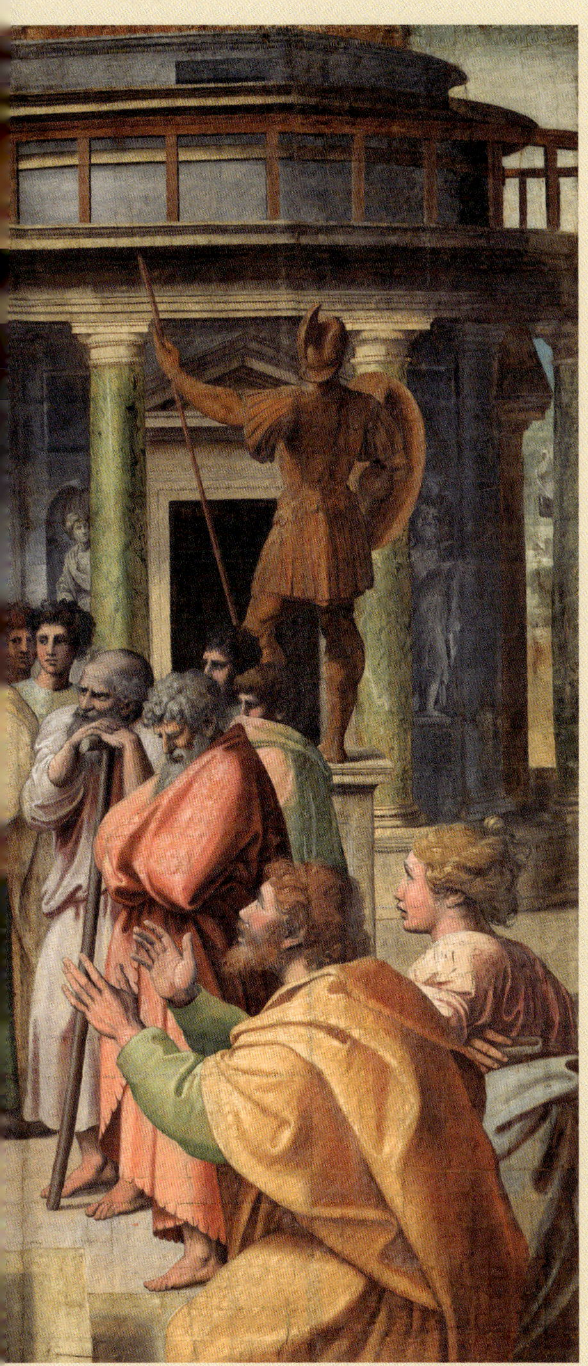

Paul Preaching on the Areopagus in Athens and the Conversion of Dionysius Areopagita and Damaris, 1515/16
Tapestry cartoon, gouache on paper, 343 × 442 cm (135 ⅛ × 174 ⅛ in)
London, Victoria and Albert Museum (on loan from the Royal Collection)
(Detail page 226)

Page 258/259
Temporary presentation of Raphael's tapestries in the Sistine Chapel, 2020

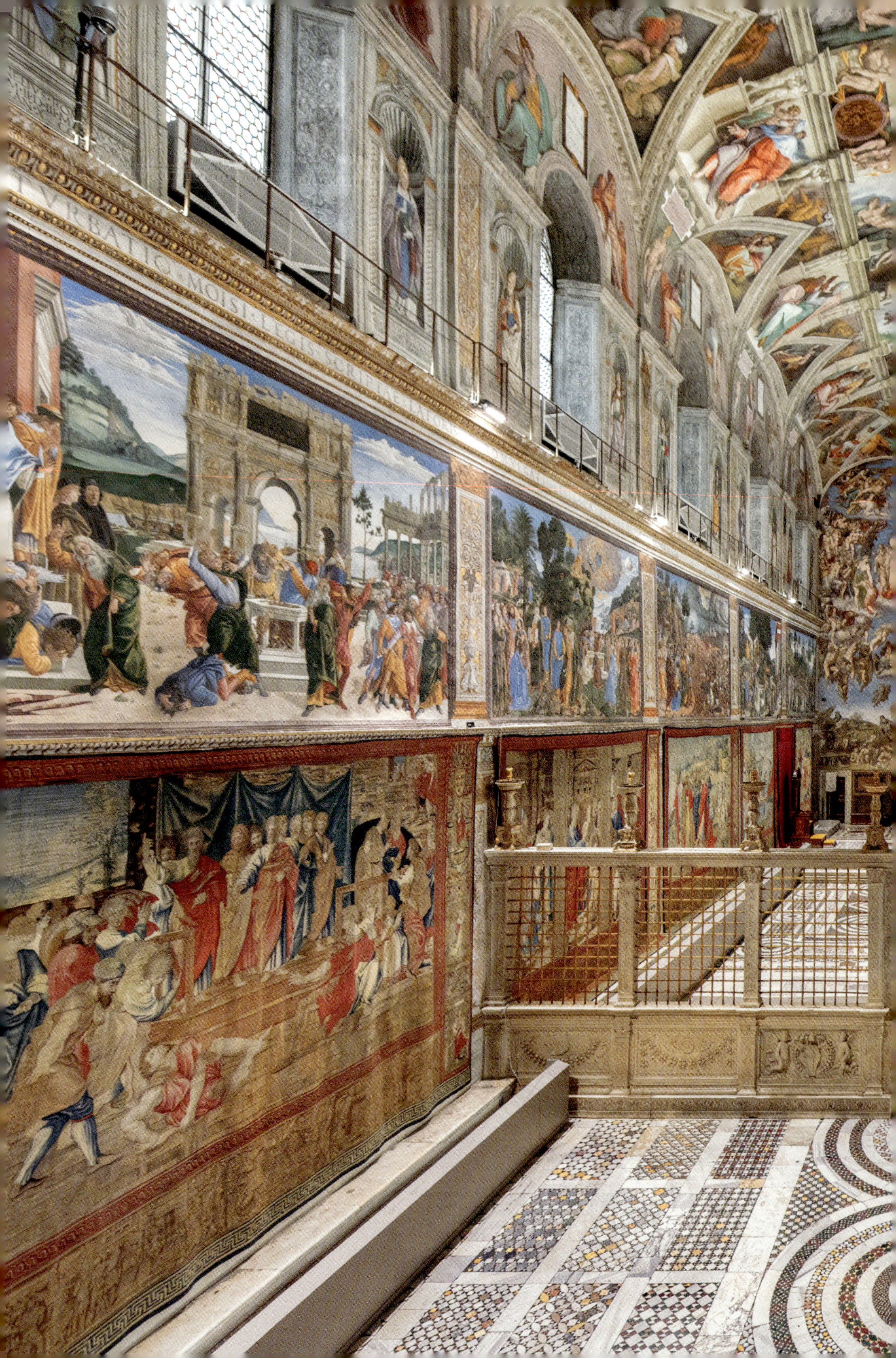
TVRBATIO · MOISI · LEGIS · SCRIPTAE · LATORIS

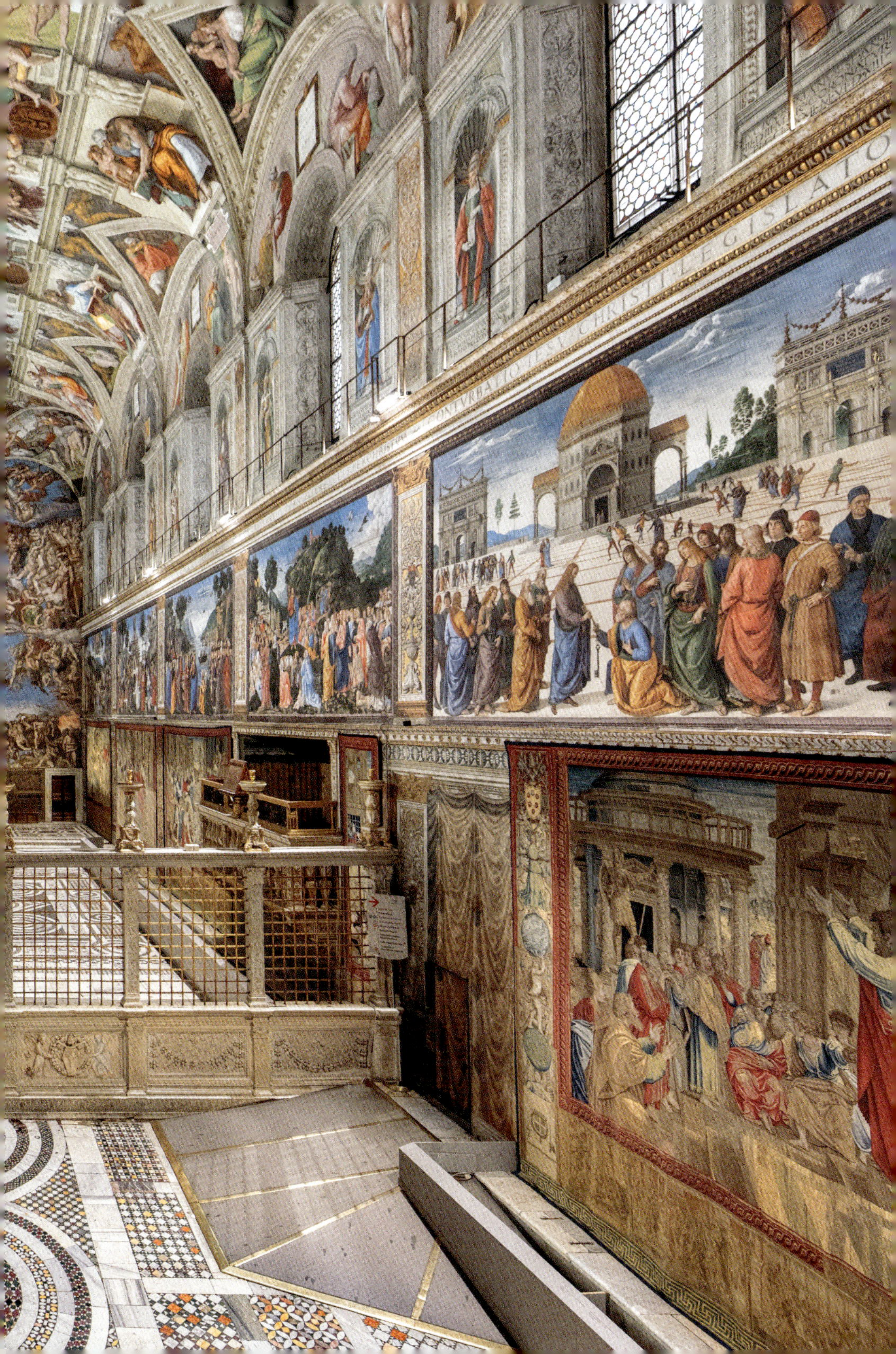
CONTVRBATIO IESV CHRISTI LEGISLATO

V.

Sacred World: The Roman altarpieces

1511/12–1520

Michael Rohlmann

"I had heard it said about Raphael so often before that it is not apparent from his works at first sight how beautiful they are ... but I must confess that his Madonna here shook me to the very core of my soul ... The heavenly is trimmed so close to the human that a copy can become very human."

PHILIPP OTTO RUNGE, 1801

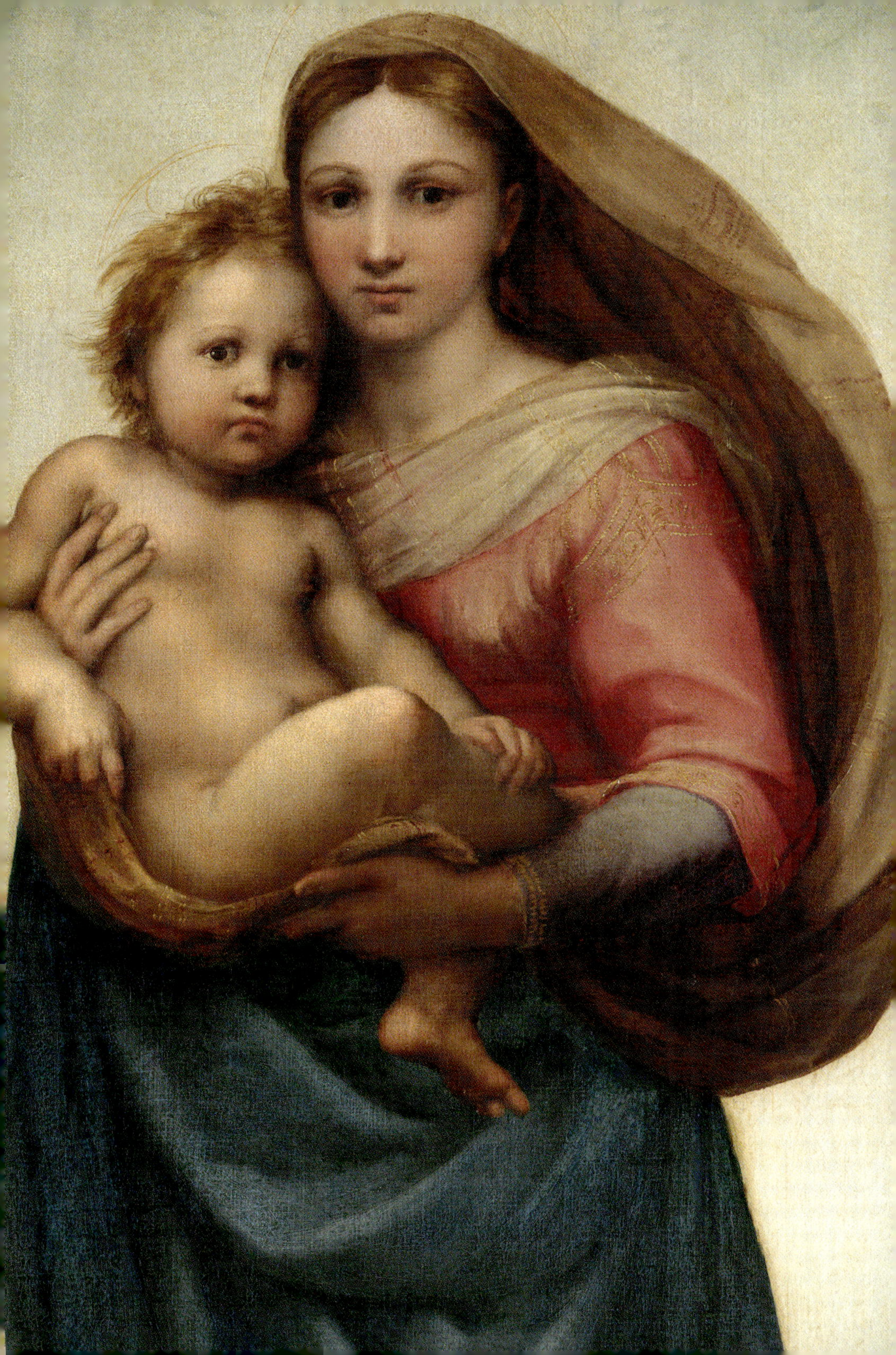

The adorning of altars with paintings was how Raphael's artistic career had begun. He continued the series of his altarpieces in his Roman years, too. It was this medium, in particular, that secured his painting a public presence in Rome and beyond. He produced altarpieces for Rome, Piacenza, Naples, Bologna, Palermo, L'Aquila, and even Narbonne in France. The Curia's underlying strategy seems to have been to surround the art produced by Raphael at the papal court – and thus indirectly the papacy itself – with an aura of religious venerability, and to spread this in major cities within the Papal States as well as among politically relevant rival powers. To the faithful, Julius II and Leo X's painter gave objects of devotion of otherworldly beauty, exalted presence, powerful visual rhetoric, and a new level of intellectual ambition. In several paintings, moreover, Raphael alluded to the Pope directly or indirectly through particular motifs. This was the case in the earliest of his Roman altarpieces, which he produced immediately after completing the Stanza della Segnatura. It was commissioned around 1511/12 by Sigismondo de' Conti (1432–1512), who was Julius II's secretary and a close confidante of the pope. The donor himself appears in the picture in robes that clearly proclaim him a member of the Curia. The work is known as the *Madonna di Foligno* (p. 262; Cat. P58) after the location in which it was later housed.

The painting was originally intended for the main altar of the Franciscan church of Santa Maria in Aracoeli. In Rome at that time, the permanent installation of a painting on a high altar was highly unusual, for special liturgical reasons that went back to early Christian traditions (de Blaauw 1996). In the large old basilicas, the main altars stood on a raised podium and above the entrance to a *confessio*, in such a way that the priest could only celebrate Mass facing the congregation from behind the altar. Many Roman churches also had a bishop's throne for the Pope at the end of the apse. The line of sight between altar and throne was not permitted to be obstructed by a retable. There were no such constraints in Santa Maria in Aracoeli, however, and Raphael's painted altarpiece could therefore be installed on the far side of the high altar. His representation had to perform a dual task: it had to combine the interests of the Franciscans with those of the donor. For the first time, Raphael moves away from the established standard arrangement of a group of saints gathered around the enthroned Madonna in an architectural setting. Instead, he locates the saints in a landscape and shows the Virgin and Child floating on clouds above them like a celestial apparition. He thereby follows earlier, isolated examples by artists such as Ghirlandaio and Perugino. Most importantly, however, this compositional solution enabled him to take up the local founding legend of Santa Maria in Aracoeli, on whose site Emperor Augustus was said to have experienced a vision of the Madonna floating in front of the sun. This vision was depicted in the vast apse fresco by Pietro Cavallini (died *c.* 1330) above the high altar. In Raphael's painting, the

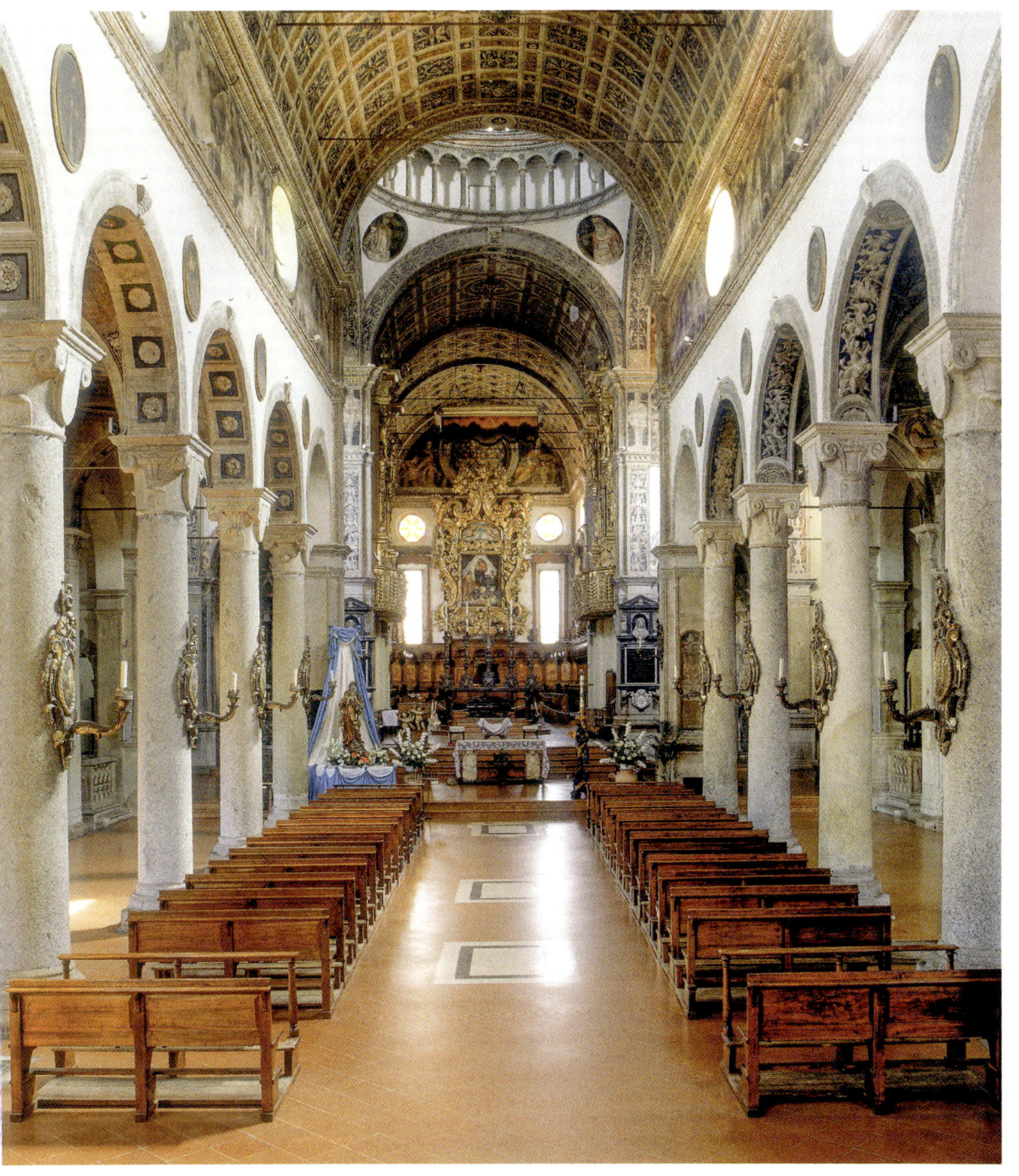

Page 261
Detail from **Sistine Madonna (Madonna and Child with Saints Sixtus and Barbara)**, *c.* 1512/13
(see ill. p. 291)

Interior of San Sisto in Piacenza with a copy of the *Sistine Madonna* in a baroque frame

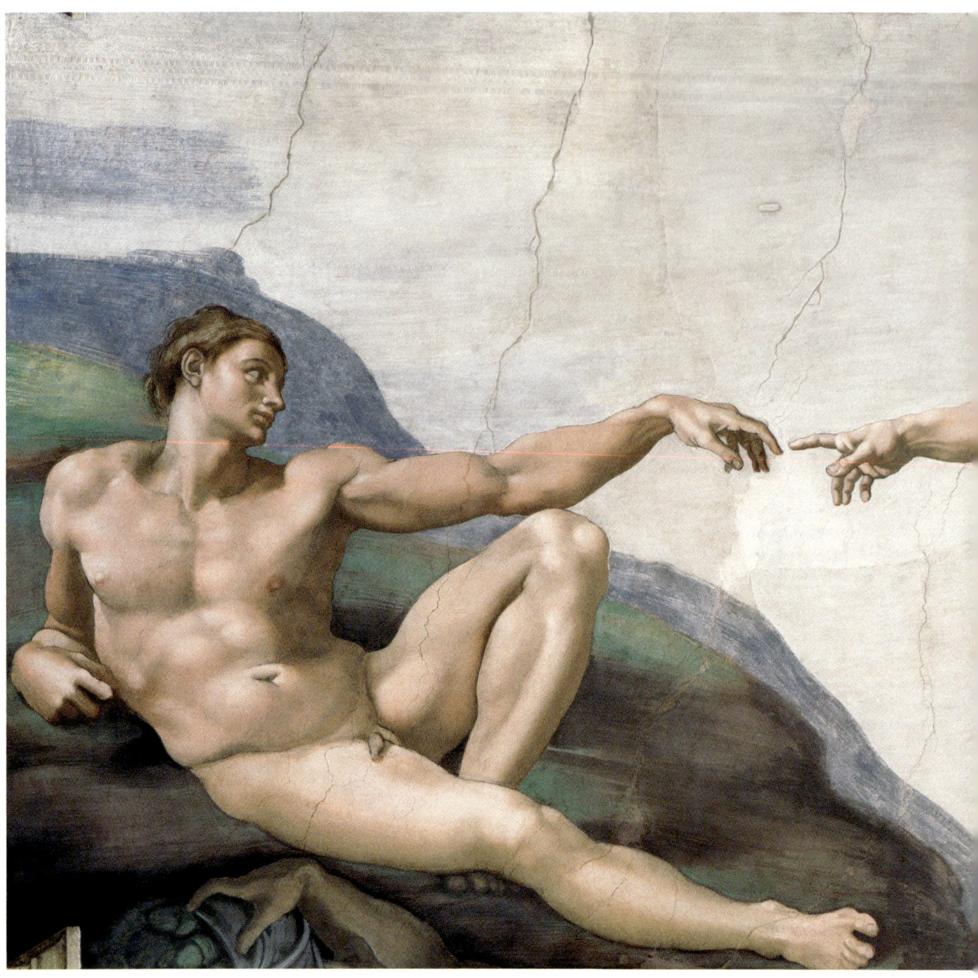

pictorial geometry and narrative elements form a sealed unit and the attention is focused on the Madonna. The luminous disc of the sun behind her is echoed in the semi-circular upper edge of the picture. Below, the circle is completed by the arrangement of the heads of the figures. On the left, John the Baptist, as the old joint patron saint of the church, looks out at us and points with an athletic right arm towards the celestial apparition, at which the other four figures at ground level are already gazing. Francis, the patron saint of the Franciscan Order, kneels humbly in front of John. As if the successor to the

Michelangelo Buonarroti, **Sistine Ceiling: Creation of Adam**, 1510
Fresco, 260 × 570 cm (102 3/8 × 224 3/8 in). Vatican City, Musei Vaticani, Cappella Sistina

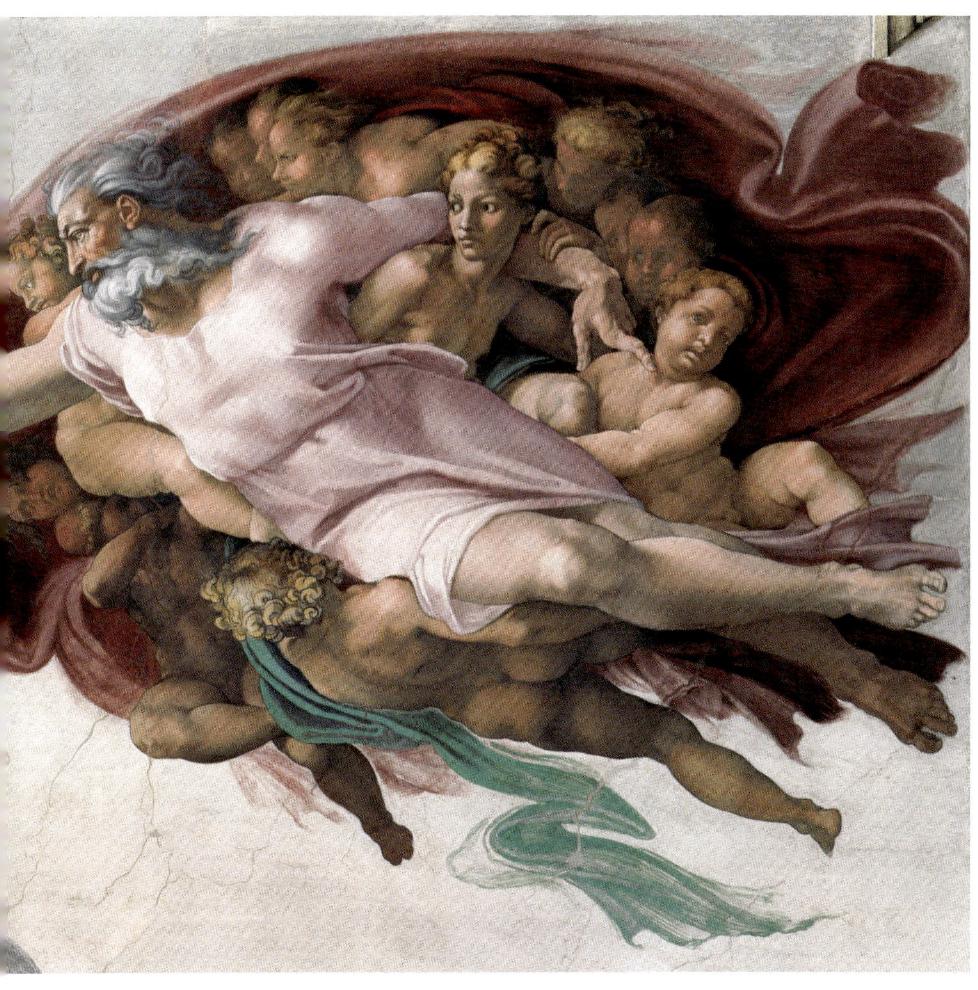

biblical preacher of repentance, with whose name he was originally christened, Francis, too, holds a cross. With his other hand he seems to want to draw the attention of the Virgin Mary and her son to the Franciscans and other members of the congregation occupying the choir stalls in front of the altarpiece. The wound visible in his hand – the sign of the stigmata – testifies to his religious merit as one who shared the sufferings of the crucified Christ, and provides hope that his gesture of intercession will be successful. While the two saints on the left mediate in both directions between the vision in the picture and the viewer outside, on the right the communication is internal. In a type of representation widespread among tomb paintings in Rome, Saint Jerome commends the donor Sigismondo de' Conti to the celestial apparition. He is thereby visibly successful:

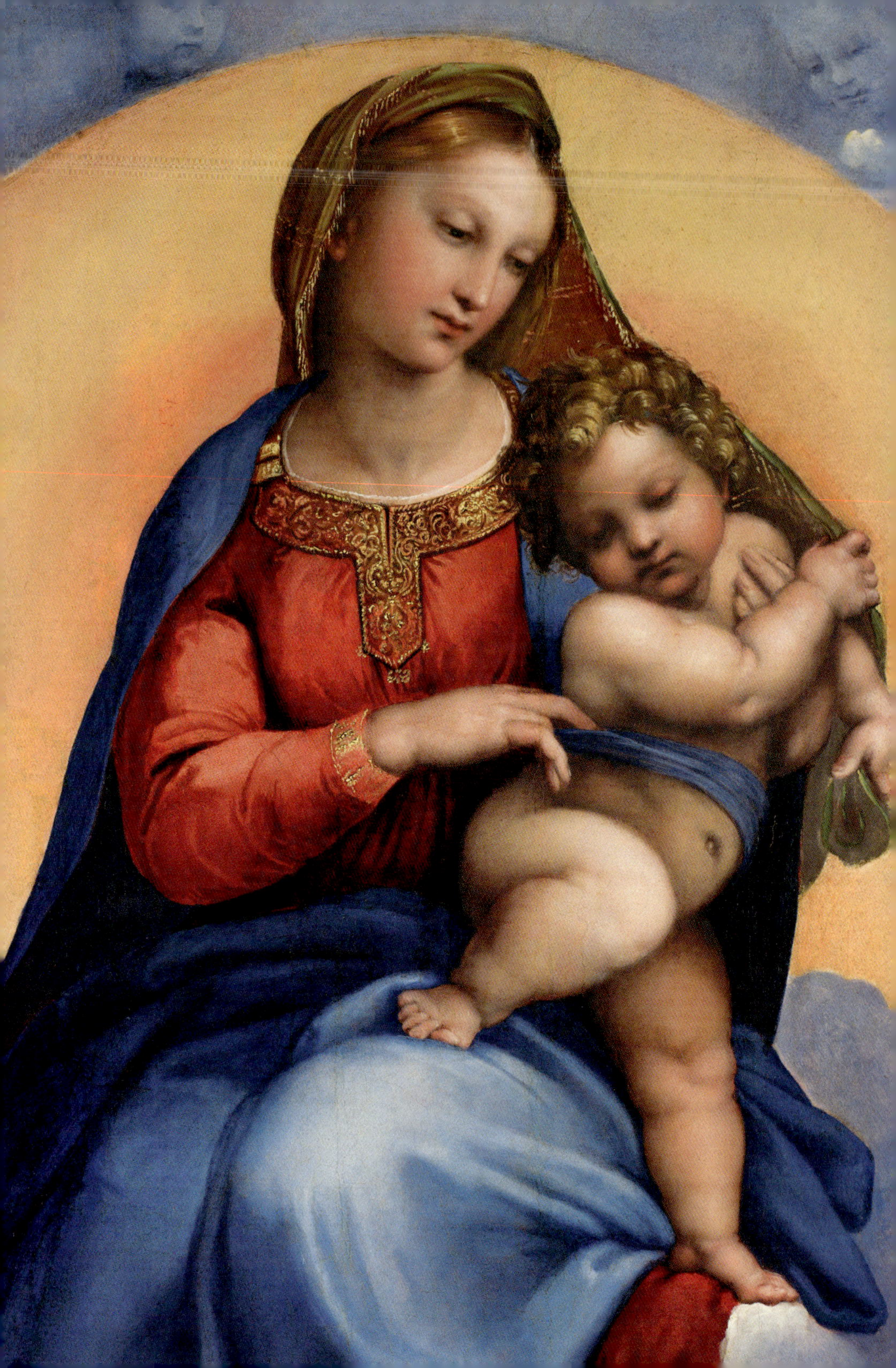

the Child's attention, and the salvation it brings, is already directed towards the donor, as the Infant shows by climbing down. In the Madonna group, Raphael cites figures from paintings by his two great contemporaries: the Virgin from Leonardo's Florentine *Adoration of the Magi* (p. 271) and the clambering Child from Michelangelo's *Doni Tondo* (p. 269). Raphael thus seems to wish to assert the status of his Madonna in terms of aesthetic tradition, perhaps also vis-à-vis a highly revered Byzantine Marian icon also housed in the church.

Jerome not only presents the donor to the Madonna, but also gestures with his extended right hand towards a winged naked boy holding an antique wooden writing tablet in the central foreground. In place of the music-making angels often shown at the Virgin's feet in altarpieces (cf. Raphael's *Madonna del Baldacchino*, p. 151; Cat. P44), Raphael invents a highly poetic motif, which invited multiple interpretations (see Rohlmann 2021, 2022b). In Raphael's day, one interpretation related to the donor would have leapt to the fore. As personal secretary to Julius II, Sigismondo de' Conti recorded the Pope's acts of governance in written documents and formulated the Della Rovere's politics, as it were, in papal briefs. De' Conti wears his ceremonial robe of office in the altarpiece and has himself commended not by his name saint, but by Jerome, the patron saint of papal secretaries (Jerome was considered the first secretary to a pope). The writing tablet may thus be understood as the attribute of both saint and donor and as the medium of their work. It takes the ancient form of a *tabula ansata*, a tablet with handles, probably in keeping with the antique atmosphere of the site on the Capitoline Hill where Augustus received his vision. The putto looks like the brother of the geniuses on the ceiling of the Stanza della Segnatura, who carry similar tablets (pp. 186/187; Cat. F3.1a–d). Like Apollo in Raphael's *Parnassus* (p. 184 b.; Cat. F3.1k), he looks heavenwards with a rapt expression, as if he, too, were receiving divine inspiration. The wooden writing tablet is to the genius what the wooden-bodied stringed instrument is to the leader of the Muses. *Numine afflatur* ("breathed upon by the spirit"), the *Parnassus* motto for divine inspiration, is illustrated in the case of the *Madonna di Foligno* putto by the light of the sky: a rainbow in the landscape behind also encompasses the putto. A celestial body with a blazing tail seems to be arcing downwards in the direction of his head, where the curly locks above his forehead gleam golden. An upturned gaze of inspiration and a blank writing sheet are also combined, moreover, in Raphael's portrait of the learned humanist and papal librarian Inghirami (1470–1516, p. 335; Cat. P52).

Detail from **Madonna di Foligno (The Virgin Mary and Child with Saints John, Francis, Jerome and the donor Sigismondo de' Conti)**, *c.* 1511/12
(see ill. p. 290)

Sigismondo de' Conti had been famous as a poet since his youth – Raphael's father Giovanni Santi praises him as such in his rhymed *Chronicle*. Pietro Bembo later admired the elegance and luminous purity of his style. His rise to the position of personal secretary to the Pope was the culmination of his life as a humanist and writer. Raphael's painting wishes to show that the divine inspiration of the poet is necessary in order to express, in the medium of text, the will of Christ's earthly representative. The work of the papal secretary appears elevated, in Raphael's altarpiece, into a religious, sacred sphere. Jerome's gesturing hands link the genius of inspired writing with Sigismondo's head. Just as the wound in Francis's hand lends weight to his intercession, so the writing tablet presented by Jerome and the putto symbolises Sigismondo's achievements during his lifetime. Jerome presents it as an argument before God, in order to secure the salvation of the donor's soul. Sigismondo was perhaps already dead when the picture was completed; his sunken face could have been painted from a death mask (Jones/Penny 1983). He was buried in the apse near the high altar in 1512.

Raphael's *Sistine Madonna* (p. 291; Cat. P59) was probably a direct commission from Julius II and was intended for the high altar of the newly completed Benedictine abbey of San Sisto in Piacenza. In June 1512, after the withdrawal of the French, the city submitted itself to papal rule and was incorporated into the Papal States. The Della Rovere had a long association with the monastery, and the endowment of the altar may be understood as a particular token of papal pardon for his new subjects. In addition to the Virgin and Child, Raphael needed to show only two saints: Sixtus, as patron saint of the church, kneels opposite Saint Barbara, whose relics were preserved in the church. Raphael was consequently able to adapt a compositional type developed in Florence for high altarpieces, which dispenses with an earthly setting and shows the Madonna and saints floating in clouds. Whereas the *Madonna di Foligno* was required to portray the celestial apparition as a vision appearing to multiple figures on earth, in the *Sistine Madonna* the entire picture transforms into a celestial vision experienced by the viewers themselves. A parapet at the bottom, and tied-back curtains hanging from a slightly sagging pole at the top, seem to belong to our imperfect reality and reinforce the illusion of the apparition of clouds and light. In his *Madonna del Baldacchino* (Cat. P44), Raphael had already shown green curtains being drawn back by angels in order to allow the saints and ourselves a view of the Virgin and Child. On the high altar, as the place where the major public celebrations of Mass were held, the visionary character of the picture was intended to suggest that God's presence was even greater here than on the private altars. The compositional type thus served to establish a hierarchy of the space within the church.

For the wide and clear Renaissance building, Raphael successfully creates, with his *Sistine Madonna*, a composition that is convincing even when seen from a distance and

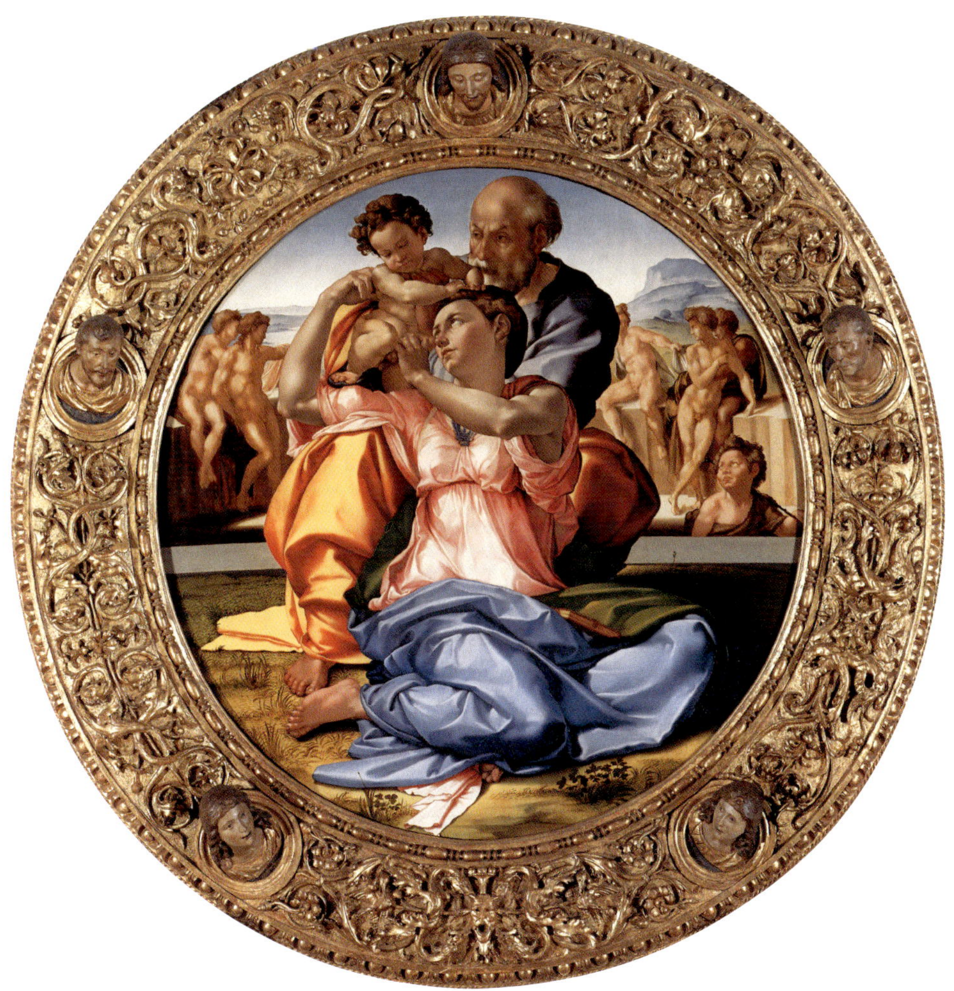

Michelangelo Buonarroti, **Holy Family with the Infant St John (Doni Tondo)**, *c.* 1504
Dia. 91 × 80 cm (35 7/8 × 31 1/2 in). Florence, Gallerie degli Uffizi

in which the simplicity of the pyramid of figures is married with the most delicate feel for animation, rhythm, transitions and the balancing of opposites (Hetzer 1947). The monumental floating Madonna steps forward with a simple majesty and quiet nobility. Seen in sharp silhouette, advancing and descending out of divine light among angelic spirits and hazy clouds, she dominated and filled the expanse of the church interior. The kneeling saints sinking into cloud, one oriented upwards and the other downwards, frame her path, whereby Saint Sixtus on the left is clearly characterised as an intermediary.

He points outwards into our world and intercedes with the divine figures on behalf of the viewer. At the same time, with the gestures of his hands he also connects himself with us. The beatified Pope Sixtus II (died 258) was the name saint of Sixtus IV, Julius II's uncle. Raphael has decorated his vestment and tiara with acorns and oak leaves, emblems of the Della Rovere family (in Italian, *rovere* means "oak"). Julius II thus claimed for himself the role of papal intercessor on behalf of his newly won territory of Piacenza: it was suggested to the inhabitants that, now they were part of the Papal States, Pope Julius II would act as intermediary ensuring their salvation. Indeed, Raphael's painting shows that the Pope's efforts have already been successful: only in this one altarpiece does Raphael's Madonna walk towards us; only here do mother and child look out at us. Their large eyes are wide open and, owing to the proximity of their respective heads, appear as a double pair, making their gaze powerful even at a distance. The attention signalled by the divine gaze and the drawing closer of the double figure carries the promise of salvation (see Rohlmann 2012).

It was the German painter Julius Schnorr von Carolsfeld (1794–1872), with his artist's eye, who noted that Raphael was alluding, in his juxtaposition of mother and child, to a masterpiece by Michelangelo. The idea of the billowing mantel surrounding the outline of the figure on the right, and the pose of the nude figure with regard to the torso and angled arm on the left, are both taken from the *Creation of Adam* (pp. 264/265). In Raphael's imagination, God and Adam reaching towards each other in Michelangelo's fresco find their supreme resolution in the Virgin Mary cradling her incarnate divine Child, who is Christ the New Adam.

Below the majestic apparition, the two little angels propping themselves on the parapet with childish unconcern were a source of delight even in the sixteenth century, captivating and touching eyes and hearts (Don Felice Passero: "invaghiscono et allettano gli occhi e 'l core"). Raphael has perhaps alluded here in light-hearted fashion to Piacenza and the meaning of its name (Latin *placentia*, pleasure) and wanted to give corresponding pleasure to its citizens with this motif.

Raphael's art of adapting his design of gatherings of saints to the context of the altarpiece in question is confirmed by a comparison with the *Madonna del Pesce* (p. 293; Cat. P63), possibly executed around 1513/14. The painting was intended not for the high altar of a vast church, but for a small, windowless burial chapel that was attached as part of an annex building to a side chapel in San Domenico, the church of the Dominican Order in Naples. The private, narrow space was reflected in the close grouping of the saints in an earthly setting, in a quiet, almost intimate, atmospheric scene. On the left, the beautiful Archangel Raphael gently and tenderly introduces the young, shyly awestruck Tobias with his fish to the Madonna. Flanking the throne on the right is the benevolent elderly Saint Jerome. The Child turns his attention away from the latter in order to greet

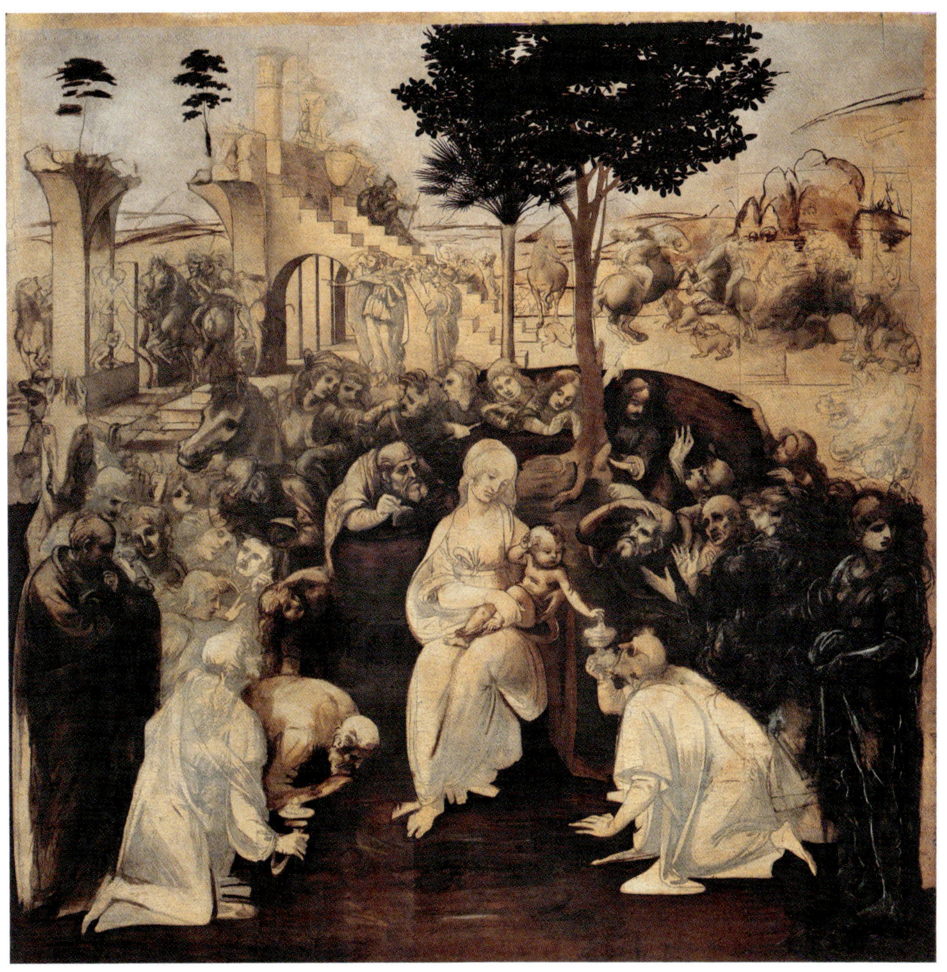

Leonardo da Vinci, **Adoration of the Magi**, 1481/82
Oil and tempera on panel, 243 × 246 cm (95 ⅔ × 96 ⅞ in). Florence, Gallerie degli Uffizi

the new arrivals on the left. The traditional quiet gathering of the saints here transforms itself into a narrative, as it were. Visitors entering the side chapel turned left to enter the burial chapel, where they could move up close to the picture of the Virgin and Child. The introduction by Archangel Raphael represented within the picture, thereby became their own, orchestrated by the art of Raphael the painter. Between Tobias, who has dropped to one knee on the left, and Jerome on the right, already kneeling on the Virgin's podium, an empty step rises in the foreground: an invitation to the viewer to kneel, in their imagination, before the Madonna.

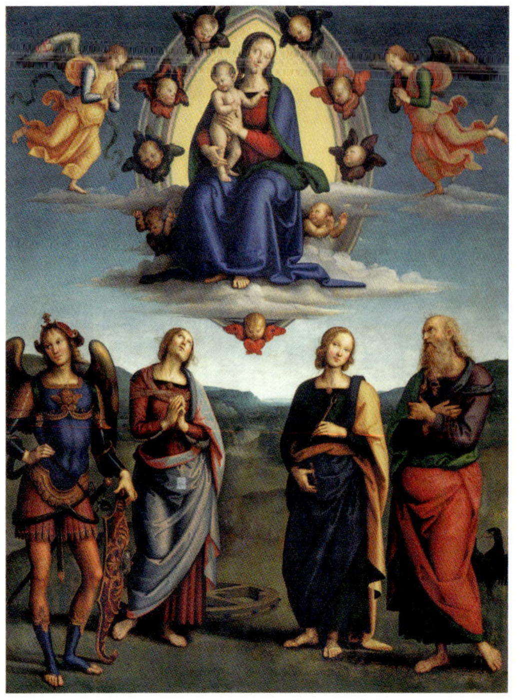

The two saints on either side of the Virgin and Child make clear reference to the history of the chapel's endowment. In 1509 the rights to the long-existing chapel were acquired by Girolamo del Doce, who probably also specified that it should be dedicated to his name saint Jerome (Stumpel 1990). The Del Doce were one of the leading old families of the Neapolitan nobility; Girolamo's grandfather Carluccio had been a royal advisor with the title Maresciallo del Regno. The Del Doce chapel led off a side chapel which housed a miracle-working crucifix associated with Thomas Aquinas (*c.* 1225–1274). In the years around 1500, numerous Neapolitan nobles installed tombs and made endowments in this chapel with its special treasure. Probably in 1518, the patronage of the Del Doce chapel passed to Girolamo's cousin, Giovan Battista. After the latter died in 1519, his widow had tombs built in the burial chapel for him and his father, Rainaldo. Probably around 1522/25, the chapel interior was redecorated in Roman Renaissance forms (Naldi 1997). With its weapons and military trophies, the architectural décor was thereby tailored to Rainaldo and Giovan Battista, who distinguished themselves as soldiers. Raphael's painting is dated stylistically to around 1513/14 and hence may have been commissioned by Girolamo, whose name saint appears in the picture. The group of Tobias and the angel can be understood as an allusion to the name Del Doce (Duce, Duca, from the Latin *dux*). In the biblical Book of Tobit, Tobias's father assigns the angel to his son as a leader

Pietro Perugino, **Virgin and Child with Saints Michael, Catherine, Apollonia and John the Evangelist**, *c.* 1497/1500
Oil on panel, 330 × 265 cm (129 ⅞ × 104 ⅓ in)
Bologna, Pinacoteca Nazionale (altarpiece from San Giovanni in Monte)

Lorenzo Costa, **Coronation of the Virgin with Saints Victor, John the Baptist, Augustine, John the Evangelist, Jerome and Sebastian**, 1501
Oil on panel, 283 × 165 cm (111 ⅜ × 64 ⅞ in). Bologna, San Giovanni in Monte

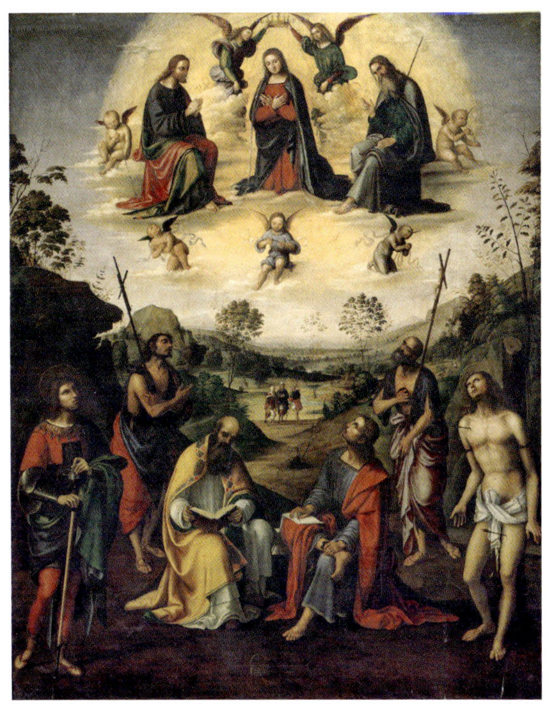

and guide *(dux)*. In inimitable fashion, Raphael has visualised the angel's leading and guiding role as the main motif of the group. By turning from Jerome's book towards the group of Tobias and the angel, the Infant Christ links, as it were, the donor's baptismal name with his family surname.

How the Neapolitan nobleman managed to commission an altarpiece from Raphael, we do not know. Raphael was at that time painter to the Medici Pope Leo X and it is highly unlikely that he could have supplied a picture intended for Naples, ruled by the Spanish viceroy, without Medici approval. The iconography of the two saints could in two places be understood as possibly containing an allusion to the Pope. Firstly, the story of Tobias and the angel is associated with healing: Tobias, with the help of the angel, brings back a fish as a medicine that will restore his father's sight. The Medici (in Italian, "medical doctors") as healers was a standard theme of papal panegyric under Leo X, including in altarpieces. Secondly, Jerome's lion (in Italian, *leone*) might call to mind the Pope's Italian name of Leone X.

Both may have struck Raphael and contemporary viewers as a fortunate or inconsequential coincidence. In the case of another detail, however, it is perhaps harder to see it as such. Raphael took the ends of the arms of the Virgin's throne from the throne of an antique statue of Jupiter, one he had already referenced in his Florentine *Madonna del Baldacchino* (Cat. P44; Shearman 1977). But neither in the antique throne nor in Raphael's Florentine altarpiece is the arm support topped by a golden-brown sphere as in the *Madonna del Pesce*. Here it shines prominently out against a dark background, and the angle of the Child's gaze and gesture even seems to be directed exactly towards it. Did Raphael wish to refer, via this sphere, to the golden *palle* or balls of the Medici coat of arms – and thus to the Pope associated with healing and the lion (cf. the ball on Leo's throne, p. 337; Cat. P79)? If so, Raphael's painting would be a particularly outstanding example, in terms of its concentration, of the play upon heraldic symbols and the meaning of names that was so popular and widespread in Renaissance culture.

Bologna received a Raphael altarpiece through the agencies of Leo X's Curia. Elena Duglioli dall'Olio (1472–1520) was a charismatic Bolognese who had led a life of virginal chastity even during her marriage. She experienced mystical visions, heard angelic music, wrote a theological treatise on spiritual life and Christian perfection, and quickly came to be considered a saint by her contemporaries. High-ranking members of clergy sought contact with her, including the later Leo X as cardinal legate under Julius II. Her theological advisor was Pietro Ritta da Lucca, a canon regular of the Lateran at the Bologna church of San Giovanni in Monte. Here, around 1513/15, following an experience that she understood as divine inspiration, Elena commissioned the construction and decoration of a new chapel. She was assisted in this enterprise by the Florentine Cardinal Lorenzo Pucci (1458–1531), a confidante of Leo X, and in particular by his nephew Antonio Pucci (1485–1544). It was evidently they who arranged for Raphael to supply the altarpiece, whose original Roman frame is still preserved in the chapel today (p. 294).

The chapel was consecrated to Saint Cecilia, upon whom Elena had chosen to model her life, as Cecilia had also lived chastely in her marriage. Cardinal Alidosi (*c.* 1455–1511) gave Elena a bone from the saint's arm, which she donated to the chapel when it was finished. Raphael's altarpiece, *Saint Cecilia with Saints Paul, John the Evangelist, Augustine and Mary Magdalene* (p. 295; Cat. P65), departs from the standard formula of the *sacra conversazione* insofar as the central position in the group of saints standing in a landscape setting is awarded to Cecilia, the patron saint of the chapel, rather than to the usual Virgin and Child. Cecilia is symmetrically surrounded by four saints. Above her, the heavens open and a circle of singing angels becomes visible. The altarpiece is precisely coordinated with the chapel architecture. The proportions of the retable correspond with those of its wall field, the vertical saints flank Cecilia in the same way as the pilaster groups surround the chapel, and at the top the angels form a circle like the cupola.

The two saints at the back are looking at each other. They are John the Evangelist, the saint to whom the church was dedicated, and Saint Augustine, whose Rule the canons at the church followed. The joint presence of these two saints makes it clear that San Giovanni in Monte is run by the canons regular of the Lateran. The same pairing is also found in the church's high altarpiece (p. 273), for example. The front two saints are conceived as opposites. On the left, the monumental Paul stands completely immersed in meditation, holding letters to the Corinthians and a sword. Dignity, religious ethos, seriousness and concentration perhaps made him a figure of identification for the high-ranking clergy associated with Elena dall'Olio. Mary Magdalene on the right looks actively out at the viewer and at the same time has only just stepped into the scene – as if inviting us to join the circle around Cecilia/Elena as well. Perhaps the Penitent Magdalene addressed herself in particular to Elena's "spiritual daughters", i. e. her female followers. Mary Magdalene carefully holds out a jar of ointment as her attribute towards Cecilia, whereby the motif is framed and further accentuated by Augustine's hands. Hartt recognised this jar, undoubtedly correctly, as an allusion to Elena's surname dall'Olio ("oil"). The donor family is thus symbolically presented to the chapel's saint.

Cecilia herself is the centre of a narrative line of visual argumentation whose complexity is unprecedented in the history of altarpiece painting. Raphael shows the saint in a golden wedding garment reconstructed on the basis of early Christian visual sources, which she wears over a hair shirt according to legend. As an expression of her chastity, Cecilia had turned away from the earthly music played during her marriage ceremony and had sung inwardly to God alone. Raphael replaces this inner singing by the saint with her listening to an angelic choir, towards which she turns with her gaze lifted heavenward. Cecilia appears in rapture and ecstasy, focused wholly on the divine. The effect is amplified by the devaluation and destruction of earthly musical instruments – a mise-en-scène invented by Raphael. Thus Cecilia lowers a portative organ, some of whose pipes are sliding out. A still life of secular musical instruments already lies on the ground at her feet. As the tools of lowly dance music, they are symbols of earthly pleasure. The instruments are damaged and transitory. At the same time, they are brought within tangible reach of the viewer by their virtuoso painterly suggestion of materiality. The angels in heaven, on the other hand, dissolve like spirits, grow blurred and fade into divine light. The celestial apparition is distinguished from the earthly sphere through the mode of painting. The divine eludes human ability to see and represent it (Stoichita 1995; Kleinbub 2011).

The painting has been understood, probably correctly, in the context of neo-Platonism. According to this interpretation, Raphael refers in Cecilia to the ascent of the soul from matter to the divine world of ideas. The viewer is invited to a visual meditation on earthly and heavenly things, on the virtues of the individual saints, and on various paths to spiritual life, knowledge of God and Christian beauty. Perhaps Elena was aiming for a visual pendant to her later treatise on how to live a spiritual life and attain Christian perfection *(Brieve et signoril modo del spiritual vivere e di facilmente pervenire alla christiana perfection).*

The theme of visionary experience at the centre of Raphael's painting was already firmly established in San Giovanni in Monte. Perugino's altarpiece in the neighbouring chapel showed two of four saints gazing up at an apparition of the Virgin Mary (p. 272), while in the main altarpiece by Lorenzo Costa (1460–1535), no fewer than five out of six saints cast their eyes heavenwards (p. 273). The reason for this probably lies with the dedication of the church to Saint John as the visionary Seer of the Apocalypse. Thus he is represented in the large circular window in the entrance wall, designed by Francesco del Cossa (*c.* 1435–1477), looking up at an angel appearing in the sky. Raphael's retable competed with such images. Does his altarpiece reflect this in the juxtaposition of heavenly and earthly music as two art forms, of which one is merely worldly craft, the other divinely inspired? *Numine afflatur*: this claim by the poets was one that Raphael had already asserted for himself as a painter in *Parnassus* (Cat. F3.1k). Whatever the case, in Bologna his *Saint Cecilia* became the aesthetic manifesto of a painting that had ascended from mere imitation of nature to inspired ideal.

Within the series of altarpieces produced by Raphael in Rome, a transition gradually takes place from the representation purely of assemblies of saints to narrative themes. It is a development that also concerns the genre of the altarpiece as a whole. Its reasons were unlikely to have been purely artistic, but were more probably connected with changes in the requirements placed on devotional art. In an epoch of the dawning Reformation and of Catholic reform efforts, the task of the paintings on the altar was no longer to line up figures to be venerated in the manner of icons, but to place more emphasis on communicating the contents of faith in a didactically narrative fashion. In place of the timeless fiction of combinations of idols, the aim was to portray a realistic and credible slice of reality. The viewer was thereby to be convinced of the truth of the representation and emotionally drawn into the events it showed. In his Roman treatments of the standard type of altarpiece, Raphael had gradually enriched the assemblies of saints in terms of content and visual rhetoric and in doing so deepened the viewer's experience of the picture. He then turned, in a number of altarpieces, to biblical themes, whereby in the earliest example he was able to draw upon his first attempt at an emotionally moving treatment, in a retable, of an episode from the life of Christ, completed even before he came to Rome.

In 1508 the *"magnifico"* Giacomo Basilicò (died 1517), a wealthy jurist with connections to the court, had endowed a church and monastery dedicated to Santa Maria dello Spasimo in Palermo. He was thereby fulfilling the wishes of his wife, who had died in 1500. The church lay directly outside the old city walls and served as a house for Olivetan monks from Santa Maria del Bosco, a Benedictine abbey located near Calatamauro, deep in the heart of Sicily. Construction work dragged on over many years: in 1533 the church was still unfinished and the vaulting of the nave, planned in 1535, was never carried out (Vesco 2007/08). Not long after this, work on the monastery was halted altogether in favour of a new fortification system for the city. Today the church survives as a ruin.

How Basilicò succeeded in commissioning an altarpiece of *Christ Carrying the Cross* (p. 299; Cat. P71) from Raphael, is likewise unknown. An engraving made in 1517, the year of Basilicò's death, by Agostino Veneziano (*c.* 1490–*c.* 1540), shows the composition of the painting. A rich marble frame for the work, carved by Antonello Gagini (1478–1536) in

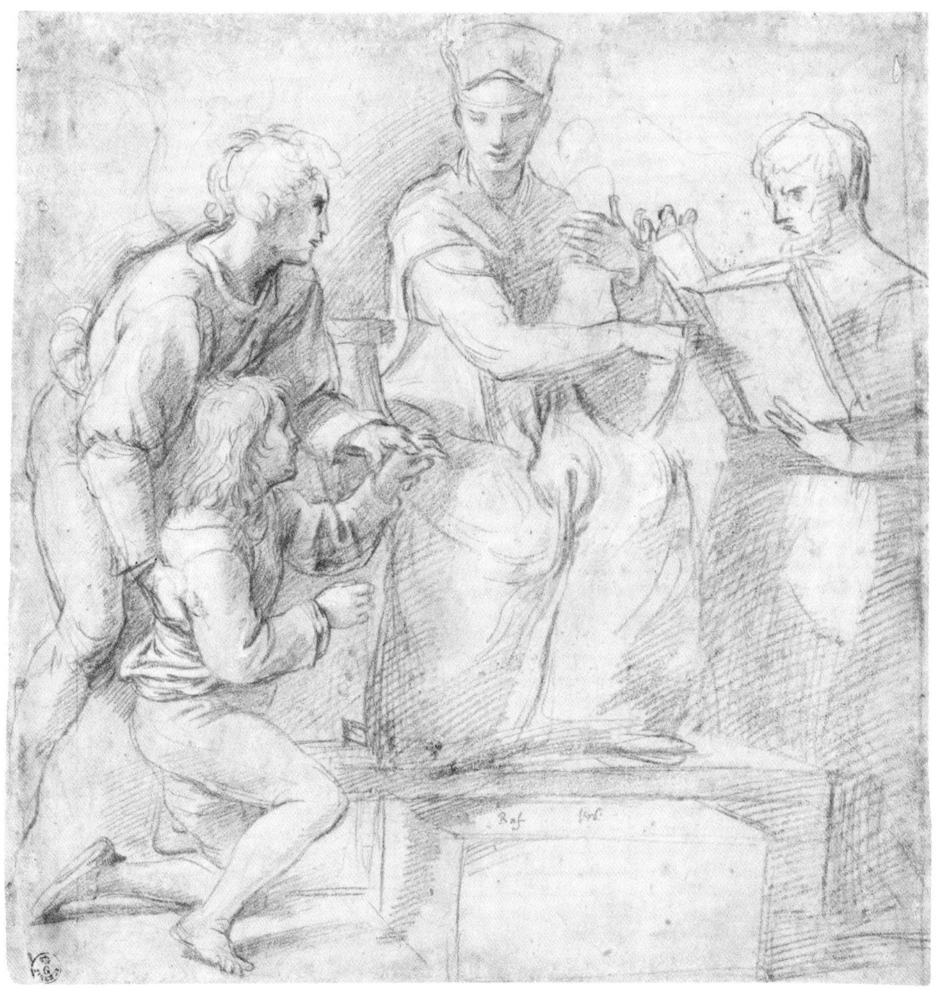

Study for the *Madonna del Pesce*, 1512
Red chalk, chalk and remnants of white heightening over stylus, 26.8 × 26.4 cm (10 ½ × 10 ⅜ in)
Florence, Gallerie degli Uffizi, Gabinetto dei Disegni e delle Stampe

Palermo, was rediscovered in fragments by Spadaro (Spadaro 2013), making it possible to attempt a reconstruction of the elaborate frame architecture (p. 298). As usually the case with Gagini, the heavy retable construction had to be built into the wall. Contrary to what has been stated in the Raphael literature to date, Raphael's altarpiece therefore cannot have been intended for the church's high altar, because in the centre of the corresponding wall in the main choir chapel there is a doorway. Moreover, when Gagini's altar is cited – in 1520 and again in 1534 – as the model on which further works are to be based, the corresponding documents clearly locate it in Basilicò's chapel in the church ("como quillu di lu Spasimo in la cappella di lu quondam magnifico Jacopu Basilicò"; "in la cappella di lu quondam magnifico Jacopo Basilicò intra la ecclesia di Sancta Maria di lo Spasimo"). The elongated side chapel was accessible from the right transept and lay south of the choir.

The *"spasimo"* to which the church is dedicated, and which is also the subject of Raphael's altarpiece, refers to the pang of agony experienced by the Virgin at the sight of Christ carrying his cross on the road to Calvary. The sacred topography of Jerusalem was evidently meant to be transferred to Palermo. Just as Santa Maria dello Spasimo lay just outside one of Palermo's city gates, a church of the same name stood on the Via crucis directly in front of the Jerusalem city gate. It marked the place where Mary encountered her son, who had fallen under the weight of the cross. Raphael bases his pictorial invention on Dürer's woodcut *Christ Carrying the Cross* (p. 298), a source he had already used for his tapestry cartoon *The Stoning of Saint Stephen* (p. 223; Cat. T5). He thereby transforms the meeting between Christ and Veronica – Dürer's theme – into one between son and mother. He also expands upon his model in terms of narrative scope and dramatic intensity, and by means of animated bodies *all'antica* rectifies the rigidity of its Northern figural world. The course of the road to Calvary can be followed in Raphael's painting from the city gate on the right towards the left and then into the central background, where an empty space on a distant hill awaits Christ's cross. The meeting between Christ and Mary takes place with both having fallen to the ground in similar poses. The Virgin's compassion *(compassio)* is thus made visually clear. Raphael clearly orients himself here towards his earlier Baglioni *Entombment of Christ* (p. 152; Cat. P35a), which also provides the basis for further motifs (narrative path away from, or in this case towards Calvary hill in the distance; contrasting groups of women and muscular male figures). In focussing the viewer's attention on the two expressive, weeping faces of Christ and Mary with their painted tears, Raphael follows a pictorial type found in Early Netherlandish devotional diptychs, which united the two sorrowing figures in an intimate pair of portraits. In Florence and Rome, for example, such Flemish combinations of Christ as the Man of Sorrows and the Virgin as the Mater dolorosa were known and sought after. Raphael expands the close-up of the devotional painting into a large-scale history painting.

Raphael complements the pair of mother and son with a second constellation of figures in which the scene is one of dramatic conflict in place of harmony. Muscular figures inspired by antique statuary oppose each other. The powerful man seen in rear view on the left is attempting to drag Christ further along the road. His pose is based on that of one of the *Horse Tamers* on the Quirinal. Where the statue had to subdue a wildly rearing horse, Raphael's figure tugs with equal force at the fallen Christ – in what thus becomes an exhibition of excessive violence. Beside him, a man carrying a lance seems to be pushing down even harder on the cross burdening Christ. But Simon of Cyrene, his eyes blazing with wrath like a hero of antiquity, opposes this brutal action: seizing the cross in his powerful grasp, he lifts its heavy weight off Christ's shoulders. The marble model for his figure, the so-called *Pasquino*, stood on a bend on the old main road in Rome. It shows a Greek hero carrying a fallen soldier away from the battlefield. Just as the Virgin Mary could serve as a female figure of identification and meditation, so Simon could serve as a male one. He invites the viewer to also take up Christ's cross in real life (Krems 2002). The grip of Simon's outstretched arms thereby seems like an answer to the imploringly outstretched arms of Mary. Perhaps the donor saw himself and his deceased wife mirrored in these two figures.

Issuing orders over the scene in the foreground is a Roman soldier, who is riding out of the gate on the right with his baton extended in a commanding gesture. State authority makes its appearance in the picture, just as Raphael had already introduced it in the *Judgement of Solomon* (Cat. F3.1h) in a constellation of figures whose poses establish those, too, of the kneeling Mary, the man seen from behind, and Simon. Next to Simon, a shouting face stares in fear, full of incomprehension, at the baton held out by the cruel captain. On the left, too, a bearded rider looks critically back at the scene, as if a counter-figure to the captain. Simon's intervention to help Christ is reflected on his armour. The mounted soldier thus carries not only the banner of power, but also the image of the good deed. As a consequence of what he has seen, compassion appears on the Roman's face. The narrative told by the major figures ends here: in this transformation and conversion to human compassion, Raphael shows the effect he hopes that his painted altarpiece will also achieve.

Raphael's *Visitation* (p. 303; Cat. P99) was destined for a personal friend, for whom the artist had also designed a palace in Rome and whom he later appointed as executor of his will. Giovanni Battista Branconio dell'Aquila (1473–1522), originally from Abruzzo, had made his career in Rome as a goldsmith and cleric, rising to become an attendant and confidant of Leo X. In his native L'Aquila, his family had built its palace right opposite the parish church of San Silvestro. In 1517 it evidently acquired the left-hand chancel of the three-nave basilica as a family chapel. The altar was dedicated to the "Visitation". That same year, Giovanni Battista's father Marino set aside money in his will for a Marian painting, whose execution was to be arranged by Giovanni Battista (Desideri 2018). An inscription on Raphael's altarpiece names Marino as the donor. The iconography of the painting, however, celebrates above all the name saint of Giovanni Battista's mother, Elisabetta. In the picture, Saint Elizabeth, who is pregnant with John the Baptist (the name saint of Giovanni Battista), greets Mary, who has come to visit her and is herself pregnant with Christ. Raphael shows the two women giving each other their right hand – a motif familiar from antiquity

(Gardner von Teuffel 2013). This sign of solidarity and friendship is portrayed as the centre of the pictorial message. In a background scene, the meeting of the women is repeated by the following generation, namely by their children not yet born in the foreground. John baptises Christ, who is declared the Son of God by a conspicuous divine apparition. Perhaps John's service to Christ makes reference to the service performed by Giovanni Battista for Pope Leo X. Branconio had skilfully campaigned for the Medici Pope's election (Zapperi 1972). Branconio was even permitted to incorporate motifs from the Medici coat of arms into his own family crest. With this coat of arms, Branconio's service to and friendly relations with the Medici pope remained permanently present in the chapel, too. In his invention of the figures in the *Visitation*, Raphael follows his design for *Enea Sylvio Piccolomini Presents Eleanor of Portugal to Emperor Frederick III* (p. 302) for the Piccolomini Library in Siena. The final painting was executed, at least in part, by Raphael's workshop.

Raphael's last great altarpiece, by contrast, is entirely autograph. The commission for the *Transfiguration* (p. 305; Cat. P85) must have come from Cardinal Giulio de' Medici in 1516. In 1515 Giulio had been given the important archdiocese of Narbonne, located in southern France, as a benefice and evidently wished to be represented in its cathedral via the donation of an altarpiece. The benefice and donation were part of Leo X's political shift towards France (Tewes/Rohlmann 2002). In January 1517 a second painting was already under discussion in Rome. Giulio commissioned Sebastiano del Piombo (*c.* 1485–1547) with an altarpiece representing the *Raising of Lazarus* (p. 285), which was planned as a rival piece to Raphael's work and was also destined for Narbonne cathedral. Sebastiano's retable, for which Michelangelo contributed some of the preliminary drawings, was completed in 1519. Raphael probably began working on his painting only in 1518 and had almost completed it by the time he died in 1520. In April 1520 both pictures were shown together in Rome for comparison. Giulio subsequently had Sebastiano's painting sent to Narbonne as planned, but Raphael's work never reached its intended destination. In 1523 Giulio eventually donated it to San Pietro in Montorio as the high altarpiece. This Roman church was under the patronage of the Spanish royal family: the Medici had now turned its political focus towards the new world power of the Habsburgs.

As early preparatory drawings show, the theme of Raphael's representation was initially only the Transfiguration of Christ (p. 284): Jesus, who has taken three disciples with him up to the top of Mount Tabor, begins to shine with a celestial light and is accompanied by an apparition of Moses and Elijah. This revelation was intended to strengthen the

Raphael and Workshop, **Madonna del Pesce (Madonna and Child with the Archangel Raphael, Tobias and Saint Jerome)** (detail), *c.* 1513/14

(see ill. p. 293)

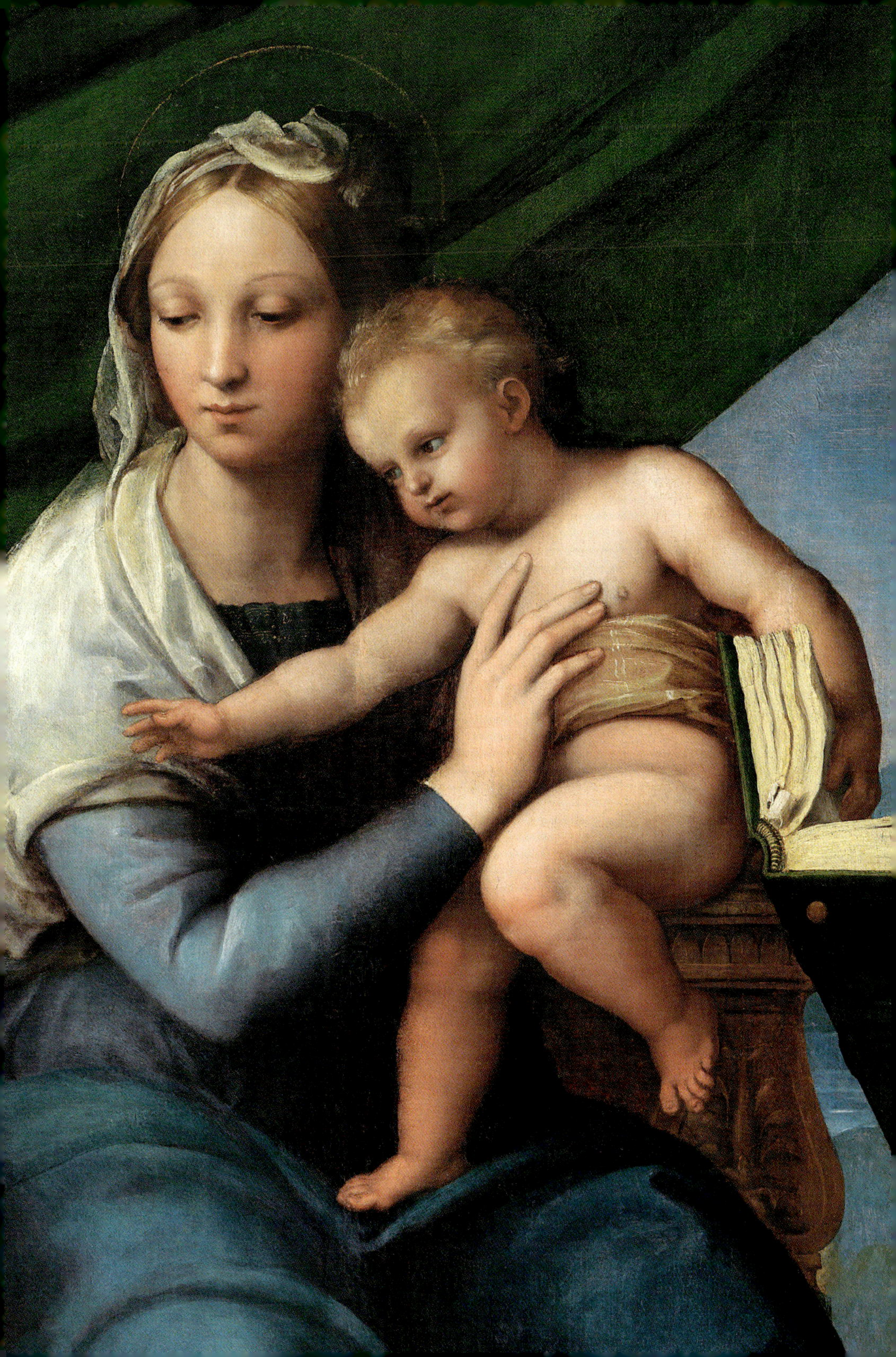

disciples' faith in Christ's divine nature before the Passion. In a second step in the genesis of the composition, the Transfiguration on the mountain is joined by another scene. The Bible reports that Jesus, having come back down from the mountain and rejoined the disciples who had not accompanied him, proceeded to heal a possessed boy. This latter had been brought to the apostles in the hope of healing while Jesus was still on the mountain. Without the Saviour, however, the disciples were unable to cure the boy on their own. It is this first, vain request for healing that fills the lower half of Raphael's painting. The artist thus preserves the unity of time in his two-part composition: the events on top of the mountain and those at its base take place simultaneously.

The two halves of the picture are composed with contrast in mind. The Transfiguration above is dominated by harmonious geometry and symmetry, a delicately coordinated palette, and a clear, solemn, light-filled order with the floating figure of Christ radiating out on all sides from its centre. Reigning below, on the other hand, are dramatic agitation, solid corporeality and a variety of violent movements and affects, as well as pronounced overlappings. The throng splits into two diagonals. Strong colours shine abruptly out of deep, dark shadows. This stylistic difference not only results in the two halves mutually reinforcing one other in their effect, but it corresponds, in an aesthetically consummate fashion, to the religious content of the painting: bright heavenly splendour shines out over earthly darkness, potent force over need and helplessness, glory over misery. Yet within this contrast, a subtle connection also make itself heard: two apostles are pointing upwards. The man gesturing on the left takes up the diagonal position of the floating Moses, while on the right the figures clustered around the possessed boy take up that of Elijah. Below, the apostles react in fear to the boy's epileptic seizure. This is transformed above into the sinking to the ground of the disciples dazzled by the transfigured Jesus. Christ and the boy are thus related to each other as figures of contrasting transformations.

Johann Wolfgang von Goethe (1749–1832) was the first to describe the unity formed by the two so different halves of the picture: "How can one separate the upper and lower? The two are one: below, the suffering and the needy, above the potent and charitable, both interrelated and interacting" (translated from: *Italienische Reise*, Berlin 2011, pp. 486 f.). The omnipotence of God, showing itself in the Transfiguration of Christ, rises above earthly suffering as consolation and hope of salvation. In the linking of above and below, in the relationship between Christ and the possessed boy, the viewer recognises what is still hidden from those in the lower half of the painting, and what only the pointing figure in the red mantle, as if in a trance, seems to suspect: Jesus will cure the boy, and suffering will be overcome by God. The question below is answered above (Justi 1870). And this answer radiates out in the outsize figure of the transfigured Christ, floating towards us against the illuminated clouds as the only figure shown *en face*, above the earthly individual case depicted below and into the world of the viewer.

How richly and eloquently Raphael has conceived figures and groups! Glaringly modelled in the light, the heroic figure of a woman seen from behind captures our attention and introduces us to the scene. With her gaze and gesture she connects left and right and directs the apostles and ourselves towards the boy who is to be cured. A number of apostles are sitting on the left, where they seem to be encamped. The group of standing figures on the right, with the possessed boy, have come to them, not the other way round. In a virtuoso piece of painting, the seated figure in the immediate foreground on the left seems to reach one foot and hand out of the pictorial plane into our reality, as if we could enter the world of the picture from here. He has turned away from reading his open book in order to watch what is happening. Raphael thus implies that, in his painting, he has turned the text to be read in the Bible into a visible pictorial reality. Behind the seated man, four apostles merge into a continuously evolving row: the crouching figure seen from behind is simply pointing, while the man standing next to him points and at the same time lays one hand on his breast in an assuring manner. The next holds both hands to his breast, and the last, who is again seated, raises both hands palm outwards in front of his chest. But contrasts, too, are established: the wide open, demanding eyes of the boy's father on the right are answered at the same height on the left by the closed eyes of the man pointing to Christ. The possessed boy makes contrasting gestures with his arms: in the case of the hand extended downwards, the fingers are spread wide in a parrying gesture. The hand stretched upwards, by contrast, seems to be receptively open, as if the boy were unconsciously already sensing the divine healing arriving from above.

For the design of his *Transfiguration*, Raphael drew inspiration from numerous existing works. With regard to the two-zone layout, reference has rightly been made to the *Coronation of the Virgin* (p. 51; Cat. P11a), the *Disputa* (p. 185 t.; Cat. F3.1) and *Parnassus* (p. 184 b.; Cat. F3.1k). Cosimo Rosselli combined a scene of Christ on a hilltop and a subsequent healing of a sick man in a fresco at the centre of one of the long walls inside the Sistine Chapel: Christ, seen frontally, delivers the Sermon on the Mount, while below and to the right, closer to the viewer, a leper is presented to the apostles and Christ to be cured. Even if Rosselli's scenes are set side by side in a landscape format, a clear conceptual and compositional kinship with the *Transfiguration* can be seen (Rohlmann 2022a). Raphael borrowed figures in the lower part of the picture from his own *Expulsion of Heliodorus* (p. 196 t.; Cat. F3.2a) and *Blinding of Elymas* (Cat. T7), but also – and in some places as direct quotations – from Leonardo's *Adoration of the Magi* (p. 271) and *Last Supper*, as well as from the *Laocoön* antique statuary group (p. 358). Raphael only decided to turn the apostle seated front left towards the viewer at a late stage in the design process.

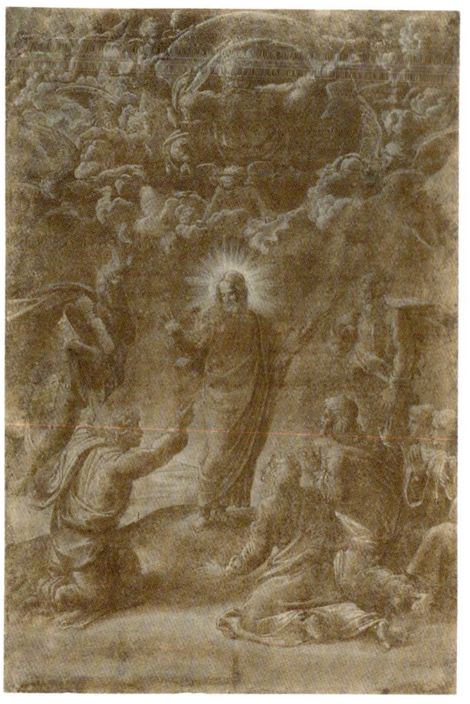

He has evidently varied here the figure of the seated Jupiter in the fresco of *Venus before Jupiter* in the Loggia di Psiche of 1518 (p. 404; Cat. F11e). Just as the nude Venus approaches Jupiter with a request, so the female figure seen in rear view in the *Transfiguration* approaches the apostle – and only at this point receives her naked shoulder. For the upper part of the picture, Raphael used his design drawings for a Resurrection of Christ that was never carried out (cf. KMOF 470).

The two outer apostles who have sunk to the ground before Christ are cited almost literally from another source (Rohlmann 2022a). The rear-view figure of James and the reclining figure of John seen from the front take up, in mirror image, the two apparitions of God in Michelangelo's *Creation of the Sun, Moon and Plants* on the Sistine ceiling (p. 289). The showing of God's buttocks represented a spectacular break with decorum by Michelangelo, and Raphael's allusion to it in James is abundantly clear. In Michelangelo's fresco, the gesture of shading the eyes against dazzling light is made by one of God's companions. Raphael replaces the sun illuminating the figures in Michelangelo with the light phenomenon of the transfigured Christ. Having faithfully followed Michelangelo's image of God in the ceiling frescoes of the Stanza d'Eliodoro (pp. 198/199; Cat. F3.2g–k), Raphael here appears to be criticising it. In the *Transfiguration*, Michelangelo's God figures become men who are dazzled by the beauty and splendour of Raphael's Christ and fall down before him. Artistic competition *(paragone)* has here taken visual form: Michelangelo's figures seem to pay homage to Raphael, as it were. The full force of this becomes clear when we remember that Michelangelo himself stood behind

Workshop of Raphael, **Copy of the first design for the *Transfiguration***, 1516–1518
Pen with wash, heightened with white, on dark brown prepared paper, 40.3 × 27.5 cm (15 7/8 × 10 7/8 in)
Vienna, Albertina

Sebastiano del Piombo, **Raising of Lazarus**, 1517–1519
Oil on panel, 381 × 289.6 cm (150 × 114 1/8 in). London, The National Gallery

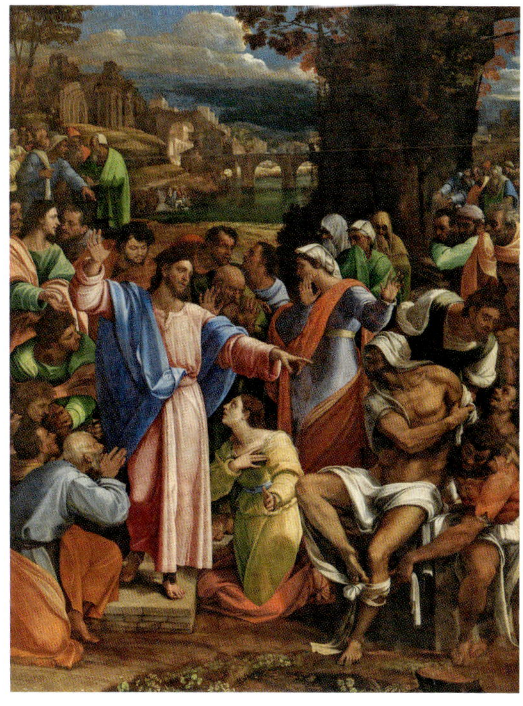

Sebastiano's *Raising of Lazarus,* the rival commission to Raphael's *Transfiguration*, and had supplied drawings for its main figures.

Giulio's double commission for Narbonne cannot be reduced to a competition between artists, however. In line with the client's wishes, the two altarpieces had to relate to one another in content and form. It has therefore been suspected, no doubt correctly, that the expansion of Raphael's *Transfiguration* theme to include the scene of the possessed boy may be understood as a reaction to this additional commission newly awarded to Sebastiano. Only via the dramatic conflict around the sick boy can Raphael offer a dramatic narrative comparable to Sebastiano's *Raising of Lazarus* (p. 285, and artistically trump his rival in terms of gestures and facial expressions. Above all, however, the two altarpieces now relate to each other in terms of content. As Weil-Garris Posner recognised, both take up the theme of *Christ medicus* (Christ as healer) and in so doing illustrate the panegyric addressed to Medici rulers. In formal terms, the two healing episodes seem to be coordinated in their composition, with apostles and family/populace grouped separately on opposite sides. In both cases, monumental apostles crowd together on the left, a woman kneels prominently in the middle and requests that healing be given, and on the right the person to be healed is physically supported from behind. Corresponding to these formal parallels is a more profound relationship, previously overlooked, between the two biblical events: just as the apostles were unable to heal the possessed boy because Christ was not with them, the sick Lazarus died because Christ did not arrive in time. A situation with its roots in Christ's absence is remedied in both episodes after his appearance. Raphael and Sebastiano thereby show different moments in the narrative situation. In Raphael's picture, the plea for a cure is being made while Christ is still absent, while in Sebastiano the request has already been met by the Saviour, who has finally arrived: the miracle takes place and Lazarus is raised from the dead. The two altarpieces appear like two phases of a single act.

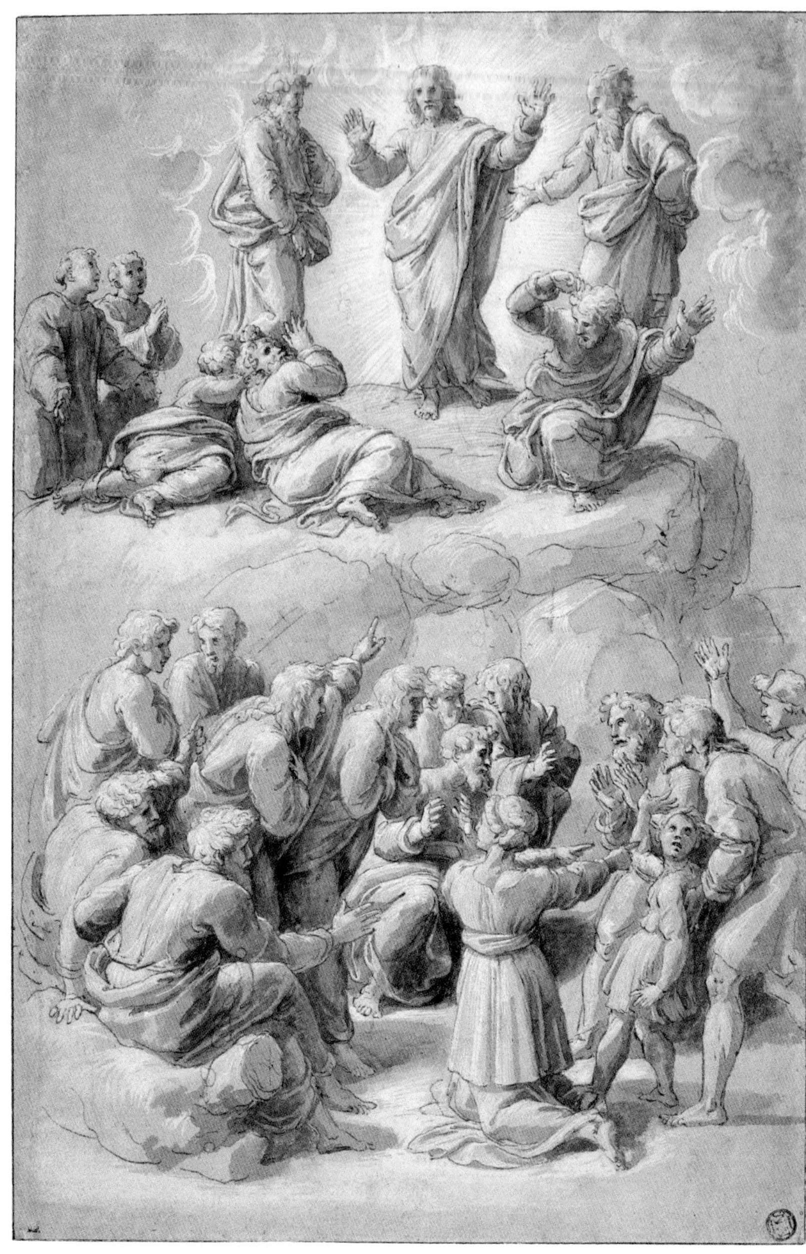

Raphael (most likely), ***Modello* for the *Transfiguration***, 1518
Pen and brown ink, with wash, over black chalk underdrawing on beige prepared paper, white heightening reinforced at a later date, 41.4 × 27.4 cm (16 ¼ × 10 ¾ in)
Paris, Musée du Louvre, Département des Arts graphiques

Where inside the cathedral of Narbonne were the altarpieces intended to be installed? Construction of the Gothic church of St-Just-et-St-Pasteur had begun in 1272, but only the choir, ambulatory and apse chapels were completed. The themes of the *Transfiguration of Christ* and the *Raising of Lazarus* corresponded to the dedications of none of the altars in the church at that time. Since the eighteenth century, a copy of Sebastiano's painting, together with a fragment of the original wooden frame, has been on display in St Martin's chapel on the north side of the apse. The original was evidently housed in St Michael's chapel to the south. It must thereby have stood forward of the altar wall, since the picture in its frame is too wide for one section of wall alone (the painting measures 381 × 289.6 cm [150 × 114 ⅛ in]). Since Raphael's painting is of similar dimensions (405 × 278 cm [159 ½ × 109 ½ in]), some art historians have concluded that it was also intended for a side chapel. It is unlikely, however, that Giulio commissioned altarpieces for two of the apse chapels that were both unsuitably large and whose relationship, in terms of form and content, would furthermore have lost its effectiveness if the two paintings had been installed in different chapels.

Other Raphael scholars have also suggested that the *Transfiguration* was intended for the high altar of the cathedral. In 1510 this had been dedicated to the Virgin Mary and probably also to the patron saints Justus and Pastor. The old high altar was decorated with sculptural reliefs of the Life of Mary and also with figures of the two martyr saints. The two shrines to the saints lay behind the altar on an elevated platform supported by columns. The ensemble possibly dated back to the Middle Ages. In the late seventeenth century, the altar area was raised and redesigned. It was now furnished with an elaborate tabernacle décor. In 1695 the new altar was dedicated to the Virgin Mary and Saints Justus and Pastor (Narbonne 1901).

The idea that Raphael's *Transfiguration* was destined for the high altar is supported by a strange motif on the edge of the painting: in the left-hand background, two petitioning figures have drawn close to the summit of the mountain. It has been possible to identify them as the two patrons of the cathedral, the young martyrs Justus and Pastor. Their liturgical feast day coincided with that of the Transfiguration. It therefore seems probable that Raphael's representation of the two saints and the higher-ranking Christian festival associated with them was indeed intended for the high altar, the place where the two patron saints were particularly venerated within their church. Giulio must consequently have planned to remodel the old high altar. The large dimensions of Raphael's painting also point to a high altarpiece. Its width (278 cm [109 ½ in]) is similar to that of the exquisite fourteenth-century *Parament of Narbonne* (286 cm [112 ⅝ in]), which once served as a temporary altar hanging in the cathedral. Iconographically, too, Raphael's painting was, with its theme of glory and apparition in the upper zone, appropriate for a high altar (cf. Raphael's high altarpieces pp. 290, 291; Cat. P58 and P59). The clear celestial figures are patently calculated to be viewed from afar, and Christ's body and eyes are proportionally magnified.

But for which location, then, was Sebastiano's panel intended? Although it corresponds to Raphael's painting in format, it lacks the triumphal theme designed to be seen from a distance. One possible place for its installation presents itself in particular. In the inner choir, the central arcade is blocked by a masonry choir screen, so that the back of today's high altar is not visible. Originally, however, another altar dedicated to Saint Catherine lay behind the old high altar ("retro altare majus"). In 1614 it was redecorated with painting. The space between the high altar and the choir screen must therefore have been accessible. This means that the back of Raphael's *Transfiguration*, if the painting had been installed on the high altar, would have been visible from the altar dedicated to Saint Catherine. It would therefore have been necessary to decorate the exposed back of the retable in its frame. A second painting offered a solution to this and would thereby have created a double-sided high altarpiece.

Free-standing double-sided altars had been known in Rome since Giotto (1267/76–1337) and Masaccio/Masolino (1383–1447). Siena cathedral boasted the famous double-sided high altarpiece by Duccio (*c.* 1255–1319). In San Francesco al Prato in Perugia, a double-sided high altarpiece stood between the church's two altarpieces by Raphael. Around 1500, the type was used in Florence in the case of free-standing high altarpieces by Ghirlandaio and Filippino Lippi/Perugino. The reconstruction of Raphael and Sebastiano's panels as a double-sided high altarpiece is supported by the fall of the light in both paintings: the scenes they show are namely lit from opposite sides, the *Transfiguration* from the left, *Lazarus* from the right. The viewers of the Raphael altarpiece would thus have been the members of the cathedral chapter, congregated in the choir stalls in front of the high altar and filling the entire choir area. They could have recognised themselves in Raphael's apostles: just as the disciples were reliant on the healing power of their absent leader, Christ, so the chapter might be seen as dependent on the actions of its Medici archbishop living in distant Rome. In the *Transfiguration*, the figure of *Christus medicus* and, with him, the absent Medici archbishop shone out into his cathedral clergy.

The *Raising of Lazarus*, by contrast, would have been visible from the direction of the ambulatory behind the choir. Built into the arcades on either side of the central axis were the tombs of past archbishops (more would be added later). Sebastiano's *Raising of Lazarus* would have faced fittingly towards an area lined by burial monuments, and in this sepulchral context promised Resurrection to those interred there. In the first adjacent arcade to the north lay Giulio's immediate predecessor, Cardinal and Archbishop Guillaume Briçonnet (1445 [?]–1514); his Renaissance tomb bears the date 1523. Giulio appointed

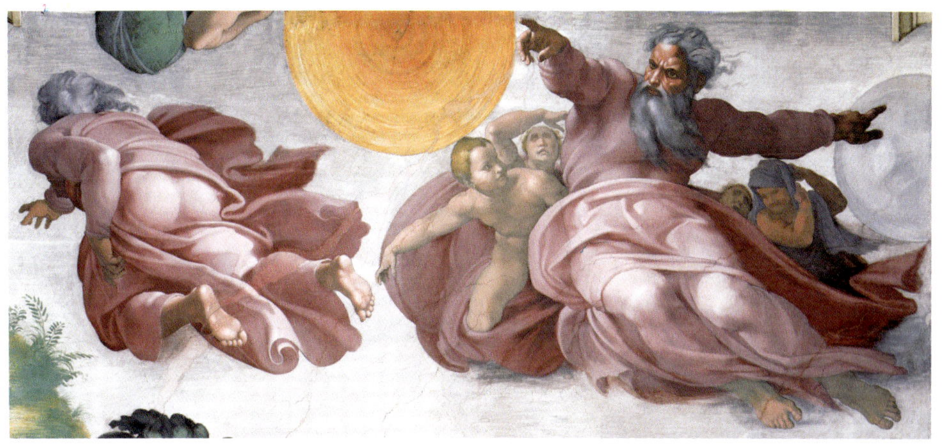

Michelangelo Buonarroti, **Sistine Ceiling: Creation of the Sun, Moon and Plants**, 1510
Fresco, 260 × 570 cm (102 3/8 × 224 3/8 in). Vatican City, Musei Vaticani, Cappella Sistina

Briçonnet's nephew Michel as administrator of the diocese. As from 1516, Briçonnet's sons were based in Rome as French envoys. Perhaps Giulio included them in the planning for the altarpiece commission; perhaps he even catered to their interests with an addition of Sebastiano's *Lazarus* to the high altarpiece. Whatever the case may be, Raphael's *Transfiguration* forms such a closely coordinated unity with Sebastiano's *Lazarus* that a reconstruction of their intended installation as an ensemble seems compelling. Since neither Raphael's painting nor a copy executed by his workshop reached Narbonne as a new high altarpiece, however, the existing altar area in the cathedral choir was never remodelled and Sebastiano's panel, as the only one delivered, was placed in one of the surrounding chapels.

Rome, on the other hand, thus received its second Raphael altarpiece. The series of "Roman" altarpieces that had begun with the *Madonna di Foligno* ended, in the *Transfiguration*, with a work that united the two previous main types of altarpiece in a single panel: the upper half of the picture shows a company of saints as if for veneration in the manner of an icon, while the lower zone is filled with an emotionally moving biblical scene. Raphael's goal is clear: to carry the altarpiece genre to an innovative new pinnacle. In the complexity of its argumentation, rhetorical brilliance, drama, painterly richness and beauty, the *Transfiguration* towered above everything that had gone before.

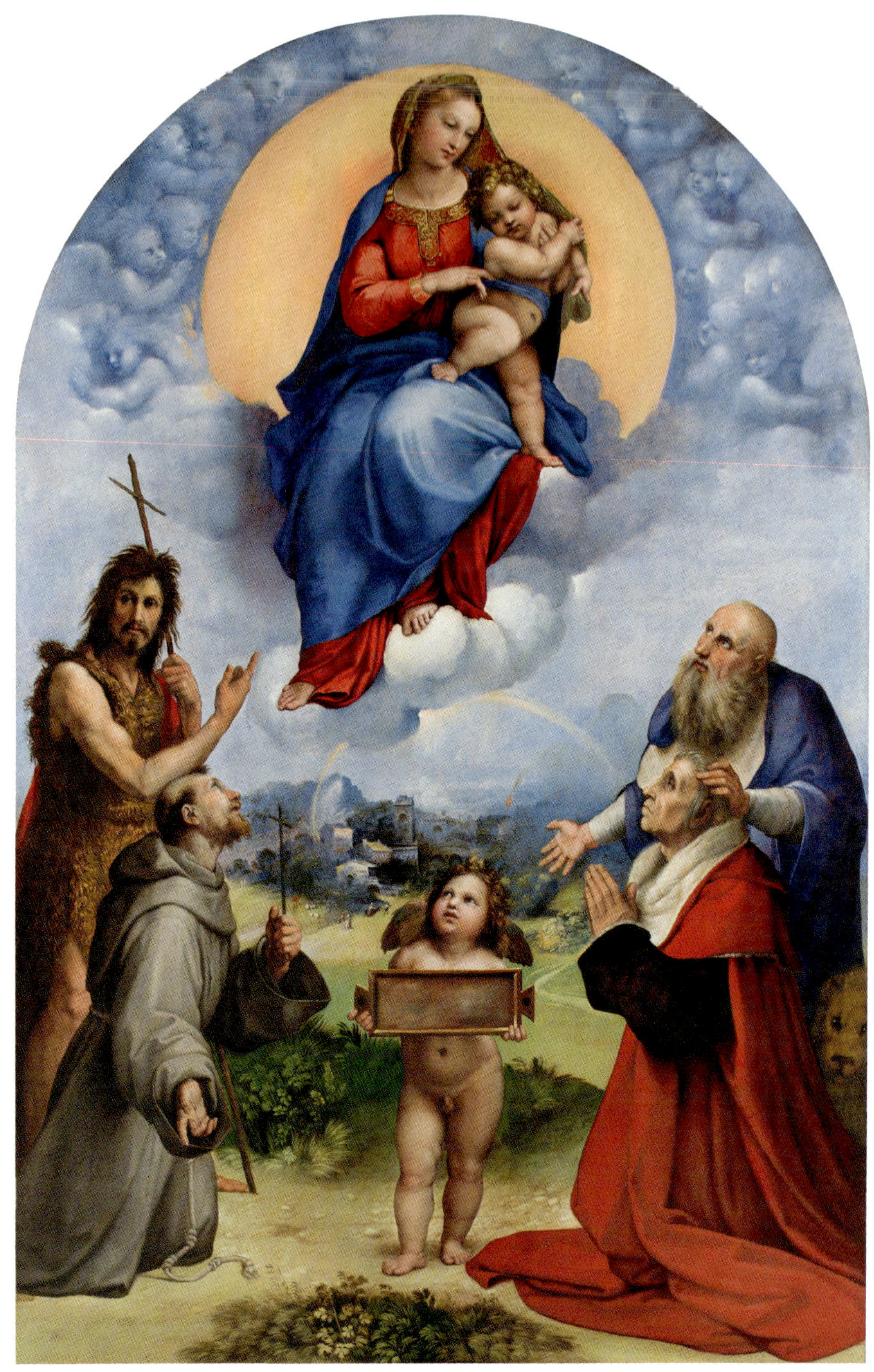

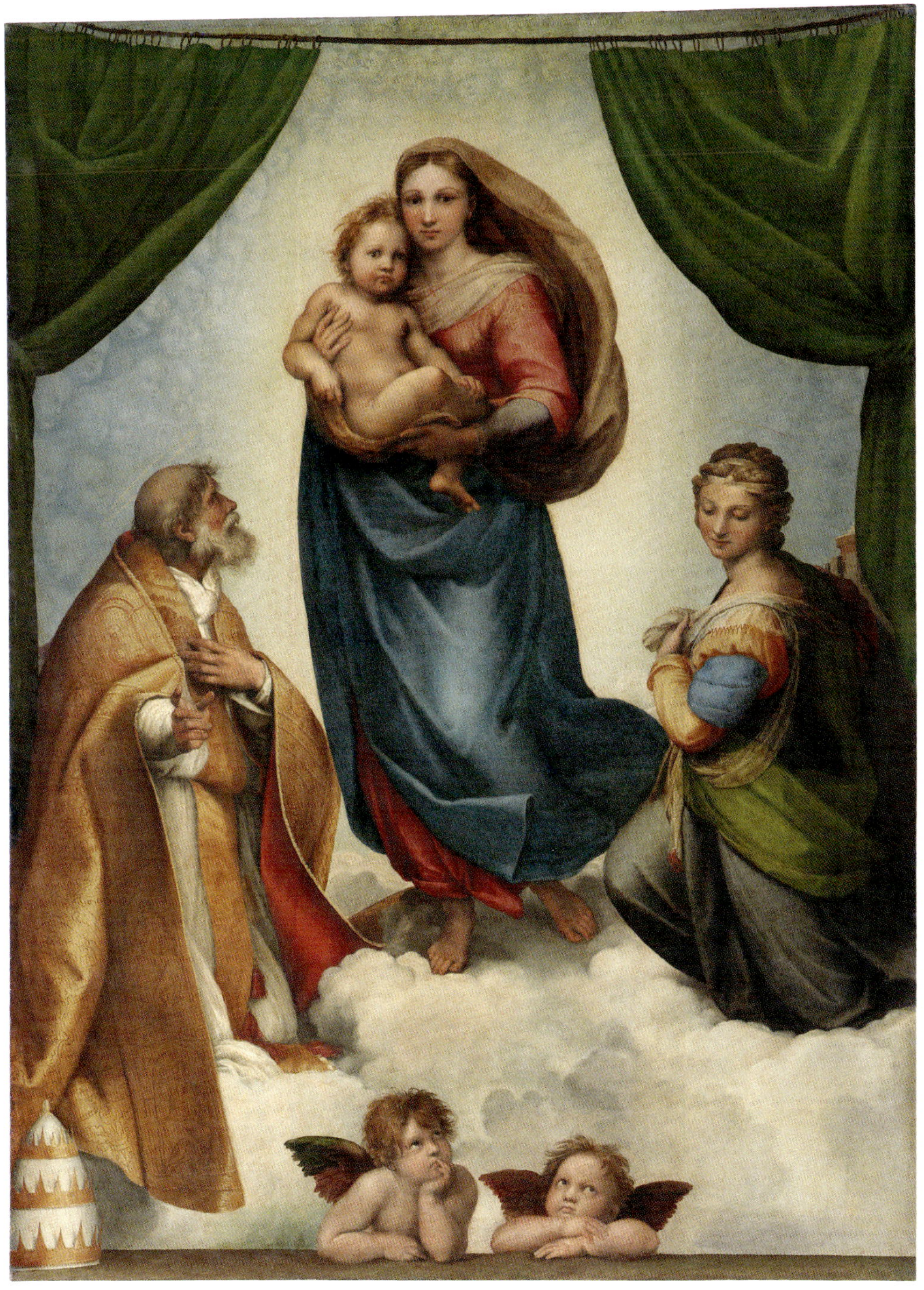

Page 290
Madonna di Foligno (The Virgin Mary and Child with Saints John, Francis, Jerome and the donor Sigismondo de' Conti), *c.* 1511/12
Oil on panel, transferred to canvas, 301 × 198 cm (118 ½ × 77 7⁄8 in)
Vatican City, Musei Vaticani, Pinacoteca
(Detail page 266)

Page 291
Sistine Madonna (Madonna and Child with Saints Sixtus and Barbara), *c.* 1512/13
Oil on canvas, 269.5 × 201 cm (106 1⁄8 × 79 1⁄8 in). Dresden, Gemäldegalerie Alte Meister
(Detail page 261)

Study for the *Madonna del Pesce*, 1512
Brush, with white heightening, over black chalk underdrawing, 25.8 × 21.3 cm (10 1⁄8 × 8 3⁄8 in)
Edinburgh, Scottish National Gallery

Raphael and Workshop, **Madonna del Pesce (Madonna and Child with the Archangel Raphael, Tobias and Saint Jerome)**, *c.* 1513/14
Oil on panel, transferred to canvas, 215 × 158 cm (84 5⁄8 × 62 ¼ in)
Madrid, Museo Nacional del Prado
(Detail page 281)

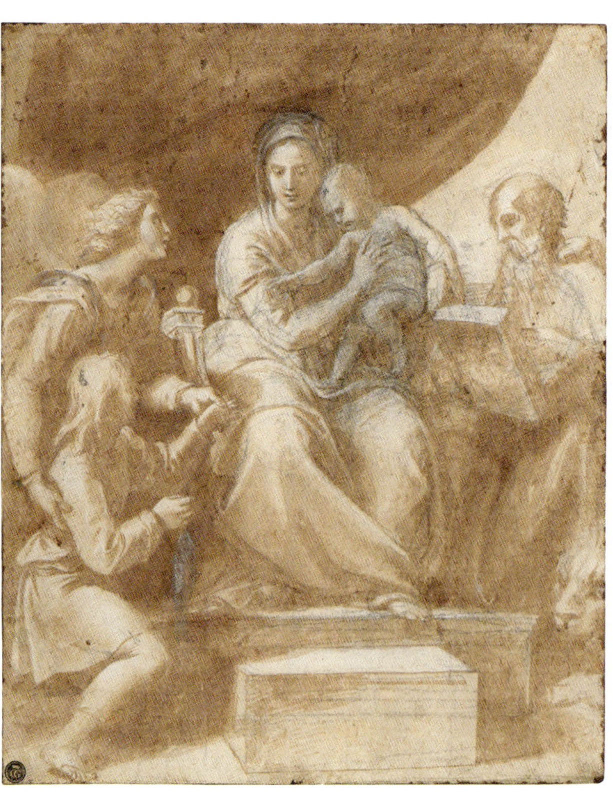

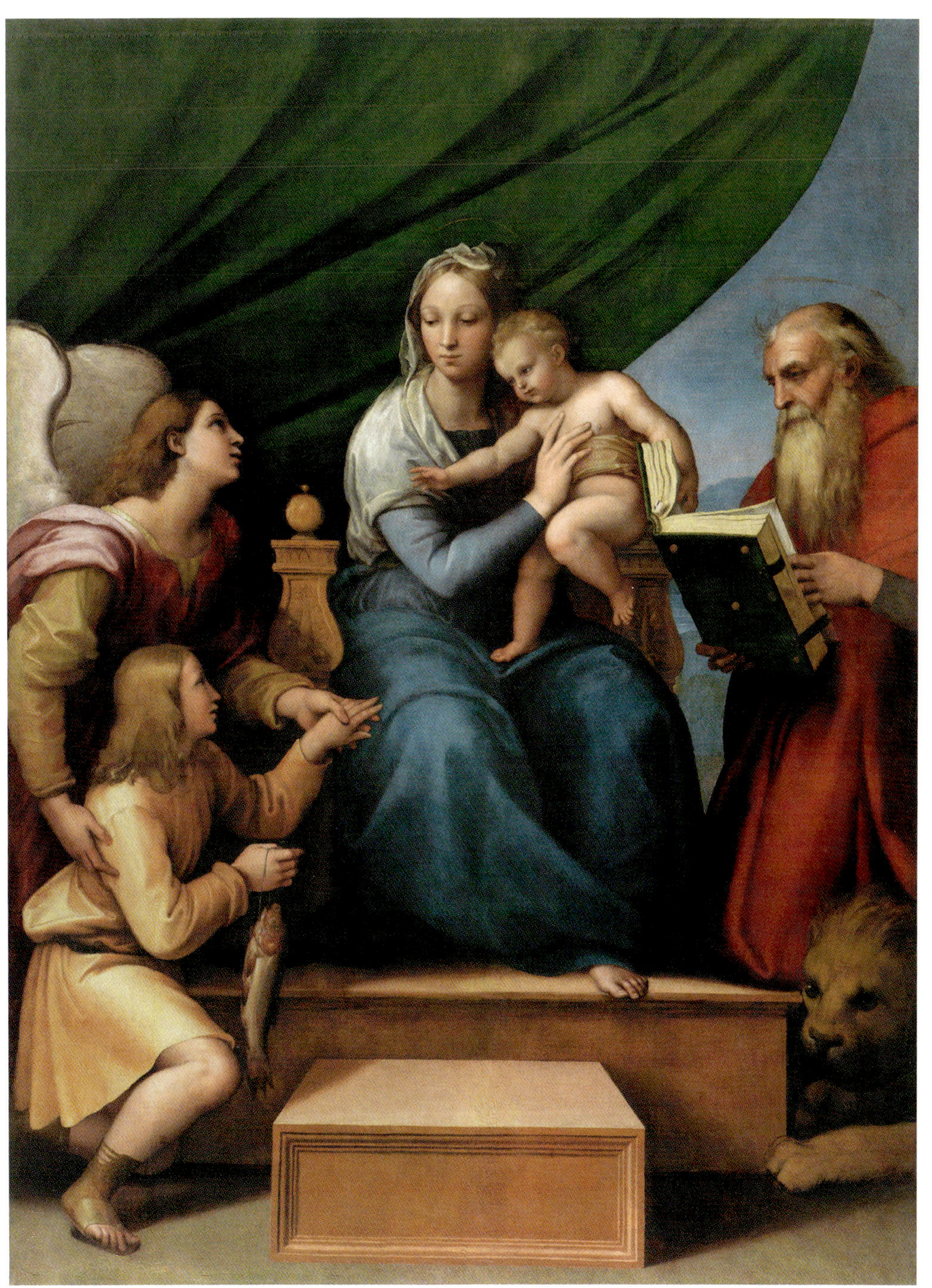

San Giovanni in Monte, Bologna:
View of the Cappella di Santa Cecilia with a copy of *Saint Cecilia*

Saint Cecilia with Saints Paul, John the Evangelist, Augustine and Mary Magdalene, *c.* 1514
Oil on panel, transferred to canvas, 238 × 150 cm (93 ¾ × 59 ⅛ in). Bologna, Pinacoteca Nazionale
(Detail pages 296/297)

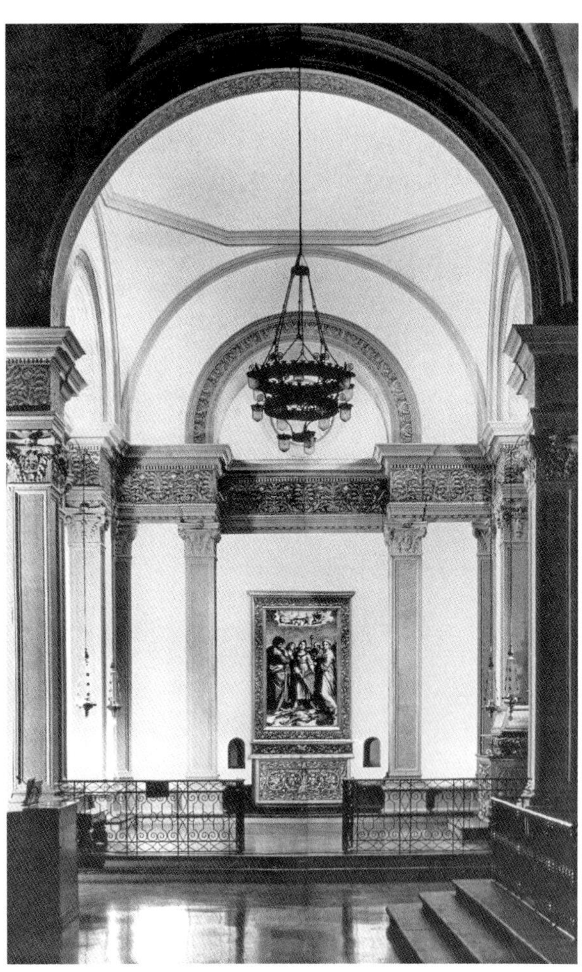

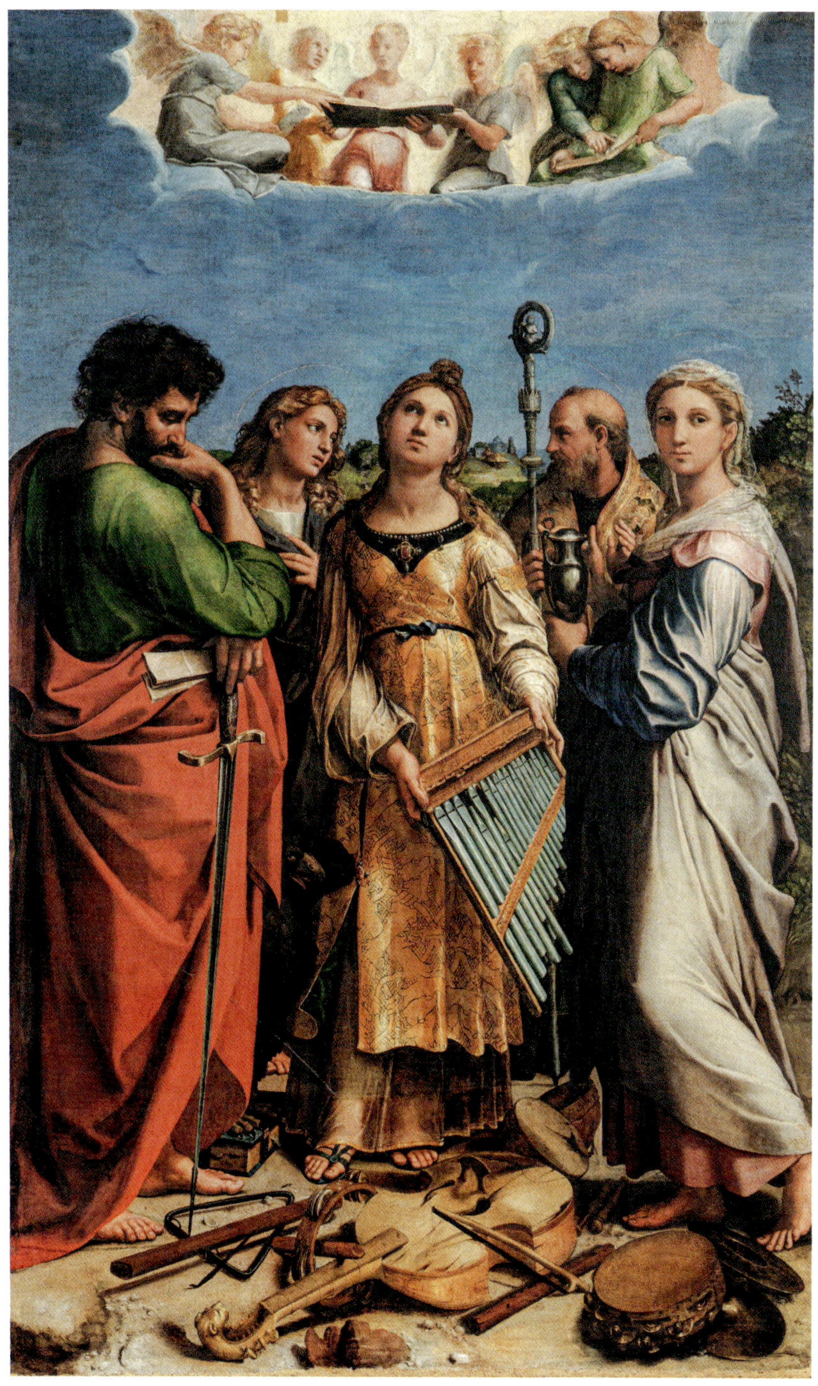

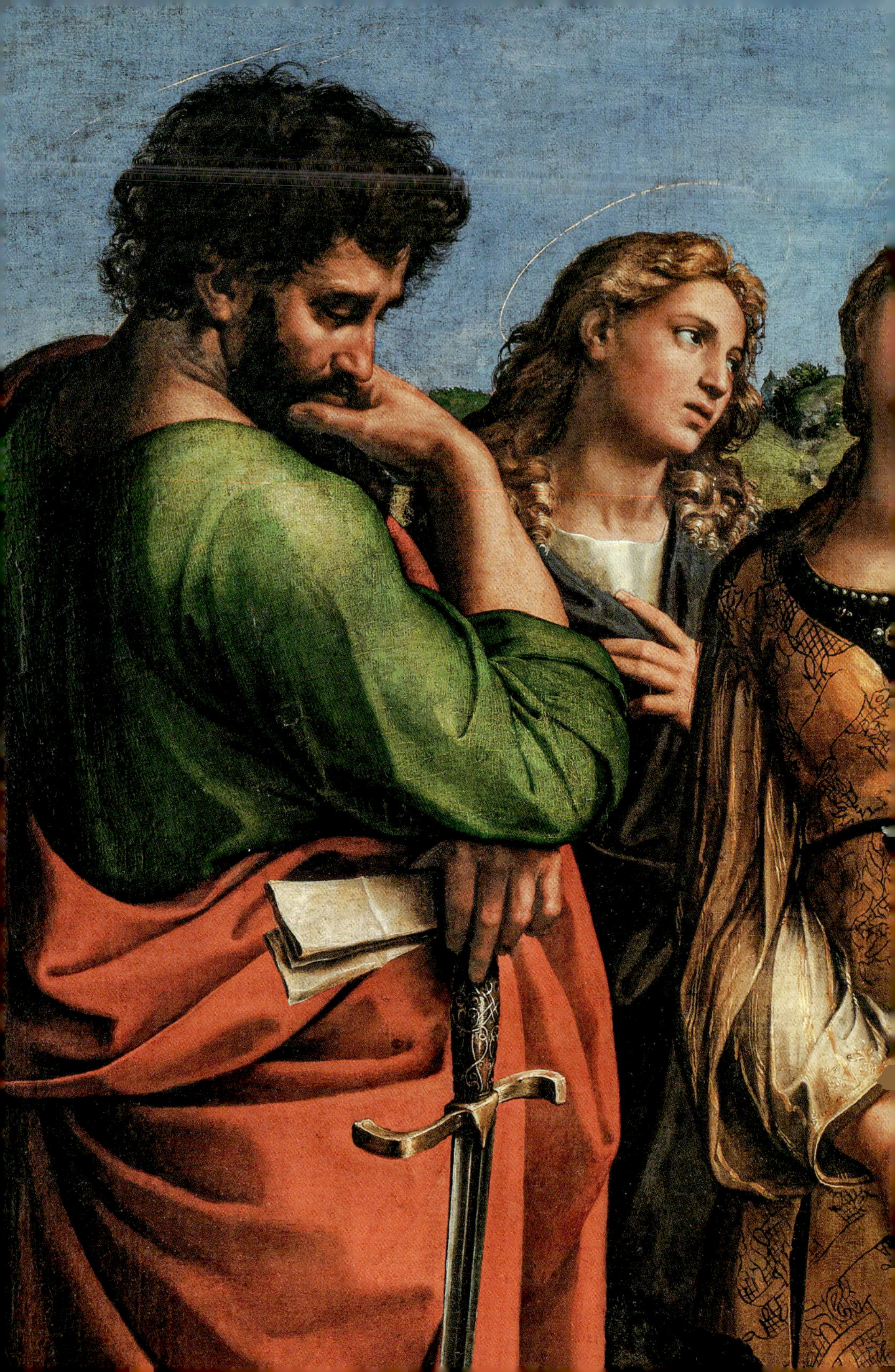

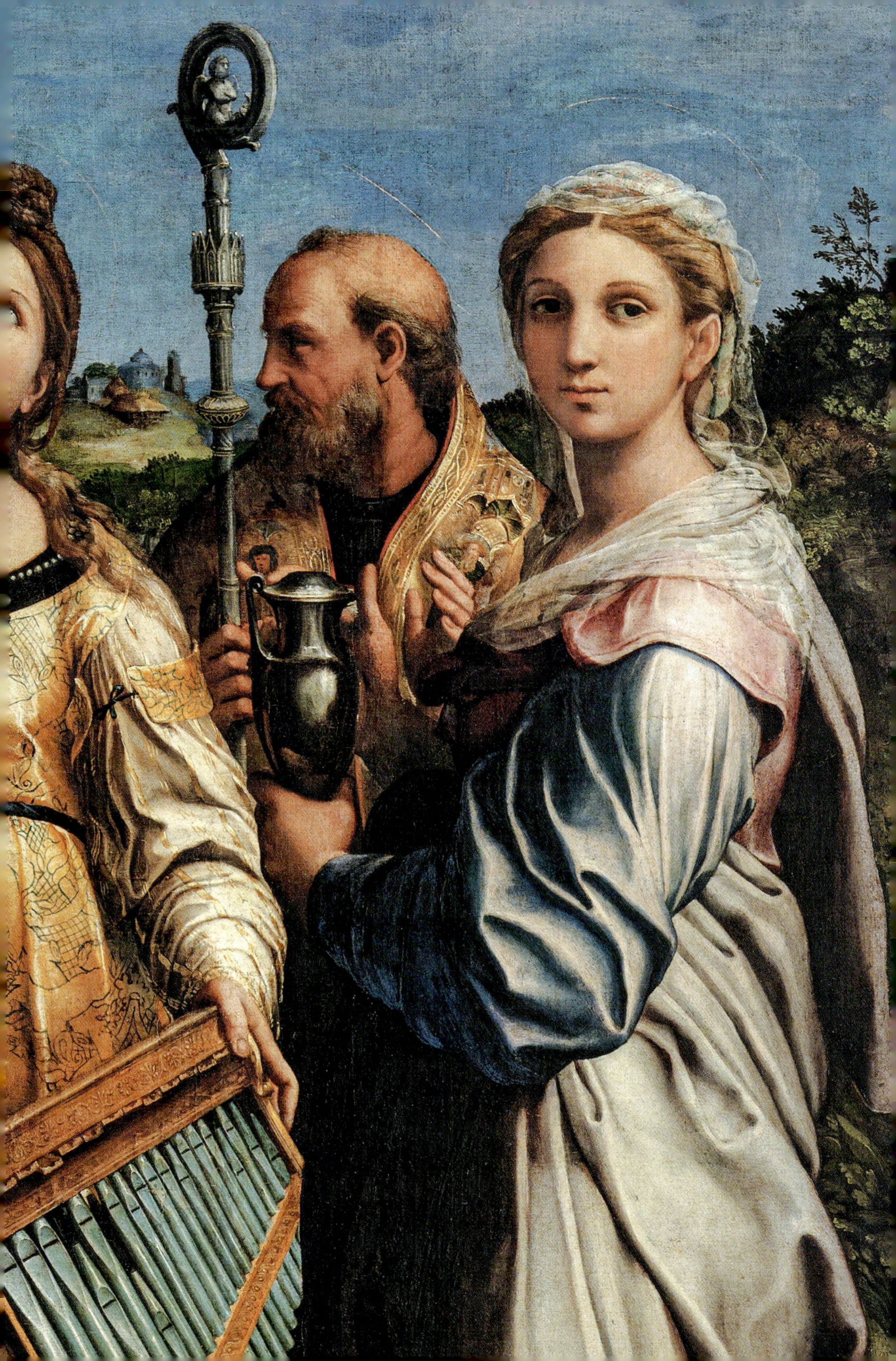

Antonello Gagini, **Marble frame for Raphael's *Christ Carrying the Cross***, before 1520
Palermo, Santa Maria dello Spasimo
(reconstruction with Raphael's altarpiece)

Albrecht Dürer, **Christ Carrying the Cross (Large Passion)**, *c.* 1498/99
Woodcut, 38.8 × 28.2 cm (15 ¼ × 11 ⅛ in)
Nuremberg, Kunstsammlungen der Stadt Nürnberg

Raphael and Workshop, **Christ Carrying the Cross (Lo Spasimo di Sicilia)**, *c.* 1516–1518
Oil on panel, transferred to canvas, 318 × 229 cm (125 ¼ × 90 ⅛ in)
Inscription: *RAPHAEL VRBINAS*
Madrid, Museo Nacional del Prado
(Detail pages 300/301)

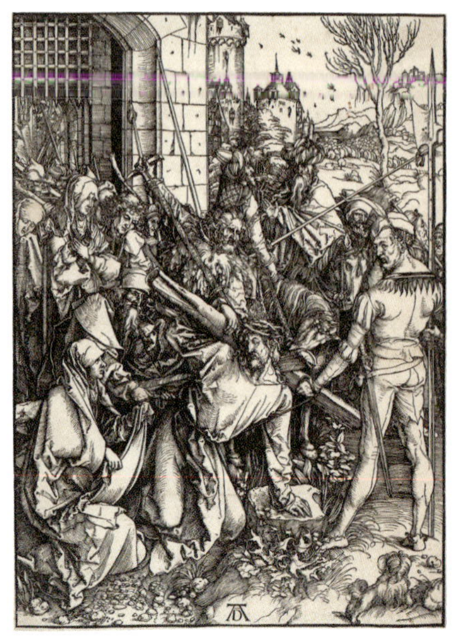

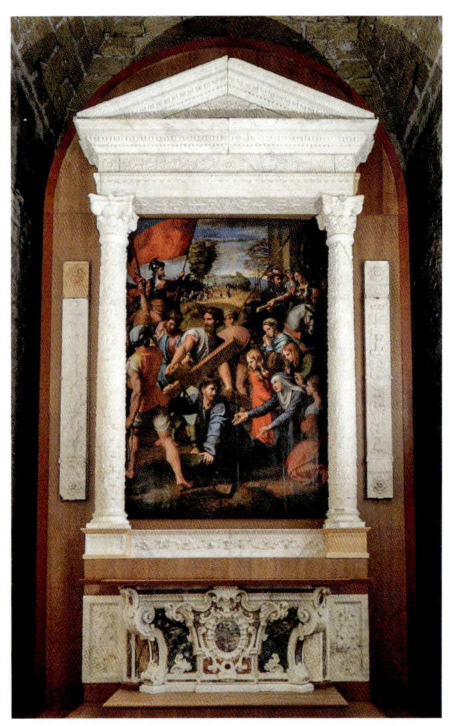

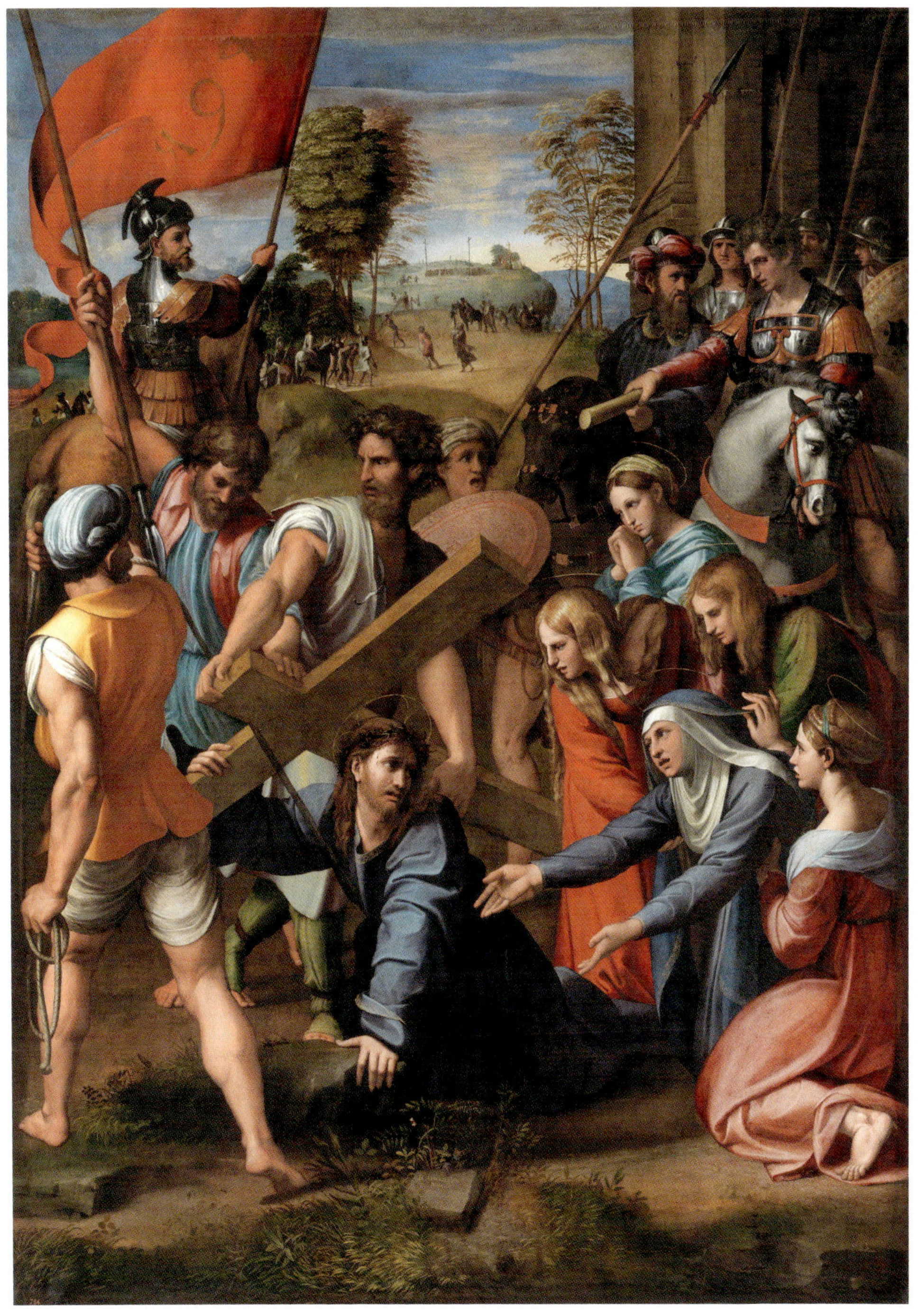

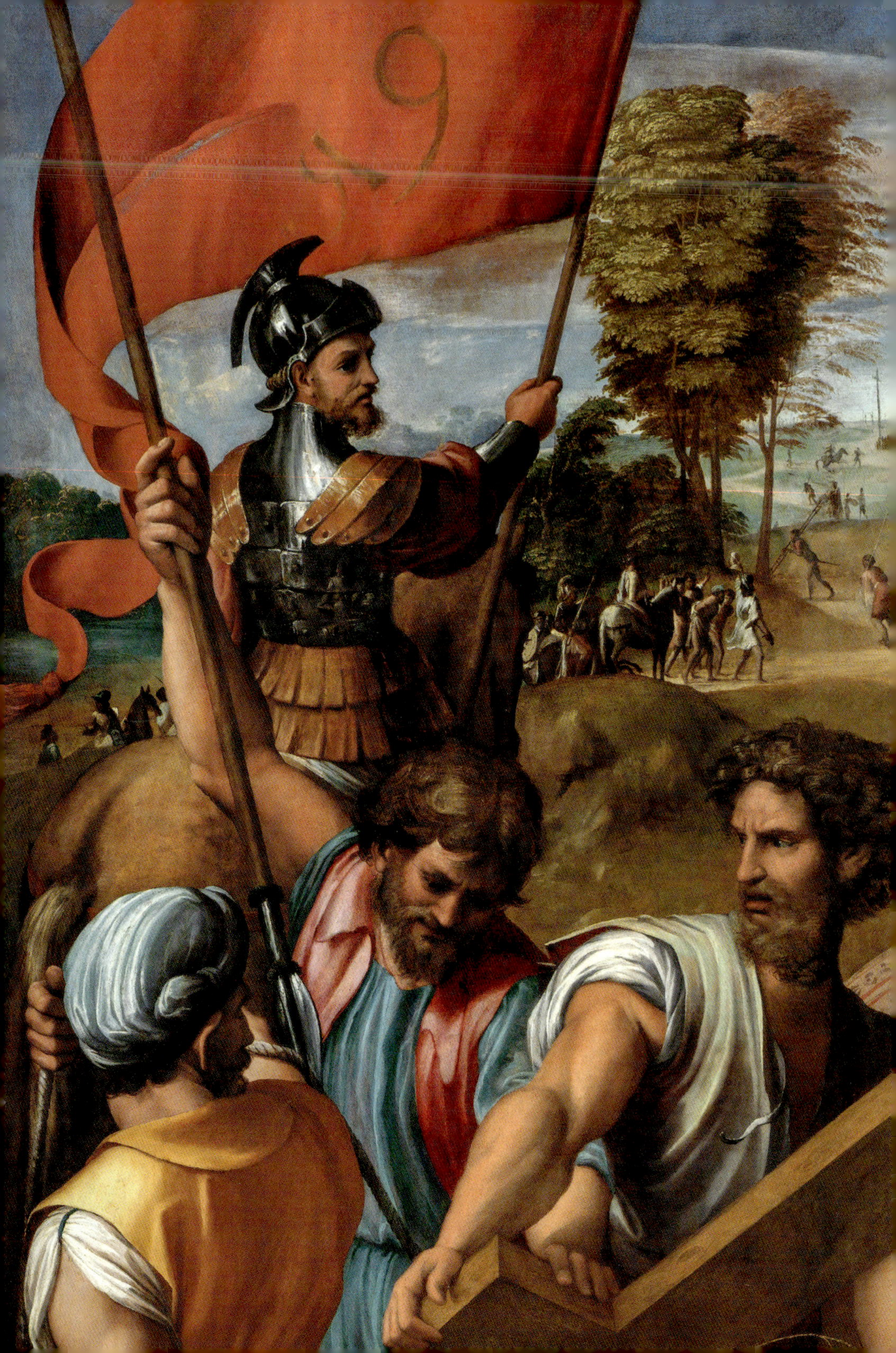

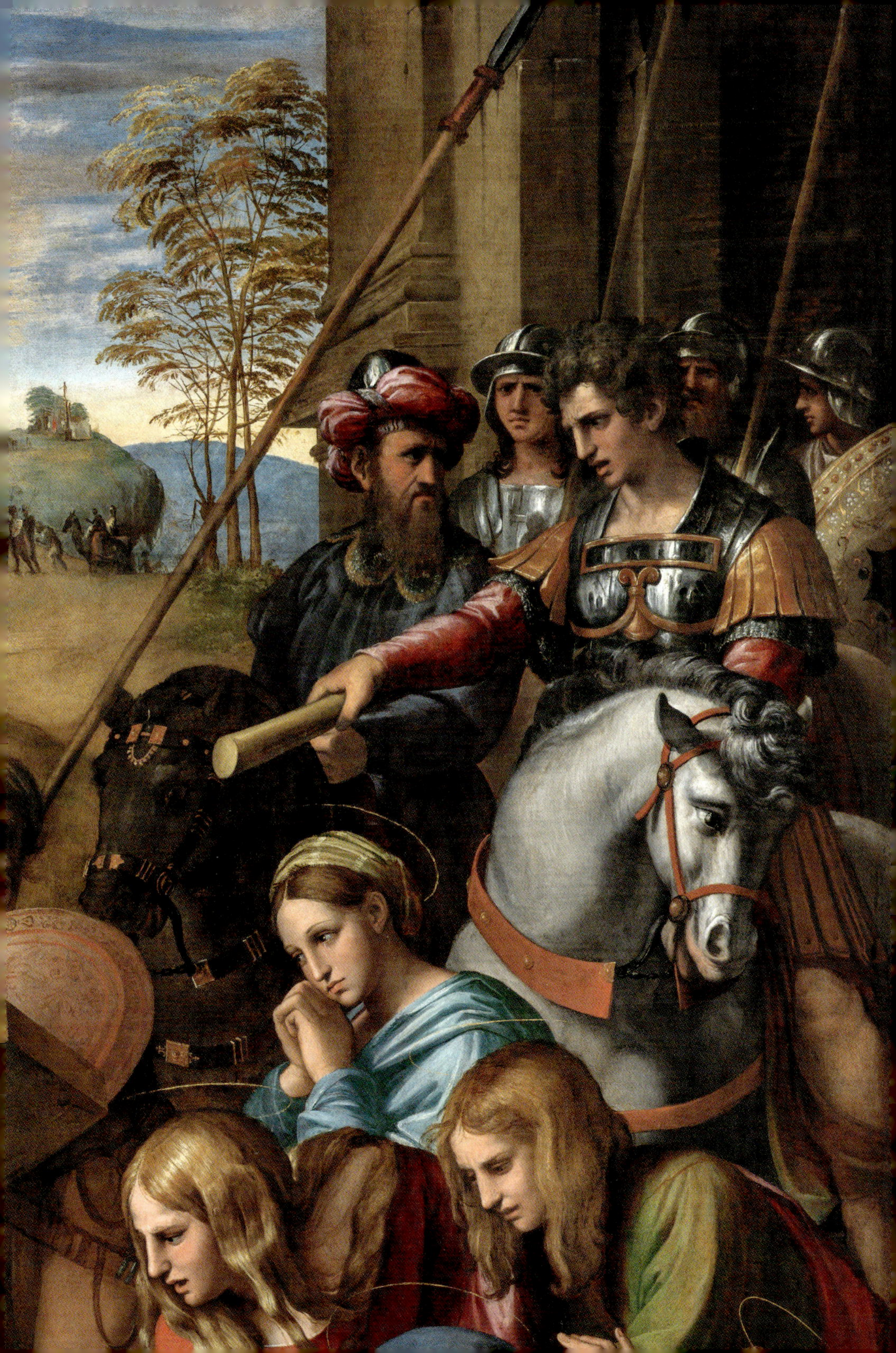

Enea Sylvio Piccolomini Presents Eleanor of Portugal to Emperor Frederick III, 1503
Pen with brownish wash, heightened with white,
over traces of black chalk and stylus, 55.9 × 42.1 cm (22 ⅛ × 16 ⅝ in)
New York, The Morgan Library & Museum

Raphael, Giulio Romano and Giovanni Francesco Penni (?), **The Visitation**, *c.* 1517
Oil on panel, transferred to canvas, 200 × 145 cm (78 ¾ × 57 ⅛ in)
Later inscription in gold lettering below left and below centre:
RAPHAEL VRBINAS: // MARINVS BRANCONIVS. F. F.
Madrid, Museo Nacional del Prado

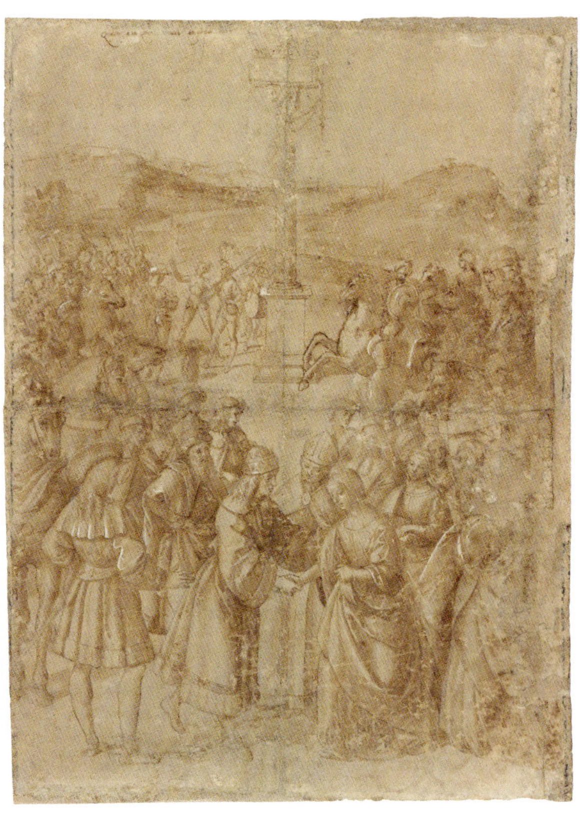

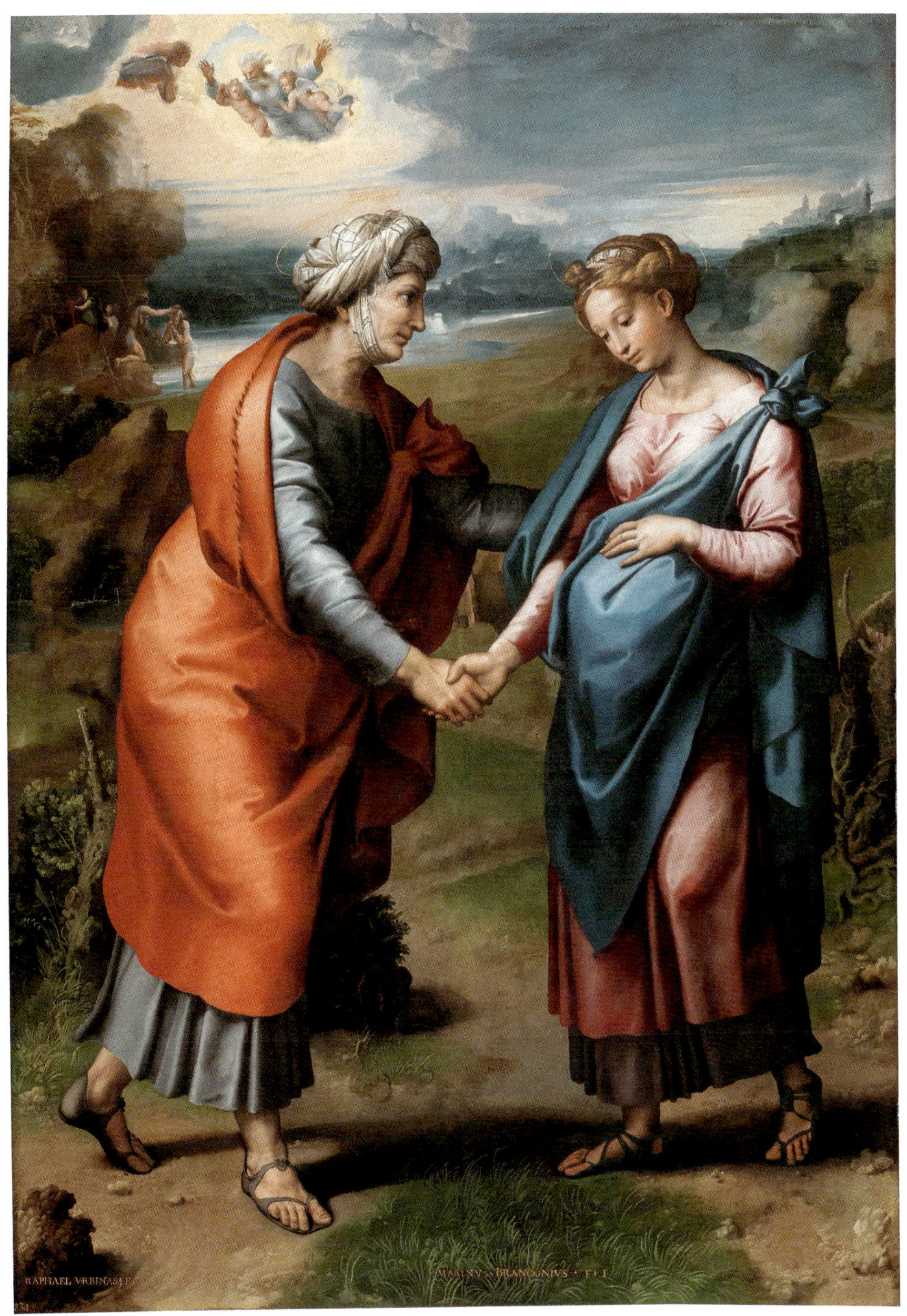
RAPHAEL VRBINAS
MARINVS BRANCONIVS

Two Apostles, 1518/19
Red chalk over stylus, 32.9 × 23.2 cm (12 7/8 × 9 1/8 in)
Chatsworth House, Collection of the Duke of Devonshire

The Possessed Boy and his Father, 1518/19
Red chalk over stylus underdrawing, 28.6 × 19.3 cm (11 1/4 × 7 5/8 in)
Milan, Pinacoteca Ambrosiana

Transfiguration, *c.* 1516–1520
Oil on cherry wood, 405 × 278 cm (159 1/2 × 109 1/2 in)
Vatican City, Musei Vaticani, Pinacoteca
(Detail pages 306/307)

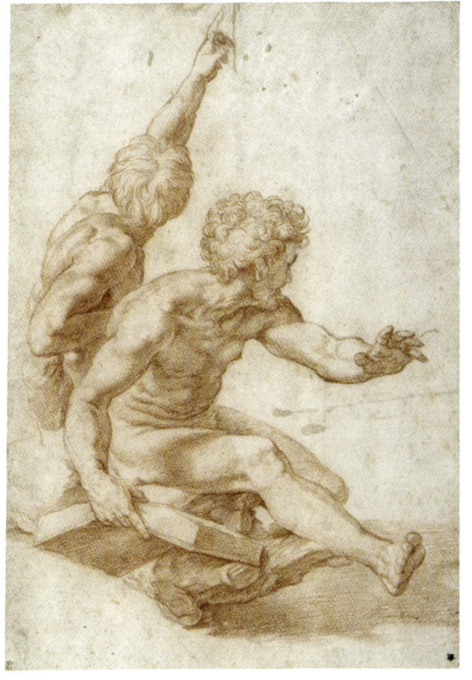

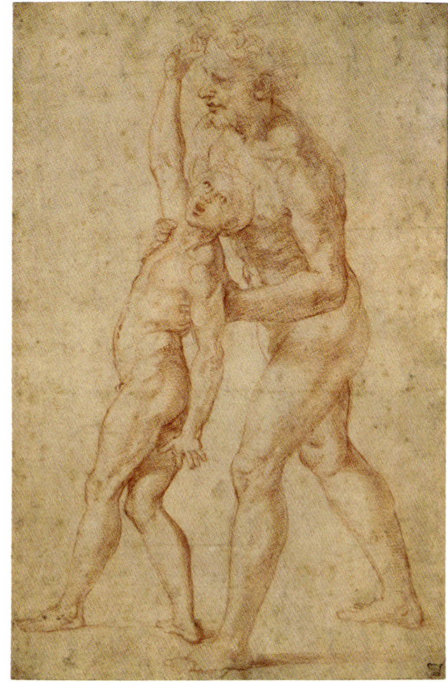

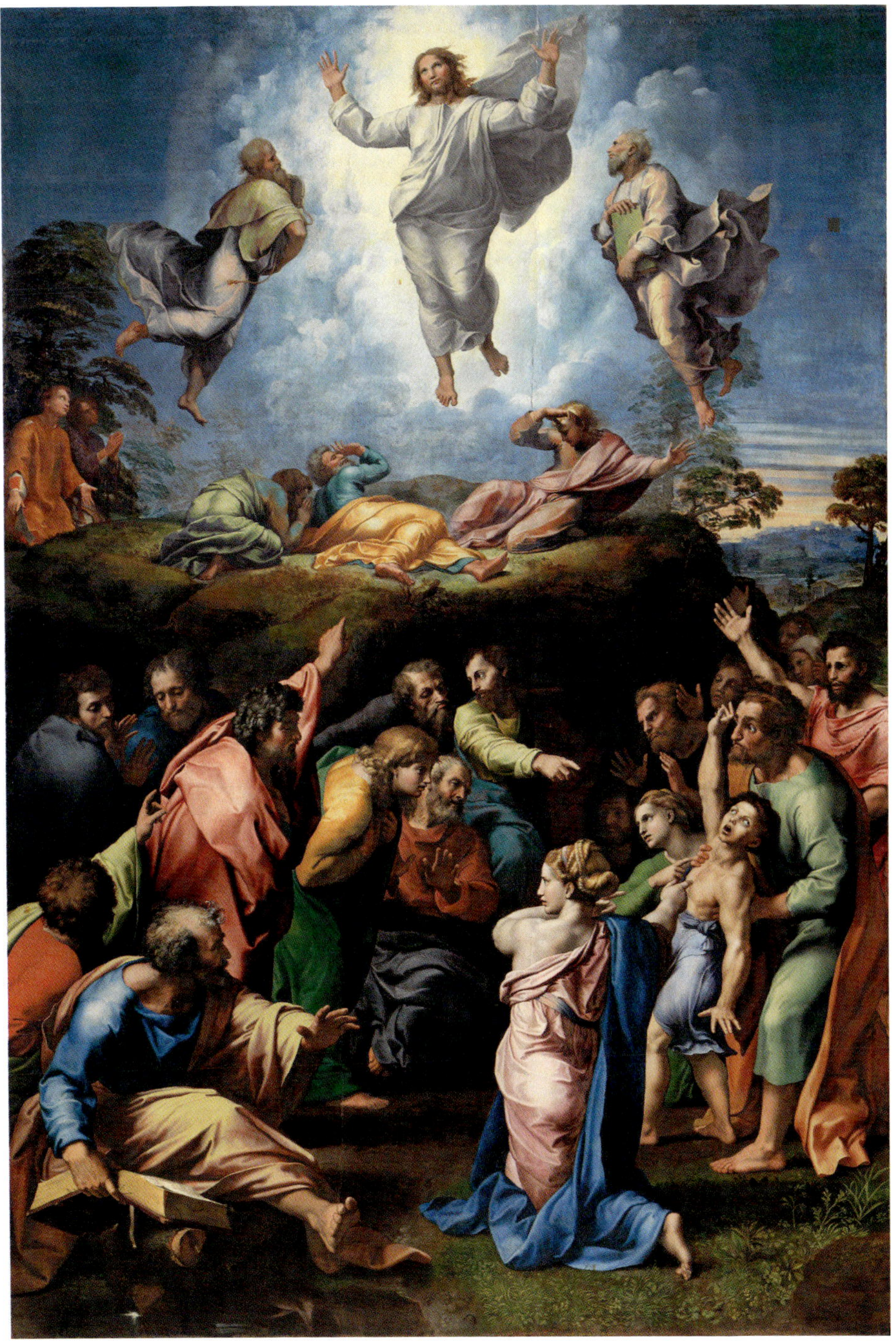

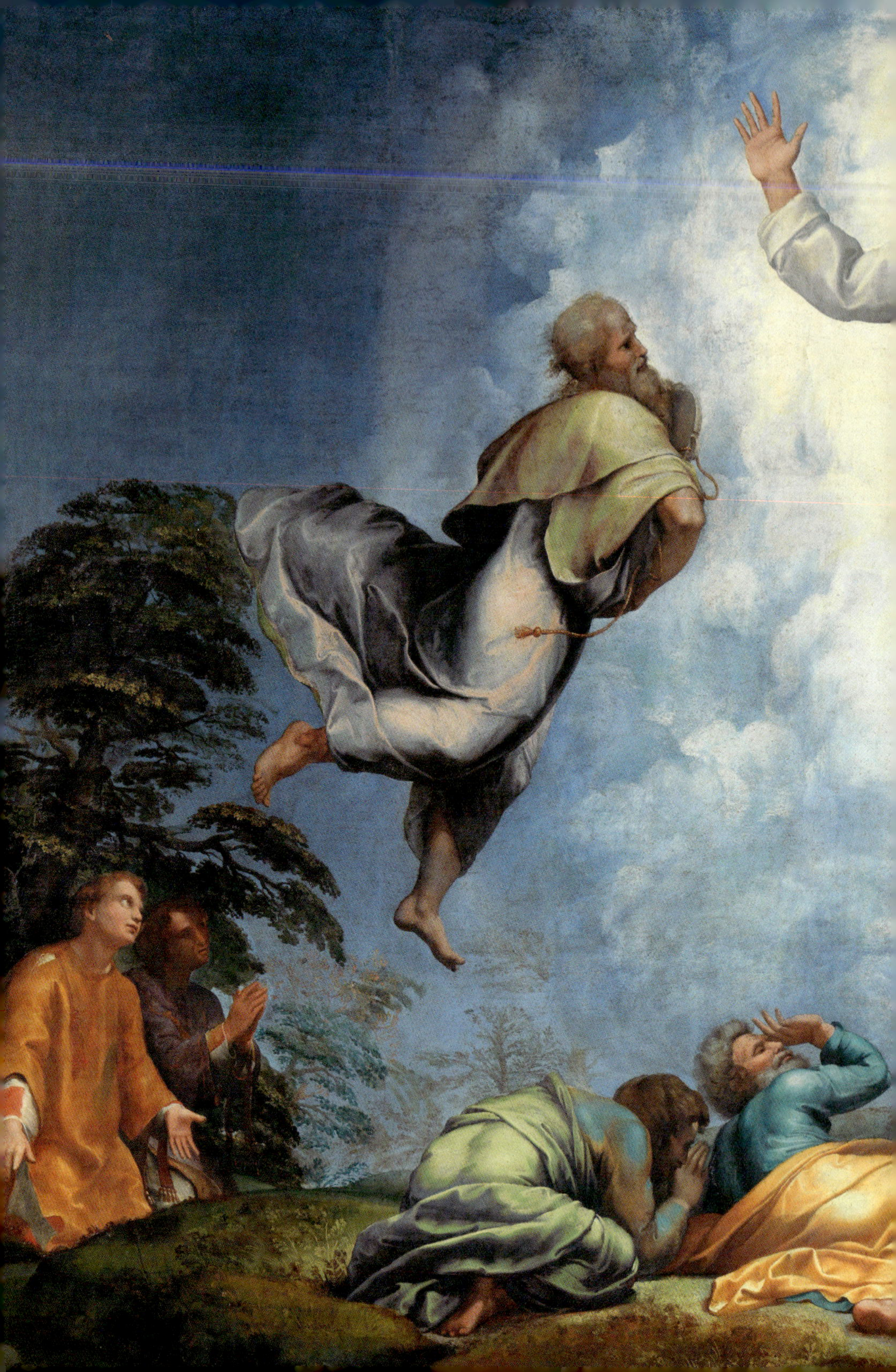

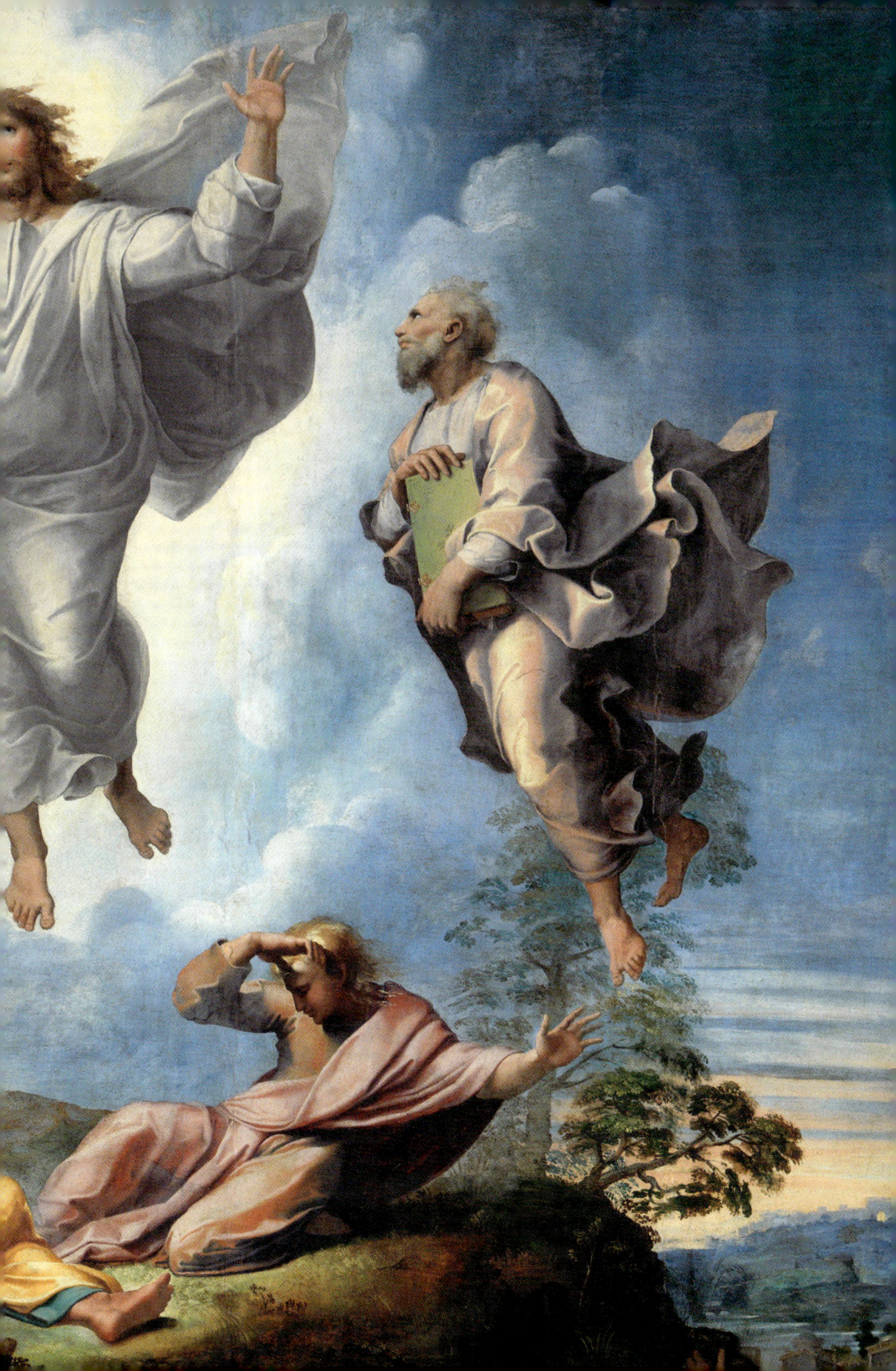

VI.

Secular and Sacred Images: Roman portraits and devotional paintings

1510–1520

Michael Rohlmann

"His portraiture transports us to such a world. From the dome of the skull, through the folds of dress and drapery, down to the hands and the base on which the figure is placed, as a statue on a pedestal, there is a stability and immobility which brings to mind the eternity of matter. The figure seems to have existed before the painter had created it."

GIORGIO DE CHIRICO, 1920

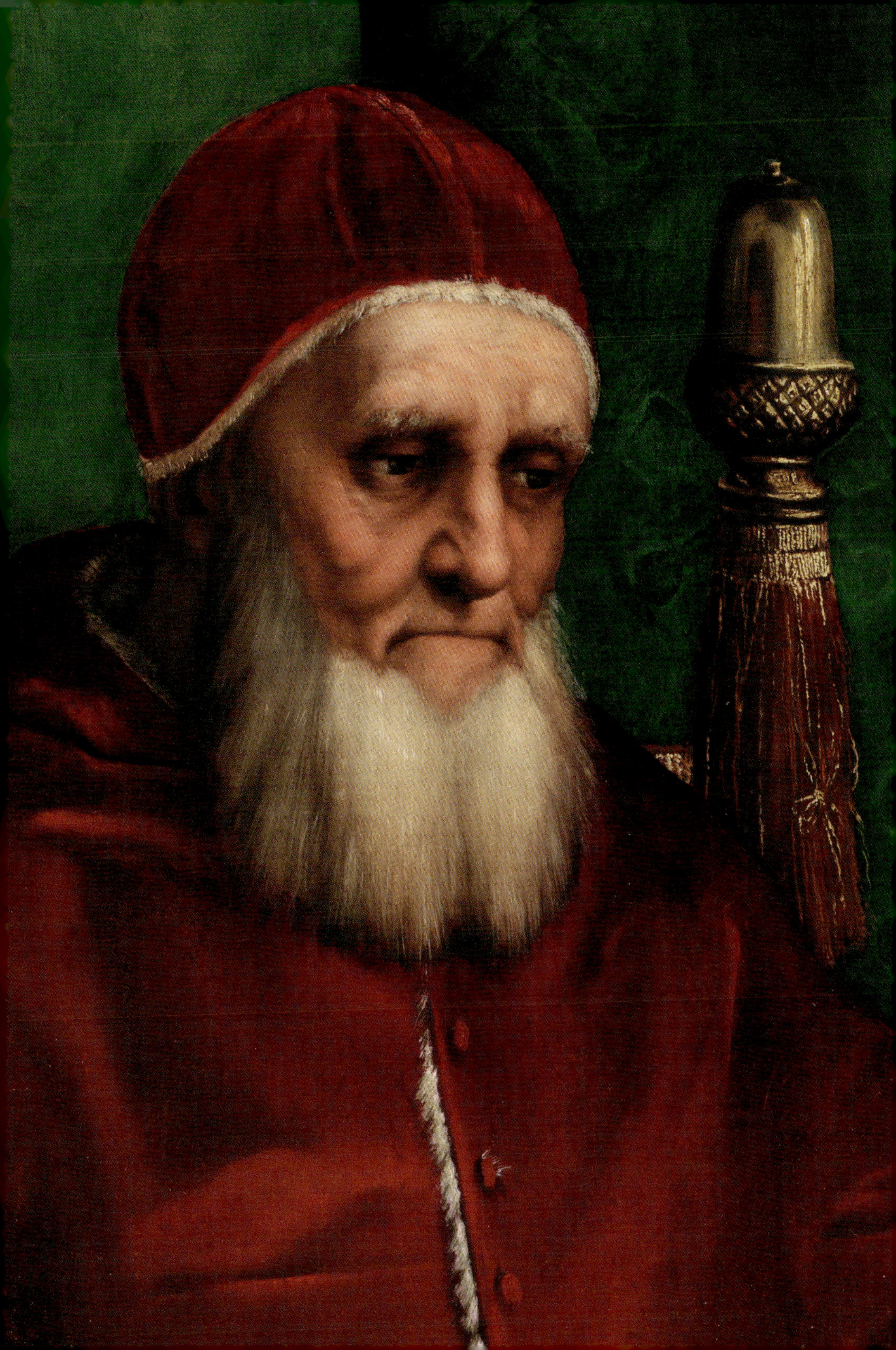

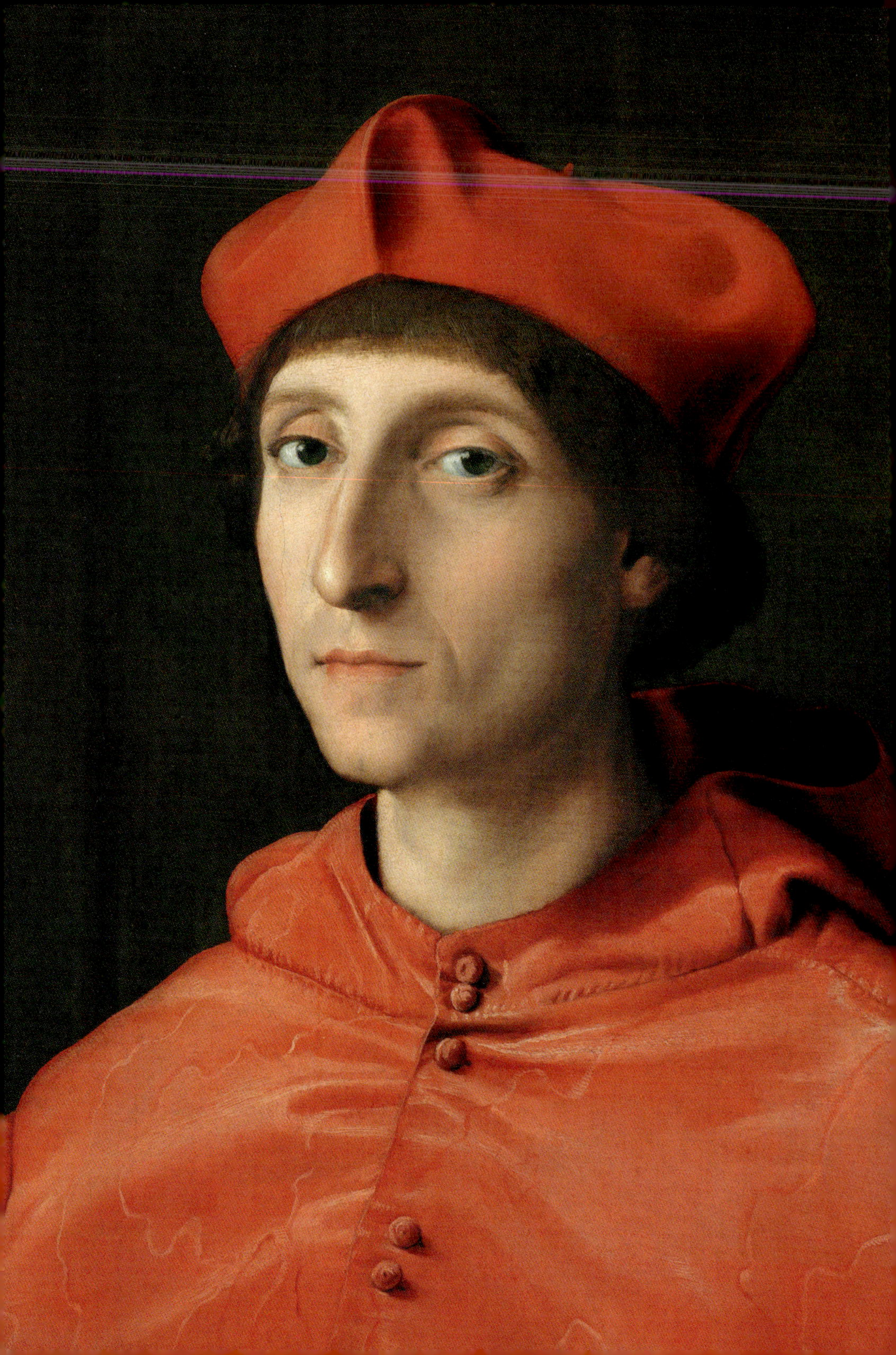

Roman portraits

Raphael's Roman paintings were not confined to the papal palace and to the public locations of altars inside the chapels and churches of Rome, Italy and beyond. They also included isolated examples of panel paintings in two genres in particular which were destined for the private sphere, for the domestic apartment or the palazzo. Those in Rome who belonged to the Pope's closest colleagues or to Raphael's intellectual circle of friends had the best chance of receiving a painted portrait from the Urbino artist. In the case of almost every sitter, their identity is still known today. As evidenced by documentary sources, Raphael's portraits were discussed by the Curia and among friends. Interest in the genre grew. Some portraits were evidently copied while still in Raphael's workshop. Raphael responded to this rise in the significance of portraiture: not only do the sizes of his Roman portraits increase substantially compared with those of his Florentine period, but the views they show are also broadened according to a hierarchical ranking. The sitter appears more powerful, more dignified, more present and more alive. Each picture thereby gains greater individuality. In each portrait, Raphael evidently rethought anew the basic type he had brought with him from Florence, varied it and dismantled it, in order to find an appropriate and representative visual solution for each social class, each character and each person. The sitters seem to speak from the paintings in a richer and more diverse way.

Portrait of a Cardinal in the Prado (p. 334; Cat. P51) is probably the earliest of Raphael's extant Roman portraits. The calm and clear geometric severity of the composition, and the upright pose set solidly into the rectangular frame, convey the impression of a church dignitary of lofty, steadfast dignity, focused determination and noble self-possession. The dominant red of his *mozzetta* (short cape) and biretta (peaked cap) echoes in muted tones in his lips. The white of his eyes, which look out at us with an alert gaze, is repeated in the sleeve of his left arm, which extends forward to the aesthetic boundary along the lower edge of the picture and keeps the world of the viewer at a distance. In the corners of his mouth lies the faint glimmer of a smile. The fabrics are painted with a breathtaking attention to detail: the pleats in the finest linen, the shimmer of the silk, the different seams, even the varying angles of the buttons – the upper ones have been pulled round to face us by the tension of the cape. The sitter thus exudes a captivating presence simply

Page 309
Detail from **Portrait of Pope Julius II**, *c.* 1512/13
(see ill. p. 336)

Detail from **Portrait of a Cardinal**, *c.* 1510
(see ill. p. 334)

through his being. The verism with which the materials are represented lends the facial features, too, the impression of being true to life. Naturalness, close likeness and the appearance of being alive were the categories singled out for praise by contemporaries writing about Raphael's portraits.

The poet, humanist, canon and director of the Vatican Library Tommaso Inghirami is seated behind his desk (p. 335; Cat. P52). The corpulent, rotund scholar with his fine fingers was wall-eyed, a condition that Raphael does not conceal, but which he tones down: Inghirami's good eye, too, is gazing "heavenwards" and so mitigates the unsettling cast of his other eye. An upturned gaze was a visual formula that signified inspiration, and was one that Raphael employed in his *Parnassus* for both Apollo and Homer (Cat. F3.1k). Inghirami's diverging eyes show that the poet draws his strength not from outer looking, but from an inner seeing. The white and black of his eyes find an echo in the blank sheet and the ink pen. Inghirami appears to be waiting for inspiration, which his beautiful hands will then put down on paper. One arm rests on the sheet and the other on a large book, which is lying open in front of the poet and is propped up at a slight angle for reading. Inghirami thus bases his writing, so to speak, on a work already written. Raphael evidently wishes to show that poetry is founded on the reading of earlier authors. The aim was to emulate the great masters of antiquity and to rise above their *imitatio* to *aemulatio*. Through divine inspiration – thus Raphael's portrait appears to proclaim – Inghirami is able to compete with the ancients. With this painted theory of poetry and emulation, Raphael was perhaps also reflecting upon his own activity as a portraitist: like a poet, he takes pre-existing material – i. e. the natural appearance of his sitter – and transforms and transfigures it in painting thanks to his inspiration.

Raphael's portrait of *Pope Julius II* (p. 336; Cat. P60) is a sensation in the history of portraiture and shaped the representational convention for Church dignitaries for centuries to come. The Pope is afforded a larger panel and seen in a somewhat wider view than the cardinal and the canon; there is space around him. The picture is painted with a freer hand and the brushwork and application of paint appear much richer and more differentiated, so that the portrait assumes greater animation. The shine and shimmer of the fabrics, the flesh with its greater modelling in colour, the gleaming reflections on the metal, the beads of light on the gold threads, the light refracting in precious gemstones, the ermine lining of the *camauro* cap and *mozzetta* cape, whose fine hairs even stray out from behind two buttons – all of these are aesthetic flourishes which add to the viewer's enjoyment.

The representation of a seated figure in three-quarter length was something with which Raphael was familiar from the Studiolo in the palace at Urbino, with its series of paintings of scholars (p. 17). He had already painted such figures himself – in a smaller

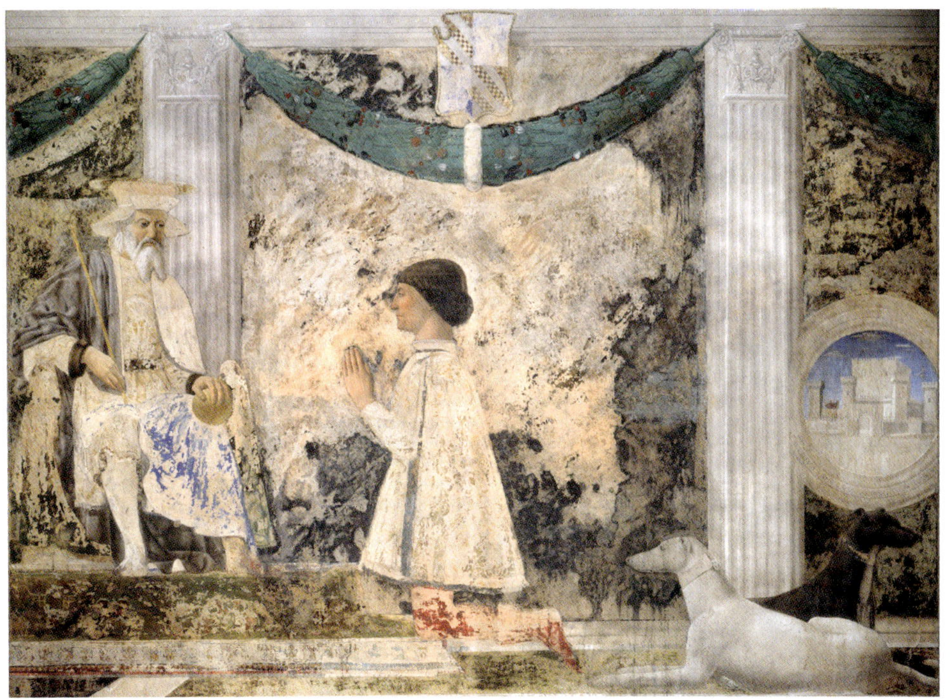

Piero della Francesca, **Sigismondo Pandolfo Malatesta Praying before Saint Sigismund**, 1451
Fresco, 237 × 345 cm (93 ¼ × 135 ⅞ in). Rimini, Tempio Malatestiano

format – in Madonna pictures. For the pose of the white-bearded elderly man, the slight inclination of his head and the arrangement of his arms and hands, Raphael seems to be looking back to Piero della Francesca's 1451 fresco *Saint Sigismund* in Rimini (p. 313), in which the holy ruler is seated opposite Sigismondo Malatesta (1417–1468), who kneels in prayer before him. The compositional formula is assigned to an emperor (IMPERATOR), too, in the Mantegna tarot cards, which Raphael had undoubtedly seen in his father's house (p. 314). The Pope's facial features are based on the same preparatory drawing (KMOF 382) as was used for the portrait of Julius in *Gregory IX Affirms the Decretals* (Cat. F3.1s). But whereas in this latter the Pope appears in full regalia with tiara and pluvial, his portrait shows him in modest, everyday pontifical dress, lined with fur as usual in winter (Bölling 2013). As viewers, our gaze fall upon the sitter as if we were observers standing to one side in an audience with the pontiff. The portrait thus suggests the context in which a close-up view of the Pope was possible in real life. The golden acorns decorating the throne allude to the family name of the Della Rovere pope and at the same time

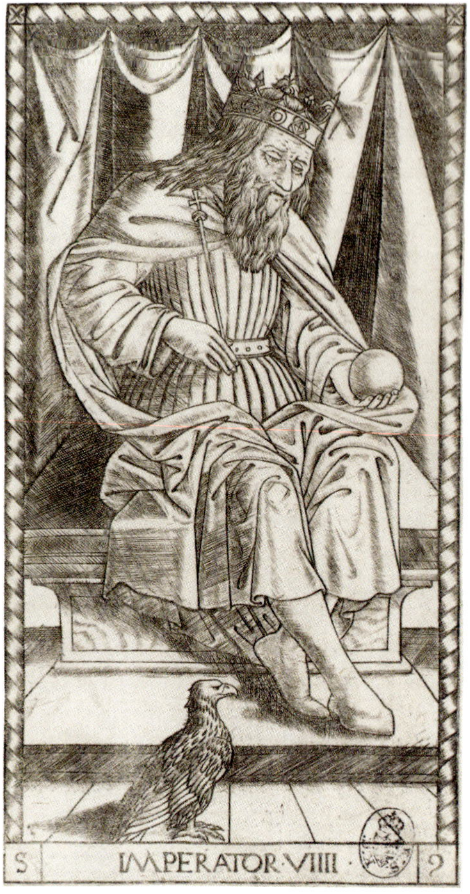

call to mind acorns as the mythical food of a primeval golden age that has now returned. It is also possible that Raphael has here depicted an authentic piece of papal furniture.

Instead of official pomp, Julius shows character: in his portrait, he is wearing a beard. This was the appearance he presented in Rome from summer 1511 to spring 1512. He let his beard grow as a sign of penitence and mourning following military defeats and insisted that he would not have it shaved off until the French had been expelled from Italy. In Raphael's portrait, the beard lends Julius the aura of a dignified elderly man, a prophet and patriarch. The Pope does not look out at the observer, but casts his shadowy eyes downwards into the unknown. His mouth is closed in a firm and serious manner. His cheeks are flushed and his forehead is brightly lit. Raphael has created the image of a noble, worried, fatherly thinker and has thus deliberately parried the idea, propagated not just by the Pope's enemies, of Julius as an irate warmonger whose person sows terror *(terribilità)*. The apparent verism of Raphael's *Julius II* thereby contains a programmatic message. As Sigismondo de' Conti, the Pope's secretary, declared, Julius was protected by divine providence so that he could restore not only Justice to the Roman papacy, but also *veritas*, truth and integrity.

In autumn 1513 the news was reported that the painting was on public display in the Roman church of Santa Maria del Popolo. In the octave of the feast of the Nativity of the Virgin (8 September), the painting was placed on the high altar, where the venerated icon of the Madonna attributed to Saint Luke could also be seen. The Della Rovere

Master of the S-Series set of "Mantegna Tarocchi Cards", **The Emperor (Imperator)**, *c.* 1470 (?)
Engraving, 17.3 × 9.3 cm (6 ¾ × 3 ⅔ in). Staatliche Kunstsammlungen Dresden, Kupferstich-Kabinett

popes had bestowed their particular patronage upon the church as a family endowment and also used it for large and politically significant ceremonies. In a tradition started by Sixtus IV, on the feast of the Nativity of the Virgin the Pope paid a visit to Santa Maria del Popolo in person. On the first such feast day after Julius's death, Raphael's portrait had to substitute for the real-life presence of the Pope (Rohlmann 2003). Whether the portrait was painted for Santa Maria del Popolo, however, or whether Julius only donated or bequeathed it to the church, is unknown. In December 1511, Julius gave a portrait painting of himself to the Roman church of San Marcello in fulfilment of a vow. Likewise in 1511, a German student mentions another portrait of the Pope in the papal palace at Bologna, where it hung over the door leading into the papal apartments ("der papa Julius, der da auf ain prust pildt gemacht was und stayndt ob der thuer, da man in des pabst stanzen gangen ist").

Raphael's large group portrait of Pope Leo X with his cardinal-nephews Giulio de' Medici and Luigi de' Rossi (1474–1519) also played a deputising role (p. 337; Cat. P79). In 1518 it had to be executed in a great hurry and sent to Florence, in order to hang above the table of the bridal couple at the belated celebration, held on 8 September, of the wedding of Leo's nephew Lorenzo de' Medici (1492–1519) to the French princess Madeleine de la Tour d'Auvergne (1495–1519). The marriage itself had taken place previously in Amboise and was part of the Medici's close alliance with France. With French help, the family was to be promoted to the European aristocracy. Leo and Giulio appeared at the celebration in Florence only in Raphael's portrait, but Luigi de' Rossi attended in person. Appointed a cardinal in 1517, de' Rossi, who had been born in Lyon and held French benefices, embodied the Medici connection with France as no other cardinal. In Raphael's portrait, he looks out of the picture into the world of the observer. At the wedding celebration, he thus mediated in person and via the painting between the Florentine guests and the – absent – heads of the Medici Curia. In other words, the portrait presented the French bride and her entourage with a special Francophile point of contact in the Curia (Tewes/Rohlmann 2002). The portrait was later installed over a door in the Medici family palace in Florence, where it served as a permanent reminder of the family's success in distant Rome and its rise to the papacy and cardinalcy.

The artist devoted greater attention to the figure of Leo at the design stage than to those of the cardinals and a clear preliminary underdrawing has been discovered only beneath the pope. The hierarchy of their respective offices is thus reflected in the process of creating the picture. But the two cardinals must have been planned from the beginning. The background architecture was painted on a green ground in which spaces were left blank for all three figures. In 2020 the homogeneous conception of the group portrait – long doubted – was confirmed by the findings of a restoration project

(Ciatti/Schmidt 2020). Raphael's painting is part of a long tradition of papal group portraits, including the fresco portraits of Sixtus IV and Julius II in the Vatican. But whereas Sixtus could still surround himself entirely with his own relatives, Julius already appears with members of the Curia from outside his own family (Cat. F3.1p). Nepotism as a concept of government had lost public acceptance after the experiences with the Borgia Pope Alexander VI. For Leo X to show himself exclusively with Medici relatives would by this date, therefore, have been socially acceptable only if the portrait were hung in the private family palace. The visual celebration of the Medici's success in the Roman Curia found its appropriate place within the family sphere. The same was later the case, too, with *Paul III and his Grandsons* by Titian (*c.* 1488/90–1576), which follows in the footsteps of Raphael's portrait (Rohlmann 2003, 2007).

The balanced composition of the three Medici exudes a solemn stillness. The colours of the family coat of arms echo in the gleam of red and gold. Raphael ennobles the fat and ugly figure of the Medici pope by means of the splendour of sumptuous heavy robes and renders the fleshy expanse of his face, too, with a soft delicacy. He reproduces the material properties of still-life elements in virtuoso fashion: the papal chair is crowned by the reflecting ball *(palla)* of the Medici coat of arms. In the fifteenth century, the Medici were granted the right to incorporate the French *fleur-de-lys* into one of the balls in its shield, as a mark of distinction and special favour from the king of France. The *palla* in Raphael's portrait also reveals the reflection of a cross-shaped window, a detail that could also be interpreted in heraldic terms – as if the family in Rome were now filled with the Christian symbol of salvation. Leo's hand touches a magnificent illuminated Bible (the original manuscript is today preserved in Berlin [p. 319]). In representational tradition, the written word of God was usually assigned as an attribute to pictures of popes. A sacred and magical significance lay in touching the Bible: it established the contact between the Pope and God (cf. p. 230 t.; Cat. F3.3a). Along with the message of the Gospel as the core of Christianity, the task of spreading God's word, and sovereignty over its interpretation, also rest in Leo's hands. Next to the book, Raphael arranges a small bell and the magnifying glass used by the extremely short-sighted pope (p. 318). If the magnifying glass alludes to looking at and absorbing what is written, the bell stands for action and the issuing of instructions – the spread and active implementation of the read message, as it were. The fact that Leo X is gazing into the distance can only signify that he is lost in inner seeing: a higher vision that defies earthly power of sight. In Raphael's painting, the portrait gains a new wealth of language and invites intellectual interpretation.

The Curia also included members of Raphael's circle of friends, some of whom were humanists, literary figures or diplomats. On 3 April 1516, Pietro Bembo wrote from Rome to Cardinal Bibbiena (1470–1520) in Fiesole that he would be travelling the following day with Andrea Navagero (1483–1529), Agostino Beazzano (*c.* 1490–1549), Baldassare Castiglione and Raphael to Tivoli. They wanted to look at the old, new and beautiful things to be found there. Raphael painted all of the above-mentioned. He had made a portrait of Bembo (a work that today appears lost) while still in Urbino, and Bembo considered having Raphael paint him a second time in Rome, too, in view of the portraits that Raphael was making of his friends. Raphael's *Portrait of Cardinal Bibbiena* (p. 338; Cat. P70) follows the type of the *Portrait of a Cardinal* (p. 334; Cat. P51) today housed in the Prado. But Bibbiena's upper body is positioned at a more pronounced angle and his left forearm in its pale sleeve is set back from the lower edge of the picture. His right hand is included in the picture, holding a letter addressed to the Pope. His apparently more generously sized *mozzetta* drapes itself in animated folds. The pathos of aliveness fills the representation. Raphael combined Navagero and Beazzano into a double portrait (p. 342; Cat. P68). The painting belonged to Bembo and the two sitters thus look out at their friend. Bembo later gave the painting to Beazzano. The portrait was a representation and medium of friendship. It recalled times spent together in Rome, even if their paths subsequently diverged. With his art, the painter is a mediator of friendship and at the same time part of it himself.

The portrait of Baldassare Castiglione (p. 349; Cat. P69) is a miracle of lively presence, poised elegance and warm sympathy. Parallels have rightly been drawn between Raphael's painting and Castiglione's *Il Cortegiano (The Courtier)*: the artist has translated the ideal of the noble courtier, conceived by Castiglione, into painting and in so doing simultaneously illustrated the author and his work. Raphael has confined his palette almost entirely to blacks, greys and browns. This allows the colours of the sitter's flesh to radiate all the more warmly out of his friendly face and quietly folded hands. The body is detached from the vertical sides of the picture and casts a remote shadow in the background. Castiglione thus appears as a free, independent individual. The handle of a sword or dagger identifies him as a member of the aristocracy. In front of his chest, fine white linen billows forth beneath a garment of stiff, dark fabric, so that the portrait seems to breathe. The broad hat not only conceals the sitter's baldness but also responds to the similarly rounded, closed silhouette of his trunk. Thus emphasised, the head rises above the body in its own right. It is very slightly inclined to one side. How overwhelming the impact of those beautiful blue eyes! Castiglione's soul seems to radiate out of them. In a touching elegy, the author imagines the effect of his portrait on his distant wife and child – how it might comfort his wife during his absence, how she might laugh and joke with it, speak to it and seem to get a reply, and how their young son might recognise his father and address his babbling talk to him.

On 19 April 1516, Bembo wrote to Bibbiena that Raphael had just finished a portrait of "our Tebaldeo" ("il nostro Thebaldeo"), i. e. the poet Antonio Tebaldeo (1463–1537).

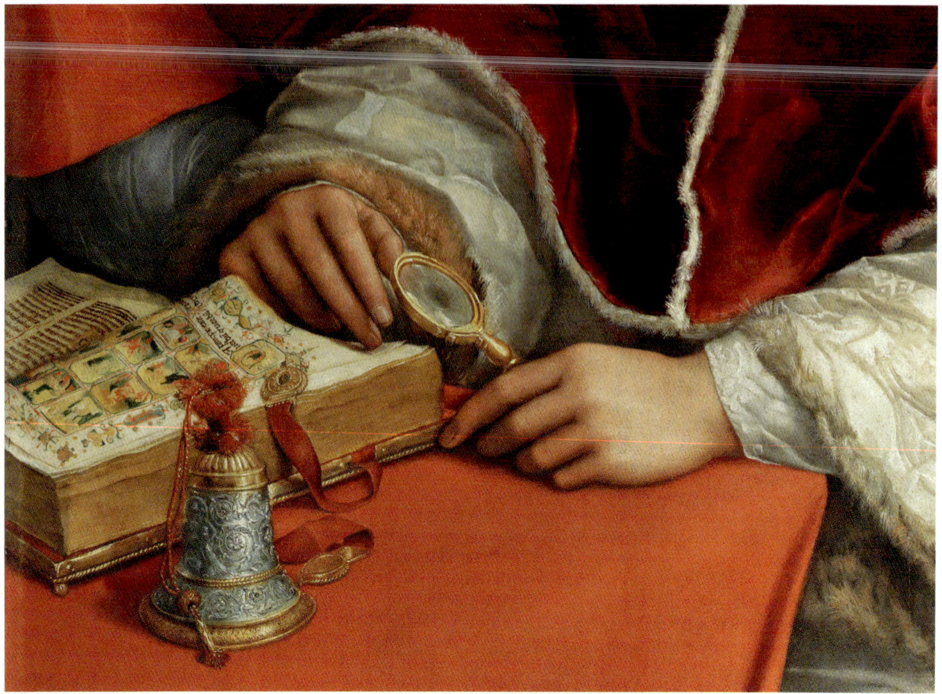

According to Bembo, it made Raphael's portraits of Castiglione and the deceased Giuliano de' Medici (1479–1516) look – in terms of their resemblance to the sitter – as if they had been painted by one of Raphael's young workshop assistants ("d'uno de' garzoni di Raphaello"). The portrait of Antonio Tebaldeo (Cat. P67), which has come down to us only via copies, was a gift from Raphael to his friend. Tebaldeo responded by composing a sonnet in which he compares painting and poetry in their goal of being able to confer immortality.

In Raphael's Paris self-portrait with a companion (*Double Portrait of Two Young Men*, p. 343; Cat. P83), friendship and fellowship become the theme of the visual narrative.

Detail from **Pope Leo X with Cardinals Giulio de' Medici and Luigi de' Rossi**, *c.* 1518
(see ill. p. 337)

Cristoforo Oriminia, **The Passion of Christ and the Last Judgement**
from: *Biblia Latina* (so-called *Hamilton Bible*), 1350–1360
Illuminated manuscript on parchment, 37.5 × 26.5 cm (14 ¾ × 10 ⅜ in)
Staatliche Museen zu Berlin, Kupferstichkabinett

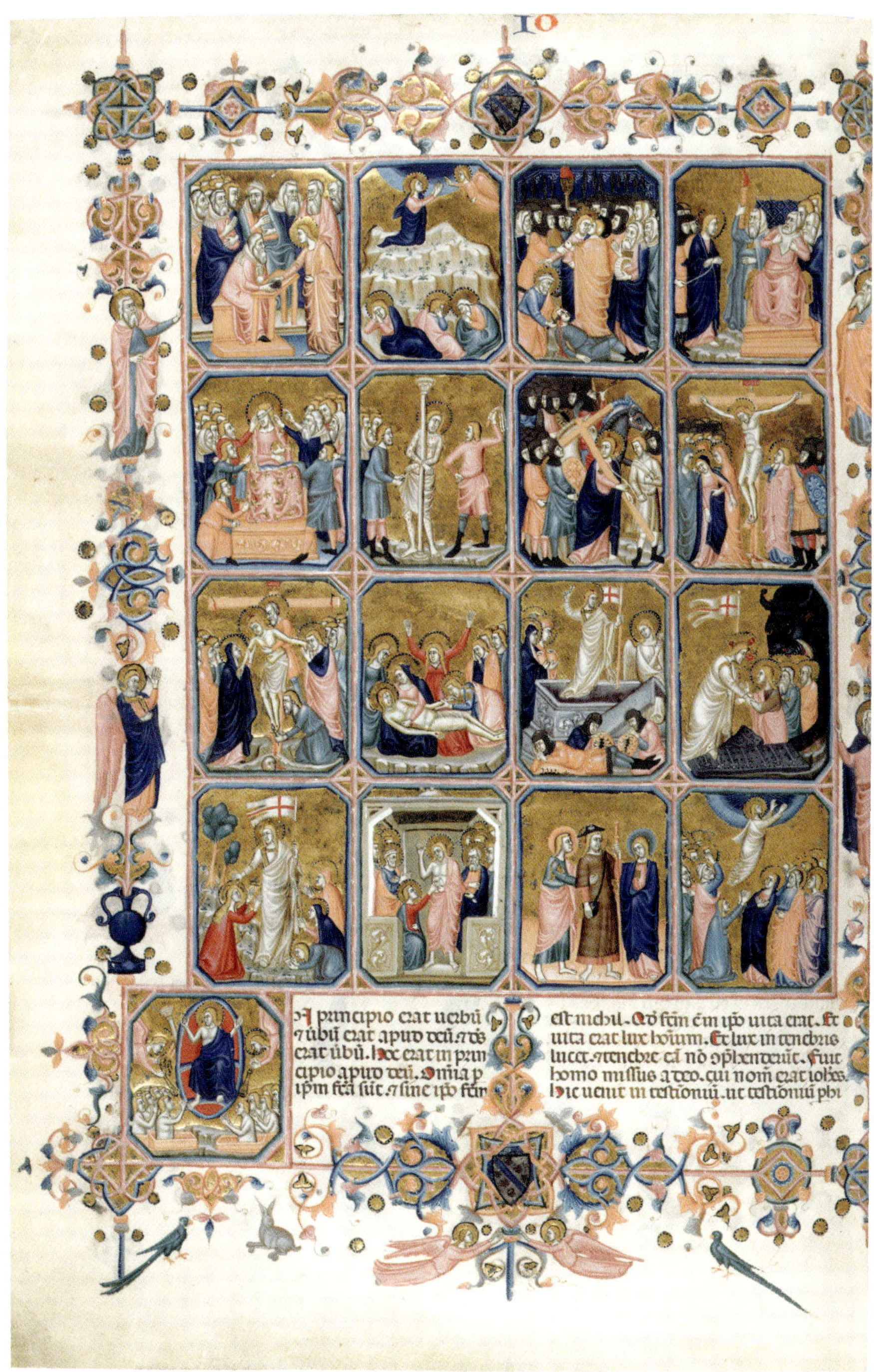
Io
In principio erat uerbū
7 ūbū erat apud deū. 7 dš
erat ūbū. Hoc erat in prin
cipio apud deū. Omnia p
ipm fcā sūt. 7 sine ipo fcm
est nichil. Qd fcm ē in ipo uita erat. Et
uita erat lux hoīum. Et lux in tenebris
lucet. 7 tenebre eā nō cōprehenderūt. Fuit
homo missus a deo. cui nomē erat iohes.
hic uenit in testimoniū. ut testimoniū phi

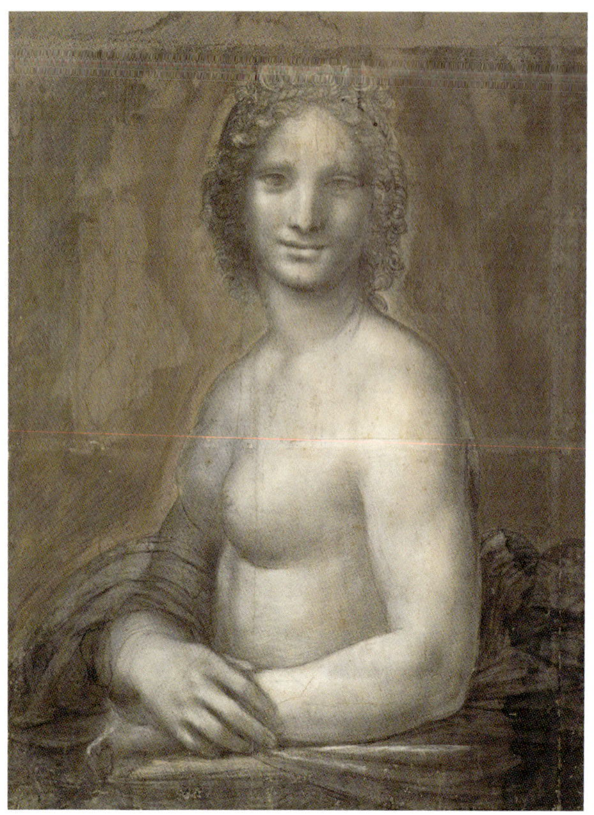

A bearded man points out of the painting at the viewer and at the same time looks back towards Raphael, as though wishing to draw his attention to the picture's audience. As if in reply, Raphael lays his hand on his companion's shoulder in affirmative acknowledgement and indeed looks directly out at us. Between the viewer and the two young men in the painting, who seem to have been brought to life, a three-way association is thus forged in which the traditional roles of painting and observer appear reversed. Just as the identity of Raphael's companion has yet to be established with certainty, so the occasion for the portrait and its deeper meaning remain tantalisingly unclear. The portrait of the young banker Bindo Altoviti (p. 346; Cat. P72) shows a handsome young man with golden locks and full lips. As viewers, we are standing to the right of the sitter. The picture invites us to accompany the good-looking Bindo side by side, shoulder to shoulder, eye to eye.

The representation of Giuliano de' Medici, brother of Leo X, is more conservative and perhaps only survives in the form of a copy (p. 352; Cat. P66). The borrowing of the pose and hand position from Leonardo's *Mona Lisa* caters to the taste of the sitter, who was Leonardo's patron and close friend in Rome at that time. In the background, a curtain has been drawn back to reveal a view of Castel Sant'Angelo. Giuliano is evidently in Raphael's Vatican loggias. A link is thus established between the secular head of the

Leonardo da Vinci (Workshop?), **La Joconde nue**, *c.* 1515/20
Charcoal and lead white, 74.8 × 56 cm (29 ½ × 22 ⅛ in). Chantilly, Musée Condé

Medici and the Roman papal fortress. Although Leo had appointed Giuliano as leader of the papal troops, Giuliano does not appear as a military figure in his portrait: arms and armour are missing.

Giuliano's nephew Lorenzo de' Medici appears with greater pomp and not with Roman identity (p. 348; Cat. P75). He presents himself as a prince in sumptuous dress. In 1515 in Milan he rivalled even the king of France in the costliness of his clothing ("in vestirsi"). At the start of 1518, the Duke of Urbino sent the portrait to his future bride in France. He thereby seems to have orientated himself towards French fashion ("ritratto del Duca Lorenzo vestito alla francese"), but at the same time identifies himself, by means of the heraldic Medici colours of red and gold, as a member of the papal family that has been Francophile for generations. At the wedding in Amboise, the bride Madeleine de La Tour d'Auvergne must have been disappointed: it is reported that the Duke had to arrive by carriage on account of his syphilis. The bride, far too beautiful for the groom, married the disease along with her new husband.

Only a few of Raphael's friends were married. The celibacy of the clergy and the only temporary presence of diplomats and humanists at the papal court had given rise to a male-dominated society, specific to Rome, in which women were often assigned the role of lovers, concubines or courtesans. The portraits of demure wives and mothers with which Raphael had fulfilled the wishes of husbands and the demands of family-oriented society in Florence, are consequently lacking in the artist's Roman oeuvre. Raphael himself did not marry. In a letter to his uncle dated 1 July 1514, Raphael mentions the latter's repeated attempts to arrange a marriage for the painter in Urbino. Raphael justifies his resistance by pointing out the large income he is earning with his art in Rome and insists that he can easily find a *"mamola bella"*, i. e. a pretty girl, in Rome.

Here Cardinal Bibbiena wanted him to marry one of his own female relations, namely his great-niece Marietta. Raphael seems to have finally agreed to this match, but Marietta apparently died shortly before the wedding. Raphael's friend Tebaldeo wrote a poem for her tomb, and Raphael left instructions in his will for a memorial inscription to be mounted next to his own tomb. Vasari later wrote that Raphael delayed the wedding because he was hoping that Leo X would make him a cardinal as a reward for painting the Sala di Costantino. Vasari also reports that Raphael indulged his sexual appetites in immoderate fashion and that his mistress lived with him in his house; he only sent her away shortly before his approaching death, entrusting her to the care of a workshop assistant and providing her with the financial means to lead a respectable life. Raphael – according to Vasari – also painted her in a portrait. The *Donna Velata* (p. 350; Cat. P64) indeed shows an idealised face, of a kind similar to that used by Raphael in his *Sistine Madonna* (p. 291; Cat. P59) and *Saint Cecilia* (p. 295; Cat. P65).

Raphael's *Donna Velata* is a masterpiece of sensual beauty and finely tuned colour harmony. In a play between concealing and revealing, a veil falls around the dark hair and soft, warm flesh of a young woman, framing her outline. Large eyes look seductively at the male viewer and a gentle smile plays around the red lips. In a display of painterly bravura, the billowing white, gold-trimmed Atlas silk of the puffed sleeve spills towards us, as if inviting us to reach in and touch it. Deep pleats serve to draw men's eyes and stimulate their imagination. The beautiful sitter touches her own hand to her breast and heart as if in a protestation of love. Her index finger thereby reaches through the opening in the neckline of her bodice and presses delicately against the pleats of her fine undergarment, through which her skin shimmers. The bows fastening the fabric at the shoulder are prominently shown and the garment is thus highlighted as one to be opened.

The eroticism of *La Fornarina* (p. 351; Cat. P84) is less subtle. The beautiful sitter resembles the young woman with the veil but is now semi-naked. With one hand at her breast and the other over her pubic area, she touches herself delicately as if wanting to arouse herself for the observer at whom she gazes (Clark 2005). In a preliminary drawing for the Wedding Banquet of Psyche and Cupid (p. 323), the naked Psyche holds her hands in exactly the same position. Just as the female nude in *La Fornarina* looks out at the viewer, Psyche gazes into the eyes of her adored, the god of love, who is reclining beside her. As in the *Donna Velata*, La Fornarina's dark hair is adorned with a single pearl, which hangs down like a pendant. This attribute of Venus, however, is joined by a bracelet inscribed RAPHAEL VRBINAS. By placing his signature on this love token, Raphael deliberately plays with identifying himself not only as the painter of the portrait, but also as the lover of its sitter. It has been suggested that the artist was furthermore seeking, in *La Fornarina*, to rival the love poetry of Petrarch (1304–1374) or even to propagate erotic inspiration as the basis of his art. But perhaps we must imagine the painting also serving a less intellectual function in the life of Curial Roman male society and its courtesan culture. With *La Fornarina*, Raphael tried his hand at a new genre of erotically arousing painting. A few years earlier in Rome, Leonardo had already produced his own painting of a naked woman in a portrait format, *Leda* (p. 320).

Only in the case of Raphael's *Portrait of the Vicereine of Naples* (p. 353; Cat. P78) do we know the circumstances surrounding its execution and the function of the finished painting (Fritz 2002). Raphael painted the portrait of Doña Isabel de Requesens i Enríquez de Cardona-Anglesola (1498–1534), a celebrated beauty, on the basis of drawings made by one of his pupils, whom he had sent to Naples for this purpose. Cardinal Bibbiena wished to present the portrait to Francis I (1494–1547) as a gift during a diplomatic mission to France. The French king's interest in beautiful young women, both in the flesh and in art, was well known. The portrait was successful: Alfonso d'Este (1476–1534), then residing

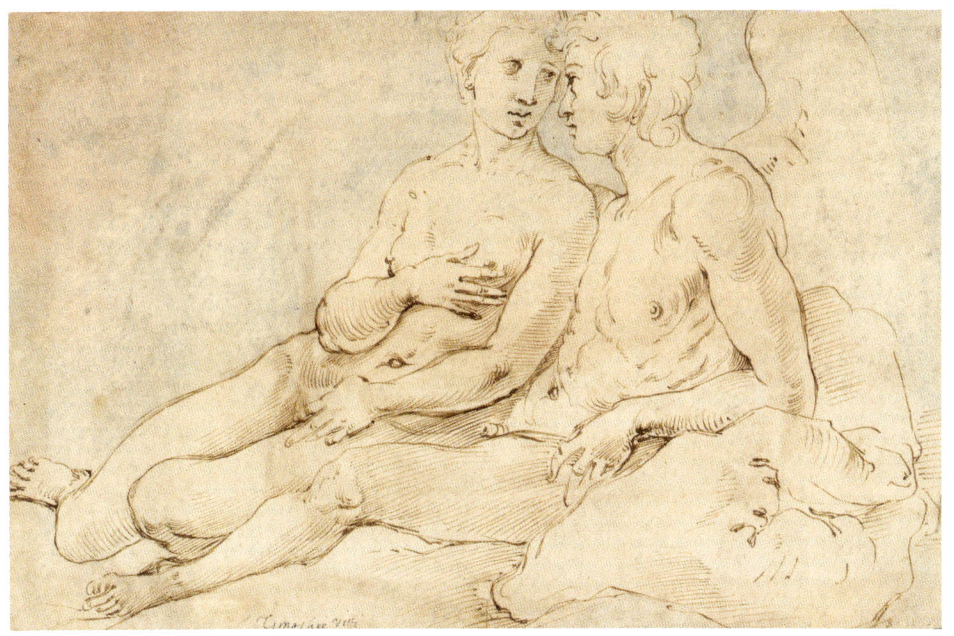

Raphael (copy?), **Cupid and Psyche, preliminary drawing for the *Marriage of Cupid and Psyche* in the Villa Farnesina**, *c.* 1517/18
Pen, 17.5 × 27 cm (6 ⅞ × 10 ⅝ in). Vienna, Albertina

at the French court, immediately asked to be sent the cartoon so that he could have a copy of the painting made. In Raphael's portrait, the Vicereine appears in three-quarter length – as only the Pope before her had. She sits enthroned in a palace interior as a magnificently dressed Queen of Beauty. With the instrument of the virginal behind her, the art of music finds its way into the representation as a pictorial motif. Even deeper in the background, a woman enjoys the view from a loggia into the far distance. Raphael's painting invited its viewers, too, to take pleasure in looking at a beautiful sight, in a *bel-vedere*.

Devotional pictures

Alongside portraits, devotional pictures were the second genre of paintings commissioned or purchased from Raphael to adorn private interiors. The enormous size to which Raphael enlarges this genre in some of the Roman examples supports the idea that these served as altarpieces in domestic and palace chapels. Such chapels were more numerous in Rome, with its many cardinal households, than in Florence. The most common motif of Raphael's devotional paintings remained the Virgin and Child, the Virgin's style of dress evolving to suit the Roman fashion. The fine veil of the Florentine Madonnas is seen one last time in the *Madonna di Loreto* (p. 357; Cat. P57), after which Mary wears turban-like headscarves, pale and white, in one case red, several times with coloured stripes, and often finely trimmed with ornamental stripes of gold. Only the standing *Madonna dell'Impannata* (p. 367; Cat. P56) has pulled her blue cloak up over the back of her head: here Raphael has taken into account the usual custom in the case of standing Madonna figures in Florence, the painting's destination. The representation is only very rarely confined to the Virgin and Child. They are almost always joined by the Infant John and subsequently by Joseph and other relations. The Holy Family grows to four, five and even seven persons. The composition thereby becomes ever more sophisticated.

For the Child, Raphael finds a powerful, dynamic pose, evidently inspired by the antique *Laocoön* statue (p. 358), which he varies three times in the *Madonna Aldobrandini* (p. 356; Cat. P49), the *Alba Madonna* (p. 359; Cat. P55) and the *Madonna dell'Impannata* (p. 367; Cat. P56) (Brock 2011). It allows the Child to oscillate between leaning in towards his mother and turning towards the outside. In the *Alba Madonna*, Christ and John the Baptist in clasping a small wooden cross contemplate their future sacrificial deaths even as children. This allusion to suffering is reinforced by the pose of the Infant Christ, which is borrowed in mirror image from that of the dying *Laocoön*. After the sculpture's discovery in 1506, the *Laocoön* was regarded in the Renaissance era as a perfect example of the representation of suffering.

In the *Madonna Aldobrandini* and *Alba Madonna*, the heads of mother and child are mutually aligned and chime magnificently together. In both cases, their twin gazes are turned towards the Infant Baptist, with whom Jesus establishes indirect physical contact via a flower and a cross-staff respectively. Both pyramidal compositions of supreme harmony and delicacy of colour are perfectly matched to their respectively rectangular and circular formats. Backgrounds become interesting. In the *Alba Madonna* nature unfolds in all its extraordinary loveliness, while in the *Madonna Aldobrandini* views through the windows open left and right onto the built landscape – Raphael had apparently seen Memling's *Pagagnotti Virgin and Child*. In the *Impannata*, the everyday motif of the window covered with thin cloth (It. *impannata*) even gives the painting its name.

The much-copied *Madonna di Loreto* (Cat. P57) is highly unusual. The Virgin holds out a veil over the Christ Child. In her *Revelations*, Saint Bridget of Sweden described how Mary uncovered the Infant so that the shepherds could see his body and sex (cf. KMOF 442). Raphael develops this into a tender play between mother and child, which makes

Detail from **Portrait of Bindo Altoviti**, *c.* 1516–1518
(see ill. p. 346)

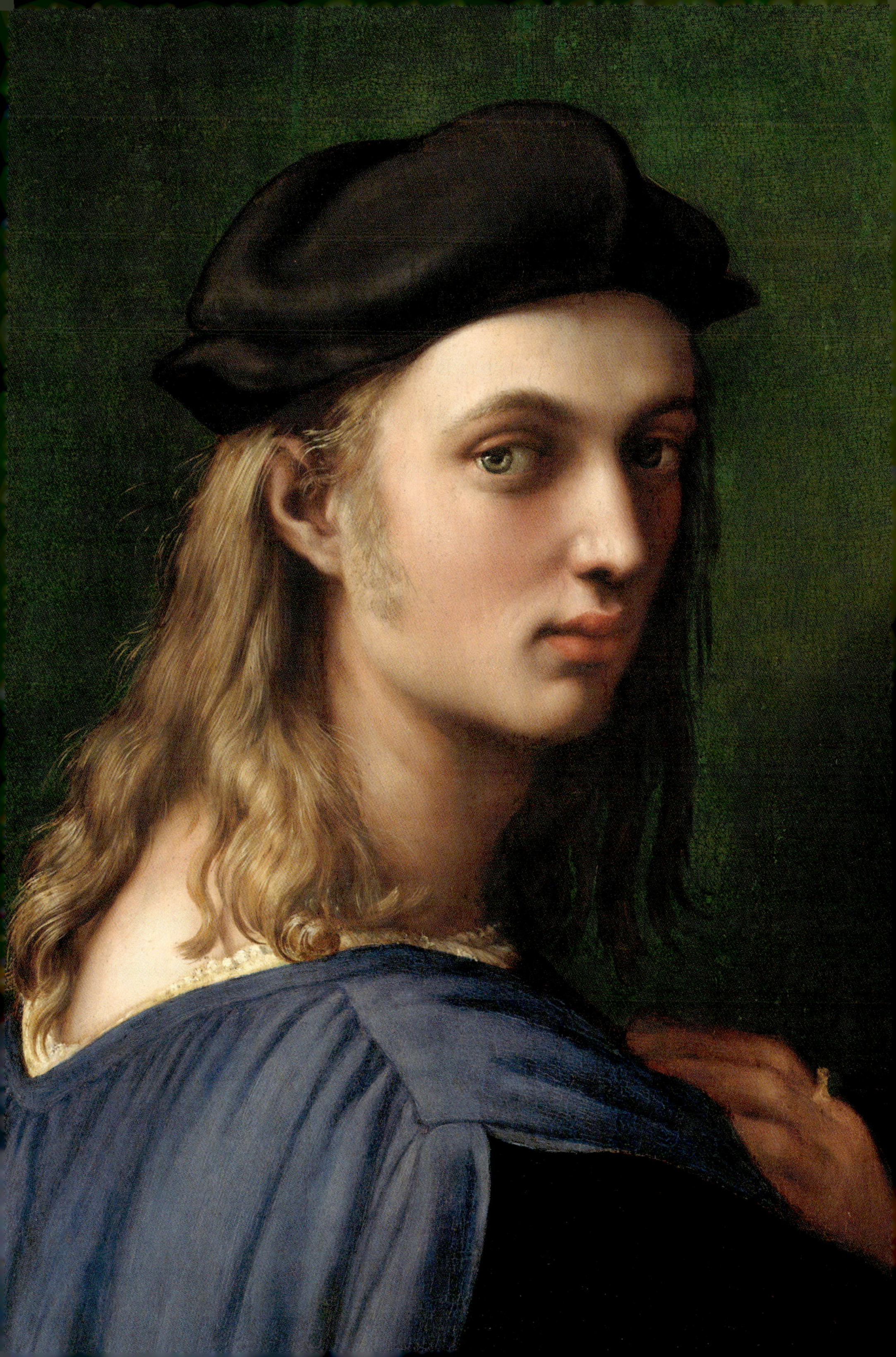

the viewers themselves the witness to a revelation. In the sixteenth century, the painting was located in the Roman church of Santa Maria del Popolo and on feast days was presented on pillars together with Raphael's portrait of *Julius II* (Cat. P60). It is possible that Julius II also donated or bequeathed Raphael's *Madonna di Loreto* to the church.

The tight-knit groups of three in close-up view in the *Madonna della Seggiola* (p. 362; Cat. P62) and *Madonna della Tenda* (p. 363; Cat. P61) are related. In the *Madonna della Seggiola*, the heads of mother and chubby child nestle snugly together. The way in which Raphael has married this representation of oneness and closeness with the circular tondo format has always been admired. Everything fuses into ever new curves, bends and arches. This wonderful inner cohesion culminates in the dual gazes of mother and child, whose two pairs of eyes look out at the observer. Inside the picture, the Infant John in the background mirrors our own looking. He is all yearning, rapturous wonder. Never have we seen the ten fingers of praying hands pressed together with such exquisite unevenness by a child oblivious to all around it! Similar naturalness is suggested on the left by the materiality of the colourful patterned shawl and the shimmering of its fringe and the upright. Nowhere else does Raphael allow us to experience the presence of the Virgin as so human and so close.

In the rectangle of the *Tenda*, the connection between mother and child has loosened. The Child's legs are splayed along the lower edge of the picture. His hand – hidden behind his mother's shawl in the *Madonna della Seggiola* – here reaches across to the left. His gaze is directed upwards to the right, where the edge of the curtain leads diagonally up to the top right-hand corner of the picture. The Virgin's head is turned in profile and lifted away from that of the Child. Mary no longer clasps her son with her hands one on top of the other. Fingers now extend to the right and her left arm embraces the Baptist, too. Thus John's head, rather than the Virgin's, is now brought close to that of the divine child. Instead of the viewer, it is now John, within the picture, who receives attention. The cross seems to spring out the heads of both children. John communicates to Christ a preview of the Passion.

Later full-figure Holy Families amplify and vary the throng of bodies in space to give them ever greater wealth and complexity. Artistic effects become more important. The surrounding space thereby assumes increased significance as a pictorial motif. The horizon shifts upwards. The landscape is allowed to unfold on a larger scale. It is no longer subordinate to the figures as a gentle background foil, but acquires its own weight as the place of action. Raphael seeks painterly effects and dramatic moods in his figures' surroundings. Atmospheric lighting, darkness, rocks and bizarre ancient ruins combine to form a heroic world with an abundance of naturalistic details. In it the figures, too, become more monumental and their appearance more imposing. The groups are conceived in sculptural terms and varied and combined in ever new ways. In the *Madonna del Divino Amore* (p. 373; Cat. P95), *La Perla* (p. 375; Cat. P81), *Madonna della Quercia* (p. 374; Cat. P82) and *Madonna della Gatta*, often attributed to Giulio Romano but probably begun in Raphael's workshop (p. 331; see Cerasuolo 2017), the Infant Jesus sits astride his mother's thigh in each case in an only slightly modified pose. *La Perla*, the *Madonna della Quercia* and *Madonna della Gatta* thereby show the almost identical groups of mother, child and cradle from different angles, while *La Perla* and *Madonna della Gatta* also include Mary's elderly female companion. A model was evidently posed in such a way as to present a beautiful and artistically attractive view from different sides. Or did Raphael also base the figure of the Virgin upon the antique seated statue of a Muse (p. 330; Ginzburg 2009)? In the *Madonna della Quercia*, the work's artistic character is heightened by faithfully reproduced *vedute* of ancient buildings as well as by identifiable antique sculptures, set out in front of Joseph as if in a garden of antiquities. Mary's hand, hanging casually down in front of them, is pure elegance. Beneath Mary's close-fitting garment, we can make out her navel and nipples. Such eroticisation of the Virgin runs parallel to religious Petrarchan love poetry and, like this latter, took up the themes of beauty and love associated with the mystical bride in the biblical Song of Songs. Yearning oscillates between earthly and heavenly desire and was intended to lead the soul of the male viewer to the love of God (see Cropper 1976; Vaccaro 2001). Perhaps the painting was intended for Agostino Chigi, the collector of antiquities and Raphael's great Roman patron of sensual art. For Chigi, Raphael designed an entire cycle of frescoes on the theme of how the soul may ascend to heaven through love (Cat. F11). One of Chigi's heraldic devices was the eponymous oak tree (It. *quercia*) beneath which the Holy Family is gathered.

Known recipients of Raphael Madonnas are Bindo Altoviti, Leonello or Alberto da Carpi, Bishop Lodovico Canossa (1475–1532), Bishop Federico Fregoso (*c.* 1480–1541) and Cardinal Bibbiena. In 1518 several Raphael paintings on religious themes were also sent to the French king as gifts from Leo X and his nephew Lorenzo de' Medici. The circumstances surrounding these paintings are particularly well documented. In 1518 Lorenzo travelled to the Loire in person not only to marry Madeleine de la Tour d'Auvergne but also, beforehand, to represent the Pope as godfather to the new-born heir to the French throne. To mark the wedding, the infant's parents, in other words the royal couple, were to receive suitable gifts of paintings. But the pictures did not arrive until months later. Francis I received a large representation of a powerful and monumental Saint Michael the Archangel vanquishing Satan (p. 381; Cat. P76). Saint Michael was the patron saint of France and its rulers. The king was also the head of the French chivalric Order of Saint Michael, named after the angel; Raphael had already depicted Saint Michael as a member of the Order many years earlier in Urbino, for Francesco Maria della Rovere (p. 97; Cat. P16a).

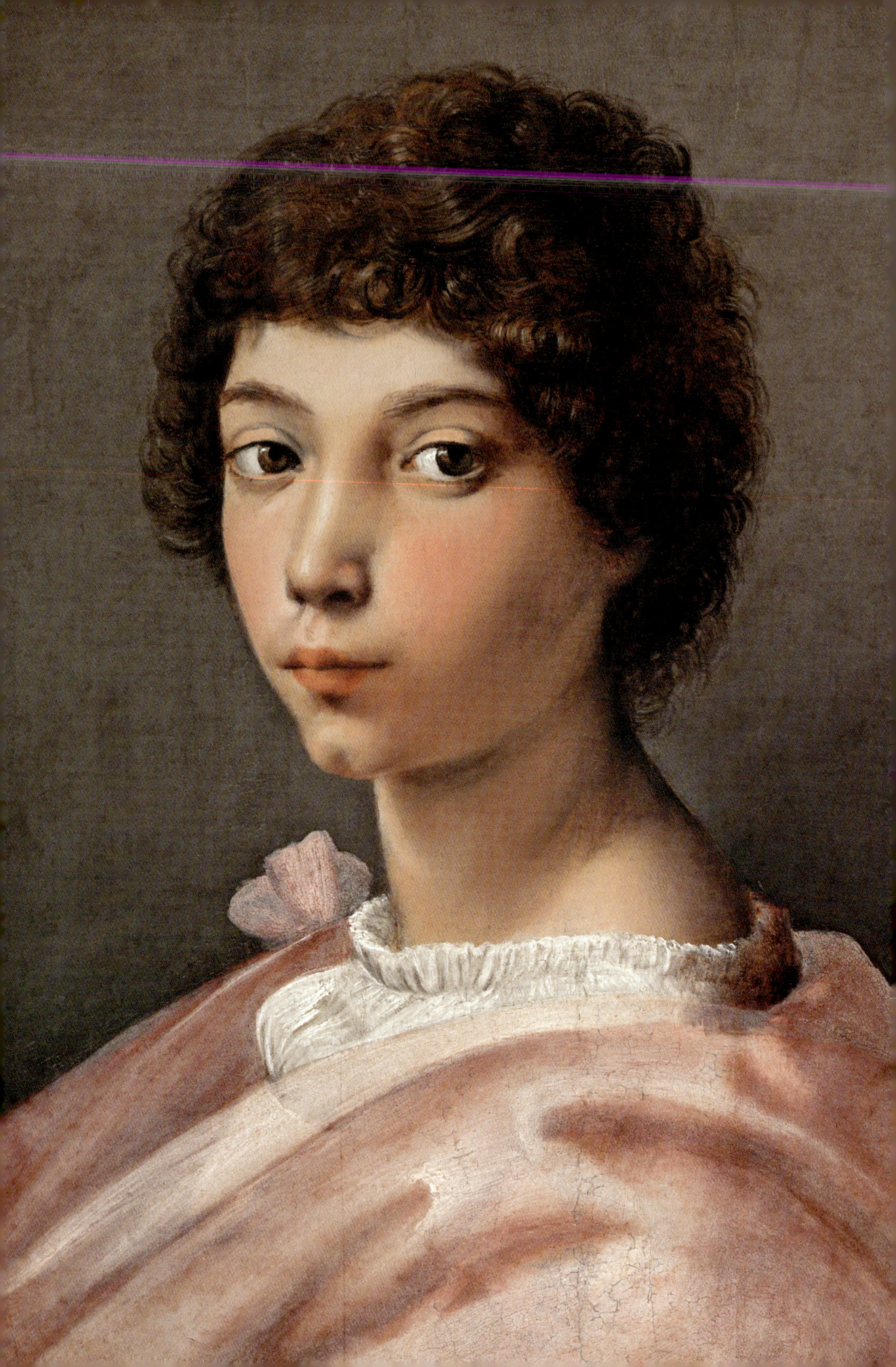

Francis I wore a small image of Saint Michael in front of his chest as part of the collar of the Order. In 1515 he had offered Giuliano de' Medici admission to the Order and later granted membership to Lorenzo. Perhaps the Pope also hoped that the gift of the picture would remind the king, as the most Christian defender of the faith, of his pledge to take military action against the Turks. In the painting, the Christian champion appears in a pose as artful as it is elegant. His *figura serpentinata* rotation triumphs over the hideously contorted body of the devil crushed beneath his foot. The angel is no longer dressed as a medieval knight, but as an ancient Roman soldier. The devil is likewise lent an antique note: he has the face of a satyr. From a high mountain, we look down on a broad coastal landscape. In conjunction with the fiery glow between the rocks, this gateway to Hell calls to mind an Italian volcano. Would Francis I have seen in this an allusion to Vesuvius and Naples? For Francis I as for his predecessors, however, dominion over the kingdom south of the Papal States would remain unattainable.

Raphael's *Holy Family* (p. 371; Cat. P77) was intended for the French queen. The representation of Elizabeth visiting the mother and child celebrates the birth of the French dauphin. The costly stone-tiled flooring, the carved wooden cradle rather than a wicker one, the motif of flowers being strewn, the increased number of figures and the large-scale format elevate the painting – as befitting the high status of the royal family – above Raphael's other late Holy Families. Raphael shows the child Jesus reaching up towards his mother in a very particular pose. The aim, clearly, is to create a visual parallel between the posture of the child and that of the archangel in the *Saint Michael* picture. The agile child looks like the pendant – in mirror image and rotated through 90 degrees – of the powerful adult. A connection is thus forged between the newborn dauphin, whom the Child Jesus is intended to call to mind, and the king represented by Saint Michael. In the boy rising up out of the cradle, the hoped-for later heroic victor already appears. Raphael has thus closely linked the two works intended for the royal couple.

The painting *Saint Margaret* (p. 382; Cat. P103) was perhaps intended for the king's sister, Marguerite d'Angoulême (1492–1549), since it shows her name saint. The serpent-like dragon is vanquished by a delicate young female saint walking forwards. Holding her martyr's palm like an artist's brush or pencil, she places its tip against the beast's clawed paw. The painted roar issuing from its spectacularly yawning jaws seems subjugated to the might of this light, effortless gesture.

In a probably later version of the theme (p. 383; Cat. P106), the artistic showpiece of the dragon's gaping maw, presented to the viewer, is repeated. Here the saint uses a

Raphael and Giulio Romano (?), **Portrait of a Young Man** (Detail), *c.* 1518
(see ill. p. 347)

small crucifix as her weapon. With her body turned, the woman surrounded by the serpent's writhing coils herself assumes the artistic pose of a *figura serpentinata*. Apparently executed for a Benedictine abbot and thus a male patron, the painting shows Margaret's clothing lying particularly close against her beautiful body.

Two cardinals each received pictures of a handsome young John the Baptist in a forested wilderness, gesturing towards the cross of the Passion (pp. 384, 385; Cat. P100, P101). A simple, tall wooden crucifix is roughly propped up against a fallen or broken tree. A symbol of hope and redemption is thus planted on top of an image of death and decay. Pompeo Colonna may have commissioned the Uffizi *John* in 1517 to mark his elevation as Cardinal. A youthful prophetic admonisher imitates the pose of the antique *Laocoön* (Schmidt 2003). Just as the Ancient Greek priest sought to warn the Trojans of impending danger, so the beautiful hermit calls us to repentance and conversion. The veneration of John the Baptist was part of Colonna family tradition. Pompeo began his clerical career under his uncle, Cardinal Giovanni Colonna, and succeeded him in office as a Colonna cardinal. He furthermore named his son, too, Giovanni. Colonna later gave the painting to his doctor, who had requested it by way of thanks for curing the Cardinal of an illness. Jacopo Berengario da Carpi, physician and famous anatomist, will have appreciated Raphael's painting as the visualisation of an ideal male physique.

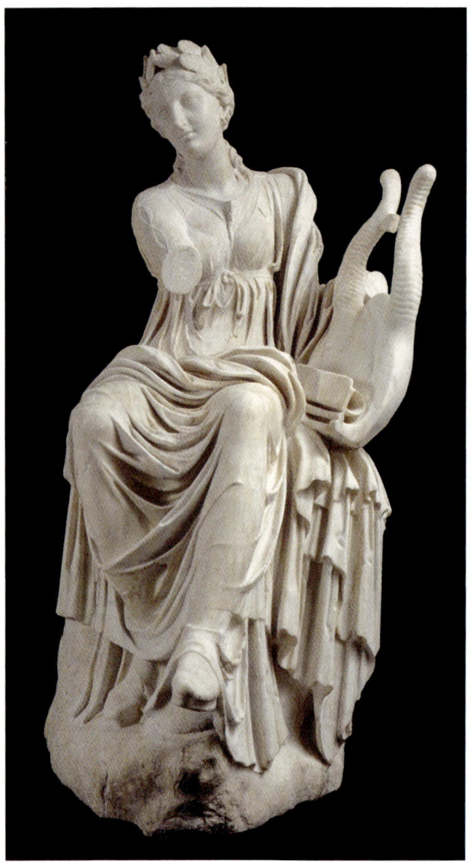

A jewel of artifice among Raphael's Roman devotional panels is the small painting known as *The Vision of Ezekiel* (p. 387; Cat. P74). Above a mountain and in front of a distant landscape receding far into the depths, the clouds open to reveal a divine apparition, which appears vast in relation to the tree below. Raphael has here borrowed from an antique relief in which Jupiter is enthroned in the sky. To the eagle on whose wings Jupiter is carried, however, he adds the bull, the lion and the angel and thus creates a group

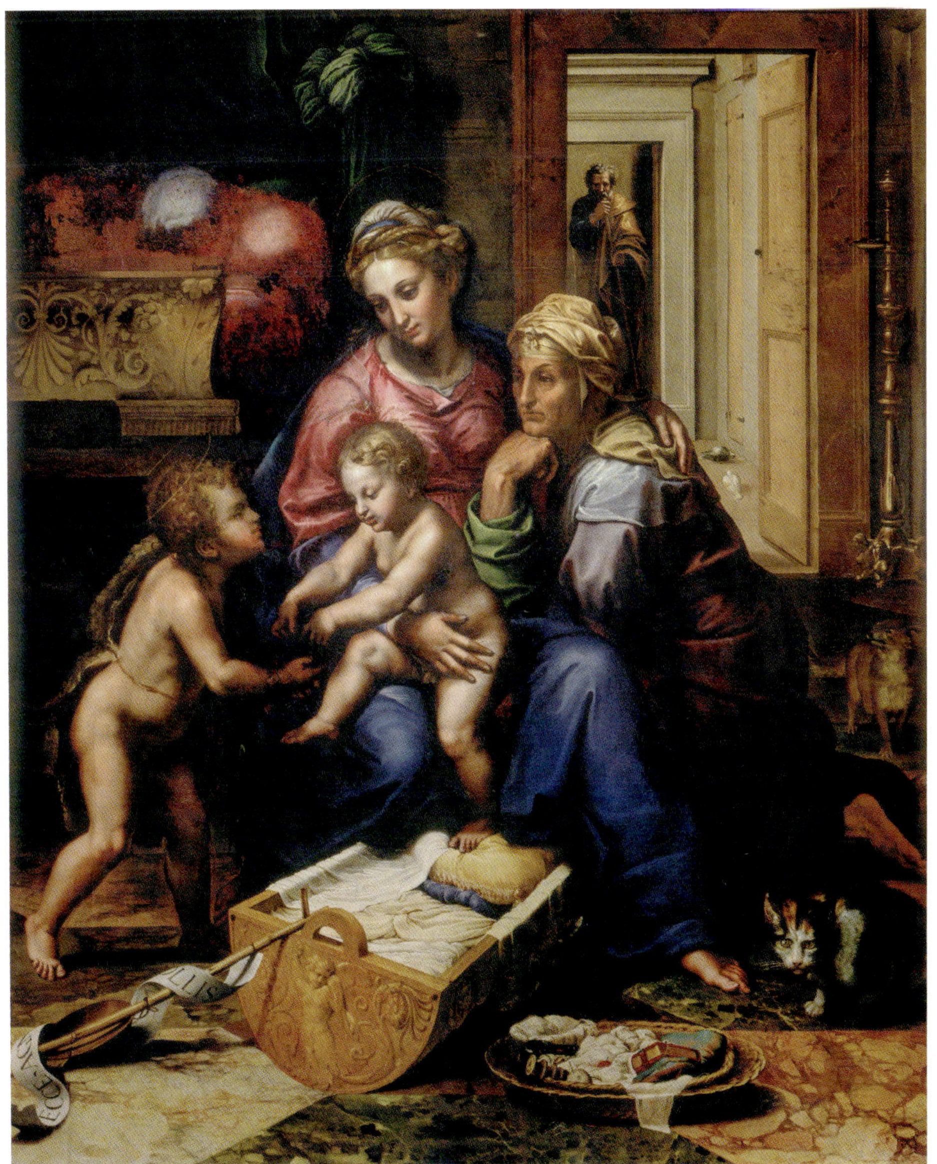

Antique seated figure of the Muse Terpsichore, *c.* AD 130
Marble, height 150 cm (59 ⅛ in). Madrid, Museo Nacional del Prado

Workshop of Raphael (Giulio Romano), **Madonna della Gatta**, *c.* 1520
Oil on panel, 171 × 147 cm (67 ⅓ × 57 ⅞ in)
Naples, Museo e Gallerie Nazionali di Capodimonte

comprising the four symbols of the Evangelists. Raphael spans the vision tightly across the rectangular format: God's raised arms point in the direction of the upper corners, the bull's foreleg and the lion's paw and God's raised leg towards the lower corners. What Raphael thereby conveys to the viewer in the medium of the painting is mirrored within the picture in the tiny figures far below: celestial light falls upon one of the spectators gathered on a hilltop. But whereas this latter can perceive only dazzling rays, the viewer of the painting experiences the vision of God directly and is shown its Christian message: God extends his arms – supported by angels, so that they do not sink – in eternal blessing over the land. Raphael has captured this blessing permanently in the rectangle of his painted panel. For its Bolognese buyer, the picture was a way of securing God's grace enduringly for himself and his household.

With Raphael's portraits and devotional pictures, painted fellow occupants, so to speak, took up residence in the private homes of their owners. Raphael's painting lent them animation and seeming presence. But the pictures were more than simply imaginary points of contact, incarnations of absent friends or saints promising salvation: in the form of portraits and devotional panels, Raphael's art also contributed to aesthetic pleasure in the private sphere. Just one Roman patron succeeded – like the popes – in going a step further and transforming his apartments wholly into a realm of art, namely by having the walls of his palace decorated with frescoes by Raphael. Not until this commission did Raphael find the opportunity to become a great painter of antique myths and sensual female beauty.

Detail from **Woman with a Veil (Donna Velata)**, *c.* 1512–1518 (?)
(see ill. p. 350)

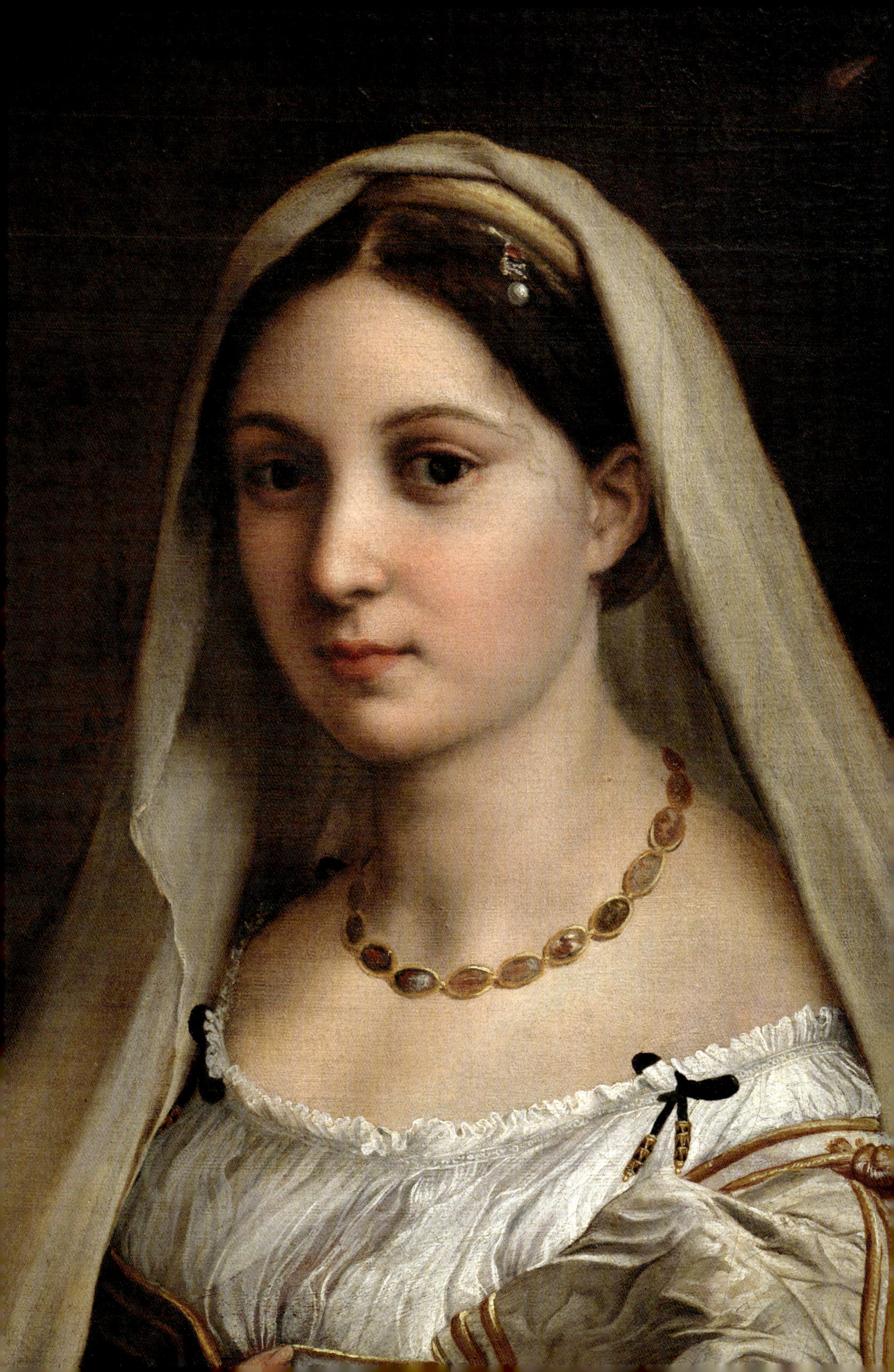

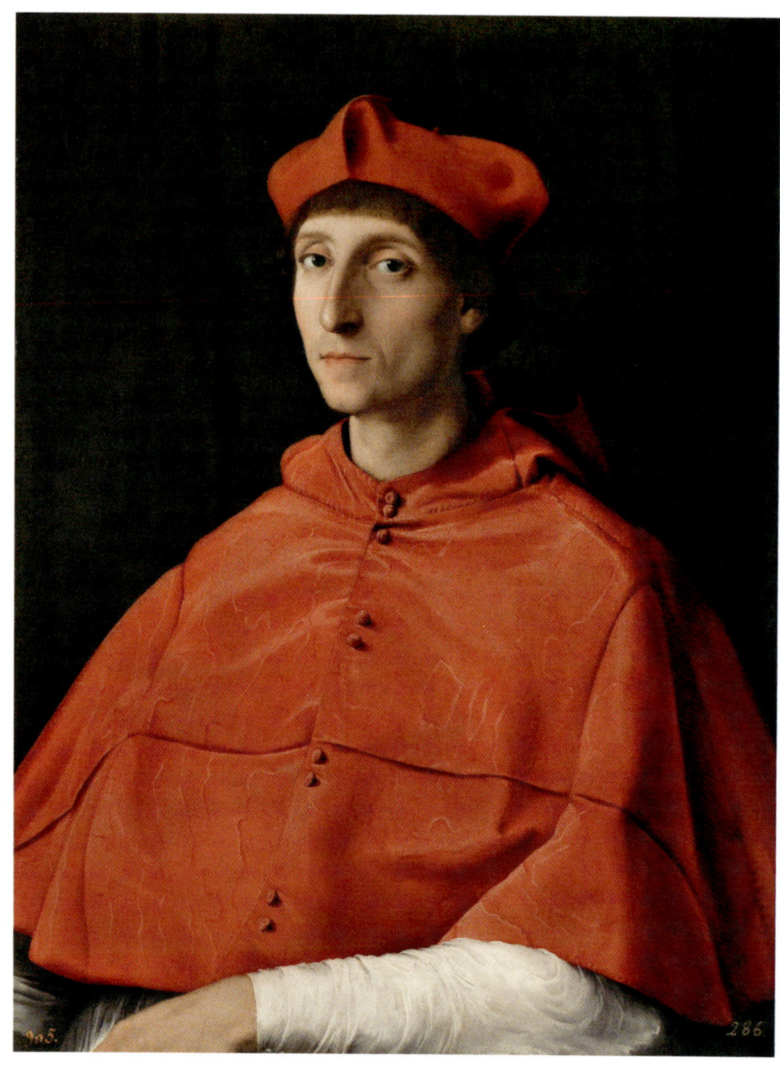

Portrait of a Cardinal, *c.* 1510
Oil on panel, 79 × 61 cm (31 ⅛ × 24 ⅛ in)
Madrid, Museo Nacional del Prado *(Detail page 310)*

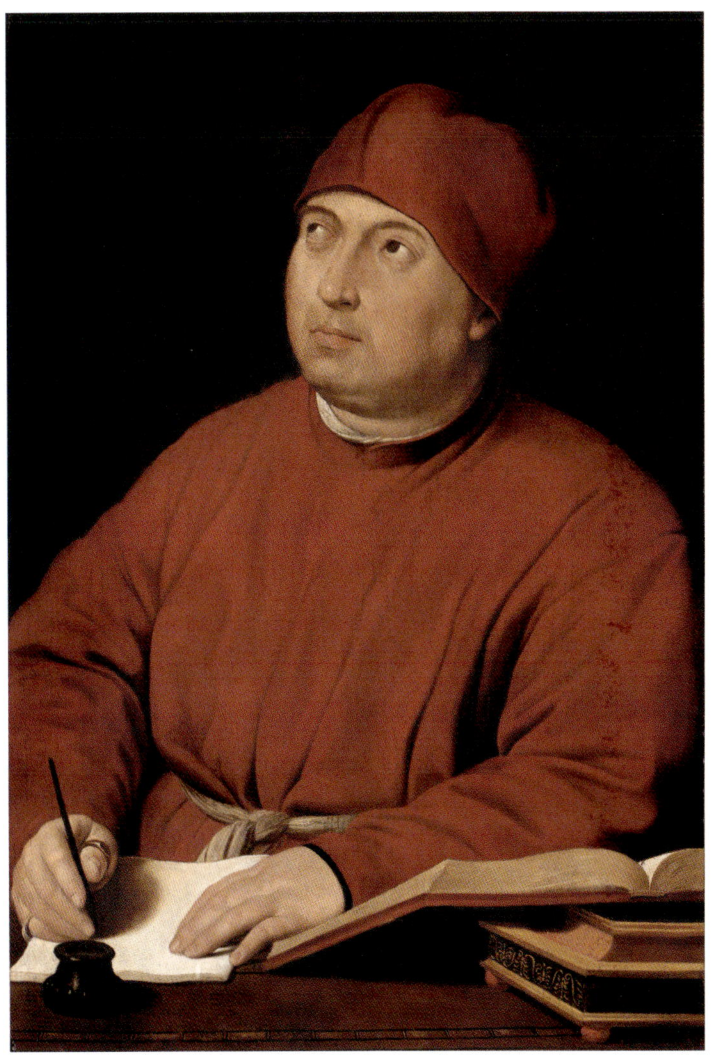

Portrait of Tommaso Inghirami, *c.* 1510/11
Oil on poplar panel, 89.9 × 62.8 cm (35 ⅜ × 24 ¾ in)
Florence, Galleria Palatina, Sala di Saturno

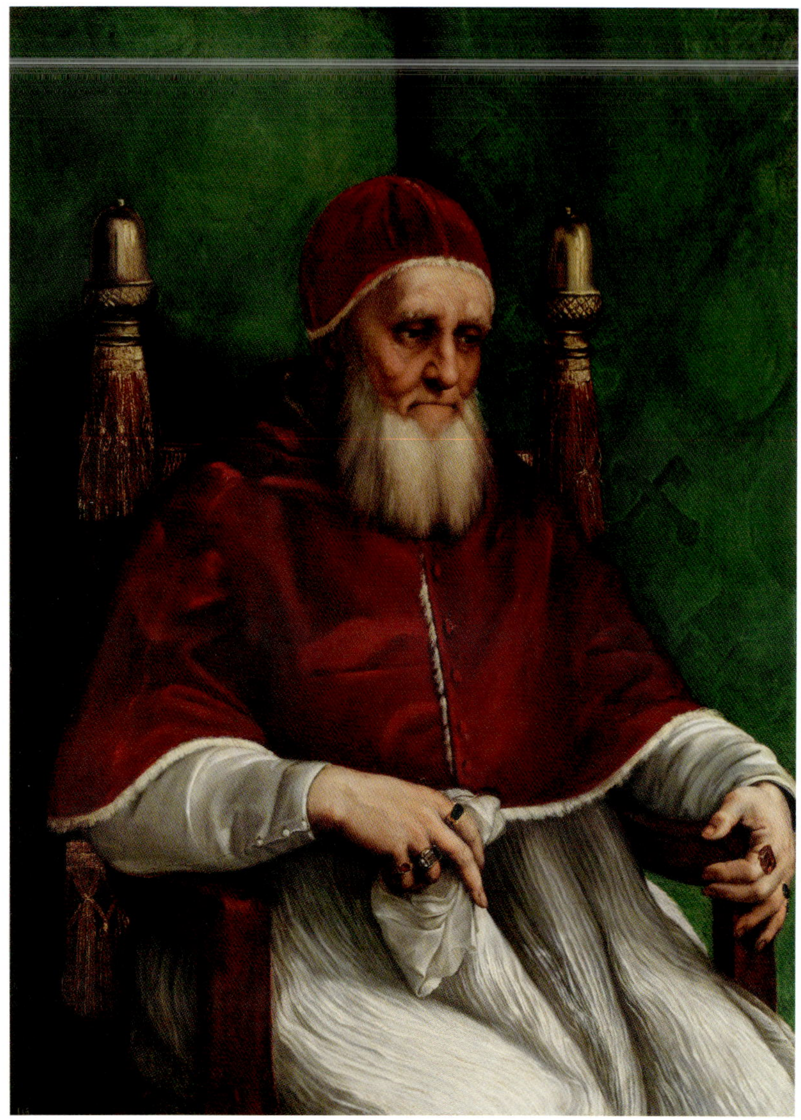

Portrait of Pope Julius II, *c.* 1512/13
Oil on poplar panel, 108 × 80.7 cm (42 ½ × 31 ¾ in)
London, The National Gallery *(Detail page 309)*

Pope Leo X with Cardinals Giulio de' Medici and Luigi de' Rossi, *c.* 1518
Oil on poplar panel, 155.2 × 118.9 cm (61 ⅛ × 46 ¾ in)
Florence, Gallerie degli Uffizi *(Detail page 318)*

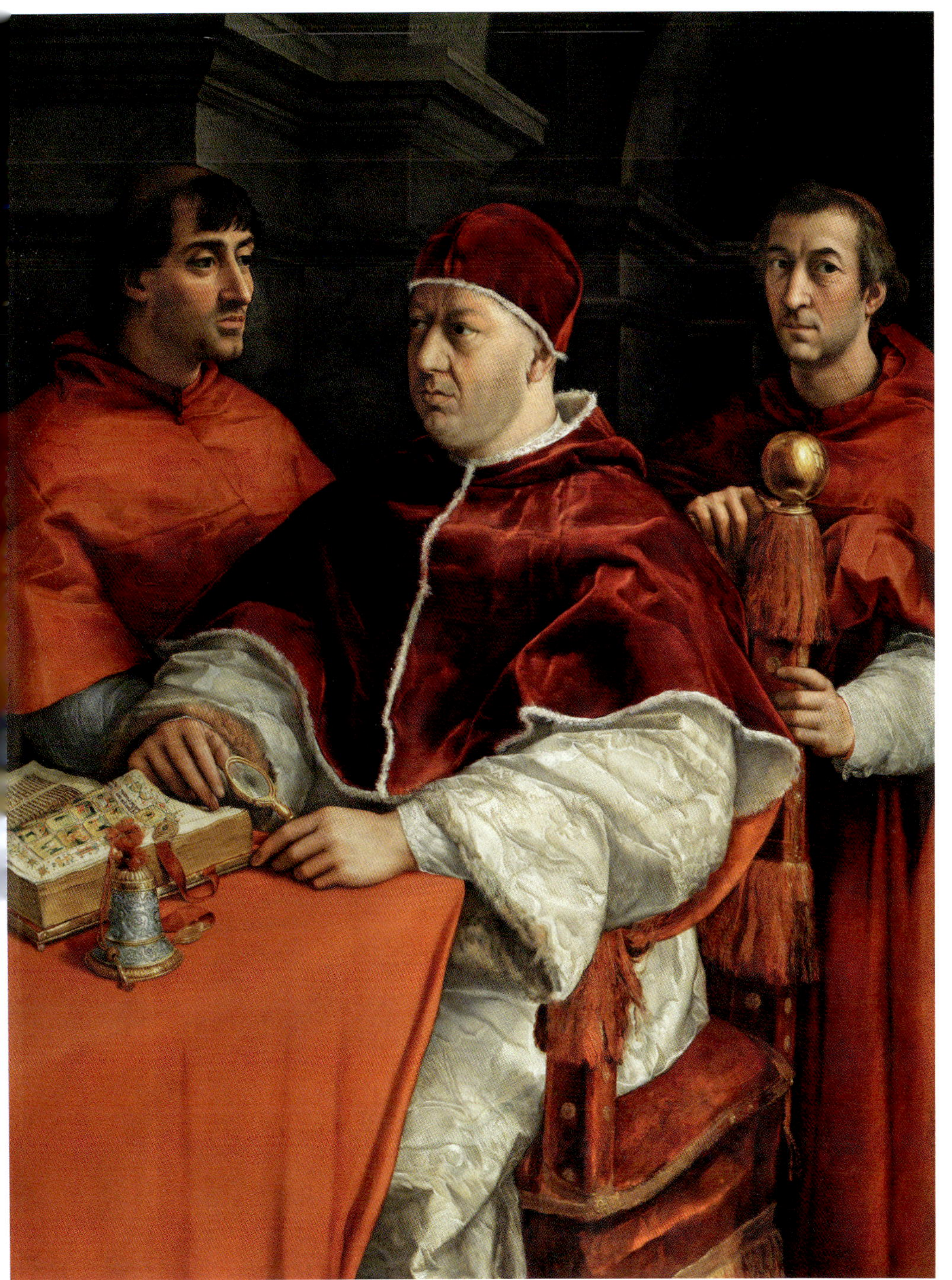

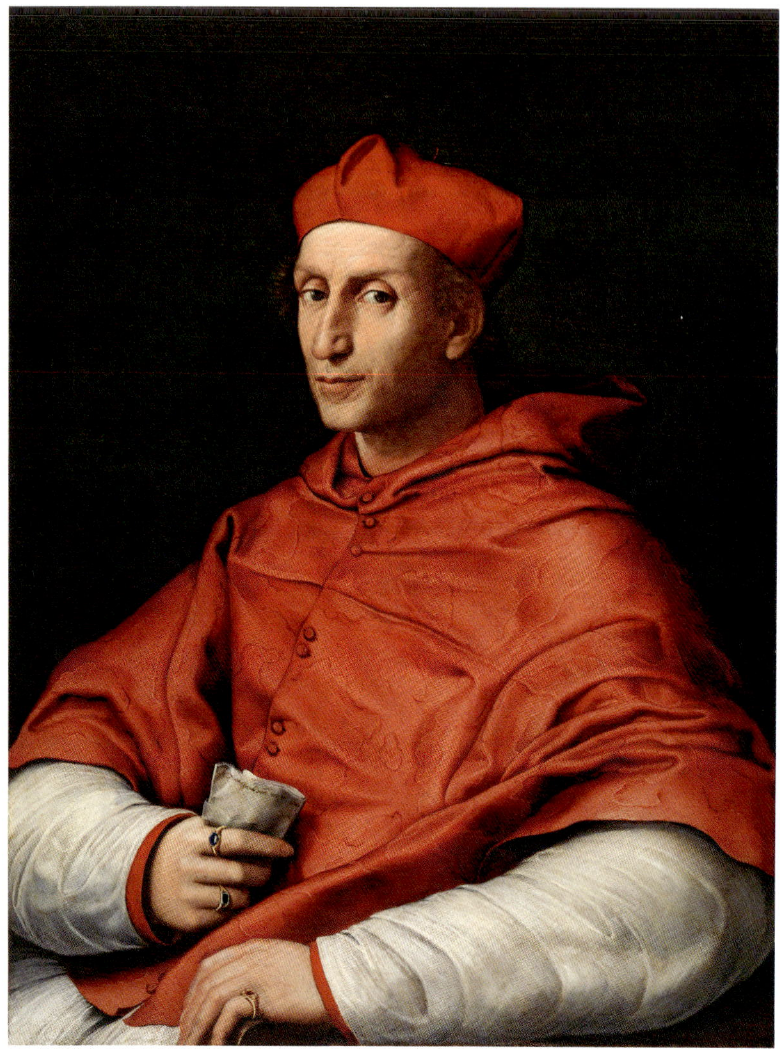

Raphael and Workshop, **Portrait of Cardinal Bernardo Dovizi da Bibbiena**, *c.* 1516/17
Oil on canvas, 85 × 66.3 cm (33 ½ × 26 ⅛ in). Florence, Galleria Palatina

Raphael (and assistants?), **Portrait of Cardinal Alessandro Farnese**, *c.* 1510/11
Oil on panel, 138 × 91 cm (54 ⅓ × 35 ⅞ in). Naples, Museo e Gallerie Nazionali di Capodimonte
(Detail pages 340/341)

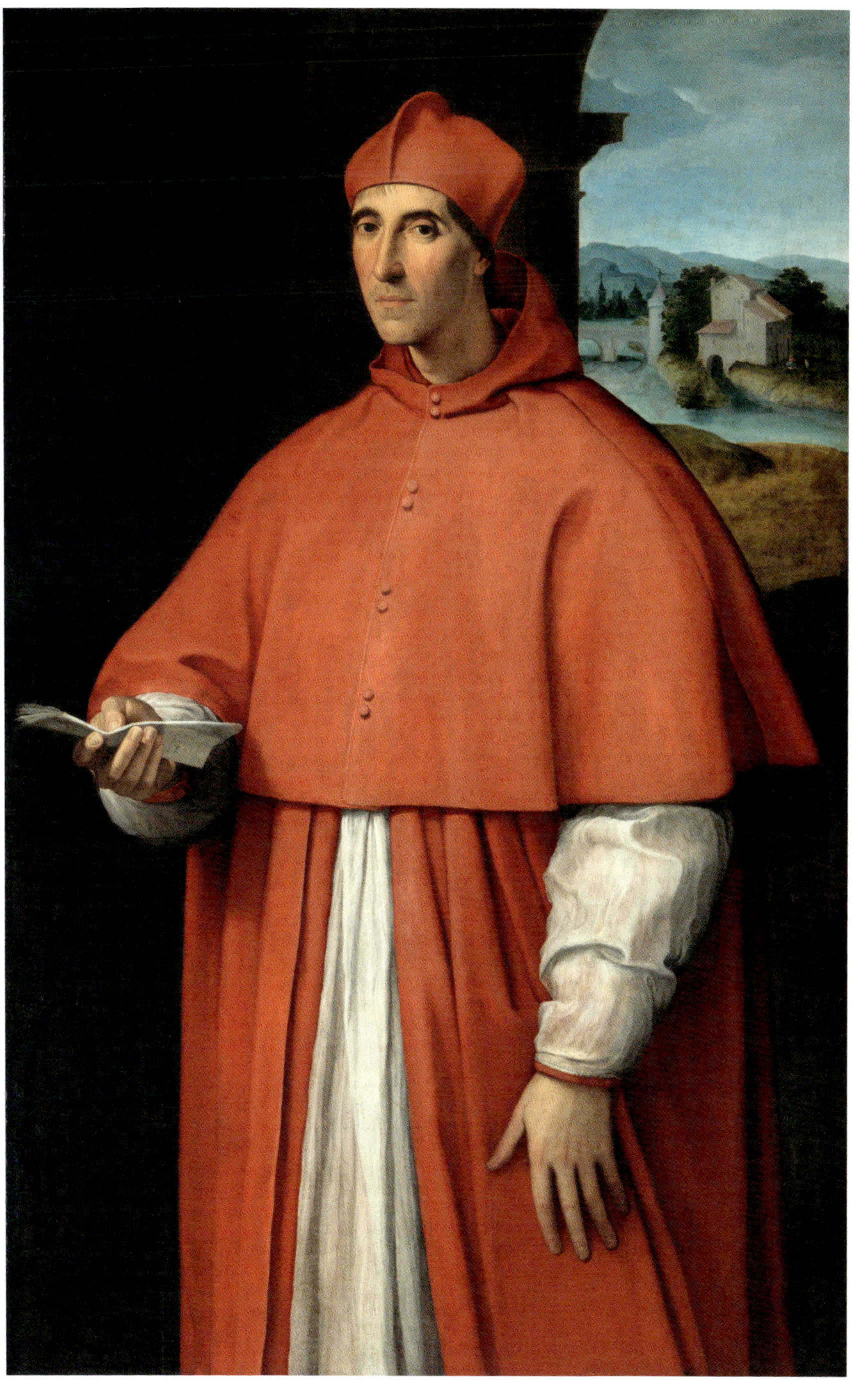

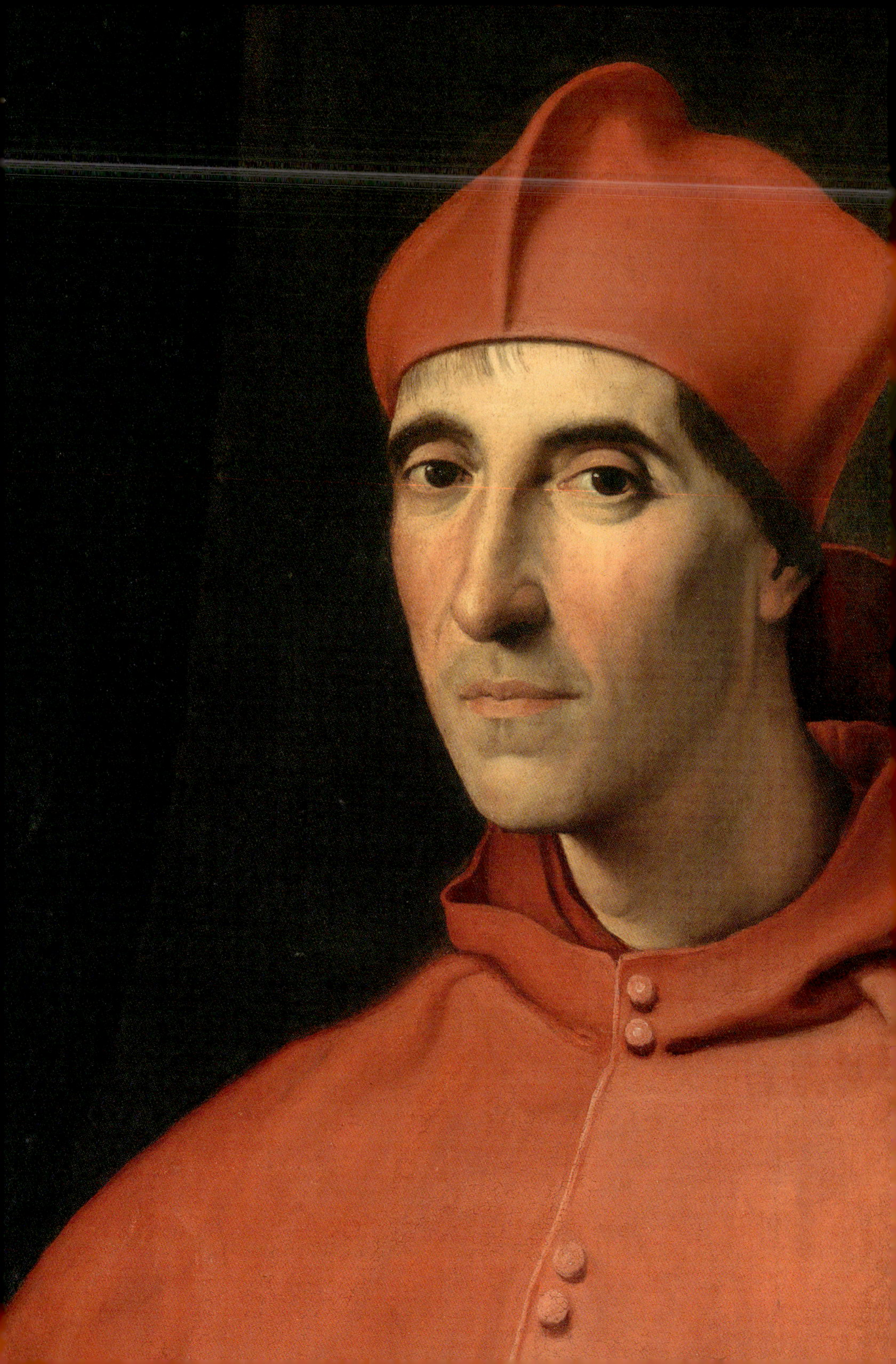

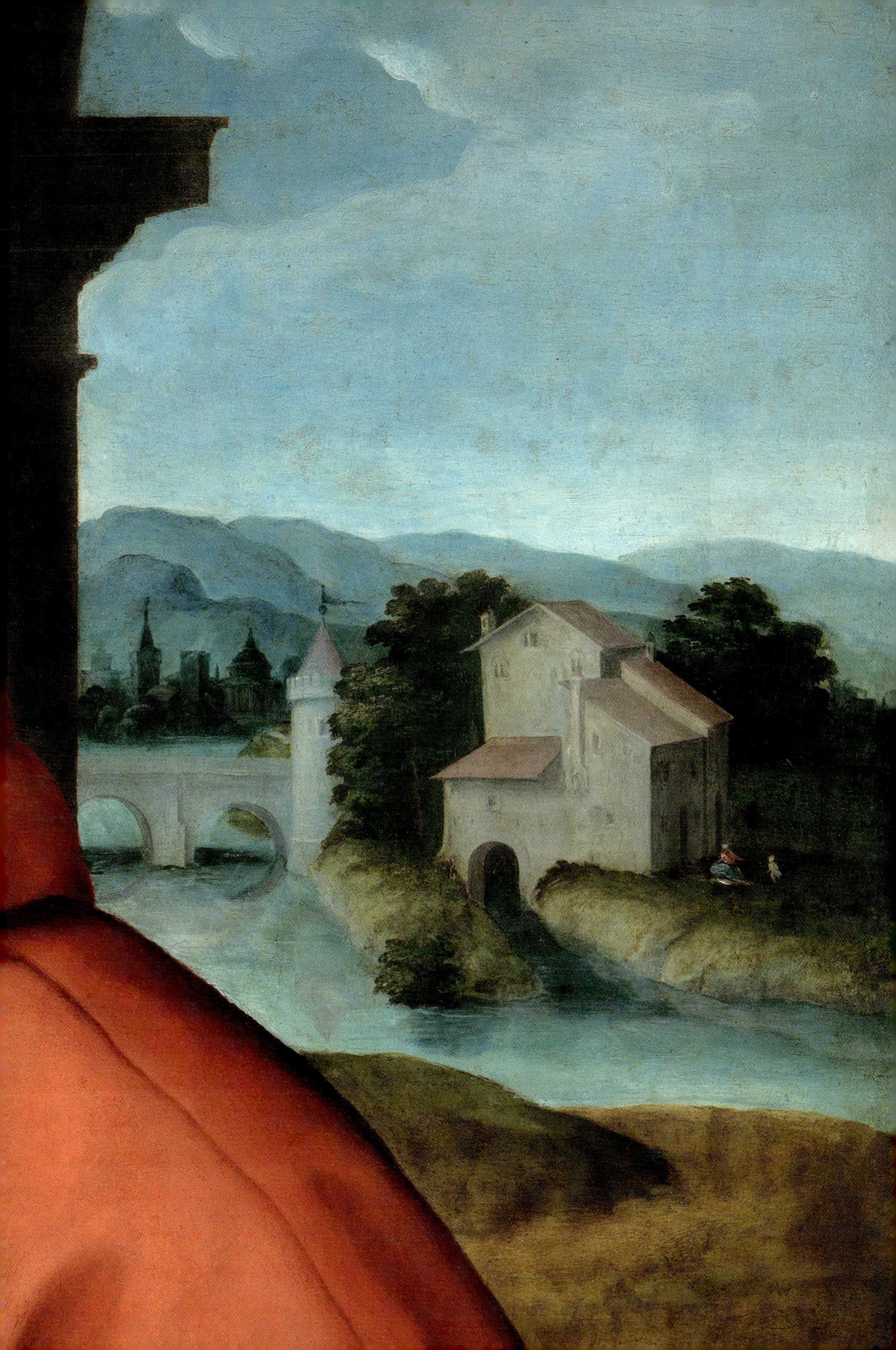

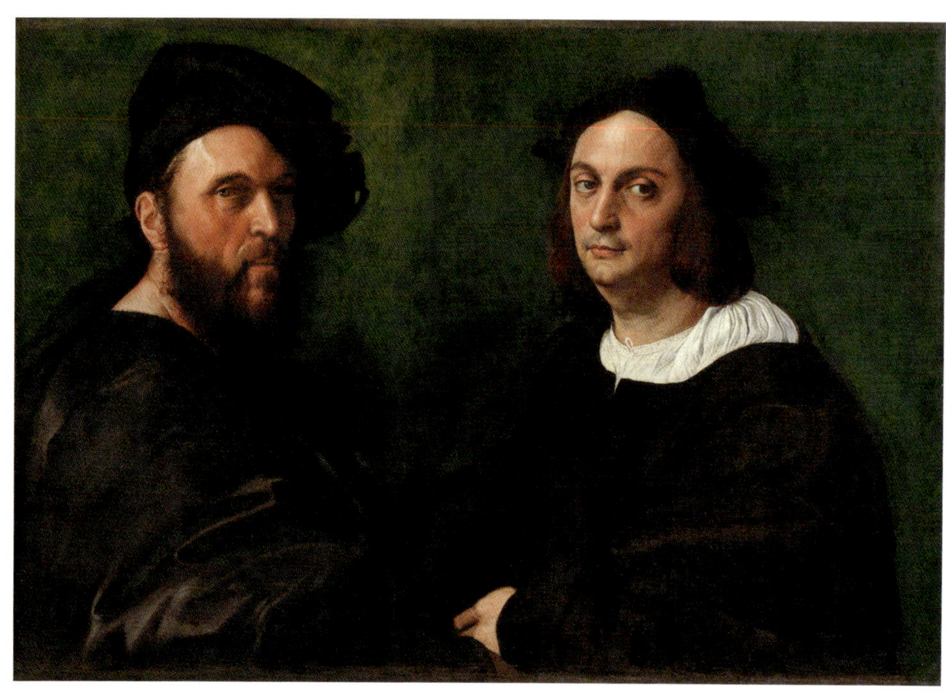

Portrait of Andrea Navagero and Agostino Beazzano, *c.* 1516
Oil on canvas, 77 × 111 cm (30 1/3 × 43 3/4 in). Rome, Galleria Doria Pamphilj

Double Portrait of Two Young Men, *c.* 1518–1520
Oil on canvas, 99 × 83 cm (38 7/8 × 32 2/3 in). Paris, Musée du Louvre
(Detail pages 344/345)

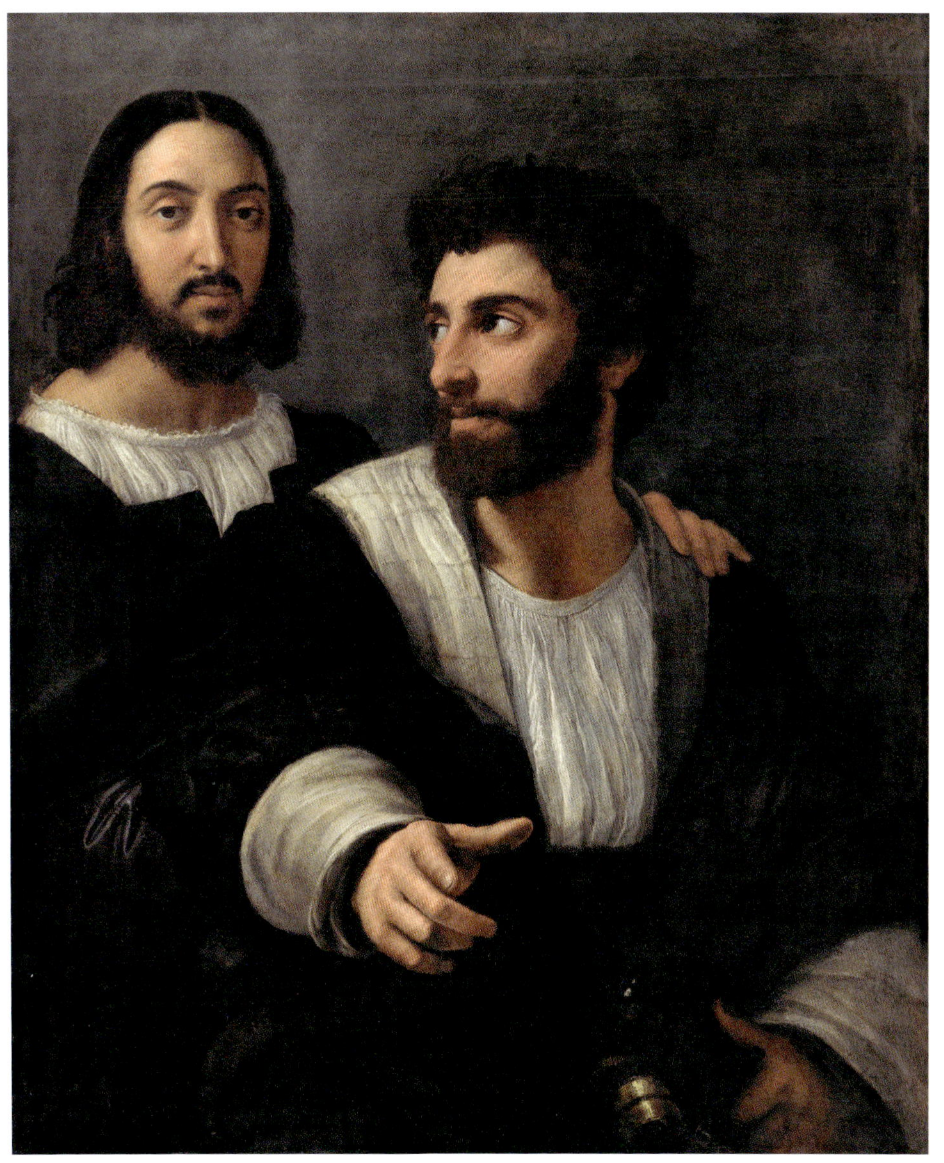

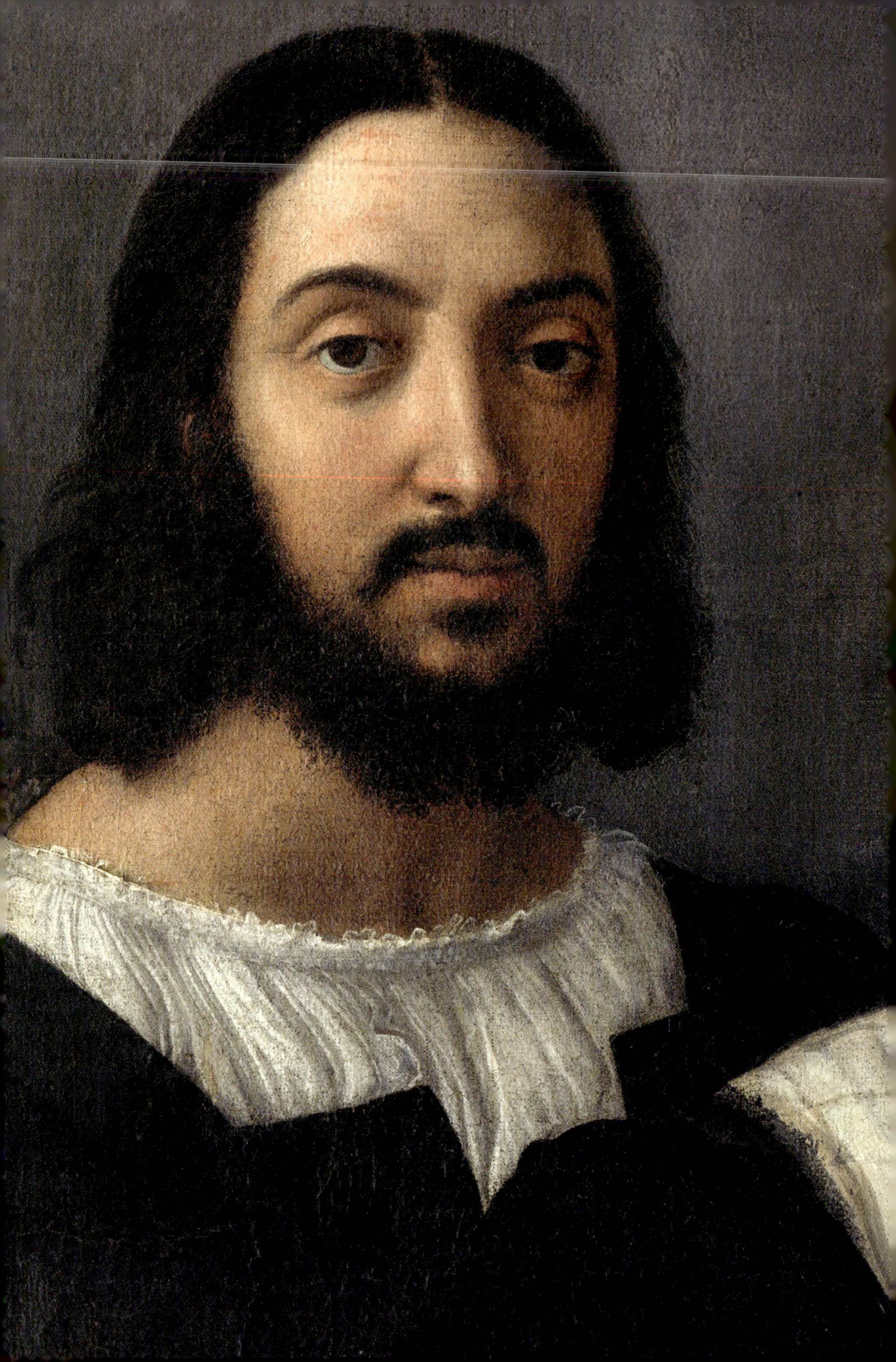

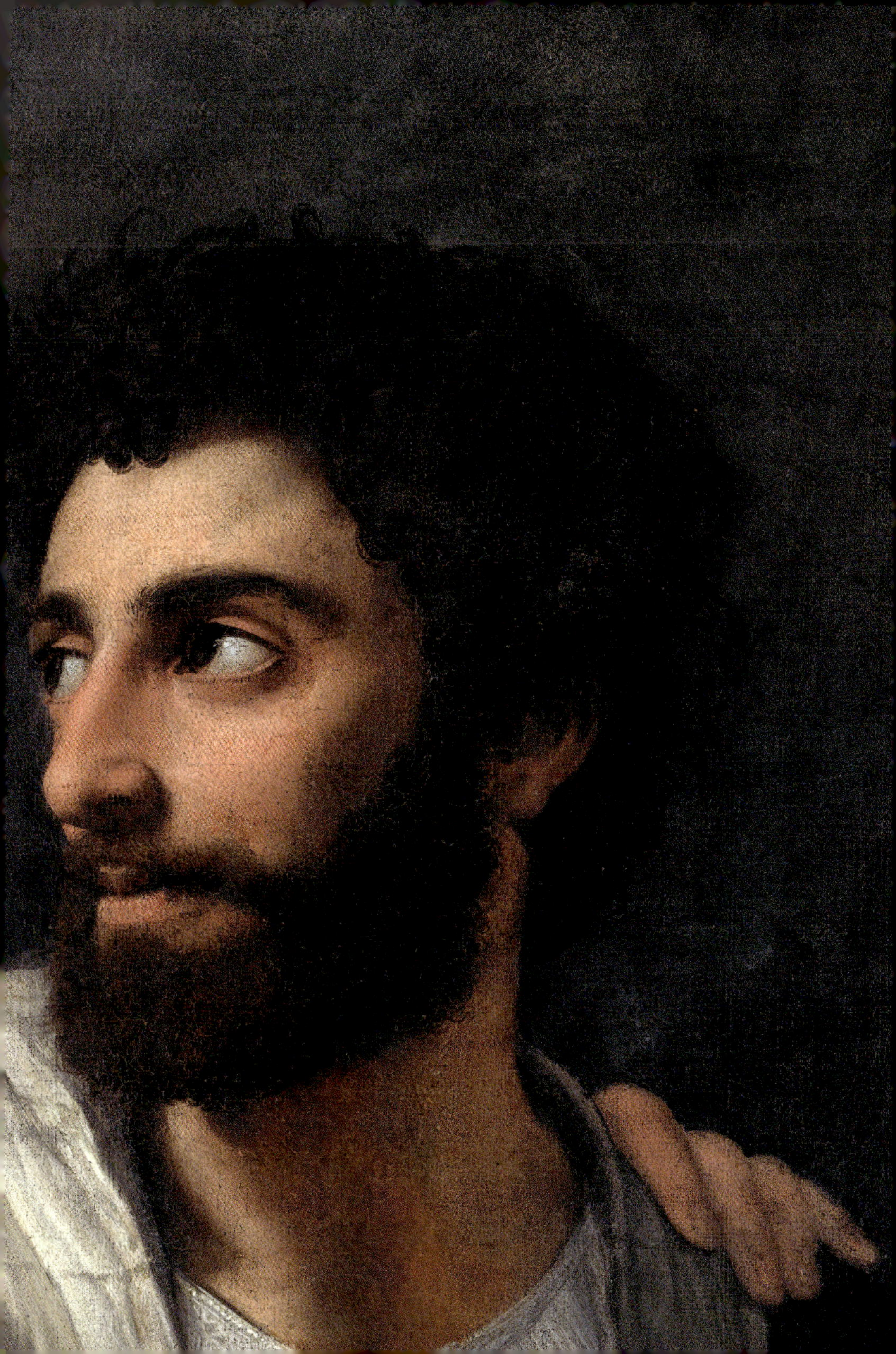

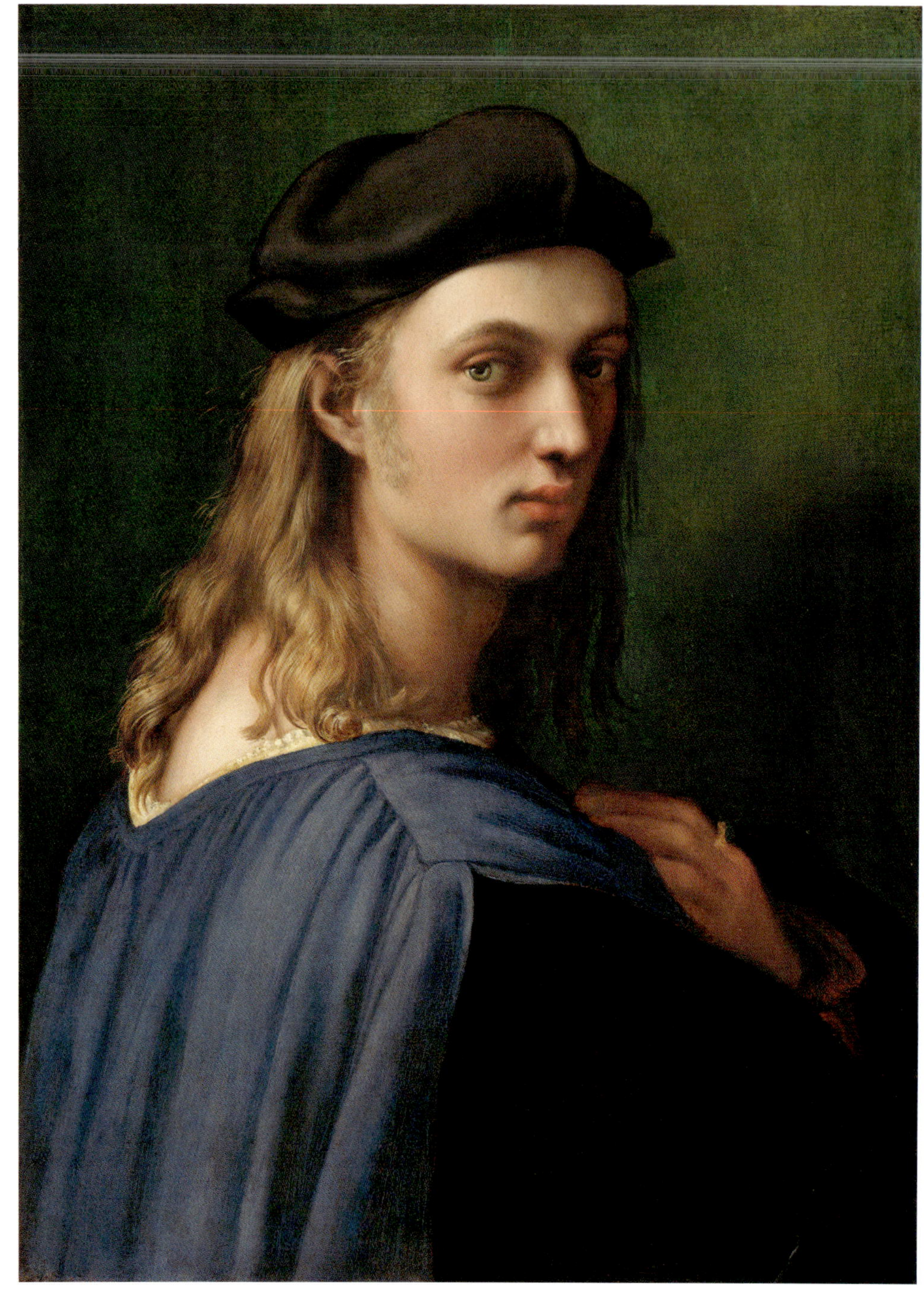

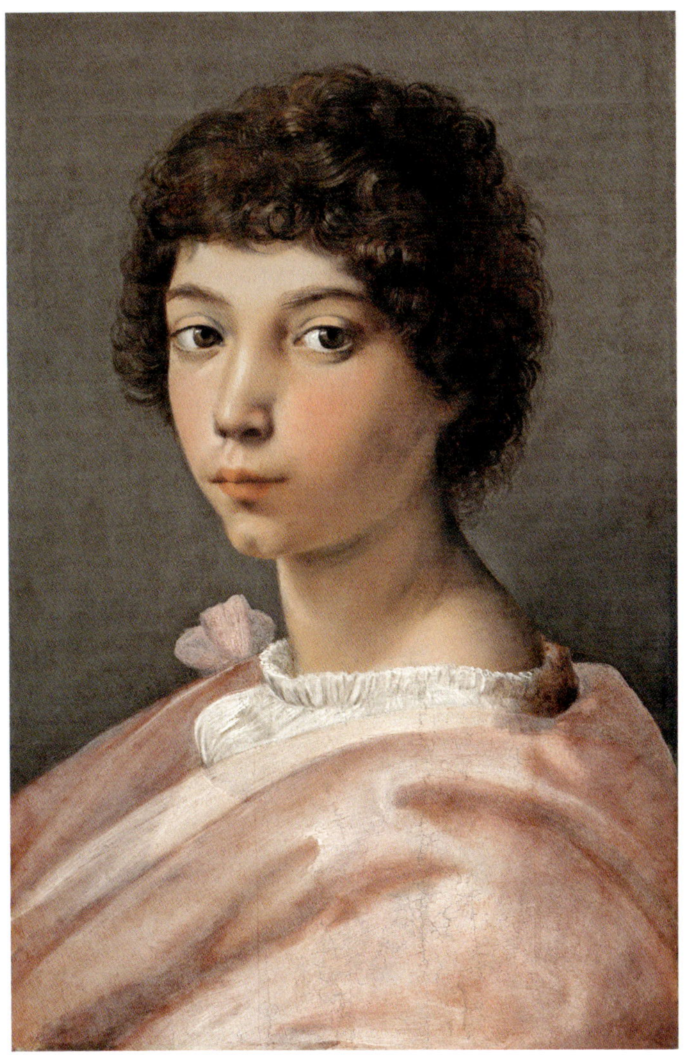

Portrait of Bindo Altoviti, *c.* 1516–1518
Oil on panel, 60 × 44 cm (23 5/8 × 17 1/3 in). Washington, D.C., National Gallery of Art
(Detail page 325)

Raphael and Giulio Romano (?), **Portrait of a Young Man**, *c.* 1518
Oil on poplar panel, 43.8 × 29 cm (17 1/4 × 11 3/8 in). Madrid, Museo Nacional Thyssen-Bornemisza
(Detail page 328)

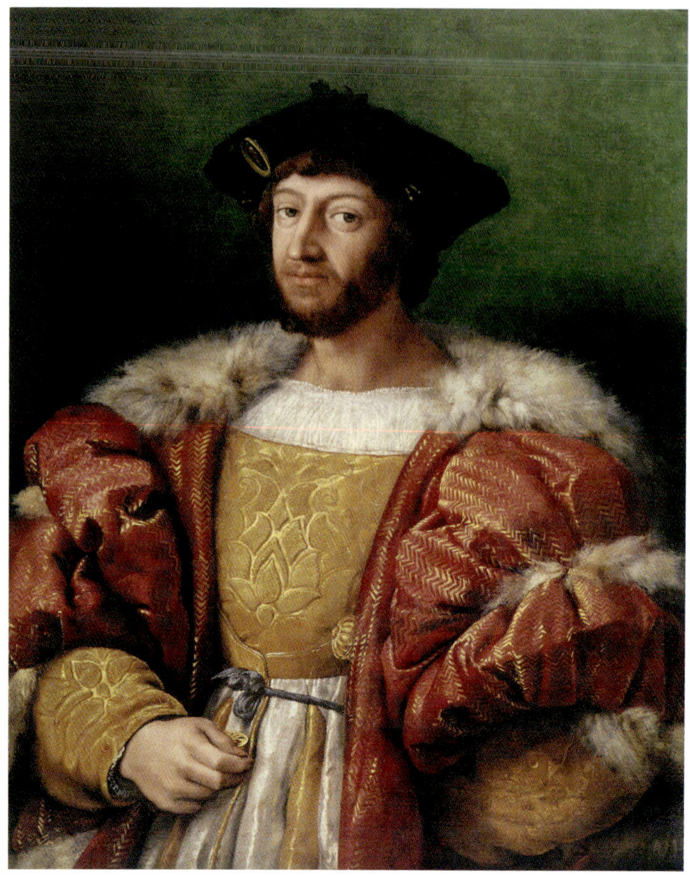

Portrait of Lorenzo de' Medici, 1518
Oil on canvas, 97 × 79 cm (38 ¼ × 31 ⅛ in)
Unknown private collection (formerly Ira Spanierman Collection, New York)

Portrait of Baldassare Castiglione, *c.* 1516/17
Oil on canvas, 82 × 67 cm (32 ¼ × 26 ⅜ in). Paris, Musée du Louvre

Page 350
Woman with a Veil (Donna Velata), *c.* 1512–1518 (?)
Oil on canvas, 77.5 × 59.5 cm (30 ½ × 23 ⅜ in). Florence, Galleria Palatina
(Detail page 333)

Page 351
Portrait of a Young Woman (La Fornarina), 1519/20
Oil on poplar panel, 85.5 × 61.5 cm (33 ⅔ × 24 ¼ in). Inscription on the armband: *RAPHAEL VRBINAS*
Rome, Galleria Nazionale d'Arte Antica

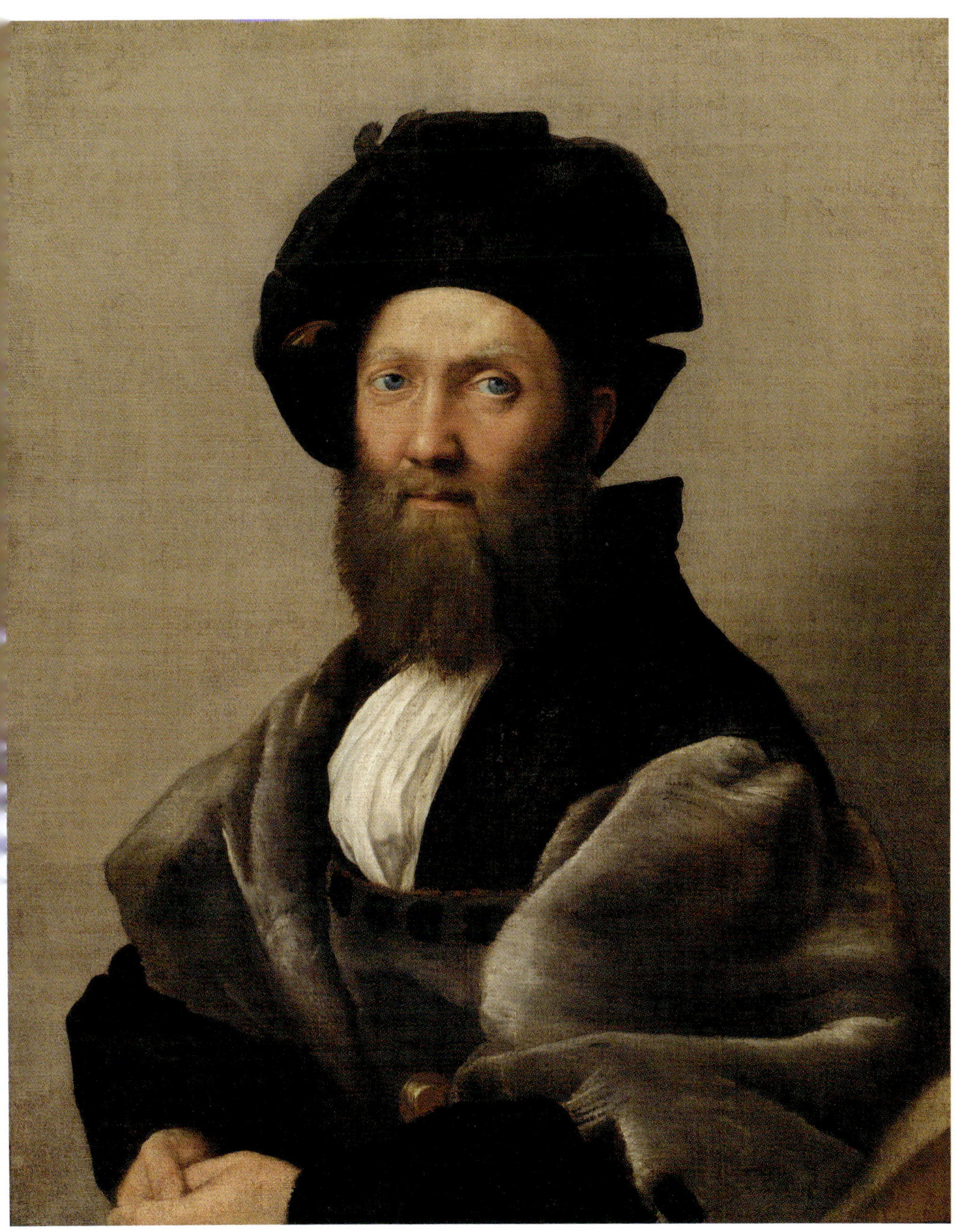

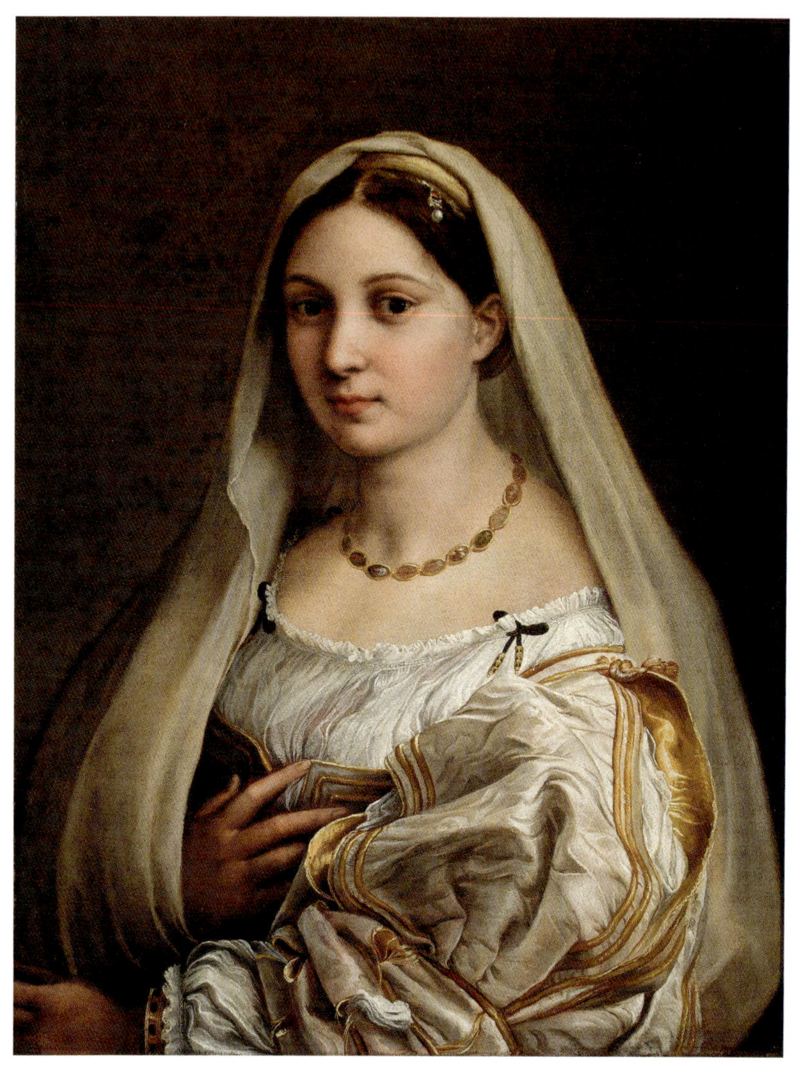

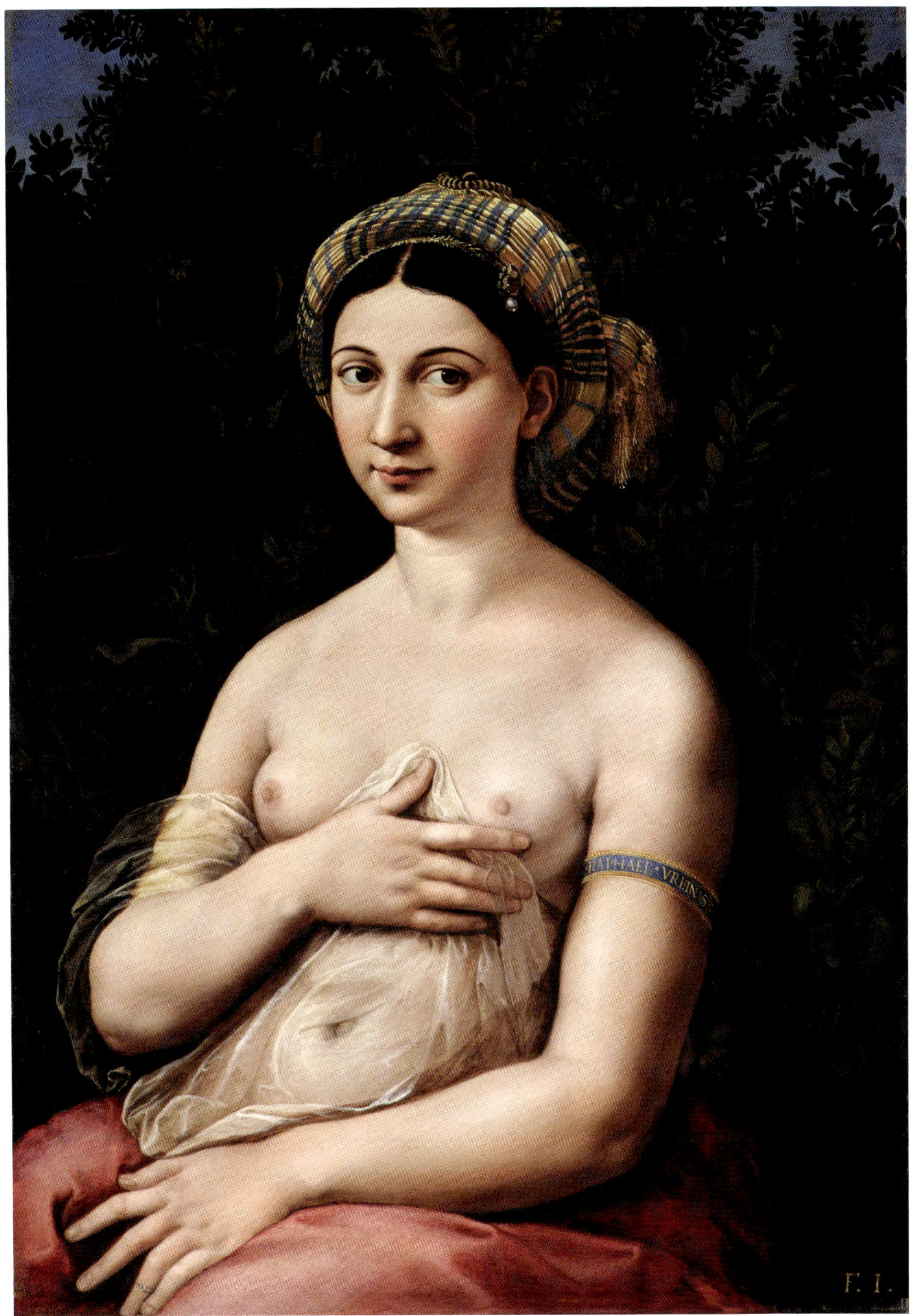
RAPHAEL · VRBINAS
F. I.

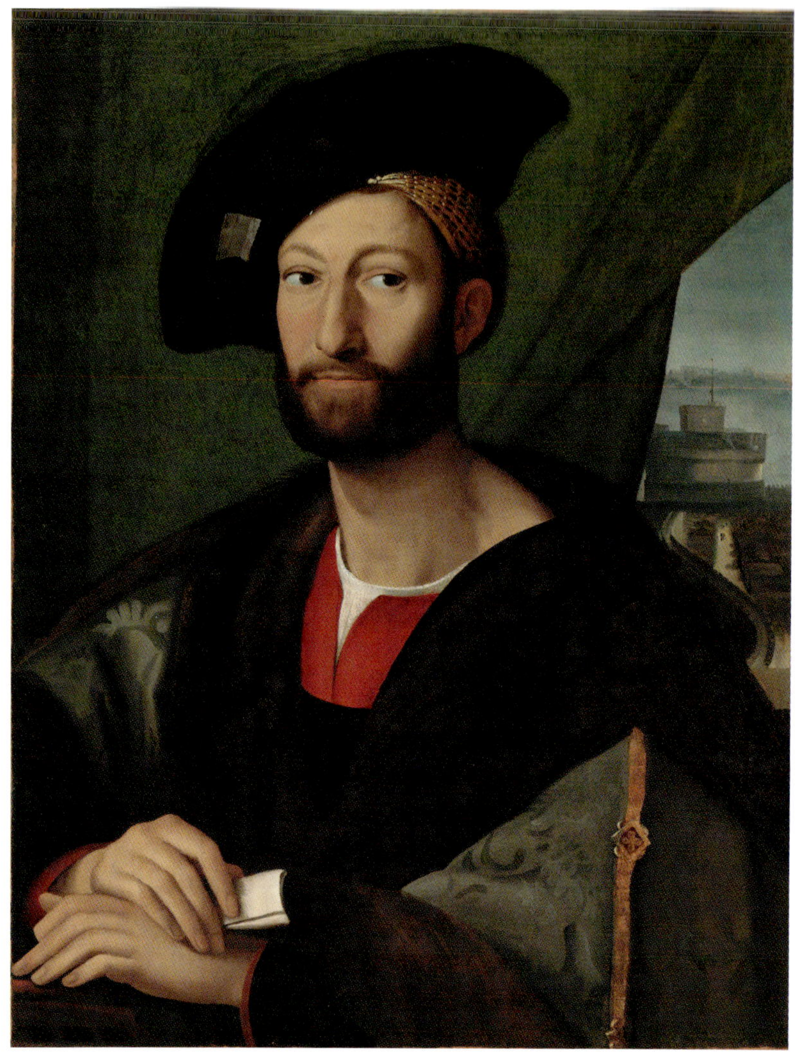

Raphael and Workshop, **Portrait of Giuliano de' Medici**, *c.* 1514/15
Tempera and oil on canvas, originally mounted on panel, 83.2 × 66 cm (32 ¾ × 25 ⅞ in)
New York, The Metropolitan Museum of Art, The Jules Bache Collection, 1949

Portrait of the Vicereine of Naples, Isabel de Requesens i Enríquez, *c.* 1518
Oil on panel, transferred to canvas, 120 × 95 cm (47 ¼ × 37 ⅜ in). Paris, Musée du Louvre
(Detail pages 354/355)

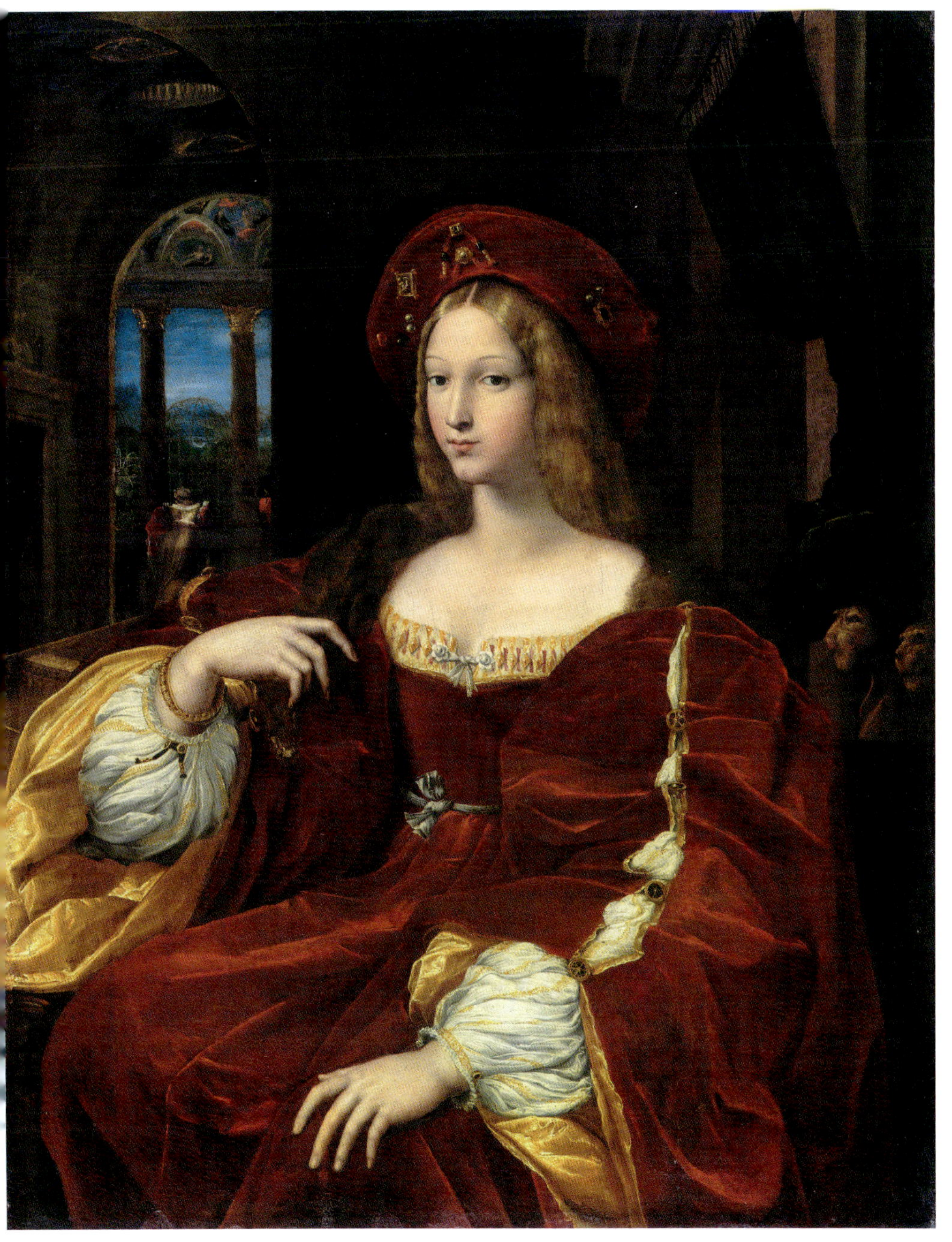

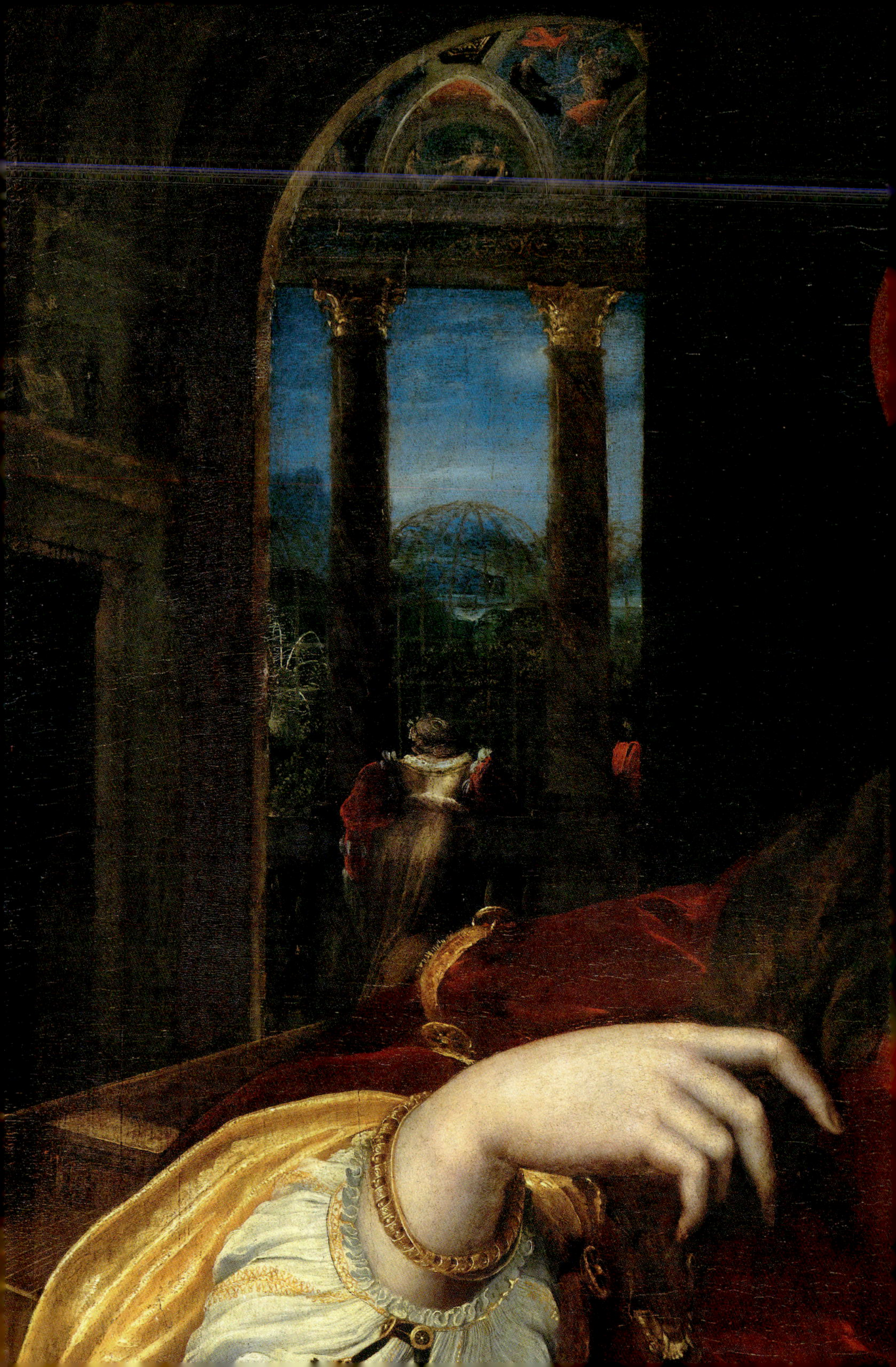

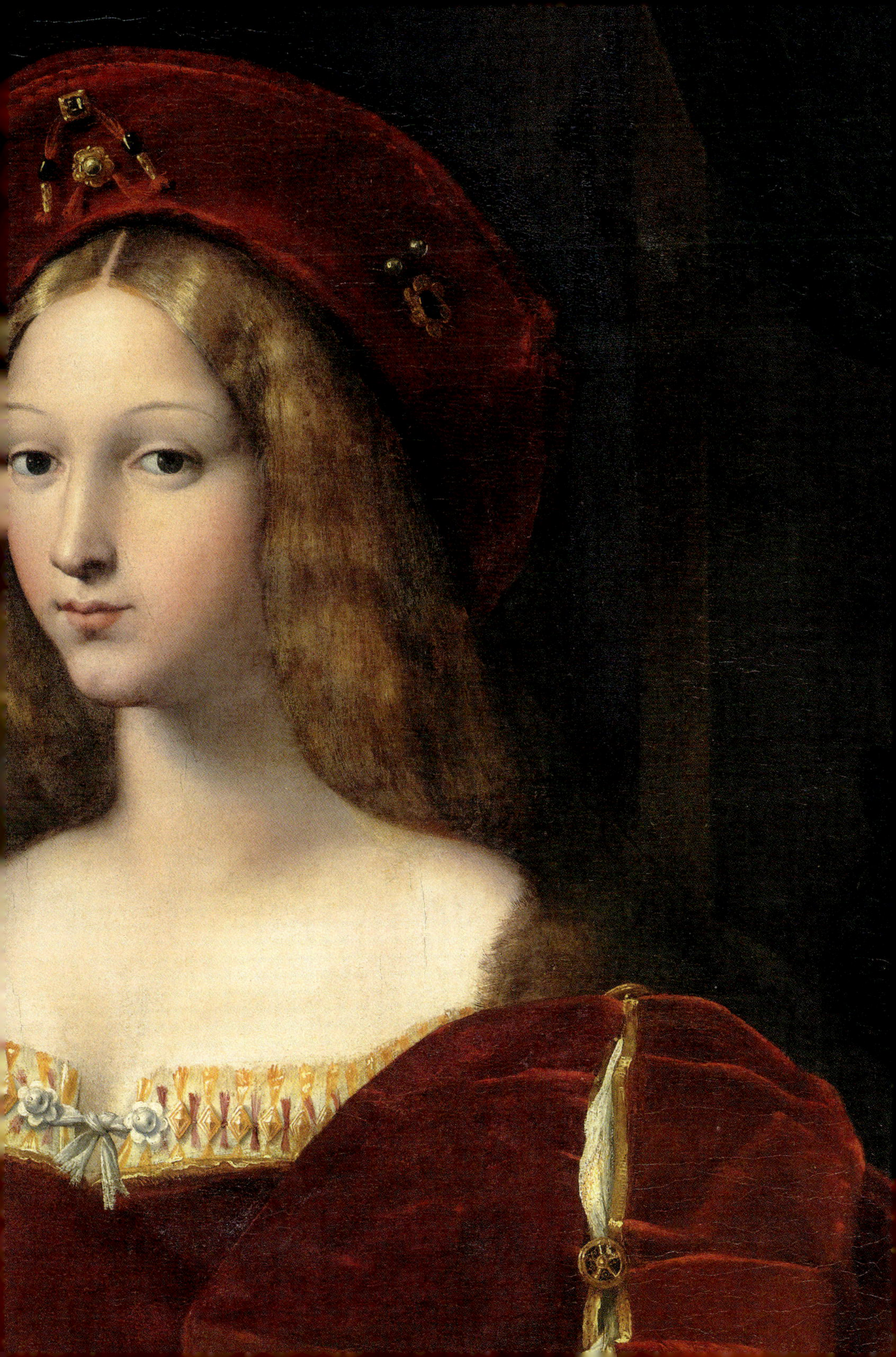

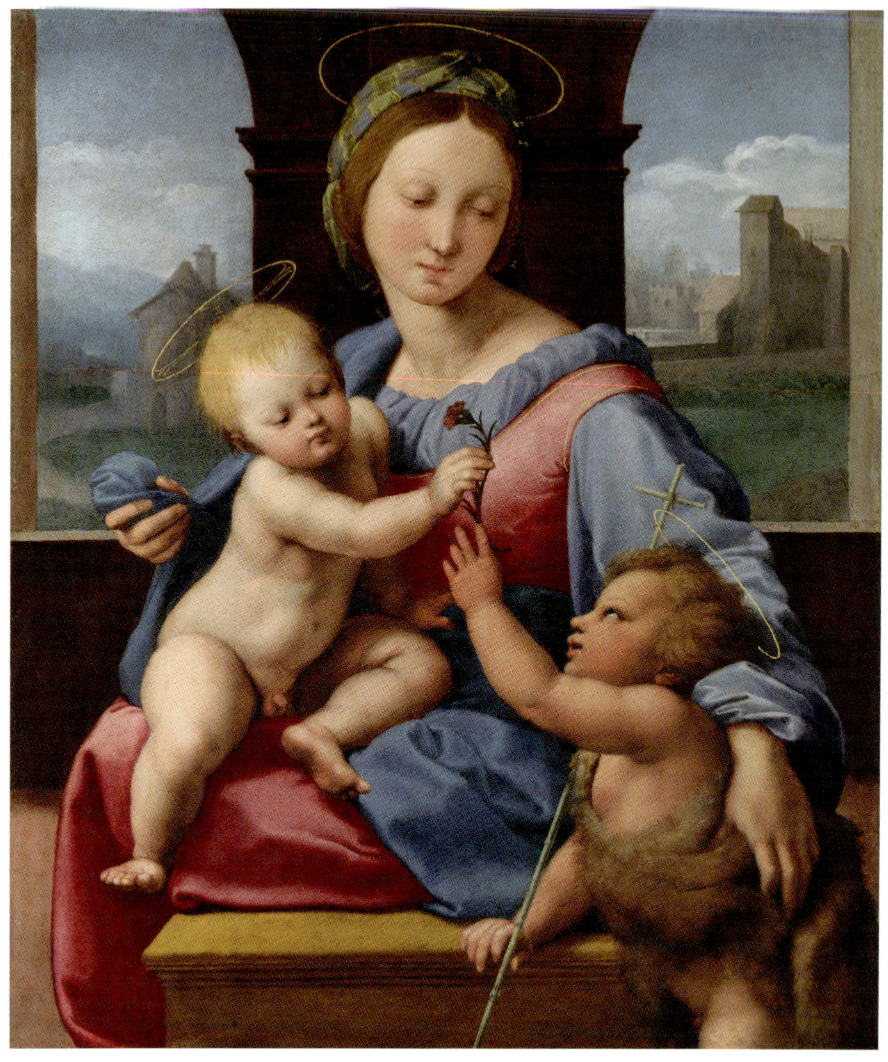

The Garvagh Madonna (The Madonna and Child with the Infant John the Baptist/Madonna Aldobrandini), *c.* 1510
Oil on panel, 38.9 × 32.9 cm (15 ⅓ × 12 ⅞ in). London, The National Gallery

Madonna del Velo (Madonna di Loreto, The Holy Family), *c.* 1511/12
Oil on poplar panel, 120 × 90 cm (47 ¼ × 35 ⅜ in). Chantilly, Musée Condé

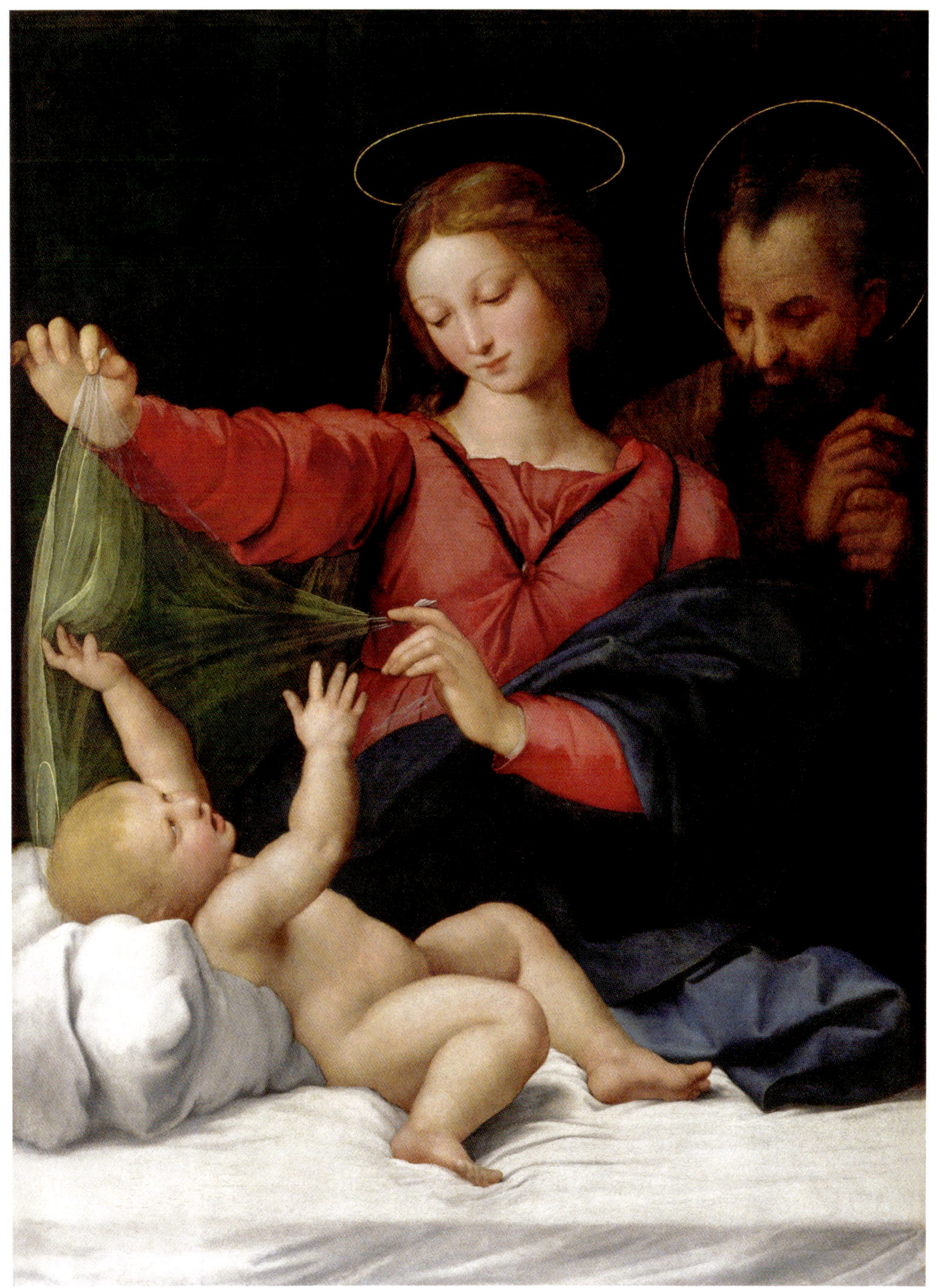

Athanadoros, Hagesandros and Polydoros of Rhodes
Laocoön group, late 1st cent. BC (?)
Marble, height 242 cm (95 ¼ in). Vatican City, Musei Vaticani,
Belvedere courtyard of statues

The Alba Madonna (Madonna and Child with Saint John the Baptist), *c.* 1511
Oil on panel, transferred to canvas, tondo, dia. 95.3 cm (37 ½ in)
Washington, D. C., National Gallery of Art, A. W. Mellon 1937

Page 360
Raphael and Workshop, **Virgin and Child with the Infant Saint John (Madonna with a Diadem)**, *c.* 1514
Oil on panel, 68 × 48.2 cm (26 ¾ × 18 ⅞ in)
Paris, Musée du Louvre

Page 361
Raphael and Workshop, **The Holy Family Meeting the Infant Saint John the Baptist (Madonna del Passeggio)**, *c.* 1517
Oil on panel, 90 × 63.3 cm (35 ⅜ × 24 ⅞ in)
Edinburgh, Scottish National Gallery, Bridgewater Collection Loan

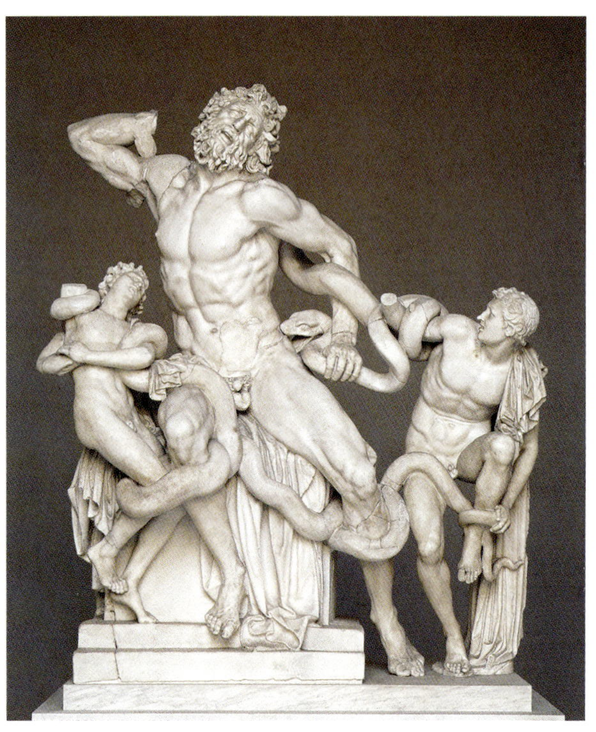

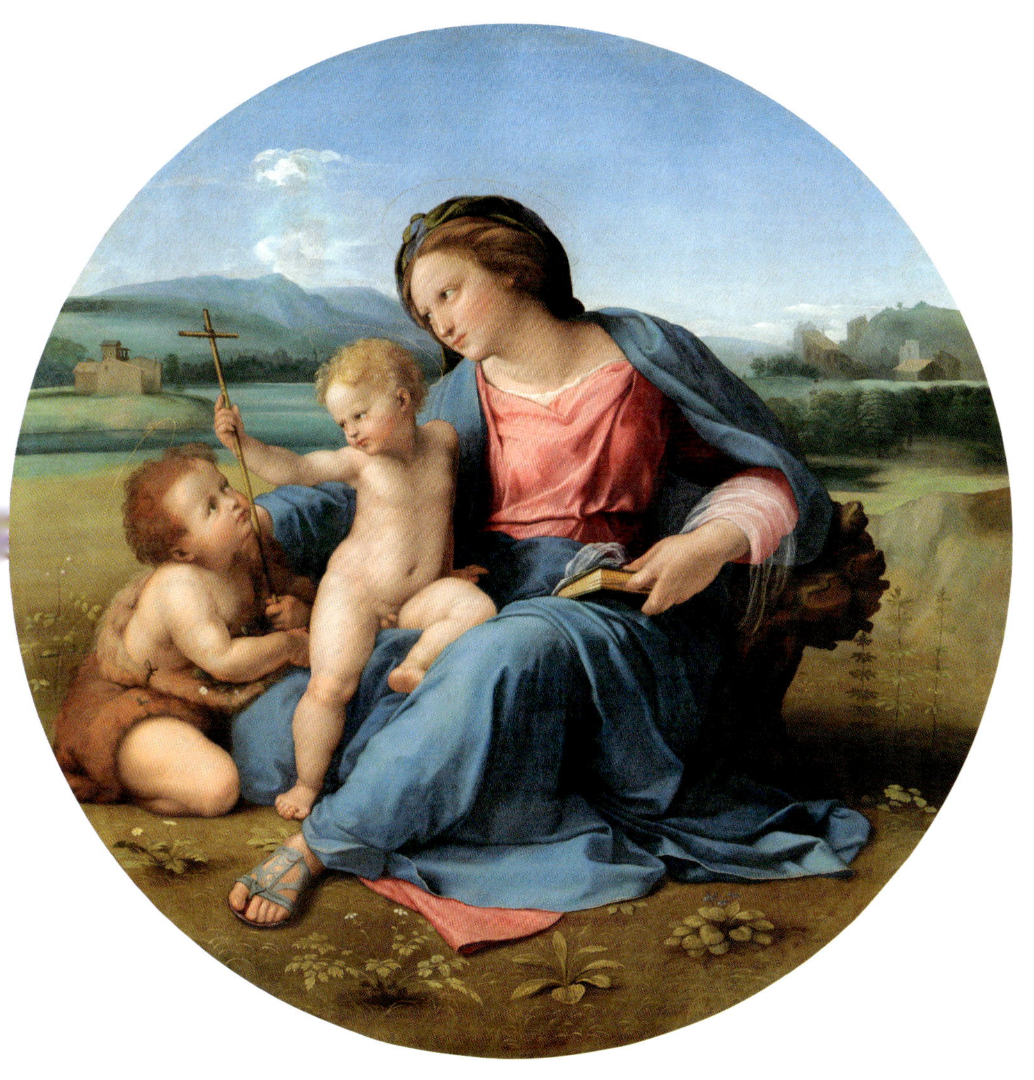

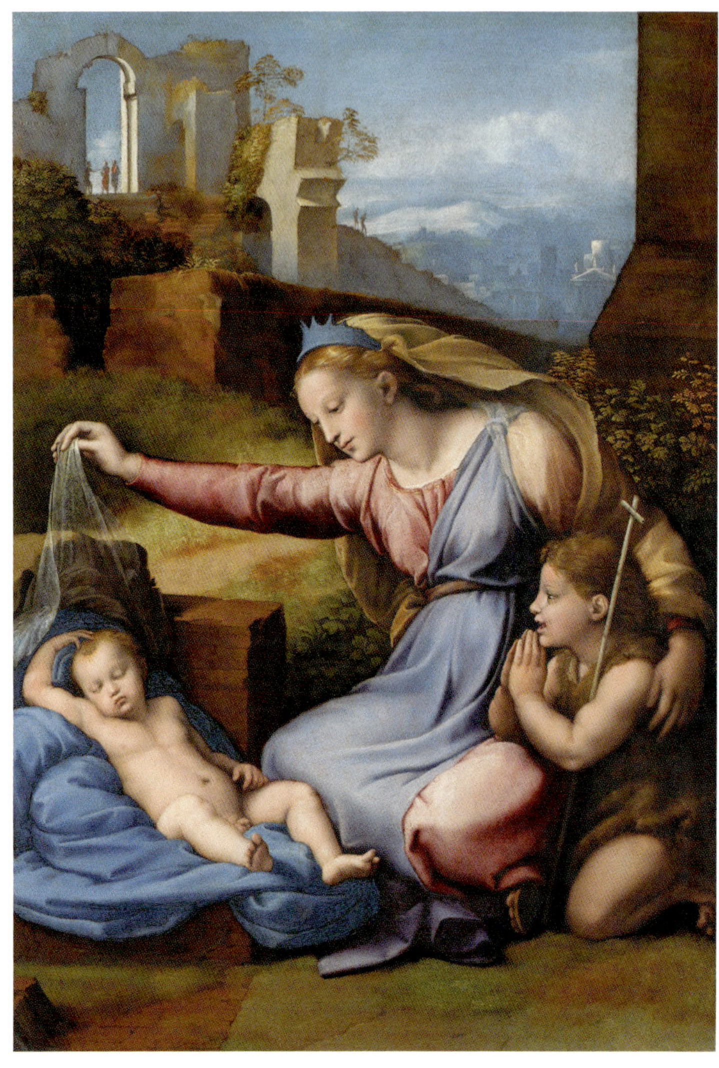

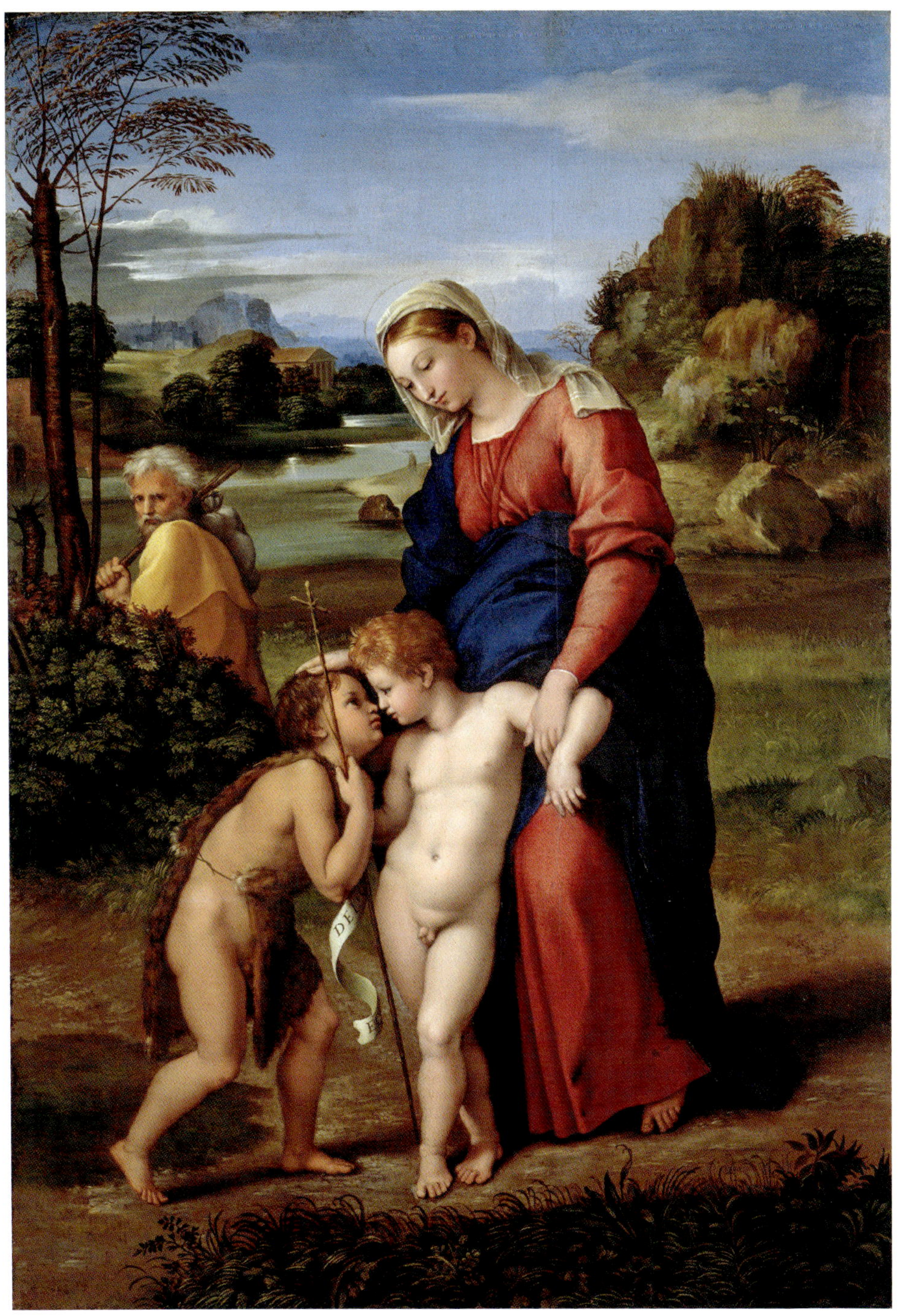

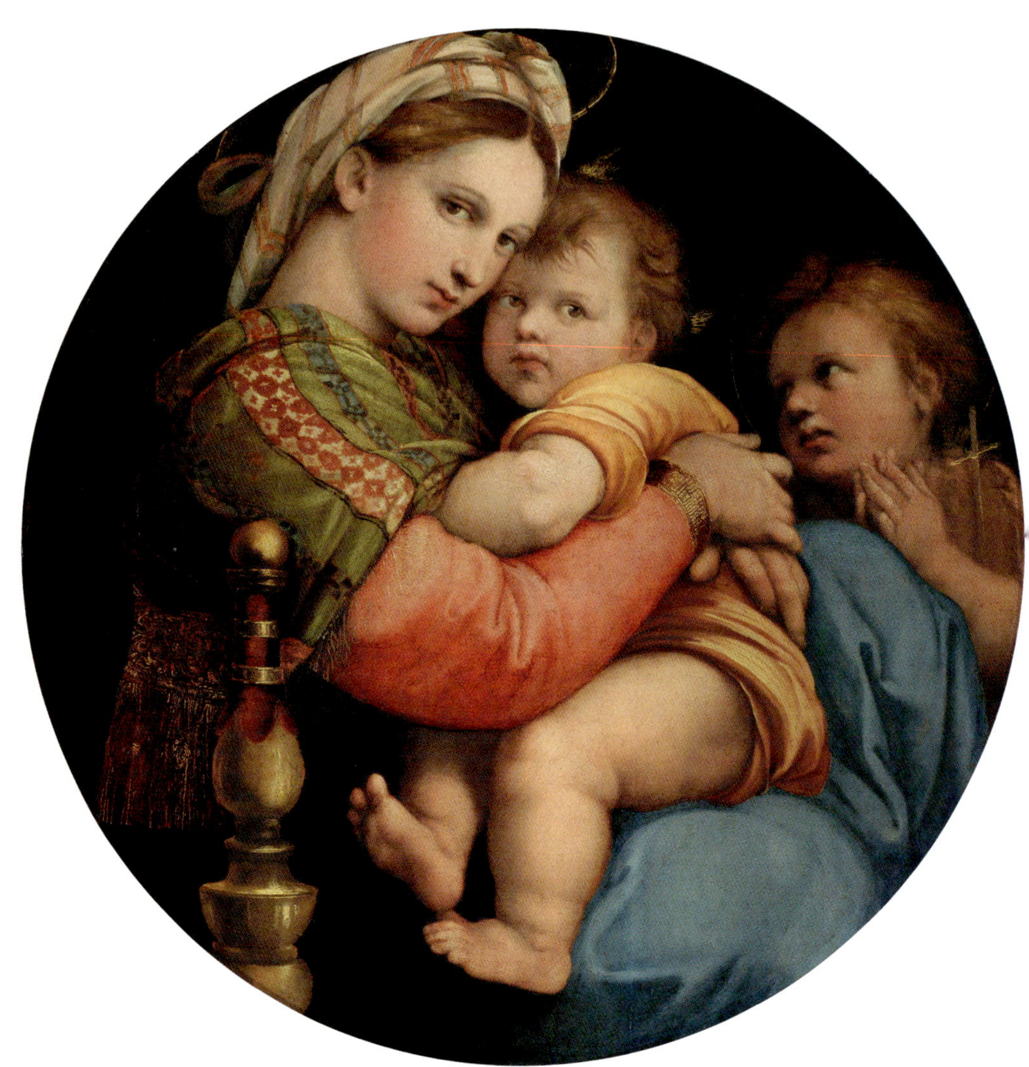

Madonna della Seggiola (Madonna with the Christ Child and the Infant Saint John), *c.* 1512–1514
Oil on poplar panel, tondo, dia. 71 cm (27 ⅞ in)
Florence, Galleria Palatina, Sala di Saturno

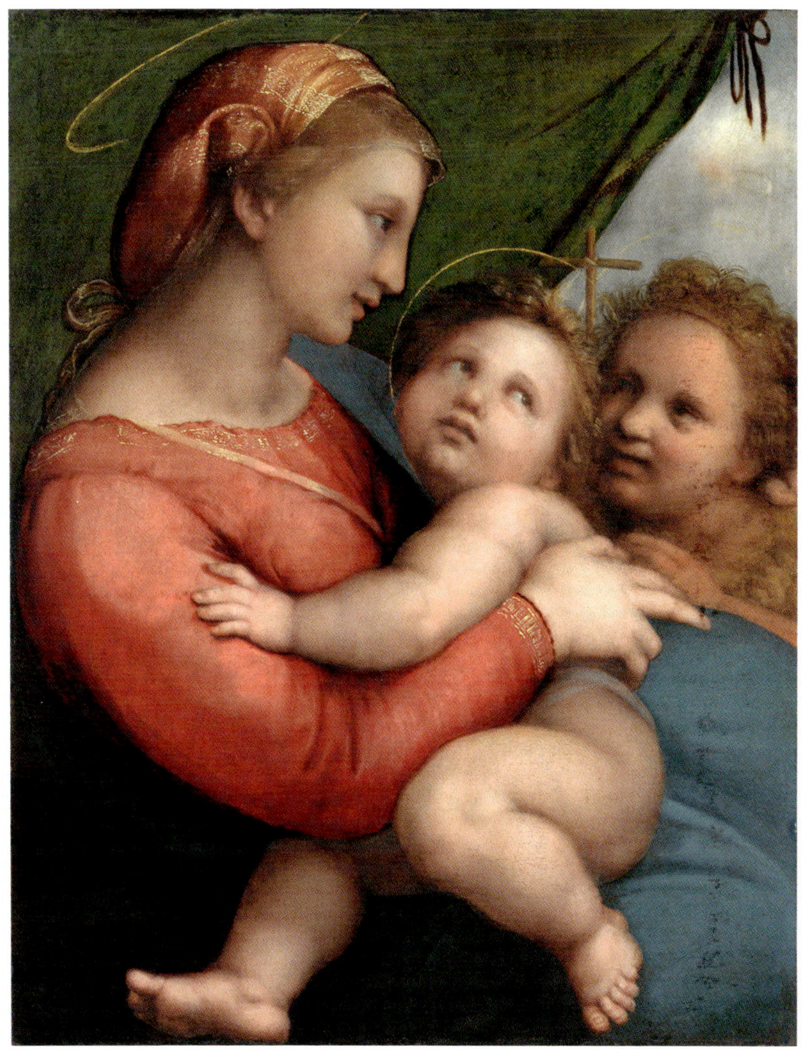

Madonna della Tenda (The Virgin Mary and Child with the Infant Saint John), *c.* 1512–1514
Oil on poplar panel, 65.8 × 51.2 cm (25 ⅞ × 20 ⅛ in)
Munich, Bayerische Staatsgemäldesammlungen, Alte Pinakothek

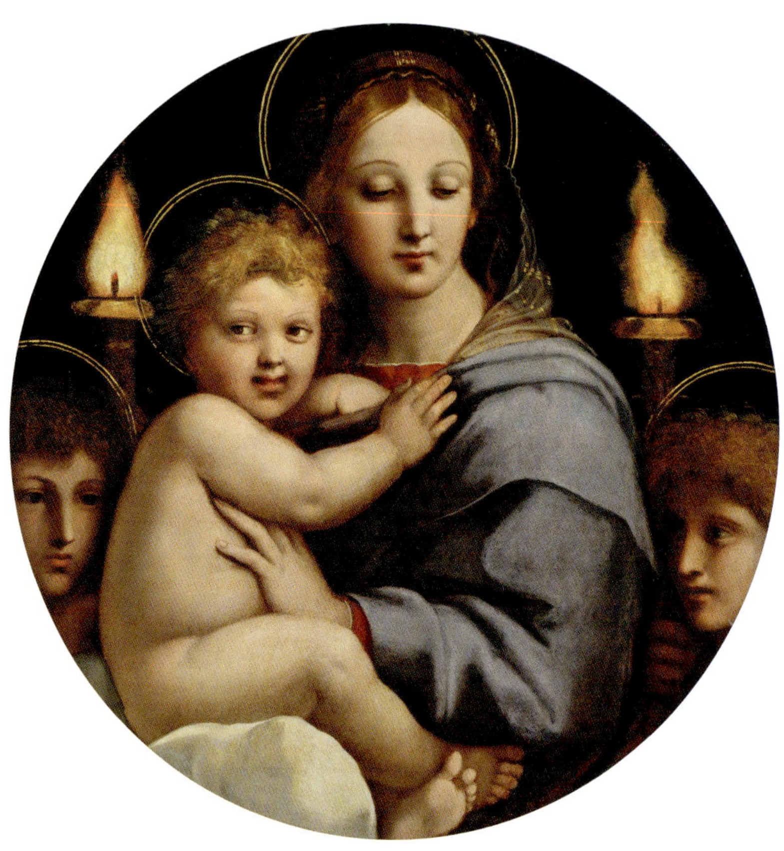

Raphael and Workshop, **Madonna of the Candelabra**, 1513/14
Oil on panel, tondo, dia. 65.7 × 64 cm (25 ⅞ × 25 ¼ in)
Baltimore, The Walters Art Museum

Raphael and an unknown assistant, **Madonna with the Book (Madonna del Libro)**, *c.* 1512
Oil on panel, 35.7 × 24.2 cm (14 ⅛ × 9 ½ in). Florence, Galleria Palatina

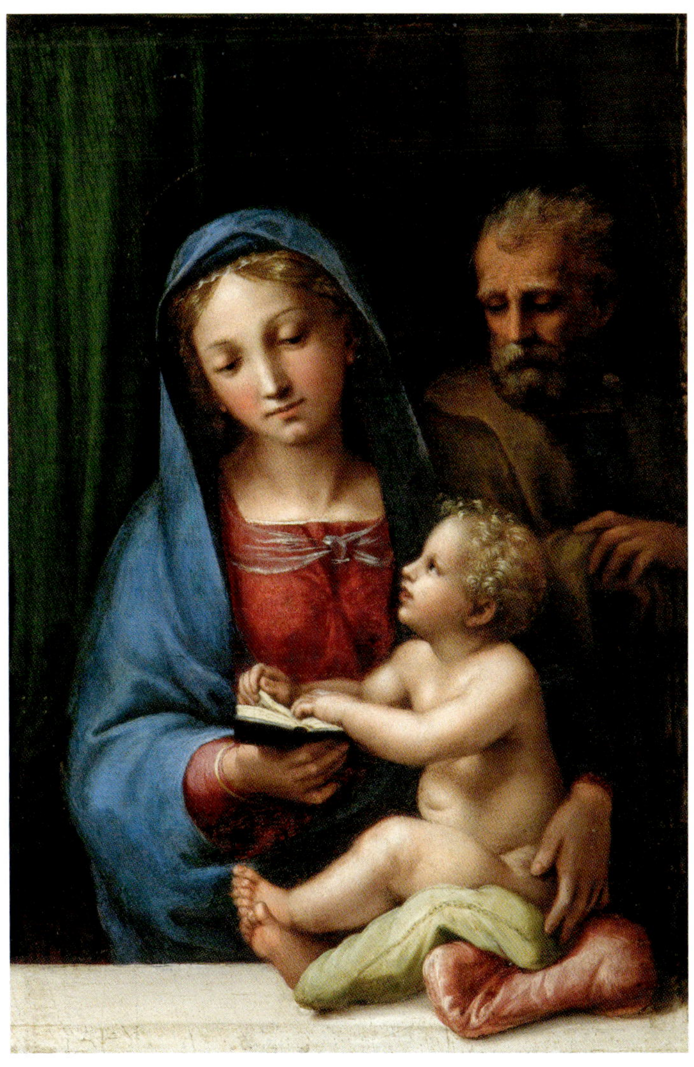

Virgin and Child with Saint Elizabeth, study for the *Madonna dell'Impannata*, 1511
Silverpoint with white heightening on greyish-brown prepared paper, 21 × 14.5 cm (8 ¼ × 5 ¾ in)
Windsor Castle, Royal Library

Madonna dell'Impannata (Madonna and Child and Saint John the Baptist, Saint Elizabeth [?] **and Saint Catherine** [?]), *c.* 1511–1515 (?)
Oil on poplar panel, 160 × 127 cm (62 ⅞ × 50 in). Florence, Galleria Palatina

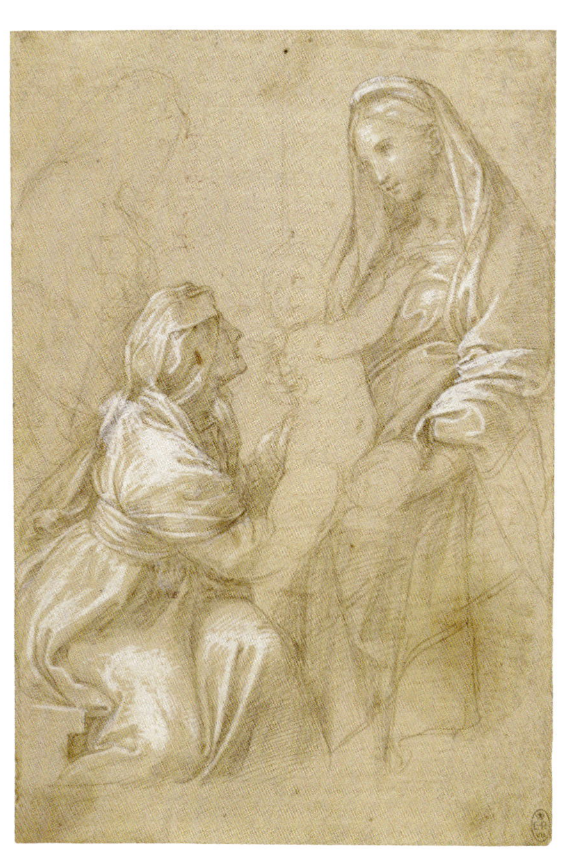

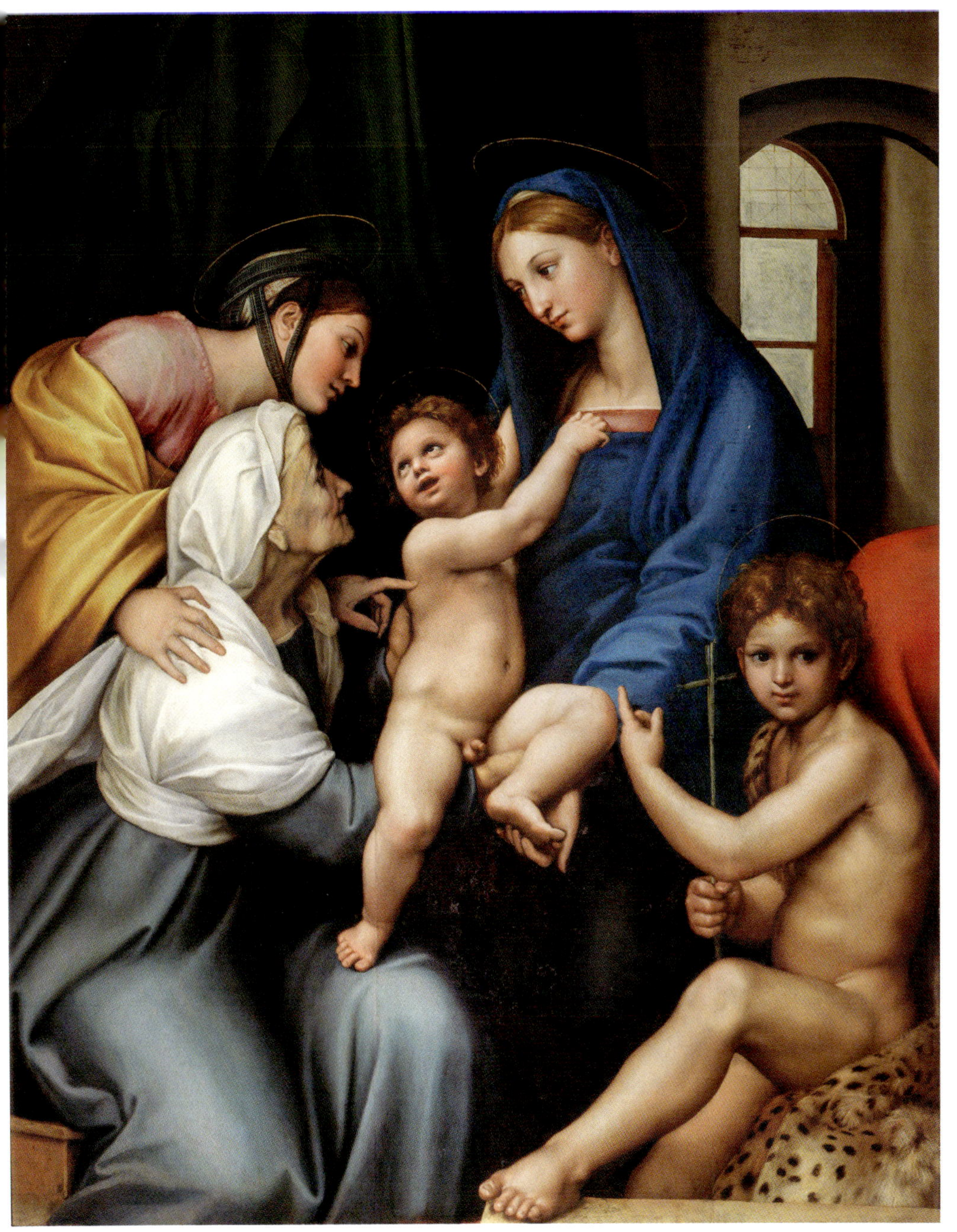

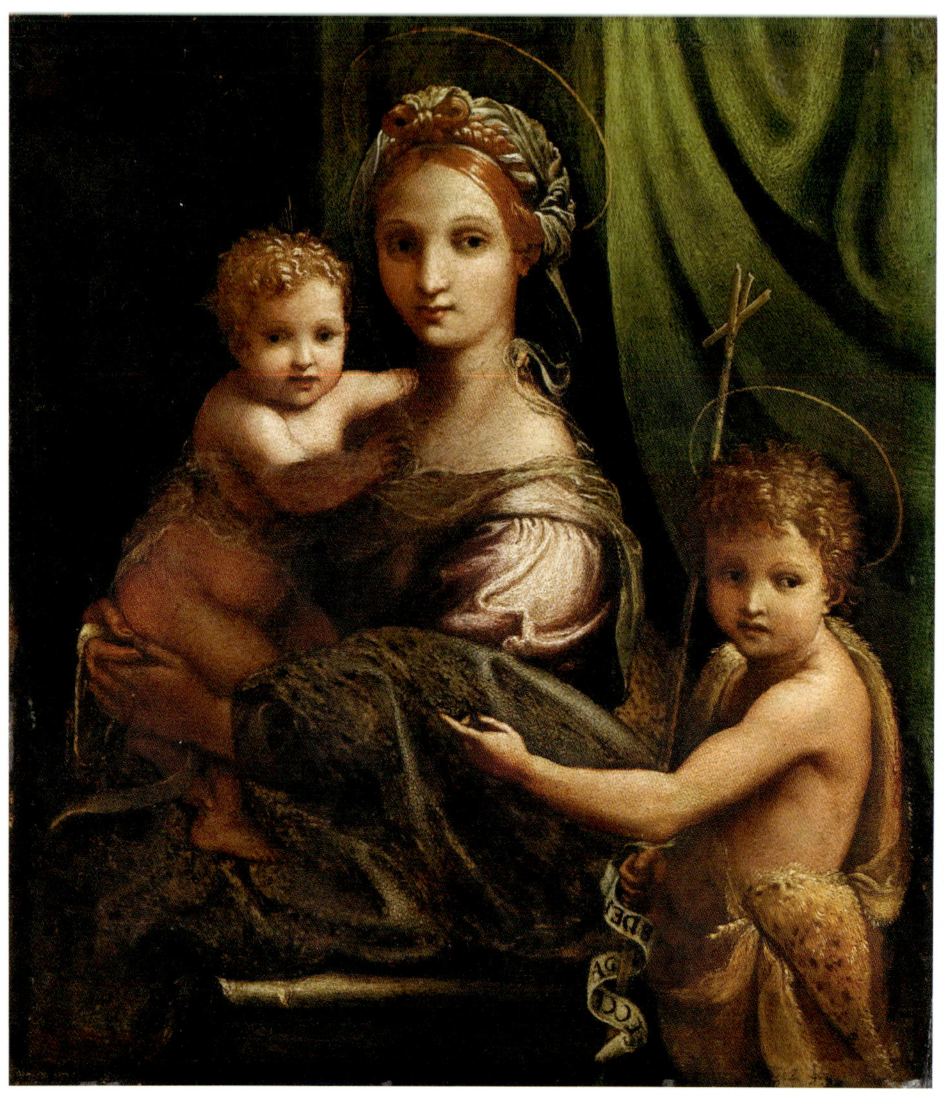

Raphael and Giulio Romano (?)
Virgin and Child with the Infant John the Baptist (La Madonnina), *c.* 1515/16
Oil on panel, 29 × 25.4 cm (11⅜ × 10 in). Inscription on the banderole: *ECC[E] AGN[V]S DEI.*
Paris, Musée du Louvre

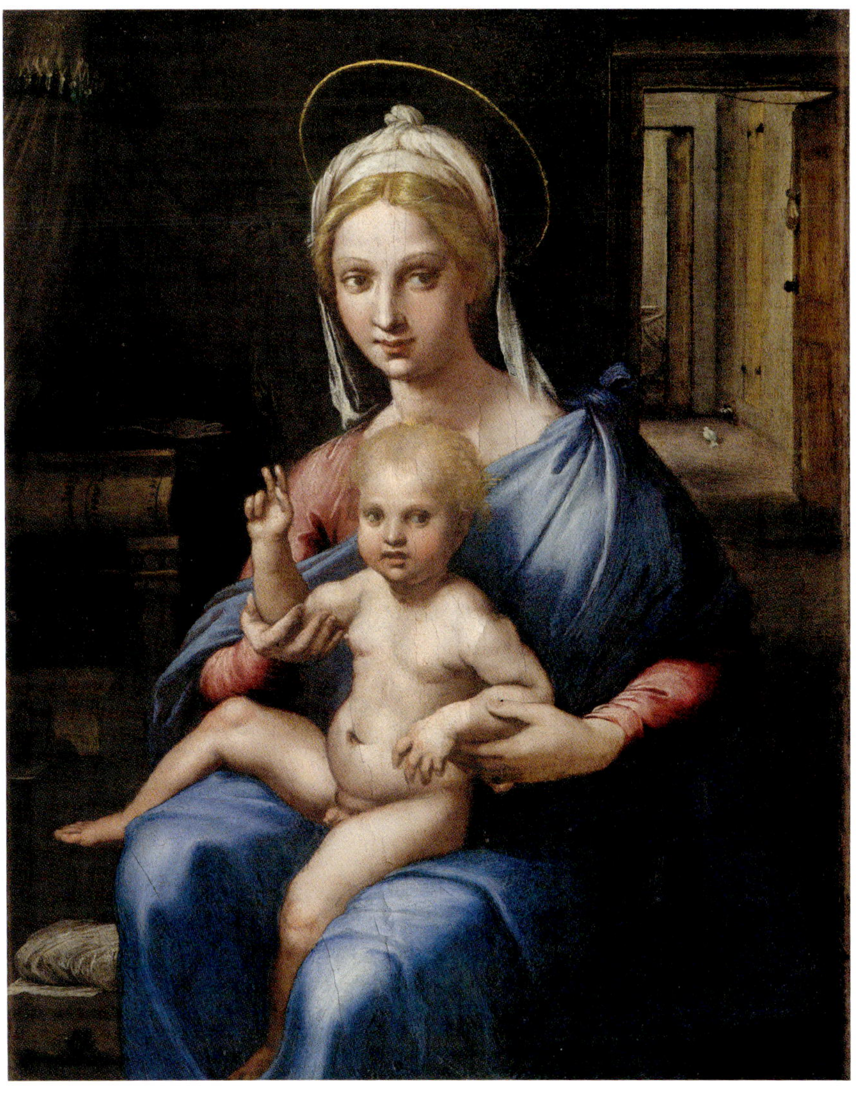

Raphael and Giulio Romano
Hertz Madonna, *c.* 1516/17
Oil on canvas, 36 × 30.5 cm (14 ⅛ × 12 ⅛ in)
Rome, Galleria Nazionale d'Arte Antica

Drapery studies for the figure of the Virgin, 1517/18
Red chalk over stylus, 33.6 × 21.4 cm (13 ¼ × 8 ⅜ in)
Florence, Gallerie degli Uffizi, Gabinetto dei Disegni e delle Stampe

Raphael and Workshop
Holy Family with Saint Elizabeth and the Infant Saint John the Baptist (Holy Family of Francis I), 1518
Oil on panel, transferred to canvas, 207 × 140 cm (81 ½ × 55 ⅛ in)
Inscription: *RAPHAEL. VRBINAS. PINGEBAT. M. D. X. VIII.*
Paris, Musée du Louvre

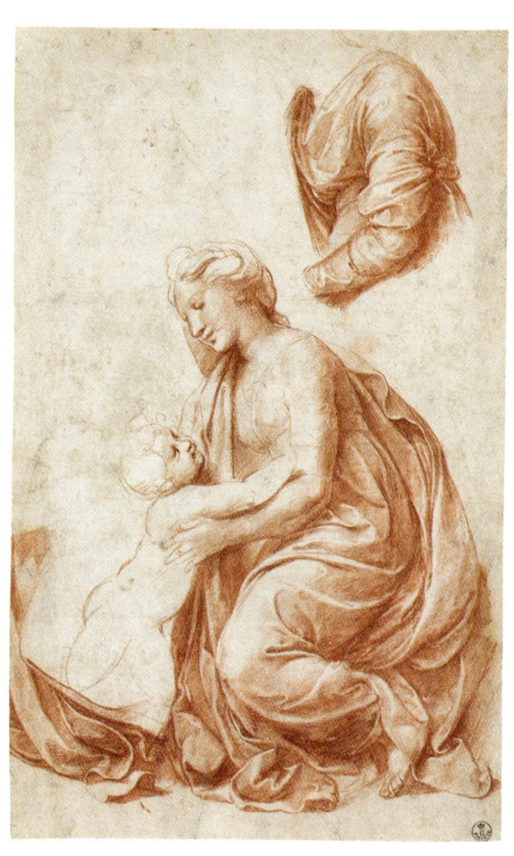

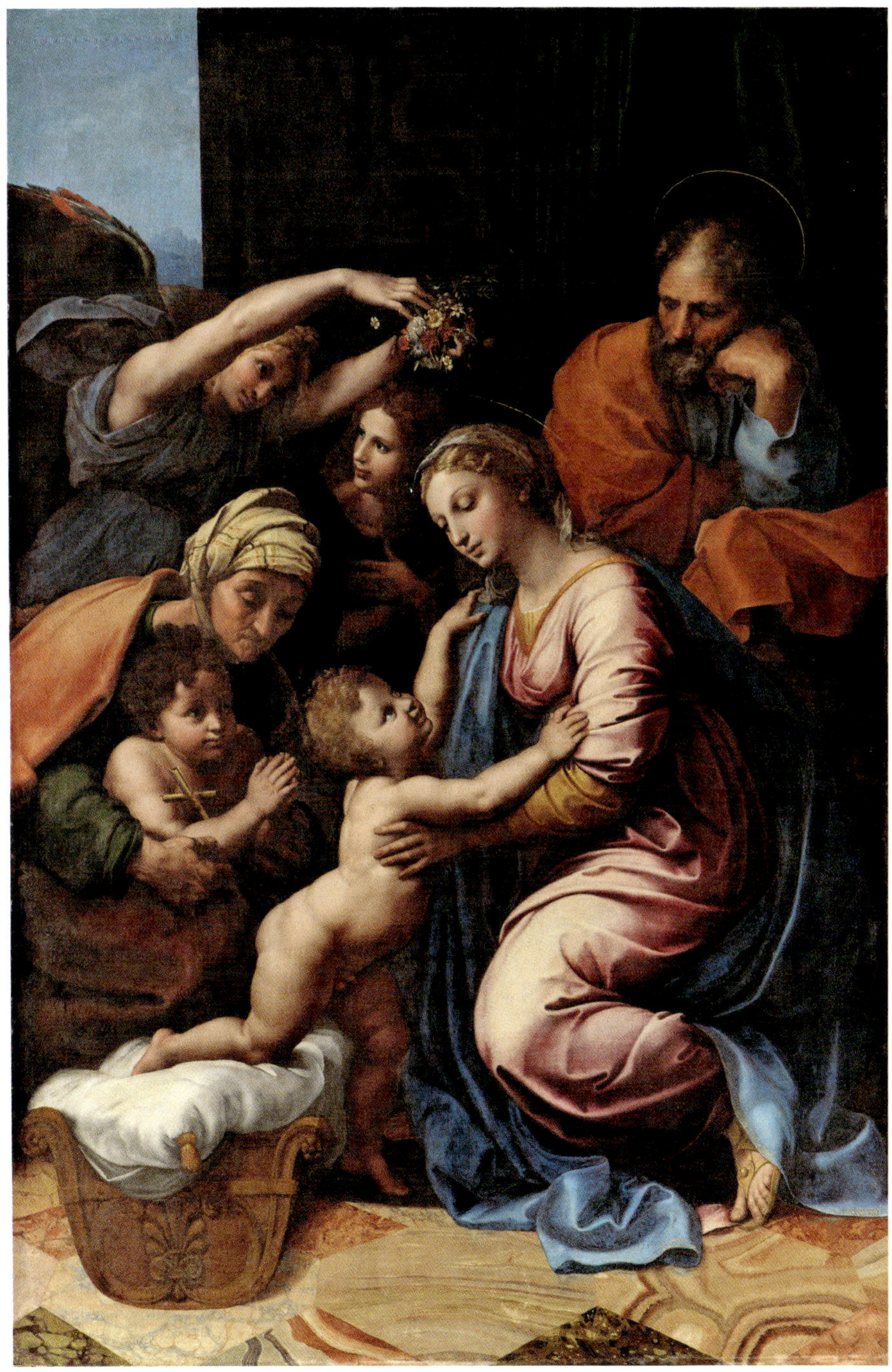

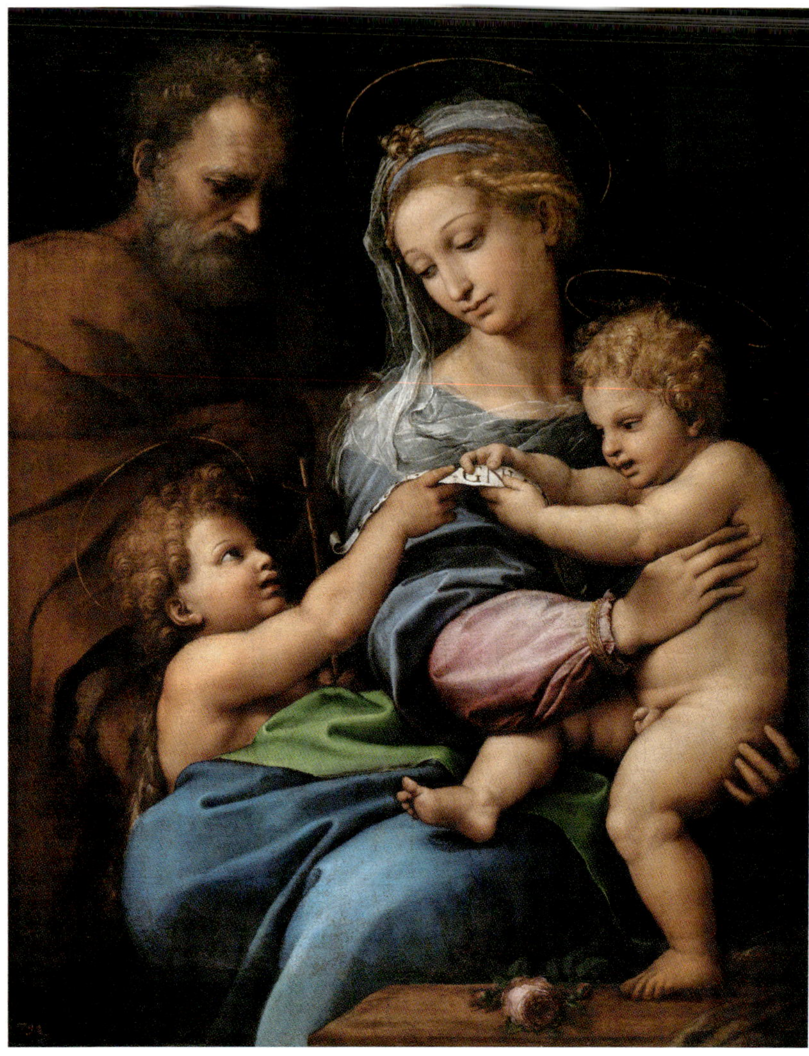

Raphael and Workshop, **Holy Family with the Infant Saint John (Madonna della Rosa)**, *c.* 1517/18
Oil on panel, transferred to canvas, 103 × 84 cm (40 ½ × 33 ⅛ in)
Madrid, Museo Nacional del Prado

Raphael and Giovanni Francesco Penni (?), **Madonna del Divino Amore**, *c.* 1516
Oil on panel, 140 × 109 cm (55 ⅛ × 42 ⅞ in)
Naples, Museo e Gallerie Nazionali di Capodimonte

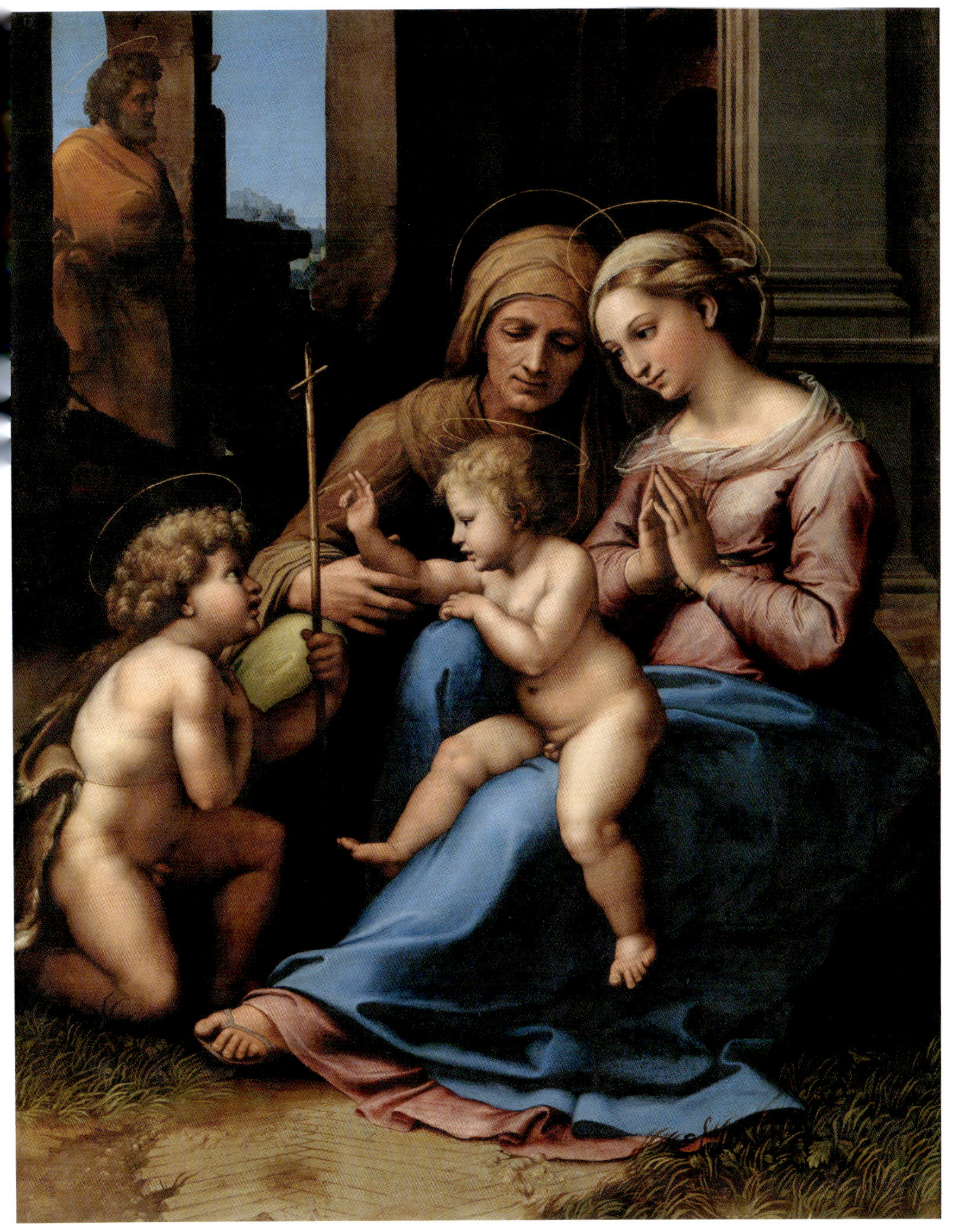

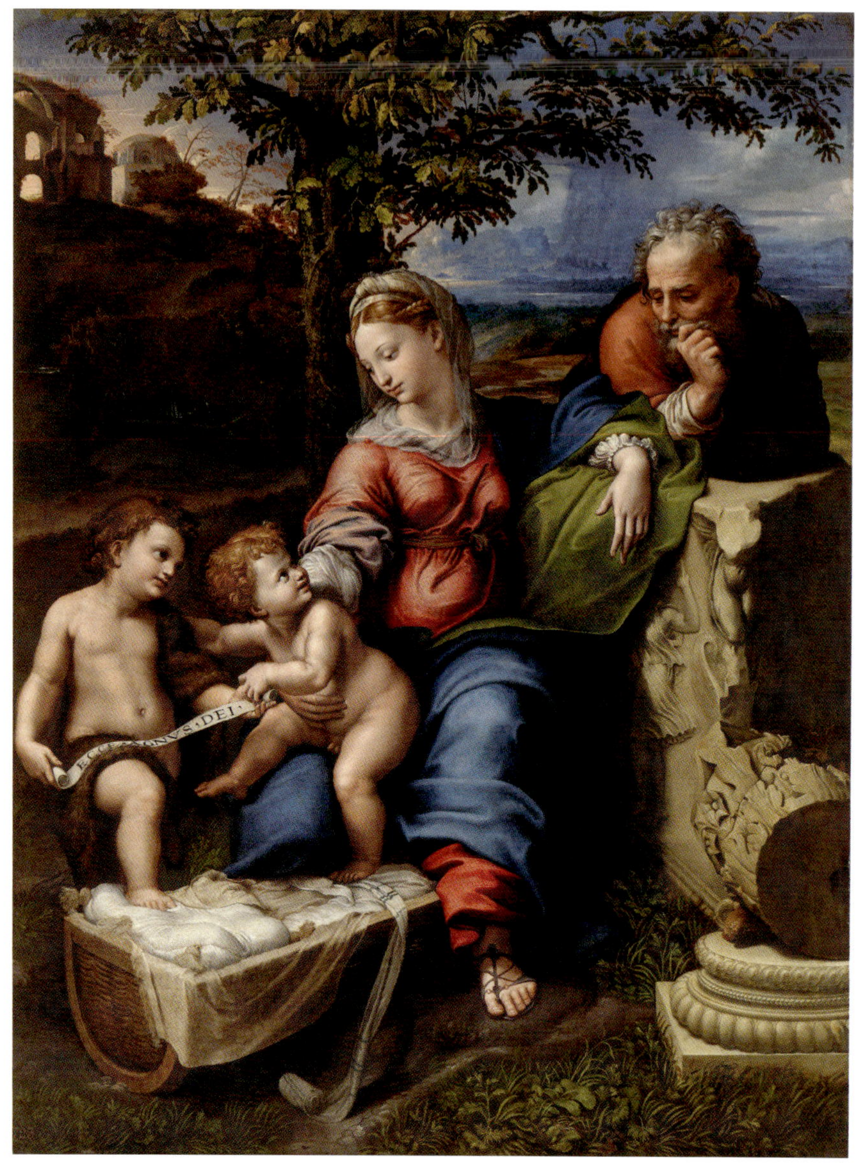

Raphael and Workshop (Giulio Romano)
The Holy Family with an Oak Tree (Madonna della Quercia), *c.* 1518/19
Oil on poplar panel, 144 × 109 cm (56 ¾ × 42 ⅞ in)
Inscription on the banderole: *ECCE AGNUS DEI*
Madrid, Museo Nacional del Prado

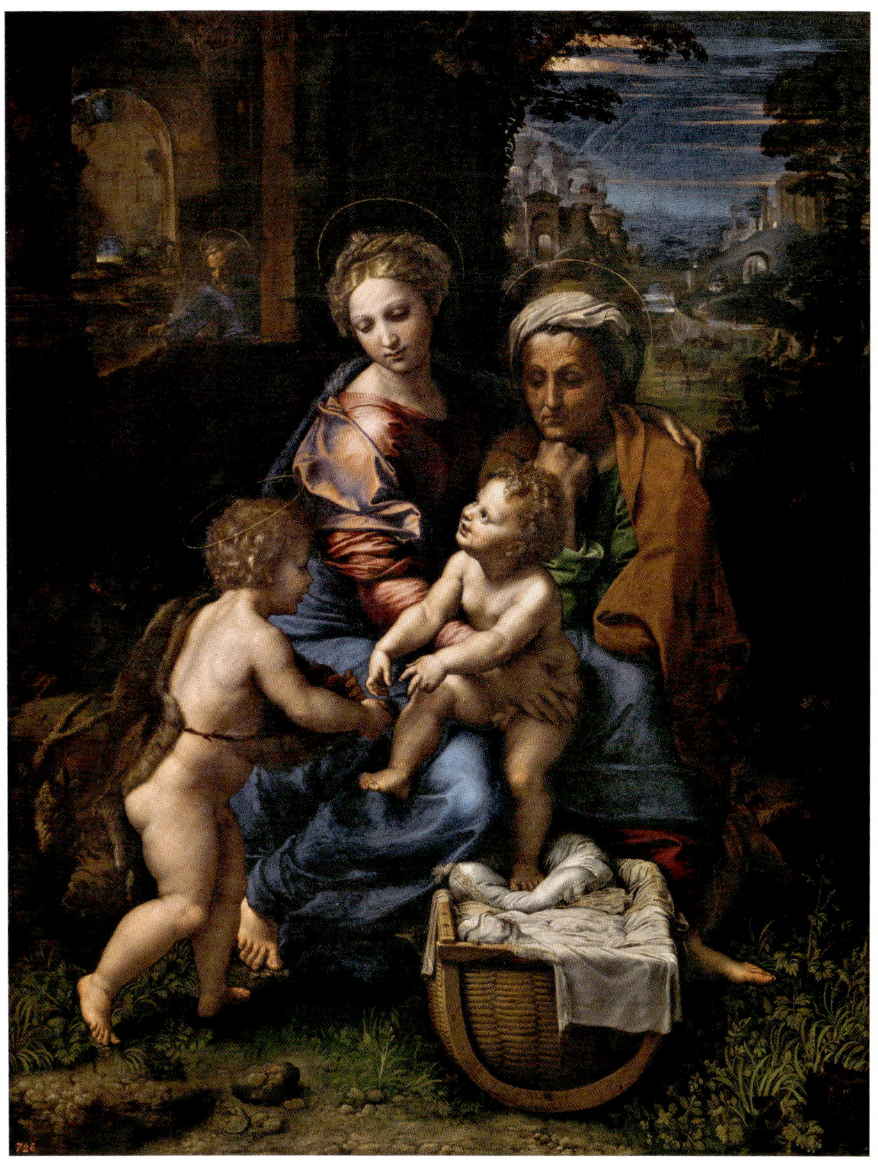

Raphael and Workshop (Giulio Romano)
The Holy Family (La Perla), *c.* 1518/19
Oil on poplar panel, 144 × 115 cm (56 ¾ × 45 ¼ in)
Madrid, Museo Nacional del Prado

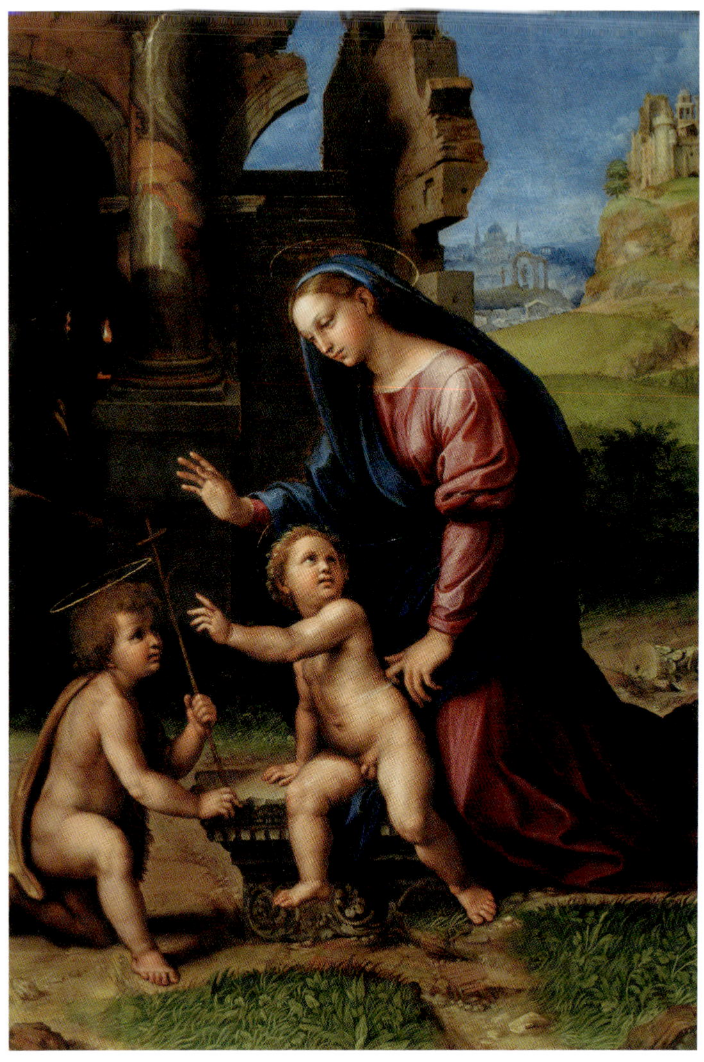

Raphael and Giovanni Francesco Penni (?), **Holy Family with the Infant John in a Landscape (The Bankes Madonna/Madonna delle Rovine)**, *c.* 1516/17
Oil on panel, 76 × 53 cm (29 ⅞ × 20 ⅞ in). Dorset, Kingston Lacy

Raphael and Workshop, **Holy Family with the Infant Saint John the Baptist**, *c.* 1512–1514 and later
Oil on poplar, 154.5 × 114 cm (60 ⅞ × 44 ⅞ in). Vienna, Kunsthistorisches Museum

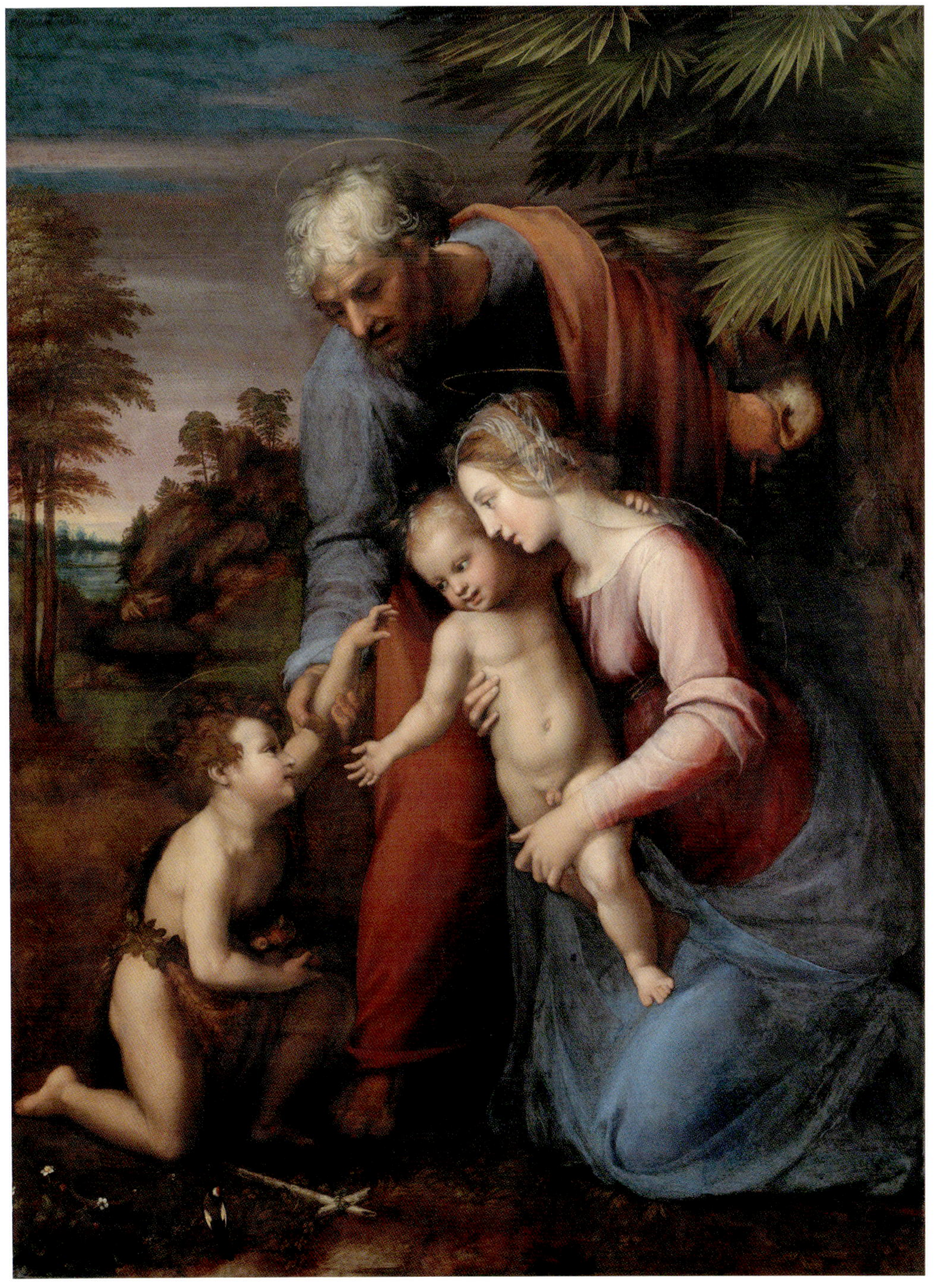

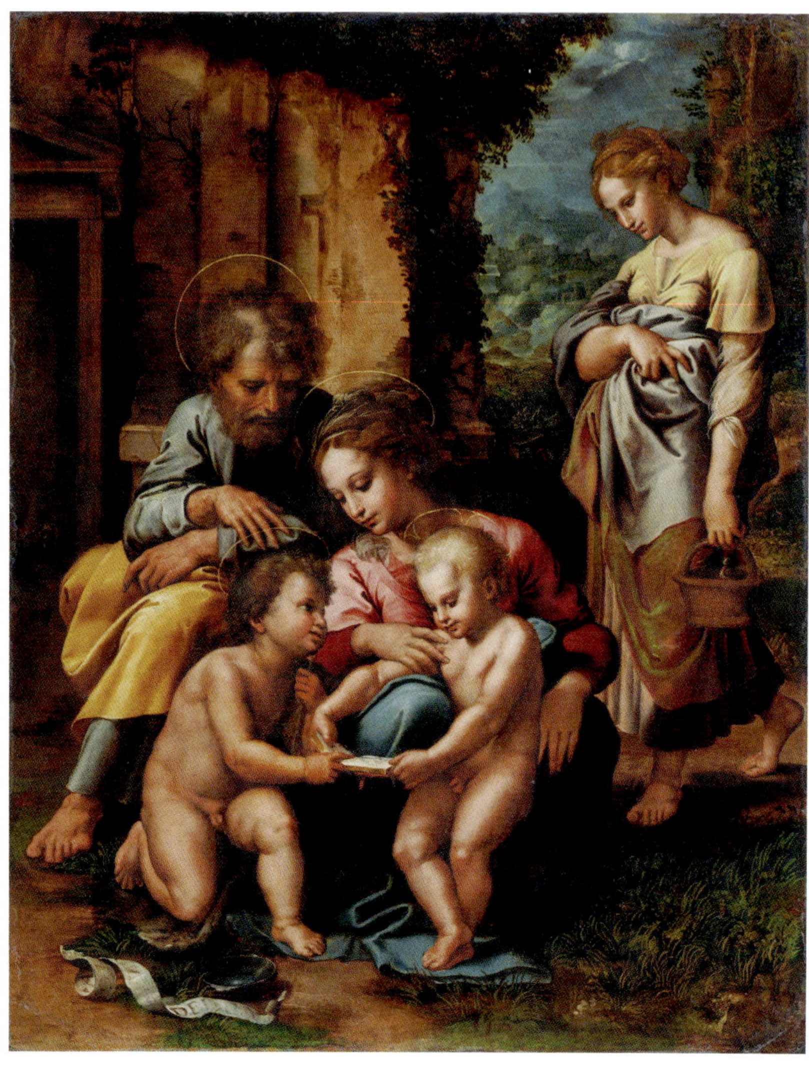

Raphael and Giulio Romano, **Holy Family (Madonna Spinola)**, *c.* 1520
Oil on panel, 77.5 × 61.9 cm (30 ½ × 24 ⅜ in)
Inscription on the banderole: *ECC[E] A[GNVS] DEI EU U.*
Los Angeles, The J. Paul Getty Museum

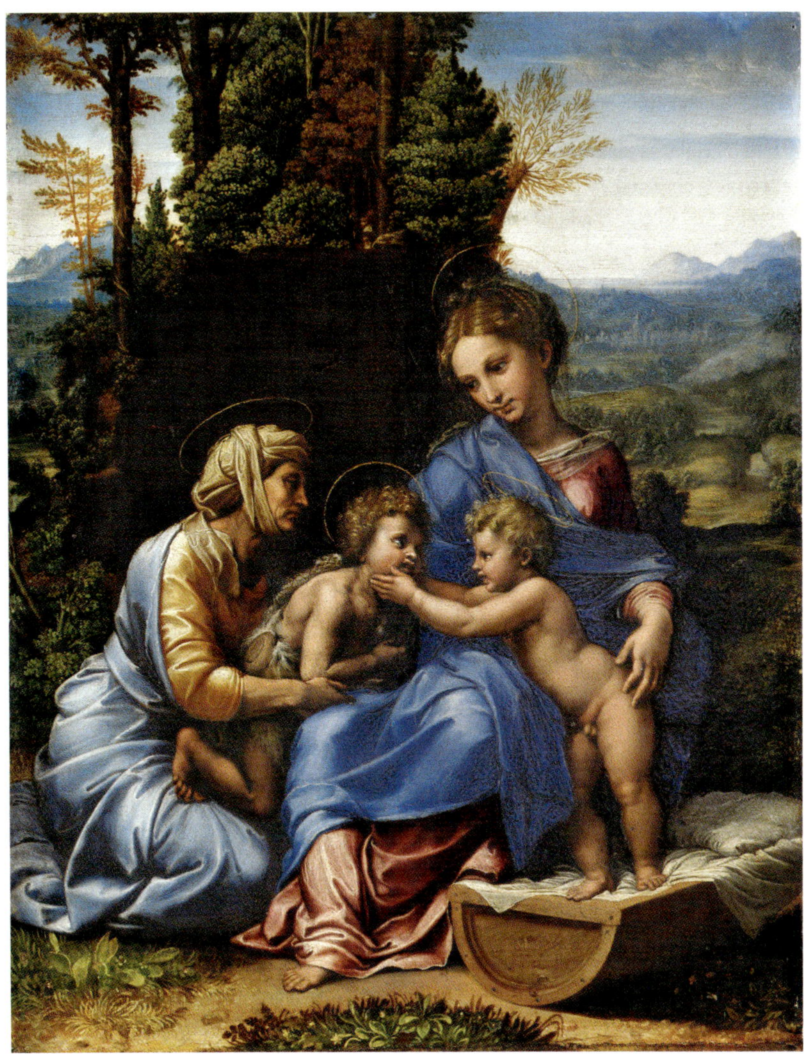

Raphael and Giulio Romano
Small Holy Family (Madonna Piccola Gonzaga), *c.* 1517/18
Oil on panel, 38.6 × 29.5 cm (15 ¼ × 11 ⅝ in)
Paris, Musée du Louvre

Raphael (most likely), **Saint Michael**, 1518
Pen, with wash and heightened with white, over chalk underdrawing, squared in chalk, 41.7 × 27.7 cm (16 ⅜ × 10 ⅞ in)
Paris, Musée du Louvre, Département des Arts graphiques

Raphael and Workshop, **Saint Michael Vanquishing Satan**, 1517/18
Oil on panel, transferred to canvas, 268 × 160 cm (105 ½ × 62 ⅞ in)
Inscription: *RAPHAEL. VRBINAS. M. D. X. VIII.*
Paris, Musée du Louvre

Page 382
Raphael and Workshop, **Saint Margaret**, 1518
Oil on panel, transferred to canvas, 184 × 116.5 cm (72 ½ × 45 ⅞ in)
Paris, Musée du Louvre

Page 383
Raphael and Giulio Romano, **Saint Margaret**, *c.* 1519
Oil on panel, 192 × 122 cm (75 ⅝ × 48 ⅛ in)
Vienna, Kunsthistorisches Museum

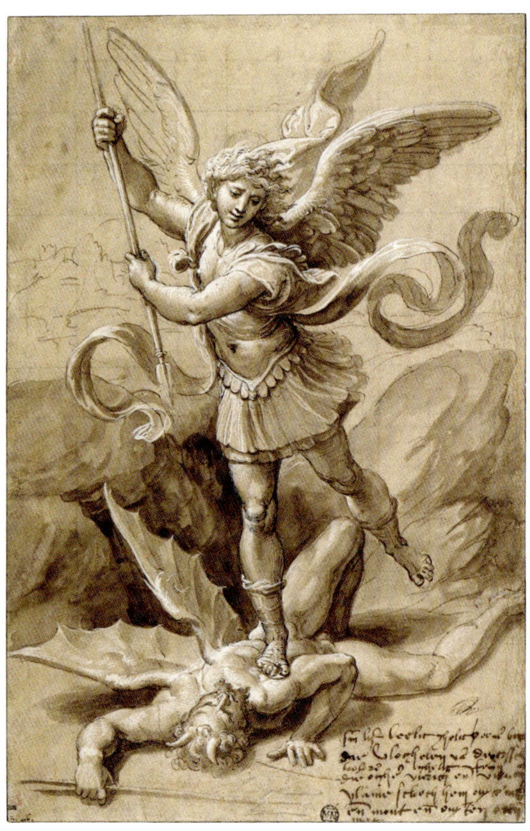

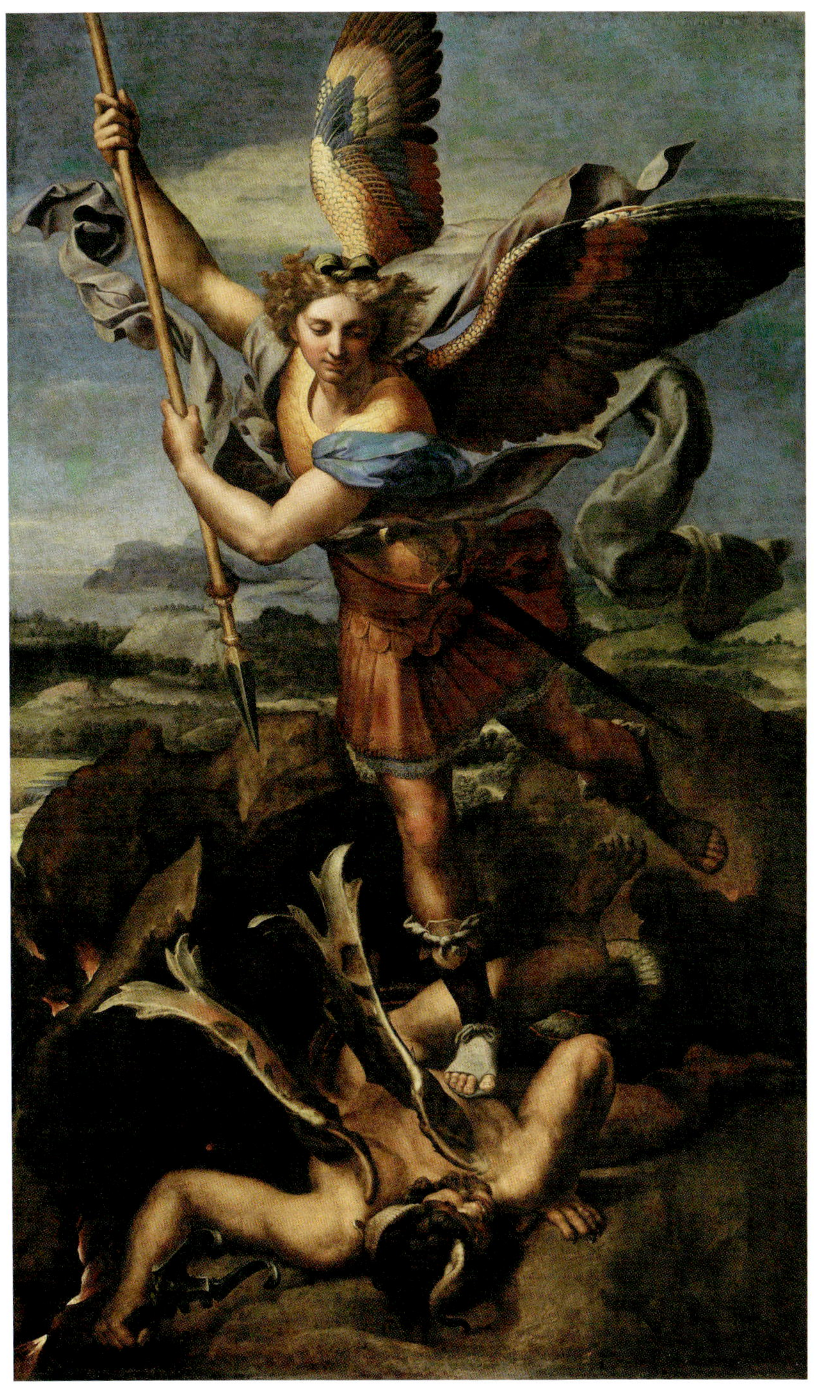

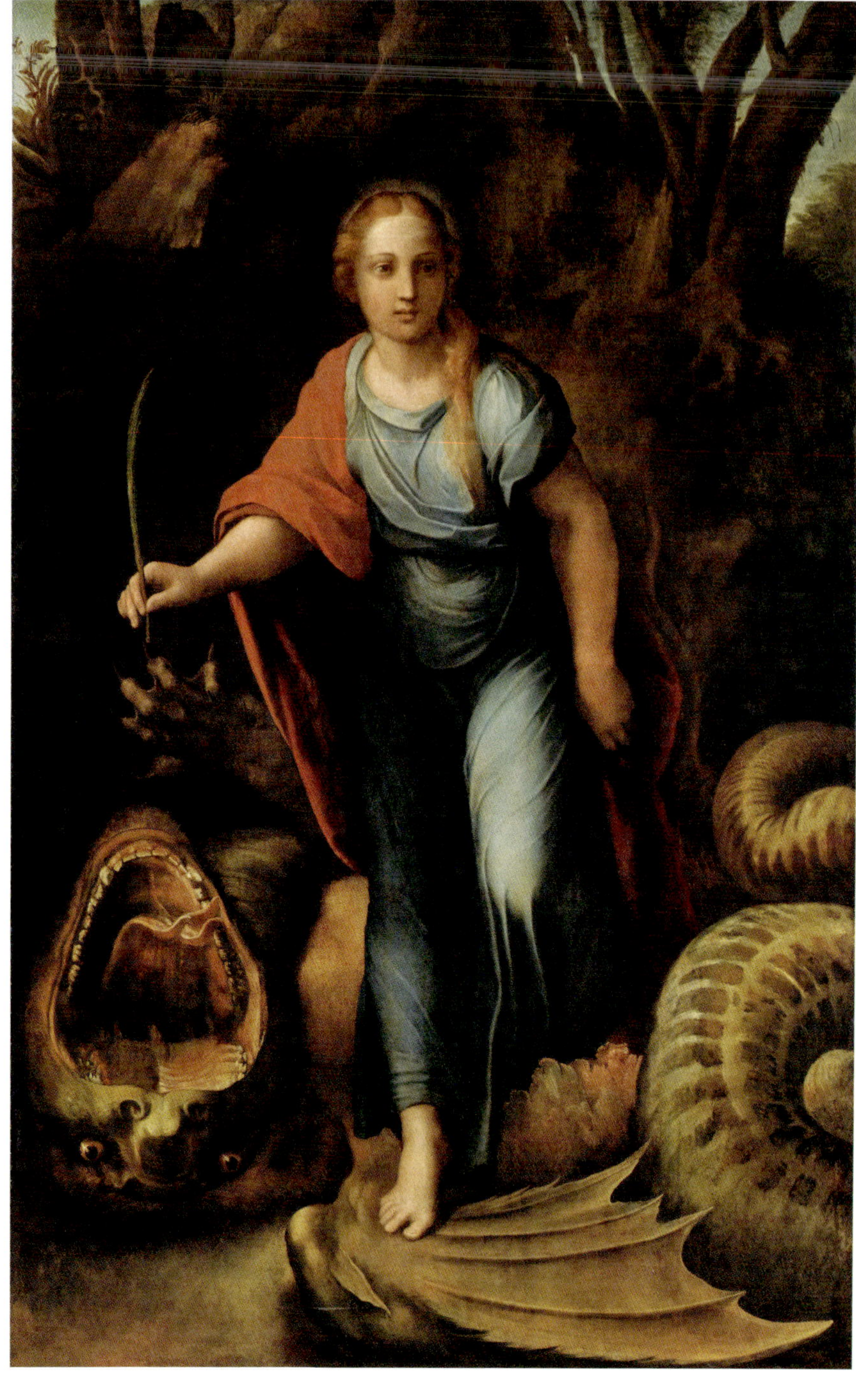

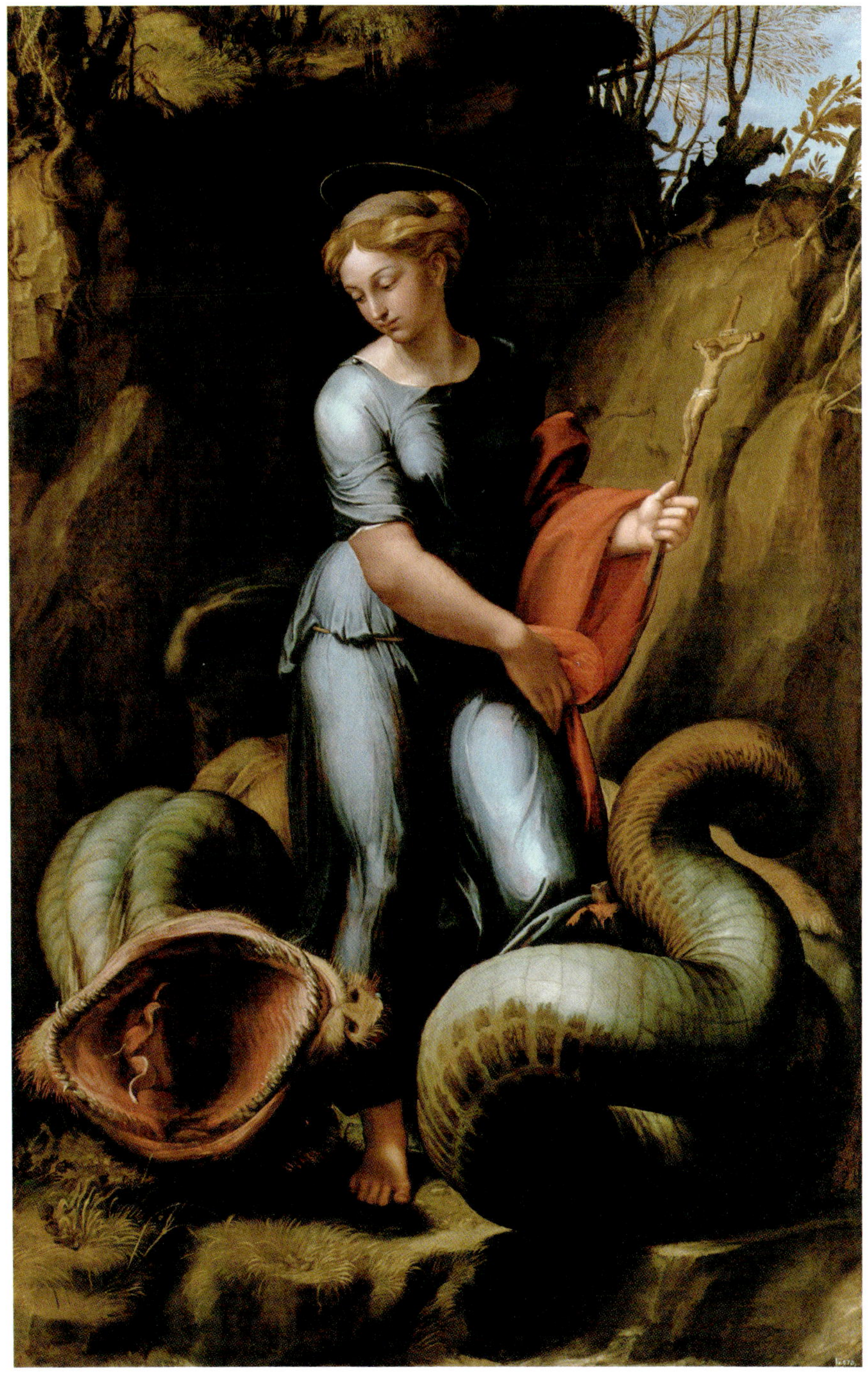

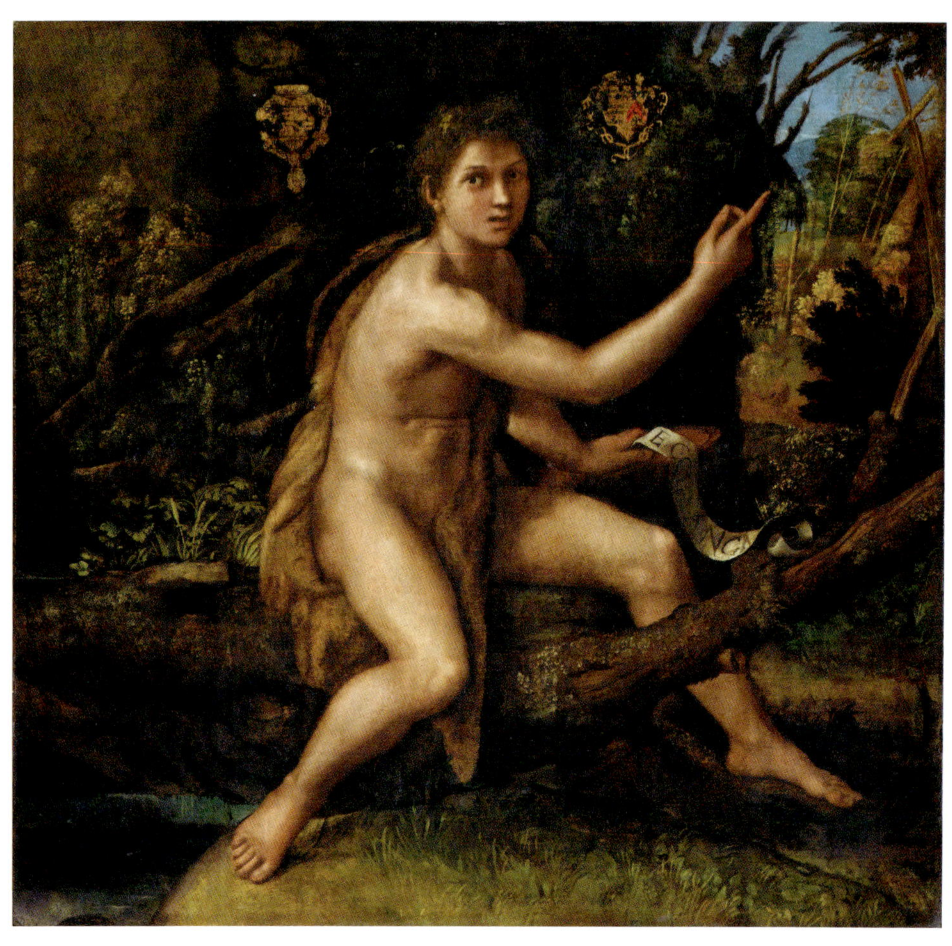

Raphael and Workshop, **Saint John the Baptist**, *c.* 1517
Oil on panel, transferred to canvas, 135 × 142 cm (53 ⅛ × 55 ⅞ in)
Paris, Musée du Louvre

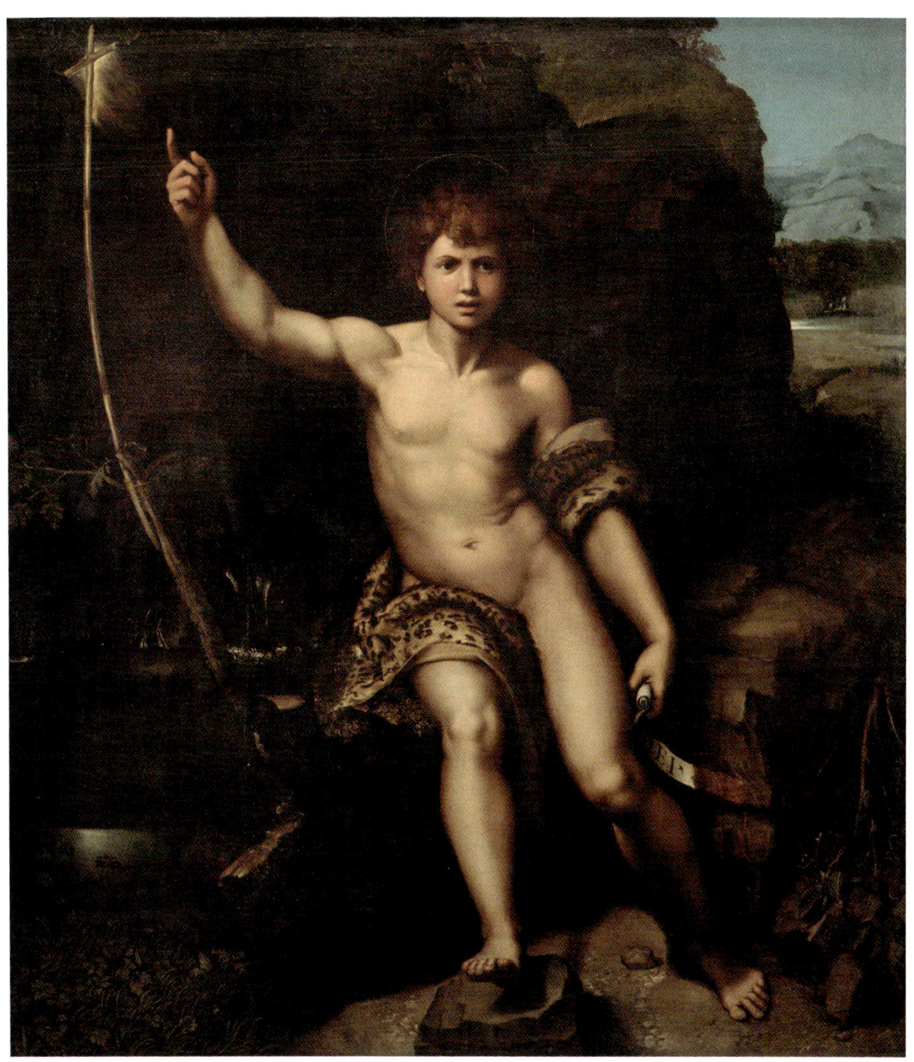

Raphael and Workshop, **Saint John the Baptist**, 1517/18
Oil on canvas, 163 × 147 cm (64 ⅛ × 57 ⅞ in)
Florence, Gallerie degli Uffizi

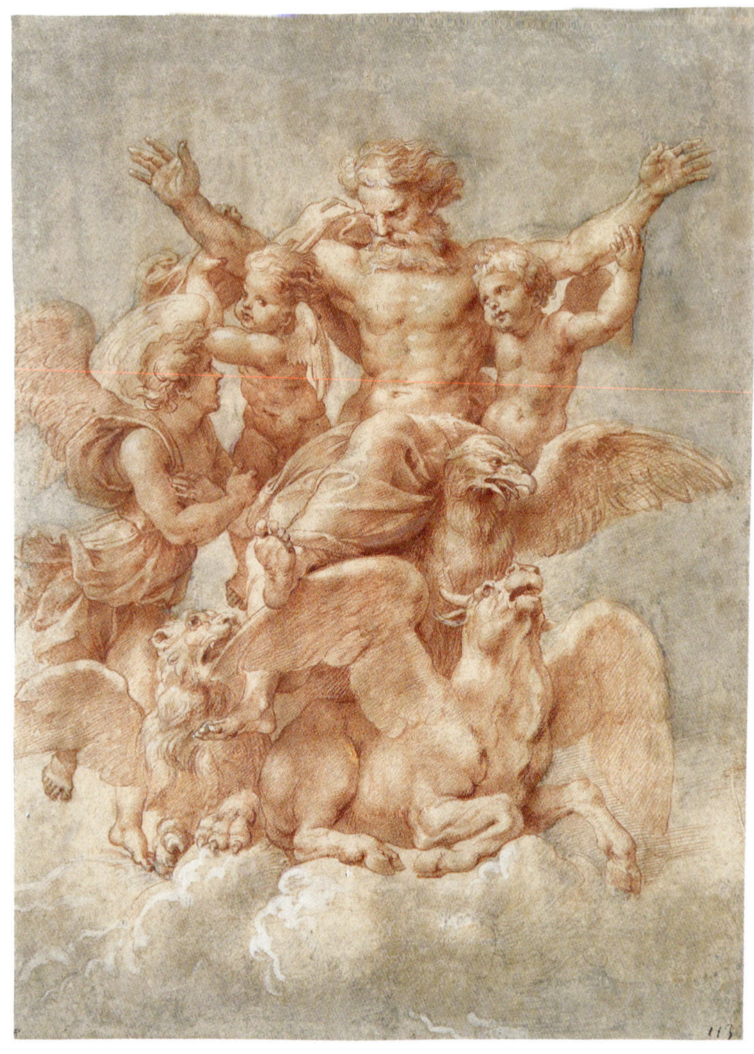

Raphael, retouched by Rubens (?), **The Vision of Ezekiel**, 1516
Black and red chalk with grey wash, heightened with white, 30 × 22.5 cm (11 ¾ × 8 ⅞ in)
Florence, Fondazione Horne

The Vision of Ezekiel/The Vision of Saint John (?), *c.* 1518
Oil on panel, 40.7 × 29.5 cm (16 ⅛ × 11 ⅝ in)
Florence, Galleria Palatina, Sala di Saturno

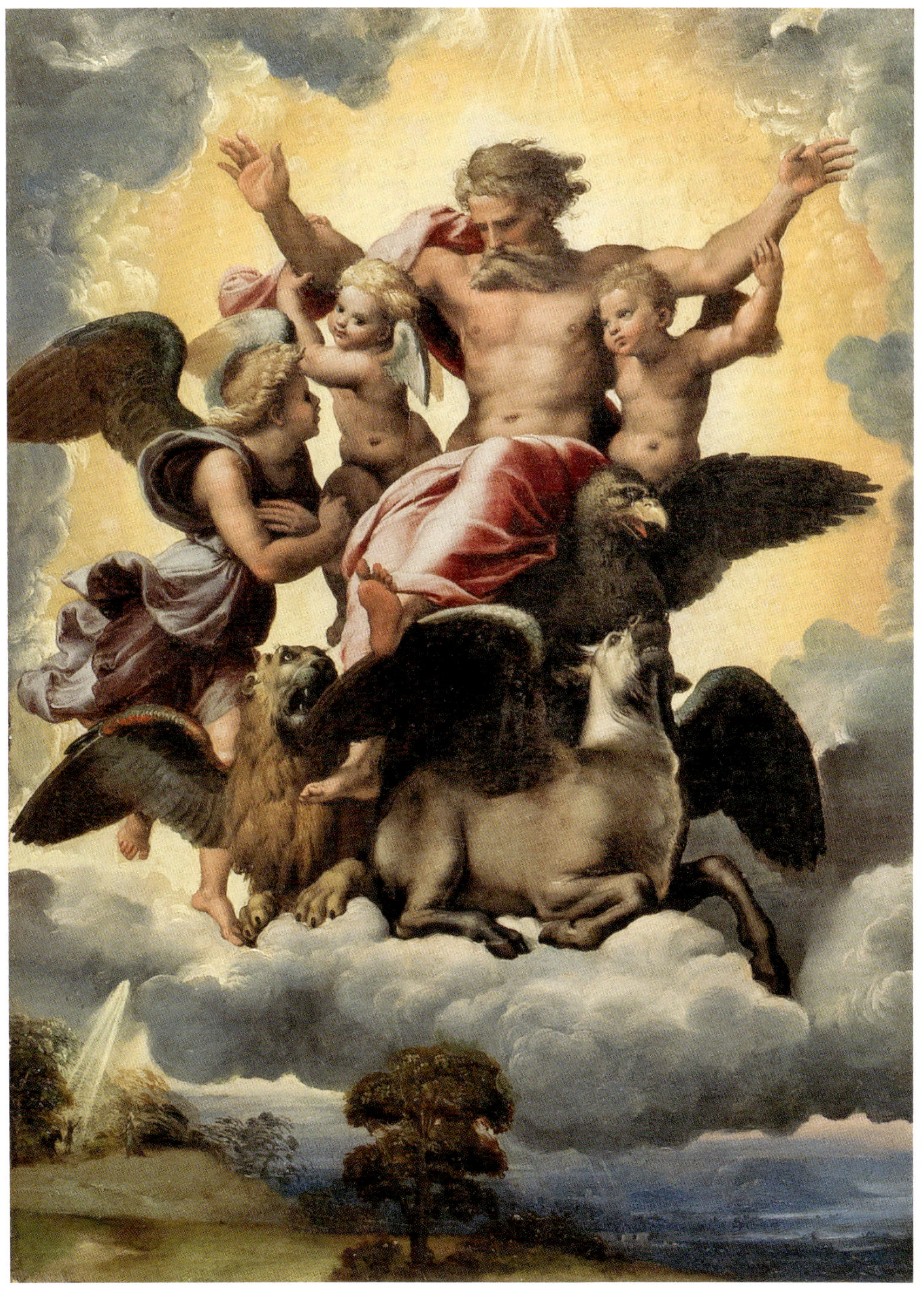

VII.

The World of Antiquity: Beauty and desire, literature and scholarship

1512–1518

Michael Rohlmann

"Raphael, divine man! It is you
who by degree elevated me to the antique!
It is you, sublime painter!"

JACQUES-LOUIS DAVID, 1793

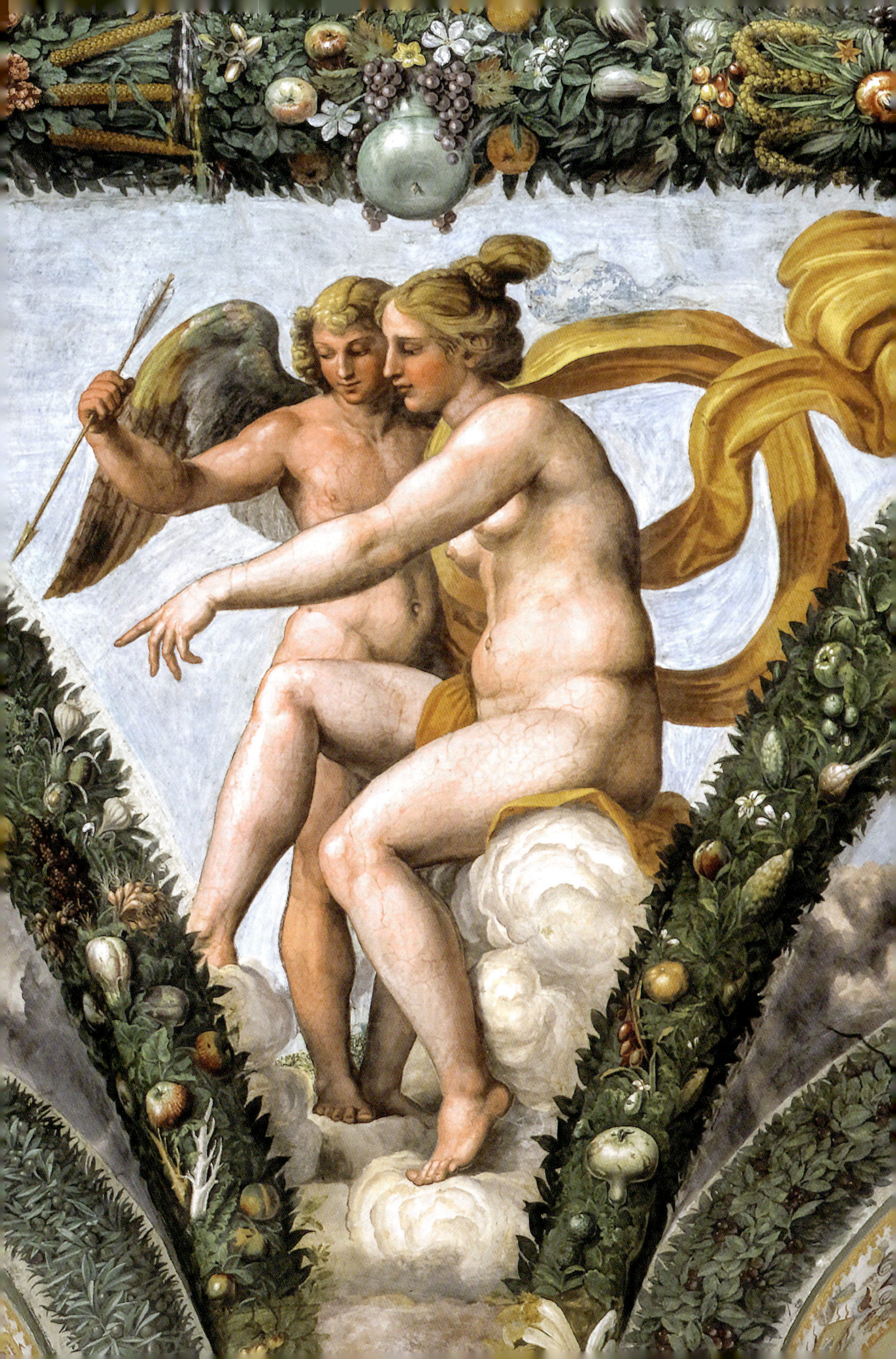

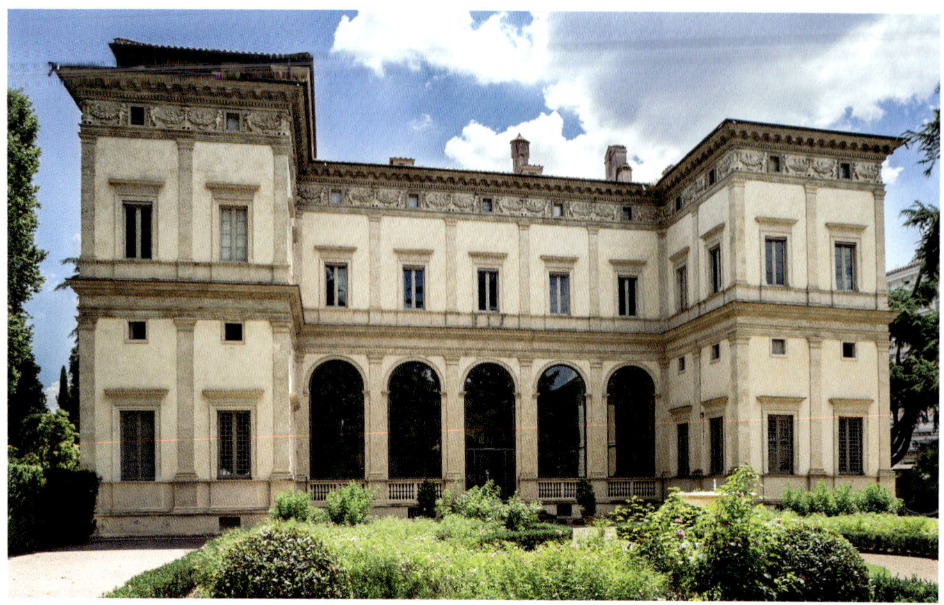

The opportunity to create a large-scale representation of antique myths and sensual nudes presented itself to Raphael for the first time in the luxury villa of Agostino Chigi. The merchant and banker was the richest Roman of his day. His large villa on the new Via Lungara, on the right bank of the Tiber, was completed in 1511. The building, today called the Villa Farnesina (after later owners), lies between the slopes of the Janiculum hill and the Tiber River, directly in front of the Trastevere city wall. It was designed by the painter and architect Baldassare Peruzzi (1481–1536), who – like Chigi himself – originally came from Siena. The villa was surrounded by a wide garden leading down to the banks of the Tiber. Antiquities and a wealth of paintings adorned the complex. Chigi not only hosted his famous banquets here, with guests drawn from Roman curial society, but declared this "place of leisure" the new focal point of his life. Poets under Chigi's

Page 389
Loggia di Psiche: **Venus and Cupid**, 1518
Fresco

View of the façade of the Villa Farnesina, Rome

Loggia di Psiche: **Cupid and the Graces**, 1518
Fresco

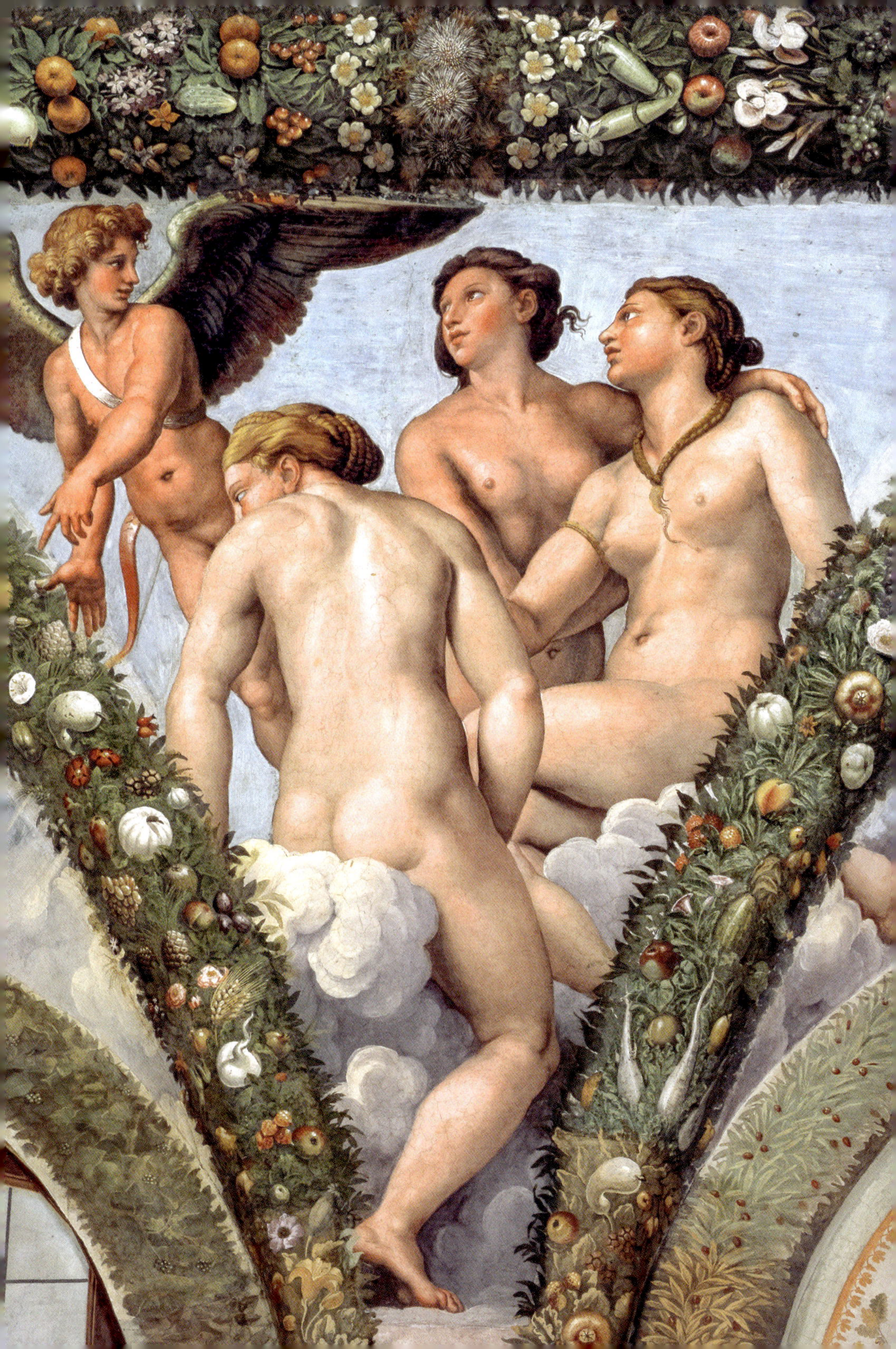

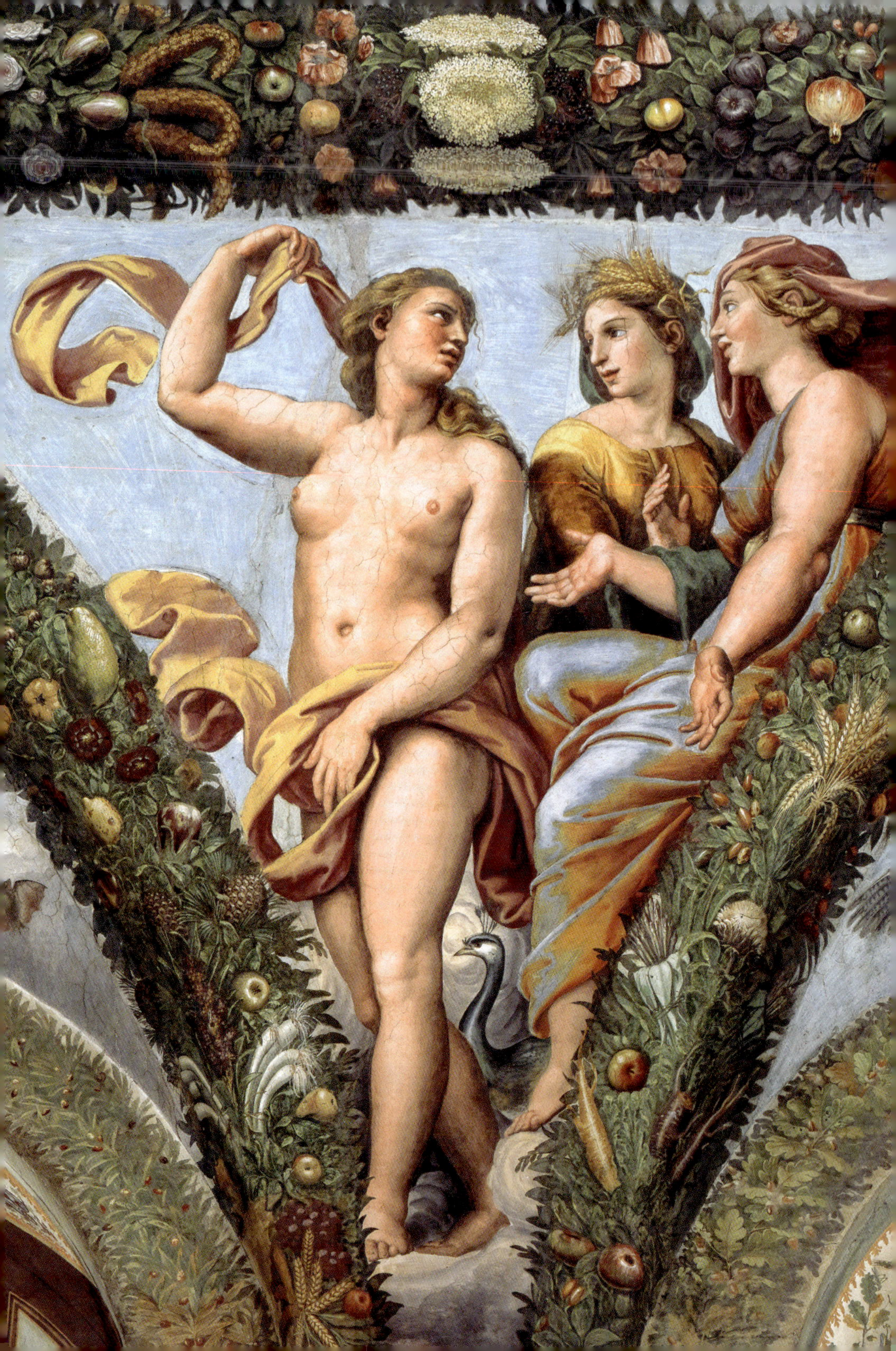

patronage praised the villa as a palace of Venus and Cupid and proclaimed that here the gods of antiquity had once again returned to Rome. Peruzzi embarked on the task of decorating the complex with frescoes. A few remnants and some copy drawings are all that survive of a chiaroscuro façade painting, whose themes were taken from antique mythology. One scene on the ground floor was particularly well known for the erotic appeal of its close-up representation of an amorous Mars and Venus (Turner 2017). Peruzzi decorated Chigi's study and office with a frieze of mythological scenes running below the wooden ceiling. The high point of Peruzzi's painting in the villa was the frescoing of the vault in the east loggia, which faces onto the garden and the river. Within a painted framing system, planetary gods, signs of the zodiac and constellations in mythological images combine to form a representation of the heavens exactly as they appeared at the moment of Chigi's birth. The programme was evidently inspired by Chigi's large family coat of arms, originally depicted in the centre of the vault, in which a star rises over hills. In the lunettes beneath this astrological vault, Sebastiano del Piombo, whom Chigi had brought from Venice to Rome in 1511, painted mythological air and bird scenes from the *Metamorphoses* by Ovid (43 BC–17 AD). This painted glorification of the view from the loggia – of nature and the sky, of stars, birds, the riverbank and the water – is complemented by two large wall frescoes: above the door at the southern end of the longitudinal wall, the giant *Polyphemus* executed by Sebastiano looks out at the sea from under trees (p. 419). The focus of the mighty shepherd's gaze and romantic yearning can be found in the adjacent mural field, painted by Raphael. Here the beautiful nymph Galatea rides in her shell chariot over the water, surrounded by her entourage. The three sections of wall following the *Voyage of Galatea* (p. 421; Cat. F10) remained undecorated under Chigi. The altogether five mural fields were all separated in the same fashion by pilasters and could each have been filled with a stand-alone picture. Instead, however, the frescoes in the first two fields combined into a double scene whose contents were mutually related, and in so doing robbed the pilaster frames of their function as the demarcations between separate subjects. The double picture by Sebastiano and Raphael did not allow itself to be extended into a visual sequence through the addition of further love scenes. This was the conclusion reached in the seventeenth century, too, when the three remaining wall sections were filled with a continuous landscape view, extending Galatea's sea to the right towards another shore, mountains and plains.

Loggia di Psiche: **Venus before Ceres and Juno**, 1518
Fresco

A look at Peruzzi's ceiling frescoes explains why Chigi had only the two left-hand sections of the loggia wall decorated. Sebastiano and Raphael's double picture appears beneath the planetary image of Venus overhead and thereby underscores her central importance, among all the other planetary gods, for the villa's owner and for the villa's function. Polyphemus, Galatea and her amorous entourage are thus declared astrological children of Venus. Chigi shows that, of all the possible aspects of his birth horoscope painted on the vault, only the one represented by the goddess of love is to be granted a role here. The presence of the pair of pictures thus stands in direct parallel to the descriptions by the poets, who were simultaneously lauding the building as the residence of Venus and Cupid. The intended relationship between the wall and ceiling frescoes is reinforced by affinities between their forms and motifs: Raphael's naked nymph standing in a seashell clearly rivals Peruzzi's goddess of love. In his representation of Venus wringing out her hair, Peruzzi had in turn based himself on the *Venus Anadyomene* by the antique painter Apelles (4th century BC), a work known only from a literary description, and had thus reconstructed a lost masterpiece of Greek painting. Rome's literati regularly compared Raphael with Apelles, the mythical master of grace. With his *Galatea* below the *Venus Anadyomene*, Raphael has invited this comparison himself.

Sebastiano and Raphael's double picture has a poetic quality and invites multiple interpretations. Art-historical scholarship was perhaps not the first to see a connection between the wealthy Polyphemus's yearning for love and Chigi's own attempts to woo first the Duke of Mantua's daughter, and second – this time successfully – a young Venetian beauty. In the loggia opening out onto nature, the giant's gaze at the water could be understood as a mythical exaltation of the real view of the Tiber that could be formerly enjoyed from here. Moreover, Sebastiano shows the huge Polyphemus sitting and resting, holding a flute and contemplating beauty. Like Chigi and visitors to the villa, he is giving himself over to leisure *(otium)*, the arts and the pleasure of looking. In his position above the door leading into the interior of the villa, he becomes a figure of identification for the patron as for every viewer. The giant's frescoed dog seems to be a portrait and originally probably lay as a *trompe l'œil* right on top of the actual lintel. Raphael made the horizon higher in the *Galatea* than in Sebastiano's fresco, in order to be able to distribute his figures more clearly and harmoniously within the space. In this way, he demarcates his sea picture from the fictional reality of Sebastiano's shore scene. This allows us to see Polyphemus, who in the myth gazes enraptured at the sea nymph with whom he has fallen in love, at the same time as someone who is looking at a painting and who is a lover of Raphael's art. In the antique story, the giant's yearning remains unfulfilled: Galatea pays no heed to his courtship. Like Raphael's painting, the beautiful nymph remains at a far remove. The central topos of the great tradition of Italian love poetry is thereby invoked: the eulogistic

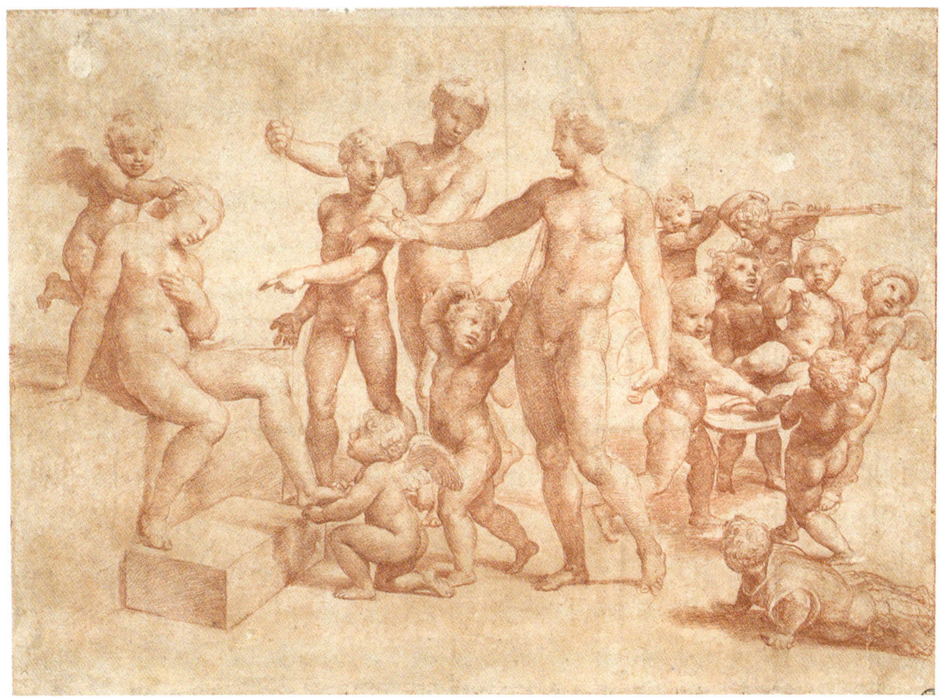

Marriage of Alexander and Roxane, compositional study for Agostino Chigi's bedroom in the Villa Farnesina, 1517
Red chalk over metal stylus underdrawing, piece of paper inserted top right, 22.9 × 31.2 cm (9 ⅛ × 12 ¼ in). Vienna, Albertina

description of, and appeal to, the unattainable beloved. Sebastiano's *Polyphemus* becomes the model for the poets and artists working for Chigi, and Raphael's *Galatea* the successor to Dante's Beatrice and Petrarch's Laura.

What distinguishes Raphael's painted Petrarchan love sonnet? It is the harmony of the sea creatures, pairs of lovers and winged cupids who encircle the beautiful nymph like rhymes, and who reply to each other left and right, front and back, above and below. Galatea herself appears in the particularly artistic, twisting pose of a *figura serpentinata* and thereby follows the *Leda* (p. 69) with which Leonardo had introduced this motif for the female nude. But unlike Leda, Raphael's Galatea takes possession of her surroundings with her turning motif and seems to set the beings playing around her, too, into a broad circular motion. The whole picture is thus interwoven with harmonious movement.

Raphael enriches his pictorial invention with motifs – the passage across the sea, the wheel, wings, the draperies billowing like sails in the wind, the restless state, and above

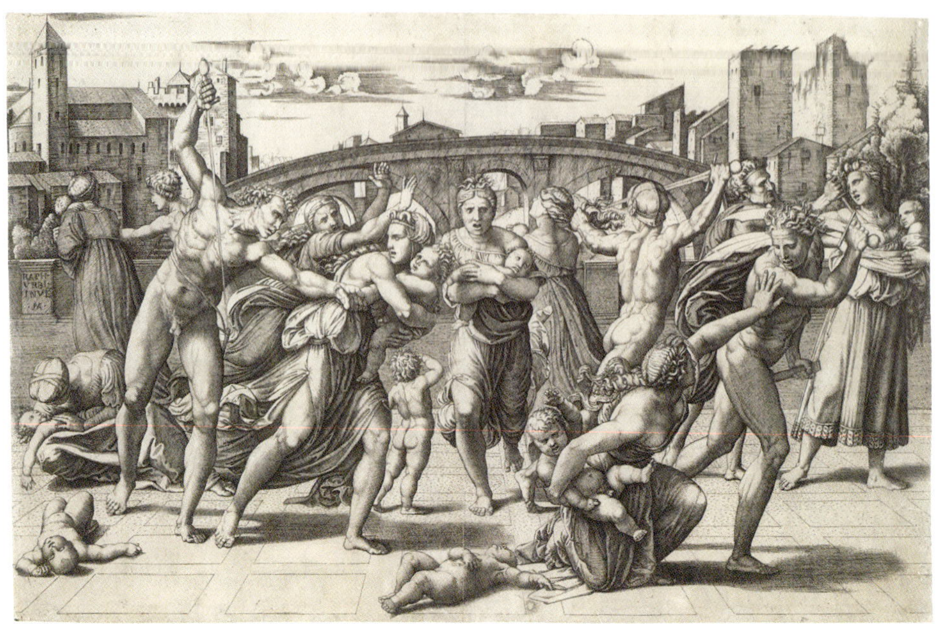

all the hair streaming away from the face of Galatea, a nymph and the swimming boy – that belong to the thematic sphere of *fortuna* and *occasio*, of luck and fortune and of the favourable opportunity that presents itself, hastens away or is to be seized (Thoenes 2019). In a motif that dominates the picture, Galatea's wind-swept hair is set against, accompanied and in this way amplified by her red draperies. All of this may allude, in the first instance, to the opportunities that present themselves in matters of love and which are to be firmly seized or alternatively which quickly disappear. Going a step further, however, we might also recognise here a fundamental principle of life and action: Chigi, as an entrepreneur of the early modern period, pursued the business opportunities that presented themselves to him boldly and watchfully, keeping an eye out like Polyphemus and grasping hold like the Triton in the foreground. Painted below Chigi's horoscope, in other words, might be the principle with which – starting from the personal aptitudes, circumstances and conditions mapped out in the stars – life was to be mastered.

For Raphael himself as a painter, *Galatea* also seems to have been a representation of her artistic process of creation. In *Parnassus* (p. 184 b.; Cat. F3.1k), by incorporating his own portrait Raphael had claimed for himself, too, the higher inspiration of the poets, the *numine afflatur* of being "breathed upon by the spirit". A text purporting to be a letter from Raphael to Castiglione, published for the first time only in 1554, declares that Raphael is raising his thoughts to higher things ("io mi levo col pensier più alto") and

Marcantonio Raimondi after Raphael
The Massacre of the Innocents, *c.* 1510
Copperplate engraving,
27.4 × 42.7 cm (10 ¾ × 16 ¾ in)
Vienna, Albertina

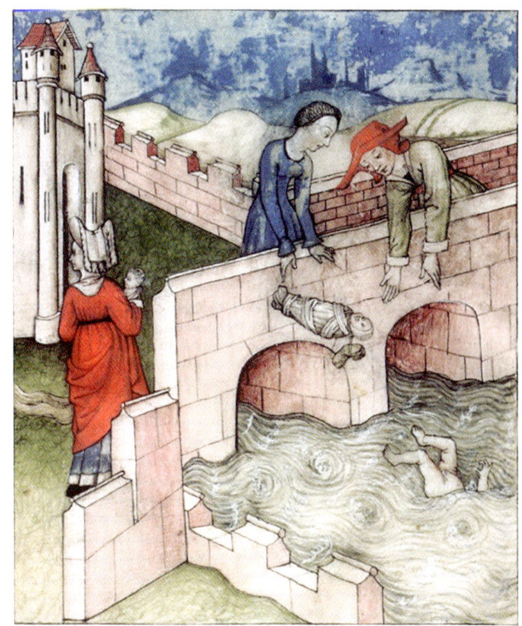

Mothers throwing their children into the Tiber (founding history of the Santo Spirito hospital in Rome), *c.* 1450–1467
Illuminated manuscript on parchment
from: *Histoire en image de la fondation de l'Hôpital du Saint-Esprit de Dijon*,
inv. Arch. hosp., A H4, fol. 7
Dijon, Centre Hospitalier Universitaire

that for the representation of Galatea he has used not models from nature but a certain idea that came into his mind ("io mi servo di certa Iddea che mi viene nella mente"). Raphael's Galatea, his personification of beauty, with her billowing robes and hair, indeed seems seized by divine inspiration. The transported gaze of her sparkling eyes is raised above the sensual cavorting around her into the bright sky. It is the look of inspiration worn by Apollo and Homer in *Parnassus*. Thus Galatea is also a child of Apollo, the god of the arts, who appears directly above her in the spandrel painted by Peruzzi and who likewise gazes heavenward as he makes music. In this context, the *amorini* who are aiming their love darts at Galatea perhaps took on an additional meaning. As *spiritelli*, winged spirits of inspiration, they send their arrows down from heaven. Raphael claimed a higher inspiration in and for his fresco and thus demarcates himself and his art from Sebastiano del Piombo's emphatic imitation of nature and from the lower pipe music of the creature of nature, Polyphemus.

A few years later, Chigi embarked on a second decoration campaign in his villa. It was evidently undertaken in conjunction with his planned wedding: in 1519 he married his long-time lover, a young Venetian woman of low birth with whom he already had several children. In 1518 Raphael's workshop frescoed the vault of the villa's entrance loggia on the basis of designs by the master. The subject was the love story of Cupid and Psyche (Cat. F11) told by Apuleius (*c.* 123–after 170 [?]). Unlike in Raphael's fresco in the

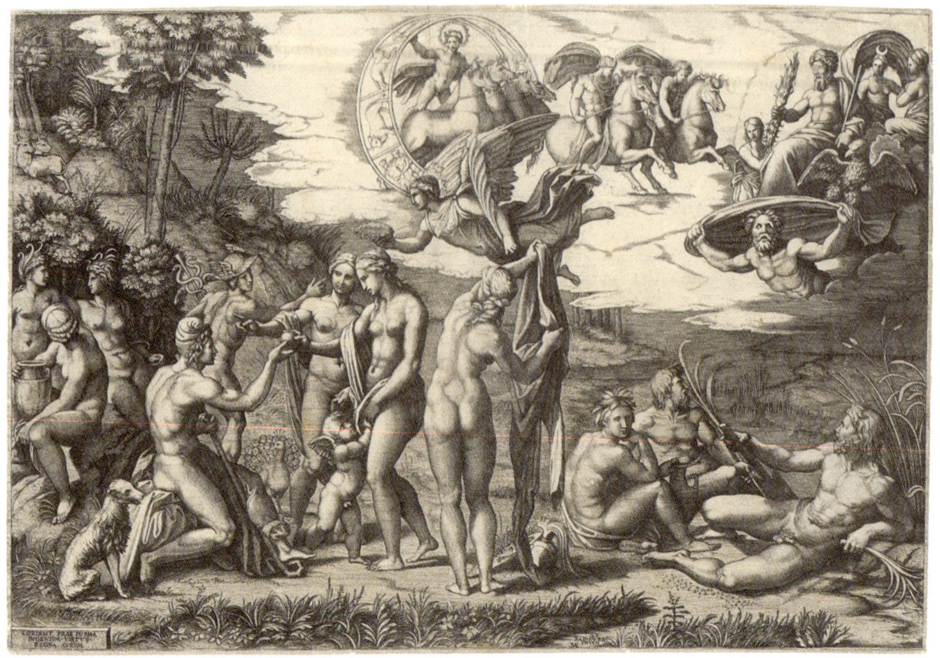

Marcantonio Raimondi after Raphael, **The Judgement of Paris**, *c.* 1513/14
Copper engraving; 1st state, 29.4 × 43.7 cm (11⅝ × 17¼ in). Vienna, Albertina

garden loggia, here the pictorial narrative does not remain distanced from the world of the viewer; instead, we enter the space of the story ourselves, becoming, as it were, a witness and a participant in the narrative. The loggia above our heads seems to be completely filled with mythological figures and the events unfold around us.

Through Raphael's design, the vault is transformed into the fiction of a garden pergola open to the heavens. Between framing festoons of fruits and vegetables, sensual naked figures float life-size against a sky of an originally much stronger blue. Moving with comfortable ease, they effortlessly fill the awkward, slanted and curved spaces of the triangular fields of the vault. Famous is the art with which Raphael portrays the female nude from all sides for the delectation of viewers from Roman male society. Thus the women must turn and stretch; they may get excited, fawn over and nestle up to one another. A further feast for the eyes is provided by the boundless variety of exotic as well as native plants and fruits, together with birds and mythical creatures of all different kinds. In the lunettes, erotes carrying attributes they have seized as booty from the gods proclaim the general theme of love that conquers everything and everyone – even celestial deities.

In the spandrels, the gods debate Psyche's fate. Worshipped on earth for her extraordinary beauty, she presented a rival to Venus. The goddess of love therefore wished to have Psyche punished by Cupid, but he himself fell in love with the beautiful mortal. Psyche was transported to his palace, where Cupid joined her at night. Intrigue, separation and flight, wanderings, the wrath of Venus and various trials had to be overcome before the council of the gods finally bestowed immortality upon Psyche and allowed her to marry Cupid at the banquet of the gods. In keeping with their location on the loggia ceiling, the frescoes show only the parts of the story that take place in heaven. Pain, fear, adversity and suffering are omitted. In the centre of the vault, the large, wide concluding scenes of the *Council of the Gods* and the *Wedding Banquet* (pp. 422/423; Cat. F11l and 11m) are rendered as simulated tapestries, but otherwise with no differentiation from the other spandrel figures in terms of figural scale, staging or the representation of clouds and sky. By emphasising the fictional character of seemingly antique works of tapestry, Raphael avoided having to show extreme, visually disrupting foreshortenings corresponding to the location of the scenes high overhead. At the same time, he plays with the perception of the viewer and challenges us to distinguish between different levels of reality.

For the viewer entering the loggia, the story begins on the left: with her outstretched arm pointing towards the outside world, Venus is indicating to her son Cupid the figure of Psyche, whom we must supply in our imagination (p. 389; Cat. F11a). Visitors who followed her gesture and looked leftwards, away from Chigi's palace, into the distance, would formerly have seen the historical centre of Rome with its Banchi district on the other side of the Tiber. This was where Chigi had lived before moving into the love palace of his villa. The painted story is thus activated by the viewer's own reality and world of experience, as if Cupid is to seek the universally admired Psyche in Rome itself. In the next spandrel, the loveliest of the entire sequence, Cupid in turn gestures outside the pictorial field. He wants to show Psyche, who has now been brought to his palace, to the Three Graces, so that they may serve his new beloved (p. 391; Cat. F11b). Cupid points downwards in the direction of the loggia's left-hand end wall. From here, a door opens onto the adjacent garden loggia with its wall fresco of Galatea (pp. 418, 419), the highly famed ideal of female beauty. In the fresco, Raphael had staged Galatea like a naked goddess of love with seashells, amorini and pairs of lovers. In comparison to the Venus painted on the ceiling above her by Peruzzi, Galatea could thus claim superiority. For the viewer in the entrance loggia, the naked nymph might represent a playful allusion to Psyche, who had been worshipped by the people as the new Venus, aroused the jealousy of the goddess of love as a result, and who was now in Chigi's palace of love. With Cupid's pointing gesture, Raphael thus incorporated the villa's existing decoration, executed a few years earlier, into his new cycle. The case is similar for the right-hand end wall of the Psyche loggia. The pictorial narrative at this point omits Psyche's flight, her trials and tasks, efforts and adventures. A door in this wall led into Chigi's office and study, which Peruzzi had had decorated with a pictorial frieze depicting the Labours of Hercules, together with other mythological scenes in which the protagonists are threatened by dangers, punishments, violence, pain and death. What here mirrored, in myth, the adversities faced by Chigi, the villa's owner, in his life in commerce, could also represent the travails and sufferings of Psyche.

A particular attraction of Raphael's Psyche frescoes lies in the mischievous, surprising connections that are orchestrated between the divine protagonists and the vegetal motifs in the framing garlands. Thus Mercury, the messenger of the gods, (p. 415; Cat. F11f), who is calling all to search for Psyche and appears to be flying into the loggia, indicates with his raised arm towards a pornographic detail composed of a marrow, aubergine and a split-open fig. This is perhaps an allusion to the erotic pleasures which Mercury, in Apuleius's text, promises as a reward to the finder of the wandering Psyche.

Mounted at the centre of the festoons in the middle of the vault is a large golden shield bearing the coat of arms of the Della Rovere pope Julius II. It stems from the period in which the villa was built. Raphael's new frescoes integrate the shield into the pictorial fiction and create the illusion that it is fastened to the pergola with ribbons. Julius had formerly taken Chigi into his family and granted him the right to incorporate the Della Rovere coat of arms into his own. In line with the Italian meaning of their name, the Della Rovere used the oak tree as their heraldic device. Oaks and acorns were omnipresent during Julius's pontificate and the central motif of papal panegyric. The oak was a symbol of strength and the tree of the supreme god, Jupiter. Acorns were considered the food of humankind during the golden age of the distant past. The gods of the loggia frescoes, too, are interested in acorns as the fruits of the heraldic main motif at the centre of the ceiling decoration. Thus Cupid not only gestures the Graces towards Psyche, who is invisible to the viewer, but also points with his index finger to three acorns in the garland beside him (p. 391; Cat. F11b). One of the Graces is already looking at these acorns, while her two companions seem to have discovered further acorns above Cupid's head and wings. Venus, sinking pleadingly before Jupiter, indicates with her open hand towards a cluster of acorns (p. 404; Cat. F11e). As Psyche presents Venus with the jar signalling her completed task, the goddess of love's line of sight extends to acorns in the framing festoon (Cat. F11h). The palm of the hand that Venus raises above Psyche

Loggia di Psiche: **Venus in Her Chariot**, 1518
Fresco

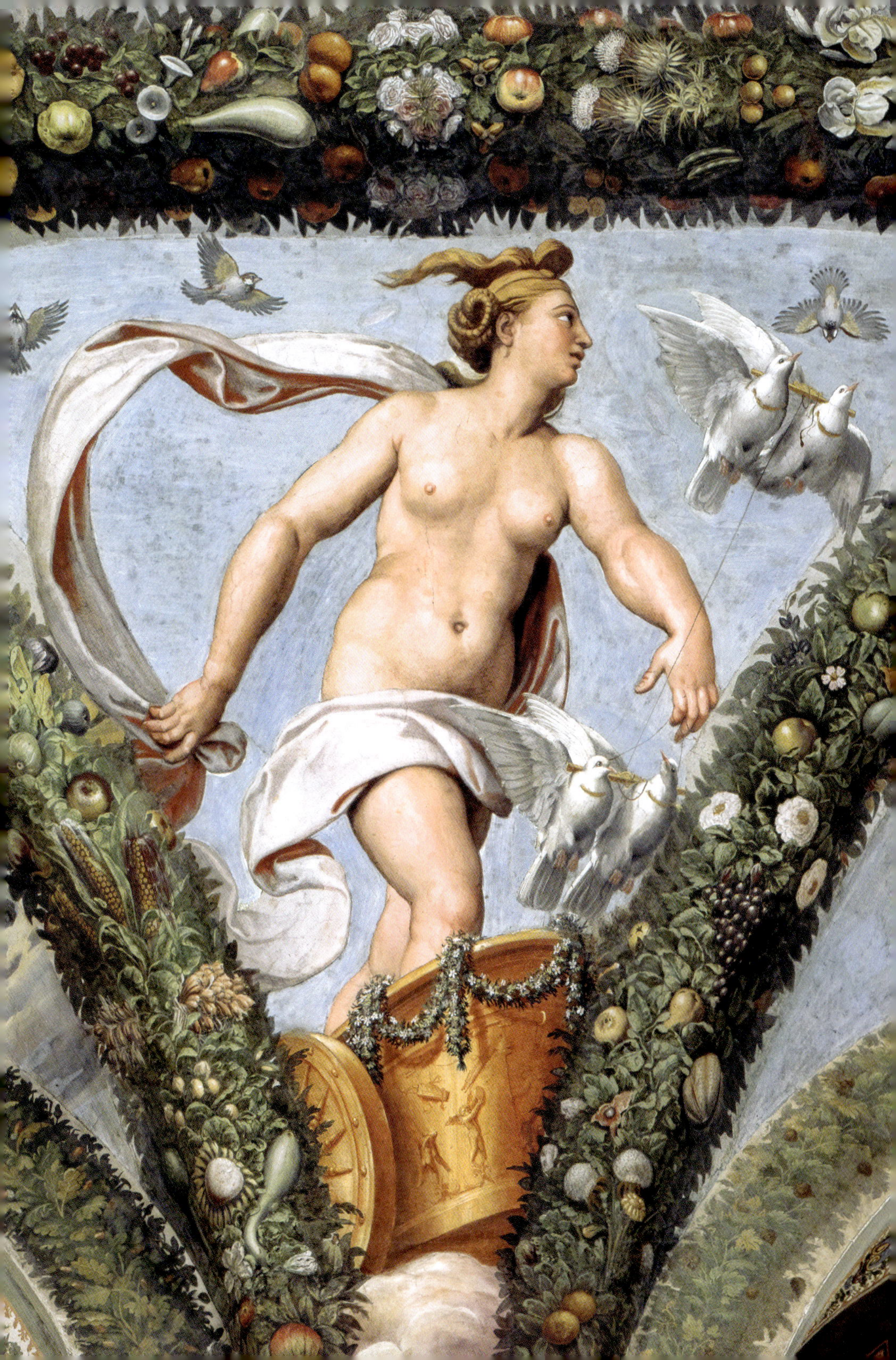

faces towards acorns. Jupiter's gaze, as he kisses Cupid, can likewise be extended in the direction of acorns (Cat. F11j). As Mercury carries Psyche up to the heavens, she, too, looks upwards to acorns, which appear in a cluster precisely where the divine messenger touches the garland with his staff and hand (Cat. F11k). In the centre of the ceiling, lastly, a parallel is established between the oak motif – conferred upon Chigi – of the coat of arms surrounded by an oak wreath, and ambrosia, the drink of the gods. Bacchus, erotes and Ganymede serve the drink at the banquet of the gods (pp. 426/427; Cat. F11m), and Psyche is granted immortality with the cup of ambrosia handed to her by Mercury at the council of the gods (pp. 424/425; Cat. F11l).

The story of Cupid and Psyche is an allegory of love (Latin, *amor*) and the soul (Greek, *psyche*): in love, the human soul raises itself up to the gods. Contemporary viewers were able to interpret Raphael's painted allegorical story in different ways, relating it for example to their own self or to Chigi's bride. If they based their reading upon the central coat of arms and the acorns, they would have seen, in the ascent of Psyche's soul to the gods, a parallel with Chigi's social ascent into the papal family of the oak tree and acorns – as if Chigi's soul had risen to a Delle Rovere world of gods.

In 1518, when the loggia frescoes were executed, an overt panegyric in praise of the Della Rovere oak was problematic in Medicean Rome. In 1516 Pope Leo X had ousted Julius's nephew Francesco Maria della Rovere as ruler of Raphael's native Urbino and replaced him with his own nephew, Lorenzo de' Medici. Only a long and costly war against Francesco had brought Lorenzo dominion in Urbino. It is a sign of Chigi's self-confidence and power that he celebrated his connection with the Della Rovere in the decoration of his villa – even if in the form of an entertaining game of hidden clues for his palace guests to discover and solve. In 1518 Raphael himself thus had the opportunity not only to publicly praise the Medici, and in particular Lorenzo, to the French royal house in gifts of art, but at the same time to express his loyalty – in a discreet and witty manner – to his old Della Rovere patrons, who had been driven into exile by the Medici.

Apart from Chigi, none of Raphael's other clients received large-format mythological paintings. But even for Chigi, Raphael left the execution of the frescoes in the Loggia di Psyche almost entirely to his workshop. Raphael prepared a depiction of the Marriage of Alexander the Great and the Persian princess Roxane, evidently planned for Chigi's bedroom, in compositional studies (p. 395 and KMOF 539). The representation was intended to reconstruct a lost antique painting by Aetion (4th century BC), documented in a detailed literary description (ekphrasis) by the author Lucian (*c.* AD 120–after 180). But Raphael's design was not implemented. In his execution of the fresco, Sodoma relied largely on his own invention. From 1513/14 onwards, the Duke of Ferrara tried for years to obtain from Raphael a large painting of the Triumph of Bacchus. But in this case, too,

Raphael ultimately produced only a drawing (Vienna, Albertina, inv. 444). The Duke's envoy was fobbed off again and again.

In the Vatican Palace, Cardinal Bibbiena, at least, was able to enjoy the small-format scenes in an antique style that Raphael had designed for his *Stufetta* (pp. 432, 433; Cat. F7.2). This small private room, in which Bibbiena took his sweat baths, imitated ancient forerunners in its function and furnishings. The main pictures show sensual female nudes, mostly in association with water motifs. Venus appears in different poses and from different angles. Love scenes show tender intimacies and are also embellished with isolated pornographic details (Turner 2017). The cycle leads from the birth of Venus to a man ejaculating. Raphael had the scenes reproduced in the form of prints (with the exception of the final scene with Hephaistos, which was evidently too risqué). Printmaking was the medium in which Raphael's designs for antique motifs and myths were widely disseminated and through which they could reach the hands of those who did not number among the few fortunate recipients of his paintings.

Prints served Raphael, like Mantegna and Dürer before him, as an important means of spreading the fame of his art. Raphael seems to have organised the deployment of the medium in systematic fashion and to have exploited it commercially (Bloemacher 2016). He thereby relied above all on Marcantonio Raimondi (1475–1534). Raimondi had previously created engravings on humanist themes for the learned circles of his hometown, the university city of Bologna, and subsequently made copies of Dürer prints in Venice. In Rome he began publishing pictorial inventions by Raphael. He thereby often reproduced motifs and compositions that Raphael had developed for panel paintings or frescoes. Raphael evidently systematically gave Raimondi access to his compositional drawings – even if these latter frequently underwent further changes during their execution in the medium paint. Among this body of prints, a small number of representations stand out for their exceptional degree of artistic sophistication. They were designed by Raphael specifically for printmaking. In them, Raimondi has delivered masterpieces of the art of engraving and printing. It appears that in these cases, too, Raphael started from frescoes on which he was working: their execution evidently fired his imagination in other directions, inspiring him to continue working on individual motifs and ideas and then to expand them into new themes and spectacular artistic inventions. In these, he was able to leave behind the contexts within which the original commission was to be executed.

The earliest example is a biblical subject, *The Massacre of the Innocents* (p. 396). Preliminary drawings show that Raphael developed the subject out of studies for his small ceiling fresco *The Judgement of Solomon* (Cat. F3.1h). There, the soldier standing over a dead child and threatening to kill the living one as a mother tries to prevent him from doing so becomes the starting point for a panoramic view of the New Testament massacre

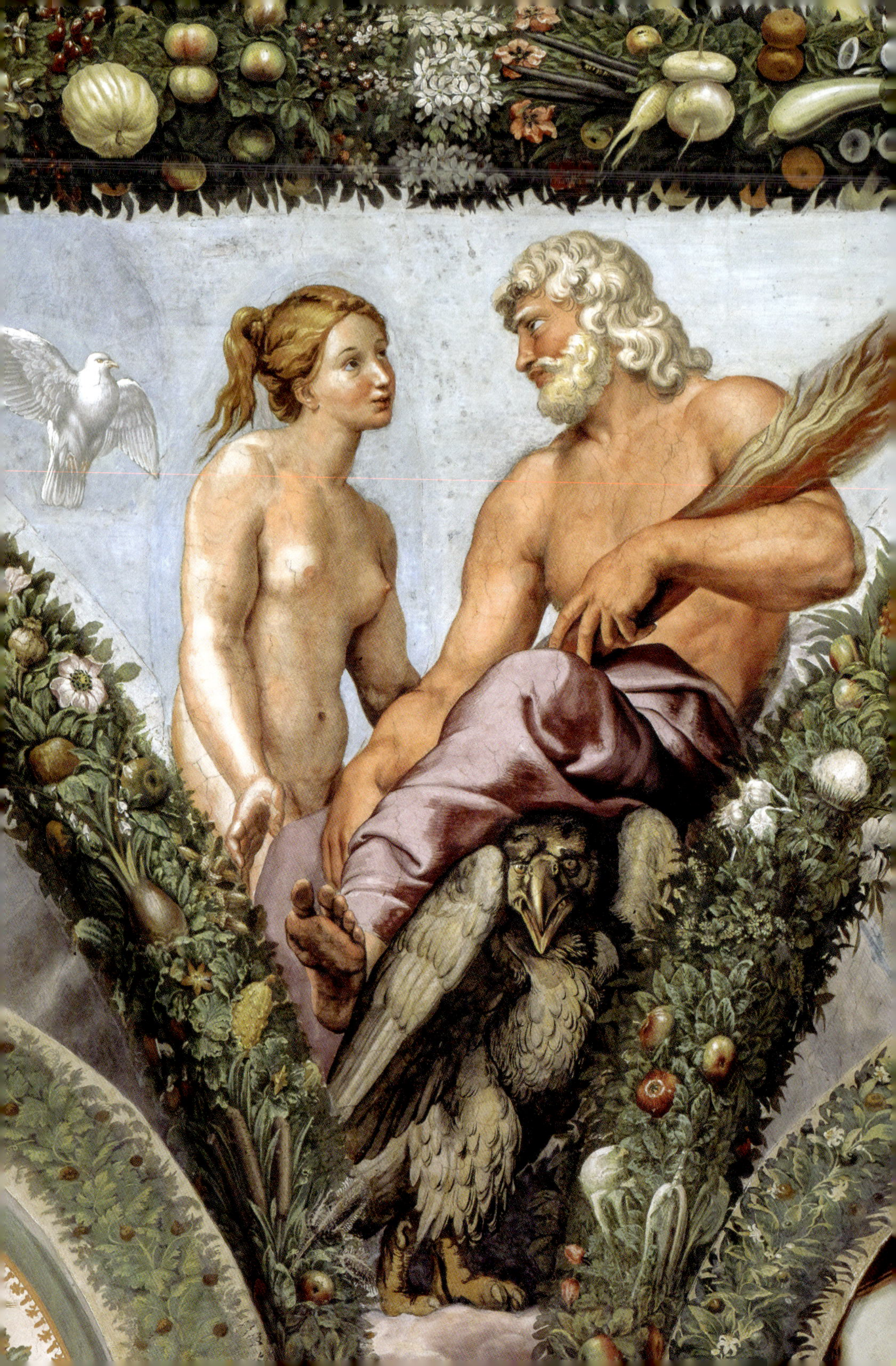

in Bethlehem. Raphael multiplies the situations of fighting and murder into a choreography of cruelty. By means of deliberately difficult artistic challenges and motifs of shocking horror, it was plainly his ambition to outstrip the Florentine tradition of battle scenes, and here above all Michelangelo's *Battle of Cascina* (p. 74). Michelangelo's central figure of a man plunging forward and shouting a warning is transformed into the mother holding her dead child in her arms and hastening towards us with an imploring expression. Unlike Michelangelo, Raphael arranges the tumult of bodies in violent movement not in rows but as a large circle rotating around the central figure. In *Galatea* (Cat. F10) he will then have the sea creatures, some of them in related poses, circle around the nymph; there, however, the central figure likewise adopts a twisting pose and in so doing heightens the aesthetic cohesion to a perfect harmony. The cityscape in the background of the *Massacre of the Innocents* is laid out to match the figural composition. The vedutà of Rome with the Ponte Giudeo (Ponte Fabricio) and Tiber Island has evidently been borrowed from a sketchbook and then adapted to the narrative scene, with the wide arched bridge spanning and structuring the figural composition.

An anti-Jewish tendency perhaps lies in the representation of the Ponte Giudeo (the "Bridge of the Jews") as the background to the massacre ordered by the Jewish king Herod. In Renaissance Rome, however, the association of the Tiber, the bridge and infanticide could have held another topical significance. The combination of motifs might namely be understood as a reference to the pressing moral and social problem of the abandonment and killing of unwanted, illegitimate children. It was because infants were being killed and tossed from bridges into the Tiber that the popes established their largest social institution, the Ospedale di Santo Spirito – thus the hospital's founding legend (p. 397). It not only took in foundlings but also cared for the poor and sick, pregnant women, pilgrims and others in need. Sixtus IV, the uncle of Raphael's papal patron, Julius II, had the hospital entirely renovated and even had the new building depicted in the Sistine Chapel. He also had the interior decorated with fresco cycles illustrating the history of the institution's foundation and the story of his own life. On the end wall, four scenes showed the victims' path from their birth to the presentation of their corpses to the Pope. In between, women were shown killing their newborns and throwing them from the Tiber Bridge into the river. The decorative scheme on this area of wall was subsequently largely destroyed by a Crucifixion fresco inserted at a later date. Its contents can be reconstructed on the basis of inscriptions, however, and from an older representation of the story of the

Loggia di Psiche: **Venus before Jupiter**, 1518
Fresco

hospital's foundation in a French miniature (Presciutti 2015). The theme of the Massacre of the Innocents provided a biblical archetype of every kind of infanticide. Raphael would have become acquainted with this idea at the latest in Florence, whose prominent foundling hospital was called the Ospedale degli Innocenti. As the "Hospital of the Innocents", it established a link between the Massacre of the Innocents and the Florentine newborns who had been abandoned or killed. The biblical mothers desperately trying to save their children were held up to contemporary perpetrators as models of maternal love. If Raphael and Raimondi, in their copper engraving, relocate the Massacre of the Innocents to the Tiber and bridge in Rome, it is probably because their representation, too, is intended as an admonishing appeal to society.

An inscription declares that Raimondi's *The Judgement of Paris* is an invention by Raphael (p. 398). Composition and narrative are clearly borrow from the representation of the theme on two damaged Roman sarcophagi, from which the overall layout and individual ancillary figures were taken. In a spirit of comparative criticism, Raphael combines motifs from both in order to develop a new, idealised antique-style representation. He does not reconstruct an antique relief, but invents a new idealised reality of sensual beauty in landscape and celestial clouds (Fehl 1983). Raphael has replaced the main characters of the Trojan prince and the three goddesses, who have asked him to judge which of them is the fairest, with new inventions. Unlike in the antique reliefs, all three goddesses appear naked. The intention was evidently also to infuse the scene with great eroticism. Raphael's starting point was thereby the double fresco with Polyphemus and Galatea in Chigi's villa (Cat. F10). He turns the shepherd Polyphemus, who marvels at the beauty of the nymph, into Paris the shepherd, who is likewise enjoying the sight of naked women. Resting beside each of them is their sheepdog. Raphael fuses the formal model of the position of Polyphemus's legs (one calf crossed over his shepherd's crook!) with the upper body of the Triton clasping a nymph between Polyphemus and Galatea. The three goddesses present themselves from different angles, so that the viewer of the print, too, can enjoy their beauty from all sides. As in *Galatea*, the female figure on the left is seen from the front (Juno/the Naiad in the foreground), the figure in the centre turning to one side (Venus/Galatea), and the right-hand figure from behind (Minerva/the rear Naiad). Later, in *Cupid and the Graces* (Cat. F11b) and throughout the series of Psyche frescoes, Raphael would reprise the theme of sequences of beautiful female nudes seen from multiple angles. An inscription accompanying *The Judgement of Paris* proclaims that reason, virtue, power and gold seem insignificant next to beauty.

The engraving celebrates beauty and at the same time aesthetic judgement (Damisch 1996). Paris, awarding the prize of the golden apple to Venus, is the figure of identification in the picture for the male viewer, who – like Paris – is also meant to study

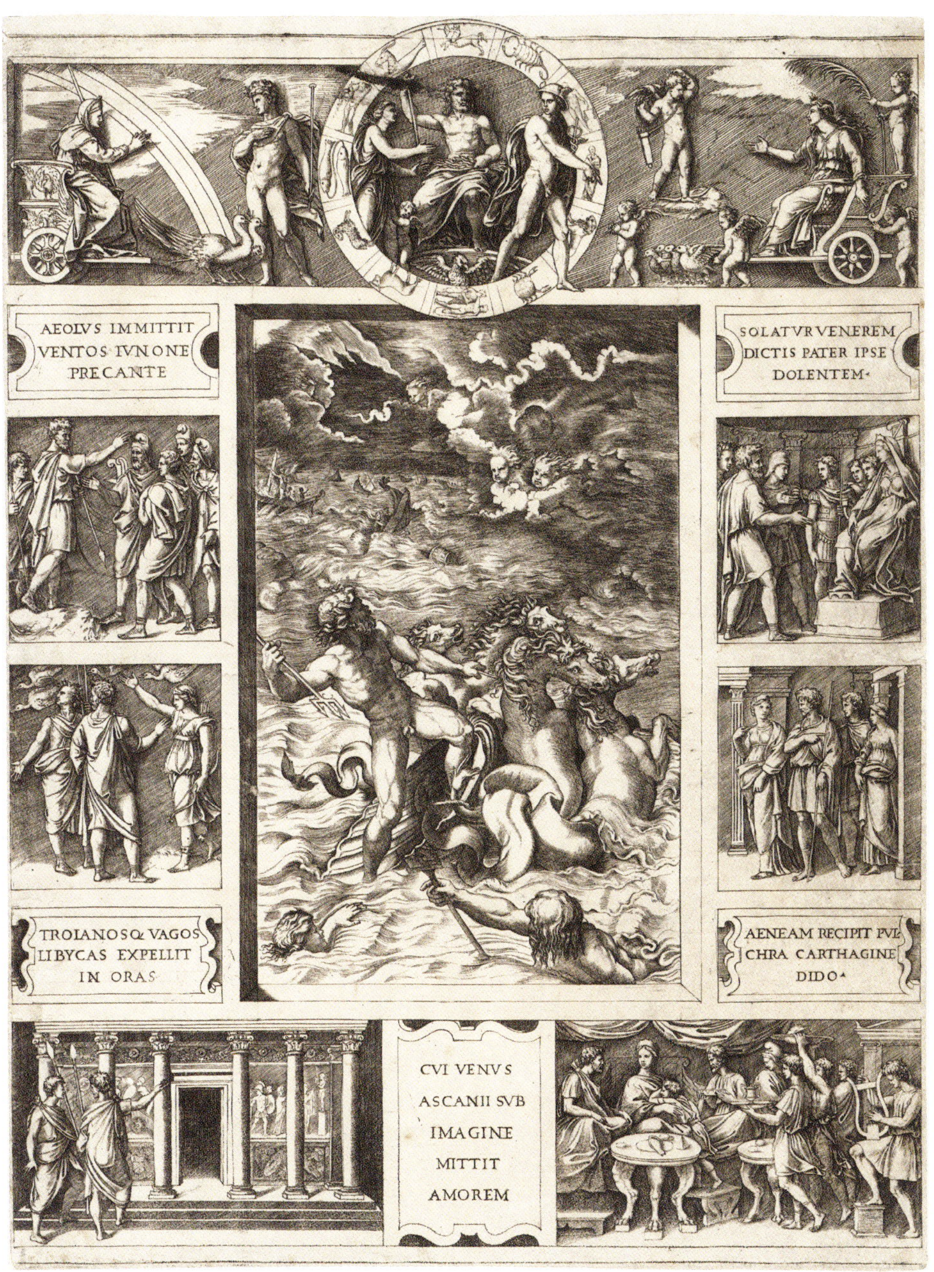

Marcantonio Raimondi after Raphael, ***Quos Ego***, *c.* 1515–1518
Copper engraving, 43.3 × 32.9 cm (17 ⅛ × 12 ⅞ in). Vienna, Albertina

and appreciatively compare the motifs portrayed. Raphael's above-mentioned letter to Castiglione, whose authenticity is disputed, plays with motifs from the story of the Judgement of Paris: Raphael is sending Castiglione several drawings on a theme invented by the latter, because he doesn't want to be the one who makes the final choice. In similar fashion, the three goddesses leave it up to the judgement of Paris to decide which of them wins the prize as the fairest. In Raphael's composition, moreover, Paris – and the viewer – can hone their powers of judgement not only on the three goddesses, but also on the many different nymphs reposing to the left and right of the standing goddesses (Viljoen 2019). With regard to Galatea, Raphael adds: in order to paint one beauty ("una bella"), he needs to look at several. And this on the condition that Castiglione is with him and picks out the best one. Unfortunately, however, beautiful women and good judgements – thus the letter – are both in short supply. Raphael plays here with a topical legend, according to which the ancient Greek painter Zeuxis (5th/4th century BC), for his representation of a beautiful woman, combined the best parts of various young women of Croton. Raphael and Raimondi's *Judgement of Paris* is, in a sense, a rival design to the model, lent shape in *Galatea*, of an artist who obtains beauty from higher inspiration ("certa Iddea che mi viene nella mente"). *The Judgement of Paris* praises aesthetic judgement acquired through comparison and the principle of selection *(electio)*. It is to this that Raphael and Raimondo's engraving itself owes its form, since Raphael used critical comparison and the combination of various sources for its composition.

In his fresco *Fire in the Borgo* (p. 231 t.; Cat. F3.3l), Raphael placed the victims of the catastrophe and their suffering – conveyed through a rich variety of emotional states and reactions – in the near foreground, while showing the Pope delivering his saving blessing like a small, distant apparition in the background. In the group formed by the man who is carrying his aged father out of the fire, accompanied by his son, Raphael makes a visual allusion – aimed at his literary-minded audience – to Virgil's account of the escape of Aeneas from burning Troy. Old father Anchises is also a portrait of Cosimo de' Medici, the famous progenitor of the papal family. Just as Cosimo had been expelled from Florence in 1433, so Pope Leo X, while still a cardinal, had been forced to flee his native city in 1494. The Medici then found a new home as a papal family in Rome. In the copper engraving *The Plague in Phrygia* (also known as *The Morbetto*; p. 410), Raphael repeated and varied formal and content-related motifs from the *Fire in the Borgo* in order to illustrate a scene taken directly from *The Aeneid*. The catastrophe here is a plague. The Trojans, who had fled their home, were directed by the god Apollo to return to the land of their ancestors. They mistakenly believed they had found their old homeland on Crete. Here, however, they are struck by a plague. One night, the images of the penates, i. e. the household gods, appear to the sleeping Aeneas in the moonlight streaming in through a window and bring him a comforting message. They explain that the true land of his ancestors is not Crete, but Italy. There a future, dominion and a great empire await the hero and his people. As in the *Fire in the Borgo*, different groups afflicted by suffering fill the foreground in *The Plague in Phrygia*. Once again the ruins of the Roman Forum serve as the setting; once again steps in the background lead up to a distant vision of holy figures who are bringing aid. The motif of flight to a new homeland, only a sub-theme of the *Fire in the Borgo*, here becomes the central element of the story. Raphael competes with Virgil's verses, which are at the same time inscribed in the engraving. He furthermore cites and varies existing models from ancient as well as contemporary art.

Raphael offers a haunting visual description of the plague. Light effects are deployed in magnificent fashion to convey the atmosphere. On the left, in the nocturnal glow of the torch, man and beast discover the dead carcasses. As if in a second step in the narrative, the plague also claims human victims on the right and thereby also in the more immediate foreground. The horror increases in broad daylight. After the discovery of the plague victims on the left, the reactions on the right range from utter despair to flight, seeking to shield oneself and offering assistance. A man tries to save a child from the lethal danger of touching its dead mother and to keep it away from the corpse's breast. Here Raphael has introduced an antique topos into his composition, as he did with the Aeneas group in the *Fire in the Borgo*. According to Pliny (AD 23–79), Aristides of Thebes – a Greek artist of the 4th century BC whom Pliny credits as the first to depict human emotions and feelings – executed a painting of the sack of a city. In this work, a child could be seen crawling towards the breast of its fatally wounded mother as she lay dying. Raphael was able to study the motif of the woman in a marble statue of a Dead Amazon, discovered in 1514 in Rome (Wouk 2016/17).

In *Quos Ego* (p. 407), Raphael and Raimondi take the *paragone* (artistic competition) with Virgil's poetry pursued in *The Plague in Phrygia* to a climax (Kleinbub 2012; Ciccuto 2016; Faietti 2020). For Aeneas's journey, Raphael entrusts himself, as it were, to the guidance of Virgil, beside whose pointing hand he had portrayed himself in the *Parnassus*. Inspired by antique reliefs (*Tabulae Iliacae* or "Iliad tablets"), which structure the various scenes from the story of Troy into a pictorial system (Nees 1978), images and texts combine here, too, into an extremely skilful ensemble. It illustrates the events of Book One of *The Aeneid* from beginning to end. In the centre, within what looks like a stone-carved frame decorated with fictive pictorial reliefs and tablets bearing inscriptions, we see a view of the dramatic and linguistic high point of Book One: mighty Neptune rises from the depths to quell the violent winds and storm that have threatened and devastated the Trojan fleet. The scenes and inscriptions around the sides complement the central scene by explaining what has gone before (Juno, top left, sends out the wind god Aeolus) and what

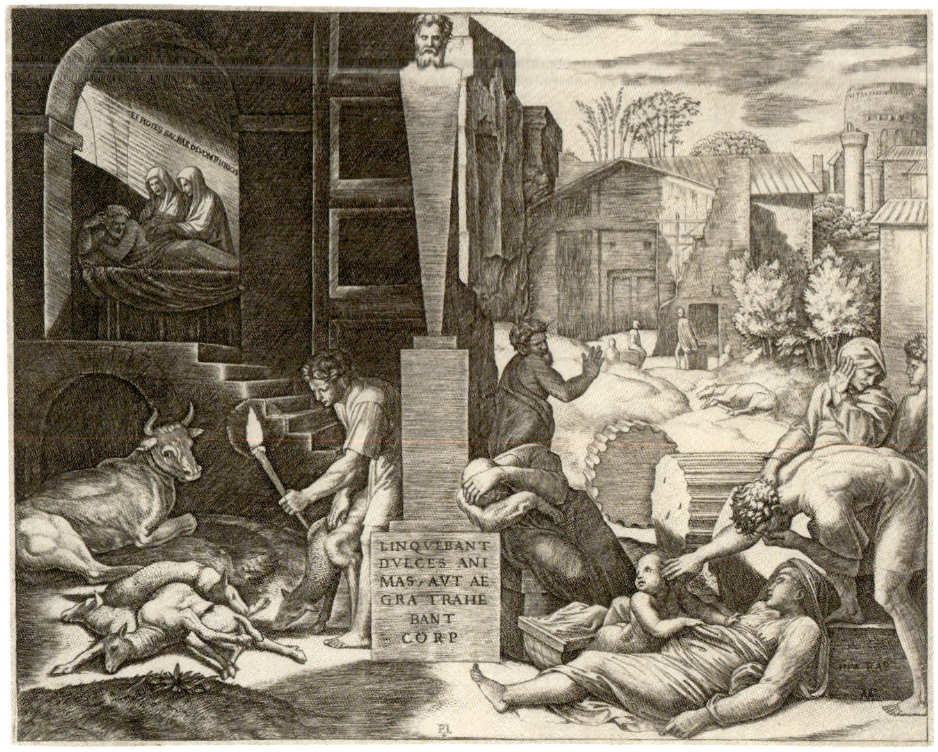

Marcantonio Raimoindi after Raphael, **The Plague in Phrygia ("The Morbetto")**, *c.* 1514–1516
Copper engraving, 20 × 25.5 cm (7 7⁄8 × 10 1⁄8 in). Vienna, Albertina

happens afterwards (the Trojans have landed in Carthage). The episodes on the frame are composed in the manner of antique reliefs. In the scene below left, two figures contemplate the narrative reliefs decorating a temple building, while on the right a poet-singer playing an instrument performs at a banquet. The two media of pictorial relief and text shown in the frame are thus reflected in the representations themselves and appear side by side as if for comparison. The vista in the centre demarcates itself clearly from the relief character of the surround insofar as it appears to show a real-life scene. Spatial depth, storm clouds, waves, the raging sea, movement and drama are conveyed with supreme artistry. Virgil's famous description of the tempest and Neptune's intervention, voiced in extraordinarily colourful and vivid language, makes readers feel that they are witnessing the event at first-hand and experiencing all its danger, violence and terror. Raphael and Raimondi give visibility to this imagination – as if we should read Virgil's word painting when looking at the engraving and compare text and image motif by motif. Who achieves the greater effect?

The significance of antiquity for Raphael as a painter is as rich as it is diverse; we need think only of his representation of antique subjects, his absorption of motifs from antique statues and reliefs, his imitation of antique compositional formats as well as antique stylistic forms of relief narrative, his reconstruction of lost antique paintings and of works surviving in damaged form or in fragments, his borrowing from antique organisational forms of multi-part pictorial ensembles, his observance of antique rules of art, and even his attempt to reconstruct antique painting techniques. Quotations from antiquity and the rivalry with antiquity thereby make up an ever larger part of his Roman oeuvre. In places he develops a positively antiquarian style (see Farinella 2021).

Raphael's engagement with surviving works of antiquity is also documented in a series of written sources. In 1515 Leo X made Raphael "prefect" in charge of all antique marble and stone ("praefectus marmorum et lapidum omnium") found and excavated in and around Rome. His aim was to give Raphael, who in 1514 had been appointed architect of St Peter's, the right to acquire any materials that could be useful in the construction of the new cathedral. Leo X also instructed that no antique stones carrying inscriptions were to be destroyed without Raphael's permission, since their preservation might be worthwhile "for the cultivation of literature and for improving the elegance of the Latin language" ("ad cultum litterarum Romanique sermonis elegantiam excolendam"). In 1516 Raphael travelled with his poet and humanist friends to Tivoli to look at antiquities, among other things. That same year, he placed an ancient statue of Venus in Cardinal Bibbiena's *Stufetta*. In 1517 he advised the Duke of Ferrara on the purchase of antique sculpture. The Duke was interested in acquiring the so-called *Letto di Policleto*, an antique relief that served Raphael several times as a visual source. In 1518, after the death of Gabriele de' Rossi and contrary to the provisions of his will, Raphael tried to appropriate his collection of antiquities for the Pope (Christian 2002). In 1519 Raphael suggested to the Pope that a broken obelisk discovered in the Mausoleum of Augustus should be erected on St Peter's Square. From Constantinople, Raphael was sent a drawing of a column base which Agostino Veneziano then turned into an engraving. Raphael also owned antiquities himself, for example mentioning a statue of the Greek poet Philemon, and envisaged a courtyard of statuary in the planned rebuilding of his house (Christian 2004). As an architect, Raphael devoted himself to the in-depth study of antique architectural theory. Fabio Calvo (*c.* 1450–1527) translated the treatise on architecture by Vitruvius (died 15 BC) into Italian for him. Raphael, who had taken the learned elderly Calvo into his home as a fatherly instructor, annotated the manuscript in his own hand. Raphael cited several antique written sources when describing his planned villa for Giulio de' Medici (Villa Madama, Cat. A12), which was to be an idealised reconstruction of a work of ancient Roman architecture.

Calvo and the antiquarian Andrea Fulvio (*c.* 1470–1527) assisted Raphael on a major project entrusted to him by Leo X. Raphael was commissioned to produce a set of plans showing a reconstruction of ancient Rome. With the help of Castiglione, he composed a literary and didactic letter to the Pope, which was probably intended to serve as a *proemium* (preface) to the work (Di Teodoro 2020, 2021). In it, Raphael presents himself as a scholar who has devoted a great deal of study to both the ancient sources and the ancient ruins ("studiosissimo di queste antiquitati"). Today, he writes, the noble homeland, once queen of the world, has been reduced to a corpse. Barbarians had ravaged and destroyed the ancient city with iron and fire. But popes, too, bear some of the blame: the new Rome of today has been built with mortar made from ancient marbles. It is now the duty of Pope Leo to take care of "the little that remains of this ancient mother of Italian glory and greatness" ("quello poco che resta di questa anticha madre de la gloria e grandezza italiana"). In this way, the competition with the ancients will be kept alive and their quality can be achieved and surpassed. When examining surviving ancient remains, Raphael notes, it is necessary to compare styles in order to distinguish the older from the more recent.

Raphael uses the example of the Arch of Constantine in order to demonstrate his artist's eye – accurately recognising quality and differences in style – and to convey to Leo the difficulty of the undertaking. Among the arts under Constantine, he considers that architecture maintains its quality, whereas sculpture has already deteriorated and is without art or good design. The reliefs reused on the Arch, dating from the time of Trajan (AD 53–117) and Antoninus Pius (AD 86–161), on the other hand, are "most excellent, and perfect in style" ("excellentissime e di perfetta manera"). Raphael also explains to the Pope the means with which he wishes to represent Rome's ancient buildings. He even develops his own instrument for measuring. The drawings are to show three views of each building: the ground plan, the exterior elevation and the interior section.

Raphael died before this project could be completed. Humanists and scholars mourned not only the artist's death, but also the fact that this marvel of a resurrection of ancient Rome remained unfinished: only one of the fourteen regions of Rome had been mapped. An impression of what was planned and lost is conveyed by a few Raphael drawings of antiquities. An accurate drawing of one of the antique horses from the large marble *Horse Tamers* on the Quirinal is annotated with hand-written measurements (KMOF 531). Raphael drew the interior of the Pantheon and in doing so sought to conceal medieval additions (Nesselrath 1982, 1986, 2008).

View of the Roman Forum, 1512
Silverpoint with white heightening on greyish-brown prepared paper, 21 × 14.1 cm (8 ¼ × 5 ½ in)
Windsor Castle, Royal Library

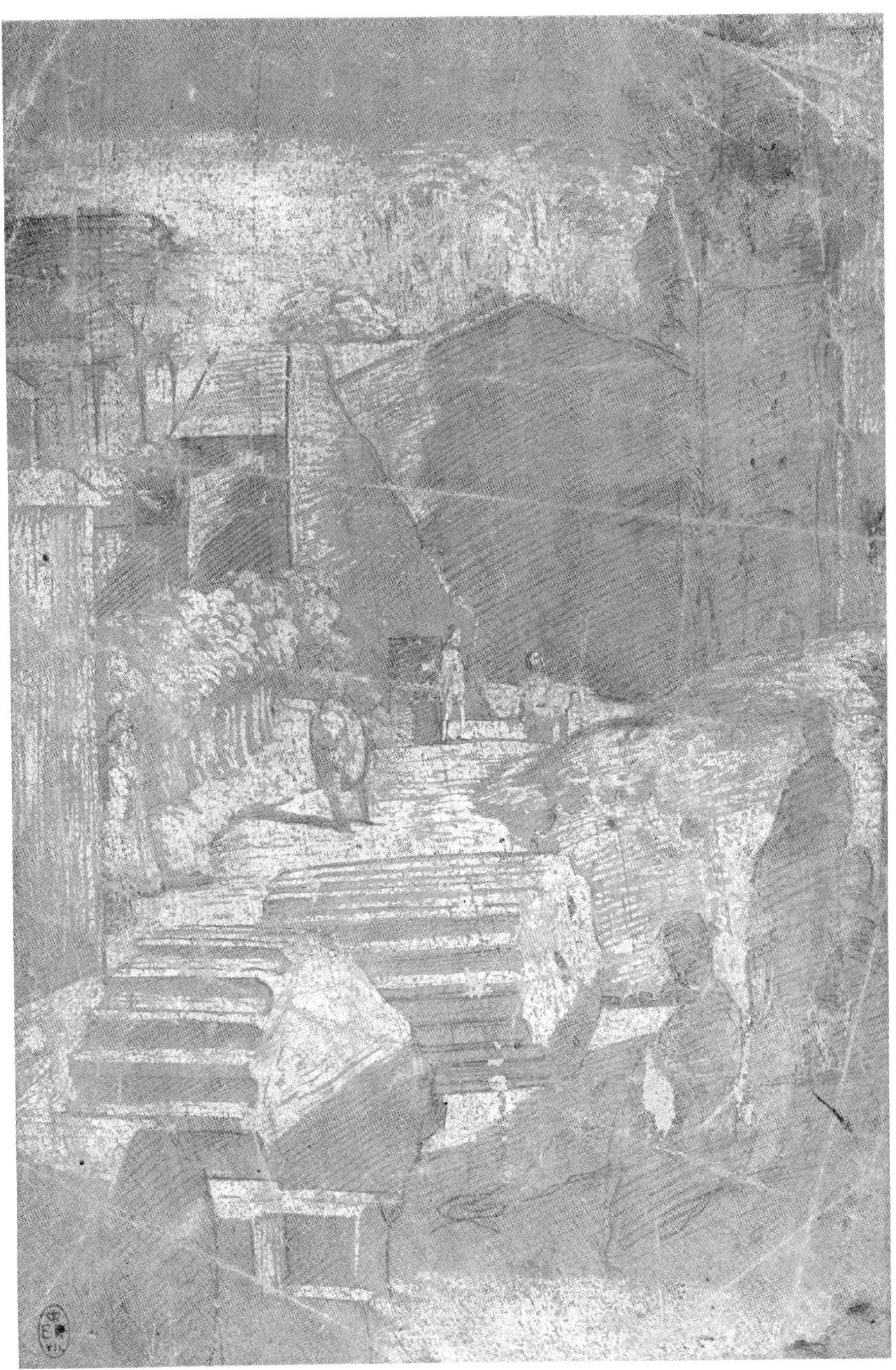

Raphael and Leo X's passion for antiquity, and the task of preserving and defending the remains of ancient Rome which Raphael assigns to the papacy in the preface to his Rome plan, have also left their traces in Vatican frescoes. When Raphael's text draws attention to the threat to the ruins posed by barbarian fury, iron and fire ("quel barbaroso furore, e 'l ferro e il fuoco") and exhorts the popes to defend these poor relics of Rome like fathers and protectors ("come padri e tuttori, deveano diffendere queste povere reliquie di Roma"), Leo X will have been reminded of Raphael's fresco *Leo I and Attila* (p. 197 t; Cat. F3.2g). There, in the role of Leo the Great, he himself halted the invasion of the wild Hun hordes. The hillsides were already burning. The ruins of ancient Rome visible behind the Pope, including the Colosseum, obelisk and aqueduct, were threatened. In the *Fire in the Borgo* (p. 231 t.; Cat. F3.3l), the fire in the foreground has destroyed authentic monuments of ancient Rome. It is Leo IV, alias Leo X, who stops the fire and thereby saves not only the fleeing citizens but also the ancient buildings from complete destruction. In his text addressed to Leo X, Raphael couches his intention of preserving ancient Rome in architectural drawings in the context of *pietas*, the dutiful devotion that each owes their parents and homeland ("pietate verso li parenti e la patria"). Aeneas, who saved his father, his son, the figures of the old household gods and finally the surviving Trojans, was regarded as the epitome of *pietas*. Insofar as Raphael's fresco references the actions of Aeneas in the foreground of the ruins, it elevates the saving of antiquities into the sphere of *pietas*. The fresco not only demands the conservation of Rome's ancient ruins, but also ensures their preservation itself: ancient Roman architectural elements are depicted in the *Fire in the Borgo* even more precisely than in *Leo I and Attila* and are thus already saved here for posterity – under the Pope's blessing – by Raphael.

Raphael's letter describes the destroyed ancient Rome as a corpse ("cadavero"). In *The Plague in Phrygia*, animal and human cadavers lie in the foreground. Raphael associates them with a vedutà of Roman ruins. Between the dead woman and the dead horse some distance behind her, overturned column drums also lie on the ground. Horror and grief over the dead people and animals are thus combined with the feelings of the antiquarian in the face of the cadaver, also represented here, of ancient architecture (Wouk 2016/17). As if the plague had carried off not only animals and humans, but also the city and buildings of antiquity. In his Roman oeuvre, Raphael is one of the great poets who, starting with Petrarch, mourn the demise of ancient Rome, and at the same time a visual artist who demands, secures and celebrates the survival and renewal of antiquity.

Loggia di Psiche: **Mercury**, 1518
Fresco

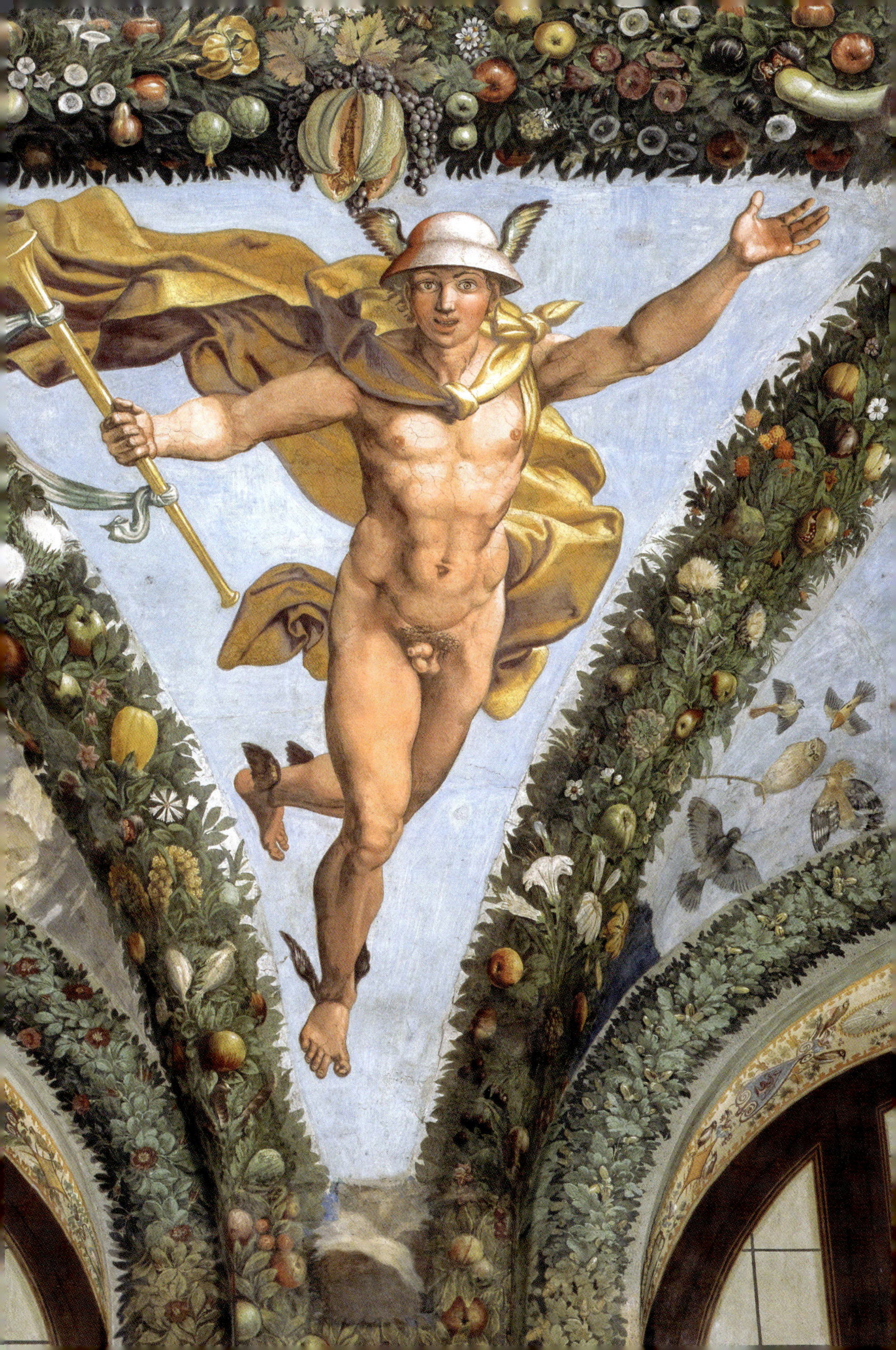

Loggia di Galatea
Loggia di Psiche

Villa Farnesina

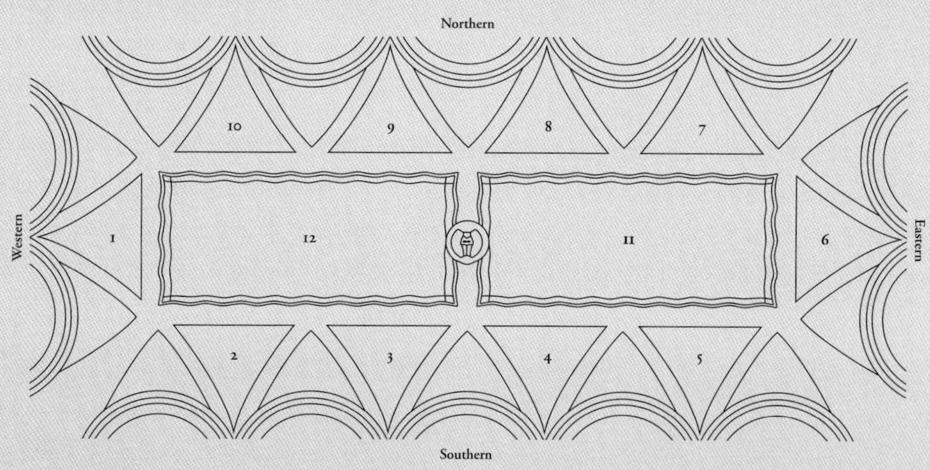

Loggia di Psiche

1 Venus and Cupid
2 Cupid and the Graces
3 Venus before Ceres and Juno
4 Venus in Her Chariot
5 Venus before Jupiter
6 Mercury
7 Psyche, Borne by Amoretti
8 Psyche before Venus
9 Cupid before Jupiter
10 Mercury and Psyche
11 Council of the Gods
12 Banquet of the Gods at the Marriage of Cupid and Psyche

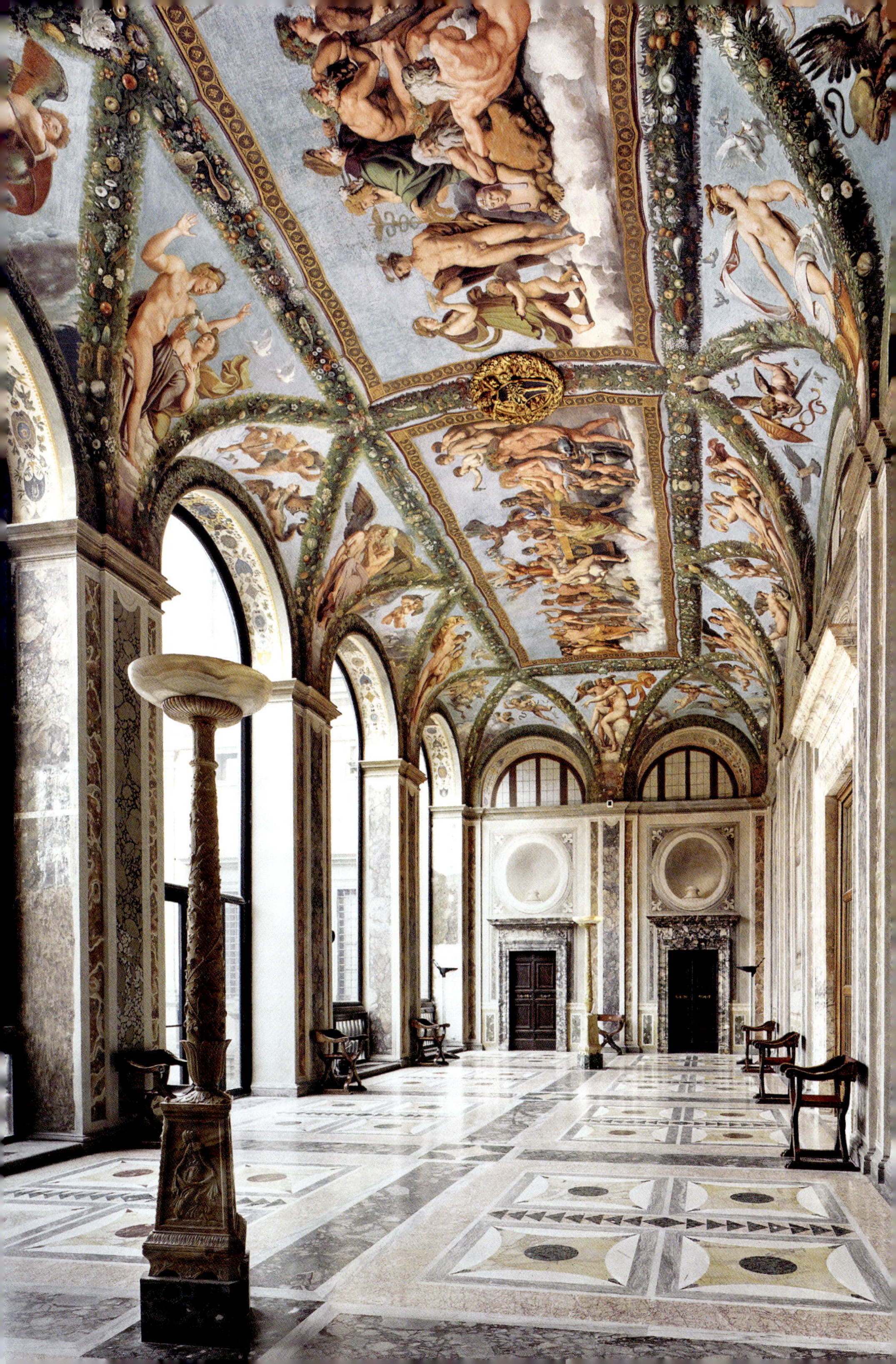

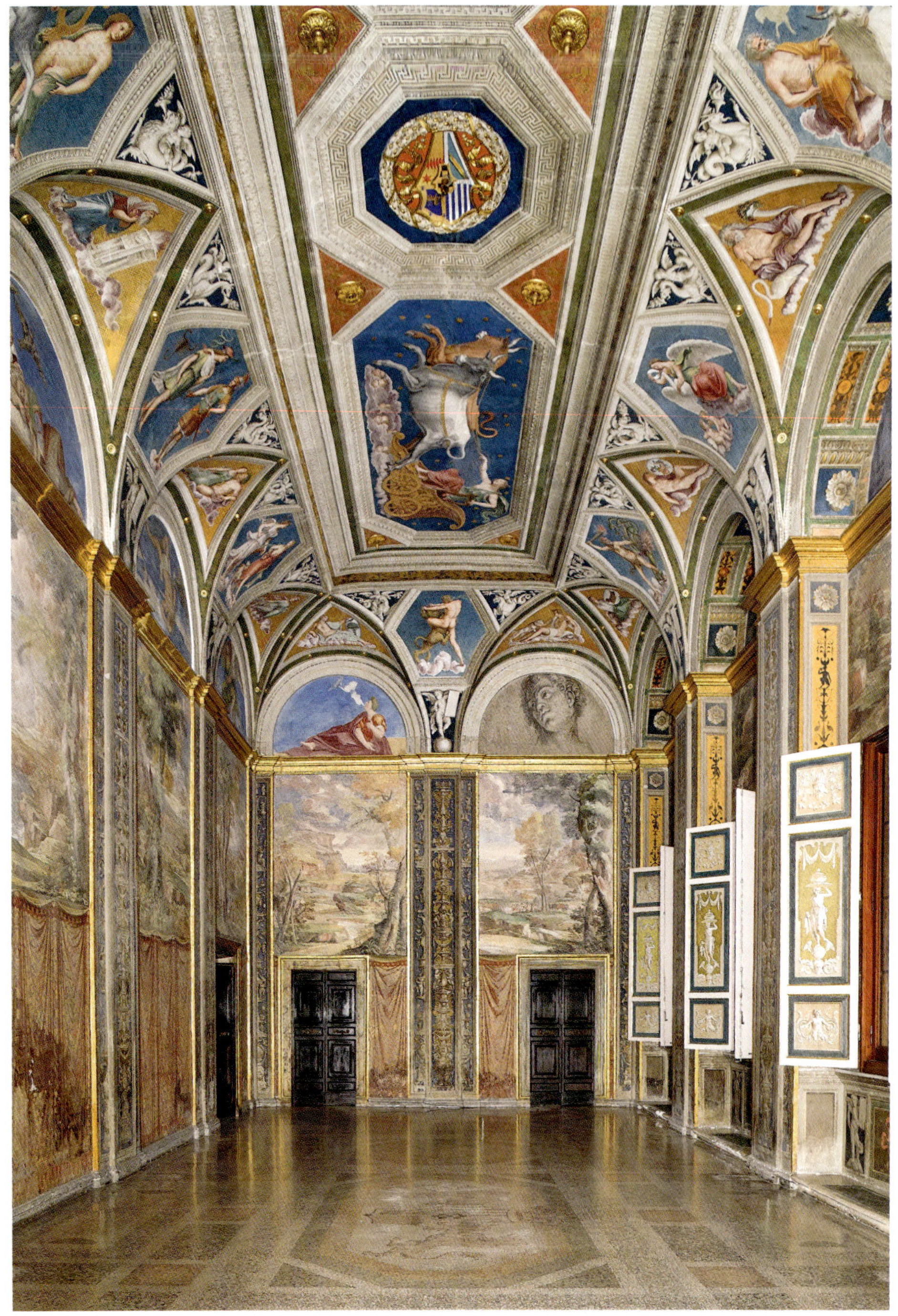

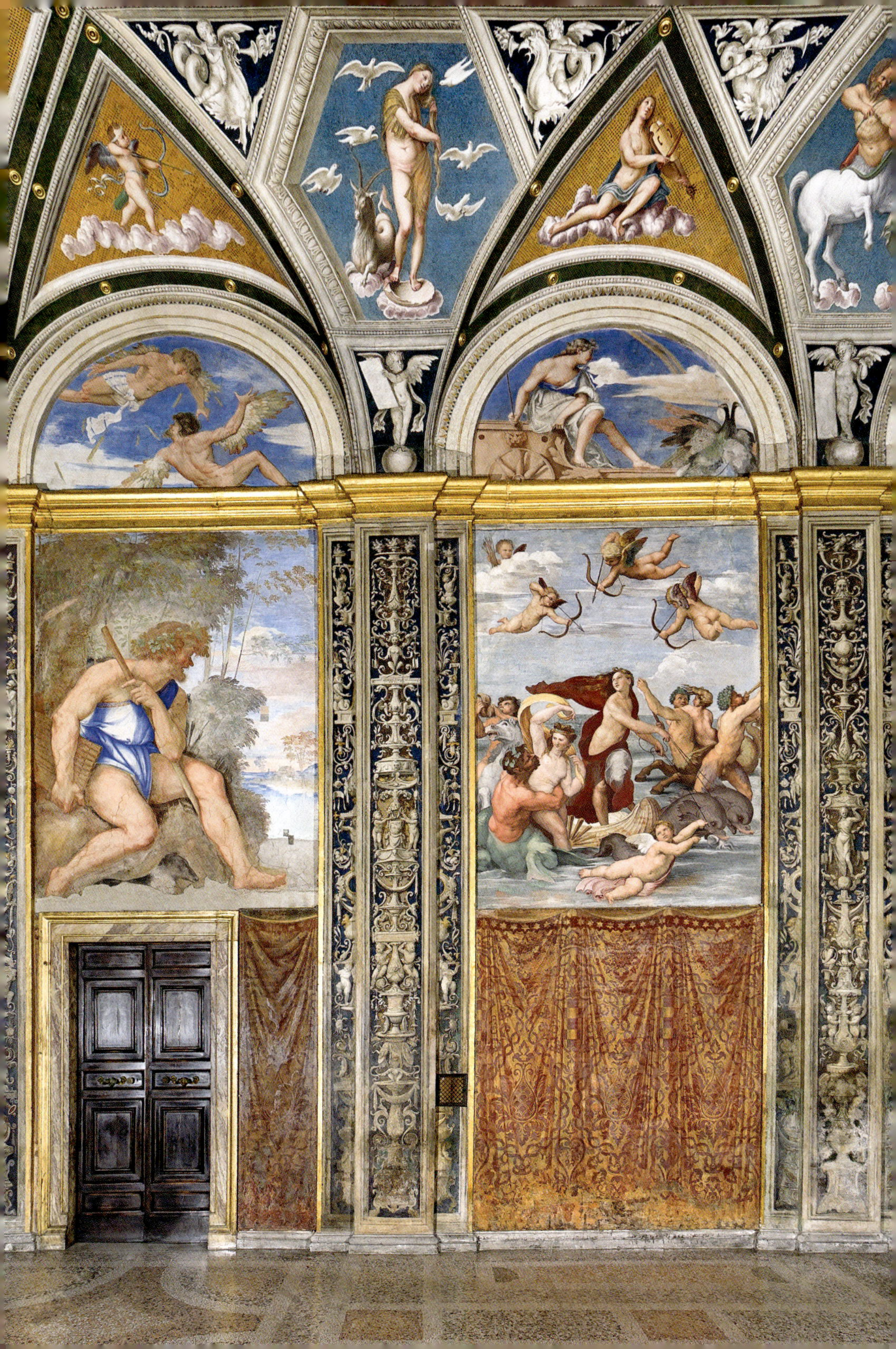

Page 417
Villa Farnesina: Loggia di Psiche

Page 418
Villa Farnesina: Loggia di Galatea

Page 419
Villa Farnesina: Wall with Polyphemus (Sebastiano del Piombo) and Galatea (Raphael) in the Loggia di Galatea

Circle of Raphael, **Pan and Daphnis**, 16th cent.
Pen and ink, 25.6 × 14.9 cm (10 ⅛ × 5 ⅞ in)
London, British Museum, Department of Prints and Drawings

Loggia di Galatea: **The Voyage of Galatea**, *c.* 1512
Fresco, 295 × 225 cm (116 ⅛ × 88 ⅝ in). Rome, Villa Farnesina

Pages 422/423
Ceiling of the Loggia di Psiche with the **Council of the Gods** (right-hand half of the ceiling) and **Banquet of the Gods at the Marriage of Cupid and Psyche** (left-hand half of the ceiling), 1518
Frescoes. Rome, Villa Farnesina *(Details pages 424–427)*

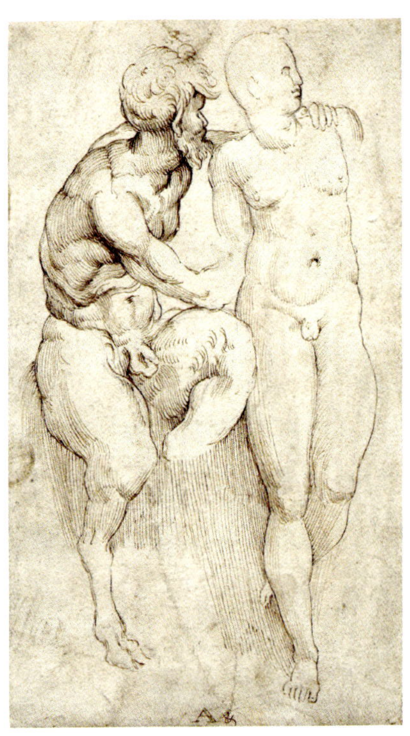

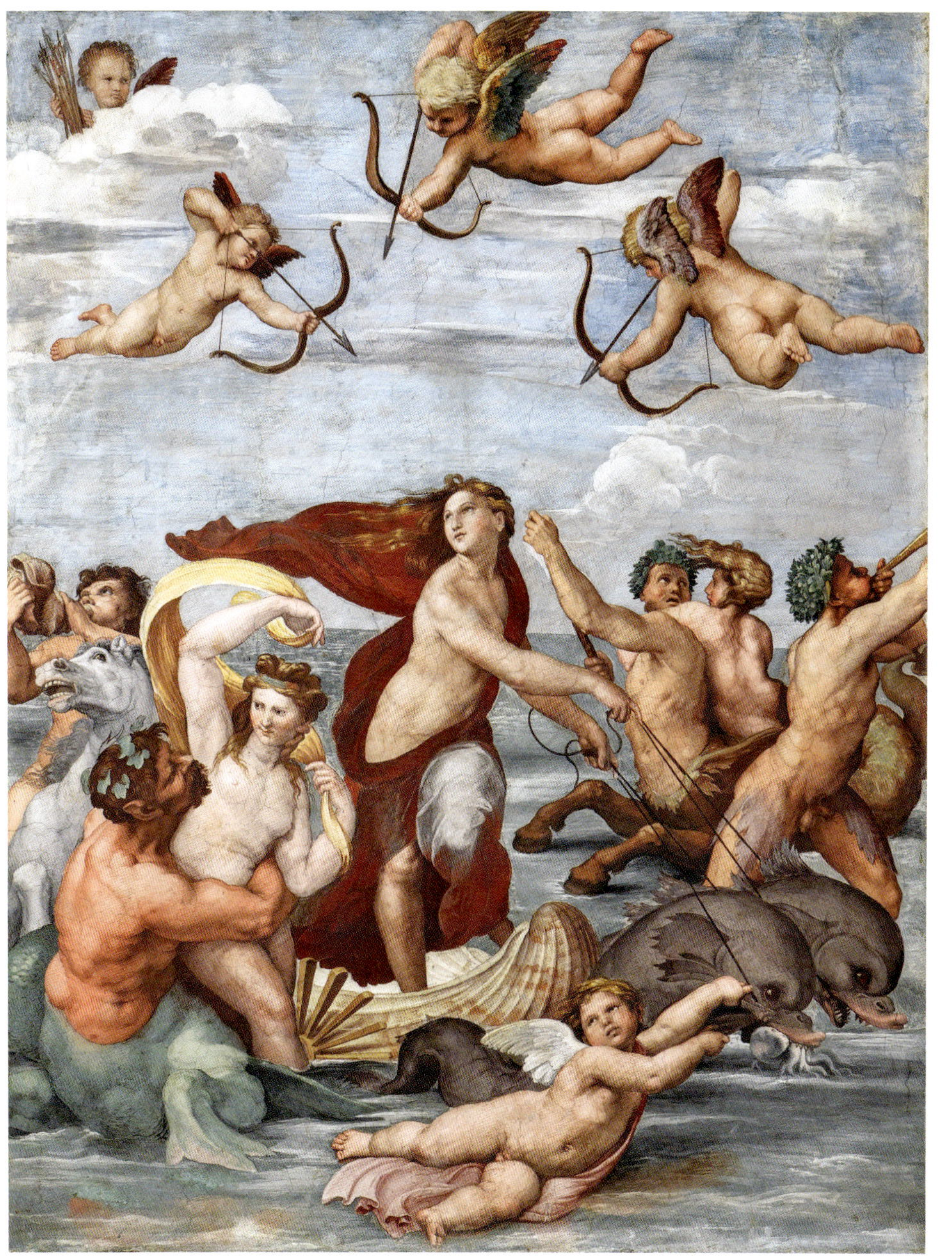

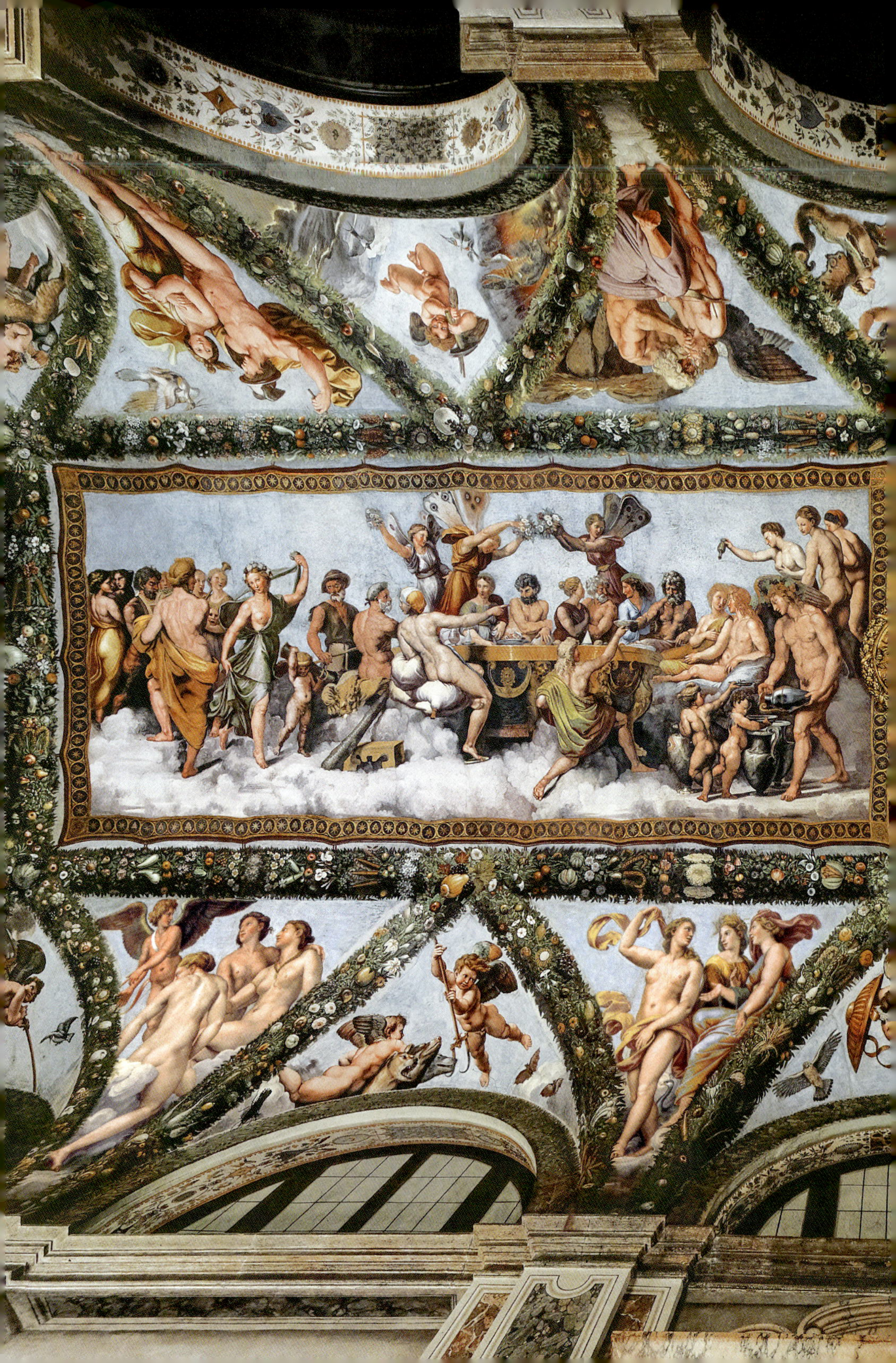

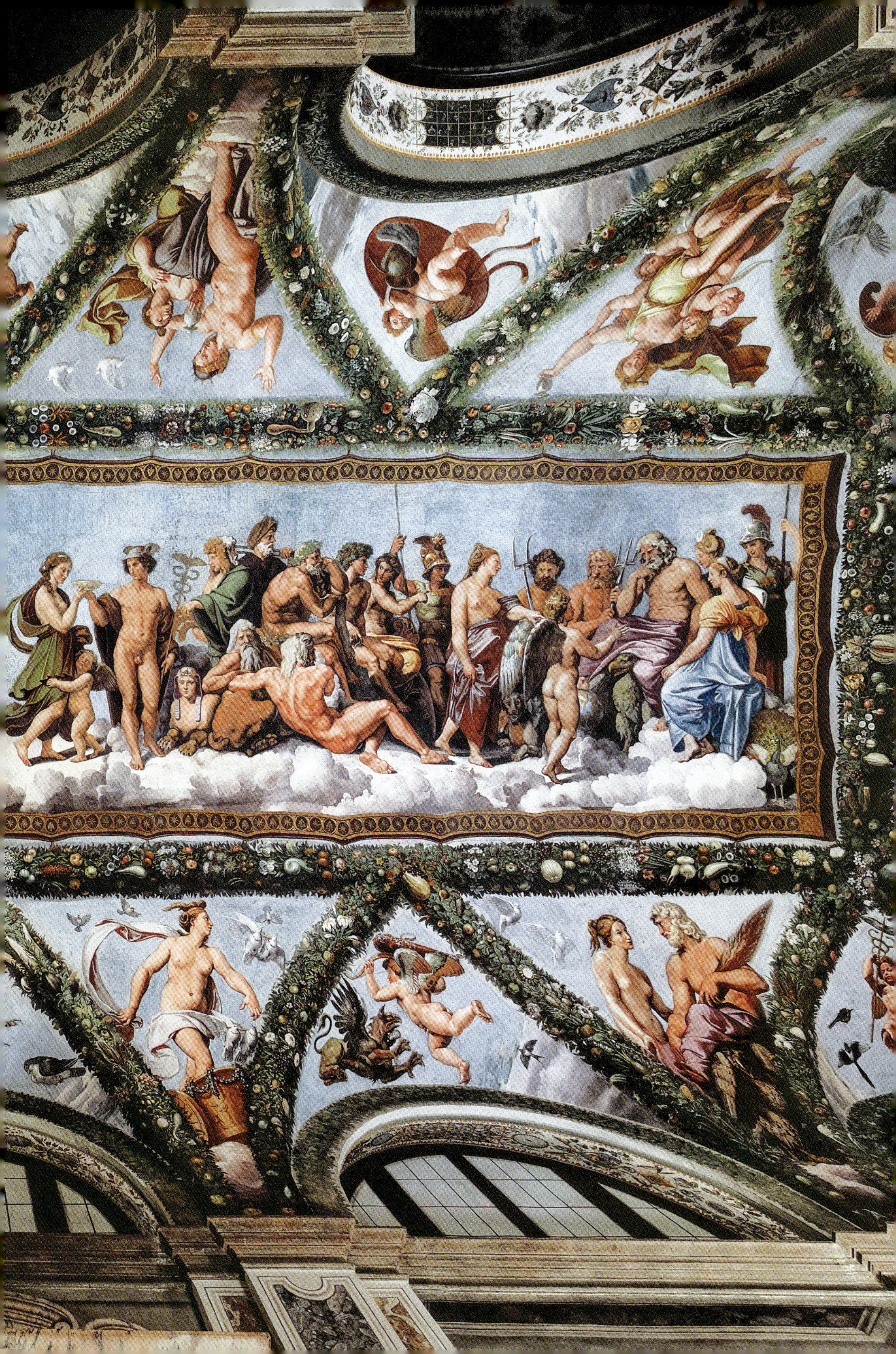

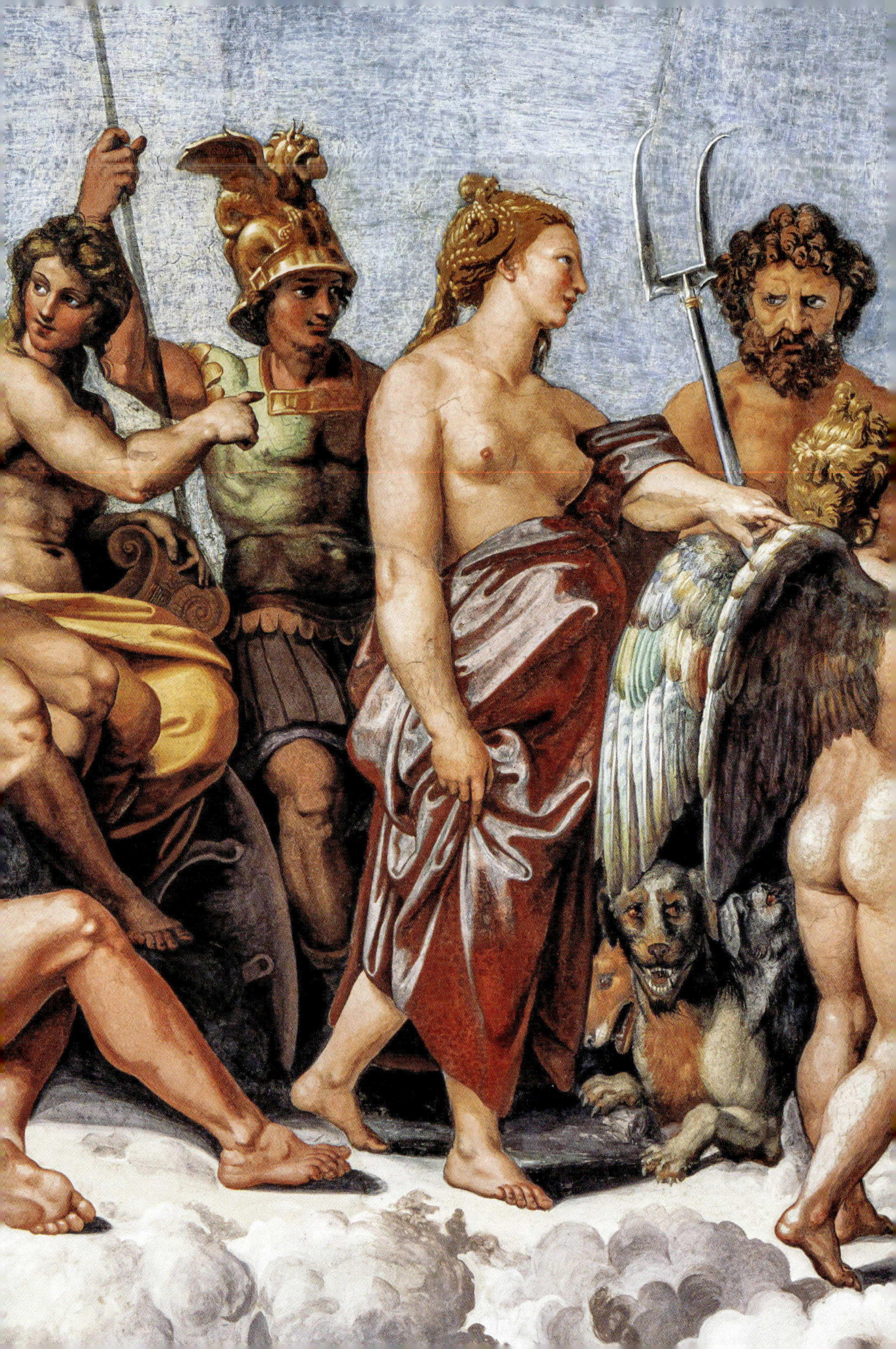

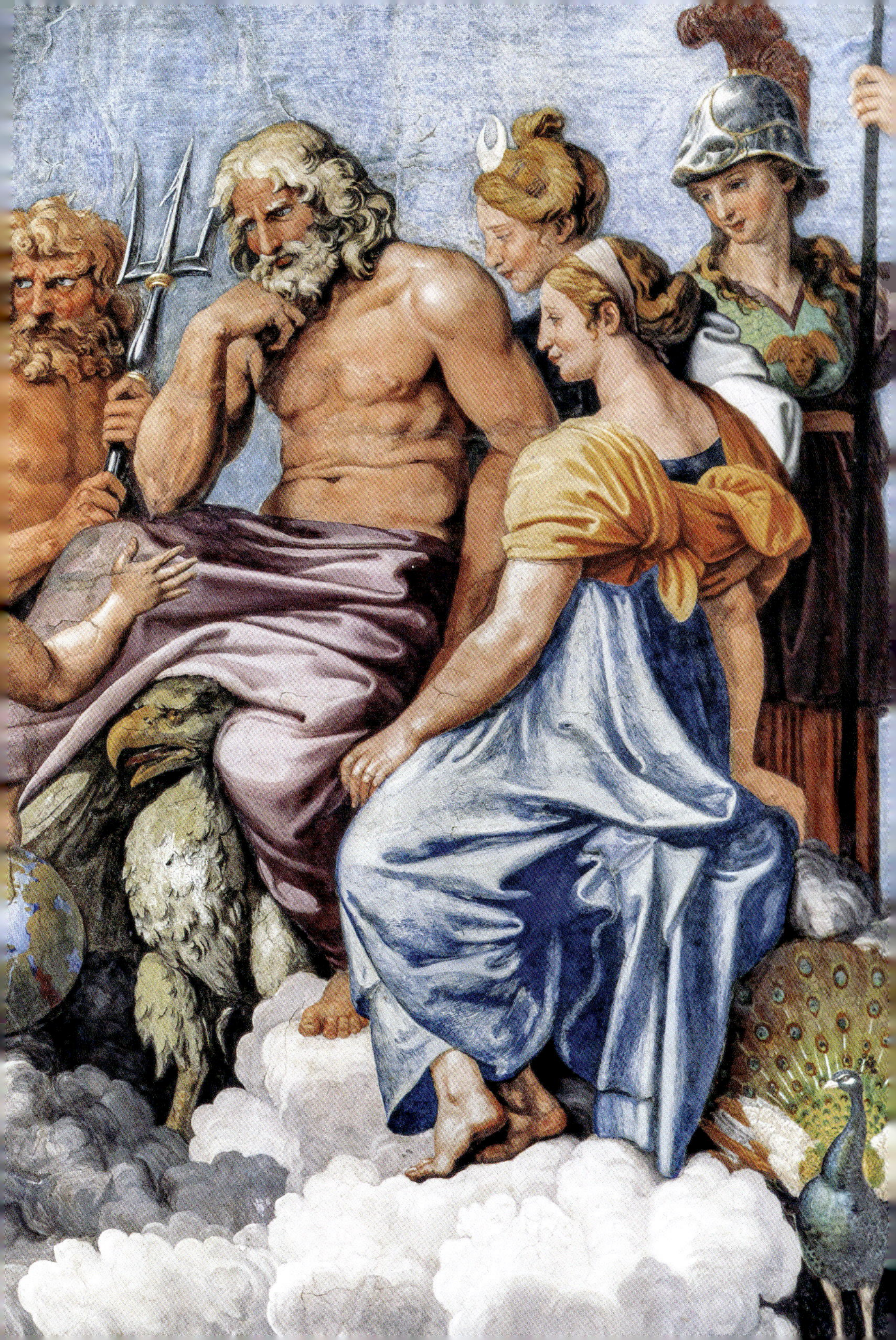

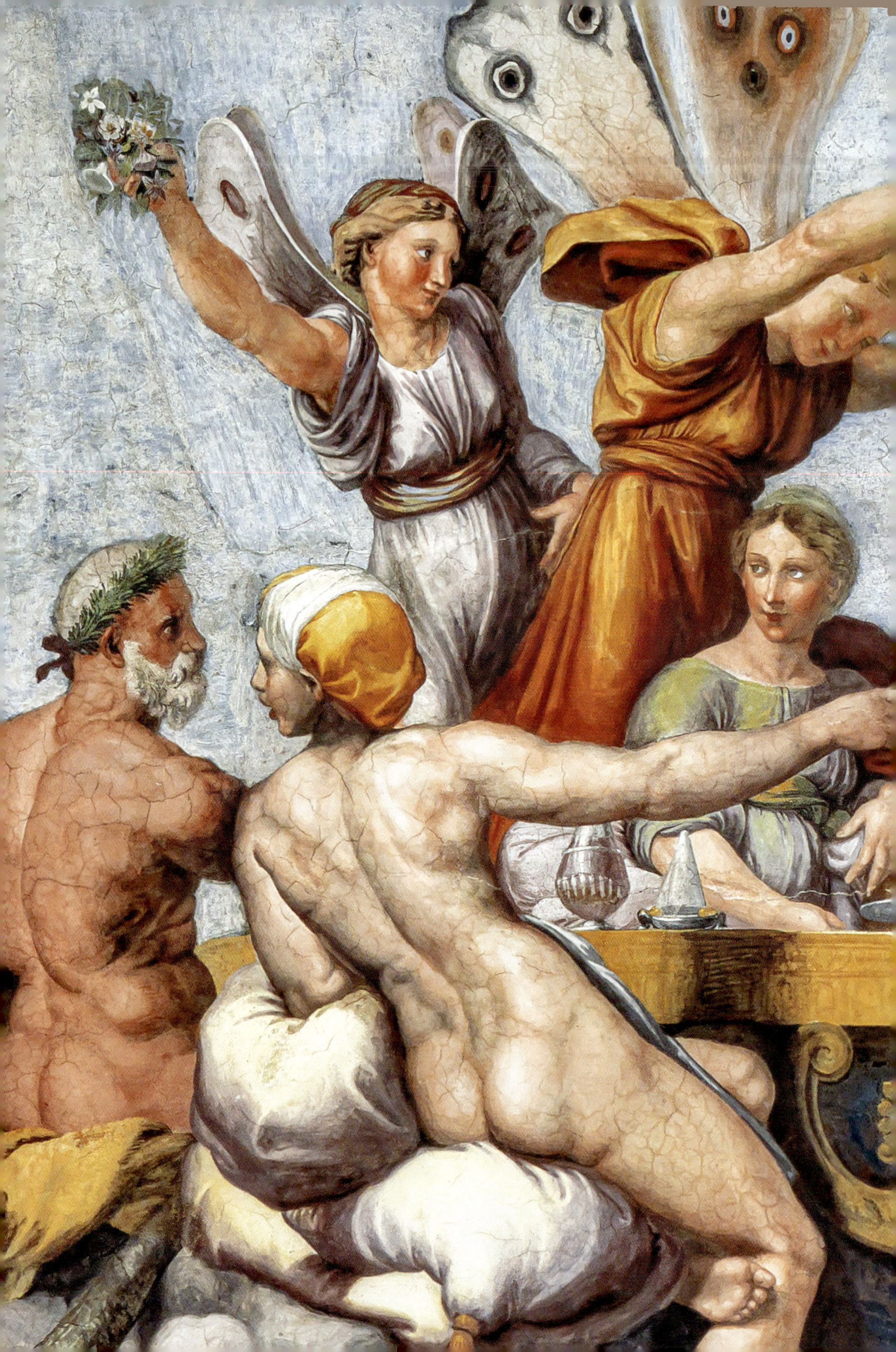

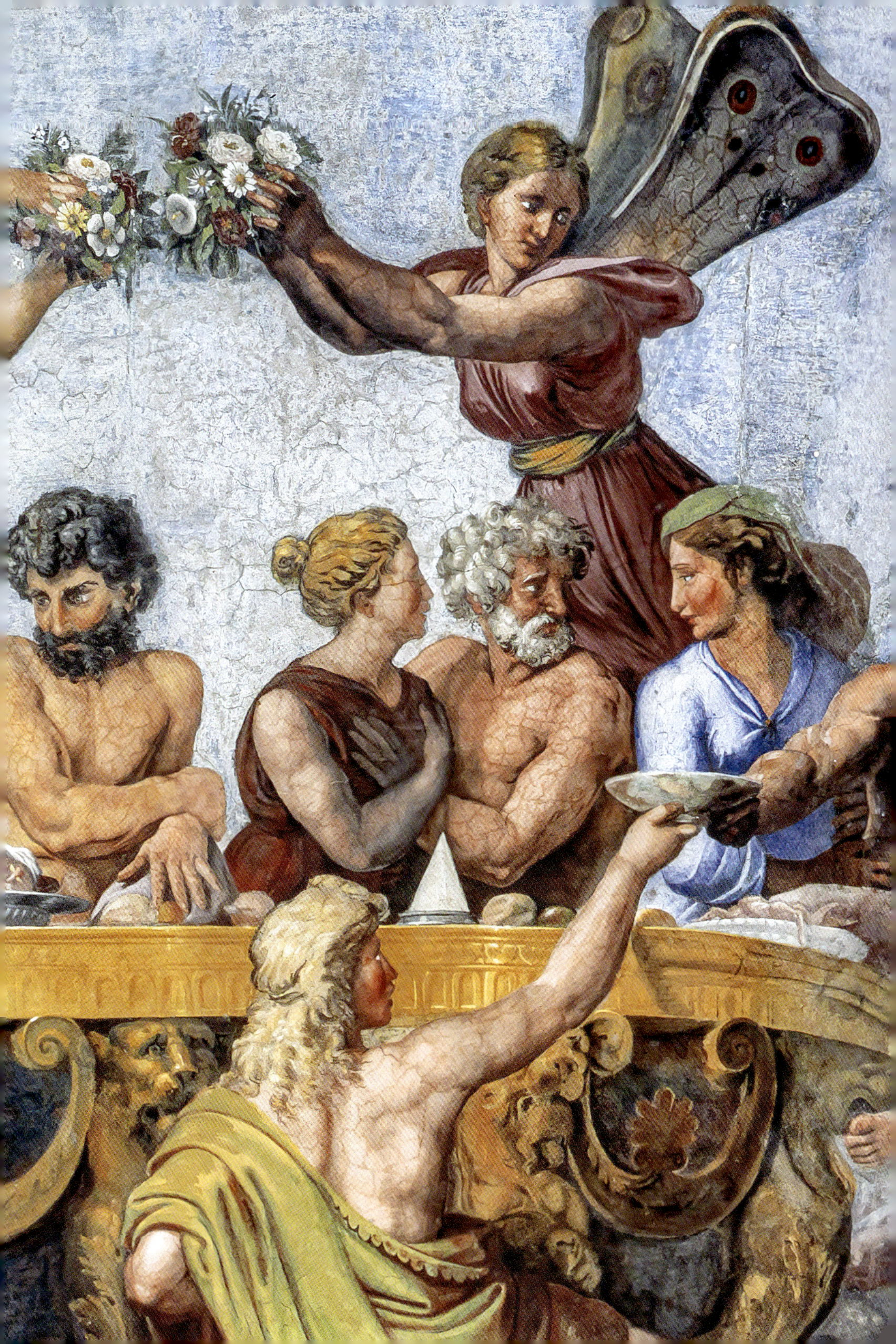

Cardinal Bibbiena's Loggetta and *Stufetta*

Musei Vaticani

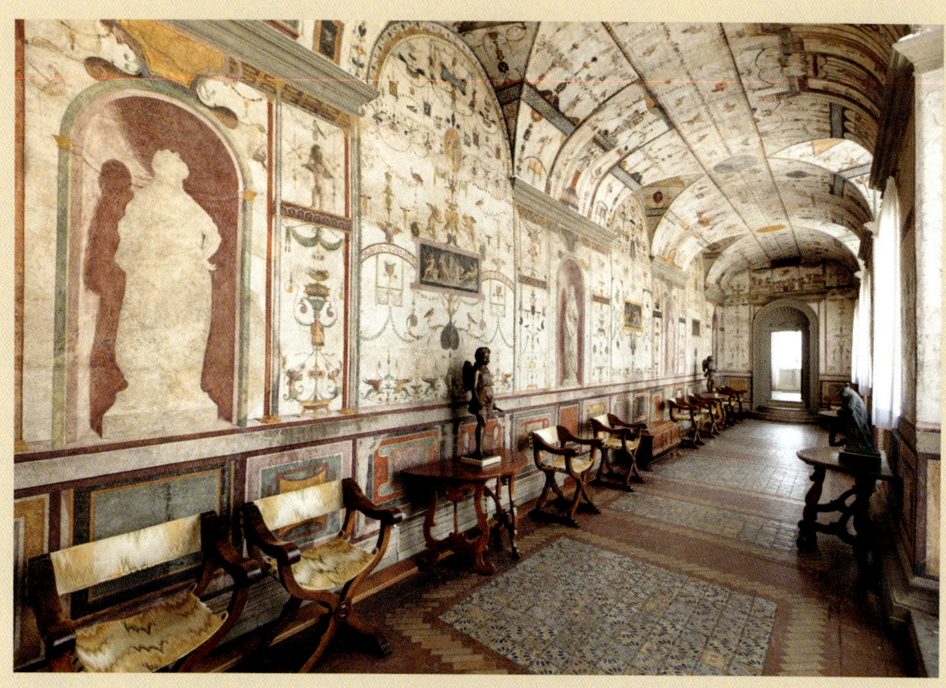

Pages 428–431
Interior view of the Loggetta and details of the wall decoration, 1516
Frescoes. Vatican City, Musei Vaticani

Pages 432–433
Interior view of the *Stufetta*, ceiling and details of the wall decoration, 1516
Frescoes: 2.5 × 2.5 m (9 ⅞ × 9 ⅞ in), height 4.34 m (170 ⅞ in)
Vatican City, Musei Vaticani

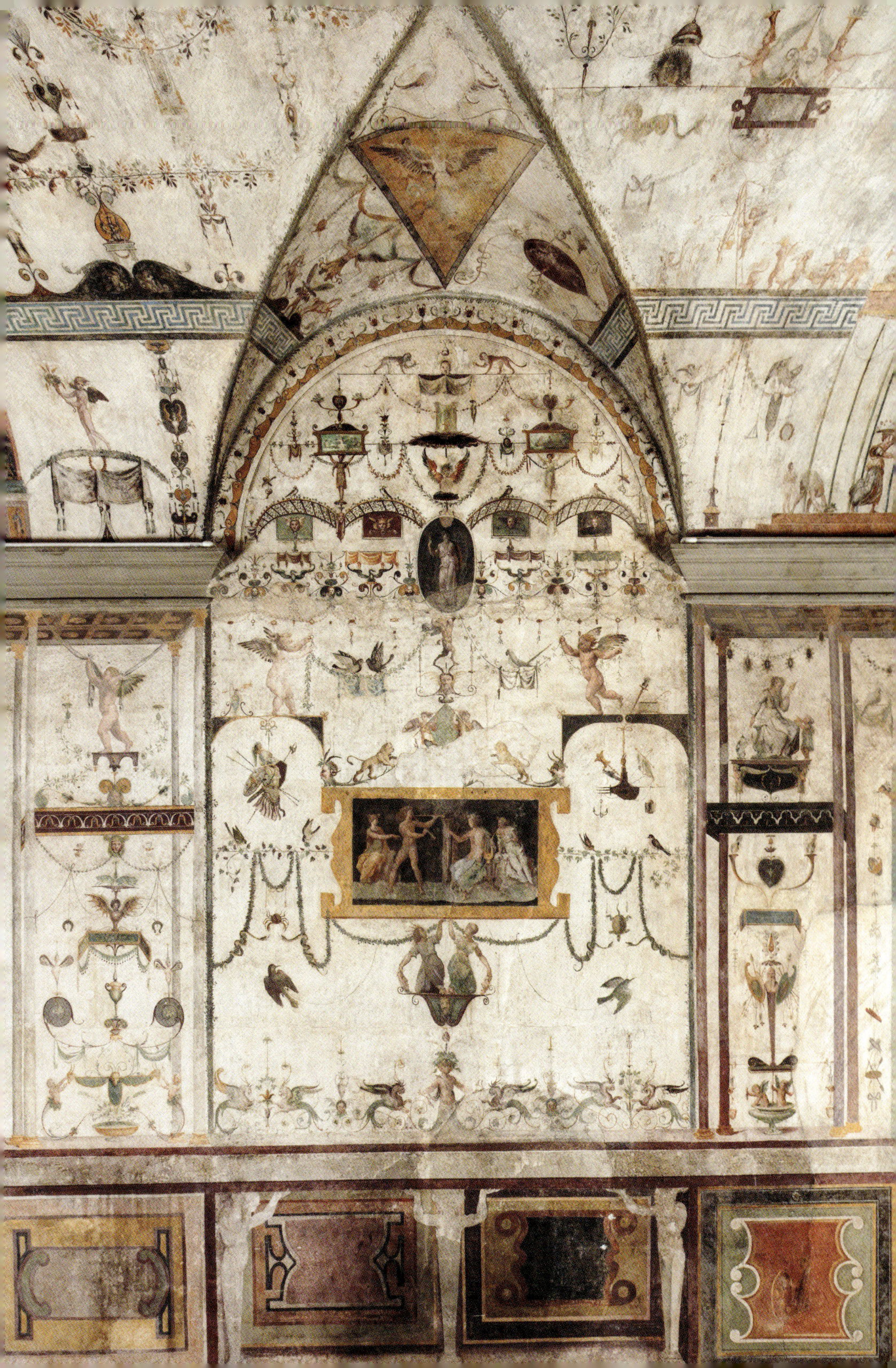

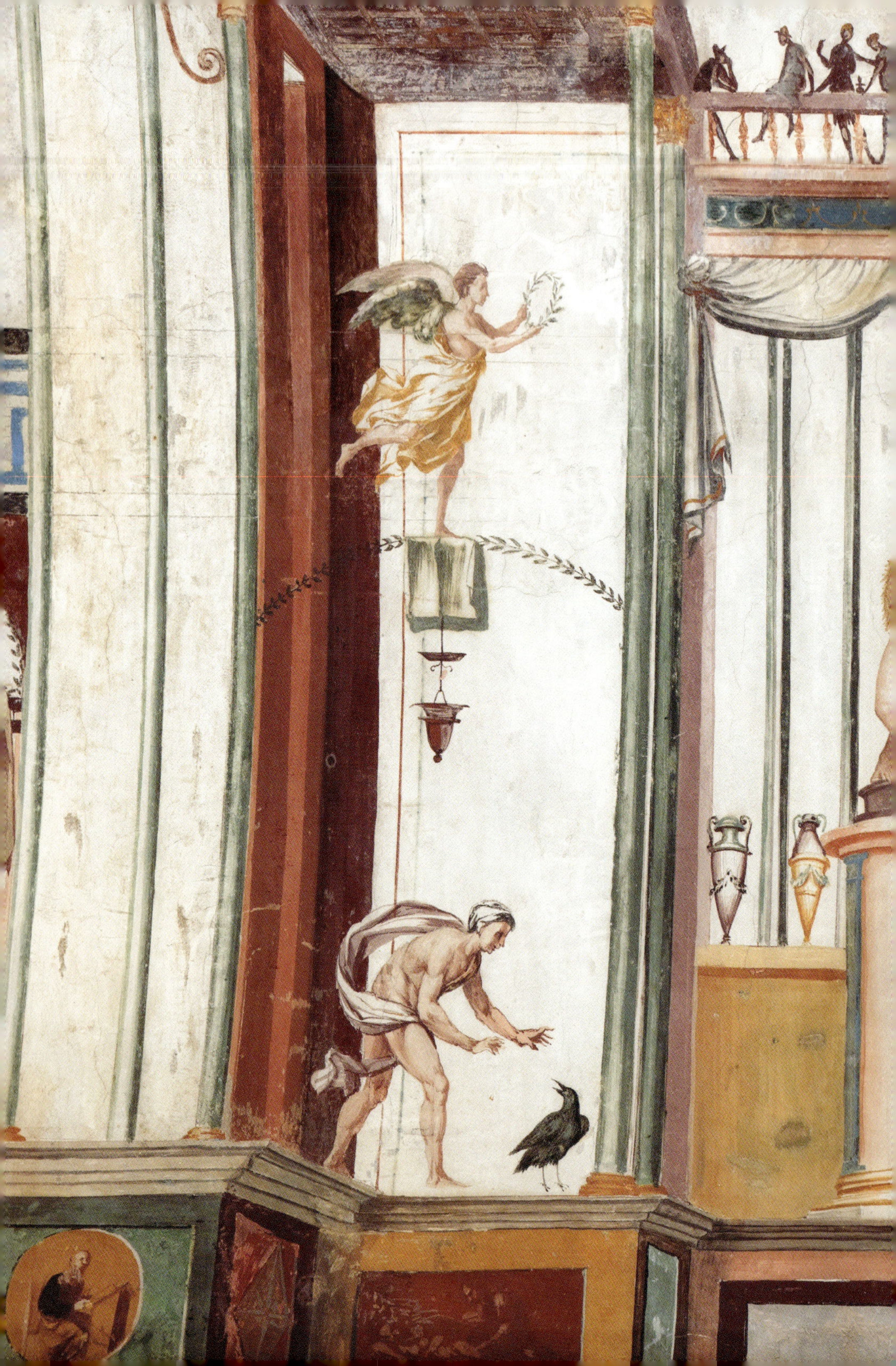

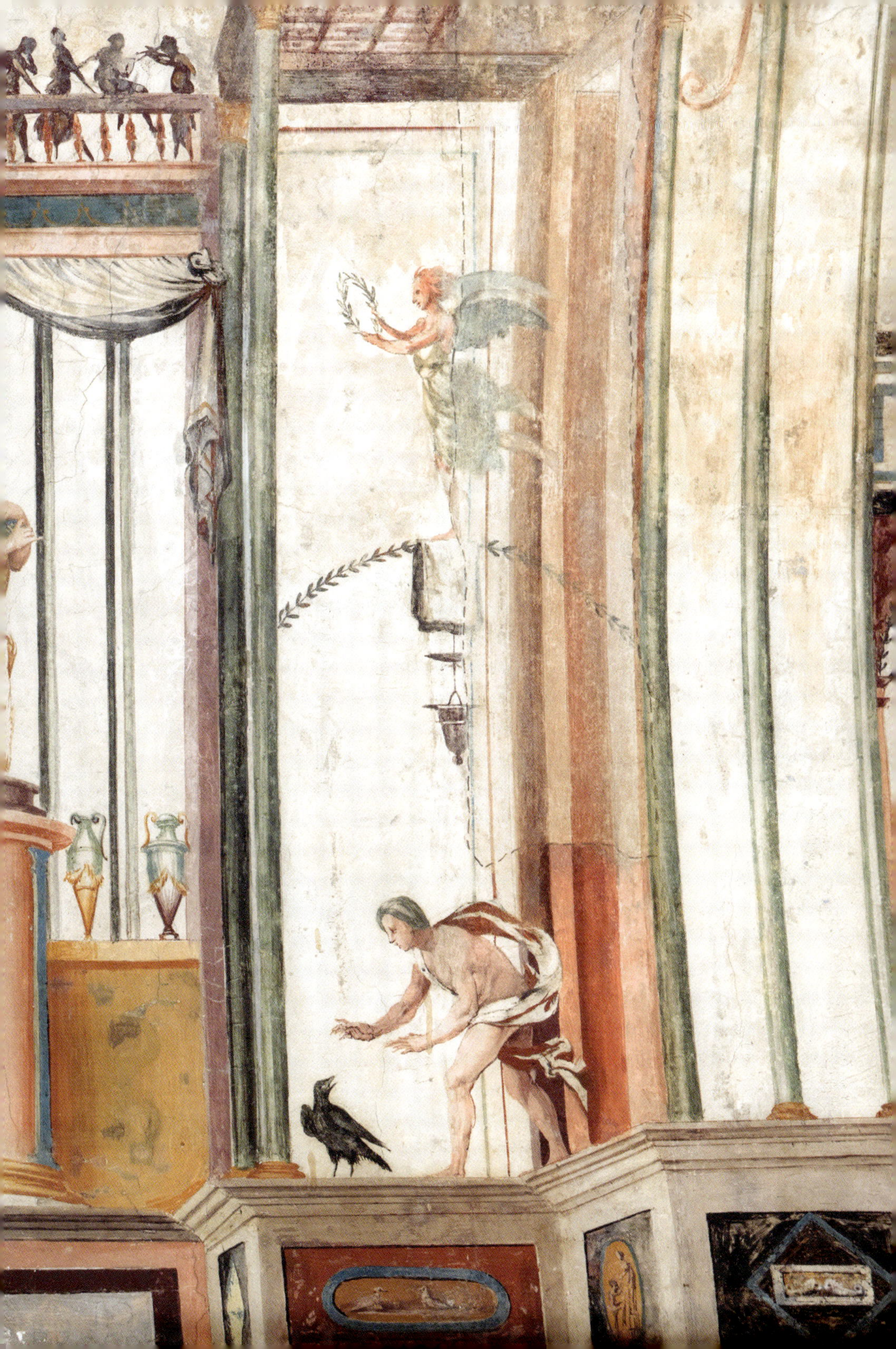

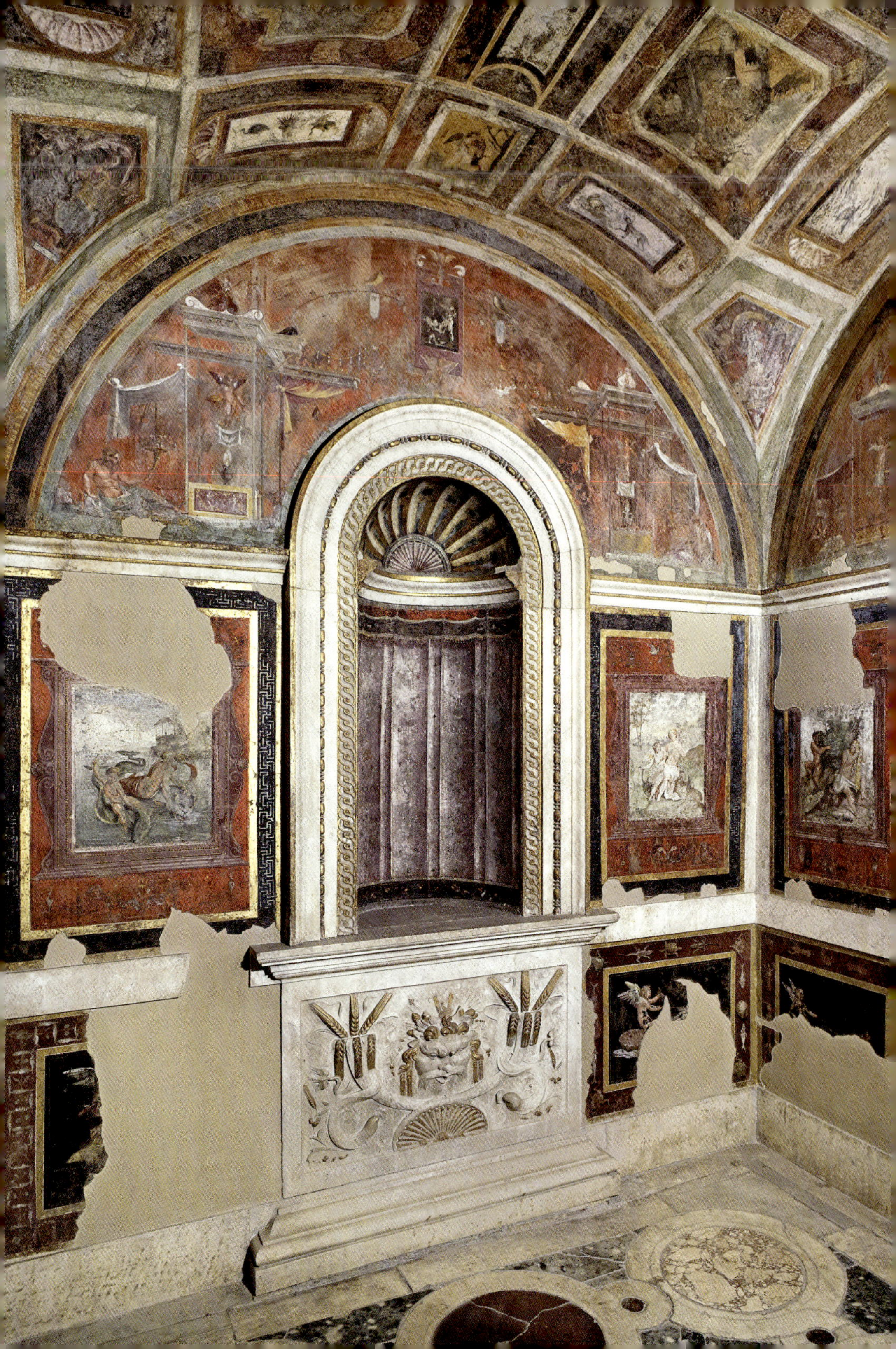

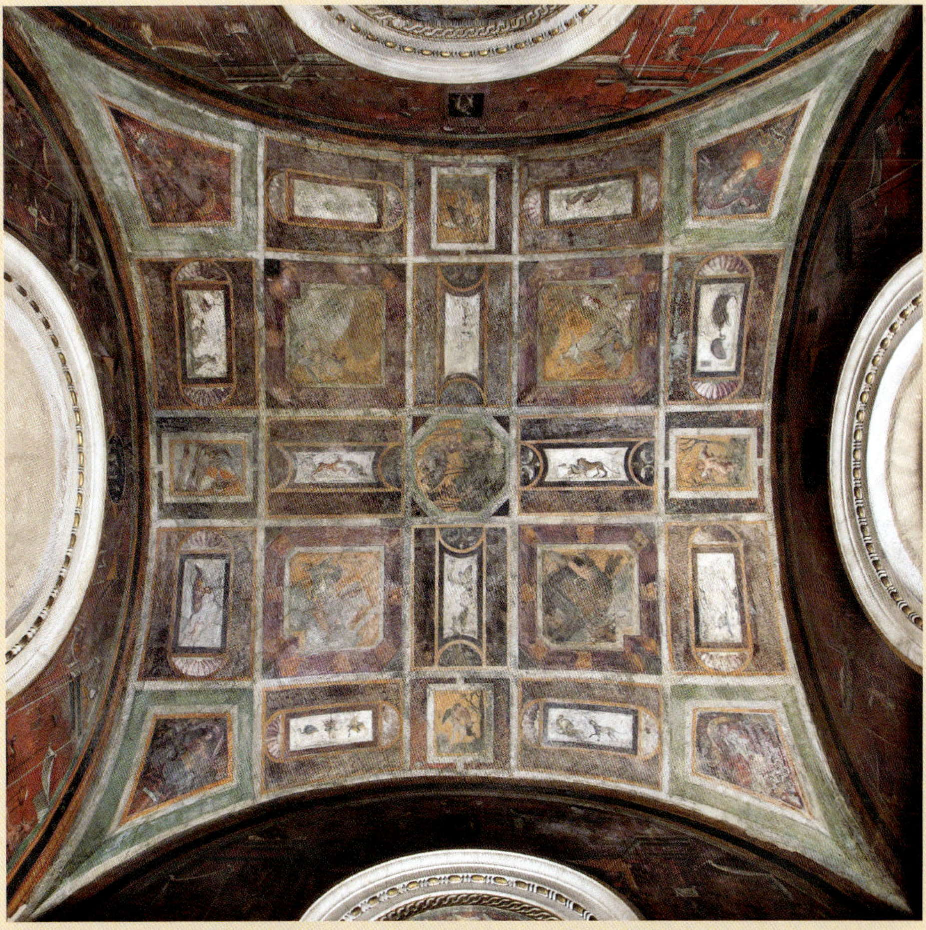

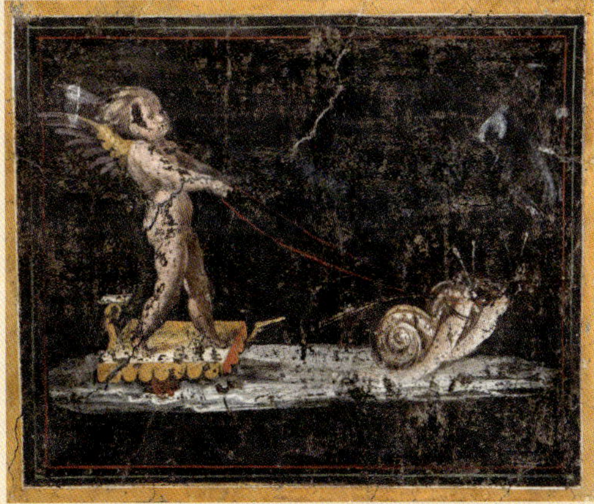

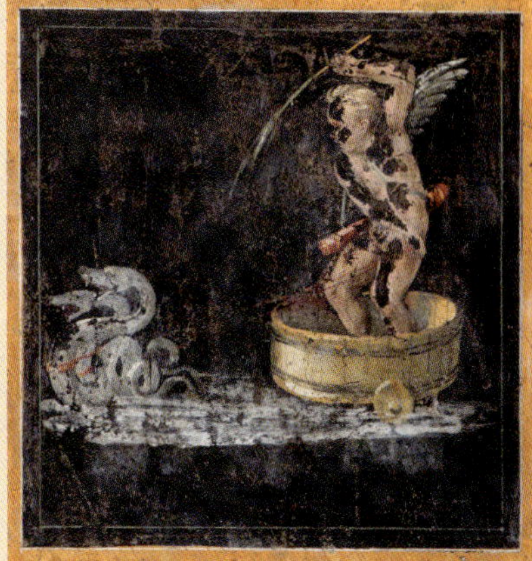

Aphrodite and Eros (Aphrodite d'Este), 1st cent. BC (?)
Marble, height 114 cm (44 ⅞ in)
Vienna, Kunsthistorisches Museum, Antikensammlung

Raphael and Giulio Romano
Picture Cover of Cardinal Bibbiena's *Small Holy Family* with the *Allegory of Abundance (Dovizia)*, *c.* 1517/18
Oil on panel, 38.4 × 31.3 cm (15 ⅛ × 12 ⅓ in). Inscription: *RAPHAEL VRBINAS.*
Paris, Musée du Louvre

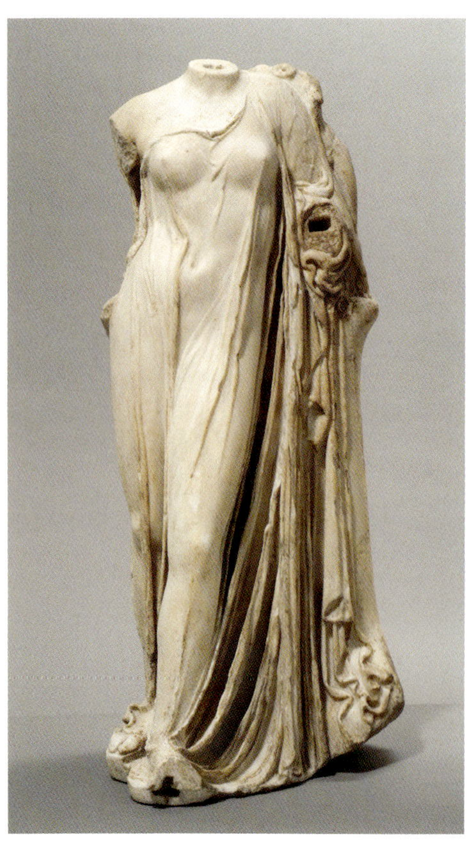

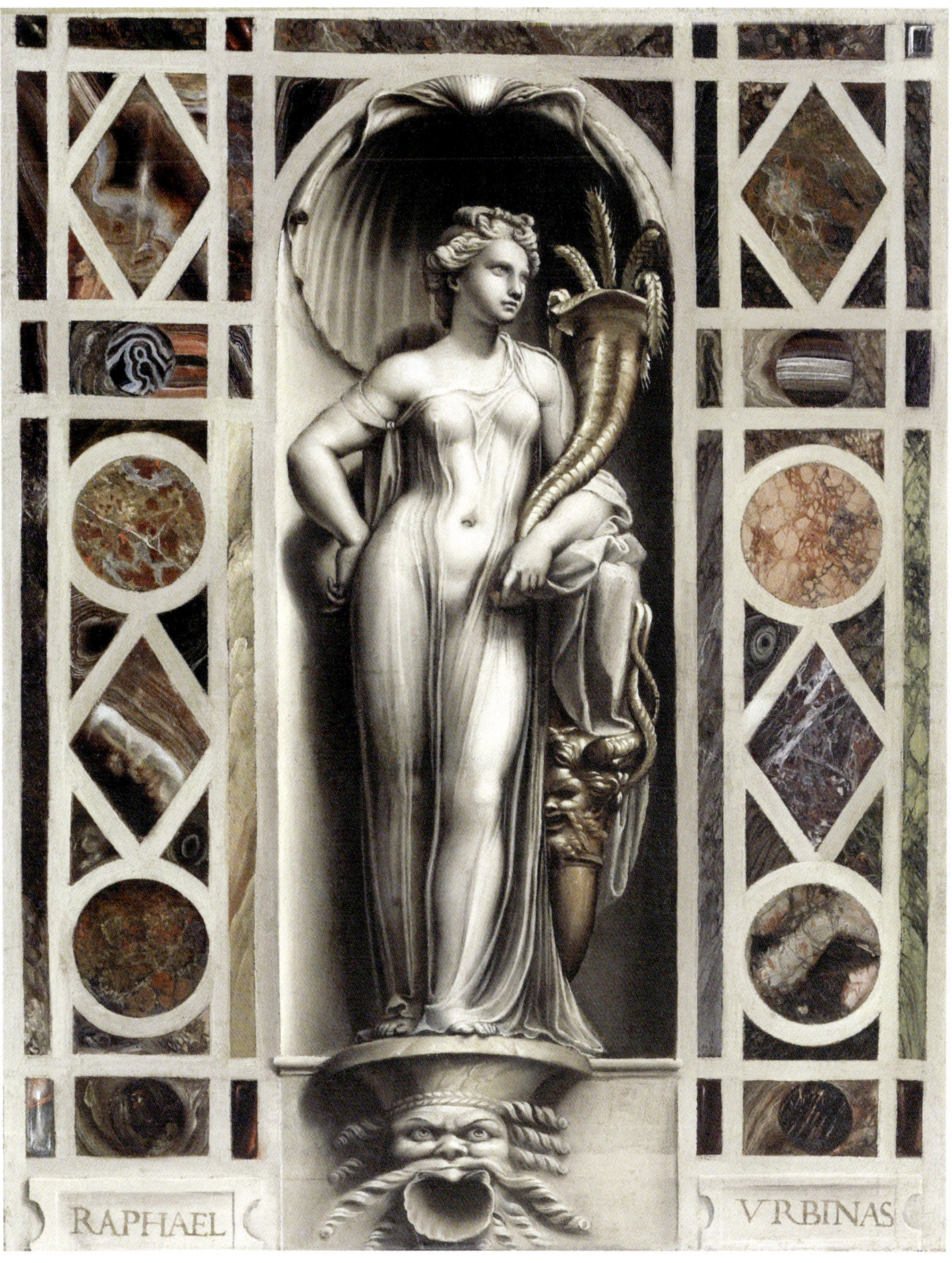
RAPHAEL
VRBINAS

VIII.

Large-Scale Decoration Projects: Chapels, loggias and the Sala di Costantino

1512/13–1520

Michael Rohlmann

"With all his extraordinary art Raphael is nevertheless artless; a superabundant charm of free, unconstrained, fresh natural life has been poured out over his works."

ADOLPH MENZEL, 1836

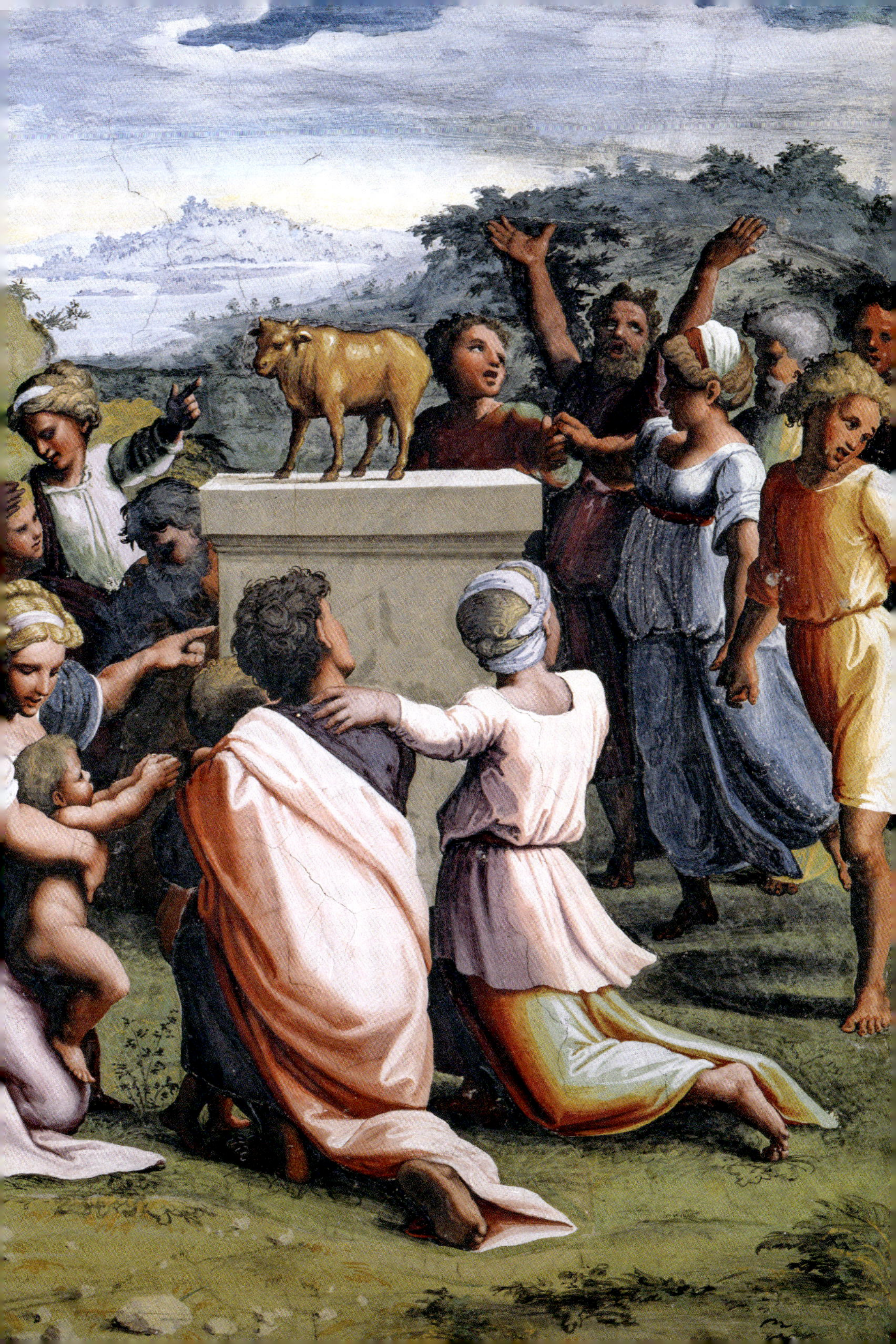

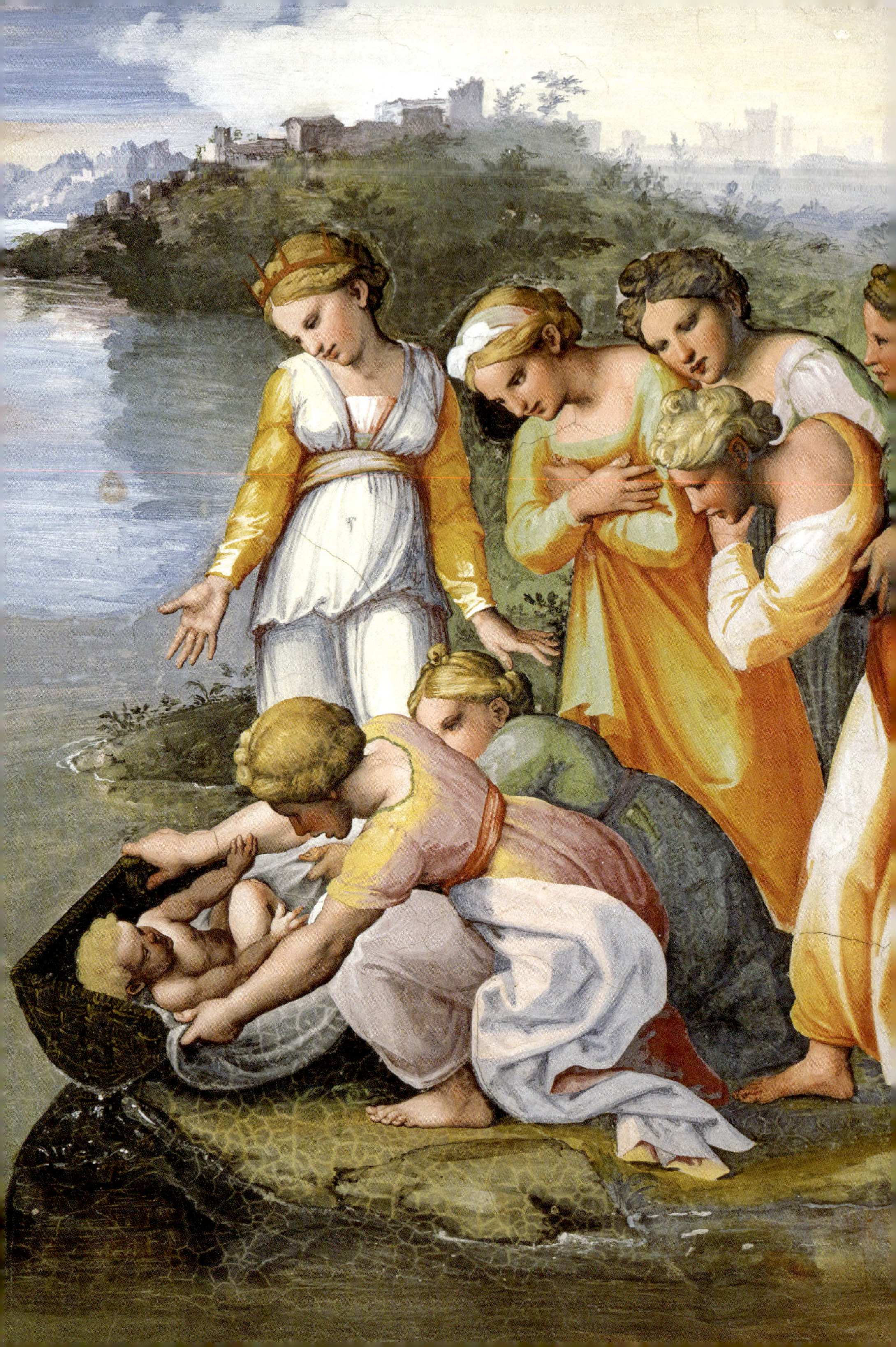

Over the course of his years in Rome, Raphael gradually advanced from producing or designing paintings to visualising their staging and spatial context as well. In some cases, he designed not only the frame of his pictures, but also their architectural surroundings. Raphael no longer planned individual paintings alone, but also entire interiors to go with them. In 1514 Pope Leo X had appointed Raphael architect of St Peter's. Other clients commissioned designs for palaces and churches. The ever-increasing number and ever greater scope of these projects required the training and organisation of a large workshop in order to be able to delegate and share out tasks. In many of his major projects, Raphael will have confined his direct involvement in the conception and production of design drawings, or even simply sketches, which were then further developed and executed by colleagues.

His design activity was directed not just at painting and architecture, but also at sculpture and tapestry. Raphael thereby increasingly aimed at a mixing of genres. Architecture and furnishings, painting and surroundings were to harmonise in overall spatial ensembles. We can trace Raphael's development during this period by examining some of his decorative schemes for chapels, in which he strove for syntheses of painting and sculpture. The pier chapel of Johannes Goritz (*c.* 1455–1527) in the Roman church of Sant'Agostino was located on a pillar of the central nave and comprised an altar, a niche containing a marble altar sculpture, and a fresco above it (pp. 474, 475; Cat. F8). The sculptural group of the *Virgin and Child with Saint Anne* is by Andrea Sansovino, the crowning fresco by Raphael. Showing the prophet Isaiah, it is closely related to the altar and sculpture in its content and form. Sansovino's marble group became the annual centre of a literary competition in which Goritz's poet friends praised and celebrated the statues and the holy figures they represented. The verses were then affixed to the chapel like votive offerings. Raphael's *Isaiah* served as a legitimising focal point for this tradition. Isaiah, too, presents us and the sculpture with a scroll containing a message directed at the saints. As a prophet, a divinely inspired seer and an author, he is a biblical forerunner of the religious poets *(vates)*. In the fresco offered to the statue, the painter Raphael has at the same time joined the ranks of the poets and contributed his own art to their competition. In a similar *paragone*, Raphael competes in an astonishing way with Sansovino's sculpture, too: just as the marble unfolds in three dimensions, so the painted prophet achieves a particular spatial effect for the viewer: wherever we stand in front of the fresco, Isaiah's bare knee and his scroll are always facing towards us. As we walk past,

Page 437
Detail from **Adoration of the Golden Calf (Moses Shatters the Tables of the Law)**, *c.* 1518/19

Detail from **The Finding of Moses on the Nile**, *c.* 1518/19

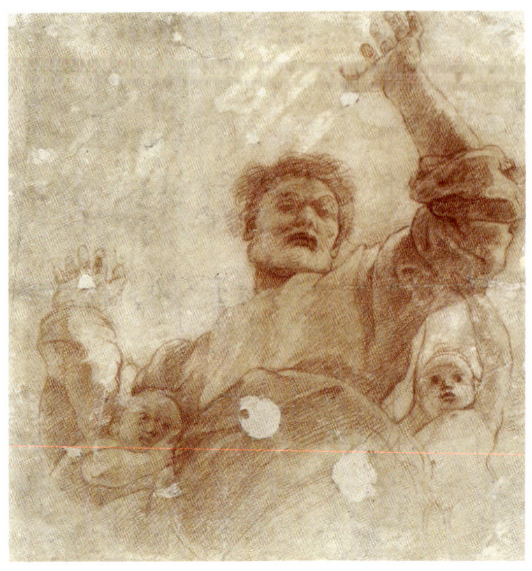

we not only experience the three-dimensionality of the sculpture, but the painted prophet above it seems to move his leg and scroll, and so turn on the spot.

For the upper section of Agostino Chigi's wall chapel in the Roman church of Santa Maria della Pace, Raphael designed two pictorial registers showing seated sibyls below and standing prophets above (p. 477; Cat. F9a, 9b). Raphael seems to have brought in Timoteo Viti to paint the prophets, but evidently executed the beautiful, arching line of sibyls himself. Sibyls and prophets, with their written messages, combine into a theologically sophisticated, erudite programme that revolves around the theme of the Resurrection. Thus the four prophesies by the sibyls allude to the following themes (in chronological order of redemption from left to right): resurrections effected by Christ on earth, Christ's own resurrection, the resurrection of the dead upon Christ's return at the Last Judgment, and the eschatological new Golden Age of the Saved. One of the two prophesies in the upper register is also incorporated into the series by the pointing gesture of an angel. Lactantius (*c.* 250–*c.* 320), the source of the citations from the sibyls, had linked the word of the Bible with the corresponding sibylline prophecy. Unfortunately, the original architectural framework of the frescoes, and the altar niches and plinth wall originally intended to appear below them, have either not been preserved or were never carried out. As the chapel's altarpiece, Raphael planned an oil painting showing the Resurrection of Christ. The oil painting, whose illusion of reality would have surpassed that of the fresco, would have allowed what was merely announced by the sibyls and prophets to become a seemingly real-life event. The altar retable was to be flanked right and left by bronze tondi showing *Christ in Limbo* (Cat. F9c) and *Christ and the Doubting Thomas* (Cat. F9d).

God the Father with Angels, 1513/14
Red chalk over stylus underdrawing, 20.9 × 21.4 cm (8 ¼ × 8 ⅜ in). Oxford, Ashmolean Museum

Luigi da Pace after designs by Raphael, **God the Father as Creator** (Detail), 1516
Cupola mosaic. Rome, Santa Maria del Popolo, Cappella Chigi

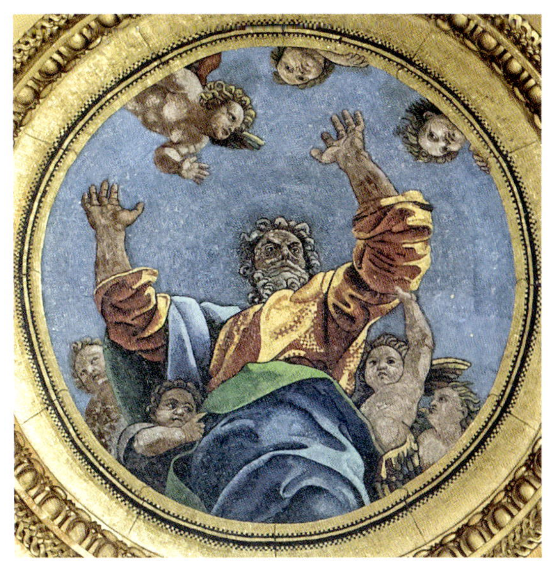

These reliefs, too, were designed by Raphael himself (KMOF 399, 401–403). They are today preserved in Chiaravalle Abbey, near Milan. Like Thomas, the viewer could have felt the reality of the Risen Christ in a tactile way.

In Agostino Chigi's burial chapel in Santa Maria del Popolo in Rome, the variety of media is increased yet further (Cat. A1). The intention here was for the visitor to be able to walk into a three-dimensional *Gesamtkunstwerk* by Raphael. The architecture, which borrows from Donato Bramante and motifs from the Pantheon, was designed by Raphael in its structure and forms of decoration. The chapel was clad in coloured marble in the antique style – for the Renaissance, an innovative and exceptionally luxurious choice. Oil painting was probably planned for the altar. The Venetian specialist Luigi da Pace was engaged to execute the mosaics on the vault, drum and pendentives of the dome. Working from designs by Raphael, he had finished the representations in the vault by 1516. Raphael engaged the Florentine sculptor Lorenzetto (1490–1541) to execute his designs for the marble statues in the corner niches and for bronze reliefs. The chapel decoration was only finally completed by Bernini (1598–1680) in the seventeenth century. Its original overarching intellectual concept remains the subject of some dispute. The scenes in the dome unite to form a coherent composition. Above the real windows of the drum, fictive views of the heavens open up in the vault and revolve around a central oculus that likewise seems open to the sky. In the central mosaic, God guides the course and position of the planets with the help of angels in the lateral fields (p. 441). But the gaze and commanding gesture of the figure of God, seen in foreshortening, are felt throughout the entire chapel. God's attention, as if palpably present, is directed at all below: the chapel visitors, Lorenzetto's statues of the prophets Jonah and Elijah – both rescued by God – in the niches, and also Chigi himself, buried beneath the cupola and awaiting resurrection. God spreads his arms in blessing out over the world, creation, the history of salvation and the chapel building, so that he may sanctify Raphael's great antique-style decoration as once he did the house of Mary, the Casa Santa of the Madonna of Loreto, to whom the chapel was dedicated.

Raphael's loggias (pp. 479–493; Cat. F6), completed in 1519, carried the wealth, variety and concentration of interior decoration to a high point of hitherto inconceivable quality and form. The covered walkway, which ran in front of the papal apartments and was open to the east, offered a breathtaking view of the city of Rome and the countryside. Leo X used the walkway for relaxation and pleasure, but also received visitors here. The loggia furthermore led from the large entrance stairway past the living and ceremonial rooms directly to the Sala di Costantino, used for official receptions, and on to the Stanze. As a designer, Raphael was faced with the difficult task of setting an equivalent interior décor against the uniquely magnificent panorama. The floor was paved with coloured majolica. The richly structured wall and niche architecture created by Raphael was filled with antique statues. These stood in tabernacles against a painted blue sky and were surrounded by *trompe l'œil* garlands of fruit. Birds appear to have flown in from outside and are perched on the fruit – an allusion to an antique legend according which illusionistic grapes painted by Zeuxis were so convincing they attracted birds. Sumptuous wood carvings filled the doors of the loggia. All the structural elements are covered by a colourfully detailed skin of playful decorative fields and ornamental motifs. Raphael's colleague Giovanni da Udine (1487–1564) had succeeded in recreating the ancient Roman technique of fine stucco marble. Imitation antique reliefs thus also appeared alongside painted *grotteschi.* The visitor gazes in amazement at a world of motifs from nature, mythology, ancient works of art and sporadically, too, the daily life of artists and Pope: figures, plants, animals, arrangements of musical instruments, models of virtue, love scenes, gods, seers, personifications, and fantastical creatures of all kinds. Who could ever put into words the visible profusion of imagination, wealth and freedom? Grotesques and stuccoes demonstrate superabundance and offer a compendium of nature, culture and history. This acted like an invitation to compare the view inside the loggia with that out onto the gardens, countryside and the eternal city of Rome. In the ornamental framework of the loggia decoration, this vedutà of the wider world was dismantled, as it were, into small individual elements. Ancient Roman interior decoration was here not only brought back to life, but surpassed.

The decorative scheme is lent order and solidity by the principle of symmetry, which organises the framing elements and ornaments on pillars, in the individual bays and through the entire sequence of rooms. A rhythm of closed ornamental surfaces and fictive views through architecture to the sky overhead is established on the vaulted ceilings. Four paintings and their picture frames are seemingly built into each of the thirteen bays. Thus the loggia appears not only as a pseudo-antique hall of sculpture, but at the same time as a replica of a *pinacotheca,* i.e. an ancient gallery of paintings, as described by Philostratus (*c.* 165/70–244/49), for example. The pictures are thereby executed in a free, lively, open

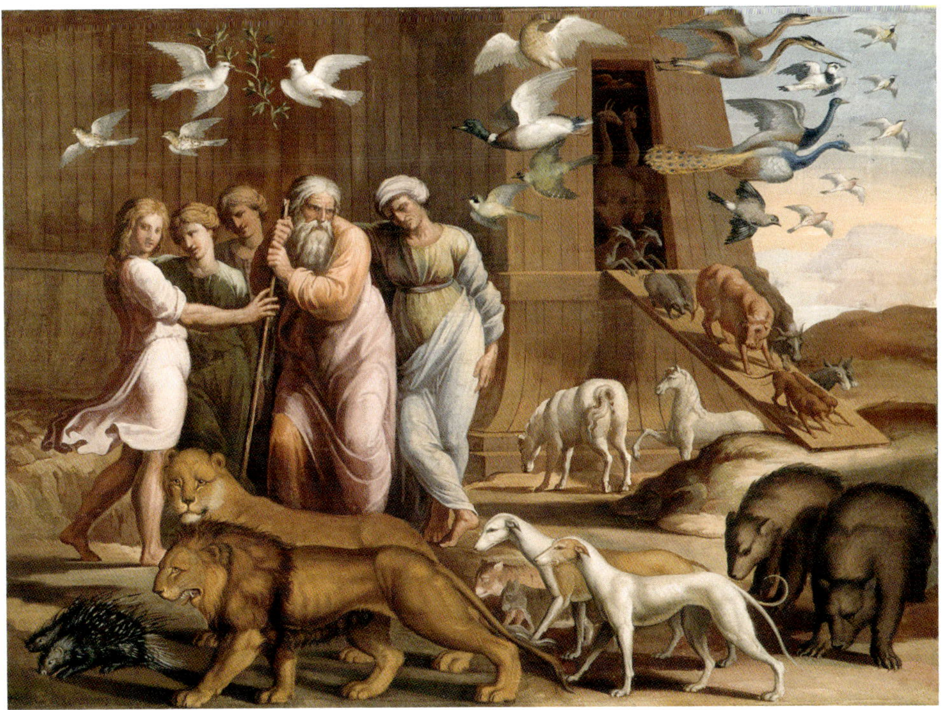

Christoph Unterberger (copy after Raphael's loggias), **The Animals Leaving Noah's Ark**, *c.* 1779–1787
Tempera on canvas. St Petersburg, Hermitage, Loggias of Catherine II

manner that likewise invited comparison with surviving antique wall painting. In their narrative style, too, the scenes take up from antique painting and in two cases even include river gods. But the subject of the representations comes from biblical antiquity: it is the story, beginning with Creation, of the predecessors of the popes as leaders of the faithful. The series runs from God, via Adam and Eve, Noah, Abraham, Isaac, Jacob, Joseph, Moses, Joshua, David and Solomon, right up to Christ. The world of nature and pagan antiquity evoked in the wall zone is thus subordinated to the history of salvation depicted in the vault, and in this way appropriated for Christianity.

The loggia's magnificent real-life view of the sky and nature is taken up and reflected in delightful ways in the biblical frescoes and their painting. Pictures such as *Jacob's Meeting with the Daughters of Laban at the Well* (pp. 488/489; Cat. F6.6b) and the *Finding of Moses* (p. 438; Cat. F6.8a) are early masterpieces of mood landscapes. Atmospheric effects appear again and again in the pictures. Sun, moon and stars rise in the sky, nocturnal darkness covers the land. Clouds gather, a storm rages, rain pelts and lightning flashes. The distant horizon turns a delicate pink with the dawn; a cheerful midday light gives way to an evening ambiance. Shade cools in the heat of the afternoon; a full moon illuminates the night with golden light. We see the sea, rivers and lakes, the foam of the waves and the calm, mirror-like surface of the water, the bubbling of the spring, the splashing waterfall and the quiet sprinkle of the fine fountain jet. Shores are flat or rocky; stones and pebbles lie on earthy ground. Plains, meadows and forests meet; bushes and individual groups of trees appear as if within reach or rise up out of the mist. Young tree trunks grow next to gnarled old ones, tender greenery next to gnarled stumps. In the distance, blue mountains gleam and snowy peaks glitter. Cities lie on hilltops or on flat land, in some cases surrounded by walls and with gates that lead inside. Castles grow out of rocky cliffs, buildings tumble down or are newly constructed. Fires are blazing, too, and cracked walls topple. Temples soar beside palaces, huts prop themselves against ruins, colourful tents are erected. Meadows are criss-crossed by paths and fences. A herd grazes, sheep huddle close together, sleep, drink at the well, or move off along a narrow path into the distance. We can make out people on foot and on horseback, labourers with their tools and ships on the water. Soldiers march, children play, a pack animal is driven, a farmer sows, a traveller rests, a dog dozes, a rabbit crouches. The frescoes show the richness of the world and life as it once presented itself from the second-storey loggia.

How the real-life landscape is viewed, and even how attention is directed towards it, are recurring themes in these ceiling frescoes. Again and again, we are offered a vista of nature from an elevated point of station. Thus the experience of looking out of the loggia is directly transformed into view. In the Creation scenes, God looks down at the earth from above (Cat. F6.1b and c). Flying overhead, he appears to Abraham and Isaac and in each case gestures across the landscape (p. 445; Cat. F6.4c and p. 486; Cat. F6.5a). From heaven, God sees and blesses the sleeping Jacob below; a staircase of angels serves to connect them (p. 487; Cat. F6.6a). God, on top of the rock, gazes down in blessing at his thirsting people (Cat. F6.8d). Moses looks down from an elevated standpoint full of wrath upon the sinful people (p. 437; Cat. F6.9b), and carries down and shows them God's law from the mountaintop (p. 457; Cat. F6.9d).

But the connection between the pictorial world and the elevated loggia situation is even closer. Insofar as Abraham has twice stepped outside his house onto a forecourt, he seems to anticipate the situation of the Pope, who has walked out into the loggia from inside the Vatican. And just as the forecourt is bounded to the rear – where the land drops away – by a fence, so a balustrade runs along the far side of the loggia (Cat. F6.4b and c). Eve, too, sits in front of her original cabin, and here, too, a fence runs along behind her (Cat. F6.2c). Noah stands in front of the door of his ark to watch the departing procession of animals

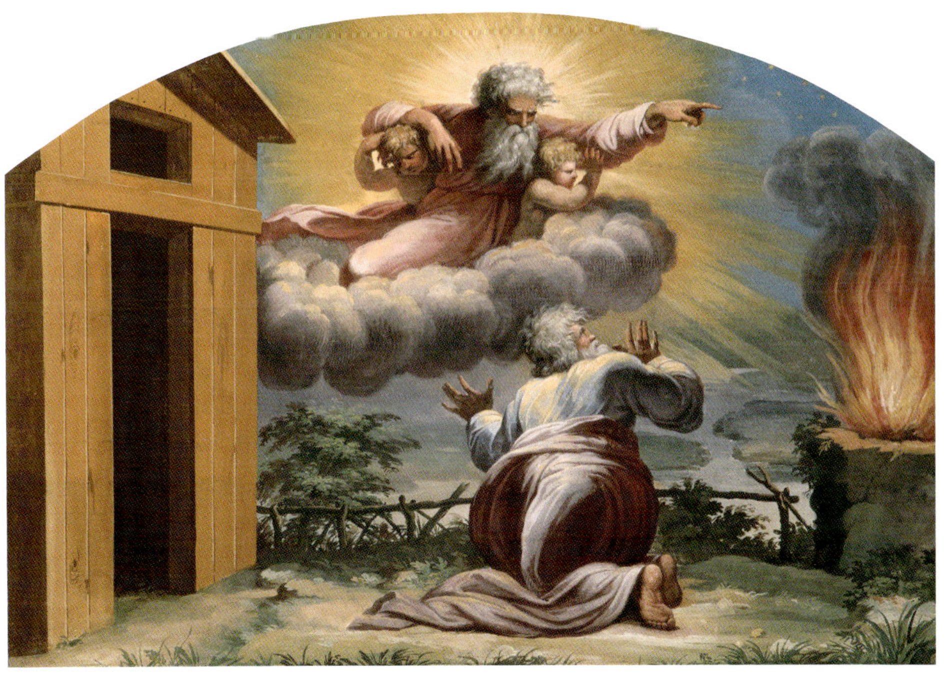

Christoph Unterberger (copy after Raphael's loggias), **God's Covenant with Abraham**, *c.* 1779–1787
Tempera on canvas. St Petersburg, Hermitage, Loggias of Catherine II

(Cat. F6.3c). Moses and the people leave their tents to look outside (Cat. F6.9c). Even the view of a lower-lying landscape from an open-sided pillared arcade – in some cases incorporating a balustrade, as in the Vatican – can be found in the frescoes. With this recurring key motif, the Vatican loggia itself becomes part of the visual narrative, as it were. Joseph interprets the Pharaoh's dreams in the room of a palace opening onto a loggia. Behind the balustrade, a river flows away into the far distance (p. 491; Cat. F6.7d). King Solomon's palace, too, offers a view of nature through pillared arcades. From here the Queen of Sheba has entered the throne room (p. 471; Cat. F6.12d). The wise ruler directs construction work on his temple from above (Cat. F6.12c). From the interior setting of the Anointing of David, we look through a window into an anteroom that is open to the outside world – in the same way as people inside the papal apartments looked out of the windows through the loggia (Cat. F6.11a). Isaac and Rebecca tenderly embrace in a loggia through whose opening a distant landscape appears below. Soft, comforting moonlight falls on the intimate scene from above and through the balustrade. The couple are spied on by the king from his vantage point high up in the loggia (p. 451; Cat. F6.5c).

From a multi-storey pillared loggia – almost a copy of the Vatican loggias – King David catches sight of Bathsheba bathing on a terrace (p. 449; Cat. F6.11c).

The loggia frescoes link the view of nature, countryside and people with the office and mission of the Pope in multiple respects. Here, beside an unimpeded view of the sky and the landscape, the pictures showed the Pope that God is present in nature and has become visible within it again and again. It is here that God spoke with his emissaries: in heavenly apparitions, pillars of cloud, through signs given by the sun and moon, and through the appearance of stars. But landscape also appears as an area of dominion, as the destination of migration, as the promised new homeland, as property to be distributed. The Promised Land is assigned by lot in front of Joshua and indicated by gestures (Cat. F6.10d). Behind the Anointing of David, the land over which the young shepherd is to reign can be seen through the window (Cat. F6.11a). The view of the landscape looking down from above is assigned to the ruler and represented as useful for his activity. God himself rules, insofar as he separates land and water from above and creates the animals below him (Cat. F6.1b and d). Just as God soars over his creation, so the Pope in his loggia elevates himself above his dominion. Watching from above, God sees when Jacob, Moses and his people are in need and gives his blessing several times from above (p. 487; F6.6a, F6.8d). Moses presents the tablets of the Law to his subjects from above (Cat. F6.9d), but it is from above, too, that he witnesses the offense and guilt of his people (p. 437; Cat. F6.9b). Joseph counsels the pharaoh in front of the view out over his dominion. A parallel is established between the two arcade openings onto the landscape and the two dreams that refer to the future abundance of the land (p. 491; Cat. F6.7d). The ruler's view of the state of his country is necessary for its well-being and for his own forward-planning government. From his raised vantage point, King Solomon can observe his workforce and issue instructions (Cat. F6.12c). King David inspects his army as it marches beneath his high loggia. From here, however, he is also seduced by the view of Bathsheba's naked beauty. It is a warning image that sets limits on the pleasure of looking (Cat. F6.11c). The event that takes place during Lot's escape from Sodom offers an antithesis to the Pope surveying good Christian Rome: looking at the burning city of sin results in Lot's wife turning into a pillar of salt (p. 486; Cat. F6.4d).

In addition to the view from the loggia, however, Raphael's pictorial cycle also thematises other functions of the loggia space. This was where the ruler wished to rest and relax. In the lost first picture in the plinth zone on the loggia's end wall, the viewer formerly saw God resting on the seventh day of Creation, sanctifying this day of rest (Cat. F6.1e).

Detail from **Triumph of David**, *c.* 1518/19

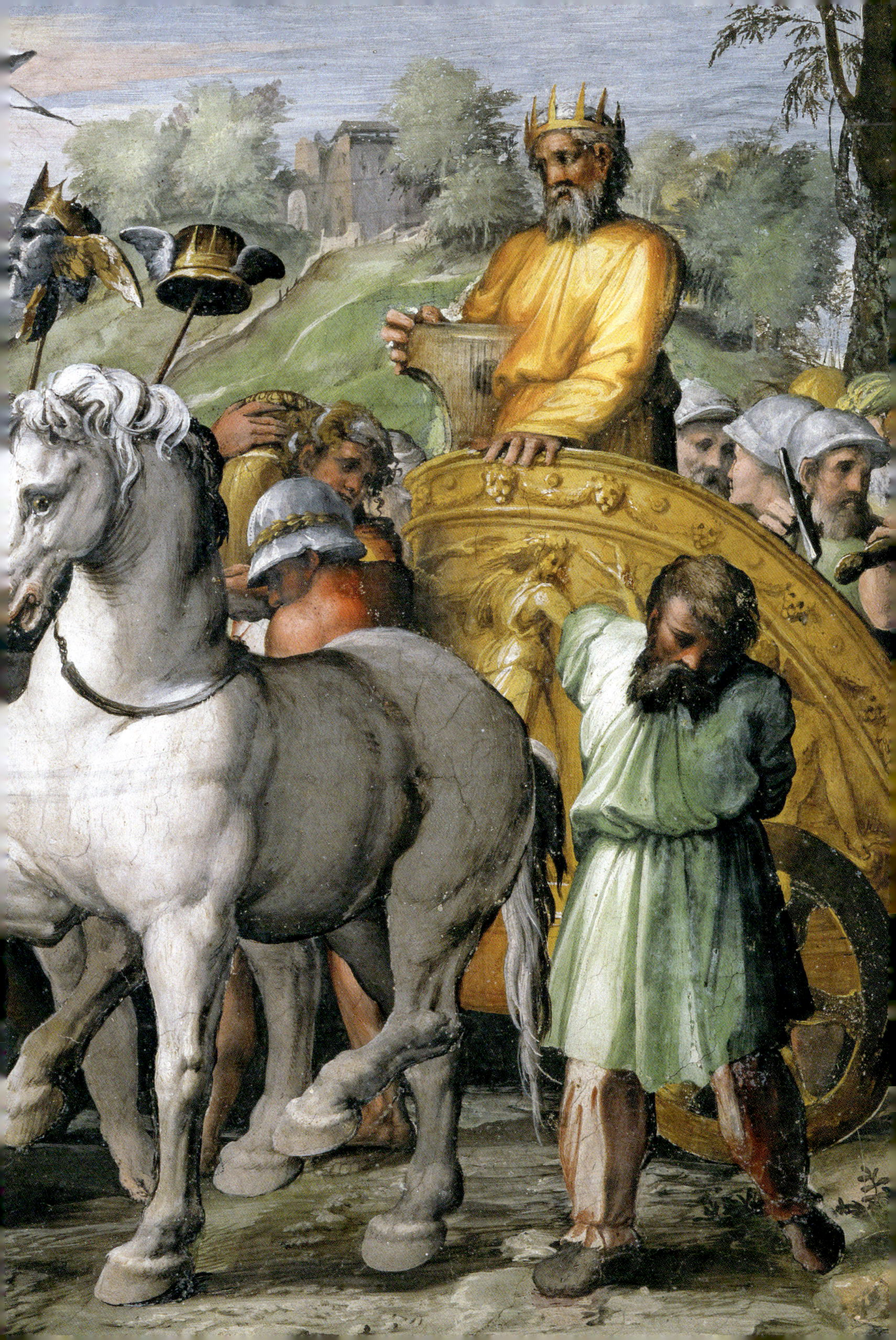

Noah, too, rests after the Flood. He props himself on his staff in front of the ark, while his wife leans against him. They lose themselves in the sight of the departing animals (p. 443; Cat. F6.3c). Rebecca rests in the shade in front of the city (p. 486; Cat. F6.5a). United with Isaac in the nocturnal loggia, she gives herself over to pleasure (Cat. F6.5c). Jacob slumbers and dreams outdoors in nature (p. 487; Cat. F6.6a). Leisure aside, the Pope also used the loggia for private audiences, meetings, discussions and negotiations. Models of these interactions were offered by scenes such as *Appearance of theThree Angels to Abraham and Sarah* (Cat. F6.4b), *Abraham and Melchisedek* (p. 483; Cat. F6.4a), *Isaac Blesses Jacob* (p. 487; Cat. F6.5b), *Joseph Tells his Brothers His Dreams* (pp. 492/493; Cat. F6.7a), *Joseph Interprets the Pharaoh's Dreams* (p. 491; Cat. F6.7d), *Solomon and the Queen of Sheba* (p. 471; Cat. F6.12d), the *Adoration of the Shepherds* (Cat. F6.13a), the *Adoration of the Magi* (Cat. F6.13b) and the *Last Supper* (Cat. F6.13d). Again and again homage is paid, talks are held, and gifts presented.

The rich biblical cycle not only illustrates the various ways in which the loggia could be used, but at the same time references the rest of its decoration. Thus the flora and fauna depicted in grotesques, framing frescoes and stucco works are also found in the biblical frescoes. The wide array of animals, including exotic species, shows itself as fashioned and blessed by God at Creation. Here, as in the framing ornamentation, the fauna of the earth is lined up before us (pp. 480/481; Cat. F6.1d). Noah, as the ancestor of the popes, unites and safeguards the animals in his ark. After the Flood, he and his family are gladdened by the sight of them, just as loggia visitors delight in the many small animal motifs in the wall decoration (p. 443; Cat. F6.3c). Noah sacrifices animals in order to thank God for this salvation (p. 483; Cat. F6.3d). Good shepherds, like the Pope, look after their flock and ensure their sheep are watered (pp. 488/489; Cat. F6.6b). Jacob brings a large herd of animals back to his homeland (p. 490; Cat. F6.6d). Even Christ seems to turn lovingly towards the ox after his birth (Cat. F6.13a). Eve receives flowers from one of her children, Adam grows crops (Cat. F6.2c). At the Nativity, angels bring garlands of flowers (Cat. F6.13a). Even fantastical beasts proclaim the fresco decoration to be God's Creation: the unicorn, siren and dragon belong among the inhabitants of Paradise just like the ostrich, elephant and rhinoceros (pp. 480/481; Cat. F6.1d). The painted Bible also offers space for antique personifications: a river god with a tiger and a fruit vase reclines in the foreground of *Zadok Anoints Solomon* (Cat. F6.12a). Jugs have faces in the story of Abraham (p. 483; Cat. F6.4a), and tables have leonine legs in the stories of Isaac and David (p. 487; Cat. F6.5b, 6.5d; F6.11a). In *David's Triumph*, helmets sprout bird's wings (Cat. F6.11d), and ornamental bands decorate pillars in Solomon's palace (Cat. F6.12d).

But dangers, too, lurk in the antique world of art and fantasy. *The Fall* warns against the alluring art of a serpent ending in a woman's head, whose powers of temptation

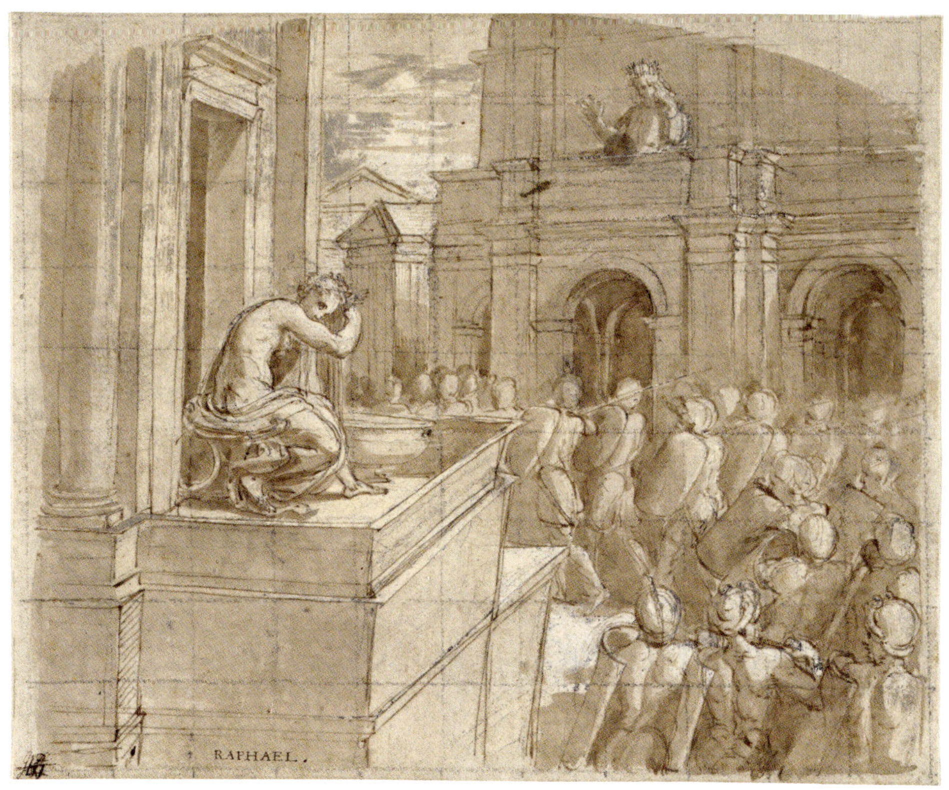

David and Bathsheba, 1516–1518
Pen and brown ink over black chalk underdrawing, with wash and heightened with white, squared in black chalk, 21.5 × 26.7 cm (8 ½ × 10 ½ in)
London, British Museum, Department of Prints and Drawings

are aided by the eroticism of the antique female nude offering herself to Adam (p. 482; Cat. F6.2a). David, too, succumbs to the sight of the naked Bathsheba as she poses in the Crouching Venus position familiar from antique statuary. The soldiers seem to be trying to protect themselves from her, as if from a siren, with their shields (Cat. F6.11c). And, of course, the Pope, like Moses, must prevent an object such as the Golden Calf being idolised and worshipped (p. 437; Cat. F6.9b).

The overwhelmingly beautiful and fantastical world of art in the loggias naturally makes it difficult to exercise a certain caution, as demanded by the Church, while enjoying their endless visual delights. It is perhaps for this reason that there stands, at the very centre of the entire cycle, an intellectualisation of pleasure. The middle bay featuring the story of Joseph – with whom Leo X, who was elected Pope when very young, liked to be compared as a way of refuting misgivings about his age – is particularly distinguished by its white and gilt stucco framework and the Medici pope's coat of arms in the centre (Cat. F6.7). Here, Leo X's youthful biblical forerunner flees before the seductive arts of a beautiful Egyptian woman, while equally beautiful female drapery figures dance around the scene in the ornamental frame. Joseph finds his mission instead in interpreting dream images in front of an audience. True to the biblical text, this leads him first into hardship and exile, but subsequently to the highest standing. Raphael shows these dreams as circular pictures-within-a-picture, floating against the sky and the painted loggia architecture. They exhibit strange combinations of motifs: sun, moon and stars gathered around a standing figure, bundles of wheat bowing down, healthy and withered ears of corn, groups of cattle (pp. 491, 492/493). They lead into the dream world of the ornament and grotesques of the real loggia architecture, where they connect with the stuccoed pictorial fields framed in a host of different ways on the walls. At its centre, Raphael's fresco cycle thus sets us the task of interpreting enigmatic representations. Joseph in the central bay seems to provide an interpretation guide for loggia visitors. This even includes instructions on how we should respond to and process the pictures: just as Joseph debates his dreams with his brothers, and the Egyptian court ponders over the Pharaoh's visionary dreams, so viewers of the loggia were supposed to discuss its strange world of motifs among each other. As if its fantastically beautiful forms concealed mysterious messages, which – like Joseph before him – the young Medici pope or his courtly inventor of images and gifted seer, the *vates* Raphael, could interpret. The task has proved as alluring as it is insoluble ever since.

From 1519, following the completion of the loggias, Raphael worked on the new decorative scheme for the large state room in the Vatican, which is located between the loggias and the Stanze. In the Sala di Costantino (pp. 494–507; Cat. F4), Raphael's art of large-scale decoration would reach its high point. Vast history paintings here combine with an organising framework that is innovatively enriched with figures from the most diverse categories and conceptually coordinated with the narrative main scenes. What Raphael has achieved here becomes clear when we look back at the directly adjacent Stanze, in which the relationship between the main frescoes and their framing decoration developed in characteristic fashion. Under Julius II, Raphael had to fill a pre-existing frame system with scenes (Cat. F3.1). This changed under Leo X in the Stanza d'Eliodoro (Cat. F3.2). On their high plinth, it was intended that the powerful impact of the new, dramatic large-scale history paintings on the walls should be given an aesthetically fitting accompanying framework. Graceful allegorical figures in monumental grisaille represent the principles of good rule by the papacy, and wealth and prosperity as the result and

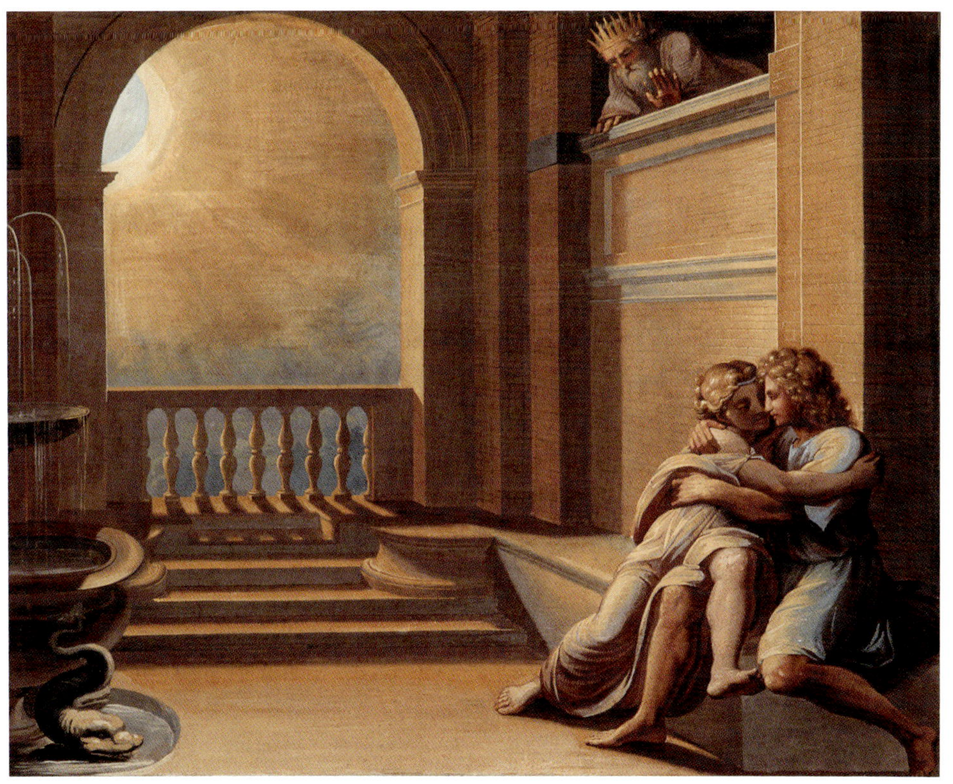

Christoph Unterberger (copy after Raphael's loggias)
King Abimelech Spies upon the Lovers Isaac and Rebecca, *c.* 1779–1787
Tempera on canvas. St Petersburg, Hermitage, Loggias of Catherine II

perpetual goal of government. Caryatids and herms lend the stone fiction of the massive, stable plinth zone a fixed rhythm across the irregular recesses of doors, windows and chimney. The antique-style supporting figures, inspired by the Erechtheion Kores on the Acropolis in Athens (Frommel 2018), carry the stage of the painted papal action playing out overhead. Here, in *The Expulsion of Heliodorus*, Raphael had portrayed himself as a litter bearer: the weight of the papal throne rests on his shoulder (Cat. F3.2a). Pictorial events and the decoration framing them combine here, in other words, in the motif of support. The famous letter purportedly written by Raphael to Castiglione also plays with the metaphorical idea of support: Raphael informs his friend that, in honouring him, the Pope has placed a great burden on his shoulders ("un gran peso sopra le spalle") – the building of St Peter's. The caryatids standing at the same height as the viewer were

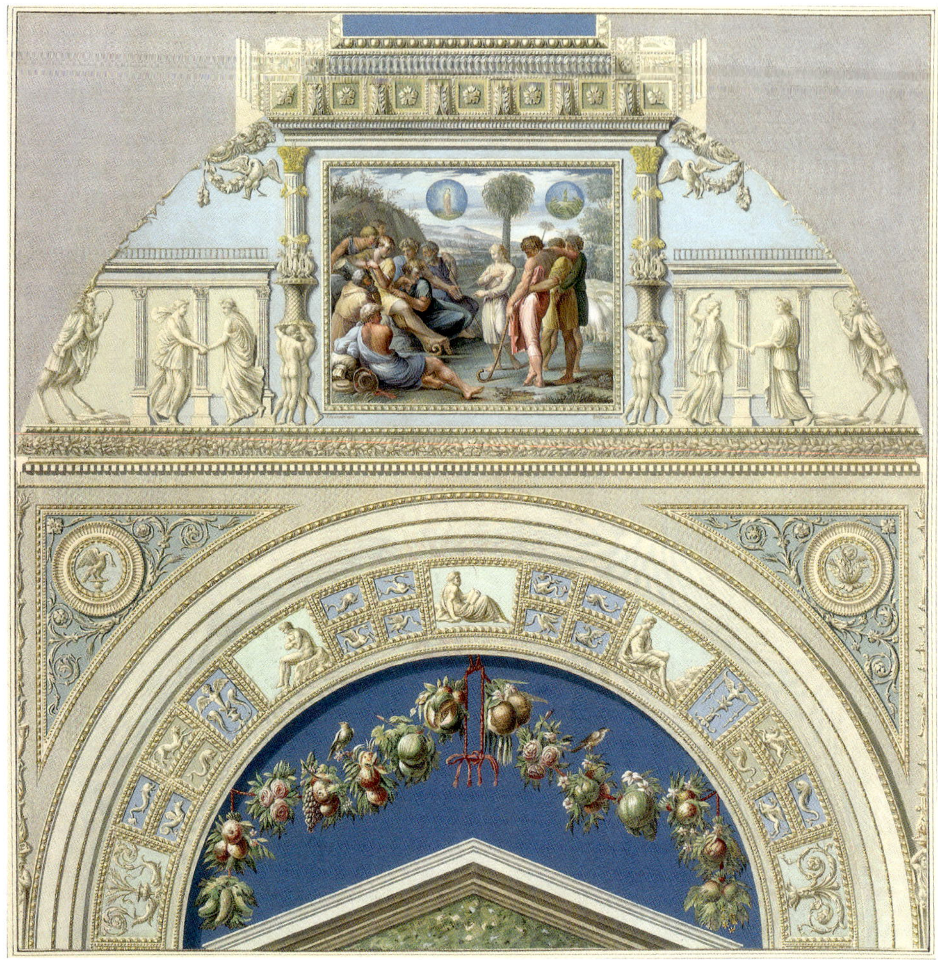

evidently intended to encourage the diplomats and members of the Curia entering the room to likewise support the Pope's policies and actions. Their graceful, casual and effortless poses furthermore proclaimed that this was an easy and pleasant task. The decoration thereby illustrates the biblical motto of the "easy yoke" which Leo X used as his device (Matthew 11: 30: "iugum enim meum suave est et onus meum leve est" – "For my yoke is easy and my burden is light").

In the Stanza dell'Incendio (Cat. F3.3), Raphael designed a plinth more richly and densely populated with figures. Now only muscular herms appear as supporting figures. They flank simulated bronze statues of rulers who had performed meritorious services for the Church and the Pope. Over the heads of these seated figures, the herms hold

Giovanni Volpato, Giovanni Ottaviani
Lunette and vault field with the representation *Joseph Tells His Brothers His Dreams*, 1776
from: *Loggie di Rafaele nel Vaticano*, 1776, vol. 2, pl. 7
Hand-coloured copper engraving,
57.6 × 56.9 cm (22 ⅔ × 22 ⅜ in)
Vienna, Albertina

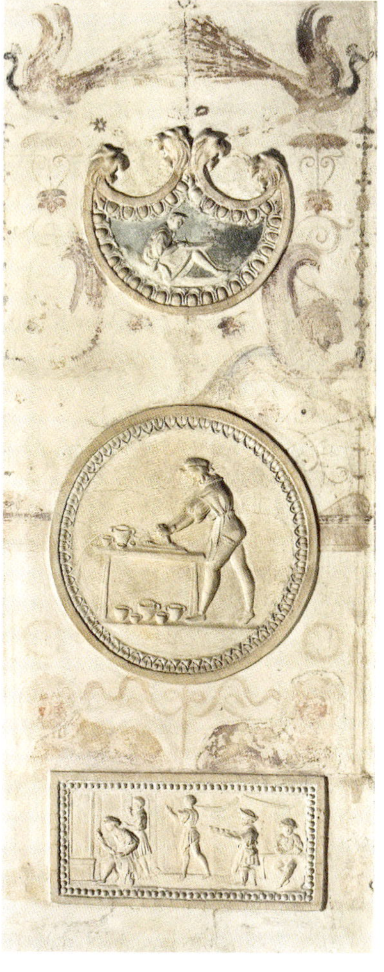

Artists at work in the loggias, *c.* 1518/19
Stucco decoration on the second pillar along the window wall
Vatican City, Musei Vaticani, Loggias

up scrolls on which the respective achievements of the individuals thus honoured are recorded. The herms in this way forge a direct visual link between the exemplary actions of the rulers and their function as pillars of the papacy. Burdens are again carried in the main frescoes, too. In the *Coronation of Charlemagne*, porters carry in heavy silver gifts for the pope (p. 230 b.; Cat. F3.3c). In the foreground of the *Fire in the Borgo*, not only is an old man being hoisted on the left and a bundle shouldered on the right, but a beautiful woman is even carrying a vase of extinguishing water on her head – like the herms below (p. 231 t.; Cat. F3.3e). Load bearers have also moved up into the surrounding decoration beside the narrative fields. In the corners, the vault consoles are supported by painted Egyptian atlas figures. Raphael had evidently studied the ancient statues, today housed in the Vatican Museums, during a trip to Tivoli in 1516. Thus the motif of the "light burden" is pursued across continents as well as back in time via Rome to Egypt. Leo's yoke *impresa* is even directly represented in the Stanza dell'Incendio's window walls, where the lightness of the yoke is playfully celebrated in the decorative grotesques.

In the Sala di Costantino (Cat. F4), finally, seated figures, caryatids and allegorical figures move right up into the main zone of decoration. In the corners of the room, eight canonised Early Christian popes appear as triumphal rulers, enthroned beneath magnificent canopies in painted stone architectural niches. They are accompanied by angelic assistants and personifications. Female and male carrying figures flanked their thrones and formerly appeared to support the huge room's flat ceiling with the yoke of Leo X. This elaborate wooden ceiling was put in before the decoration of the walls commenced. Between the papal groups, the large history paintings are seemingly hung up and rolled out as fictive narrative tapestries. They show the deeds of Emperor Constantine and the beginning of Christian rule. Borders adorned with grotesque ornamentation and Leo's *imprese* assign the fictive tapestries, too, to the Medici pontificate. In this reception hall for a large audience, the wealth, splendour and magnificence of the decoration are carried to supreme heights. Raphael plays with levels of reality and even incorporates actual reliefs into the architectural fictions of the canopied thrones on the window wall.

The first two episodes from the life of Constantine were designed by Raphael himself before his death. The cycle begins on the narrow side of the room, next to the loggias, with the *Vision of the Cross* (pp. 496/497; Cat. F4.1–4.3). Drawing upon ancient imperial reliefs and written sources, Raphael here reconstructs the *adlocutio*, i. e. the address given by the emperor to his troops before the battle. But the astonished Constantine himself becomes witness to a message, when angels appear in the sky bearing the cross and promise that this sign will bring him victory. While in the legend the heavenly vision was intended for the emperor, in the fresco the symbol of salvation is angled away from Constantine towards the right, along with the ray of light carrying the message. There, outside the fiction of the tapestry, the enthroned Pope Clement I (*c.* 50–97/101; in office from 90/92) raises his hand in greeting as if to receive the enlightening words and looks up at the celestial apparition (Cat. F4.3). Clement, however, is a portrait of Leo X, the reigning pope, who is thus inserted into the role of Saint Peter's early successor. Victory thus seems to be divinely promised to Leo, as the recipient of the message of the cross, in a crusade against the Turks that he was planning at the time. The fresco shows that a miraculous sign can effortlessly overcome different epochs and levels of reality. The celestial light falls in front of a view of Rome, which appears as part of the backdrop to the vision of the cross. It thereby brushes the top of the Mausoleum of Hadrian crowned by a statue and descends over the bridge across the Tiber to the far bank (pp. 472/473). Pope Gregory I, the Great (*c.* 540–604; in office from 590) is said to have seen an angel standing on top of the mausoleum and sheathing a bloody sword, in a sign to the pope that a deadly plague was at an end. It is to this apparition that the Castel Sant'Angelo and the Ponte Sant'Angelo (the "Castle" and "Bridge of the Holy Angel" respectively) owe their new names. The painted ray of light in the fresco thus illuminates the tip of the Mausoleum of Hadrian as a place where, in the sixth century, too, an angelic vision delivered a promise of divine rescue to the reigning pope. On the far side of the Tiber, the celestial light causes an obelisk in front of the Mausoleum of Augustus to gleam brightly. The obelisk was understood as an Egyptian representation of the sun's ray. This very obelisk had been rediscovered in 1519. The ancient representation of a celestial ray had thus been brought back to light under Leo X and a ray of light from antiquity had, as it were, reached the Pope. Raphael suggested that the obelisk should be erected in St Peter's Square. Insofar as the fresco illuminates the obelisk with the light of the vision promising victory, the ancient find is given the aura of a miracle willed by God. The obelisk itself becomes a heavenly sign. For the Medici, who believed in miraculous phenomena and prophecies, this could appear as a good omen. The fresco thus links the vision of Emperor Constantine with the apparition of the angel to Gregory I and the miraculous obelisk find of Leo X. The redirection of the promise of victory from Constantine to the Pope is given a legitimising context. The tapestry's message to the pope is answered by an opposing, humorous interjection into the reality of the tapestry scene by the papal group in the right-hand foreground. Here a dishevelled dwarf jester is pulling on his armour, looking out at the viewer and – in his role as court fool – exposing his genitals (Burke 2016). On the right, the papal virtue of Moderation *(moderatio)* holds up her attribute of a bridle in admonition, as if the pope, for reasons of decency, wished to try to rein in the artist's unseemly *capriccio.*

Leo X had commissioned Raphael to create a visual reconstruction of ancient Rome in the form of drawings. The fresco of the *Vision of the Cross* offered a foretaste of this project in its vedutà of ancient Rome (Fehl 1993). The viewpoint is thereby chosen in such a way that the observer is located in precisely the place where the Vatican and the papal palace now lie. In other words, Raphael reconstructs the vista that would have presented itself in Roman times to the viewer looking in the direction of the fresco. The location of the picture is identical to that of the events it portrays: the past is overlaid upon the present. By passing through the door in this wall into the loggia beyond, the viewer could compare the Rome of antiquity with the city of today. Here in this picture, too, the view from the loggia is celebrated and at the same time annotated. In the sky above Rome, the Pope receives heavenly inspiration. Indeed, the name "Vatican" is derived from the Latin *vaticinium.* Thus the seat of the pope was characterised from antiquity onwards as a place of divination and prophecy.

In the vast panorama of *The Victory of Constantine against Maxentius at the Milvian Bridge* (pp. 498/499; Cat. F4.5), Raphael fuses antiquarian expertise and motifs of ancient relief art with the pathos of the great Florentine battle-scene projects of Leonardo and Michelangelo (pp. 74, 98). A chaotic sea of surging and swirling bodies flows across the landscape vedutà of the battlefield. The technical difficulties of representing contorted, foreshortened and moving bodies in an endless variety of poses are mastered with supreme artistry. At the same time, the abundance of individual detail fuses into a vast, coherent whole. In the middle, Constantine rises golden bright as an upright hero from the seething mass. Overhead, angels guide him to victory and lend his calm and clear appearance a supernatural power. In front of and beneath him, Constantine's mount sends his enemies into a plunging cascade that leads, in successive stages, to the deadly river. From there Maxentius (*c.* 278–312), already sinking, looks back to the victor. Their eyes meet. Amid the horror of the carnage, Raphael makes room for tragedy. Ever since the poetic interpretation by Giovanni Pietro Bellori (1613–1696), the group in the left-hand foreground has been especially famous: an old soldier, full of sorrow and pity, bends over a young soldier and recognises in him his own son. Thus suffering and grief do not disappear in the furious mass of killing. In the imagination of the viewer, one of the victims suffers a human, tragically moving fate on behalf of all. The standard of the defeated army has slipped out of the dead man's hand. Only the standards of the victors, crowned with the cross, reach up into the sky. They stand out against the warm evening light of the setting sun and accompany the emperor's sun-like appearance on the battlefield.

The following two scenes on the west and north wall were selected and executed under Pope Clement VII. Leo X's plans for these fields emerge from a letter of 6 September 1520, written by Sebastiano del Piombo. According to this, the *Battle of Constantine against Maxentius* was to be followed by the *Parade of Prisoners before Constantine*. Like the *adlocutio* of the *Vision of the Cross* and the equestrian battle of *Constantine against Maxentius*, the theme corresponds to a narrative formula of imperial Roman triumphal reliefs: in topical fashion, the victorious emperor shows clemency – the virtue of *clementia* (clemency) – to his defeated enemies. The scene would have corresponded to the image with which Leo X is present in the room as a role portrait: as Pope Clement I, whose very name promises mildness and gentleness, he is accompanied by *moderatio* (moderation) and *comitas* (courtesy) (Cat. F4.3).

The cycle was to conclude on the window wall with the strange representation of preparations being made to kill young children so that the sick Constantine could take

Detail from **Adoration of the Golden Calf (Moses Shatters the Tables of the Law)**, *c.* 1518/19

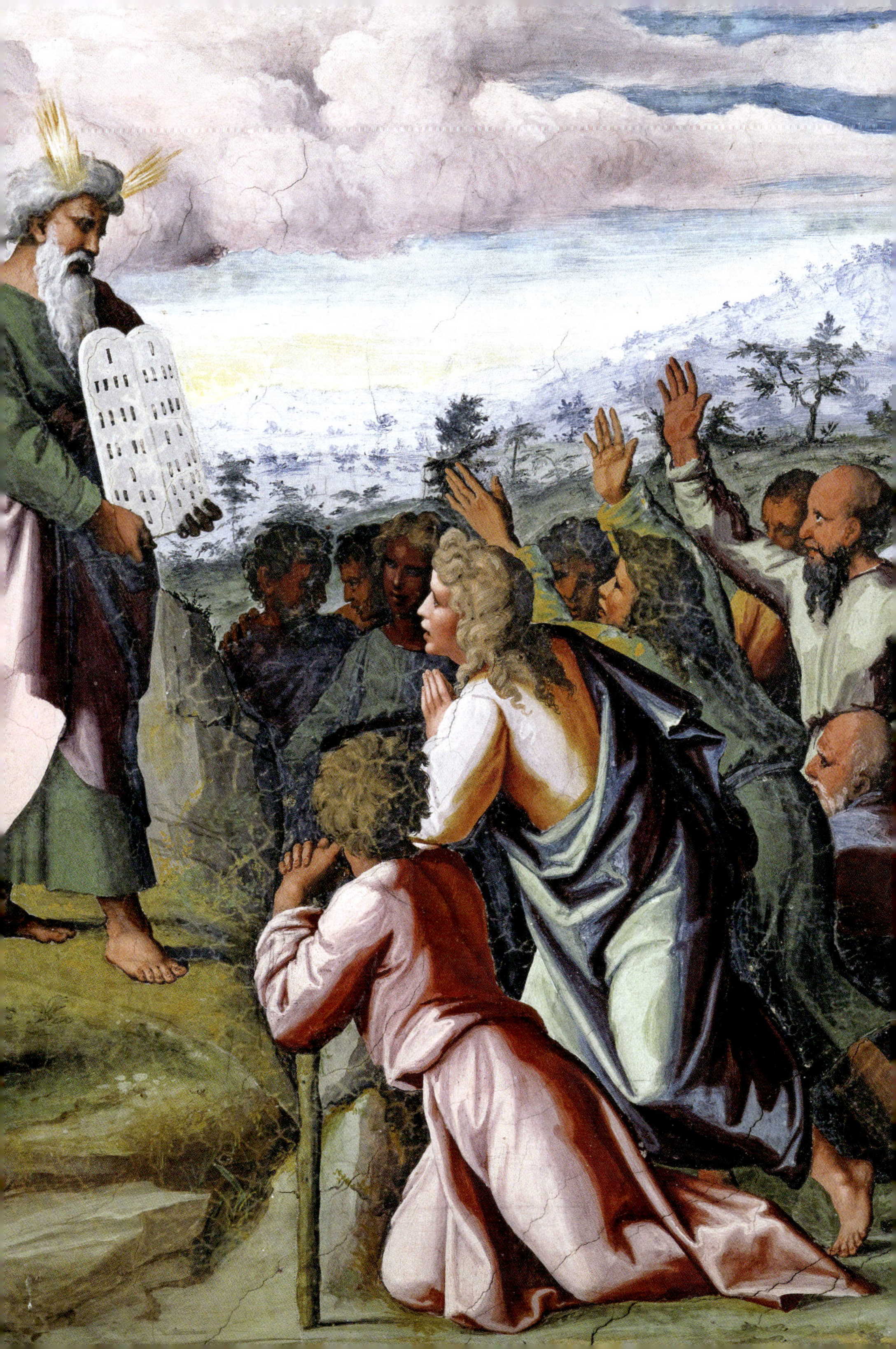

a curative bath in their fresh blood. The fresco was to show many women, infants and executioners ("el preparamento de l'incendio del sangue de quei putti, che lì intraven gono don[n]e assai e putini et manegoldi per amazarli, per far el bagno de l'Imperator Costantino"). The story is taken from the legend of Saint Sylvester. Pagan priests had recommended that the ailing emperor bathe in fresh blood as a cure for his disease. When Constantine saw the children and their distraught mothers, however, he was deeply moved and renounced his plan, and instead showered gifts on those whose lives had been threatened. He thereby extolled the virtues of Roman piety *(pietas romana)* and mercy. The *clementia* demonstrated to his own people would thus have complemented the clemency that Constantine showed to his defeated enemies (Quednau 1979).

A more compelling reason for the choice of the theme of the bloodbath and its prevention, however, seems to have been the decoration planned by Leo X for the plinth zone of the Sala di Costantino. The Pope ordered a series of twenty exceptionally sumptuous tapestries with representations of cherubs playing games *(Giochi di Putti)*. Raphael's pupil Tommaso Vincidor (1493–1536) had produced the cartoons for the tapestry weavers in 1520/21, probably basing himself on drawings by the master and by Giovanni da Udine. Although the original tapestries are lost, a number of drawings, prints and later copies give an impression of their cheerful magnificence. Philostratus had described an ancient painting that showed erotes picking apples and pursuing various forms of entertainment in an orchard. Leo's tapestries took up this antique motif and expanded it into a series of variations: in most cases, three winged putti frolic and play in front of and around festoons laden with fruit. As well as picking fruit, they also sport with a variety of animals, including a rabbit, a lion, a monkey and an ostrich. They romp around and entertain themselves, too, with papal insignia, with Leo X's *imprese* of the yoke and the ring, and with the balls of the Medici coat of arms. The entrancing cherubs are able to give themselves over entirely to innocent, carefree play. The sight of them is intended to lighten and gladden the heart. Woven in gleaming gilt and silver thread, the tapestries evoke peace, happiness, serenity and the abundance of a golden age (pp. 460, 462, 463).

The tapestries surrounded the room on all four sides. Hanging below the simulated, painted tapestries, the real ones were closer to the viewer physically, materially, and in the level of reality of their representation. Under Leo X, golden happiness seemed to envelop the present. At the same time, the putti cycle is closely linked to the world of the frescoes. It is glorified as the goal towards which the Constantine cycle and the cycle of popes aspire. One of the trios from the *Giochi di Putti* has already found its way in the scene of action as a celestial apparition in the *Vision of the Cross* (Cat. F4.2). Three winged cherubs hold up the cross, just as they flourish the papal emblems, for example, in the *Giochi di Putti*. Gleaming a yellowish red, they are aligned in terms of colour, too, with their fellows in the plinth tapestries. What in the real tapestries below had moved tangibly close, appeared to Constantine and Pope Clement I, alias Leo X, as a distant divine promise and mission. On the wall of the *Battle of Constantine against Maxentius*, the three climb as children up to the breasts of *Caritas*. Pope Urban I (died 230; in office from 222) halts retributive Justice on the side of the bloody slaughter with one hand and gestures with the other to the personification of Charity and her children as a model of virtue (Cat. F4.6). On the remaining two walls, only the papal groups on the window wall were executed under Leo X (Cat. F4.10 and 12). Here the winged putti have taken over the action in a helpful and playful way, cheerfully holding up the Pope's tiara and ring *imprese*, his vestment and writings, and drawing back the curtains of the canopy above his throne as well as in front of the fictive tapestry in the middle (p. 465). It was here that the scene of the halting of preparations for Constantine's bloodbath, in which the fate of the many children was reversed from death to deliverance and reward, was intended to appear as the conclusion of the story of Constantine. The planned Constantine cycle thus culminated in the happiness of the infants as its climax and goal. The joy of the young children was to radiate outwards from here, filling first of all the adjacent papal groups and then lending the whole room its festive and cheerful character in the gleaming and shimmering gold and silk tapestries of the plinth zone.

Looking back from the end and the plinth zone to the beginning, the heavenly message which is inscribed in Greek in the *Vision of the Cross*, and which translates literally as "in this, conquer", takes on a double meaning. Emperor and pope were to win victory not only with the sign of the cross, but at the same time, too, with the image of the happy putti who here joyfully present the cross of Christ. Just as Constantine carried the cross as his standard, so Leo planned to magic the joy of the cherubs out of the distant sky down to the floor level of the hall and into his receptions and celebrations. Under his pontificate, people were to transform back into happy children. In this way the real and painted tapestry decoration of the Sala di Costantino, its various pictorial groups and represented spheres of reality, could unite into a large, interlinking decorative and thematic unity.

On 6 April 1520, during the planning of this earthly paradise of happiness and joy, Raphael died in his Roman palazzo. His life did not end in fulfilment, but was cut short. His sudden, violent fever lasted one or two weeks. Friends reacted to the shock of his death with many words of consolation and praise for the man and his art: Raphael's fame would last forever; he would live on in his painting, in his works and in the writings of scholars and poets. His unexpected departure was Death taking his revenge: Raphael had aroused Death's anger and envy because, through art, he had given life to his figures and was thus able to conquer transience and death. Death was the reward for life begotten in art. With Raphael's death, countless lives had also died in the future works it prevented.

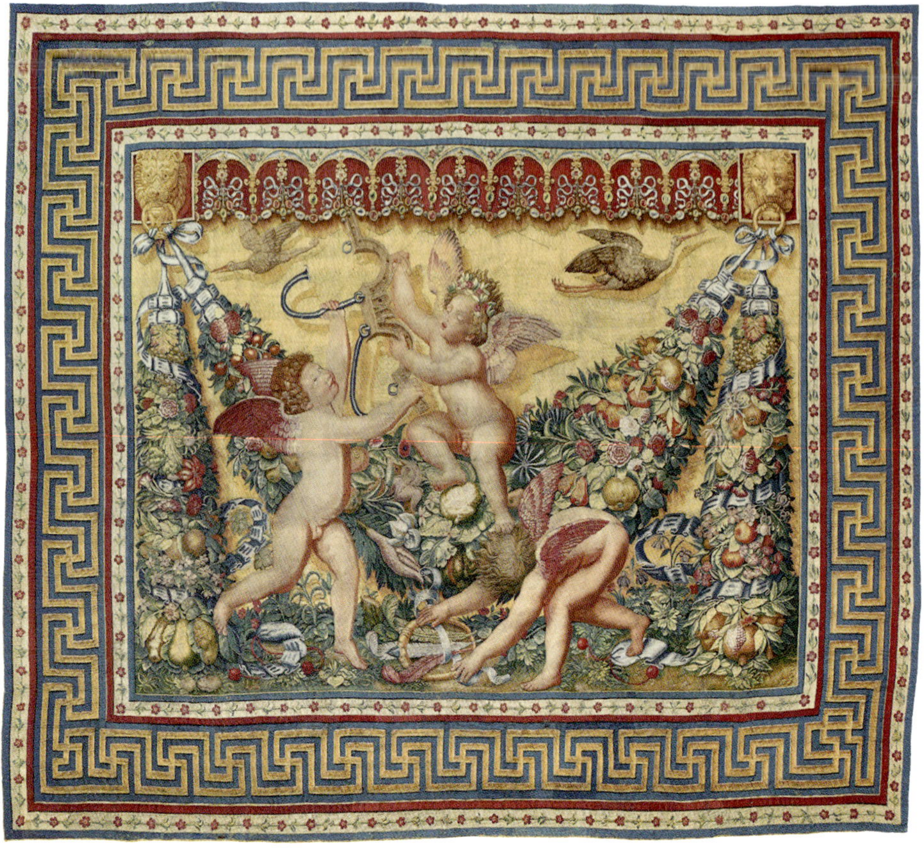

After Tommaso Vincidor, ***Giochi di Putti*: Putti with the *imprese* of Leo X**, Rome, 17th cent.
Tapestry, 274 × 301 cm (107 ⅞ × 118 ½ in). Budapest, Iparművészeti Múzeum

Because Raphael had conquered nature, it now vanquished him. But with his death, nature died at the same time. The gods punished their favourites with death; they wanted Raphael with them in heaven.

With Raphael, contemporaries wrote, a god seemed to have died. As Christ was the god of nature, so Raphael was the god of art. He died on Good Friday, the moment of Christ's death. Cracks in the Vatican Palace announced his death, just as the veil of the temple was rent in two when Christ died. Vasari describes how Raphael's body was laid out in his studio with his painting of the *Transfiguration* (p. 305; Cat. P85) at his head, presenting a sight of the dead artist and a living picture. If this was truly the case, the disciples abandoned by their master must have felt helpless, like the apostles, in the face of earthly misery. They could draw comfort, however, from the vision of the transfigured Christ: with the painting and within it, Raphael had showed his companions the power of a god of art that would radiate beyond suffering and death into the future.

Without Raphael, Rome – thus it seemed to his friends – would no longer be Rome. Rome died with Raphael. If Raphael, in his Rome plan begun for Leo X, had intended to resurrect the deceased ancient city in drawings, to bring the corpse of Rome back to life and to allow its ruins to awaken, the greatness of ancient Rome would now sink with him back into its grave. Rome's fame would fall with Raphael's death.

Raphael seems to have anticipated such thoughts and countered them, in perhaps his last work, with a poetic thought of his own. He wished to be buried in the Pantheon, the ancient building transformed into the church of Santa Maria Rotonda. For his grave, one of the old tabernacles was to be restored with coloured marble in an antique manner and filled once again with the stone sculpture of a goddess – now the Christian Madonna. It is possible that Raphael even told his sculptor, Lorenzetto, which ancient marble statue he should use as his model for a new statue of the Virgin Mary (Buddensieg 1968). Although Raphael's death spelled the end of his Rome plan, it was thus also accompanied – by way of compensation – by the restoration of an ancient ensemble, the partial restitution of an ancient interior with its ancient décor. Insofar as antiquity was reborn here, Raphael's corpse as it were breathed new life into the ill-treated cadaver of ancient Rome. This revival of antique form at his tomb might thereby serve as a pledge for his own Christian hope of resurrection (p. 469).

The day after his death, Raphael was buried in the Pantheon with great honour ("honoratissamente") and great pomp ("grandissima pompa"). A hundred torches, all carried by fellow painters, lit the funeral procession. The fame of the dead artist burns brightly right up to today, exploited and transfigured into ever new myths through the decades and centuries. Alive, Raphael knew celebrity from his youth onwards. In 1500 the seventeen-year-old was already considered famous in Urbino. Raphael had laid the foundations of his standing and reputation while still young (thus Leo X in 1514). In 1505 he was recommended as the best painter in Perugia. For Bembo in 1507, he was "un gran maestro della pittura". In 1511 reports of Raphael's great fame travelled from Rome to Ferrara. The topoi of praise increased with Raphael's death: he was worthy of immortality; the century's greatest light had gone out and its finest adornment vanished. In the mid-1500s, he was widely regarded as miraculous, magnificent and divine *(il divino Raffaello, più che divino, mirabile, miracoloso, grandissimo, eccellentissimo)* and as the lord of all painters of his era. The first examples of praise celebrating not only Raphael's art, but also his person and character, date from the artist's Roman years. He was an excellent man and there was a divine power to his genius (1516). Santi was not just his family name,

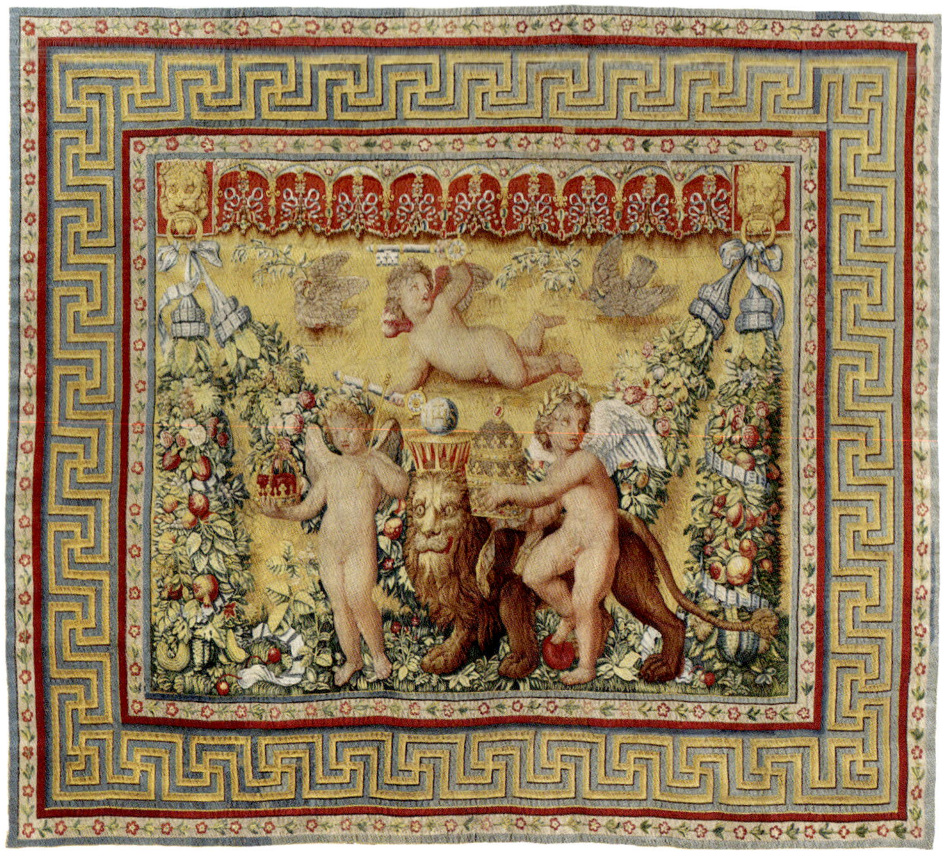

but his character and life, too, were saintly. Raphael was friendly and inspired ("gentile et ingenioso", 1519) and of unique virtue (1520). He had a graceful, noble and endearing aspect (1531). In 1542 his friend Pietro Aretino (1492–1566) attested to Raphael's amiable nature in dealing with people and praised his noble presence and fine mind. Grace, *grazia*, becomes the quality emphasised above all others in connection with Raphael and his work ("la illustre gratia di Rafaello", 1545; "il graziosissimo Raffaello", 1550). This praise reaches its high point in Vasari's *Lives* published in 1550 and again in 1568. In his *Lives of*

After Tommaso Vincidor
***Giochi di Putti*: Putti with lion and emblems of power; Putti with an ostrich**, Rome, 17th cent.
Tapestries, 286 × 310 cm (112 5/8 × 122 1/8 in), 270 × 310 cm (106 1/4 × 122 1/8 in)
Budapest, Iparművészeti Múzeum

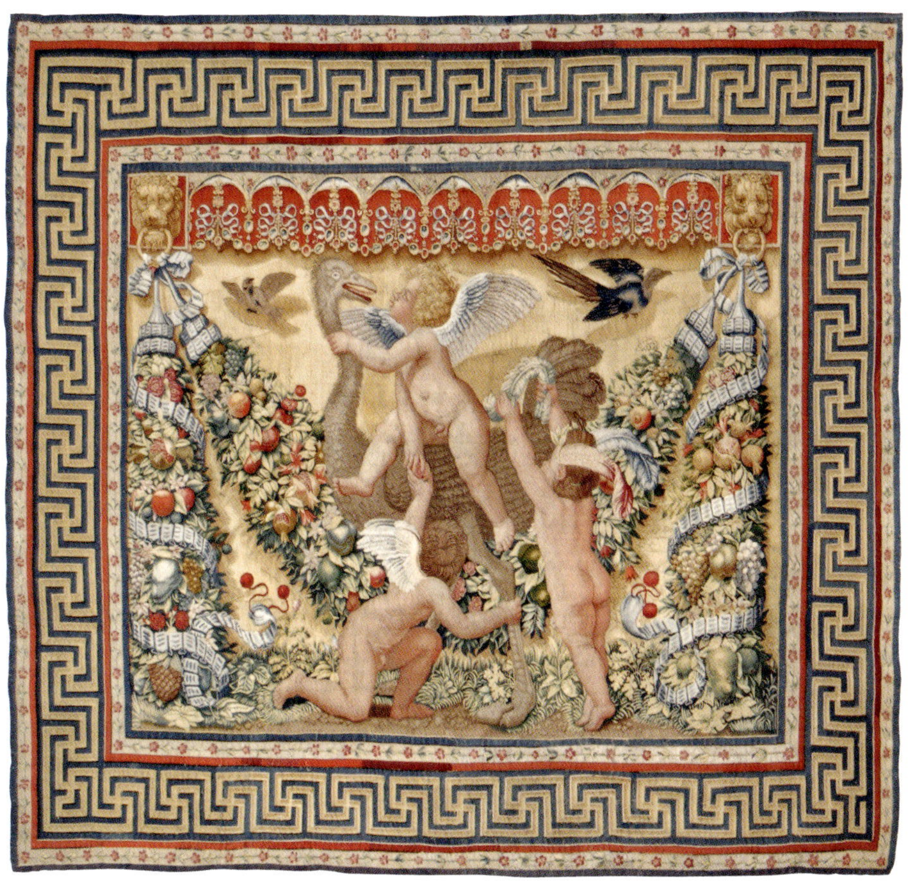

the Artists, Vasari writes that Raphael was distinguished by his modesty and goodness, loving-kindness and politeness, all the outstanding virtues of the soul, combined with grace, industriousness, a handsome appearance and courteous behaviour. He had the ability to reconcile all strife and all discord and transform them into harmony.

Alongside the poetic transfiguration and didactic stylisation of Raphael into a model of virtue, a few documents offer glimpses of more mundane and typically contemporaneous facets of Raphael's person. They show the human being behind the remote ideal. Again and again they reveal Raphael's concern for money, remuneration and possessions, his urgent desire to earn large sums and his demands for payment (see Thoenes 1997). In Urbino, he sued his stepmother for years over his father's estate – in defiance of the stipulations in the latter's will. A debtor lands in debtor's prison; Raphael attempts to appropriate a collection of antiquities, once again contrary to the provisions of the deceased's will. On the other hand, an artist colleague receives a generous loan and paintings are given away to friends. Marcantonio Michiel (1484–1552) valued Raphael's estate at his death in 1520 at the enormous sum of 16,000 ducats. As an entrepreneur, Raphael secured himself wealth and status. His paintings commanded enormous prices that not all could afford (Nelson/Zeckhauser 2018). When Gregorio Cortese asked Raphael, the "painter of our time", to carry out the decoration of the refectory at Santa Giustina abbey, the artist demanded such an exorbitant fee – explaining how difficult it was for him to leave Rome – that negotiations were dropped. Instead of "Apelles", in 1513 the planned *Last Supper* was painted by the considerably cheaper Girolamo Romanino as a future "Parrhasius" (Nagel 2011). The high prices were evidently part of Raphael's image as an artist of distinction – one he cultivated not without humour. Awaiting a visitor to Raphael's house was an antique statue, whose inscription declared it to be a portrait of the Greek poet Philemon. The statue held out one open hand towards the viewer, while clutching a scroll tightly in the other. Raphael's acquaintance Pierio Valeriano explained the gesture as a symbol of avarice *(avaritia)*: the author was only willing to hand over his work after he had been handsomely paid for it first (Daly Davis 1990, Christian 2004). A tongue-in-cheek Raphael evidently identified himself in this regard with the antique comic poet, by whom no works survive.

In line with social expectations, Raphael maintained a lifelong connection with his native region and family. He acquired property in Urbino and from his base in Rome also gave assistance to relatives, providing the son of his aunt Margherita with income and ultimately appointing him one of his heirs. Raphael's Christian faith evidently moved within the usual bounds: he was a member of a large religious confraternity in Urbino. In Rome Raphael endowed money for requiem Masses to be said in his own burial chapel. When it comes to sorrow and death, he said, it is necessary to have patience and reconcile oneself to the will of God ("bisognia avere pazientia e acordarsi con la volontà de Dio", 1508).

Raphael was a courtier. The Montefeltro had extended their patronage to him as a child. In 1508 he counted himself a servant of the court of Francesco Maria della Rovere, the new regent of Urbino ("suo antico servitore e familiare"). Letters of recommendation from the ducal family were intended to advance Raphael's career. In Rome he later left the service of the Della Rovere pope to work for the Medici. In 1515 he was possibly even a member of the household of Giuliano de' Medici. In 1511 Julius II appointed him a curial official with a regular salary. Leo X added the fixed income that went with the position of architect of St Peter's. In 1513 Raphael was considered painter to the Pope ("maestro Raphael da Urbino, pictor di N[ostro]. S[ignore]."). Together with Fra Giocondo (1433–1515), Raphael visited the Pope daily to discuss issues relating to the building of the new St Peter's. He formed friendships with other courtiers. His relationship with poets and writers was close. Pietro Bembo was busy writing to Cardinal Bibbiena when – according to the letter – first

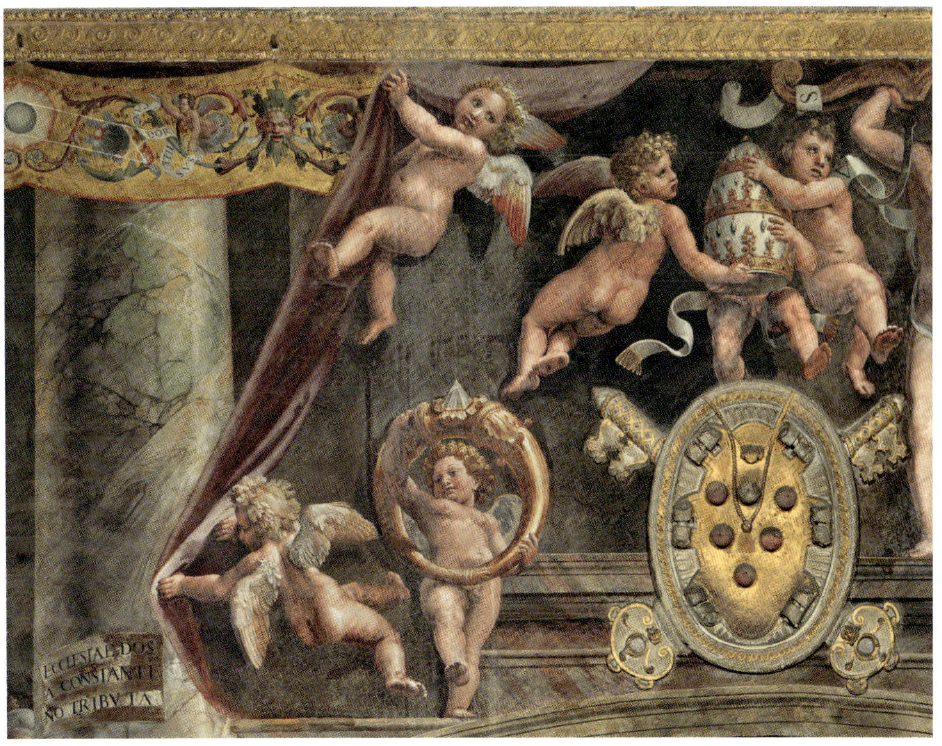

Workshop of Raphael, **Putti**, *c.* 1520/21
Fresco above the east window on the north side of the Sala di Costantino
Vatican City, Musei Vaticani

Raphael and then Castiglione called by. In Florence Raphael maintained close links with Taddeo Taddei, who in turn had connections with the ducal court at Urbino and was also a close friend of Bembo (Nova 2020). Raphael thus completed the paradigmatic ascent of a visual artist from an artisan workshop into the circle of poets, humanists and intellectuals in his own daily life. To his group of friends consisting of pupils and fellow painters, he added a second circle of friends, the poets (Hulse 1990).

Raphael's intellectual friends received paintings, in some cases as a gift. Customers who were not members of the ruler's court had much greater trouble in obtaining the works they had commissioned from Raphael. The altarpiece for the Florentine Dei family remained unfinished after Raphael entered the service of the Pope in Rome (Cat. P44). Raphael likewise stopped work on a chapel decoration in Perugia after completing only the Trinity fresco (Cat. F2). The nuns of Monteluce in Perugia had to wait over a decade for the *Coronation of the Virgin* (Cat. P107), which was supplied only after Raphael's death by his workshop. Raphael worked on a picture for Isabella d'Este only when Castiglione – as her intermediary – put pressure on him. Raphael's manners also left much to be desired in the eyes of clients whom he neglected. The envoys from Ferrara were repeatedly fobbed off and sent home, and the Duke was obliged to wait years in vain, despite having made a down payment. In 1519 one envoy was unable to speak to Raphael at his house because the artist was busy upstairs working on a portrait of Castiglione. Back in Ferrara, the Duke was incandescent with wrath: this was no way to treat one's peers. Promises had to be fulfilled – otherwise Raphael would feel the consequences of his hatred instead of his love. Raphael had lied and been deceitful, had treated him no better than an uncouth plebeian. Was Raphael's charming, polite friendliness selective?

The large number of papal commissions meant that Raphael was increasingly overloaded with work. Letters regularly speak of the fact that he had to be pressured. His personal mood also affected his productivity. When Pope Julius II lay dying, Raphael could not work for grief. Like all exceptional individuals, Raphael was melancholic (1519). Raimondo's portrait engraving shows him correspondingly reserved, sitting and thinking between his artist's palette and a blank canvas, his inactive hands hidden in his robe. The copper engraving was not made by Raphael's hands. Rather, it is the product of his mental powers of invention, which someone else then materialised in the work of art. In Rome, Raphael increasingly became an art contractor, supplying designs and overseeing projects. He had worked with other artists ever since the beginning of his career in Umbria – with Evangelista da Pian di Meleto from his father's former workshop, then with Pinturicchio and Domenico Alfani (*c.* 1479–1553). Colleagues received drawings from which to execute commissioned works. In Rome he worked alongside Sodoma and employed Lorenzo Lotto (1480–1557) and others. Under Leo X the business grew enormously and tasks were delegated to the appropriate specialists. In 1517 Raphael purchased a house near the Vatican, the Palazzo Caprini designed by Bramante – a pioneering example of High Renaissance secular architecture *all'antica*. Young artists lived with Raphael and he took in pupils like sons. He appointed Giulio Romano and Penni among his heirs. Vasari reports that, whenever Raphael made his way from his palazzo to the Vatican, he was invariably accompanied by fifty artists. The painter thus became the centre of his own court of artists ("pictorum omnium princeps", 1519; "non visse da pittore ma da principe", 1550). It is true that not everyone subscribed to this model. Raphael's rivals Michelangelo and Sebastiano del Piombo became enemies of the *principe della sinagoga* (thus Sebastiano in a letter of 2 July 1518 to Michelangelo). In 1520 Sebastiano declared that there were other demigods ("semidei") besides Raphael and his pupils. He was convinced that Raphael was scheming against him. Michelangelo rightly suspected Raphael of espionage as he worked on the Sistine Ceiling. In 1517 Baccio d'Agnolo, a confidante of Michelangelo, described Raphael as the latter's arch enemy ("suo nemico capitale"). In 1520 an unnamed Florentine painter and follower of Michelangelo saw himself stifled by Raphael out of envy ("lo tiene basso").

Raphael's mistress lived in his palace. With death looming, Raphael provided her with a secure future. But the presence of his live-in lover did not prevent the painter – according to Vasari – from pursuing sexual pleasures ("i piaceri amorosi") with no sense of moderation outside the home, too. Returning home exhausted, he was struck down by the fateful fever. Raphael concealed the cause to the doctors, and the wrong treatment that followed led him to his death. Raphael had postponed his promise to marry Bibbiena's relative, whom the Cardinal had arranged for him as a wife, for years until her death. He nevertheless had her buried in the Pantheon next to his own tomb.

The stories and legends that have sprung up around Raphael, and were related even by his contemporaries, are often inspired by the contents and formal qualities of his artistic works. Grace, sweetness, the ever-admired beauty *(venustà)* and harmony of his figures reflected back, as it were, upon their maker and also transfigured his person. Thus even upon Raphael's death it was said that the god Hephaistos had sent him the deadly, burning fever out of jealousy: for Raphael could only have created his works with the help of Venus and her Graces, and Hephaistos's wife Venus must therefore have visited him secretly. In 1554 Lodovico Dolce (1508–1568) was the first to name, above and beyond the mysterious divine grace, other key qualities of Raphael's art: the universal wealth and variety of motifs and styles, always chosen to suit the subject and appropriate to the place and occasion ("quando il soggetto lo ricercava, secondo il luogo e le occasioni"), the habitual careful study, and the combination of tastefully selective fidelity to nature with the beautiful idealised forms of antique statuary ("la bella maniera delle statue antiche"). In all of this, Raphael succeeded in the hardest task of all, namely in making the result look easy and pleasant, skilfully hiding the artistic effort involved and igniting the love of the viewer.

Perhaps the finest tribute to Raphael was written during his own lifetime by Celio Calcagnini (1479–1541). Raphael – according to Calcagnini – is very rich and is very dear to the Pope, a young man of the highest goodness and admirable talent ("iuvenis summae bonitatis sed admirabilis ingenii"). He excels in the virtues and is the prince of all painters when it comes to the theory and practice of art. He is thereby not proud, but accessible and friendly to all. He does not shun criticism or discussion; on the contrary, no one rejoices more readily than he if his views are called into doubt or disputed, since he thinks that the reward of life is to be taught and to teach ("docerique ac docere vitae praemium"). He thereby supports the elderly scholar Fabio Calvo, discusses everything with him and follows his advice (Shearman 2003). Calvo had taught the young Federico

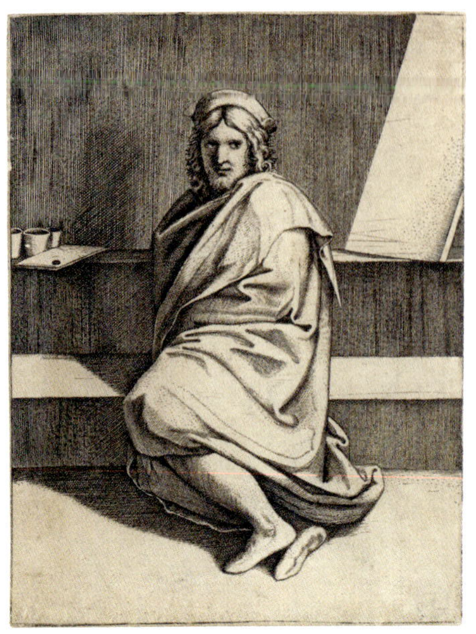

Gonzaga (1500–1540) at the Vatican under Julius II; in 1512 there is mention of a lecture on Greek, arithmetic and geometry. How long Raphael's close friendship with Calvo dated back is unknown. Calcagnini's testimony regarding the central importance that Raphael attached to discussion, learning and teaching is confirmed by Raphael's self-portraits. In the Louvre double portrait, the artist follows the gesture made by his companion and lays his hand affirmatively on his shoulder (Cat. P83). Much earlier, in the fresco of *The School of Athens* (Cat. F3.1j), Raphael and an older companion stand on the right-hand edge of the picture in conversation with leading thinkers of antiquity. And directly in front of them, the bald (It. *calvo*) geometrician is teaching his students that knowledge gained from learning advances step by step – perhaps the finest representation of the phases of pedagogical success. Like no other artist, Raphael learnt from everyone and taught many throughout his career. In his most famous painting, with its programmatic image of a past intellectual culture, he has thus also left us, as a legacy, a motto of his life: "docerique ac docere vitae praemium".

Marcantonio Raimondi, **Portrait of Raphael**, *c.* 1520
Copperplate engraving, 13.9 × 10.7 cm (5 ½ × 4 ¼ in). Staatliche Museen zu Berlin, Kupferstichkabinett

Altar tabernacle with the *Madonna del Sasso* by Lorenzetto and, beneath it, Raphael's tomb
Rome, Pantheon

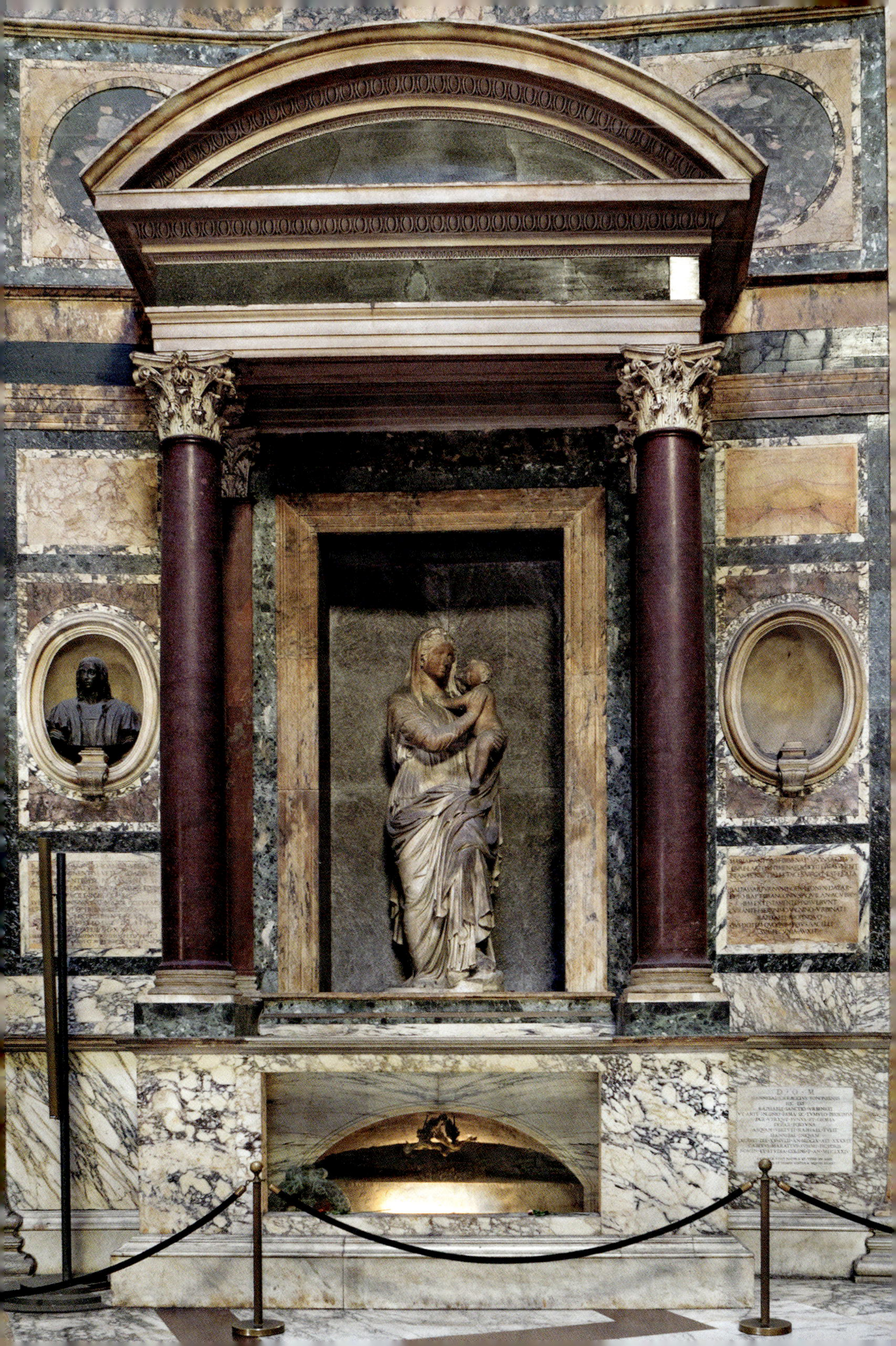
D·O·M

Detail from **Solomon and the Queen of Sheba**, 1518/19

Pages 472/473
Detail from **The Vision of the Cross of Emperor Constantine, presaging victory in the sign of the Cross**, 1520/21
(see ill. pp. 496/497)

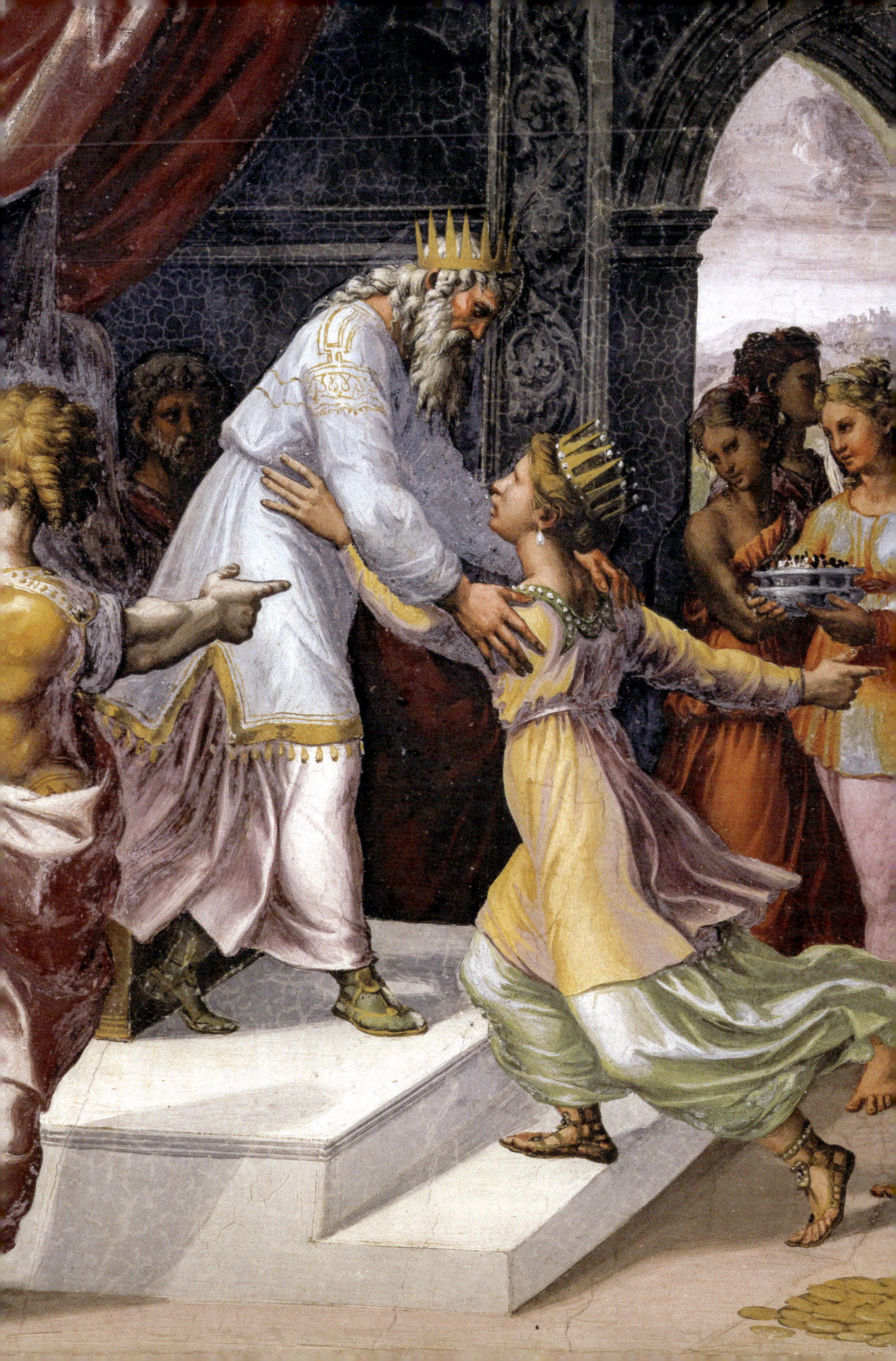

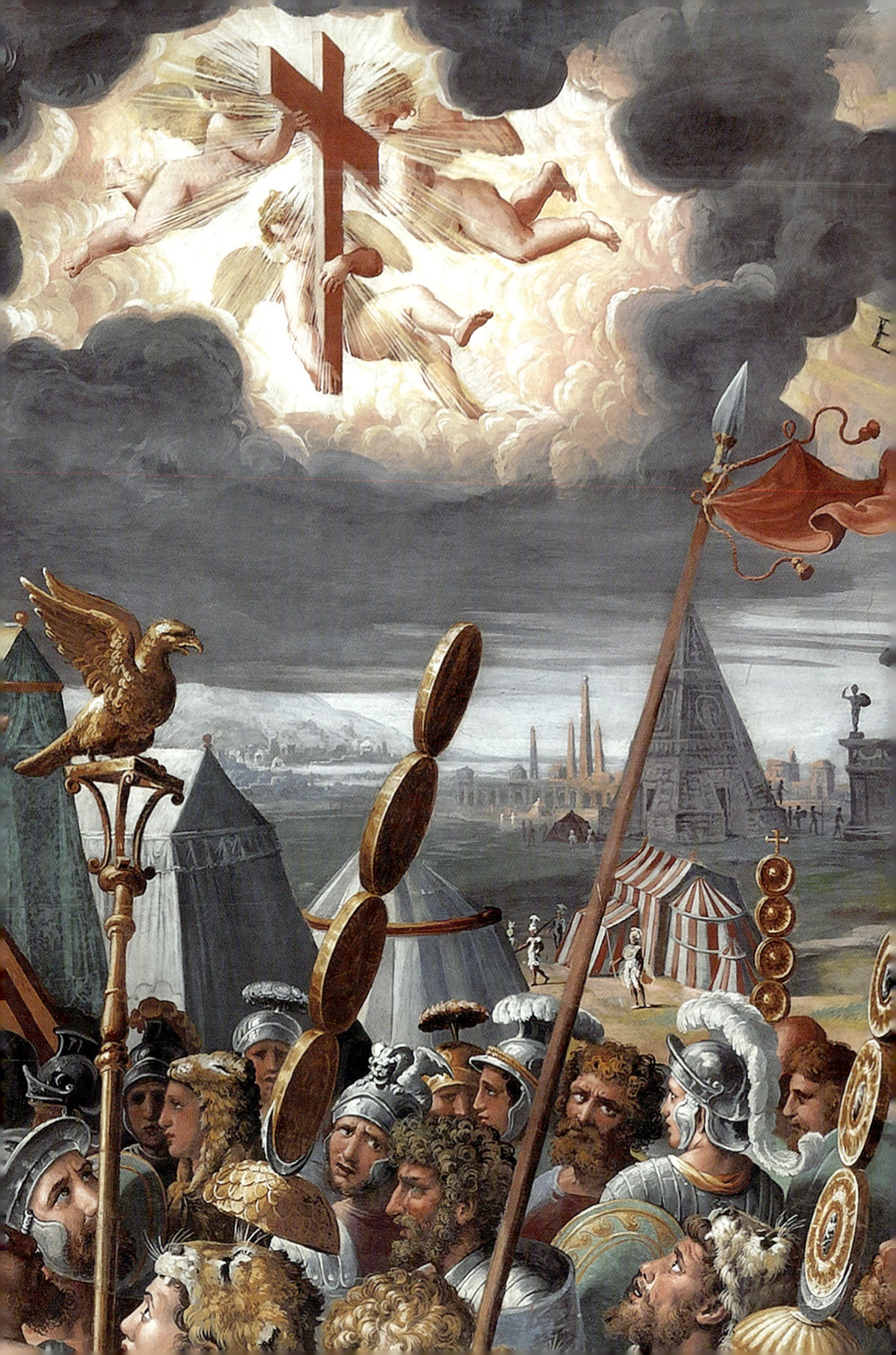

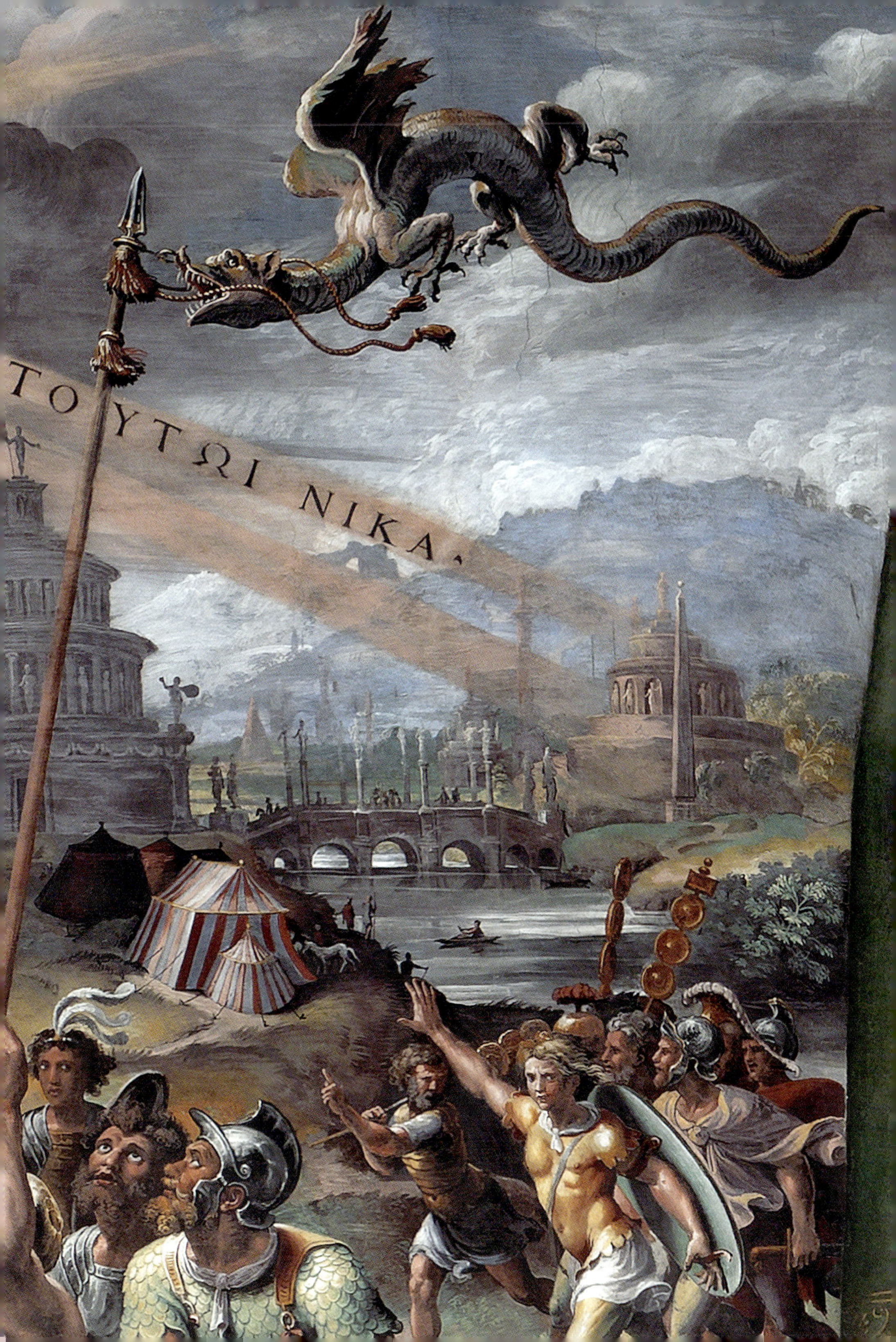

TOYTΩI NIKA.

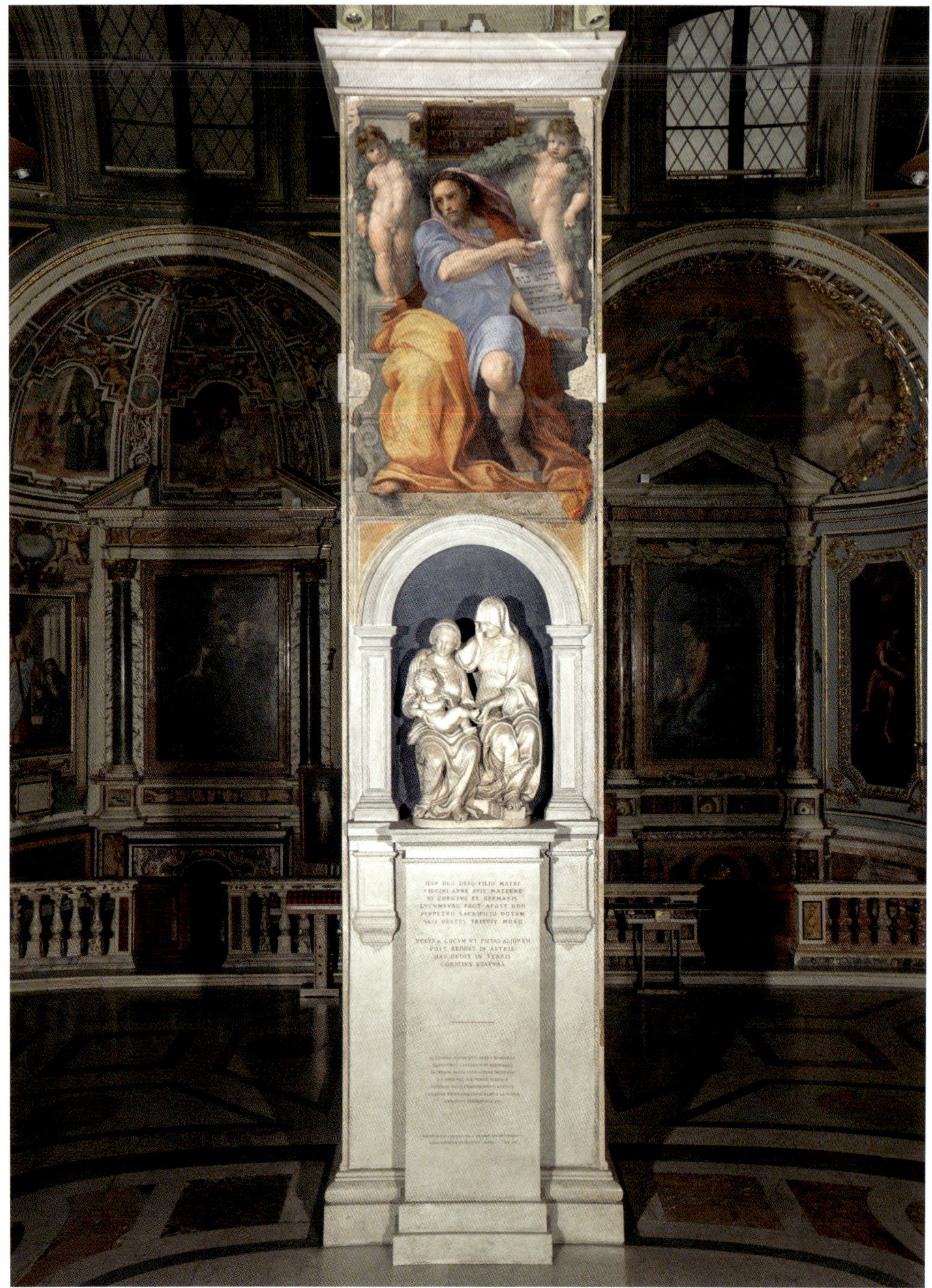
IESV DEO DEIQ FILIO MATRI
VIRGINI ANNE AVIE MATERNE
IO CORICIVS EX GERMANIS
LVCVMBVRG PROT APOST DDD
PERPETVO SACRIFICIO DOTEM
VASA VESTES TRIBVIT MDXII
VESTRA LOCVM VT PIETAS ALIQVEM
POST REDDAT IN ASTRIS
HAS DEDIT IN TERRIS
CORICIVS STATVAS

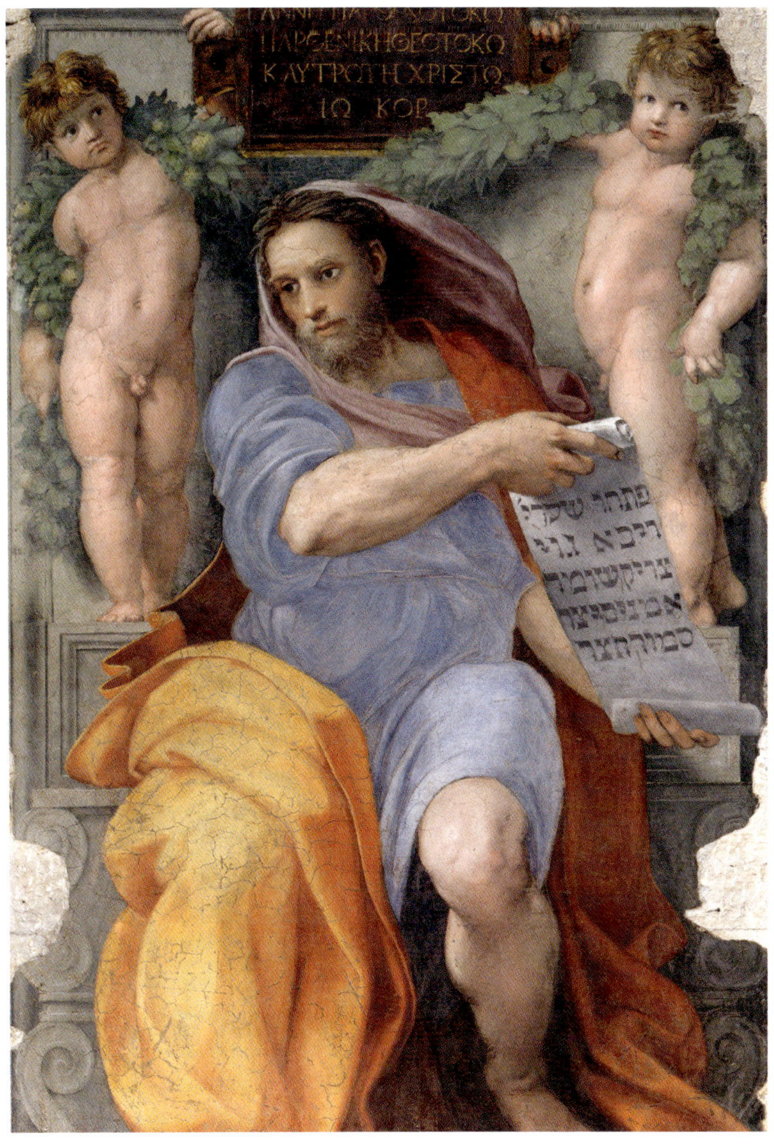

Pillar of the central nave with the representation of the *Prophet Isaiah* by Raphael and the sculptural group of *Virgin and Child with Saint Anne* by Andrea Sansovino, *c.* 1512/13
Rome, Sant'Agostino, Cappella Goritz

The Prophet Isaiah, *c.* 1512/13
Fresco, 235 × 155 cm (92 ½ × 61 ⅛ in). Rome, Sant'Agostino, Cappella Goritz

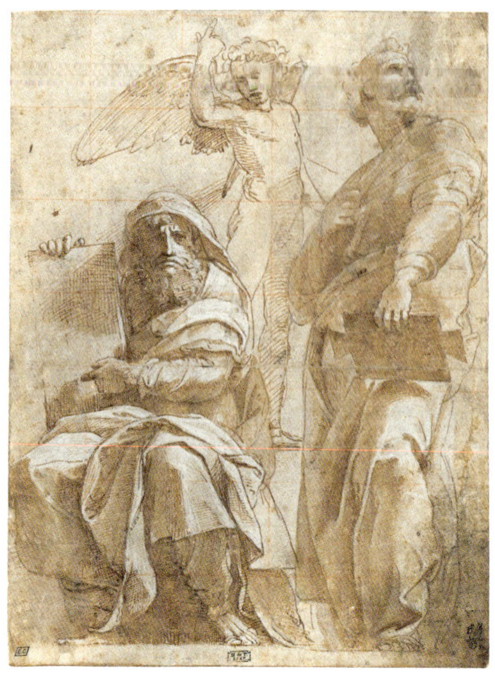

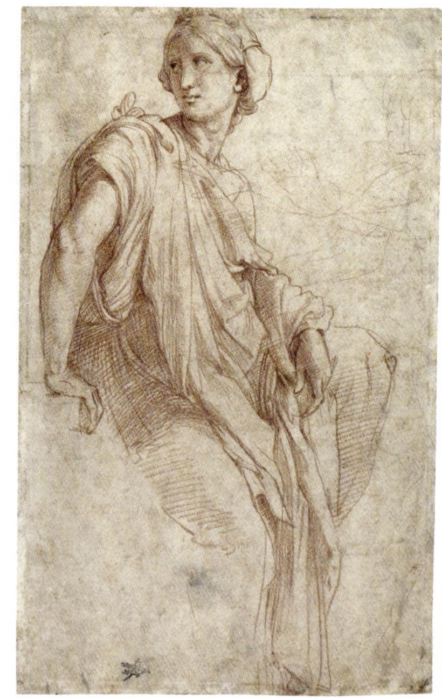

The prophets Jonah and Hosea, 1510–1512
Pen, wash, black chalk, heightened in white over lead stylus, squared with metalpoint and red chalk, 27 × 19.8 cm (10 5/8 × 7 3/4 in)
Washington, D. C., National Gallery of Art, The Armand Hammer Collection

Sibyl, 1510–1512
Red chalk over stylus underdrawing, 26.1 × 16.5 cm (10 1/4 × 6 1/2 in)
London, British Museum, Department of Prints and Drawings

The Prophets Hosea, Jonah, David, Daniel and Four Sibyls, *c.* 1512
Frescoes, width *c.* 615 cm (242 1/8 in)
Rome, Santa Maria della Pace, Cappella Chigi

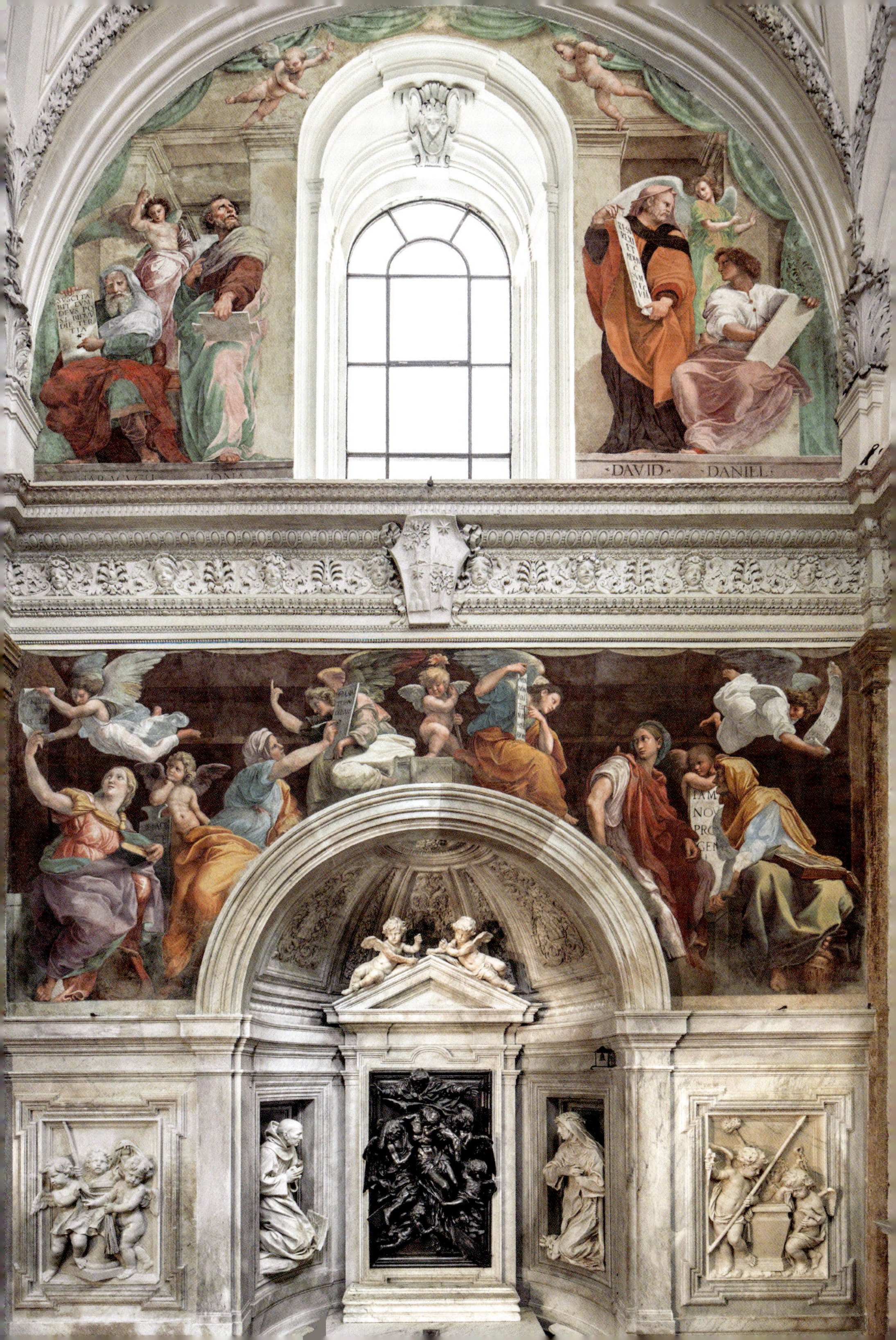

·DAVID·
·DANIEL·

Loggias

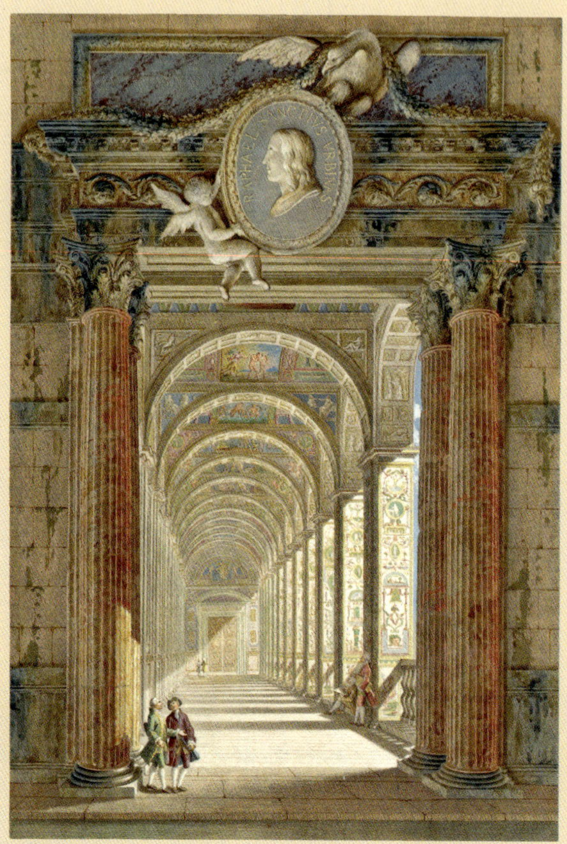

Giovanni Volpato after Pietro Camporesi
Loggias of Raphael, Frontispice of the Print Series, 1776/77
Hand-coloured copper engraving, 58.3 × 39.9 cm (22 7/8 × 15 3/4 in)
Vienna, Albertina

View of the loggia
Vatican City, Musei Vaticani

Pages 480/481
God Creates the Animals, *c.* 1518/19

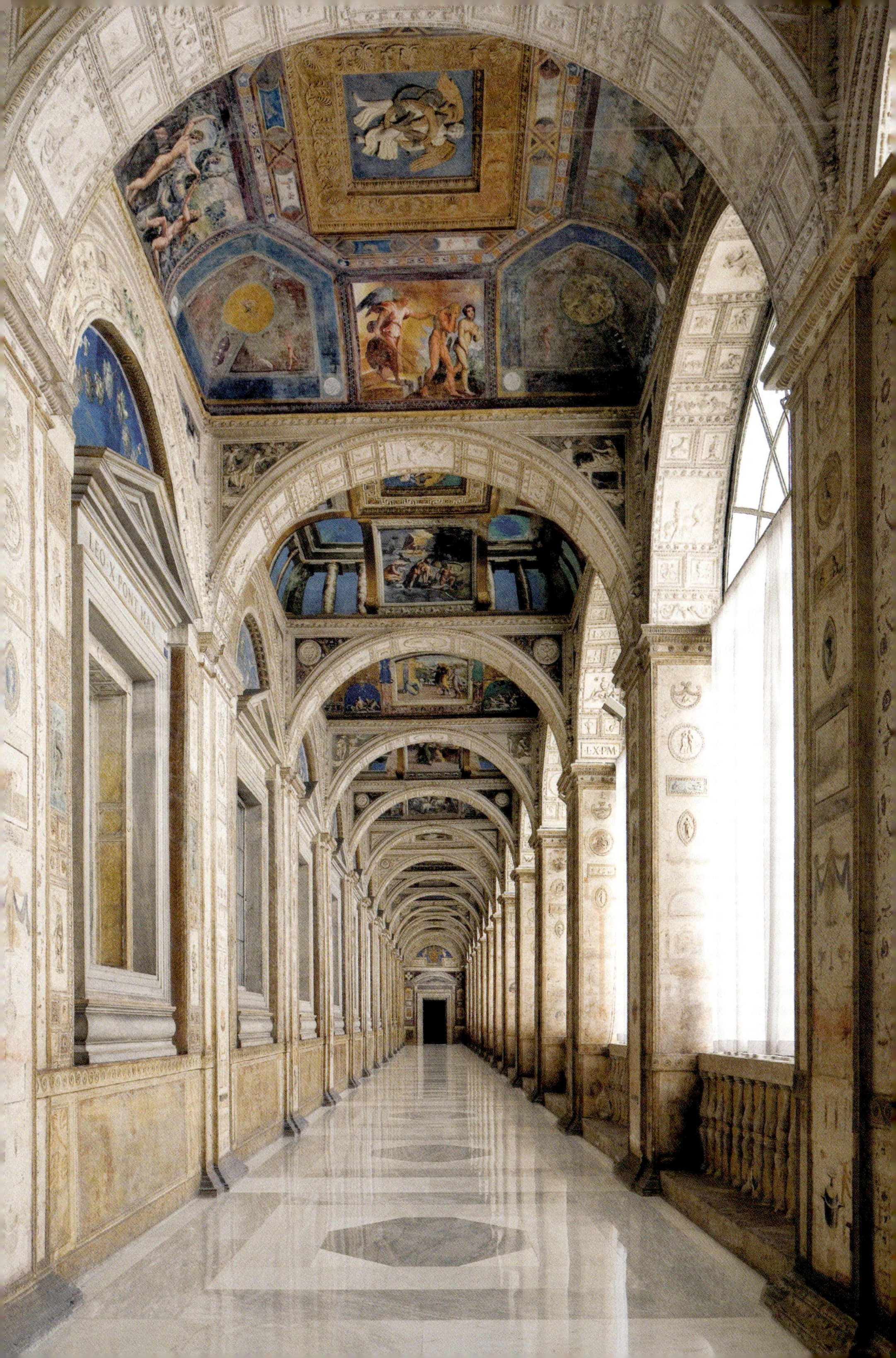
LEO X PONT MAX
L·X·P·M·

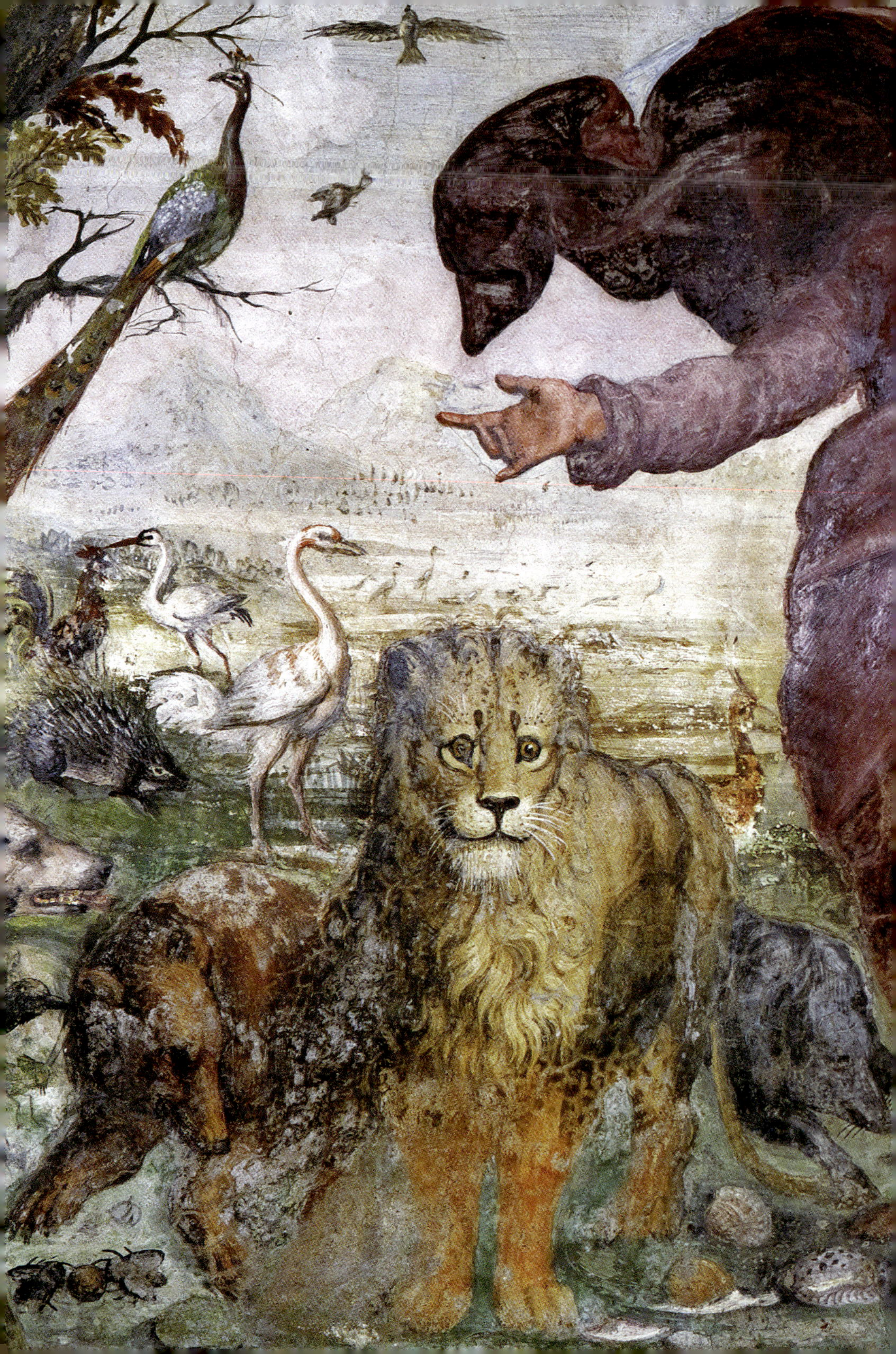

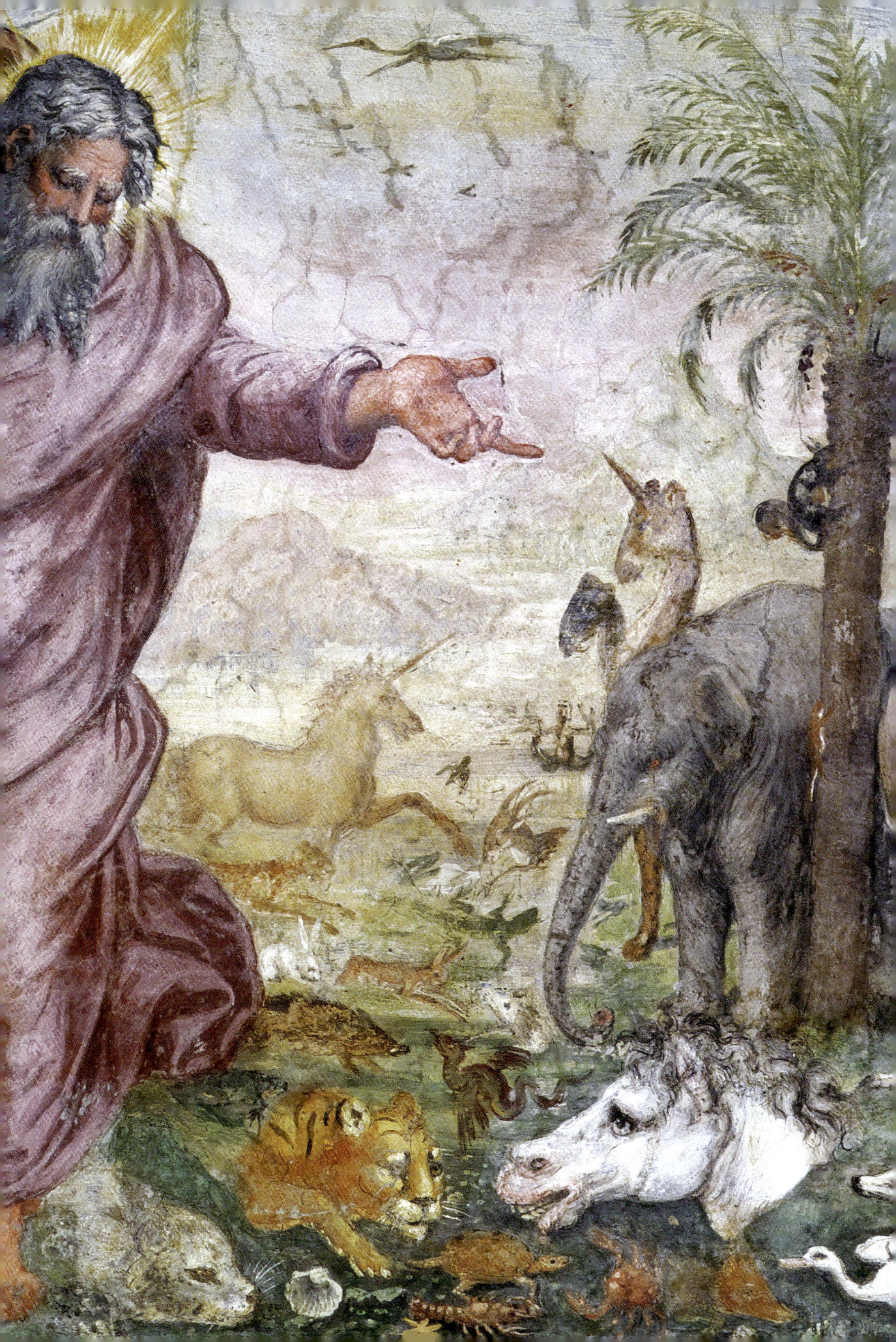

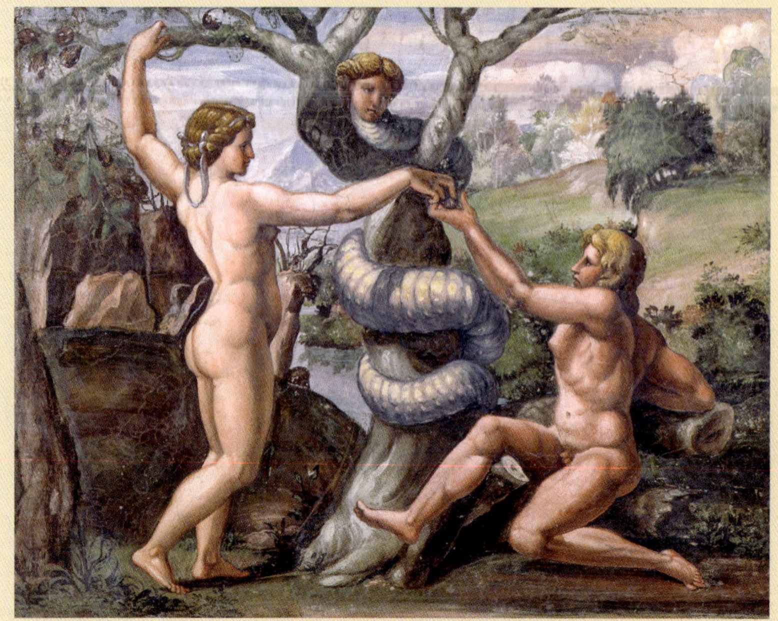

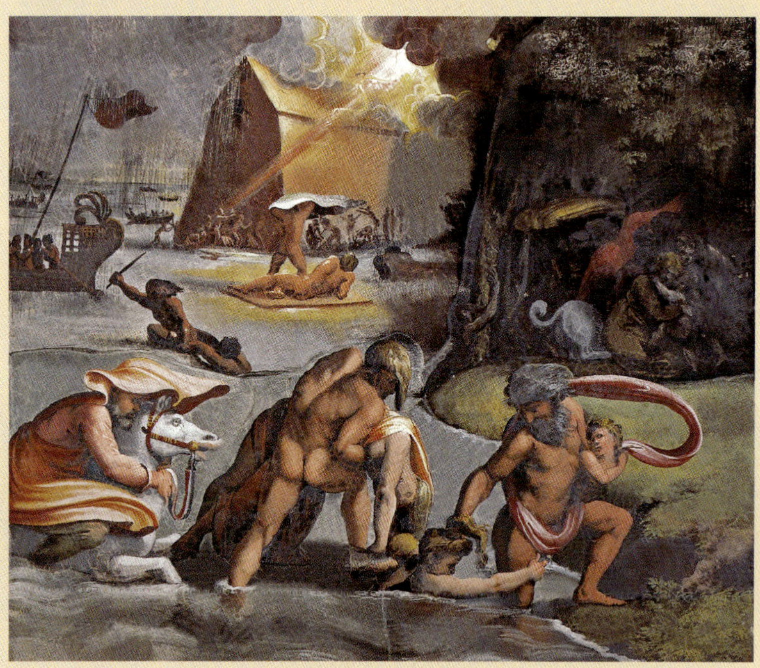

The Fall, *c.* 1518/19

The Deluge, *c.* 1518/19

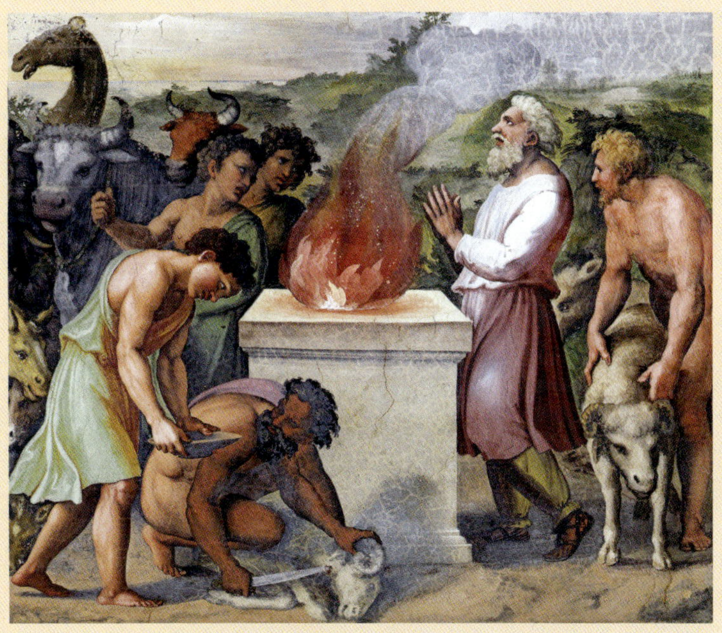

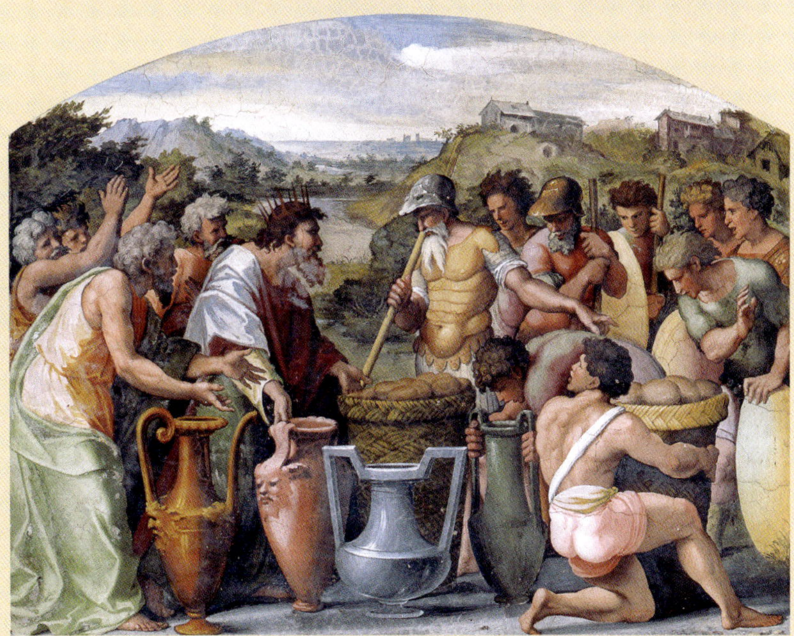

Noah's Thanksgiving Sacrifice, *c.* 1518/19
Abraham and Melchisedek, *c.* 1518/19

Pages 484/485
Noah Orders the Ark to be Built, *c.* 1518/19

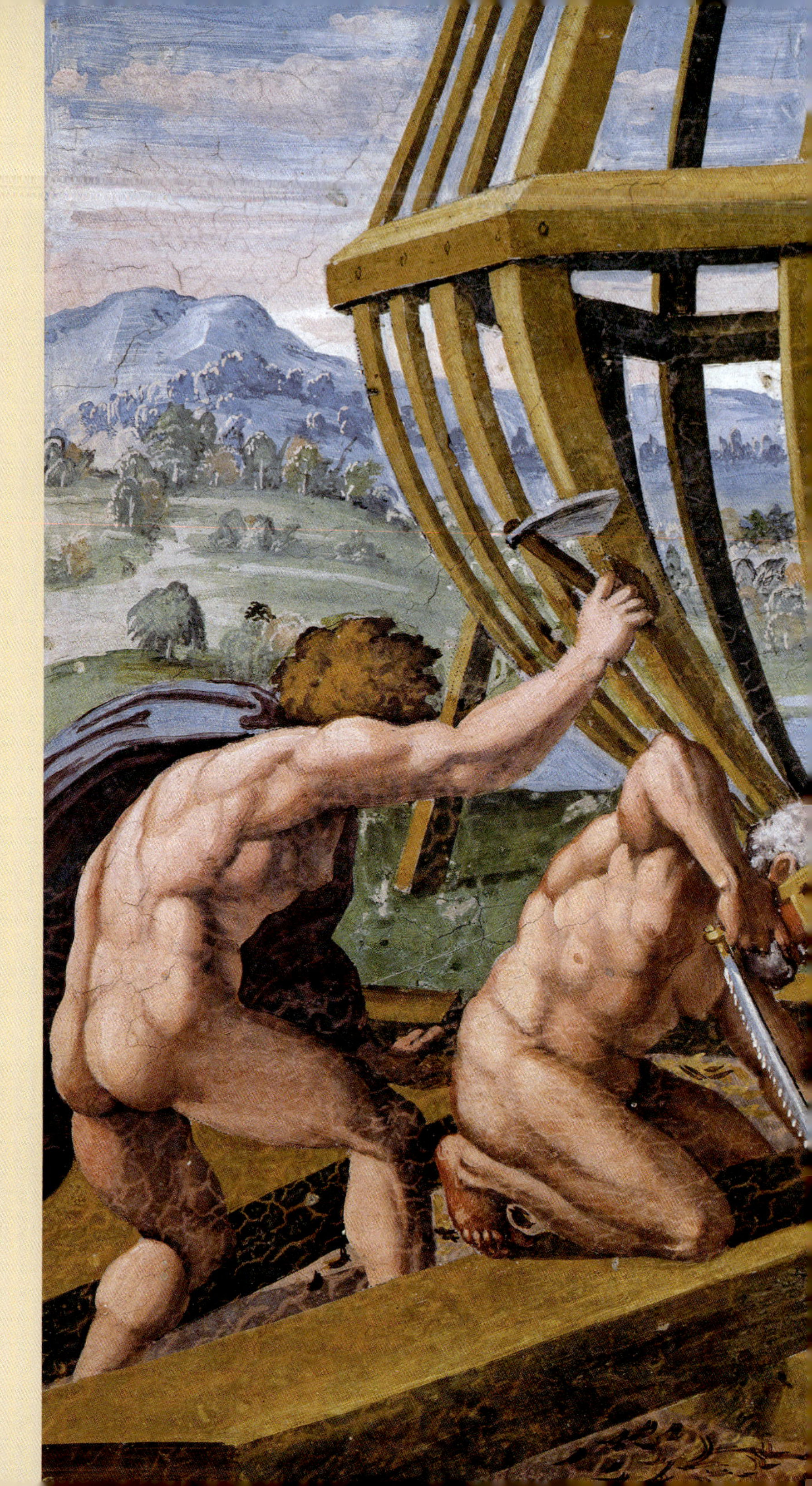

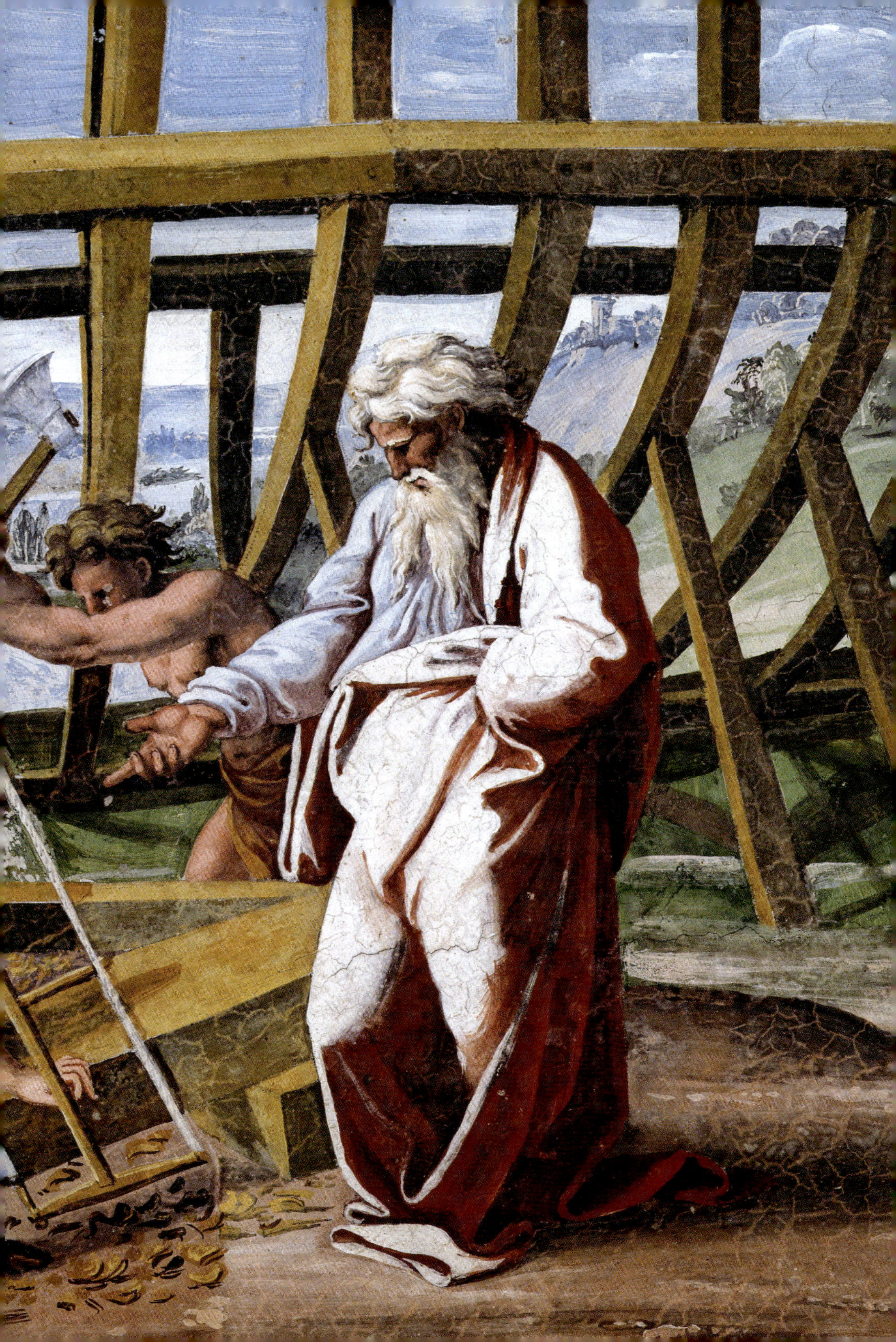

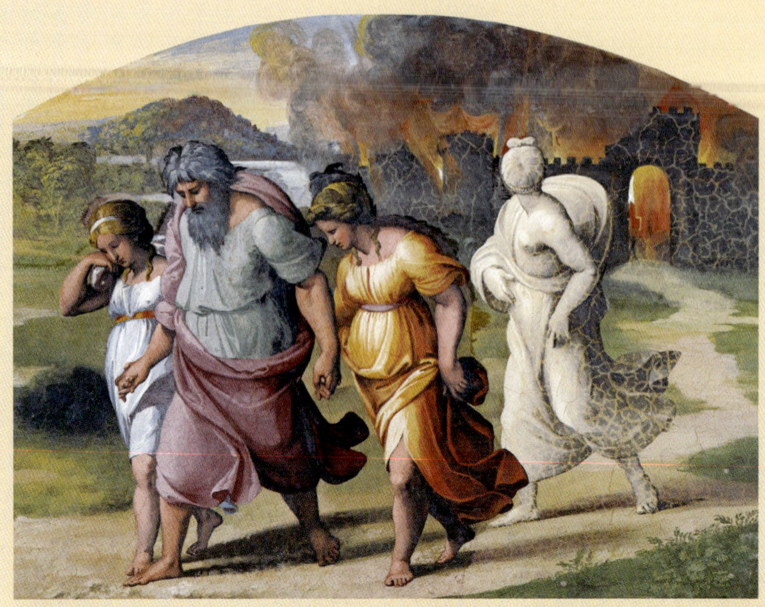

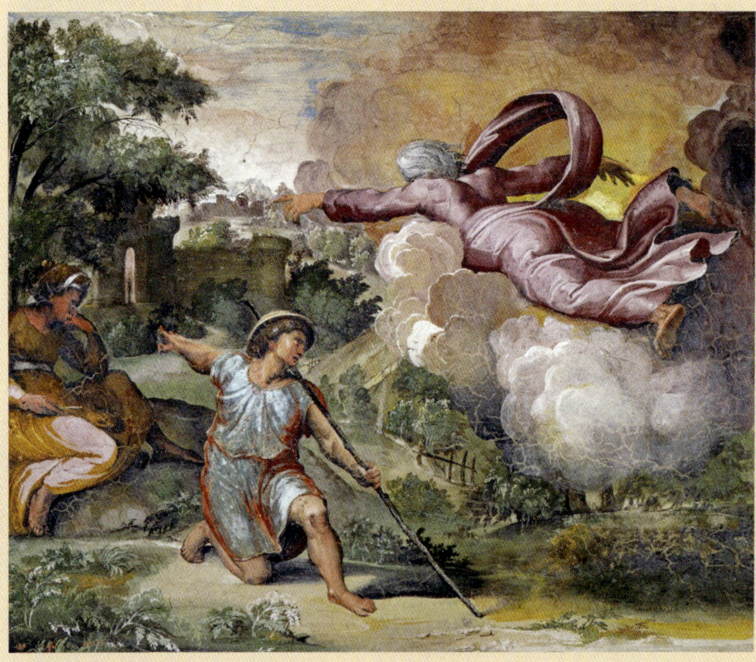

Isaac Prays to God for His Wife Rebecca, *c.* 1518/19

Lot's Flight from Sodom, *c.* 1518/19

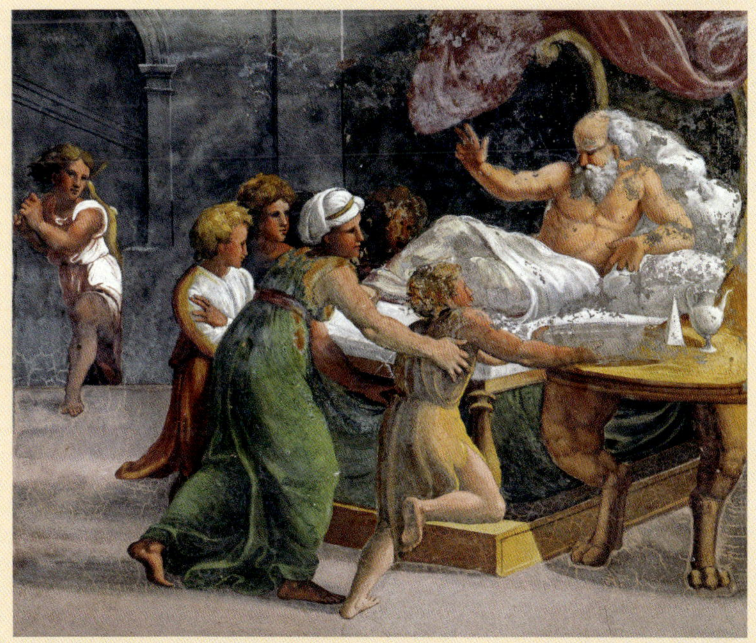

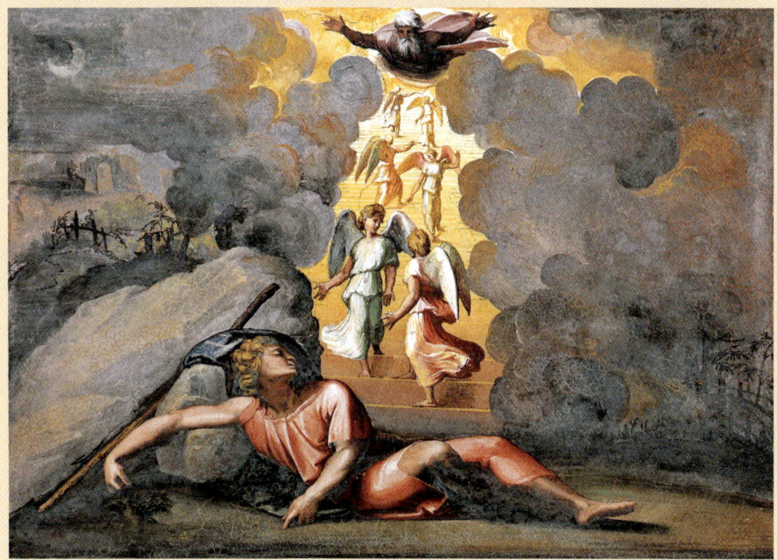

Isaac Blesses Jacob, *c.* 1518/19
Jacob's Dream of the Ladder, *c.* 1518/19

Pages 488/489
Jacob's Meeting with the Daughters of Laban at the Well, *c.* 1518/19

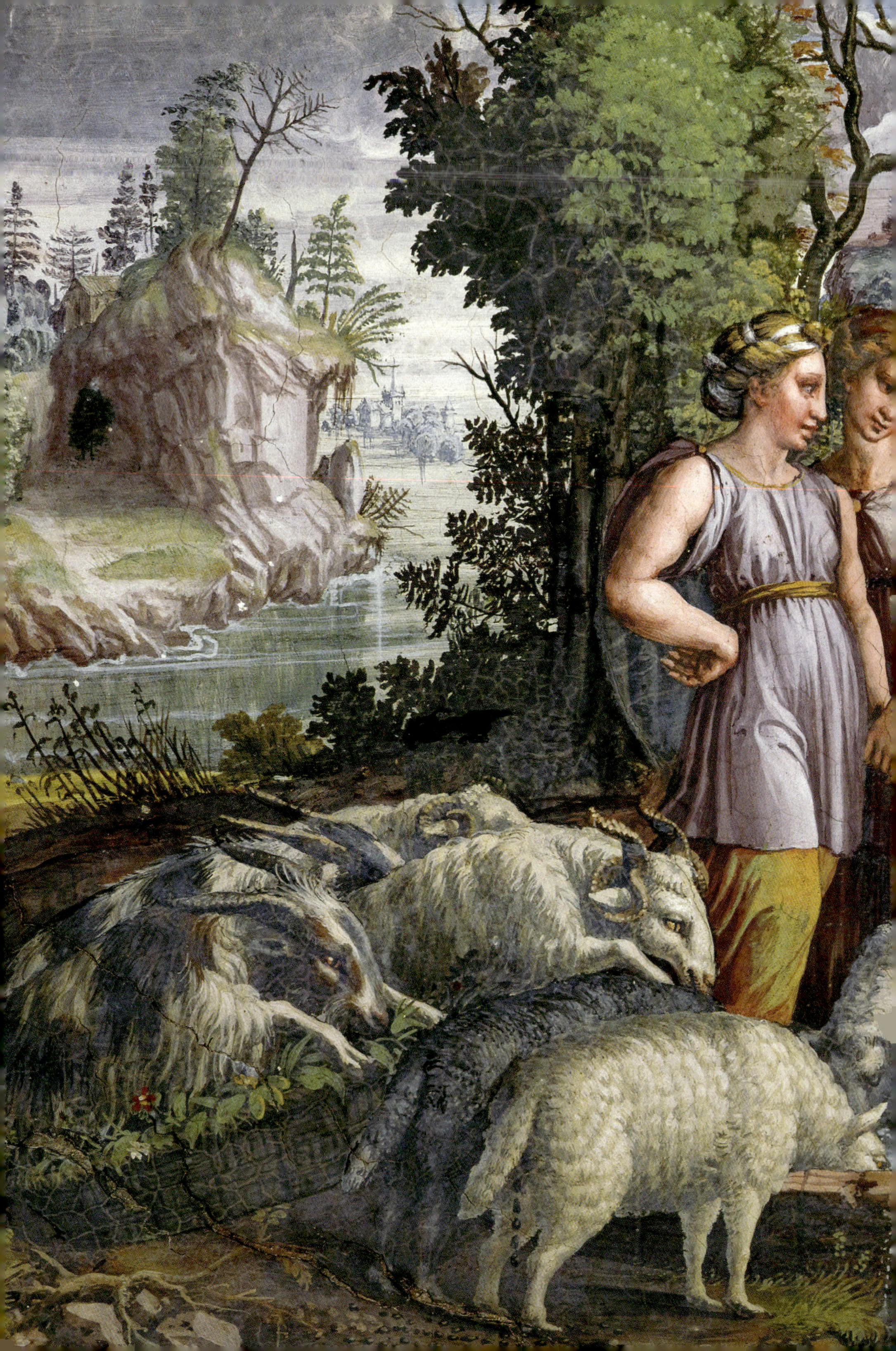

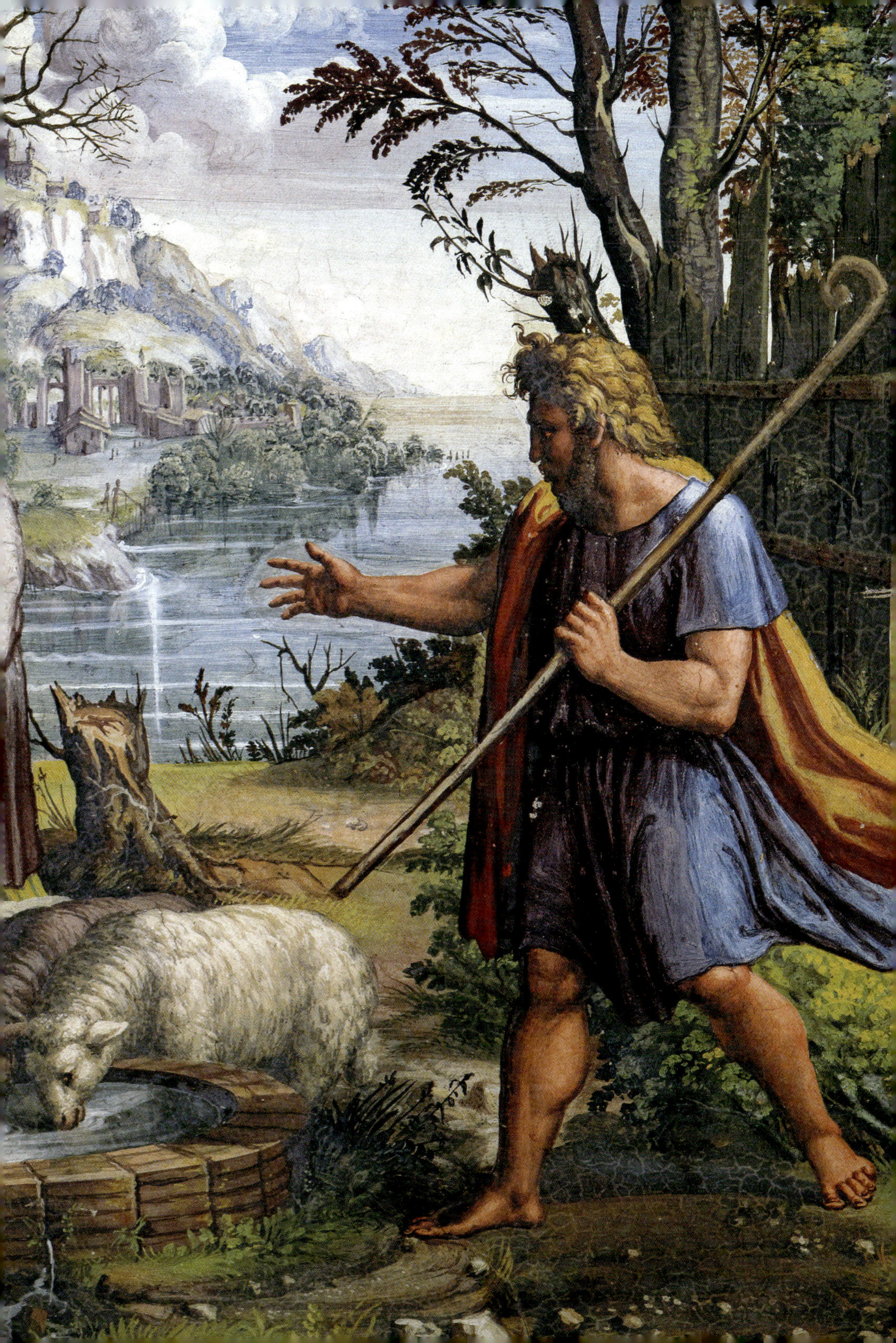

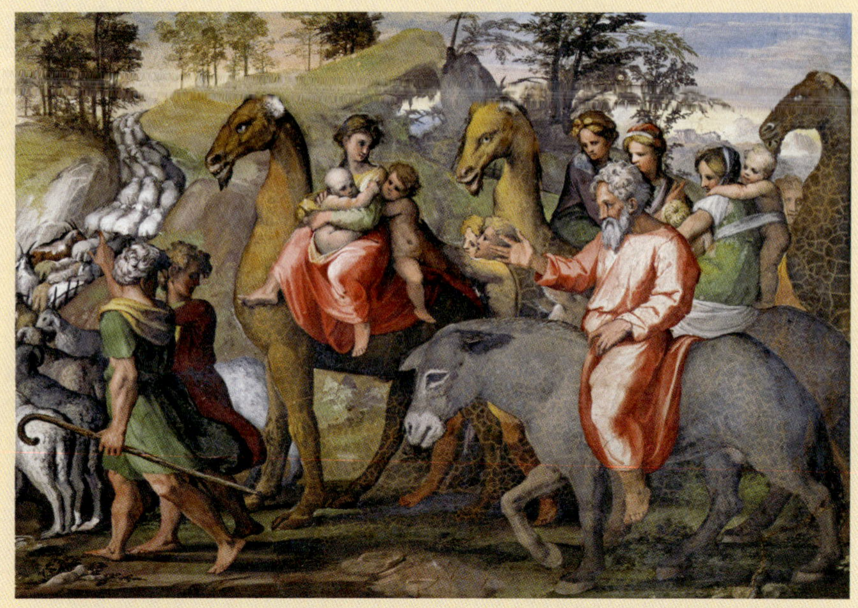

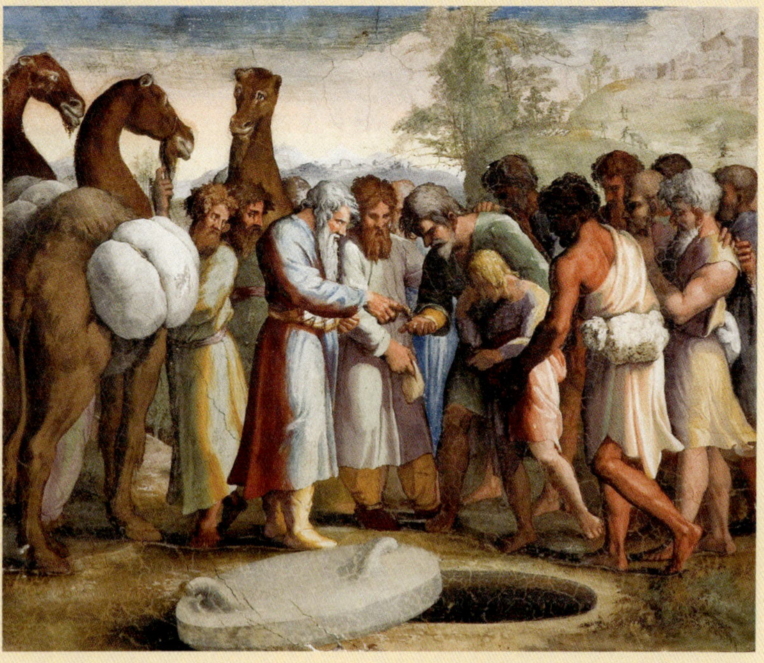

Jacob Returns to Canaan,
c. 1518/19

Joseph is Sold by His Brothers,
c. 1518/19

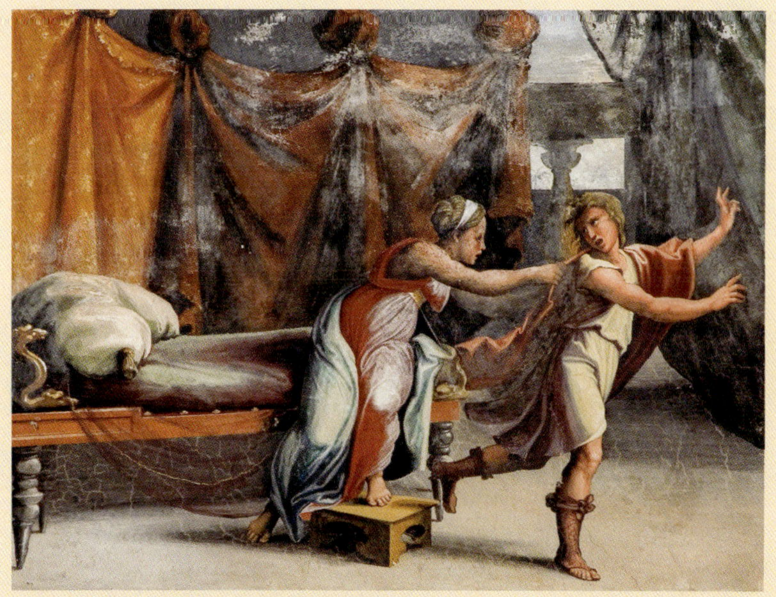

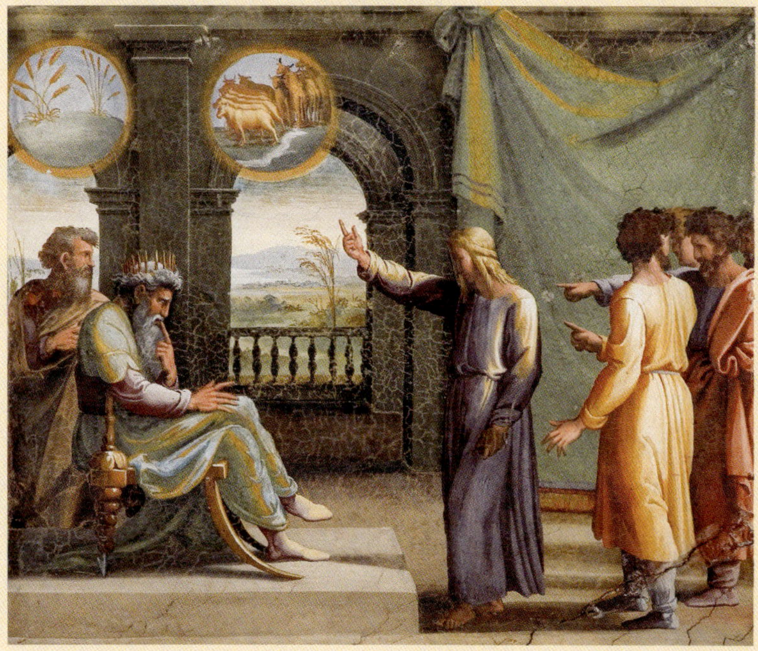

Joseph and Potiphar's Wife, *c.* 1518/19
Joseph Interprets the Pharaoh's Dreams, *c.* 1518/19

Pages 492/493
Joseph Tells His Brothers His Dreams, *c.* 1518/19

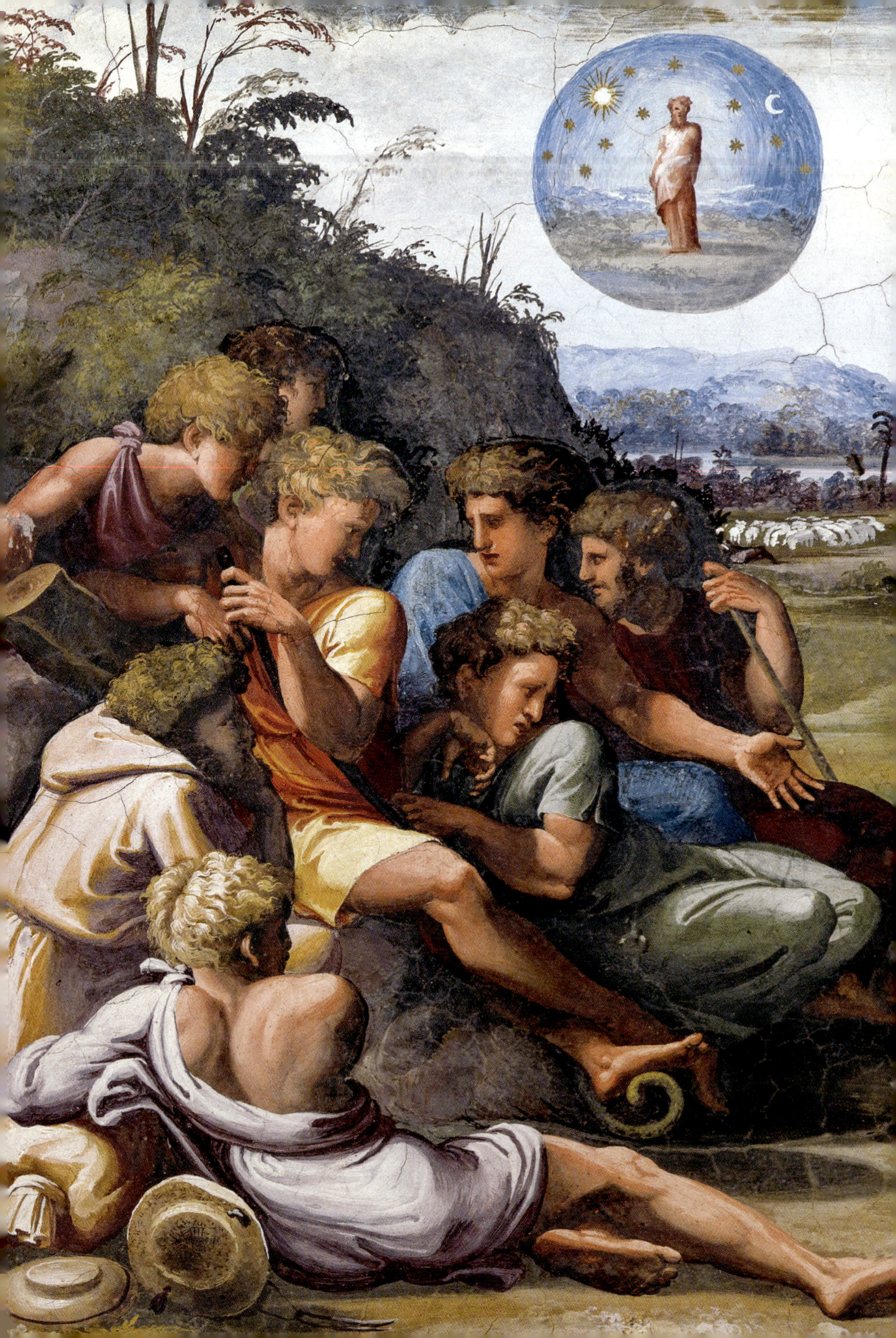

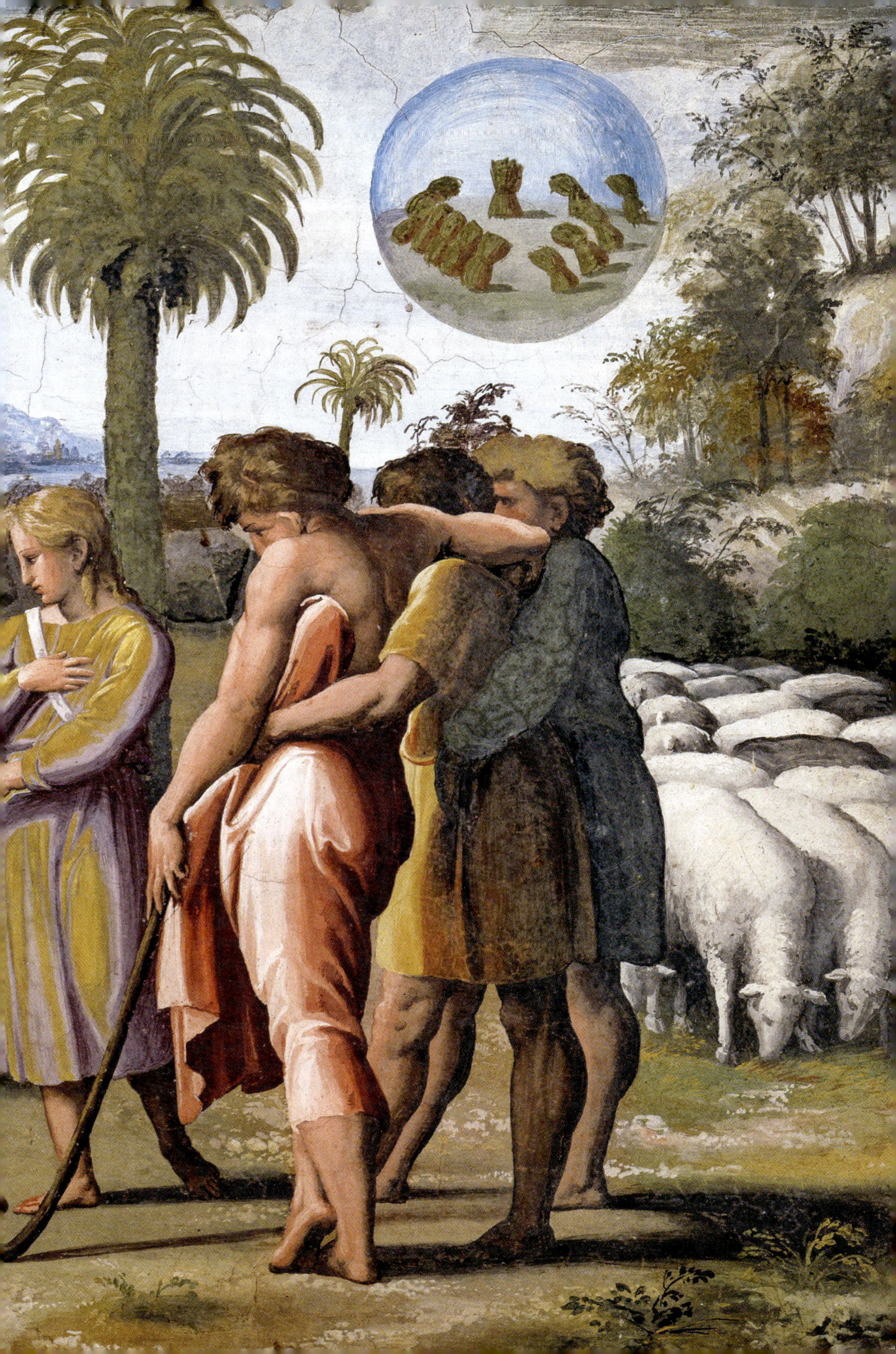

Sala di Costantino

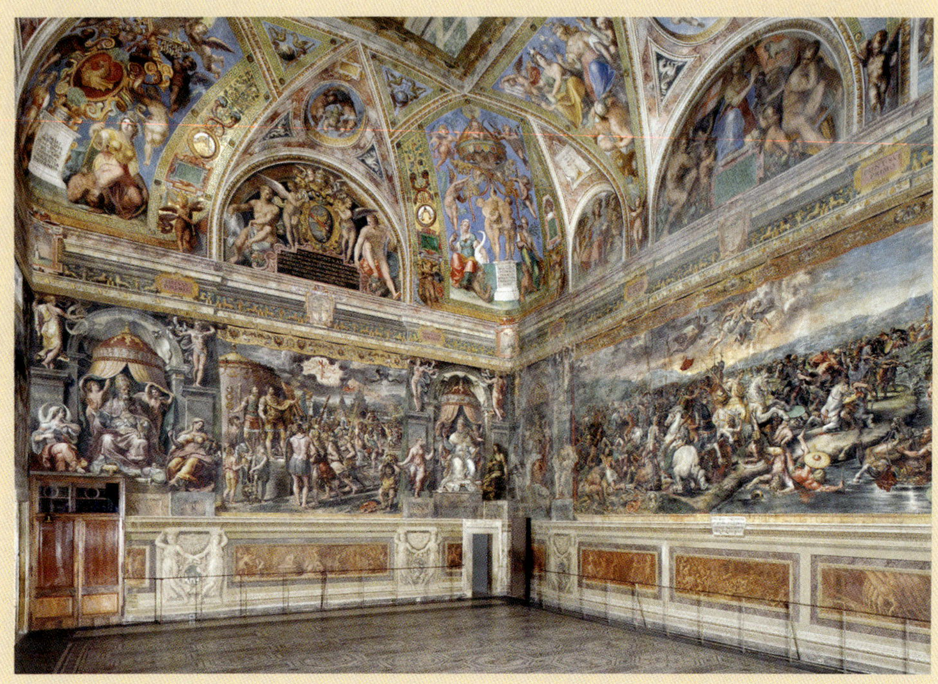

Interior view of the Sala di Costantino

Detail from **Pope Damasus I between Prudentia (Prudence) and Pax (Peace)**, 1523/24

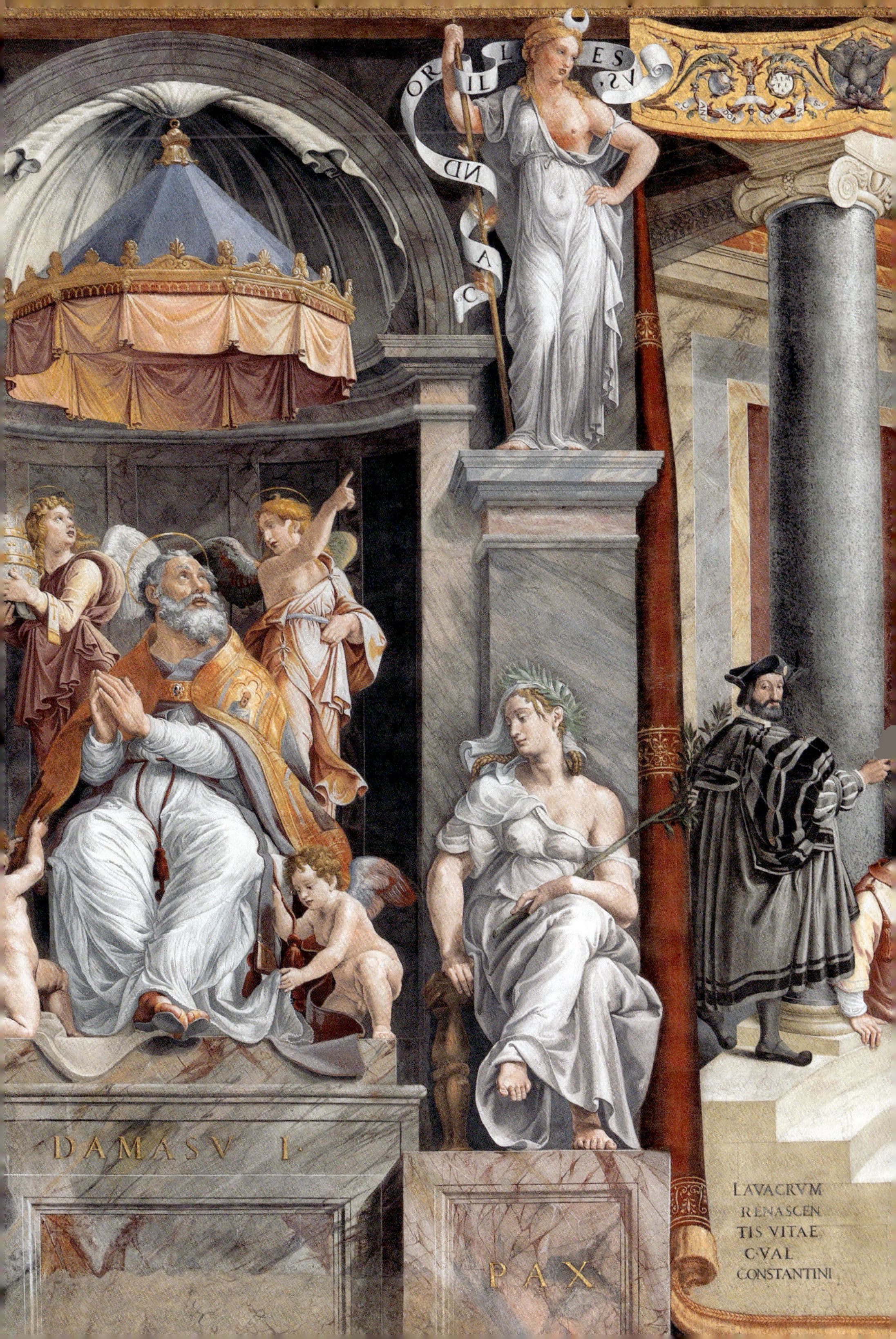
DAMASV I.
PAX
LAVACRVM
RENASCEN
TIS VITAE
C·VAL
CONSTANTINI

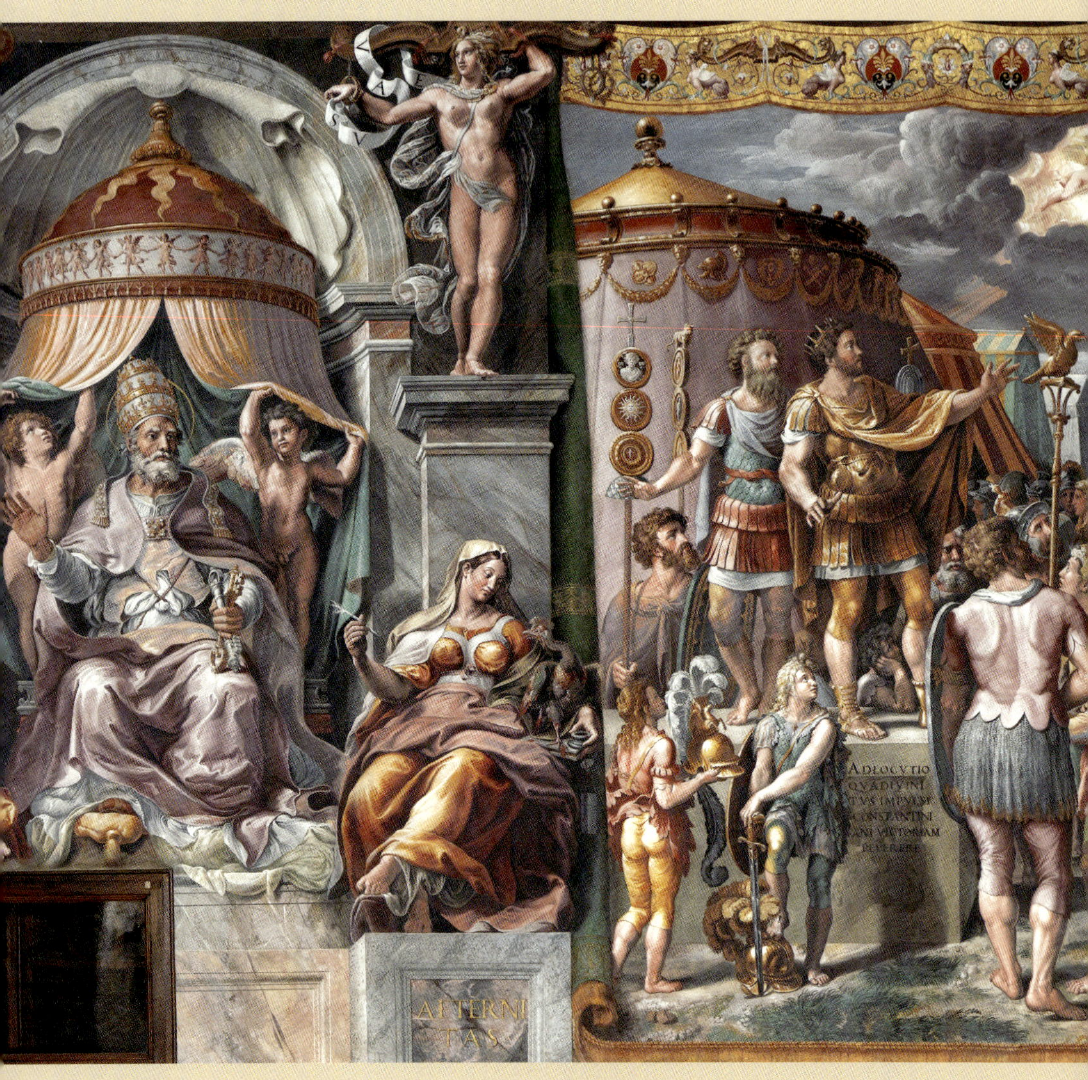

Detail from **St Peter between Ecclesia (Church) and Aeternitas (Eternity)**

The Vision of the Cross of Emperor Constantine, Presaging Victory in the Sign of the Cross, 1520/21

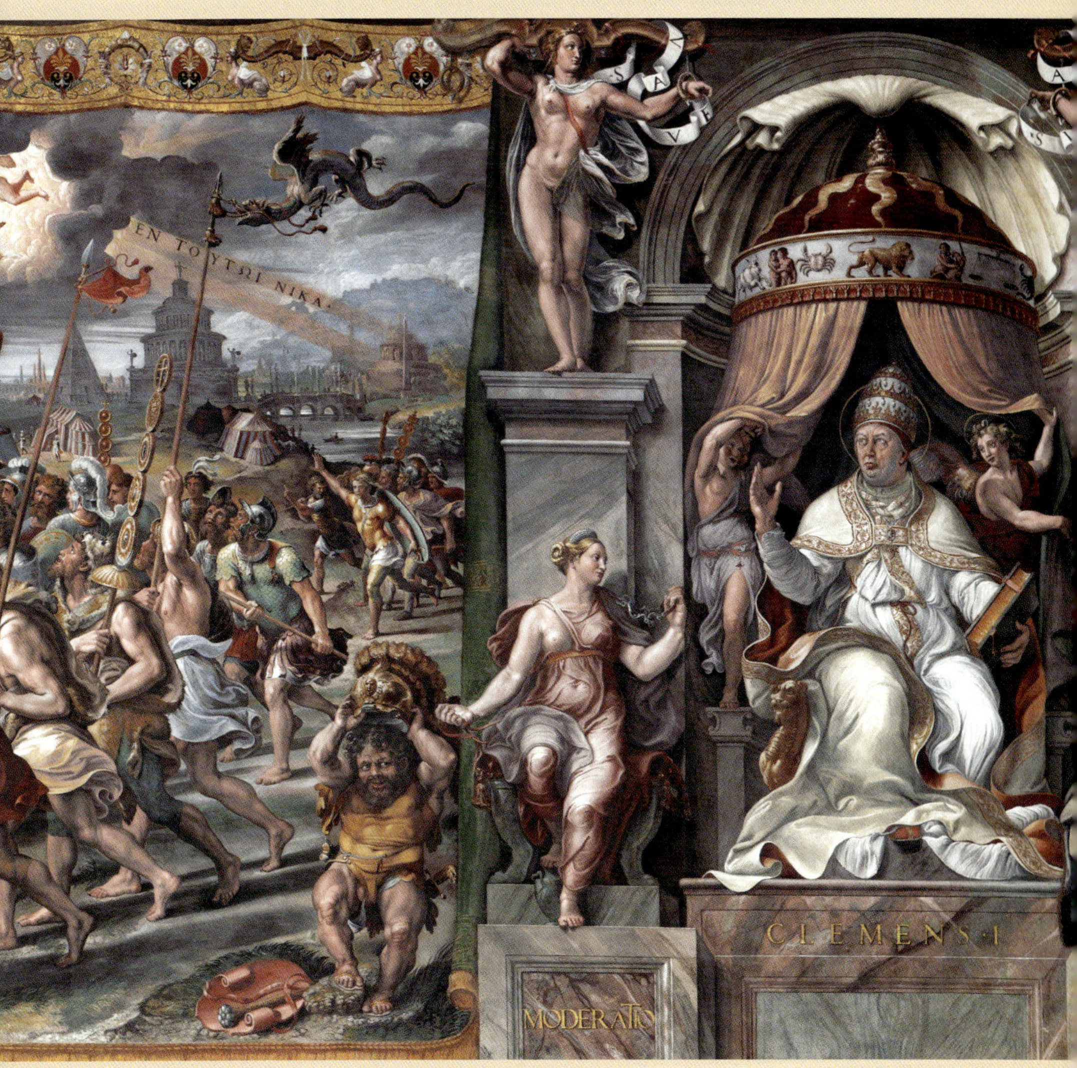

Detail from **Pope Clement I (portrait of Leo X) between Moderatio (Temperance) and Comitas (Courtesy)**, 1520/21
(see also pp. 472/473)

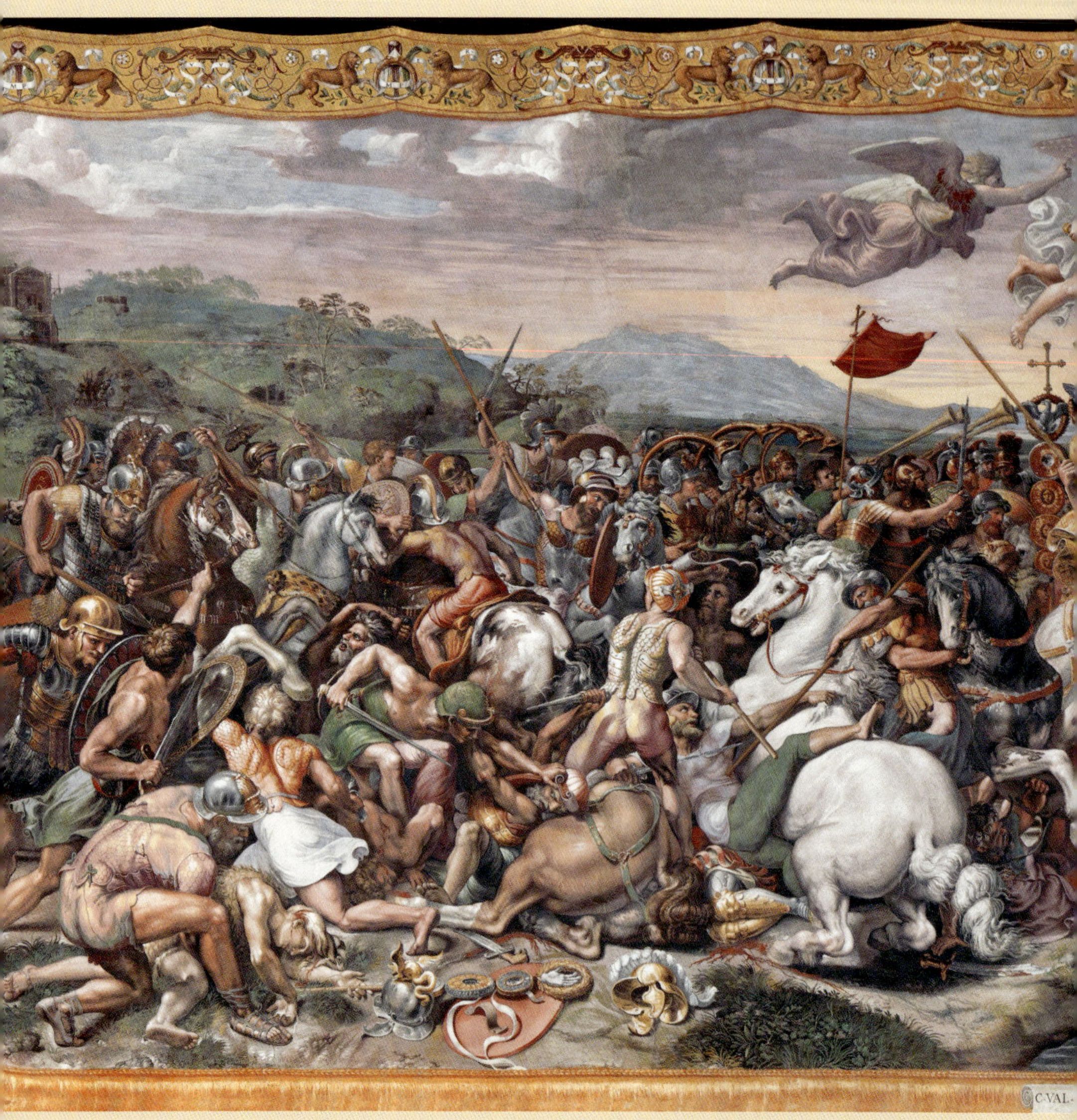

The Victory of Constantine against Maxentius at the Milvian Bridge, 1520/21
(Detail page 500)

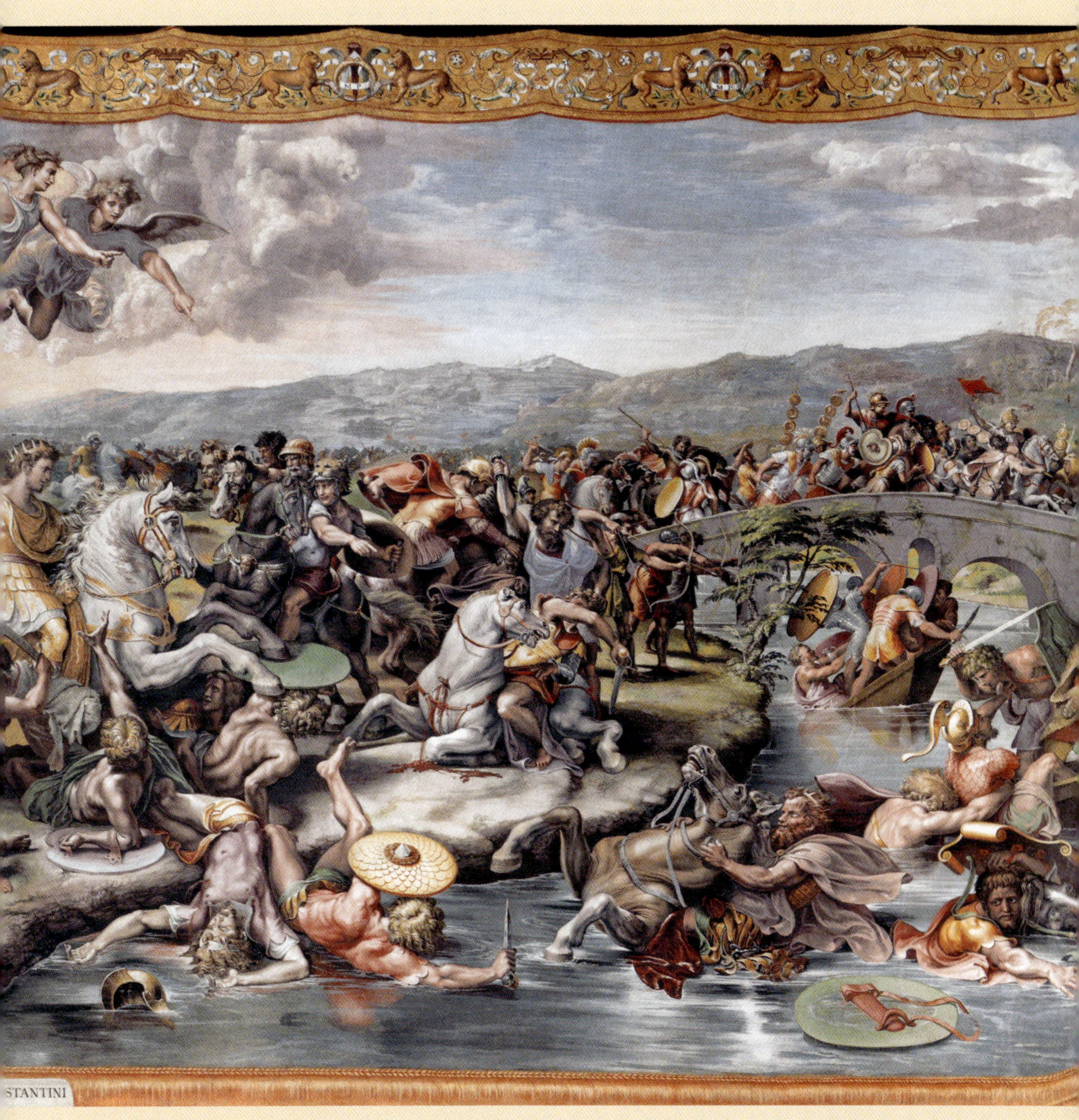
STANTINI

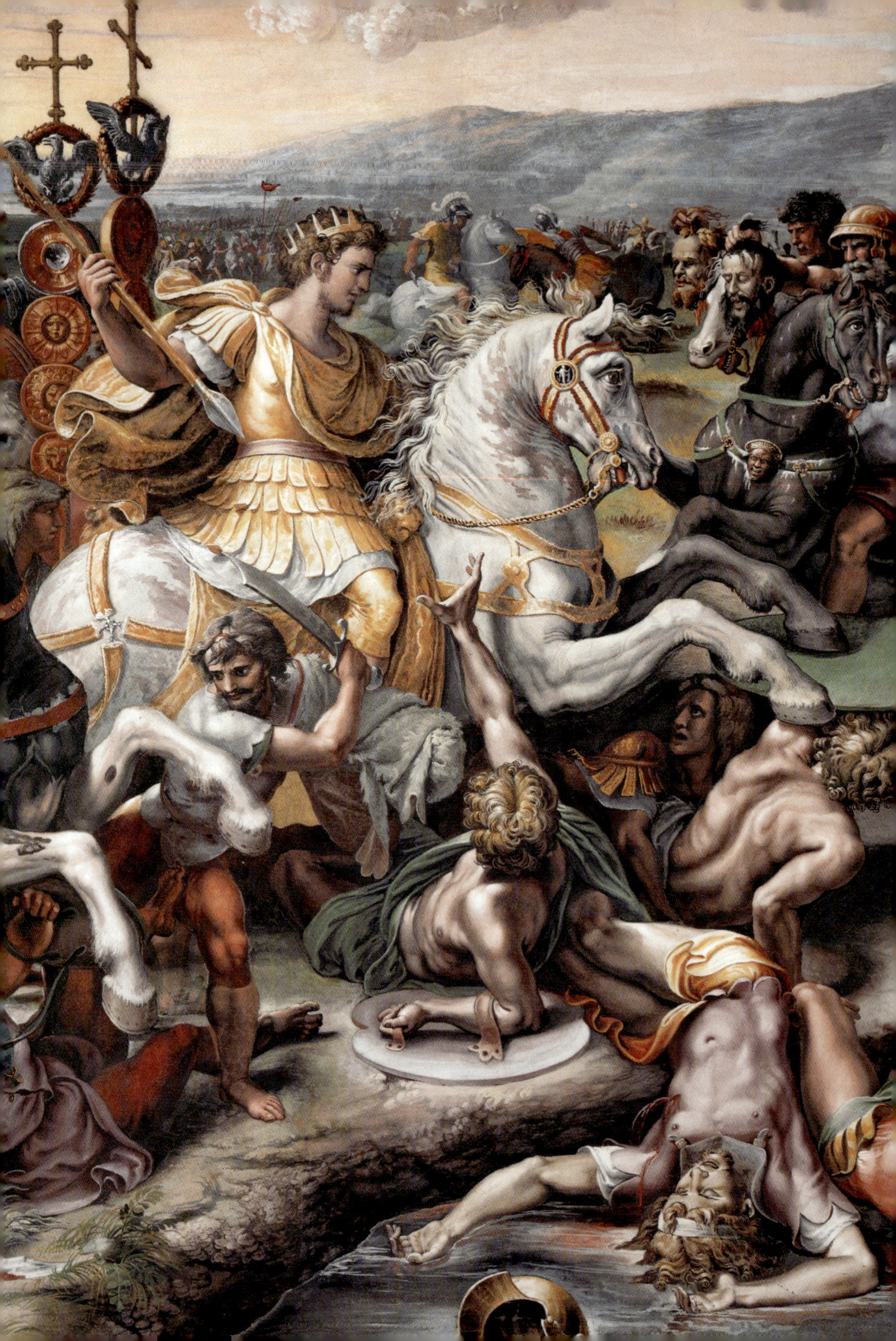

Battle of Constantine against Maxentius at the Milvian Bridge, 1519/20
Pen, with wash and heightened with white, over chalk underdrawing, squared, on support with a beige wash, 37.6 × 85.8 cm (14 ¾ × 33 ¾ in)
Paris, Musée du Louvre, Département des Arts graphiques

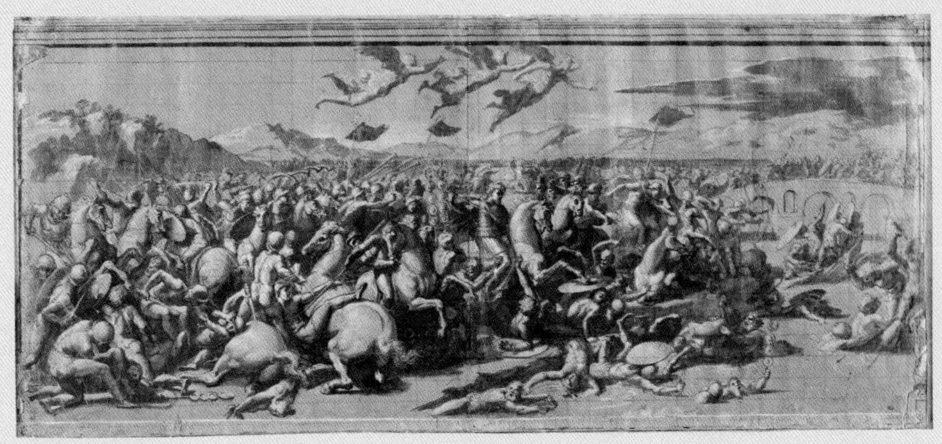

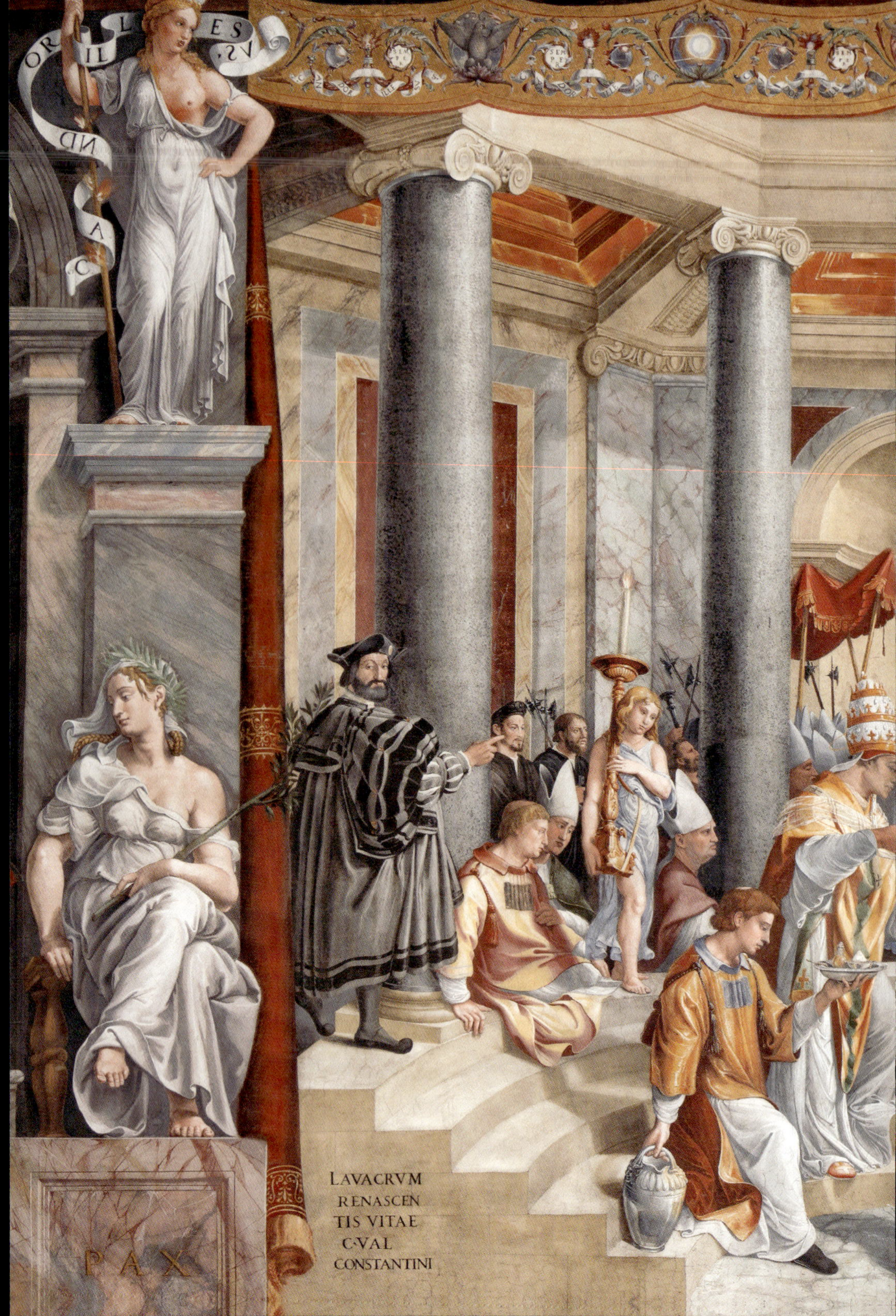
LAVACRVM
RENASCEN
TIS VITAE
C·VAL
CONSTANTINI
PAX

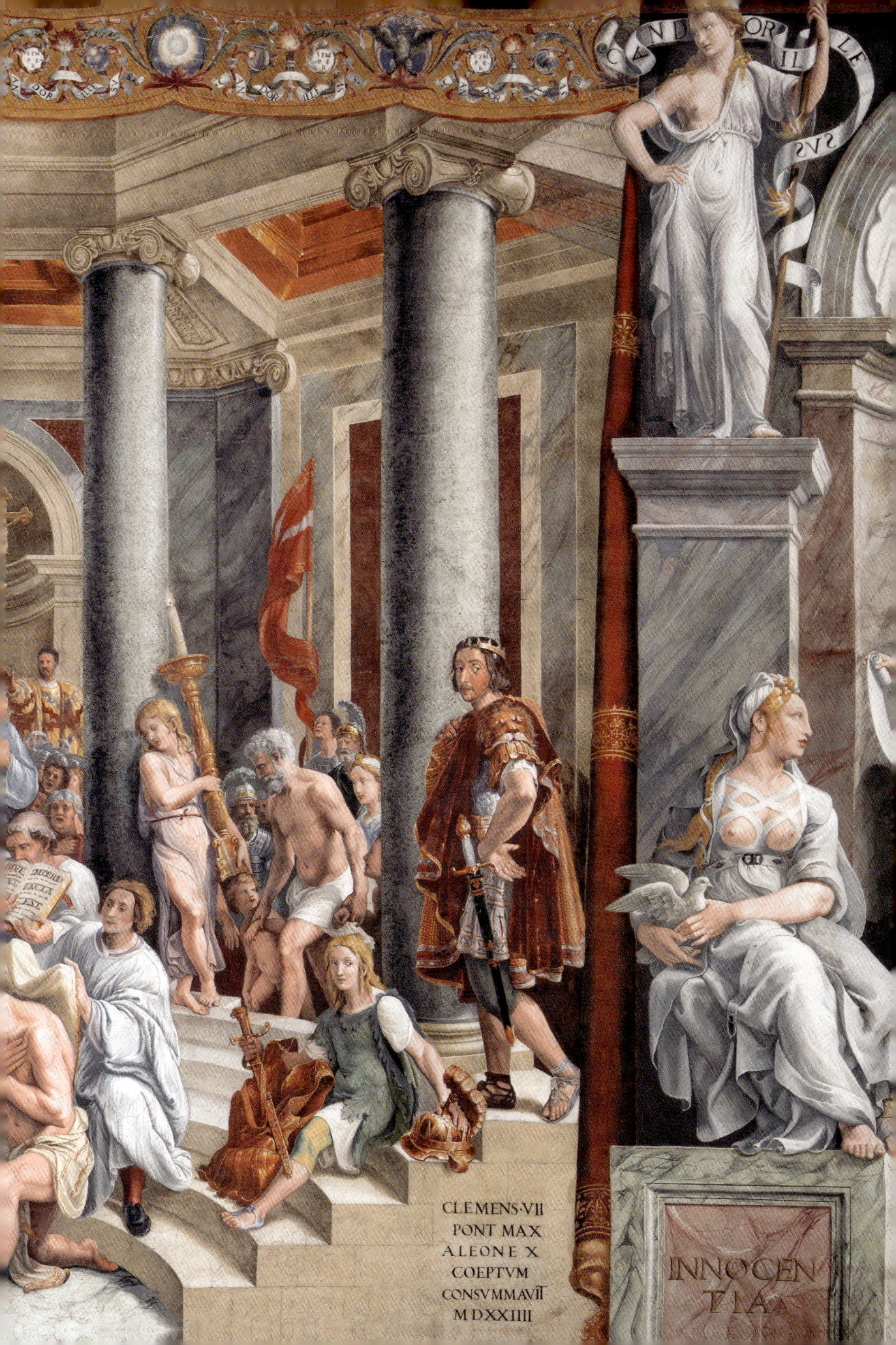
CLEMENS·VII
PONT MAX
A LEONE X
COEPTVM
CONSVMMAVIT
MDXXIIII
INNOCEN
TIA

Pages 502/503
The Baptism of Constantine by Pope Sylvester, 1523/24

Detail from **Pope Clement I (portrait of Leo X) between Moderatio (Temperance) and Comitas (Courtesy)**, 1520/21

Pages 506/507
Constantine's Donation, 1523/24

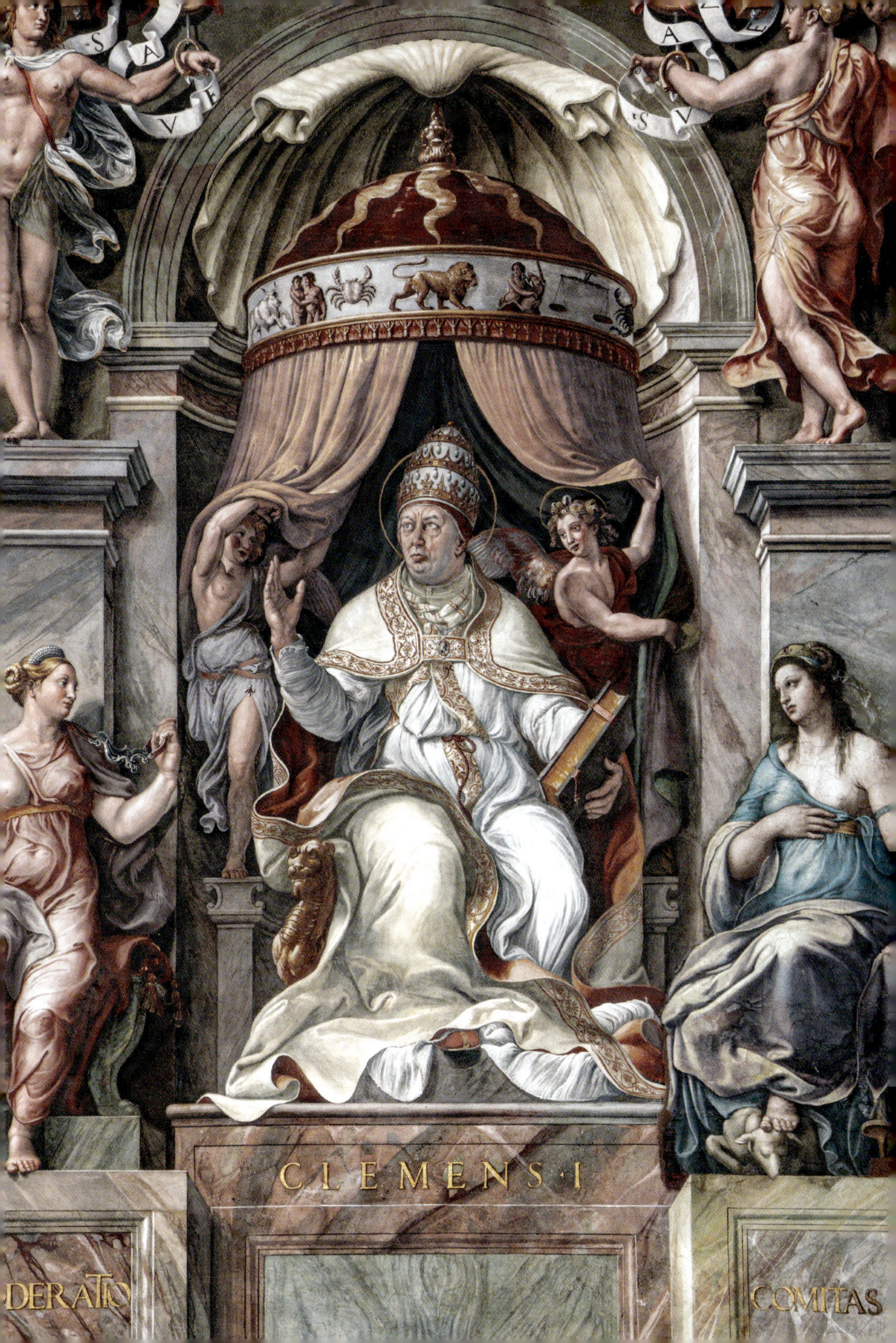
CLEMENS·I
DERATIO
COMITAS

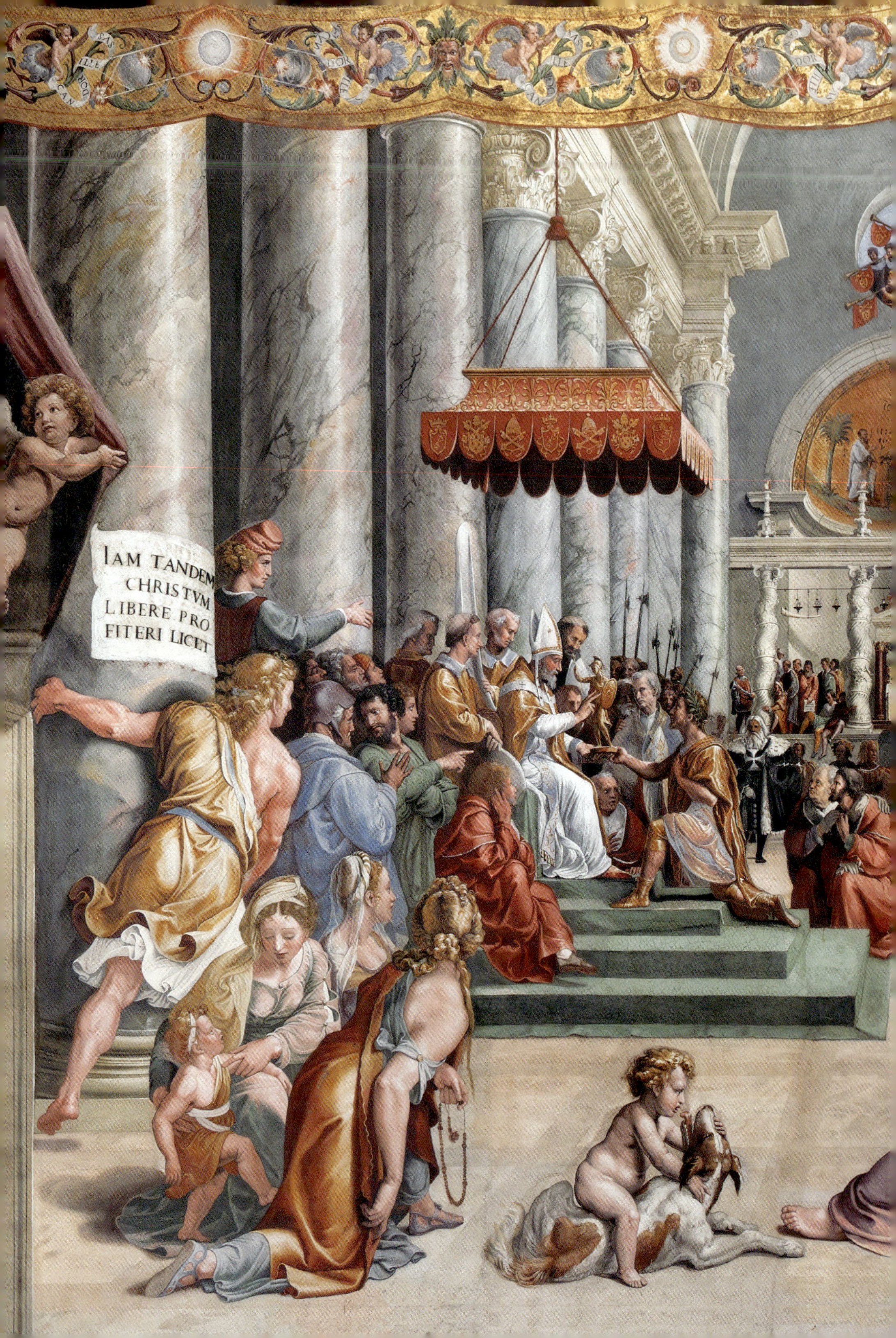
IAM TANDEM
CHRISTVM
LIBERE PRO
FITERI LICET

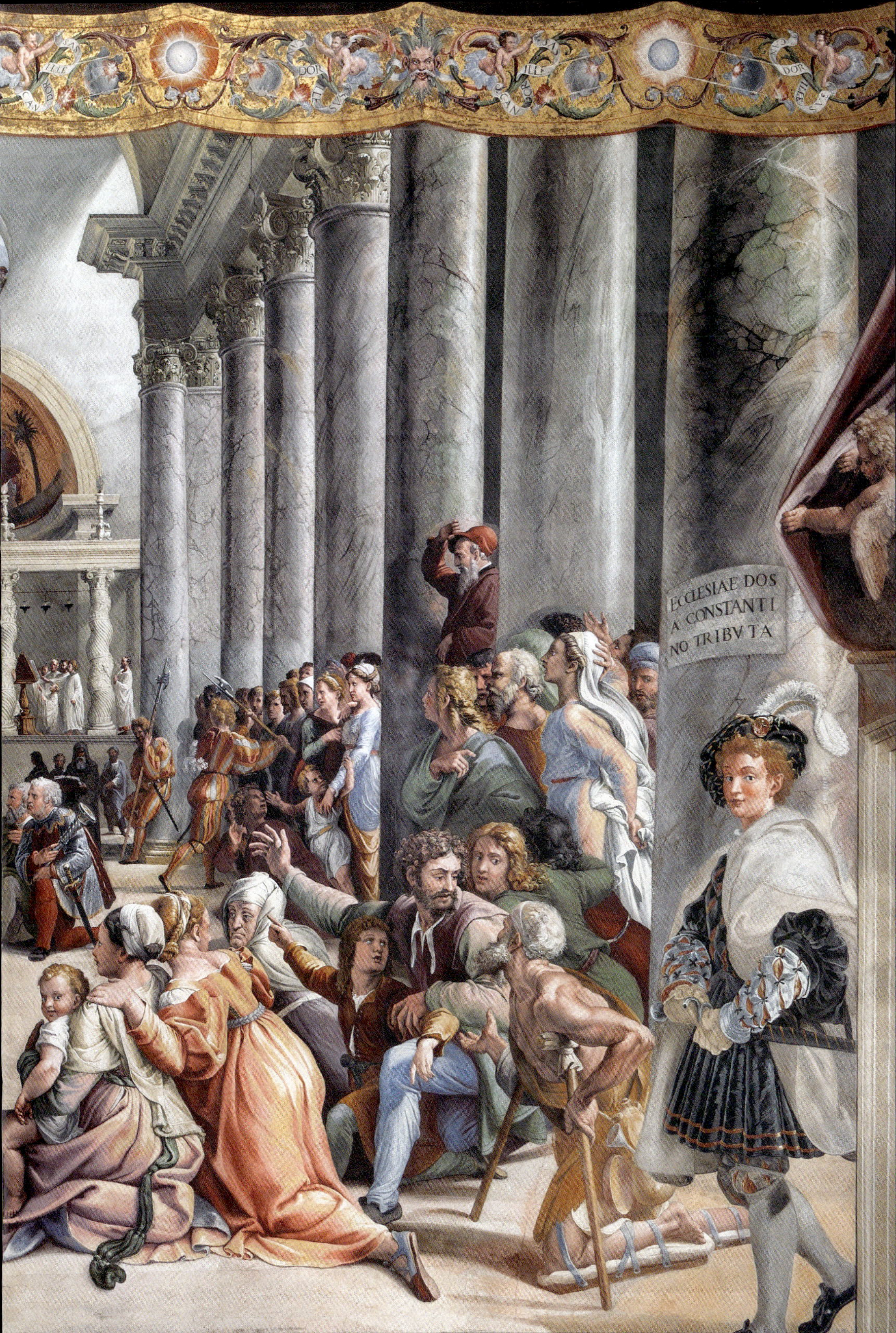
ECCLESIAE DOS
A CONSTANTI
NO TRIBVTA

Bibliography

Acidini, Cristina, *Raffaello*, Pisa 2020.

Bellori, Giovanni Pietro, *Descrizioni delle immagini dipinte da Raffaello d'Urbino nel Vaticano e di quelle alla Farnesina* (1695), Rome 1821.

Bloemacher, Anne, *Raffael und Raimondi. Produktion und Intention der frühen Druckgraphik nach Raffael,* Berlin/Munich 2016.

Città di Castello 2021/22: Marica Mercalli/Laura Teza (eds.), *Raffaello giovane a Città di Castello e il suo sguardo*, exh. cat. Città di Castello 2021/22, Cinisello Balsamo 2021.

Cosgriff, Tracy/Butler Wingfield, Kim (eds.), *Revisiting Raphael's Vatican Stanze,* London/Turnhout 2021.

Crowe, Joseph Archer/Cavalcaselle, Giovanni Battista, *Raphael. His Life and Works*, 2 vols., London 1882/85.

Dacos, Nicole, *Raffael im Vatikan. Die päpstlichen Loggien neu entdeckt*, Stuttgart 2008.

De Vecchi, Pierluigi, *Raffael*, Munich 2002.

Dohna Schlobitten, Yvonne/Bertling Biaggini, Claudia/Cieri Via, Claudia (eds.), *Himmlische und irdische Liebe. Ein anderer Blick auf Raffael*, Regensburg 2023.

Dussler, Luitpold, *Raphael. A Critical Catalogue of His Pictures, Wall-Paintings and Tapestries*, London/New York 1971.

Ettlinger, Leopold D./Ettlinger, Helen S., *Raphael*, Oxford 1987.

Farinella, Vincenzo, *Raffaello pittore archeologo. Eguagliare e superare gli antichi*, Rome 2021.

Ferino-Pagden, Sylvia, "Raffael post festum II", in: *Kunstchronik* 77, 2024, pp. 330–352.

Fischel, Oskar, *Raffaels Zeichnungen*, 8 vols., Berlin 1913–1941.

Fischel, Oskar, *Raphael*, 2 vols., London 1948 (Eng. edition).

Freedberg, Sydney J., *Painting of the High Renaissance in Rome and Florence*, 2 vols., Cambridge, MA 1961.

Freedberg, Sydney J., *Painting in Italy. 1500 to 1600*, Harmondsworth 1971.

Gardner von Teuffel 1987b: Gardner von Teuffel, Christa, "Raffaels römische Altarbilder: Aufstellung und Bestimmung", in: *Zeitschrift für Kunstgeschichte 50*, 1987, pp. 1–45.

Grimm, Herman, *Das Leben Raphael's. Zweite Ausgabe des ersten Bandes und Abschluss in einem Bande*, Berlin 1886.

Hall, Marcia (ed.), *Raphael's "School of Athens"*, Cambridge 1997.

Hall 2005a: Hall, Marcia B. (ed.), *The Cambridge Companion to Raphael,* Cambridge 2005.

Henning, Andreas, *Raffaels Transfiguration und der Wettstreit um die Farbe. Koloritgeschichtliche Untersuchung zur römischen Hochrenaissance*, Munich/Berlin 2005 (*Kunstwissenschaftliche Studien*, 125).

Hetzer, Theodor, *Bild als Bau*, Stuttgart 1996 (*Schriften Theodor Hetzers*, vol. 4).

Hiller von Gaertringen, Rudolf, *Raffaels Lernerfahrungen in der Werkstatt Peruginos. Kartonverwendung und Motivübernahme im Wandel,* Munich/Berlin 1999.

Hamburg 2021: Andreas Stolzenburg/David Klemm (eds.), *Raffael. Wirkung eines Genies*, exh. cat. Hamburg 2021, Petersberg 2021.

Jatta, Barbara/Cimino, Vittoria (eds.), *Raffaello in Vaticano. Atti del Convegno per il V centenario della morte*, Vatican City 2023.

Joannides, Paul, *The Drawings of Raphael. With a Complete Catalogue*, Berkeley, CA/Los Angeles 1983; Oxford et al. 1983.

Joannides, Paul, *Raphael*, London 2022.

Jones/Penny 1983a: Jones, Roger/Penny, Nicholas, *Raphael*, New Haven, CT/London 1983.

KMOF: Knab, Eckhart/Mitsch, Erwin/Oberhuber, Konrad, *Raphael. Die Zeichnungen*, in collaboration with Sylvia Ferino-Pagden, Stuttgart 1983.

London 2004/05: *Raphael. From Urbino to Rome / Raffael. Von Urbino nach Rom*, exh. cat. London 2004/05, ed. by Hugo Chapman, Tom Henry and Carol Plazzotta, London 2004/Stuttgart 2004.

London 2022: David Ekserdjian/Tom Henry/Matthias Wivel (eds.), *Raphael*, exh. cat. London 2022.

Madrid/Paris 2012/13: *Raphaël. Les Dernières Années/Late Raphael*, exh. cat. Madrid/

Paris 2012/13, ed. by Tom Henry and Paul Joannides, Paris 2012/London 2013.

Meyer zur Capellen, Jürg, *Raphael. A Critical Catalogue of His Paintings*, 3 vols., Landshut 2001–2008.

Müntz, Eugène, *Raphaël. Sa vie, son œuvre et son temps*, Paris 1881.

Nesselrath 2020a: Nesselrath, Arnold, *Raffael!*, Stuttgart 2020.

Oberhuber 1999a: Oberhuber, Konrad, *Raffael. Das malerische Werk*, Munich 1999.

Paolucci, Antonio/Agosti, Barbara/Ginzburg, Silvia (eds.), *Raffaello a Roma. Restauri e ricerche*, Rome 2017.

Passavant, Johann [Jean] David, *Rafael von Urbino und sein Vater Giovanni Santi*, 3 vols., Leipzig 1839/58.

Pfisterer, Ulrich, *Raffael. Glaube, Liebe, Ruhm*, Munich 2019.

Plazzotta, Carol/Henry, Tom, *The Sixteenth Century Italian Paintings, Volume 4: Raphael.* National Gallery Catalogues, London 2022 (online).

Pope-Hennessy, John, *Raphael*, London 1970.

Quednau, Rolf, *Die Sala di Costantino im Vatikanischen Palast. Zur Dekoration der beiden Medici-Päpste Leo X. und Clemens VII.*, Hildesheim/New York 1979.

Raffaello a Roma 1986: *Raffaello a Roma. Il convegno del 1983*, ed. by Bibliotheca Hertziana and Musei Vaticani, Rome 1986.

Raffaello nell'appartamento di Giulio II e Leone X, Milan 1993.

Rohlmann, Michael/Zöllner Frank/Hiller von Gaertringen, Rudolf/Satzinger, Georg, *Raffael. Das Gesamtwerk. Gemälde, Fresken, Teppiche, Architektur*, Cologne 2022.

Rohlmann, Michael, "Die Kunst des Zitats. Zu inhaltlicher Motivation und Bedeutung entlehnter Motive bei Raffael", in: *Wallraf-Richartz-Jahrbuch* 82, 2021, pp. 71–131.

Rome 2020: Marzia Faietti/Matteo Lafranconi/Francesco P. Di Teodoro/Vincenzo Farinella (eds.), *Raffaello 1520–1483*, exh. cat. Rome 2020, Milan 2020.

Rome 2023: Alessandro Zuccari/Costanza Barbieri (eds.), *Raffaello e l'antico nella villa di Agostino Chigi*, exh. cat. Rome 2023.

Schöne, Wolfgang, *Raphael*, Berlin/Darmstadt 1958.

Shearman 1971a: Shearman, John, "The Vatican Stanze: Functions and Decoration", in: *Proceedings of the British Academy* 57, 1971, pp. 369–424.

Shearman, John, *Raphael's Cartoons in the Collection of Her Majesty the Queen and the Tapestries for the Sistine Chapel*, London 1972.

Springer 1883b: Springer, Anton, *Raffael und Michelangelo*, vol. 1: *Bis zum Tode Julius II.*, vol. 2: *Seit dem Regierungsantritte Leos X.*, 2nd edition, Leipzig 1883 (1st edition Leipzig 1878).

Strobel, Anna Maria de (ed.), *Leone X e Raffaello in Sistina. Gli arazzi degli Atti degli Apostoli*, vol. 1: *Saggi e Regesto*, vol. 2: *Schede e Tavole*, Rome 2020.

Stuttgart 2001: *Raffael und die Folgen. Das Kunstwerk in Zeitaltern seiner graphischen Reproduzierbarkeit*, exh. cat. Stuttgart 2001, ed. by Corinna Höper, Ostfildern 2001.

Thoenes, Christof, *Raffael. 1483–1520*, Cologne 2005.

Thomas, Ben/Whistler, Catherine (eds.), *Raphael: Drawing and Eloquence*, Urbino 2020 (*Accademia Raffaello. Il contesto artistico*, 3).

Traeger, Jörg, *Renaissance und Religion. Die Kunst des Glaubens im Zeitalter Raphaels*, Munich 1997.

Turner, James Grantham, *The Villa Farnesina. Palace of Venus in Renaissance Rome*, Cambridge 2022.

Vasari, Giorgio, *Le vite de' più eccellenti pittori, scultori e architettori nelle redazioni del 1550 e 1568. Testo*, ed. by Rosanna Bettarini and Paola Barocchi, 6 vols., Florence 1966–1987.

Vienna 2017/18: *Raffael*, exh. cat. Vienna 2017/18, ed. by Achim Gnann, Vienna/Munich 2017.

Wagner, Christoph, *Farbe und Metapher. Die Entstehung einer neuzeitlichen Bildmetaphorik in der vorrömischen Malerei Raphaels*, Berlin 1999.

White, John/Shearman, John, "Raphael's Tapestries and their Cartoons", in: *The Art Bulletin* 40, 1958, pp. 193–221, 299–323.

Williams, Robert, *Raphael and the Redefinition of Art in Renaissance Italy*, Cambridge 2017.

Wölfflin, Heinrich, *Die klassische Kunst. Eine Einführung in die italienische Renaissance*, Munich 1899.

Zezza, Andrea/Cioffi, Rosanna/Lattuada, Riccardo (eds.), *Raffaello 500 anni dopo. Atti del convegno internazionale di studi Raffaello 1520-2020*, Rome 2024.

Imprint

EACH AND EVERY TASCHEN BOOK PLANTS A SEED!
Each year, we offset our annual carbon emissions with carbon credits at the Instituto Terra, a reforestation program in Minas Gerais, Brazil, founded by Lélia and Sebastião Salgado. To find out more about this ecological partnership, please check: www.taschen.com/institutoterra.
Inspiration: unlimited.
Carbon footprint: (almost) zero.

Want to see more? Visit taschen.com to view our current publications, browse our latest magazine, and subscribe to our newsletter.

Hohenzollernring 53, D–50672 Cologne
www.taschen.com

Translation:
Karen Williams, Dartmouth

Printed in Bosnia-Herzegovina
ISBN 978-3-7544-0347-1

Cover, pages 4–7
Disputa (details), *c.* 1509/10
Fresco, height 5.88 m (231 ¼ in), width at base 8.18 m (322 ⅛ in)
Vatican City, Musei Vaticani, Stanza della Segnatura

Pages 1–3
The Voyage of Galatea (details), *c.* 1512
Fresco, 295 × 225 cm (116 ⅛ × 88 ⅝ in)
Rome, Villa Farnesina